*When should I travel to get the best airfare?*
*Where do I go for answers to my travel questions?*
*What's the best and easiest way to plan and book my trip?*

# frommers.travelocity.com

**Frommer's**, the travel guide leader, has teamed up with **Travelocity.com**, the leader in online travel, to bring you an in-depth, easy-to-use resource designed to help you plan and book your trip online.

At **frommers.travelocity.com**, you'll find free online updates about your destination from the experts at Frommer's plus the outstanding travel planning and purchasing features of Travelocity.com. Travelocity.com provides reservations capabilities for 95 percent of all airline seats sold, more than 47,000 hotels, and over 50 car rental companies. In addition, Travelocity.com offers more than 2,000 exciting vacation and cruise packages. Travelocity.com puts you in complete control of your travel planning with these and other great features:

> **Expert travel guidance from Frommer's** - over 150 writers reporting from around the world!

> **Best Fare Finder** - an interactive calendar tells you when to travel to get the best airfare

> **Fare Watcher** - we'll track airfare changes to your favorite destinations

> **Dream Maps** - a mapping feature that suggests travel opportunities based on your budget

> **Shop Safe Guarantee** - 24 hours a day / 7 days a week live customer service, and more!

Whether you're traveling on a tight budget, looking for a quick weekend getaway, or planning the trip of a lifetime, Frommer's guides and Travelocity.com will make your travel dreams a reality. You've bought the book, now book the trip!

**Travelocity.com**
A Sabre Company

## Here's what the critics say about Frommer's:

## Other Great Guides for Your Trip:

*Frommer's New York City*

*Frommer's New York City with Kids*

*Frommer's Irreverent Guide to Manhattan*

*The Mad Monks Guide to New York City*

*The Unofficial Guide to New York City*

*Frommer's Memorable Walks in New York*

*Frommer's Manhattan by Night*

*Frommer's Born to Shop New York*

*Frommer's Wonderful Weekends from New York City*

*New York City for Dummies*

# Frommer's® 2001

# NEW YORK CITY
# FROM $80 A DAY

## The Ultimate Guide to Comfortable Low-Cost Travel

### by Cheryl Farr Leas

### with research assistance from Nathaniel R. Leas

IDG Books Worldwide, Inc.
An International Data Group Company
Foster City, CA • Chicago, IL • Indianapolis, IN • New York, NY

## ABOUT THE AUTHOR

**Cheryl Farr Leas** was senior editor at Frommer's Travel Guides before embarking on a freelance writing career. She also authors *Frommer's New York City*, as well as *California for Dummies* and *Hawaii for Dummies* (brand-new in late 2000). She has also contributed to *Frommer's USA*, Continental Airlines' in-flight magazine, *Daily Variety*, and other publications. When she's not traveling, she's at home in Park Slope, Brooklyn, with her groovy husband, Rob, and their happy dog, Monty. Feel free to write her directly at rncleas@yahoo.com.

## IDG BOOKS WORLDWIDE, INC.

An International Data Group Company
919 E. Hillsdale Blvd.
Suite 400
Foster City, CA 94404

Find us online at **www.frommers.com**

ISBN 0-02-863784-4
ISSN 8755-5433

Editor: Claudia Kirschhoch
Production Editor: Donna Wright
Design by Michele Laseau
Staff Cartographers: John Decamillis, Elizabeth Puhl, Roberta Stockwell
Production by IDG Books Indianapolis Production Department

## SPECIAL SALES

For general information on IDG Books Worldwide's books in the U.S., please call our Consumer Customer Service department at 1-800-762-2974. For reseller information, including discounts, bulk sales, customized editions, and premium sales, please call our Reseller Customer Service department at 1-800-434-3422.

Manufactured in the United States of America

5  4  3  3  1

# Contents

## 6   Great Deals on Dining   131

## 7   Exploring New York City   189

## 8 Shopping for Big Apple Bargains 264

## 9 New York City After Dark 297

## Index 339

# List of Maps

## AN INVITATION TO THE READER

In researching this book, I discovered many wonderful places—hotels, restaurants, shops, and more. I'm sure you'll find others. Please tell me about them, so I can share the information with your fellow travelers in upcoming editions. If you were disappointed with a recommendation, I'd love to know that, too. Please write to:

*Frommer's New York City from $80 a Day 2001*
IDG Books Worldwide, Inc.
909 Third Avenue
New York, NY 10022

## AN ADDITIONAL NOTE

Please be advised that travel information is subject to change at any time—and this is especially true of prices. We therefore suggest that you write or call ahead for confirmation when making your travel plans. The author, editors, and publisher cannot be held responsible for the experiences of readers while traveling. Your safety is important to us, however, so we encourage you to stay alert and be aware of your surroundings. Keep a close eye on cameras, purses, and wallets, all favorite targets of thieves and pickpockets.

## WHAT THE SYMBOL MEANS
### ✪ Frommer's Favorites

Our favorite places and experiences—outstanding for quality, value, or both.

The following abbreviations are used for credit cards:

| | | | |
|---|---|---|---|
| AE | American Express | EC | EuroCard |
| CB | Carte Blanche | JCB | Japan Credit Bank |
| DC | Diners Club | MC | MasterCard |
| DISC | Discover | V | Visa |
| ER | enRoute | | |

## FIND FROMMER'S ONLINE

**www.frommers.com** offers up-to-the-minute listings on almost 200 cities around the globe—including the latest bargains and candid, personal articles updated daily by Arthur Frommer himself. No other Web site offers such comprehensive and timely coverage of the world of travel.

# The Best of the Big Apple

**W**elcome to New York City—the only city on the planet brazen enough to call itself "The Capital of the World." New York has never been subtle, self-effacing, or coy. This is the Muhammad Ali of cities: We Are the Greatest!

It's precisely this kind of urban machismo that makes people either love New York or hate it—or both. Either you'll be enthralled by the tempo, glamour, and sheer excitement of it all, or you'll be stunned by the noise, the intimate mingling of inhuman poverty and unimaginable wealth, the smog, and the callousness that's an everyday occurrence on these city streets. If your emotional metronome swings back and forth from one moment to the next, take heart: We New Yorkers have a never-ending love-hate relationship with this awful, wonderful town. We talk endlessly about escaping for the weekend, commiserate about subways that arrive late, and bemoan the noise, the rents, the crowds, the cab drivers who don't seem to know Lincoln Center from the Lower East Side. Yet still we stay.

The questions beg to be asked: Why do we stay? And what is it about New York City that makes you, dear reader, want to join us?

Any attempt to define New York today recalls the Zen wisdom that you can't step in the same stream twice. The city is so mutable, so constantly changing that it's almost impossible to get a fix on it. Restaurants and nightclubs become trendy overnight and then die under the weight of their own popularity. (Yogi Berra had the perfect phrase for that very phenomenon: "Nobody goes there anymore; it's too crowded.") Fashions, almost by definition, change in the time it takes to try on a pair of vinyl pants. Broadway shows, exercise fads, even neighborhoods are all subject to the same Big Apple fickleness. But within this ebb and flow lies the answer: No other place keeps any of us on our toes quite like New York City. Nowhere else is the challenge so tough, the pace so relentless, the stimuli so ever-changing and insistent—and the payoff so rewarding. Simply put, New York never gets boring. Anything can happen here.

The city has a special magnetism—a charisma, if you will—that pulls in the intelligent, the creative, the determined, the overbearing, and the overblown from all over the world. Just about any language and any dialect is spoken here, from Mandarin to Brooklynese; no other dot on the map is quite so ethnically, culturally, socially, and economically diverse. This is the nerve center of world finance and trade.

The international hub of advertising, publishing, entertainment, and fashion. The creative core for the arts. The top showcase for pure celebrity. And, now as never before, a huge magnet for travelers from all over the country and around the globe, in search of a brief glimpse of it all.

You've probably heard the good news: The city is in top form, its finest in more than 50 years. The economy is up, and crime is down. Everywhere you look, things are being refurbished and the city is steadily improving. It has even become, believe it or not, *family friendly;* just look at the new peep show– and porn-free Times Square. Few alive today have ever seen the city so radiant or so manageable. New Yorkers perpetually love to wax nostalgic about the good-old, bad-old days, but the fact is that we're reveling in our own good fortune—and the success of the world's largest millennium celebration and the defeat of the Y2K bug has lent an air of invincibility to the whole package. Simply put, now is a great time to be in New York.

Visitors, pumped with curiosity about this "new" New York, are arriving by the millions, swarming the city's streets, sights, hotels, museums, restaurants, nightclubs, and theaters. The city, aglow in its millennial optimism, is welcoming them, and you, with open arms. So come—and be prepared to be overwhelmed, exasperated, delighted, and utterly charmed. That, after all, is what the Big Apple is all about.

## 1  How This Guide Can Save You Money

New York, as everyone knows, is perpetually short on space and overflowing with people. And the city's huge popularity these days means that more people are coming to visit—or to stay—than ever. It's a situation that turns the economy of supply and demand in the seller's favor, with vendors charging whatever the market will bear for goods and services. The result has been stratospheric prices, generally the highest you'll find in the country. Average hotel rates are higher than ever before in the city's history—around $200 a night—and New Yorkers don't bat an eye at dropping a hundred bucks on a modest dinner for two. If you're used to getting a simple motel room for $50 or so, the kind of basic accommodations available all over the United States, get set for a shock. With hotel occupancy rates hovering perilously close to 90%, most hoteliers laugh at the notion of giving away any hotel room for $100 or less.

That's the bad news—but there's plenty of good news to tell, too. Simply put, you *can* stay in New York City comfortably, eat well, and see and do everything you want without blowing your budget. There are plenty of great deals in every category for the intrepid traveler who knows where to look for good value and mine for discounts. And you've taken the right first step—buying this book. I've done the initial legwork for you, scouring the city from top to bottom and loading the pages that follow with the best money-saving advice, leads on the top values and bargains, and the kind of New York travel know-how that only comes with years of research and experience.

Accommodations will be your biggest hurdle. Most other aspects of New York are budgetable if you look before you leap, which is precisely how we regular New Yorkers manage to live here on regular salaries. The city tends to snag people who, exhausted, sit down at the first meal they see and end up with a huge bill—or those who stumble into a chic boutique to buy a standard replacement item or a souvenir that can be had for a fraction of the price with just a little effort. Keep an eye on the goal and you'll soon see that New York has more affordable culinary and bargain-hunters' delights than you'll have time to enjoy.

With average museum admissions hovering around 10 bucks a pop and guided bus tours starting near $25 for the basic look-see, you could spend a fortune on sightseeing and activities—but you don't have to. Start perusing these pages and you'll soon find more to see and do for free and on the cheap than you could possibly squeeze into one vacation (or two or three or four). I'm not suggesting that you skip anything that has a price tag; certain New York experiences shouldn't be missed, money be damned. But read the pages that follow and you'll know what's worth your dough—and what's not.

## THE NEW YORK–FROM-$80-A-DAY PREMISE

This premise might seem like a pipe dream, but it's not. The idea is this: With good planning and a watchful eye, you can keep your basic daily living costs—accommodations and three meals a day—down to as little as $80. This budget model works best for two adults traveling together who have at least $160 a day to work with and can share a double room (as you're probably well aware, single rooms are much less cost-efficient). This way, if you aim for accommodations costing around $100 double, you'll be left with about $30 per person per day for food (less drinks and tips).

If you want to do it even cheaper by spending even less on accommodations, I'll show you how to do that, too. But in defining this basic premise, we at Frommer's have assumed that you want to travel comfortably, with your own room rather than a hostel bunk (even if it does mean a shared bathroom), dining on good food rather than fast food at every meal. This book will also serve you well even if you don't need to keep your two-person budget to a strict $160 a day, but you want to keep the tabs down and get the most for your money at every turn.

Of course, the cost of sightseeing, transportation, and entertainment are all extras. But don't worry—I'll offer plenty of suggestions on how to keep those bills down, too. What you choose for entertainment will have a huge effect on your overall budget. If you frequent nightclubs every night, you'll come home with a lighter wallet than if you spend time taking in free concerts or browsing galleries. If you seek top-name entertainment on Broadway or the cabaret circuit, you'll pay more than if you take a risk on tomorrow's stars at an off-Broadway show or a no-cover bar. Only you know how much money you have to spend—but follow my advice, and you'll be able to make informed decisions on what to see and do so that it's money well spent. Even if you stick with freebies, the Big Apple guarantees a memorable time. After all, to the late, great Quentin Crisp, every flat surface in New York is a stage—and you're guaranteed a nonstop show.

## 2 Frommer's Favorite Affordable Experiences

- **Sailing to the Statue of Liberty.** If you have time to do only one thing in New York, this is what it should be. No monument so embodies the nation's, and the world's, notion of political freedom and economic potential more than Lady Liberty. The view never loses its power—and neither does the Manhattan skyline, which is breathtaking from this perspective. The ferry that takes you out to Liberty Island also stops at the historic federal immigration station on Ellis Island, gateway to America for nearly half of our forefathers and foremothers. The museum's exhibits illustrate, with moving simplicity, what coming to the "promised land" was all about. If you want the view but prefer to skip the tourist crowds—and the fare—consider catching the free Staten Island Ferry instead. See chapter 7.
- **Visiting the Museums.** The Metropolitan Museum of Art, the American Museum of Natural History, the Museum of Modern Art, the Whitney Museum of American Art, the Guggenheim—museum hopping just doesn't get any better than this. The number of masterworks housed in this city is mind-boggling. But

don't just stick to the biggies; New York boasts a wealth of smaller, lower-profile museums that speak to specific interests—from folk art to photography to financial history—and house some phenomenal treasures. For a complete rundown, see chapter 7—and don't miss the box "Free Culture at Big Apple Museums," which will fill you in on which ones offer free or discounted admission on select days.

- **Strolling the Neighborhoods.** One of the greatest things about New York is the distinct character of each of its neighborhoods. Rather than try to quick-scan them all, I highly recommend picking one and really getting to know it. Wend your way through the historic streets of Greenwich Village, saunter the cast-iron canyons of SoHo, or explore the lovely, trendy Flatiron District. All you really need is a map and a sense of adventure. If you prefer a little structure, consider taking one of the many excellent walking tours that are available; there's no better way to get to know a hood than with an expert at the helm. Some of the city's best guided tours are even free. See chapters 4 and 7.

- **Walking the Brooklyn Bridge.** A marvel of civil engineering when it first connected Brooklyn to Manhattan in 1883, the Brooklyn Bridge still awes even the most jaded New Yorkers. I, for one, never tire of admiring its Gothic-inspired stone pylons and intricate steel-cable webs. Get an up-close look, and some marvelous views of Manhattan, by taking the easy stroll from end to end. Start on the Brooklyn side for best effect, and consider pairing your walk with a stroll through historic Brooklyn Heights for a lovely afternoon. See chapter 7.

- **Stargazing at Grand Central Terminal.** Always a Beaux-Arts gem, this majestic 1913 railroad station received a remarkable facelift, unveiled in 1998, that has made it a must-see. Every surface glitters with renewed optimism—but none more than the masterful ceiling, once again brilliant with 24-karat gold zodiac constellations against a gorgeous blue-green sky. Walk in, throw your head back, and watch the stars gleam. See chapter 7.

- **Ogling the City's Art-Deco Marvels.** Nothing embodies the city's historic sense of optimism more so than its streamline masterpieces. And nowhere is the art-deco style more passionately realized than at Rockefeller Center, the business-and-entertainment center at the heart of Midtown. The most romantic of the city's skyscrapers, the chrome-topped Chrysler Building, is another art-deco gem; look for the gargoyles jutting out from the upper floors. And when you visit the marvelous Empire State Building, don't miss the mural in the lobby in your rush to get to the iconic observation deck. See chapter 7.

- **Wandering Central Park.** This beautiful accident of civil planning makes the otherwise uninterrupted urban jungle tolerable for workaday New Yorkers. Don't skip the chance to enjoy its wonders. Be sure to seek out Strawberry Fields, the living memorial to John Lennon. Without this great green park, I couldn't imagine life in the city. See chapter 7.

- **Watching Your Favorite Talk Show Being Taped—for Free.** If you have the forethought (to send away months in advance) or the patience (to wait in the standby line), you can watch Dave, Conan, Rosie, Sally, or the ladies of *The View* work their TV magic. If sketch comedy or sitcoms are more your speed, think *Cosby* or, the holy grail of TV audience wannabes, *Saturday Night Live*. To start planning—or for insider tips on how to score last-minute tickets—see chapter 7.

- **Dining Out.** New York is the world capital of great eating—and the true beauty of New York's restaurant scene is that you don't have to spend a fortune to eat well. You'll find cheap but dazzling Chinese in Chinatown, pastrami to die for at any number of Jewish delis, pasta and cannoli that Carmela Soprano would be proud to call her own . . . the list goes on and on. See chapter 6.

- **Watching the Curtain Rise on a Play.** There's nothing like the immediacy and excitement of a live production. Movie and TV stars know it, which is why more and more are showing their stuff on the New York stage. Make it a priority to catch a theater production while you're in town. Sure, tickets are expensive, but creative minds almost never have to pay top dollar. First of all, consider the city's wealth of affordable off-Broadway productions. Who knows? You could be the first on your block (or in your state) to catch the next *Rent*. If your heart's set on a big Broadway show, buy your tickets through the TKTS booth, where you can save 25% to 50% off face value. See chapter 9.

- **Celebrating the Holidays in the City.** Christmas and New Year's can be nightmarish times in New York, with crowds choking the entire city and every merchant in town charging top dollar. But the city can be a dream on other, less attention-grabbing holidays and a veritable bargain to boot. On Chinese New Year, a bright dragon promises great fortune ahead—and bargain-basement winter getaway rates. With the promise of summer heat keeping both visitors and city dwellers out of town, a peaceful hush comes over the city on July 4th—until the fireworks explode overhead, lighting up the night sky with patriotic flair. The huge hot-air balloons of the Macy's Thanksgiving Day Parade bring out the kid in all of us—and it's a little-known fact that some of the best hotel bargains in the city can be had over the holiday weekend away from the parade route. See "When to Go" and the "Calendar of Events" in chapter 2.

- **Taking Advantage of Freebies.** Always financially pressed in this perpetually too-expensive city, New Yorkers and visitors alike love nothing better than a bargain. But even longtime locals often don't realize just how much wonderful stuff there is to see and do that's absolutely free. Be sure to check out "Cheap Thrills: What to See & Do for Free" in chapter 7.

## 3 Best Low-Cost Hotel Bets

There's no way around it—you're going to spend more than you like on a hotel room. But lest you worry that your credit card can't handle the stress, never fear: New York has plenty of good wallet-friendly choices, and even some downright bargains, for those who know where to look. For the details on these and other affordable city hotels, see chapter 5.

- **Best Overall Value—Downtown:** It's hard to beat the **Cosmopolitan Hotel–TriBeCa,** 95 W. Broadway (☎ 888/895-9400), for value. Each of the small but comfy, modern rooms comes with its own petite but immaculate private bathroom for as little as $99 a night. The high-rent neighborhood is hip as can be and subway-convenient to the rest of the city.
- **Best Overall Value—Midtown:** No Midtown choice is better located or more consistently value-priced than the **Hotel Edison,** 228 W. 47th St. (☎ 800/637-7070), a mammoth hotel with freshly renovated, perfectly comfortable rooms for just $150 double (or $175 for four) right in the heart of the Theater District. As Gershwin himself said, who could ask for anything more?
- **Best Overall Value—Uptown:** The **Hotel Newton,** 2528 Broadway (☎ 888/HOTEL58), is the one budget hotel in the city that doesn't expect you to put up with a miniscule room or myriad inconveniences just because you don't have a king's ransom to spend. With rates running just $99 to $140 for a double with

private bathroom, you'll more than get your money's worth here—and you'll save an extra 10% if you're a AAA member.

- **Best Value for Bargain-Hunters Who Don't Mind Sharing:** If you're willing to share a hall bathroom, you'll be pleased as punch with the charming **Larchmont Hotel,** in the leafiest, loveliest part of Greenwich Village at 27 W. 11th St. (☎ 212/989-9333).
- **Best Value for Bargain-Hunters Who Do Mind Sharing: Chelsea Lodge,** 318 W. 20th St. (☎ 800/373-1116), offers the perfect compromise: You'll have an in-room sink and shower so all you have to share with your fellow travelers is a toilet in the hall. If you're willing to do that much, you'll find yourself in one of the cutest, cleanest, and most comfortable hotels in New York—and at one of the cheapest rates in town.
- **Best Service for the Budget-Minded:** The professional staff at the **Broadway Inn,** 264 W. 46th St. (☎ 800/826-6300), just might be the most helpful in the city. They're so committed to making their guests feel welcome and at home in New York that they give you a hot line number to call when you're out and about if you need directions, advice on where to eat, or any other assistance. And you thought New York wasn't friendly!
- **Best for Families:** Located on the Upper West Side, one of the city's most desirable and kid-friendly residential neighborhoods, is the **Milburn,** 242 W. 76th St. (☎ 800/833-9622), whose one-bedroom suites are the most affordable in town. A queen-size sleeper sofa in the living room makes the suites large enough to comfortably accommodate four, and a kitchenette with microwave, minifridge, and coffeemaker means Mom and Dad can save on breakfast bills. And the kids-under-13-stay-free policy softens the blow even more for budget-minded families.
- **Best for a Romantic Getaway:** Even if money were no object, I'd send you to **Country Inn the City,** on the Upper West Side on West 77th Street (☎ 212/580-4183), one of the most impeccable guest houses I've ever seen. Couples will have everything they need at hand—including plenty of privacy.
- **Best for Creative Spirits:** At the super-cool, factory-esque **Gershwin Hotel,** 7 E. 27th St. (☎ 212/545-8000), Billy Name is the house photog; what more do I need to say? There's also the brand-new **Chelsea Star,** 300 W. 30th St. (☎ 877/827-6969), where the budget-basic rooms are individually dressed in cheeky themes ranging disco to *Star Trek.* Madonna wannabes can even crash in the shrine-like room where the Material Girl herself lived just before she broke.
- **Best for Style Hounds on a Shoestring:** The **Habitat Hotel,** 130 E. 57th St. (☎ 800/255-0482), is carving out quite a niche for itself as the "upscale budget" choice among style-conscious consumers. The narrow rooms are fresh and outfitted with flair, and the neighborhood is about as high fashion as it gets.
- **Best for Gay & Lesbian Travelers:** New York is such an important center of gay life that, thankfully, virtually all of the city's hotels welcome gay and lesbian visitors. But if you're looking for like-minded folks, try the simply fabulous Hollywood-themed **Chelsea Pines Inn,** 317 W. 14th St. (☎ 212/929-1023), or the more low-key but equally welcoming **Colonial House Inn,** 318 W. 22nd St. (☎ 800/689-3779).
- **Best Freebie: Travel Inn,** 515 W. 42nd St. (☎ 800/869-4630), wins on not just one, but *two* counts. First is the free garage parking—a $25-a-day value at minimum for visitors driving to the city and free in-and-out privileges to boot. Freebie number two is for summer visitors, who can take advantage of Travel

Inn's excellent rooftop swimming pool and huge sundeck. The **Skyline Hotel** (directly below) offers similar value-minded perks.

- **Best for Disabled Travelers:** The comfortable, budget-minded **Skyline Hotel,** 725 Tenth Ave. (☎ **800/433-1982**), has 7 wheelchair-accessible rooms, ramps, and fire-safety alarms for deaf and blind visitors, plus free parking.
- **Best Splurge:** The art-deco–style **Hotel Metro,** 45 W. 35th St. (☎ **800/356-3870**), is a midpriced Midtown gem that feels much more expensive than it actually is. You'll get a surprisingly good deal, including a marble bathroom.

# 4  Best Low-Cost Dining Bets

One of the great joys of being in New York is that there's fabulous food at nearly every turn—and you don't have to be toting a gold card to pay for it. Go ethnic—Chinese, Jewish, Italian, and much, much more—to indulge in the best cheap eats you'll find anywhere. For the details on these and other terrific affordable city restaurants, see chapter 6.

- **Best for a Special Occasion:** TV chef "Molto" Mario Batali's charming **P6,** 31 Cornelia St. (☎ **212/645-2189**), manages to feel special while still remaining affordable, and his inspired pastas are more impressive than those served in much pricier restaurants around town. Book well ahead; it's worth the wait.
- **Best Spot for a Business Lunch:** If you want to impress with your New York acumen, head to the **Oyster Bar,** on the lower level of Grand Central Terminal (☎ **212/490-6650**), a New York classic that's a perfect spot to seal the deal.
- **Best Chinese:** With all the culinary wonders that Chinatown has to offer, this is a tough choice. But whenever I think about the steamy soup dumplings at **Joe's Shanghai,** 9 Pell St. (☎ **212/233-8888**), I can't help but swoon.
- **Best Affordable French:** Your best bet is **Le Pere Pinard,** 175 Ludlow St. (☎ **212/ 777-4917**), for a true slice of St-Germain. Ultra-charming—and an excellent prix-fixe lunch deal to boot.
- **Best Affordable Italian:** For the most-bang-for-your-buck Italian, the award goes to **Frank,** 88 Second Ave. (☎ **212/420-0202**), for meatballs, homemade pasta, and tomato "gravy" better than mama used to make.
- **Best Affordable Seafood:** You can't do better for your money than at **Pisces,** 95 Ave. A (☎ **212/260-6660**), where the top-quality fish is always fresh and creatively prepared. The early-bird prix-fixe dinner makes an already terrific value even more wallet-friendly.
- **Best Newcomer:** The winner is **Junno's,** 64 Downing St. (☎ **212/627-7995**), for Japanese fusion cuisine (served in a sophisticated moderne setting, no less) that's shockingly good considering its bargain-basement price tag.
- **Best Diner:** It's so nice that it hardly deserves to be called a diner. But **Bubby's,** 120 Hudson St. (☎ **212/219-0666**), does comfort food better than anybody— and the classic homestyle pies are better than Ma used to bake.
- **Best Burger and Beer:** Ask a hundred New Yorkers, and you'll get a hundred opinions. But the name that's bound to pop up most is **Corner Bistro,** 331 W. 4th St. (☎ **212/242-9502**), an unpretentious neighborhood pub where the well-charred, beefy burgers are perfect every time.
- **Best Pizza:** Pizza doesn't get any better than the coal oven–baked, fresh-mozzarella-topped pie at **Grimaldi's Pizzeria,** 19 Old Fulton St., Brooklyn Heights (☎ **718/858-4300**). If you're unwilling to travel across the river, **Lombardi's,** 32 Spring St. (☎ **212/941-7994**), has been baking up its own coal-oven pies since 1905.

- **Best Fine-Dining Bargain:** Dining values don't get any better than the **Tavern Room at Gramercy Tavern,** 42 E. 20th St. (☎ 212/477-0777), which allows you to experience one of the city's finest restaurants for a fraction of what expense-account diners pay in the main dining room. I actually prefer this friendly bistro-style alternative, which offers excellent New American food without the pretension.
- **Best All-U-Can-Eat Meal Deal: Salaam Bombay,** 317 Greenwich St. (☎ 212/ 226-9400), has reinvented the buffet with its top-quality pan-Indian lunch spread, offered daily except Saturday. You simply can't eat better anywhere in the city for just $10.95.
- **Best Breakfast:** Uptown, head to **Sarabeth's Kitchen,** 423 Amsterdam Ave. (☎ 212/496-6280), whose sophisticated homestyle cooking and sigh-inducing pastries inspire lines around the block (go early on weekends to avoid the wait). Downtown, head to TriBeCa favorite **Bubby's,** 120 Hudson St. (☎ 212/ 219-0666)—and don't be surprised if Harvey Keitel is chowing down on a monster-size omelette at the next table.
- **Best for Aspiring Cooks: Shabu Tatsu,** 216 E. 10th St. (☎ 212/477-2972), is loads of interactive fun. Come in a group to enjoy the Japanese specialty shabu-shabu, a dish you cook yourself in the hotpot of boiling water built into the center of your table. The waiters bring the plateful of raw meat and veggies, and you'll have a blast doing the rest.
- **Best Late-Night Hangout:** Half authentic-French bistro, half all-American diner, **Florent,** 69 Gansevoort St. (☎ 212/989-5779), is the hipster crowd's favorite after-hours hangout. Thanks to its good food, great people watching, and wonderful sense of humor, it's mine, too.
- **Best Dessert:** There are lots of stellar pastry chefs in town, but you'd be hard-pressed to do better than the remarkable confections at **Payard Pâtisserie and Bistro,** 1032 Lexington Ave. (☎ 212/717-5252), which is well located for a sweet-and-coffee break during a day of Upper East Side museum hopping.

# Planning Your Trip: The Basics

**2**

In the pages that follow, you'll find everything you need to know to handle the practical details of planning your trip in advance—airlines and area airports, a calendar of events, resources for those with special needs, and much more—plus time-tested advice on how to save money at every turn.

## 1 60 Money-Saving Tips

Here are some tips to help you keep your travel costs down:

1. **Buy a money-saving package deal.** A travel package that includes your plane tickets and hotel stay for one price might just be the best bargain of all. In some cases, you'll get airfare, accommodations, transportation to and from the airport, plus extras—maybe an afternoon sightseeing tour or restaurant and shopping discount coupons—for less than the hotel alone would have cost had you booked it yourself. For the lowdown on where and how to get the best package, see "Money-Saving Package Deals" later in this chapter.

2. **Buy a *New York for Less* guidebook.** The primary value in buying this guide ($19.95) is the discount card within, which offers hundreds of discounts from 20% to 50% at restaurants, attractions (including the Empire State Building and the World Trade Center observation deck), shops, theaters, and nightlife spots around Manhattan. The card is good for up to 4 people for up to 8 days and comes with a handbook detailing all the places that honor *New York for Less*. You can order *New York for Less* by calling ☎ 888/463-6753 or online at **www.for-less.com**.

3. **If you're an American Express cardholder, sign up to receive AmEx-only special offers.** American Express offers its cardholders a surprisingly good array of discounts at local and national merchants via its "Online Extras" program. By registering your AmEx card with this free program, you can receive discounts—often 20%—at restaurants, hotels, shops, attractions, and other merchants in New York and throughout the country (even in your hometown). Participants change constantly, but the list is usually extensive, and at press time included such terrific budget-minded hotels as the Comfort Inn–Central Park West and the Chelsea Star Hotel and such recommendable restaurants and bars

as Planet Sushi and the Sporting Club (see chapters 5, 6, and 9). American Express is good about keeping these offers current, but be sure to carefully check the expiration dates as well as the terms and conditions. Sign up at **www.americanexpress.com**; at the home page, click on SEE SPECIAL OFFERS under PERSONAL, which will direct you to the sign-up page.

## WHEN TO GO

4. **Choose your season carefully.** The biggest factor that will affect how much you pay for your hotel room and airfare is the season in which you travel. Prices on hotel rooms, in particular, can vary dramatically—by hundreds of dollars in some cases—depending on what time of year you visit. Winter from January to mid-April is the best season for bargains, with summer from June to mid-August being second best. Spring and fall are the busiest and most expensive seasons after Christmas, but negotiating a decent rate is doable, especially in spring. Budget-minded travelers should skip Christmas and New Year's altogether, when visitors pay top dollar for everything. Thanksgiving, however, is a little-known bargain-hunter's delight. For more on this subject, see "Money Matters" under "When to Go" later in this chapter.

## GETTING TO NEW YORK CITY
### AIR TRAVEL

5. **Plan ahead, and be flexible.** On most flights, even the shortest hops, the full fare is close to $1,000 or more, but you'll most likely pay a lot less if you buy a 7-, 14-, or 21-day advance-purchase ticket. If you stay over a Saturday night or are willing to travel on a Tuesday, Wednesday, or Thursday, you'll likely save even more. Many airlines won't volunteer this information, so be sure to ask.

6. **Always ask for the lowest fare.** Yes, reservations and travel agents should take for granted that you want the lowest possible fare—but they don't always do so. Be sure to ask specifically for the lowest fare, not just a discount fare. And, as with every aspect of your trip, ask about discounts for groups, seniors, children, and students.

7. **Consider all three airports when you're shopping around.** Fares can be markedly different depending on which airport you fly into—LaGuardia, JFK, or Newark, NJ—and none of them are that far from Manhattan. Continental, for instance, almost always has cheaper flights into Newark because it's one of their main hubs. In fact, even though it's in nearby New Jersey, Newark can often be more convenient to your Manhattan destination than the other two airports, and the public buses that run between the airport and the city are cheap and easy to use.

8. **Keep an eye out for promotional rates or special sales.** Periodically, airlines lower prices on their most popular routes, which often include New York. Check your newspaper for advertised discounts or call the airlines directly and ask whether any special deals are available. You'll almost never see a sale during the peak summer vacation months of July and August or during the Thanksgiving or Christmas seasons, but in periods of low-volume travel, you should be able to get a cross-country flight for $400 or less. Note, however, that the lowest-priced fares are often nonrefundable and have other restrictions. When you're quoted a fare, make sure you know exactly what they are before you commit.

# New York Metropolitan Area

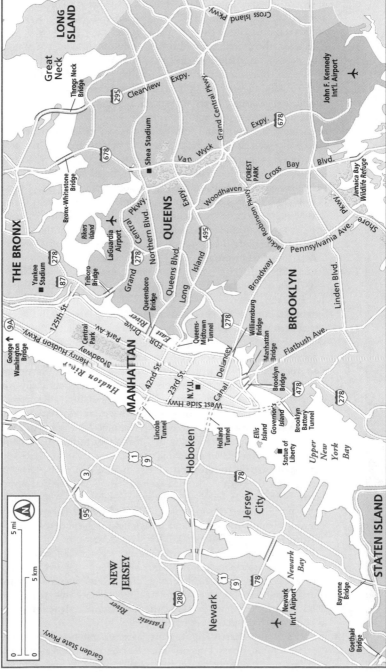

9. **Try the discount carriers, too.** When shopping the airlines, don't forget to check with the smaller, no-frills airlines that fly to New York, including Tower Air, ATA, and Spirit Airlines. You might not get the same kind of service or frequent-flyer bonuses that you will get from the majors, but you can save a lot of dough. See "Getting There," below, for a rundown of discount carriers that fly into area airports.

10. **Check for discounted fares with consolidators.** Also known as bucket shops, consolidators are a good place to find low fares, often below even the airlines' discounted rates. There's nothing shady about the reliable ones; basically, they're just big travel agents that get discounts for buying in bulk and pass some of the savings on to you. Before you pay, however, ask for a confirmation number from the consolidator and then call the airline itself to confirm your seat. Be prepared to book your ticket with a different consolidator—there are many to choose from—if the airline can't confirm your reservation. Also be aware that consolidator tickets are usually nonrefundable or come with stiff cancellation penalties.

    I've gotten great deals on many occasions from ✪ **Cheap Tickets** (☎ **800/377-1000**; www.cheaptickets.com). **Council Travel** (☎ **800/ 226-8624**; www.counciltravel.com) and **STA Travel** (☎ **800/781-4040**; www.statravel.com) cater especially to young travelers, but their bargain-basement prices are available to travelers of all ages. Other reliable consolidators include **Lowestfare.com** (☎ **888/278-8830**; www.lowestfare. com); **1-800-AIRFARE** (www.1800airfare.com); **Cheap Seats** (☎ **800/ 451-7200**; www.cheapseatstravel.com); and **1-800-FLY-CHEAP** (www. flycheap.com).

11. **Search the Internet for cheap advance-purchase fares.** Online booking services can be especially useful because they show you all the options, and some even make lower-priced suggestions on alternatives to your requested itinerary. Keep in mind, though, that it's a good idea to compare your findings with the research of a dedicated travel agent (if you're lucky enough to have one) before you buy, especially when you're booking more than just a flight. A few of the better-respected virtual travel agents are **Travelocity** (**www.travelocity.com**) and **Expedia** (**www.expedia.com**). See the "Planning Your Trip: An Online Directory" immediately following this chapter for further discussion on this topic and other recommendable sites.

12. **Sign up for e-mail notification of last-minute fare deals.** Great last-minute deals are available through e-savers, free e-mail services provided directly by the airlines. Each week, the airline sends you a list of discounted flights, usually leaving the upcoming Friday or Saturday and returning the following Monday or Tuesday. You can sign up at each airline's Web site; see "Getting There" later in this chapter for Web addresses.

    Better yet, save yourself the headache and register with **Smarter Living** (**www.smarterliving.com**). Take a moment to register, and every week you'll get an e-mail summarizing the discount fares available from your departure city. Smarter Living tracks more than 15 different airlines, so it's a worthwhile time-saver. The site also features concise lists of links to hotel, car rental, and other hot travel deals.

13. **Book a seat on a charter flight.** Most charter operators advertise and sell their seats through travel agents, thus making these local professionals your best source of information for available flights. Before deciding to take a charter flight, however, check the restrictions on the ticket: You

might be asked to purchase a package tour, pay in advance, be amenable to a change in departure date, pay a service charge, fly on an airline you're not familiar with (although this is not usually the case), and/or pay harsh penalties if you cancel—as well as be understanding if the charter doesn't fill up and is canceled up to 10 days before departure. Summer charters fill up more quickly than others and are almost sure to fly, but if you decide on a charter flight, seriously consider cancellation and baggage insurance.

14. **Look into courier flights.** They're usually unavailable on domestic flights, but it's worth checking into if you're committed to flying for as little as humanly possible. Companies that hire couriers use your luggage allowance for their business baggage; in return, you get a deeply discounted ticket. Flights are often offered at the last minute, and you might have to arrange a pre-trip interview to make sure you're right for the job. **Now Voyager** (☎ **212/431-1616;** www.nowvoyagertravel.com) sometimes has cross-country flights for as little as $199 round-trip. They also offer non-courier fares at discounts of 15% to 30%, so call the company even if you don't want to fly as a courier.

## OTHER TRANSPORTATION OPTIONS

15. **Consider taking a train or bus instead of flying.** Traveling by train or bus is usually considerably cheaper than flying. More importantly, it saves you money upon arrival and departure because you'll come right into and leave right out of Manhattan (where you want to be) without the additional cost of airport transfers. If you're as close to New York as Boston, Philly, or Washington D.C., these alternate methods can also save time, too, now that Amtrak has switched all its old Metroliner trains to the new high-speed Acela trains. Keep in mind, though, that the cheapest transportation method, the bus, can eat up a lot of time and be pretty uncomfortable.

16. **Have a flexible schedule when booking train travel, and always ask for the lowest fare.** When you're offered a fare, always ask if you can do better by traveling at different times or days. You can often save money by traveling at off-peak hours and on weekends. And don't forget to ask for discounts for kids, seniors, passengers with disabilities, military personnel, or anything else that you think might qualify you for a lower fare.

17. **Keep an eye out for fare sales.** Go to the "Schedules & Fares" page at **www.amtrak.com** and click on RAIL SALE or WEEKLY WEB DEALS, where you'll find discounts of up to 90% on select routes. If you register your e-mail address, you'll be notified of sale fares as they happen. Keep in mind, though, that if you buy a rail sale ticket, it is not refundable and cannot be exchanged.

Greyhound advertises fare sales right on its home page at **www.greyhound.com**. This national bus line usually has a number of money-saving deals, ranging from "Friends and Family Ride Free" companion deals to "Go Anywhere" fares for as little as $69.

18. **Make reservations as soon as possible.** As with the airlines, discounts on buses and trains are often based on advanced purchase. Book ahead, and you're bound to do better.

## GETTING AROUND NEW YORK CITY

19. **Don't rent a car.** Save your money; you don't need one. Driving is a nightmare and parking is ridiculously expensive (or near-to-impossible

in some neighborhoods). It's much easier to get around using public transportation.

20. **Take a bus or the subway from the airport.** You might have to allot a bit more time, but public transportation offers great savings over taxis and private car services. A shuttle bus connects JFK Airport to the A train, which whisks you right into the city for $1.50. The M60 bus comes into Manhattan from LaGuardia for the same bargain-basement price. From Newark, convenient and affordable buses can drop you off at various points around the city for around 10 bucks.

21. **Use the subway and bus to travel around the city.** The transit system is probably the city's best bargain. It's safe, relatively clean (the bus, anyway), quick, efficient, and very, very cheap. Use taxis only late at night, when trains and buses can be few and far between, or when traveling a short distance in a group of three or four, when the fare might be less than multiple subway or bus fares.

22. **Buy a MetroCard.** With the MetroCard, you can enjoy free transfers between bus and subway for 2 hours. And you can save even more money if you evaluate how you're going to use your MetroCard: If you're going to be in the city for a few days, or you're traveling in a group (up to four people can use a MetroCard at any given time), buy a $15 pay-per-ride MetroCard, which will get you 11 rides for the price of 10. If you're going to do a lot of running around the city, consider a $4 daily **Fun Pass** or a $17 **7-Day MetroCard,** each of which allows unlimited rides for the life of the card. There's one strong caveat, however: Every person has to have his or her own unlimited-use MetroCard; you can't double-up as you can with pay-per-ride MetroCards.

23. **In the daytime, walk.** No other American city is more welcoming or so rewarding to explore on foot. Walking will save you a bunch of money— and work off all the fab meals you'll no doubt buy with the savings.

## ACCOMMODATIONS

24. **Stay Uptown or Downtown.** The advantages of a midtown location are highly overrated, especially when saving money is your object. Manhattan is a petite island, and the subway can whisk you anywhere you want to go in minutes; even if you stay way Uptown, you can be at the ferry launch for the Statue of Liberty inside a half-hour. You'll get the best value for your money by staying outside the Theater District, in the residential neighborhoods where real New Yorkers live, such as Greenwich Village, Chelsea, Murray Hill, or—my absolute favorite neighborhood for space-seekers and bargain hunters—the Upper West Side. These are the neighborhoods where real New Yorkers hang out, too, so you won't want for good eats, nightlife, or good old Big Apple bustle. Or hoof it to the Financial District for big discounts on weekend stays (see tip no. 25 below).

25. **Visit over a weekend.** If your trip includes a weekend, you might be able to save big. Business hotels tend to empty out, and rooms that go for $300 or more Monday through Thursday can drop dramatically, to as low as $150 or less, once the midlevel execs have headed home. These deals are especially prevalent in the Financial District, but they're often available even in tourist-friendly Midtown. They're frequently advertised on hotel Web sites, or just ask when you call. See "Dealmaking with the Chains" in chapter 5 for tips on where to check.

26. **Watch for advertised discounts.** Scan ads in the Travel section of your local Sunday paper, which can be an excellent source for up-to-the-minute hotel deals. Also check the back of the Travel section of the Sunday *New York Times*, where the best weekend deals and other hotel bargains are usually listed.

27. **Don't be afraid to bargain.** Always ask for a lower price than the first one quoted. Most rack rates include commissions of 10% to 25% or more for travel agents, which many hotels will cut if you make your own reservations and haggle a bit. Ask politely whether a less-expensive room is available than the first one mentioned or whether any special rates apply to you. You might qualify for corporate, student, military, senior citizen, or other discounts. Mention membership in AAA, AARP, frequent-flyer programs, corporate or military organizations, or trade unions, which might entitle you to special deals as well. The big chains, such as Best Western and Comfort Inn, tend to be good about trying to save you money, but reservation agents often won't volunteer the information; you have to pull it out of them.

28. **Dial direct.** When booking a room in a chain hotel, call the hotel's local line, as well as the toll-free number, and see where you get the best deal. The clerk who runs the place is more likely to know about booking patterns and will often grant deep discounts in order to fill up.

29. **Call a travel agent.** Certain hotels give travel agents discounts in exchange for steering business their way, so if you're shy about bargaining, an agent might be better equipped to negotiate discounts for you.

30. **Shop online.** New York hotels often offer "Internet-only" deals that can save you 10% to 20% over what you'd pay if you booked by telephone. Also, hotels often advertise all of their available weekend and other package deals on their Web sites. In addition, some of the discount reservations agencies (see below) have sights that allow you to book online. And consider joining the **Playbill Online Theater Club** (**www.playbillclub.com**), a free service that offers some excellent members-only rates at select city hotels in addition to discounts on theater tickets. Theatre.com's free **Broadway Circle Club** (**www.theatre.com**) offers similar discounts to its members.

31. **Investigate reservation services.** These outfits usually work as consolidators, buying up or reserving rooms in bulk and then dealing them out to customers at a profit. They do garner special deals that range from 10% to 50% off; but remember, these discounts apply to rack rates, inflated prices that people rarely end up paying. You're probably better off dealing directly with a hotel, but if you don't like bargaining, this is certainly a viable option. Most of them offer online reservation services as well. A few of the more reputable providers are **Accommodations Express** (☎ 800/906-4685; www.accommodationsxpress.com) and **Hotel Reservations Network** (☎ 800/715-7666; www.180096HOTEL.com). Another good bet is **Hotel ConXions** (☎ 800/522-9991 or 212/ 840-8686; www.hotelconxions.com), a consolidator that handles hotels in only a few select destinations, including New York. Not only can they check pricing and availability on a number of hotels with just one phone call, they can also save you up to 60% off rack rates. Also, because Hotel ConXions has guaranteed room blocks in select properties, they can often get you into a hotel that's otherwise sold out.

**Important tips:** Never just rely on a reservations service. Do a little homework; compare the rack rates to the discounted rates being offered by the service to see what kind of deal they're offering. That way you'll know whether you're actually being offered a substantial savings or they've just gussied up the rack rates to make their offer sound like a deal. And always check the rate a reservations service offers you with the rate you can get directly from the hotel, which can actually be better on occasion. If you're being offered a stay in a hotel I haven't recommended, do more research to learn about it, especially if it isn't a reliable brand name such as Holiday Inn or Best Western. It's not a deal if you end up at a dump.

32. **If you find a rate that seems a particularly good value, book it early.** If somebody quotes you an attractive rate, don't assume it'll be there waiting for you in a month, a week, or even a day from now. Occupancy rates have shot through the roof in New York these days, and everyone, like you, is on the lookout for a decent room rate. As hotels fill up and the number of empty rooms goes down, rates go up. You can even get burned at those hotels that don't jack up their rates according to demand, because hotels often have only a limited number of rooms in a particular price category, and the most affordable ones usually go first.

33. **If you find yourself without a room at the last minute, work it to your advantage.** I never recommend coming to town without reservations; you never know when a convention or some other event can hit town and fill up the city's hotels in a snap. But if you find yourself in the city without a room, you might be able to strike quite a bargain. As the hours progress, the hotel becomes more anxious to fill empty rooms and will lower the rate to get your business. I've seen desk clerks sell $179 rooms for $79 more than once. But remember—this is a risky way to go, because if the hotel is full, you're out of luck.

34. **Be willing to share a bathroom.** For the best bargains in town, do as the Europeans do: Share a hall bathroom with your fellow travelers. Usually there are two or three bathrooms to a floor, often with separate rooms for the toilet and the shower and/or tub so all the facilities aren't tied up at once. If you can wrap your mind around this idea—it's not much different from sharing with your siblings when you were a kid—you can get a lot of bang for your buck. If you're on a tight budget, you'll be able to stay at a much nicer hotel than if you insist on a private bathroom. Many rooms even have private sinks, which means you can brush your teeth or wash your face without leaving the room. A couple of very good bargain-rate places, the Chelsea Lodge and the Chelsea Pines Inn, have private in-room showers, so the only thing you have to share is the toilet.

35. **Consider a suite.** It sounds like the ultimate splurge, but if you're traveling with another couple or your family, a suite can be a terrific bargain. They're always cheaper than two hotel rooms. The living room almost always features a sofa bed, and there's often a kitchenette where you can save money by preparing coffee and light meals for yourself. Remember that some places charge for extra guests beyond two; some don't.

36. **If you're traveling with the kids, stay at a hotel that lets them stay for free.** Most hotels add a surcharge to the nightly rate—anywhere from $10 to $25 per night—for each extra person beyond two sharing a hotel room. Ten bucks might seem like a drop in the bucket, but it can really add up. So if you're traveling with the kids, choose a hotel that lets them stay free. Age limits for free kid stays can range from 10 to 18, so you might even be able to have your teens stay with you for free. Even if the hotel usually charges for kids, it might be willing to drop this extra charge to draw you in, so always ask.

37. **Look into group or long-stay discounts.** If you come as part of a large group, you should be able to negotiate a bargain, because the hotel can then guarantee occupancy in a number of rooms. If you're planning a long stay in town (usually 5 to 7 days or more), you might qualify for a discount, so be sure to ask.

38. **If you're on a shoestring budget, book a hostel bed.** You'll have no privacy whatsoever—you'll share a room with fellow travelers from all over the world and all facilities are common—but there's no arguing with the rate. The largest hostel in the **Hostelling International–American Youth Hostels** system houses travelers in bunk-bedded rooms for $22 to $27 per person, per night. You'll save about $3 a night if you become an AYH member, which is worth looking into if you're coming to the city for an extended stay or if you plan on doing other hostel-based traveling around the world. Also consider the dorms at the better-located **Gershwin Hotel,** the **Chelsea Star,** the **Chelsea International Hostel,** the **Big Apple Hostel,** the **Aladdin Hotel,** Harlem's **Park View Hostel,** and the **Central Park Hostel & Inn.**

39. **Try the Y.** The Y isn't nearly as cheap as hostel living, but the facilities are much better. The **YMCA of Greater New York** (☎ 212/630-9600; www.ymcanyc.org) has eight residences for travelers throughout the city's five boroughs. You'll have a private room (some have private bathrooms) and access to the on-site fitness center—many feature extensive state-of-the-art equipment, pools, and a full slate of exercise classes—for absolutely free. The atmosphere is usually on the quiet side, because the Y is popular with families, older travelers, and singles. A number of Ys also feature a calendar of cultural and other events, which fosters a warm community spirit. The main Manhattan branches, all of which are extremely well located, are reviewed in chapter 5; always book as far in advance as possible, as these Ys are extremely popular. For complete information on other New York–area locations, visit the Y's Web site and click on RESIDENCES & RESERVATIONS.

40. **Do as little business as possible through the hotel.** Any service the hotel offers will come with a stiff premium. You can easily find dry cleaners or other services in most areas of Manhattan. Find out before you dial whether your hotel imposes a surcharge on local or long-distance calls; it might be cheaper to use the pay phone in the lobby instead.

41. **If you're driving into the city and will need to garage your car, check parking rates with the hotel before you book.** Many hotels negotiate discounted parking rates at nearby garages. Choose a hotel that has negotiated a good rate, or you might end up paying a fortune for parking (thereby negating any savings you've earned by booking a cheap hotel). For more on this subject, see "Deals for Visitors with Wheels: Cheap Parking Tips" in chapter 4.

## DINING

42. **Book a hotel room with a kitchenette.** Booking a room with a kitchenette allows you to grocery shop and eat some meals in. Even if you only use it to prepare breakfast, you're bound to save money on food this way.

43. **Stay at a hotel, guest house, or bed-and-breakfast that includes breakfast in the rate.** However, be sure to confirm that it's included before you book, because some city guest houses keep rates down by not offering breakfast. If breakfast is offered, ask what's included, especially if

# Homestay Sweet Homestay

New York apartment stays or homestays can be a great way to go for budget-minded travelers. They usually fall on the lower end of the price continuum and can range from spartan to splendid, and from a hosted bedroom in a private home to an unhosted, fully equipped apartment with multiple bedrooms. No matter what, you can pretty much guarantee that you'll get more for your money than if you book a regular hotel room.

The city's best-kept accommodations secret is ❂ **Homestay New York** (☎ and fax **718/434-2071;** www.homestayny.com). Lovely owner Helayne Wagner can book you into a private room with a New York City family (including her own) that regularly welcomes travelers into their well-kept home. Homes are in very nice residential neighborhoods in Brooklyn, Queens, or the Harlem section of Manhattan, but all are within a half-hour of Midtown or Downtown via subway or bus, and most are beautifully restored 19th- and early 20th-century houses. Not only can this option save you a lot of money, but it can be fun, too: Visitors are matched to hosts by age, interests, and occupation, and the carefully chosen hosts are more than happy to provide advice and assistance. This is a terrific option for adventurous travelers who want to see more of the city, and how real New Yorkers live, than the regular tourist neighborhoods will show you.

Rates run $90 to $135 single or double, with shared or private bathroom depending on the home. Most rooms have TV, air-conditioning, and a small fridge, and towels are provided. Breakfast is included daily; the price also includes a welcome dinner, plus a farewell dinner if your stay lasts 5 or more days. Also included are free MetroCards and phone cards (values depend on the length of your stay), plus a CityPass for those staying a week or more (see tip no. 51). With all these extras included,

you're used to starting the day with a hearty meal; the offerings will most likely be a limited continental breakfast.

44. **Use any coupons you can get your hands on.** The New York Convention & Visitors Bureau offers a free visitor's guide that includes discount coupons in the back. Even if you order one in advance (see "Visitor Information," below), stop into the local visitor centers while you're in town, where the wall racks sometimes have coupons and advertisements for freebies, two-for-ones, and other dining discounts. And before you leave home, check the deals offered through the **Playbill Online Theater Club** (**www.playbillclub.com**), which often include a few dining discounts; see tip no. 57 below for further details. If you use a dining discount coupon, remember to tip your waiter based on the full value of the meal; he's on a budget, too.

45. **Eat ethnic.** New York has what's probably the best collection of ethnic restaurants in the country, and the best of them offer first-class eats for low, low prices. Chinatown is always a good bet for top-quality meals for a pittance, as are the restaurants lining East Sixth Street east of Second Avenue, known as Little India. Jewish delis are first-rate in Manhattan—and the pile of pastrami can keep you well-fueled for days. New York's

Homestay New York adds up to an excellent value. What's more, tax is included, which saves you an additional 13.25% plus $2 per night over what you'd pay in a hotel. Helayne even has access to theater discounts that you can't get on your own. A 3-night minimum is requested, and no credit cards are accepted. Children 3 and over are welcome.

Additionally, these agencies can book you into a B&B room (hosted or unhosted) or an unhosted private apartment: **Manhattan Getaways** (☎ 212/956-2010; www.manhattangetaways.com) has personally inspected apartments starting at $100 a night, with a 3-night minimum stay. **Manhattan Lodgings** (☎ 212/677-7616; www.manhattanlodgings. com), also provides B&B stays and private apartments for stays lasting 3 days to 3 months, with rates starting at $90. **New York Habitat** (☎ 212/255-8018; www.nyhabitat.com), is a real estate brokerage that offers short-term apartment rentals (minimum stay 4 nights) as well as B&B stays (2-night minimum) for as low as $85 a night; accommodations are mostly in Manhattan, but some apartments are available in nice outer-borough neighborhoods, too.

*A few words of warning:* If you go this route, keep in mind that you won't have the amenities that a hotel—even a budget hotel—can usually offer, such as maid service and tour planning. In fact, many accommodations called "B&Bs" don't even offer breakfast, so be sure to ask. You'll have a host on hand to offer personal assistance if you book through Homestay New York, but otherwise you can count on being on your own. I've received complaints about agencies that offer one thing and deliver another, so get all promises in writing and an exact total up front. Try to pay entirely by credit card if possible, so you can dispute payment if the agency fails to live up to its promises.

excellent selection of pizza parlors serves up dining bargains by the slice all over town.

46. **During warm weather, picnic.** New York is full of marvelous delicatessens, greenmarkets, and gourmet groceries where you can assemble a delicious, affordable meal—almost always one much finer than you'd get for the same price at a restaurant. The city is full of small parks that serve as great picnic spots, such as Battery Park, Bryant Park, and Union Square—and don't forget Central Park, where a picnic just doesn't get any better on a nice day. If you don't feel like going through the hassle of assembling a picnic at a grocery, try take-out, which will save you the cost of the tip you'd leave if you ate in.

47. **Eat street food.** Although dirty-water hot dogs and soft pretzels still have their appeal, New York's street-food offerings have expanded considerably in recent years. You'll find vendors on street corners all over the city hawking gourmet soups, gyros, falafels, freshly baked potatoes with a variety of toppings, fresh fruit, and much more. The best vendors congregate in high-end business districts, such as around Rockefeller Center in Midtown (vendors often line up just off Sixth Avenue; 50th Street is a hot corner) and in the Financial District (the 1-block park bordered by

Broadway, Church, Liberty, and Cedar streets is a hub of good, cheap eats). Sixth Avenue is lined with open plazas where you can enjoy your alfresco lunch, and Lower Manhattan offers a wealth of even more pleasant open spaces.

48. **Fill up at lunch, when prices are generally lower.** Eating your main meal at midday and following up with a lighter dinner can save you money. Lunch prices are usually lower, and at many restaurants you'll get the same size portions you'd get at dinner anyway. This is especially good advice if you plan on splurging on a pricey meal, because fancier restaurants are often a much better bargain at lunch—especially if they offer a multi-course prix-fixe deal, which many do.

49. **Order the prix-fixe special.** Fixed-price specials that include appetizers, side dishes, and dessert (as well as beverages in some cases) will almost always get you more bang for your dining buck. Also consider all-you-can-eat deals, such as the terrific Indian lunchtime buffet at Salaam Bombay (see chapter 6).

50. **Bring your own wine.** This is a great way to save on huge wine markups. Some restaurants, even those with their own wine lists, will let you bring your own bottle if you just call and ask. At press time, places that are BYOB as policy include **Kitchenette,** the **Zen Palate** in Union Square, **Tartine, Afghan Kebab House,** and just about any restaurant in Little India; all of these places are happy to open your bottle and provide glasses. However, *always* call and ask permission in advance; never just show up with your own bottle. (The only exception to this rule is Little India, where you can just arrive with a bottle or a six-pack and ask at the door.) If the answer is "no," be gracious and accept it without argument. If the answer is "yes," be sure to ask whether a corkage fee is charged so there's no unpleasant surprise at bill time. See chapter 8 for tips on shops with good values on wine.

## SIGHTSEEING

51. **Buy a CityPass.** Pay one price ($31.75) for admission to six top attractions—the Top of the World observation deck at the World Trade Center, the American Museum of Natural History, the Solomon R. Guggenheim Museum, the Museum of Modern Art, the Empire State Building, and the *Intrepid* Sea-Air-Space Museum—which would cost you fully twice as much if you paid for each one separately. More importantly, CityPass is not a coupon book; it contains actual admission tickets, so you can bypass lengthy ticket lines. CityPass is good for 9 days from the first time you use it. It's sold at all participating attractions, and discounted rates are available for kids and seniors. If you want to avoid that first line, order your CityPass online at **www.citypass.net** or www.ticketweb.com. For phone orders, call TicketWeb at ☎ **212/269-4TIX.** Call CityPass at ☎ **707/256-0490** for further details.

52. **Take advantage of freebies.** You'll be surprised to discover how many there are to be had. Many of the best things to do and see in Manhattan are absolutely free, from walking the Brooklyn Bridge to riding the Staten Island Ferry to exploring Central Park to attending TV show tapings. Additionally, a number of organizations now offer neighborhood walking tours at absolutely no charge. And many museums and attractions that charge admission have free or pay-as-you-wish programs one day or evening a week. See these boxes in chapter 7: "Cheap Thrills: What to See

& Do for Free"; "Show Me, Show Me, Show Me: Free Walking Tours"; and "Free Culture at Big Apple Museums."

## SHOPPING

53. **Ship major purchases home.** If you're buying high-ticket items, you can often save on the exorbitant New York sales tax by having items shipped home. Depending on the laws of your state, you can pay a lesser tax or skip the duty completely.

54. **Seek out sample sales.** Garment designers and manufacturers often sell off their newest items (sometimes not even available in the store yet) for a song to raise quick cash; see "Scouring the Sample Sales" in chapter 8.

55. **Do your homework and bargain on electronic equipment.** You'll also notice a wealth of electronics stores throughout the Theater District, many suspiciously trumpeting GOING OUT OF BUSINESS sales. These guys have been going out of business since the Stone Age. That's the bait and switch; pretty soon you've spent too much money for not enough stereo. If you want to check out what they have to offer, go in knowing what going prices are on that PDA or digital camera you're interested in. You can make a good deal if you know exactly what the market is, but these guys will be happy to suck you dry given half a chance. Trust me on this: The only way you'll do well is if you know your stuff. And play hard to get; I've seen prices tumble precipitously the closer I got to the door.

56. **Always ask for a better price on anything used or vintage.** It won't always work, but a lot of vintage, antique, and collectibles dealers—even those with nice shops in high-rent districts such as SoHo and the Village—will drop their price if you're just savvy enough to ask. Always be polite, however, and don't push if you're told "no."

## PERFORMING ARTS & NIGHTLIFE

57. **Buy discounted theater tickets in advance through Playbill Online.** Joining Playbill's Online Theater Club (**www.playbillclub.com**) can yield substantial savings on theater tickets for select Broadway and off-Broadway shows. Becoming a member is free; all you have to do is register, and you'll have access to discounts that can range from a few dollars to as much as 45% off regular ticket prices. The club also offers its members excellent deals at some very nice hotels as well as a few dining discounts on occasion, and they'll even send you regular e-mail updates as the offers change. Other sites that offer similar services are **Theater-Mania** (**www.theatermania.com**), **Theatre.com's** Broadway Circle Club (**www.theatre.com**), and **Broadway.com** (**www.broadway.com**).

58. **Buy discounted same-day theater tickets at the TKTS booth.** If your heart is set on seeing a particular show, you should buy full-price advance tickets before you come to the city. But if you're flexible about what you see, check out TKTS, which sells day-of-show tickets to popular plays both on and off-Broadway for 25% to 50% off face value. See "Top Ticket-Buying Tips" in chapter 9.

59. **Take advantage of freebies.** Summertime is a great time to be in the city if you're a culture buff. Some of the city's top cultural organizations offer free outdoor events, from Shakespeare in the Park to the Metropolitan Opera. See "Park It! Shakespeare, Music & Other Free Fun" in chapter 9. But you don't have to wait until summer to enjoy yourself for free: Comb the listings in *Time Out New York, New York* magazine, the *New Yorker,*

and *The New York Times* for listings of free performances throughout the city, which can range from free dance performances to book lectures at Barnes & Noble. If you want to do some research before you arrive, hop online; see the "Planning Your Trip: An Online Directory" immediately following this chapter for useful cyber-sources.

60. **Eschew high-priced, high-profile performances for lesser-known, lower-priced surprises.** Sure, attending a performance at the New York Philharmonic or a big-name Broadway extravaganza is a must if you can afford it. But you'll save money—and maybe even enjoy yourself more—by looking beyond the obvious to lower-profile options. For instance, the nation's top music education institution, the **Julliard School,** offers a full slate of free and cheap events, from first-rate student concerts to lectures by visiting celebrities of the performing-arts world. Smaller venues such as **Bargemusic,** the **92nd Street Y,** and the **Amato Opera Theatre** offer more intimate, only-in–New York performances, sometimes by nationally known artists, at rock-bottom prices. Off- and off-off-Broadway theater is usually significantly less expensive than the shows offered on the Great White Way, and the quality doesn't have to suffer one bit.

## 2 Visitor Information

For information before you leave home, your best source (besides this book, of course) is NYC & Company, the organization behind the **New York Convention & Visitors Bureau** (NYCVB), 810 Seventh Ave., New York, NY 10019. You can call ☎ **800/NYC-VISIT** or 212/397-8222 to order the **Official NYC Visitor Kit,** detailing hotels, restaurants, theaters, attractions, events, and more. It costs $5.95 to receive the packet (payable by credit card) in 7 to 10 days, $9.95 for rush delivery (3 to 4 business days) to U.S. addresses and international orders. You can also order the guide that's the heart of the kit for free on the bureau's Web site, **www.nycvisit.com.** The Web site itself is also a terrific source of information. To speak to a travel counselor who can answer specific questions, call ☎ **212/484-1222.**

For visitor center and information desk locations once you arrive, see "Visitor Information" in chapter 4.

**FOR U.K. VISITORS** There is an **NYCVB Visitor Information Center** at 33–34 Carnaby St, London W1V 1PA (☎ **0207/437-8300**). You can order the Official NYC Visitor Guide by sending an A5-size self-addressed envelope and 52p postage to the above address. For New York–bound travelers in the London area, the center also offers free one-on-one travel-planning assistance.

### Site Seeing: The Big Apple on the Web

The NYCVB's official site, **www.nycvisit.com,** is an excellent online resource offering tons of information on the city, from trip-planning basics to tips on where to take the kids. Other privately run general-information sites also serve top-flight trip-planning tools, providing everything from a current calendar of events to the latest club schedules. The best of the bunch, by far, are **CitySearch** (**www.newyork.citysearch.com**); *The New York Times's* **New York Today** (**www.nytoday.com**); and the Web site from the legendary weekly **Village Voice** (**www.villagevoice.com**). For more details on these and other useful Web sites, see p. 46 in "Planning Your Trip: An Online Directory."

# 3 Money

You never have to carry too much cash in New York, and although the city's pretty safe these days, it's best not to overstuff your wallet. Credit cards and travelers checks are accepted almost everywhere—plastic is even accepted in the subway system now—and ATMs are almost always on hand in case you need the green stuff. Still, always make sure you have at least $20 in taxi fare on hand. And note that cash only is accepted at many of New York's most affordable restaurants.

## ATMS

Almost all New York City ATMs are linked to a national network that most likely includes your bank at home. **Cirrus** (☎ **800/424-7787;** www.mastercard.com/atm) and **Plus** (☎ **800/843-7587;** www.visa.com/atms) are the two most popular networks; check the back of your ATM card to see which network your bank belongs to (most banks belong to both these days). The city's biggest ATM networks belong to Citibank, Chase, Fleet, and HSBC banks, which belong to both networks.

In the most popular Manhattan neighborhoods, there's a bank with ATMs on every other corner or so. The only places you might have some difficulty in are more far-flung neighborhoods, such as the far East Village or far uptown in Harlem. If you don't easily spot an ATM, use the 800 numbers to locate one in your location.

New York's Consumer Affairs chief has tried to ward off additional ATM charges for consumers, but it has proven to be a losing battle. Expect to pay $1 to $2 each time you withdraw money from an ATM, in addition to what your home bank charges. Try to stay away from commercial machines, such as those in hotel lobbies and corner delis, which often charge $3 or more per transaction.

## TRAVELER'S CHECKS

Traveler's checks are something of an anachronism from the days before the ATM made cash accessible at any time. These days, they seem less necessary because 24-hour ATMs allow you to withdraw as needed. But New York is an expensive city, capable of sucking money right out of your pocket. If you're withdrawing money every day, you can really rack up those withdrawal charges, so you might be better off with traveler's checks—provided you don't mind showing identification every time you want to cash one.

You can get traveler's checks at almost any bank. **American Express** offers checks in denominations of $10, $20, $50, $100, $500, and $1,000. You'll pay a service charge ranging from 1% to 4%. You can get American Express traveler's checks over the phone by calling ☎ **800/221-7282** or 800/721-9768; you can also purchase checks online at **www.americanexpress.com**. AmEx gold or platinum cardholders can avoid paying the fee by ordering over the telephone;

### Safety Tip

Avoid poorly lit or out-of-the-way ATMs, especially at night. Use an indoor machine or one at a well-trafficked, well-lit location. Put your money away discreetly; don't flash it around or count it in a way that could attract the attention of thieves.

platinum cardholders can also purchase checks fee-free in person at AmEx Travel Service locations (check the Web site for the office nearest you). American Automobile Association members can obtain checks fee-free at most AAA offices.

**Visa** offers traveler's checks at Citibank branches and other financial institutions nationwide; call ☎ **800/227-6811** to locate the purchase location near you. **MasterCard** also offers traveler's checks through **Thomas Cook Currency Services**; call ☎ **800/223-9920** for a location near you.

If you carry traveler's checks, be sure to keep a record of their serial numbers (separately from the checks, of course), so you're ensured a refund in case they're lost or stolen.

## CREDIT CARDS

Credit cards are the way to pay in New York. They're a safe way to carry money and keep track of your expenses. **American Express, MasterCard,** and **Visa** are accepted virtually everywhere in New York. **Carte Blanche** and **Diner's Club** have made quite a comeback, especially in hotel circles, and **Discover** is also quite popular (although don't count on it being accepted everywhere). Because New York has such a heavy influx of international visitors, cards such as **enRoute, Eurocard,** and **JCB** are also widely accepted, particularly at hotels.

Still, be sure to keep some cash on hand for small expenses, such as cab rides, or for that rare occasion when a restaurant or small shop doesn't take plastic, which can happen if you're dining at a neighborhood joint or buying from a small vendor.

**THEFT**  Almost every credit card company has an emergency 800 number you can call if your wallet or purse is stolen. They might be able to wire you a cash advance off your credit card immediately, and in many places, they can deliver an emergency credit card in a day or two. **Visa's** U.S. emergency number is ☎ **800/847-2911. American Express** cardholders should call ☎ **800/233-5432** to report a lost card, but traveler's check holders should call ☎ **800/221-7282** if they have a money emergency. **MasterCard** holders should call ☎ **800/307-7309.**

Odds are that if your wallet is gone, the police won't be able to recover it for you. However, after you realize that it's gone and you cancel your credit cards, it's still worth informing the authorities. Your credit-card company or insurer might require a police report number.

## 4 When to Go

Summer or winter, rain or shine, New York City always has great things going on, so there's no real "best" time to go.

**MONEY MATTERS**  If money is your biggest concern, you might want to visit in winter, between the first of the year and early April. Sure, the weather can suck, but hotels are suffering from the post-holiday blues, and rooms often go for a relative song. In the winter of 2000, rooms at the truly comfortable Comfort Inn Midtown were going for as little as $79.

Spring and autumn are the busiest, and most expensive, seasons after holiday time. Don't expect hotels to be handing you deals, but you might be able to negotiate a good rate. Spring is generally easier than fall; many hotels consider their peak season to be the last four months of the year.

New York's spit-shined image means that the city is drawing more families these days, and they usually visit in the summer. Still, the prospect of heat and humidity keeps some people away, making July and the first half of August a significantly cheaper time to visit than later in the year, and good hotel deals are often available.

Christmas is not a good time for budget-minded travelers. If you come, expect to pay top dollar for everything. The first two weeks of December—the shopping weeks—are the absolute worst when it comes to scoring an affordable hotel room; that's when shoppers from around the world converge on the town to catch the holiday spirit and spend, spend, spend. Hotel prices go sky high throughout December, and the crowds are almost intolerable. If you'd rather have more of the city to yourself, with better chances at discount Broadway show tickets and easier access to museums and other attractions, you'll be happier visiting at another time of year.

But Thanksgiving can be a great time to visit, believe it or not: Business travelers have gone home for the holiday, and the holiday shoppers haven't yet arrived. It's a little-known secret that most hotels away from the Thanksgiving Day Parade route have empty rooms sitting, and they're usually willing to make great deals to fill them.

**WEATHER**    The worst weather in New York is during that long week or 10 days that arrives each summer between mid-July and mid-August, when temperatures go up to around 100°F with 90% humidity. You feel sticky all day, the streets smell horrible, everyone's cranky, and the concrete canyons become furnaces. It can be no fun walking around in this weather. Don't get put off by this—summer has its compensations, such as wonderful free open-air concerts and other events, as I've already mentioned—but bear it in mind. And you might luck out, as the last few summers have been downright lovely. But if you are at all temperature sensitive, your odds of getting comfortable weather are better in June or September.

Another period when you might not like to stroll around the city is during January or February, when temperatures are commonly in the 20s (–6°C) and those concrete canyons turn into wind tunnels. The city looks gorgeous just after a snowfall, but the streets soon become an ugly, slushy mess. Again, you never know; temperatures have regularly been in the 30s and mild 40s during the past few winters. If you hit the weather jackpot, you could have a bargain bonanza (see "Money Matters" above).

Fall and spring are the best times in New York (which is why they're the most expensive seasons to be here). From April to June and September to November, temperatures are mild and pleasant, and the light is beautiful. With the leaves changing in Central Park and just the hint of crispness in the air, October is fabulous—but expect to pay for the privilege of being here.

If you want to know how to pack just before you go, check the Weather Channel's online 5-day forecast at **www.weather.com** or CNN's 4-day forecast at **www.cnn.com/weather**. If you're not Net-savvy, you can also call the Weather Channel's hot line for the week's forecast at ☎ **900/WEATHER** but beware that the call costs 95¢ per minute. You can also hear today's and tomorrow's forecast by calling ☎ **212/976-1212.**

### New York's Average Temperature & Rainfall

|  | Jan | Feb | Mar | Apr | May | June | July | Aug | Sept | Oct | Nov | Dec |
|---|---|---|---|---|---|---|---|---|---|---|---|---|
| Daily Temp. (°F) | 38 | 40 | 48 | 61 | 71 | 80 | 85 | 84 | 77 | 67 | 54 | 42 |
| Daily Temp. (°C) | 3 | 4 | 9 | 16 | 22 | 27 | 29 | 29 | 25 | 19 | 12 | 6 |
| Days of Precipitation | 11 | 10 | 11 | 11 | 11 | 10 | 11 | 10 | 8 | 8 | 9 | 10 |

# New York City Calendar of Events

As with any schedule of events, the following information is always subject to change. Always confirm information before you make plans around an event. Call the venue or the NYCVB at ☎ **212/484-1222,** go to **www.nycvisit.com** or **www.newyork.citysearch.com**, or pick up a copy of *Time Out New York* once you arrive in the city for the latest details on these or other events taking place during your visit.

## January

- **Chinese New Year.** Every year Chinatown rings in its own New Year (based on a lunar calendar) with two weeks of celebrations, including parades with dragon and lion dancers, vivid costumes of all kinds, and fireworks (although the city has been cracking down on using fireworks in recent years). The year 2001 (4699 in the Chinese designation) is the Year of the Snake, and the Chinese New Year falls on January 24. Call the NYCVB hot line at ☎ **212/484-1222** or the Chinese Center at 212/ 373-1800.

- **Restaurant Week.** Look for the new winter version of the favorite summer event, which allows you to lunch for only $20 at some of New York's finest restaurants—a coup for gourmet-minded bargain-hunters. Call ☎ **212/484-1222** or check **www.restaurantweek.com** to see whether the winter event is repeated in 2001. *Reserve instantly.* Late January or early February.

## February

- ✪ **Westminster Kennel Club Dog Show.** The ultimate purebred pooch fest. Some 30,000 dog fanciers from the world over congregate at **Madison Square Garden** for the 125th "World Series of Dogdom." All 2,500 dogs are American Kennel Club Champions of Record, competing for the Best in Show trophy. Call ☎ **800/455-3647** or visit **www. westminsterkennelclub.org** for this year's exact dates (usually second or third weekend in February). Tickets become available after January 1 through **TicketMaster** (☎ **212/307-7171** or 212/ 307-1212; www.ticketmaster.com).

## March

- **St. Patrick's Day Parade.** More than 150,000 marchers join in the world's largest civilian parade, as Fifth Avenue from 44th to 86th streets rings with the sounds of bands and bagpipes, and an inordinate amount of beer is consumed (much of it green). The parade usually starts at 11am, but go extra-early if you want a good spot. Wear green and insist you're Irish if anyone asks; you are, at least for today. Call ☎ **212/ 484-1222.** March 17.

## April

- ✪ **The Easter Parade.** This isn't a traditional parade, per se: There are no marching bands, no baton twirlers, no protesters. Once upon a time, New York's gentry came out to show off their tasteful but discreet toppings. Today, if you were planning to slip on a tasteful little number— say something delicately woven in straw with a simple flower or two that matches your gloves—you will *not* be the grandest lady in this springtime hike along Fifth Avenue from 48th to 57th streets. It's more about flamboyant exhibitionism, with hats and costumes that get more outrageous every year—and anybody can join right in for free. The parade generally runs Easter Sunday from about 10am to 3 or 4pm. Call ☎ **212/ 484-1222.** April 15.

## May

- **Bike New York: The Great Five Boro Bike Tour.** The largest mass-participation cycling event in the United States attracts about 30,000 cyclists from all over the world. After a 42-mile ride through the five boroughs, finalists are greeted with a traditional New York–style celebration of food and music. Starting line is at Battery Park in Manhattan; the finish line is at Fort Wadsworth Naval Station on Staten Island. Call ☎ **212/ 932-BIKE** or visit **www.bikenewyork.org** to register. First or second Sunday in May.

- **Ninth Avenue International Food Festival.** Cancel dinner reservations and spend the day sampling sizzling Italian sausages, homemade pierogi, spicy curries, and an assortment of other ethnic dishes. Street musicians, bands, and vendors add to the festive atmosphere at one of the city's best street fairs, stretching along Ninth Avenue from 37th to 57th streets. Call ☎ **212/581-7217.** One weekend in mid-May.

- ✪ **Fleet Week.** About 10,000 Navy and Coast Guard personnel are "at liberty" in New York for the annual Fleet Week at the end of May. Usually from 1 to 4pm daily, you can visit the ships and aircraft carriers as they dock in at the piers on the west side of Manhattan and watch some dramatic exhibitions by the U.S. Marines. The whole celebration is hosted by the *Intrepid* Sea-Air-Space Museum, and kids love it. But even if you don't take in any of the events, you'll know it's Fleet Week, because those 10,000 sailors invade Midtown in their starched white uniforms. It's simply wonderful—just like *On the Town* come to life. Call ☎ **212/ 245-0072**, or visit **www.uss-intrepid.com**. Late May.

- **Washington Square Outdoor Art Exhibition.** This Greenwich Village tradition, in its 69th year, features the works of 250 artists displayed on 20 blocks in and around Washington Square Park. Call ☎ **212/982-6255.** Usually Memorial Day weekend and the following weekend and again in September.

## June

- ✪ **Museum Mile Festival.** Fifth Avenue from 82nd to 102nd streets is closed to cars from 6 to 9pm as 20,000-plus strollers enjoy live music from Broadway tunes to string quartets, street entertainers from juggling to giant puppets, and free admission to nine Museum Mile institutions, including the Metropolitan Museum of Art and the Guggenheim. Visit **www.museummile.org** or call any of the participating institutions for details. Usually the second Tuesday in June (June 12 in 2001).

- ✪ **Lesbian and Gay Pride Week and March.** A week of cheerful happenings, from simple parties to major political fund-raisers, precedes a zany parade commemorating the Stonewall Riot of June 27, 1969, which for many marks the beginning of the gay liberation movement. Fifth Avenue goes wild as the gay/lesbian community celebrates with bands, marching groups, floats, and plenty of panache. The parade starts on upper Fifth around 52nd Street and continues into the Village, where a street festival and a waterfront dance party with fireworks cap the day. Call ☎ **212/ 807-7433.** Mid- to late June.

- ✪ **SummerStage.** A summer-long festival of free or low-cost outdoor concerts in **Central Park,** featuring world music, pop, folk, and jazz artists ranging from Ziggy Marley to Yoko Ono to Morrissey. Call ☎ 212/360-2777 or visit **www.summerstage.com.** June through August.

✪ **Metropolitan Opera in the Parks.** Free evening performances are given in the city parks. Past performers have included Luciano Pavarotti and Kathleen Battle. Call ☎ 212/362-6000 or visit **www.metopera.org.** June through July.

✪ **Shakespeare in the Park.** The Delacorte Theater in **Central Park** is the setting for first-rate free performances under the stars—including at least one Shakespeare production each season—often with stars on the stage. For details, see "Park It! Shakespeare, Music & Other Free Fun" in chapter 9. Call ☎ 212/539-8750, or point your browser to **www.publictheater.org.** June through August.

• **Restaurant Week.** Lunch for only $20 at some of New York's finest restaurants. Participating places vary each year, so watch for the full-page ads in the *New York Times,* call the NYCVB at ☎ 212/484-1222, or check **www.restaurantweek.com** for the current schedule and list of participants, usually available by mid- or late May. *Reserve instantly.* One week in late June; some restaurants extend their offers through summer to Labor Day.

**July**

✪ **Independence Day Harbor Festival and Fourth of July Fireworks Spectacular.** Start the day amid the patriotic crowds at the Great July Fourth Festival in Lower Manhattan, watch the tall ships sail up the Hudson River in the afternoon. Then catch Macy's great fireworks extravaganza (one of the country's most fantastic) over the East River (the best vantage point is from the FDR Drive, which closes to traffic several hours before sunset). Call ☎ 212/484-1222 or Macy's Visitor Center at 212/494-2922. July 4.

• **Lincoln Center Festival 2001.** This festival celebrates the best of the performing arts from all over the world—theater, ballet, contemporary dance, opera, even puppet and media-based art. Schedules are usually available in mid-March, and tickets go on sale in late May or early June. Call ☎ 212/546-2656, or visit **www.lincolncenter.org.** July.

✪ **Midsummer Night's Swing.** Dancing duos head to the **Lincoln Center Fountain Plaza** for romantic evenings of big band swing, salsa, and tango under the stars to the sounds of top-flight bands. Dance lessons are offered with the purchase of a ticket. Call ☎ 212/875-5766, or visit **www.lincolncenter.org.** July and August.

• **Mostly Mozart.** World-renowned ensembles and soloists are featured at this month-long series at **Avery Fisher Hall.** Schedules are usually available in mid-April and tickets in early May. Call ☎ 212/875-5030 for information or 212/721-6500 to order tickets, or visit **www.lincolncenter.org/mostlymozart.** Late July through August.

**August**

✪ **Lincoln Center Out-of-Doors.** This series of free music and dance performances is held outdoors at **Lincoln Center.** Call ☎ 212/875-5108 or visit **www.lincolncenter.org** for this year's schedule (usually available in mid-July). August to September.

• **New York Fringe Festival.** Held in a variety of tiny Lower East Side venues for a mainly hipster crowd, this arts festival presents alternative as well as traditional theater, musicals, dance, comedy, and all manner of performance art, including new media. Literally hundreds of events are held at all hours over about 10 days in late August. The quality can vary wildly (a lot of performers use Fringe as a workshop to develop their acts and shows) and some performances really push the envelope, but you'd be surprised at how many shows are actually *good*. Call ☎ 888/FRINGENYC or 212/420-8777, or point your browser to www.fringenyc.org. Mid- to late August.

○ **U.S. Open Tennis Championships.** The final Grand Slam event of the tennis season is held at the slick new facilities at **Flushing Meadows Park** in Queens. Tickets go on sale in May or early June. The event sells out immediately, because many of the tickets are held by corporate sponsors who hand them out to customers. (It's worth it to check the list of sponsors to determine whether anyone you know has a connection for getting tickets.) You can usually scalp tickets outside the complex (an illegal practice, of course), which is right next to **Shea Stadium.** The last few matches of the tournament are most expensive, but you'll see a lot more tennis early on, when your ticket allows you to wander the outside courts and view several different matches. Call ☎ **888/OPEN-TIX** or 718/760-6200 well in advance; visit **www.usopen.org** or www.usta.com for additional information. Two weeks surrounding Labor Day.

• **Harlem Week.** The world's largest black and Hispanic cultural festival actually spans almost the whole month, including the Black Film Festival, the Harlem Jazz and Music Festival, and the Taste of Harlem Food Festival. Expect a full slate of music, from gospel to hip hop, and a lot of other festivities. Visit **www.harlemweek.com** or www.discoverharlem.com (where you'll find contact numbers relating to specific events) or call ☎ **212/484-1222** for this year's schedule of events and locations. Throughout August.

## September

• **West Indian–American Day Parade.** This annual Brooklyn event is New York's largest street celebration. Come for the extravagant costumes, pulsating rhythms (soca, calypso, reggae), bright colors, folklore, cheap food (jerk chicken, oxtail soup, Caribbean soul food), and 2 million hip-shaking revelers. The parade runs down Eastern Parkway in Brooklyn. Call ☎ **212/484-1222** or 718/625-1515. Labor Day.

○ **Wigstock.** Come see the Lady Bunny, Hedda Lettuce, Lypsinka, even RuPaul—plus hundreds of other fabulous drag queens—strut their stuff. The crowd is usually wilder than the stage acts. Wigstock outgrew its original East Village location and has been held on the pier at 11th Street on the Hudson River in recent years, but another move could be in the offing. For a preview, see Goldwyn's *Wigstock: The Movie.* For this year's information, point your Web browser to **www.wigstock.nu**, or call ☎ **800/494-TIXS** (www.boxofficetickets.com) or the Lesbian and Gay Community Services Center at ☎ 212/620-7310 (www.gaycenter.org). Labor Day weekend.

• **Washington Square Outdoor Art Exhibition.** The May event returns for Labor Day, when the works of 250 artists are displayed in and around Washington Square Park. Call ☎ **212/982-6255.** Labor Day weekend and the weekend after Labor Day.

○ **Broadway on Broadway.** This free afternoon show features the songs and casts from virtually every Broadway production performing on a stage erected in the middle of **Times Square.** Call ☎ **212/768-1560,** or visit **www.timessquarebid.org** and click on EVENTS. Early or mid-September.

- **Feast of San Gennaro.** An atmospheric Little Italy street fair honoring the patron saint of Naples, with great food, traditional music, carnival rides, games, and vendors set up along Mulberry Street north of Canal Street. Expect big crowds. And who knows? You might even spot a godfather or two. Call **212/768-9320** or visit **www.sangennaro.org** for this year's schedule. Usually 10 days in mid-September.

- **New York Film Festival.** Legendary hits *Pulp Fiction, The Sweet Hereafter,* and *Mean Streets* had their U.S. premieres at the Film Society of Lincoln Center's two-week festival, a major stop on the film fest circuit. Screenings are held in various **Lincoln Center** locations; advance tickets are a good bet always and a necessity for certain events (especially evening and weekend screenings). Call ☎ **212/875-5601,** or check out **www.filmlinc.com.** Two weeks from late September to early October.

- **BAM Next Wave Festival.** One of the city's most important cultural events takes place at the **Brooklyn Academy of Music.** The months-long festival showcases experimental new dance, theater, and music works by both renowned and lesser-known international artists. Recent celebrated performances have included Astor Piazzolla's *Maria de Buenos Aires* (featuring Piazzolla disciple Gidon Kremer) and the 25th anniversary of the Kronos Quartet. Call ☎ **718/636-4100** or visit **www.bam.org.** September through December.

## October

- **Ice-Skating.** Show off your skating style in the limelight at the diminutive **Rockefeller Center** rink (☎ **212/332-7654**), open from mid-October to mid-March (you'll skate under the magnificent Christmas tree for the month of December), or at the larger **Wollman Rink** in Central Park, at 59th Street and Sixth Avenue (☎ **212/396-1010**), which usually closes in early April.

- ✪ **Feast of St. Francis.** Animals from goldfish to elephants are blessed as thousands of Homo sapiens look on at the **Cathedral of St. John the Divine.** A magical experience; pets, of course, are welcome. A festive fair follows the blessing and music events. Buy tickets in advance, because they can be hard to come by. Call ☎ **212/316-7540** or 212/662-7133 for tickets, or visit **www.stjohndivine.org.** First Sunday in October.

- ✪ **Greenwich Village Halloween Parade.** This is Halloween at its most outrageous. You may have heard Lou Reed singing about it on his classic album *New York;* he wasn't exaggerating. Drag queens and assorted other flamboyant types parade through the village in wildly creative costumes. The parade route has changed over the years, but most recently it has started after sunset at Spring Street and marched up Sixth Avenue to 23rd Street or Union Square. Point your Web browser to **www.halloween-nyc.com** or check the papers for the exact route so you can watch—or participate, if you have the threads and the imagination. October 31.

## November

- ✪ **New York City Marathon.** Some 30,000 hopefuls from around the world participate in the largest U.S. marathon, and more than a million fans will cheer them on as they follow a route that touches on all five New York boroughs and finishes at Central Park. Call ☎ **212/860-4455,** or point your Web browser to **www.nyrrc.org.** November 5 in 2000; call for the 2001 date.

- **Radio City Music Hall Christmas Spectacular.** A rather gaudy extravaganza, but a lot of fun nonetheless. Starring the Radio City Rockettes and a cast that includes live camels. After undergoing an extensive restoration for most of 1999, spectacular Radio City itself is a sight to see. For information, call ☎ **212/247-4777** or visit **www.radiocity.com**; buy tickets at the box office or via TicketMaster's **Radio City Hotline** (☎ **212/307-1000**), or visit **www.ticketmaster.com**. Mid-November through early January.

○ **Macy's Thanksgiving Day Parade.** The procession from Central Park West and 77th Street and down Broadway to Herald Square at 34th Street continues to be a national tradition. Huge hot-air balloons in the forms of Rocky and Bullwinkle, Snoopy, the Pink Panther, Bart Simpson, and other cartoon favorites are the best part of the fun. The night before, you can usually see the big blow-up on Central Park West at 79th Street; call in advance to see whether it will be open to the public again this year. Call ☎ **212/484-1222** or Macy's Visitor Center at 212/494-2922. November 23 in 2000, November 22 in 2001.

○ **Big Apple Circus.** New York City's homegrown, not-for-profit circus is a favorite with children and everyone who's young at heart. Big Apple is committed to maintaining the classical circus tradition with sensitivity and only features animals that have a traditional working relationship with humans. A tent is pitched in **Damrosch Park** at **Lincoln Center.** Call ☎ **212/268-2500,** or visit **www.bigapplecircus.org**. November to January.

• *The Nutcracker.* Tchaikovsky's holiday favorite is performed by the New York City Ballet at **Lincoln Center.** The annual schedule is available from mid-July, and tickets usually go on sale in early October. Call ☎ **212/870-5570,** or point your Web browser to **www.nycballet.com**. Late November through early January.

## December

○ **Lighting of the Rockefeller Center Christmas Tree.** The annual lighting ceremony is accompanied by an ice-skating show, singing, entertainment, and a huge crowd. The tree stays lit around the clock until after the New Year. Call ☎ **212/632-3975** for this year's date. Early December.

○ **Holiday Trimmings.** Stroll down festive Fifth Avenue, and you'll see doormen dressed as wooden soldiers at **FAO Schwarz,** a 27-foot sparkling snowflake floating over the intersection outside **Tiffany's,** the **Cartier** building ribboned and bowed in red, wreaths warming the necks of the **New York Public Library's** lions, and fanciful figurines in the windows of **Saks Fifth Avenue** and **Lord & Taylor.** Throughout December.

• **Christmas Traditions.** In addition to the **Radio City Music Hall Christmas Spectacular** and the New York City Ballet's staging of *The Nutcracker* (see November, above), traditional holiday events include *A Christmas Carol* at the Theater at **Madison Square Garden** (☎ **212/465-6741** or www.thegarden.com, ☎ **212/307-7171** or www.ticketmaster.com for tickets). At **Avery Fisher Hall** is the National Chorale's sing-along performances of Handel's *Messiah* (☎ **212/875-5030;** www.lincolncenter.org) for a week before Christmas. Don't worry if the only words you know are "Alleluia, Alleluia!"; a lyrics sheet is given to ticket holders.

• **Lighting of the Hanukkah Menorah.** The world's largest menorah (32 feet high) is at Manhattan's **Grand Army Plaza,** Fifth Avenue and 59th Street. Hanukkah celebrations begin at sunset on December 21, 2000, and December 8, 2001, with the lighting of the first of the giant electric candles.

❂ **New Year's Eve.** The biggest party of them all happens in **Times Square,** where hundreds of thousands of raucous revelers count down in unison the year's final seconds until the new lighted ball drops at midnight at 1 Times Square. I personally don't understand it, because it's always a crowded, cold, boozy madhouse, but hey! Call ☎ **212/768-1560** or 212/484-1222, or visit **www.timessquarebid.org.** December 31.

Other unique events include **fireworks** followed by the New York Road Runner's Club's annual **5K Midnight Run** in **Central Park,** which is fun for runners and spectators alike; call ☎ **212/860-4455** or visit **www.nyrrc.org.** Head to Brooklyn for the city's largest New Year's Eve **fireworks** celebration at Prospect Park; call ☎ **718/965-8951** or visit **www.prospectpark.org.**

The **Cathedral of St. John the Divine** is known for its annual **New Year's Eve Concert for Peace.** Past performers have included the Manhattan School of Music Chamber Sinfonia, Tony-award-winning composer Jason Robert Brown (*Parade*), American soprano Lauren Flanigan, and the Forces of Nature Dance Company. Reserved tickets are $75 to $100, but general-admission seating is absolutely free. A hugely popular event, so come early. Call ☎ **212/316-7540** for information or 212/622-2133 for tickets, or go online to **www.stjohndivine.org.**

## 5 Health & Insurance

It can be hard to find a doctor you can trust when you're in an unfamiliar place. Take proper precautions the week before you depart to avoid falling ill while you're away from home. Amid the last-minute frenzy that often precedes a vacation break, make an extra effort to eat and sleep well—especially if you feel an illness coming on. It's a drag to be sick on vacation, and a head cold can make a plane flight intolerable.

### WHAT TO DO IF YOU GET SICK AWAY FROM HOME

If you worry about getting sick away from home, you might want to consider **medical travel insurance** (see "Travel Insurance," below). In most cases, however, your existing health plan will provide all the coverage you need. Be sure to carry your identification card in your wallet.

If you suffer from a chronic illness, consult your doctor before your departure. For conditions such as epilepsy, diabetes, or heart problems, wear a **Medic Alert Identification Tag** (☎ **800/ID-ALERT;** www.medicalert.org), which will immediately alert doctors to your condition and give them access to your records through Medic Alert's 24-hour hot line.

Pack prescription medications in your carry-on luggage. Carry written prescriptions in generic, not brand-name form, and dispense all prescription medications from their original labeled vials. If you wear contact lenses, pack an extra pair in case you lose one.

**FINDING A DOCTOR** If you do get sick, ask the concierge at your hotel to recommend a local doctor, even his or her own. This will probably yield a better recommendation than any 800 number would. There are also several walk-in medical centers, such as **DOCS at New York Healthcare,** 55 E. 34th St., between Park and Madison avenues (☎ **212/252-6001**), for non-emergency illnesses. The clinic, affiliated with Beth Israel Medical Center, is open Monday to Thursday 8am to 8pm, Friday 8am to 7pm, Saturday 9am to 3pm, and Sunday 9am to 2pm. A 24-hour referral service for doctors who make house calls can be reached by calling ☎ 212/737-2333.

If you have dental problems, a nationwide referral service known as **1-800-DENTIST** (☎ **800/336-8478**) will provide the name of a nearby dentist or clinic.

If you can't find a doctor who can help you right away, try the emergency room at the local hospital. Many emergency rooms have walk-in-clinics for emergency cases that are not life threatening. You might not get immediate attention, but you won't pay the high price of an emergency room visit (usually a minimum of $300 just for signing your name, plus the price of whatever treatment you receive). For a list of local hospitals, see "Fast Facts: New York City," in chapter 4.

## TRAVEL INSURANCE

There are three kinds of travel insurance: trip-cancellation, medical, and lost-luggage coverage. **Trip-cancellation insurance** is a good idea if you have paid a large portion of your vacation expenses up front (say, by purchasing a package deal). The other two types of insurance, however, don't make sense for most travelers. Rule number one: Check your existing policies before you buy any additional coverage.

Your existing health insurance should cover you if you get sick while on vacation—although if you belong to an HMO, you should check whether you are fully covered when away from home. For independent travel health-insurance providers, see below.

Your homeowner's or renter's insurance should cover stolen luggage. The airlines are responsible for losses up to $2,500 on domestic flights if they lose your luggage; if you plan to carry anything more valuable than that, keep it in your carry-on bag.

The differences between **travel assistance** and insurance are often blurred, but in general, the former offers on-the-spot assistance and 24-hour hot lines (mostly oriented toward medical problems), and the latter reimburses you for travel problems (medical, travel, or otherwise) after you have filed the paperwork. The coverage you should consider will depend on how much protection is already contained in your existing policies. Some credit- and charge-card companies might insure you against travel accidents if you buy plane, train, or bus tickets with their cards. Before purchasing additional insurance, read over your policies and agreements carefully. Call your insurers or credit-card companies if you have any questions.

Some credit cards (American Express and certain gold and platinum Visa and MasterCards, for example) offer automatic **flight insurance** for death or dismemberment in case of an airplane crash at basic limits and allow you to purchase additional coverage through them.

If you do require additional insurance, try one of the companies listed below. But don't pay for more than you need. If you need only trip-cancellation insurance, don't purchase coverage for lost or stolen property, which should be

**Travel Tip**

If you're buying a package vacation or tour, don't buy your trip-cancellation insurance from your tour operator; talk about putting all of your eggs in one basket! Buy it from an outside vendor instead.

covered by your homeowner's or renter's policy. Trip-cancellation insurance costs approximately 6% to 8% of the total value of your vacation.

Among the reputable issuers of travel insurance are **Access America** (☎ 800/284-8300; www.accessamerica.com); **Travel Guard International** (☎ 800/826-1300; www.travel-guard.com); and **Travelex Insurance Services** (☎ 888/457-4602; www.travelex-insurance.com).

## 6 Tips for Travelers with Special Needs

### FOR FAMILIES

You don't have to leave the kids home, Mom and Dad. New York is a playground for the younger set, too. There are hundreds of ways to keep the kids entertained, from kid-oriented museums and theaters to theme park-style shopping and restaurants.

For the best places to stay and eat, see "Affordable Family-Friendly Hotels" in chapter 5 and "Affordable Family-Friendly Restaurants" in chapter 6. For details on sightseeing, check out the section called "Especially for Kids" in chapter 7.

Good bets for the most timely information include the "Weekend" section of Friday's *The New York Times,* which has a whole section dedicated to the week's best kid-friendly activities; the weekly *New York* magazine, which has a full calendar of children's events in its "Cue" section; and *Time Out New York,* which also has a great weekly kids section with a bit of an alternative bent. Good Web sources for up-to-date information, advice, and Yellow-pages links to family-related services include **New York Family (www.family.go. com/Local/nyfm)**. Both *New York Family* and the *Big Apple Parents' Paper* are usually available for free at children's stores and other locations in Manhattan.

**FINDING A BABY-SITTER**    The first place to look for baby-sitting is in your hotel (better yet, ask about baby-sitting when you reserve). Many hotels have baby-sitting services or will provide you with lists of reliable sitters. If this doesn't pan out, call the **Baby Sitters' Guild** (☎ 212/682-0227; www. babysittersguild.com). The sitters are licensed, insured, and bonded and can even take your child on outings.

### FOR TRAVELERS WITH DISABILITIES

A disability shouldn't stop anyone from traveling. The Americans with Disabilities Act and state and local laws require an increasing number of buildings and other public spaces to accommodate people with disabilities, making New York more accessible to travelers with disabilities than ever before. The city's bus system is wheelchair-friendly, and most of the major sightseeing attractions are easily accessible. Even so, always call first to be sure that the places you want to go are fully accessible.

Many hotels are ADA compliant, with suitable rooms for travelers who use wheelchairs and those with other disabilities. But before you book, **ask a lot of questions** based on your needs. Many budget hotels are housed in older buildings that have had to be modified to meet requirements; still, elevators and bathrooms can be on the small side, and other impediments can exist. If you have mobility issues, you'll probably do best to book into one of the city's newer hotels, which tend to be more spacious and accommodating. See "Best for Disabled Travelers" under "Best Low-Cost Hotel Bets" in chapter 1.

Some Broadway theaters and other performance venues provide total wheelchair accessibility; others provide partial accessibility. Many also offer lower-priced tickets for theatergoers with disabilities and their companions, although you'll need to check individual policies and reserve in advance.

**GENERAL TRAVEL INFORMATION** Moss Rehab ResourceNet (**www.mossresourcenet.org**) is a great source for information, tips, and resources relating to accessible travel. You'll find links to a number of travel agents who specialize in planning trips for travelers with disabilities here and through **Access-Able Travel Source** (**www.access-able.com**), another excellent online source. You'll also find relay and voice numbers for hotels, airlines, and car-rental companies on Access-Able's user-friendly site, as well as links to accessible accommodations, attractions, transportation, tours, local medical resources and equipment repairers, and much more.

You can join **The Society for the Advancement of Travelers with Handicaps** (SATH), 347 Fifth Ave. Suite 610, New York, NY 10016 (☎ **212/447-7284;** fax 212-725-8253; www.sath.org), to gain access to their vast network of connections in the travel industry. They provide information sheets on destinations and referrals to tour operators that specialize in traveling with disabilities. Their quarterly magazine, *Open World*, is full of good information and resources.

**CITY-SPECIFIC INFORMATION** Hospital Audiences, Inc., 548 Broadway, 3rd Floor, New York, NY 10012-3950 (☎ **212/575-7676** or 212/575-7660; TTY 212/575-7673; www.hospitalaudiences.org), arranges attendance and provides details about accessibility at cultural institutions as well as cultural events adapted for people with disabilities. Services include "Describe!," which allows visually impaired theatergoers to enjoy theater events, and an omnibus program that transports people with disabilities to cultural events. This nonprofit organization also publishes *Access for All*, a guidebook on accessibility at many of the city's cultural institutions, available by calling ☎ **212/575-7663** or by sending a $5 check to the above address.

Another terrific source for travelers with disabilities coming to New York City is **Big Apple Greeter** (☎ **212/669-8159;** www.bigapplegreeter.org). Their Greeter Access Project is geared to travelers with disabilities interested in getting to know the Big Apple. All of their employees are extremely well versed on accessibility issues. They can provide a resource list of agencies that serve the city's disabled community and sometimes have special discounts available to theater and music performances. Big Apple Greeter offers one-to-one tours that pair volunteers with visitors with disabilities; they can even introduce you to the public transportation system if you like. Reserve at least one week ahead.

Other helpful organizations are the **American Foundation for the Blind,** 11 Penn Plaza, Suite 300, New York, NY 10001 (☎ **800/232-5463** or 212/502-7600); **The Lighthouse, Inc.,** 111 E. 59th St., New York, NY 10022 (☎ **800/829-0500** or 212/821-9200; www.lighthouse.org); and the **New York Society for the Deaf,** 817 Broadway, 7th floor, New York, NY 10003 (☎ TTY and voice **212/777-3900;** www.nysd.org).

**GETTING AROUND** Gray Line Air Shuttle (☎ **800/451-0455** or 212/315-3006; www.graylinenewyork.com) operates minibuses with lifts from JFK, LaGuardia, and Newark airports to midtown hotels by reservation; arrange pick-up three or four days in advance. **Olympia Airport Express** (☎ **888/662-7700** or 212/964-6233; www.olympiabus.com) provides service from Newark Airport, with half-price fares for travelers with disabilities.

A licensed ambulette company, **Upward Mobility Limousine Service** (☎ **718/645-7774;** www.brainlink.com/~phil) is a wheelchair-accessible car service that can provide door-to-door airport shuttle service as well as taxi service anywhere in the metropolitan area. Arrange airport pick-ups with as much advance notice as possible.

**Taxis** are required to carry people who have folding wheelchairs and Seeing-Eye or hearing-ear dogs. However, don't be surprised if they don't run each other down trying to get to you; even though you shouldn't have to, you might have to wait a bit for a friendly (or fare-desperate) driver to come along.

**Public buses** are an inexpensive and easy way to get around New York. All buses' back doors are supposed to be equipped with wheelchair lifts (although the city has had complaints that not all are in working order). Buses also "kneel," lowering their front steps for people who have difficulty boarding. Passengers with disabilities pay half-price fares (75¢). The **subway** isn't yet fully wheelchair accessible, but a list of about 30 accessible subway stations and a guide to wheelchair-accessible subway itineraries is on the MTA Web site. Call ☎ 718/596-8585 for bus and subway transit info, or point your browser to **www.mta.nyc.ny.us/nyct**; click on CUSTOMERS WITH SPECIAL NEEDS under GENERAL INFORMATION.

## FOR SENIOR TRAVELERS

One of the benefits of age is that travel often costs less. New York subway and bus fares are half price (75¢) for people 65 and older. Many museums and sights (and some theaters and performance halls) offer discounted entrance and tickets to seniors, so don't be shy about asking. Always bring an ID card, especially if you've kept your youthful glow.

Also mention the fact that you're a senior when you first make your travel reservations. Both **Amtrak** (☎ 800/USA-RAIL; www.amtrak.com) and **Greyhound** (☎ 800/231-2222; www.greyhound.com) offer discounts to persons over 62, and most of the major domestic airlines offer discount programs for senior travelers. Many hotels also offer senior discounts; **Choice Hotels** (which include Comfort Inns, some of my favorite affordable midtown hotels; see chapter 5), for example, give 30% off their published rates to anyone over 50, provided you book your room through their nationwide toll-free reservations number (that is, not directly with the hotel or through a travel agent). For a complete list of Choice Hotels, visit **www.hotelchoice.com**.

Members of the **American Association of Retired Persons (AARP)**, 601 E St. NW, Washington, DC 20049 (☎ 800/424-3410; www.aarp.org), get discounts not only on hotels but on airfares and car rentals, too. The AARP offers members a wide range of special benefits, including *Modern Maturity* magazine and a monthly newsletter. If you're not already a member, do yourself a favor and join.

## FOR GAY & LESBIAN TRAVELERS

Gay and lesbian culture is as much a part of New York's basic identity as yellow cabs, high-rises, and Broadway theater. Indeed, in a city with one of the world's largest, loudest, and most powerful gay and lesbian populations, homosexuality is hardly seen as an "alternative" these days; it's squarely in the urban mainstream. So city hotels tend to be neutral on the issue, and gay couples shouldn't have a problem; for particularly gay-friendly accommodations, see "Best for Gay & Lesbian Travelers" under "Best Low-Cost Hotel Bets" in chapter 1. You'll want to see "The Lesbian & Gay Scene" in chapter 9 for nightlife suggestions.

If you want help planning your trip, **The International Gay & Lesbian Travel Association** (IGLTA; ☎ 800/448-8550 or 954/776-2626; www.iglta.org) can link you up with the appropriate gay-friendly service organization or tour specialist. With around 1,200 members, it offers quarterly newsletters, marketing mailings, and a membership directory that's updated quarterly. Members are kept informed of gay and gay-friendly hoteliers, tour operators, and airline and cruise-line representatives.

*Out and About* (☎ 800/929-2268 or 212/645-6922; www.outandabout. com) has been hailed for its "straight" reporting about gay travel. It offers a monthly newsletter packed with good information on the global gay and lesbian scene. Out and About's guidebooks are available at most major bookstores and through **A Different Light Bookstore,** 151 W. 19th St. (☎ 800/ 343-4002 or 212/989-4850; www.adlbooks.com), and its Web site features links to gay and lesbian tour operators and other gay-themed travel links.

All over Manhattan, but especially in neighborhoods like the **West Village** (particularly Christopher Street, famous the world over as the main drag of New York gay-male life) and **Chelsea** (especially Eighth Avenue from 16th to 23rd streets and West 17th to 19th streets from Fifth to Eighth avenues), shops, services, and restaurants have a lesbian and gay flavor. A Different Light (above) and the **Oscar Wilde Bookshop,** 15 Christopher St. (☎ 212/255-8097; www.oscarwildebooks.com), are the city's two best gay and lesbian bookstores; both are good sources for information on the city's gay community.

## FOR STUDENTS

Many attractions and theaters offer reduced admission to students, so don't forget to bring your valid student ID and proof of age.

Your best resource is the **Council on International Educational Exchange,** or CIEE. They can set you up with an International Student ID card, and their travel branch, **Council Travel** (☎ 800/226-8624; www. counciltravel.com), the world's biggest student travel agency, can get you discounts on plane tickets and the like. In New York City at 254 Greene St., in Greenwich Village (☎ 212/254-2525); in Midtown at 205 E. 42nd St. (☎ 212/822-2700); and on the Upper West Side at 895 Amsterdam Ave. (☎ 212/666-4177).

**Hostelling International–American Youth Hostels** (☎ 202/783-6161; www.hiayh.org), has their largest hostel in New York City at 891 Amsterdam Ave, at 103rd Street (☎ 212/932-2300; www.hinewyork.org); see chapter 5 for a complete review. Reserve well ahead, because this place is always booked. You'll also find other, privately run hostels with super-cheap dorm beds reviewed in chapter 5.

## 7 Getting There

### BY PLANE

Three major airports serve New York City: **John F. Kennedy International Airport** (☎ 718/244-4444) in Queens, about 15 miles (or one hour's driving time) from midtown Manhattan; **LaGuardia Airport** (☎ 718/533-3400), also in Queens, about 8 miles (or 30 minutes) from Midtown; and **Newark International Airport** (☎ 973/961-6000) in nearby New Jersey, about 16 miles (or 45 minutes) from Midtown. Information about all three airports is available online at **www.panynj.gov.**

Almost every major domestic carrier serves at least one of these airports; most serve two or all three. Among them are **America West** (☎ 800/ 235-9292; www.americawest.com), **American** (☎ 800/433-7300; www.americanair. com), **Continental** (☎ 800/525-0280; www.continental.com), **Delta** (☎ 800/ 221-1212; www.delta-air.com), **Northwest** (☎ 800/225-2525; www.nwa.com),

Keep in mind that it's more convenient to fly into Newark than Kennedy if your destination is Manhattan, and consider that fares to Newark are often cheaper than the other airports. Newark can also be the most convenient if your hotel is in Midtown West or downtown near the World Trade Center.

**TWA** (☎ 800/221-2000; www.twa.com), **US Airways** (☎ 800/428-4322; www.usairways.com), and **United** (☎ 800/241-6522; www.ual.com).

In recent years there has been rapid growth in the number of start-up, no-frills airlines serving New York. These smaller, sometimes struggling airlines might offer lower fares—but don't expect the same kind of service you get from the majors. You might check out Atlanta-based **AirTran** (☎ 800/AIRTRAN; www.airtran.com); Denver-based **Frontier** (☎ 800/4321-FLY; www.flyfrontier.com); Detroit-based **Spirit Airlines** (☎ 800/772-7117; www.spiritair.com); Raleigh-Durham–based **Midway** (☎ 888/22-MIDWAY; www.midwayair.com); Milwaukee- and Omaha-based **Midwest Express** (☎ 800/452-2022; www.midwestexpress.com); Chicago-based **ATA** (☎ 800/I-FLY-ATA; www.ata.com); Las Vegas–based **National Airlines** (☎ 888/757-JETS; www.nationalairlines.com); and Minneapolis-based **Sun Country** (☎ 800/752-1218; www.suncountry.com). After a much-lauded launch in early 2000, the new cheap-chic airline **jetBlue** (☎ 800/JETBLUE; www.jetblue.com) has taken New York by storm with its low fares and high-end service to Buffalo, NY, and Florida; expect a significantly expanded route map by the time you're ready to fly. The nation's leading discount airline, **Southwest** (☎ 800/435-9792; www.iflyswa.com), has flights to Long Island's MacArthur (Islip) Airport (see p. 42 for transportation info into the city).

Most major international carriers also serve New York; see chapter 3 for details.

For advice on how to get the best airfare, see "60 Money-Saving Tips" earlier in this chapter.

### TRANSPORTATION TO & FROM THE NEW YORK AREA AIRPORTS

Since there's no need to rent a car for a visit to New York, you're going to have to figure out how you want to get from the airport to your hotel and back.

For complete transportation information for all three airports (JFK, LaGuardia, and Newark), call **Air-Ride** (☎ 800/247-7433); it gives recorded details on bus and shuttle companies and private car services registered with the New York and New Jersey Port Authority. Similar information is available online at **www.panynj.gov**; just click on the airport where you'll be arriving.

On the arrivals level at each airport, the Port Authority also has Ground Transportation Information counters where you can get information and book on all manner of transport once you land. Most transportation companies also have courtesy phones near the baggage-claim area.

Generally, travel time between the airports and midtown Manhattan by taxi or car is one hour for JFK, 45 minutes for LaGuardia, and 50 minutes for Newark. Always allow extra time, though, especially during rush hour, peak holiday travel times, and if you're taking a bus.

**SUBWAYS & PUBLIC BUSES** Taking the MTA to and from the airport can be a hassle, but it's the cheapest way to go—just $1.50 each way. However, keep in mind that the subways and buses that currently serve the airports involve multiple transfers and staircases; count on more hauling to your hotel (or a taxi fare) once you arrive in Manhattan. This won't work for travelers with lots of luggage, because you won't have anywhere to store it on the bus or subway train. You might not want to take the bus or the subway if you're traveling too early in the morning or late at night, as you'll be passing through some less-than-desirable neighborhoods.

For additional subway and bus information, see "Getting Around" in chapter 4.

**From/to Kennedy Airport**   You can take the **A train** to Kennedy airport, which connects to one of two free **shuttle buses** that serve all the JFK terminals. Plan on 2 hours in each direction, maybe more if you're traveling at rush hour: The subway ride from Midtown takes about 75 minutes, and you'll need another 20 to 30 minutes for the shuttle ride to your terminal; also be sure to factor in waiting time at both ends.

Upon exiting the terminal, pick up the shuttle bus (marked **LONG TERM PARKING LOT**) out front; it takes you to the **Howard Beach station,** where you pick up the A train to the west side of Manhattan. Service is every 10 to 15 minutes during rush hour and every 20 minutes at midday, and the subway fare is $1.50. If you're traveling to JFK from Manhattan, be sure to take the A train that says **FAR ROCKAWAY** or **ROCKAWAY PARK**—*not* LEFFERTS BOULEVARD. Get off at the Howard Beach/JFK Airport station and connect to the shuttle bus, A or B, that goes to your terminal (they're clearly marked, and there's usually a guide to point you to the right one). The subway can actually be more reliable than taking a car or taxi at the height of rush hour.

**From/to LaGuardia**   The **M60 bus** serves all LaGuardia terminals. When leaving LaGuardia, follow the **GROUND TRANSPORTATION** signs and look for the **M60** stop sign at the curb. The bus will take you to Broadway and 116th Street on Manhattan's west side, where you can transfer to a downtown bus or the 1 or 9 subway; you can also pick up the N subway into Manhattan by disembarking at the Astoria Boulevard station in Queens. The bus runs daily between 6am and 1am, leaving at roughly half-hour intervals and taking about 50 minutes. (From Manhattan, you can pick up the bus as early as 4:30am from Broadway and 106th Street.) Be sure to allow at least 1¼ hour, however; you never know about traffic. *Money-saving tip:* Use a MetroCard to pay your fare and you'll save the extra $1.50 it usually costs for the transfer. For the complete schedule and other pickup and drop-off points, visit **www.mta.nyc.ny.us/nyct**.

**From/to Newark**   Sorry, there's no public transportation; use one of the private bus services listed below.

**PRIVATE BUSES & SHUTTLES**   Buses and shuttle services are more expensive than using the MTA for airport transfers, but they're less expensive than taxis (but usually more time-consuming).

**Gray Line Air Shuttle** and **Super Shuttle** serve all three airports; **New York Airport Service** serves JFK and LaGuardia; **Olympia Trails** serves Newark. These services are my favorite option for getting to and from Newark during peak travel times because the drivers usually take lesser-known surface streets that make the ride much quicker than if you go with a taxi or car, which will virtually always stick to the traffic-clogged main route.

**Gray Line Express Shuttle USA** (☎ **800/451-0455** or 212/315-3006; www.graylinenewyork.com) vans depart JFK, LaGuardia, and Newark every 20 minutes between 7am and 11:30pm. They will drop you off at most hotels

# Money-Saving Package Deals

Before you start your search for the lowest airfare, you might want to consider booking your flight as part of a travel package.

Package tours are not the same as escorted tours. They are simply a way to buy airfare and accommodations (and sometimes extras such as sightseeing tours and hard-to-get theater tickets) at the same time. For New York, a package can be a smart way to go. In many cases, a package that includes airfare, hotel, and transportation to and from the airport will cost you less than your hotel bill alone had you booked it yourself. That's because packages are sold in bulk to tour operators, who then resell them to the public at a cost that drastically undercuts standard rates.

Packages vary widely. Some offer a better class of hotels than others. Some offer the same hotels for lower prices. With some packagers, your choice of accommodations and travel days can be limited. Which package is right for you depends entirely on what you want.

Here are a few tips to help you tell one package from another and figure out which one is right for you:

- **Read this guide.** Do a little homework; read up on New York. Compare the rack rates that we've published to the discounted rates being offered by the packagers to see what kinds of deals they're offering— whether you're actually being offered a substantial savings or they've just gussied up the rack rates to make their offer *sound* like a deal. If you're being offered a stay in a hotel I haven't recommended, do more research to learn about it, especially if it isn't a reliable franchise such as Holiday Inn or Best Western. It's not a deal if you end up at a dump.

- **Read the fine print.** Make sure you know *exactly* what's included in the price you're being quoted and what's not. Are hotel taxes and airport transfers included, or will you have to pay extra? Conversely, don't pay for a rental car you don't need—and you won't need one in New York. Before you commit to a package, make sure you know how much flexibility you have, say, if your child gets sick or your boss suddenly asks you to adjust your vacation schedule. Some packagers require iron-clad commitments, but others will go with the flow, charging only minimal fees for changes or cancellations.

- **Use your best judgment.** Stay away from fly-by-nights and shady packagers. If a deal appears to be too good to be true, it probably is. Go with a reputable firm with a proven track record. This is where your travel agent can come in handy; he or she should be knowledgeable about different packagers, the deals they offer, and the general rate of satisfaction among their customers.

between 23rd and 63rd streets in Manhattan or Port Authority (34th Street and Seventh Avenue) or Grand Central (42nd Street and Park Avenue) terminals if you need to catch a subway to another part of town or a train to the 'burbs. No reservation is required; just go to the ground-transportation desk or use the courtesy phone in the baggage-claim area and ask for Gray Line. Service from most major mid-Manhattan hotels to all three airports operates 5am to 9pm; you must call a day in advance to arrange a hotel pickup. The regular one-way fare to and from JFK is $19, to and from LaGuardia is $16,

**Finding a Package Deal**  The best place to start your search is the travel section of your local Sunday newspaper. Also check the ads in the back of national travel magazines such as *Travel & Leisure, National Geographic Traveler, Arthur Frommer's Budget Travel,* and *Condé Nast Traveler.*

One of the biggest packagers in the Northeast, **Liberty Travel** (☎ 888/ 271-1584; www.libertytravel.com) boasts a full-page ad in many Sunday papers. You won't get much in the way of service, but you will get a good deal. They offer great-value 2- to 7-night New York packages that usually include such freebies as a Circle Line cruise, a guided city tour, and discounts at Planet Hollywood, plus a lot of good hotels to choose from.

The major airlines offering good-value packages to New York include **Continental Airlines Vacations** (☎ 800/634-5555; www.coolvacations. com), which featured a short but strong selection of hotels at press time, among them was the Hotel Metro, one of my mid-priced favorites. **Delta Vacations** (☎ 800/872-7786; www.deltavacations.com) boasts a similarly good selection of hotels. **US Airways Vacations** (☎ 800/472-2577; www.usairwaysvacations.com) also offers a pleasing range of hotels, plus Broadway tickets as part of their list of add-on options (watch for the rental car you don't need, however). Both **United Vacations** (☎ 800/ 328-6877; www.unitedvacations.com) and **American Airlines Vacations** (☎ 800/321-2121; www.aavacations.com) have an extensive but mixed selection of hotels, so be careful where you book. **Northwest WorldVacations** (☎ 800/800-1504; www.nwa.com/vacpkg) is another option. You might want to choose the airline that has frequent service to your hometown or the one on which you accumulate frequent-flyer miles (you might even be able to pay with your trip using miles).

For one-stop shopping on the Web, go to **www.vacationpackager.com,** a search engine that will link you to many different package-tour operators offering New York City vacations, often with a company profile summarizing the company's basic booking and cancellation terms. A terrific source specifically for Big Apple packages is **New York City Vacations** (☎ 888/ 692-8701; www.nycvp.com), which can sell you a complete vacation package, including hotel stay, theater tickets, and more.

In New York, many **hotels** also offer package deals, especially for weekend stays. Some of the best deals in town are those that include theater tickets, sometimes for otherwise sold-out shows such as *The Lion King.* (Most aren't air/land combos, however; you'll have to book your airfare separately.) I've included tips on hotels that regularly offer them in chapter 5, but always ask about available packages when you call any hotel.

and to and from Newark is $19, but you can save a few bucks by pre-paying your round-trip at the airport ($28 for JFK and Newark, $26 for LaGuardia).

The familiar blue vans of **Super Shuttle** (☎ 800/258-3826 or 212/ 258-3826; www.supershuttle.com) serve all three area airports, providing door-to-door service to Manhattan and points on Long Island every 15 to 30 minutes around the clock. As with Gray Line, you don't need to reserve your airport-to-Manhattan ride; just go to the ground-transportation desk or use the courtesy phone in the baggage-claim area and ask for Super Shuttle. Hotel pickups for your return trip require 24 to 48 hours' advance booking; reservations can be made online. One-way fares are $16 to and from JFK, $15 to and from LaGuardia, and $19 to and from Newark; you'll pay full fare for the first passenger, and $9 for each additional passenger.

**New York Airport Service** (☎ 718/875-8200) buses travel from JFK and LaGuardia to the Port Authority Bus Terminal (42nd Street and Eighth Avenue), Penn Station (34th Street and Seventh Avenue), Grand Central Terminal (Park Avenue between 41st and 42nd streets), or your midtown hotel, plus the Jamaica LIRR Station in Queens, where you can pick up a train for Long Island. Follow the GROUND TRANSPORTATION signs to the curbside pickup or look for the uniformed agent. Buses depart the airport every 20 to 70 minutes (depending on your departure point and destination) between 6:30am and midnight. Buses to JFK and LaGuardia depart the Port Authority and Grand Central Terminal on the Park Avenue side every 15 to 30 minutes, depending on the time of day and the day of the week. To request direct shuttle service from your hotel, call the above number at least 24 hours in advance. One-way fare for JFK is $13 and $10 to and from LaGuardia; children under 12 ride free with a parent.

**Olympia Airport Express** (☎ 888/662-7700 or 212/964-6233; www.olympiabus.com) provides service every 5 to 10 minutes (less frequently during off hours) from Newark Airport to four Manhattan locations: 1 World Trade Center (on West Street, next to the Marriott World Trade Center Hotel), Penn Station (the pickup point is the northwest corner of 34th Street and Eighth Avenue and the drop-off point the southwest corner), the Port Authority Bus Terminal (on 42nd Street between Eighth and Ninth avenues), and Grand Central Terminal (41st Street between Park and Lexington). Passengers to and from the Grand Central Terminal location can connect to Olympia's midtown shuttle vans, which service most hotels between 30th and 65th streets. From the above departure points in Manhattan, service runs every 15 to 30 minutes depending on your pickup point; call for exact schedule. The one-way fare is $10 or $15 if you connect to the hotel shuttle; senior and citizens with disabilities ride for half-price.

## If You're Flying into Islip Airport on Southwest

Southwest Airlines, the nation's leading discount carrier, now flies into the New York area via Long Island's Islip Airport, 50 miles east of Manhattan. If you're on one of these flights, your cheapest option for getting into the city is to call **Village Taxi** when you land (☎ 516/563-4611), and they'll send over a driver to take you 3 miles to the Ronkonkoma Long Island Rail Road Station, where you can pick up a LIRR (Long Island Rail Road) train to Manhattan. The taxi fare is $5 to $8, plus tip. From Ronkonkoma, it's about a 1¹/₂-hour train ride to Manhattan's Penn Station; the one-way fare is $9.50 at peak hours, $6.50 off-peak (half fare for seniors 65 or older and kids 5 to 11). Trains usually leave Ronkonkoma once or twice every hour, depending on the day and time. For more information, call ☎ 718/217-5477 or go online to **www.mta.nyc.ny.us/lirr**.

**Classic Transportation** (☎ 800/666-4949 or 516/567-5100; www.classictrans.com) and **Legends** (☎ 888/LEGENDS or 718/788-1234) car services will pick you up at Islip Airport and deliver you to Manhattan via private sedan if you arrange for it in advance, but expect to pay $100 plus tolls and tip for door-to-door service.

Never accept a car ride from the hustlers who hang out in the terminal halls. They're illegal, they don't have proper insurance, and they aren't safe. You can tell who they are because they'll approach you with a suspicious conspiratorial air and ask whether you need a ride. Not from them, you don't. Sanctioned city cabs and car services wait outside the terminals.

**TAXIS**   Taxis are a quick and easy way to travel to and from the airports, but you'll pay for the convenience of door-to-door service. They're available at designated taxi stands outside the terminals, with uniformed dispatchers on hand during peak hours (follow the **GROUND TRANSPORTATION** or **TAXI** signs). There might be a long line, but it generally moves pretty quickly. Fares, whether fixed or metered, do not include bridge and tunnel tolls ($3.50 to $4) or a tip for the cabbie (15% to 20% is customary). They do include all passengers in the cab and luggage; never pay more than the metered or flat rate, except for tolls and a tip (from 8pm to 6am a 50¢ surcharge also applies on New York yellow cabs). Taxis have a limit of four passengers, so if there are more in your group, you'll have to take more than one cab. For more on taxis, see "Getting Around" in chapter 4.

- **From JFK:** A flat rate of $30 to and from Manhattan (plus any tolls and tip) is charged. The meter will not be turned on and the surcharge will not be added.
- **From LaGuardia.** $20 to $25, metered.
- **From Newark.** The dispatcher for New Jersey taxis gives you a slip of paper with a flat rate ranging from $30 to $45 (toll and tip extra), depending on where you're going in Manhattan, so you'll have to be precise about your destination. New York yellow cabs aren't permitted to pick up passengers at Newark. The yellow-cab fare from Manhattan to Newark is the meter amount plus $10 and tolls (about $40 to $50, perhaps a few dollars more with tip). New Jersey taxis aren't permitted to take passengers from Manhattan to Newark.

**PRIVATE-CAR SERVICES**   Private-car and limousine companies provide convenient 24-hour door-to-door airport transfers. The advantage over taking a taxi is that you can arrange your pickup in advance and avoid the hassles of the taxi line. A taxi is virtually always cheaper from JFK thanks to the flat fare; otherwise, as a general rule of thumb, expect to pay a tad less with a car service during rush hour (because there's no ticking meter), slightly more at other times.

Call at least 24 hours in advance (even earlier on holidays), and a driver will meet you near baggage claim or at your hotel for a return trip. You'll probably be asked to leave a credit-card number to guarantee your ride; you'll likely be offered the choice of indoor or curbside pickup. Curbside pickup will take about 10 minutes longer, but you'll save a few dollars. Vehicles range from sedans to vans to limousines and tend to be relatively clean and comfortable. Ask when booking what the fare will be and whether you can use your credit card to pay for the ride. There might be waiting charges tacked on if the driver has to wait an excessive amount of time for your plane to land when picking you up, but the car companies will usually check on your flight beforehand to get an accurate landing time.

If you're traveling to a borough other than Manhattan, call **ETS Air Service** (☎ 718/221-5341) for shared door-to-door service. For Long Island service, call **Classic Transportation** (☎ 800/666-4949 or 516/567-5100; www.classictrans.com). For service to Westchester County or Connecticut, contact **Connecticut Limousine** (☎ 800/472-5466 or 203/878-6867; www.ctlimo.com) or **Prime Time Shuttle of Connecticut** (☎ 800/733-8267; www.primetimeshuttle.com).

If you're traveling to points in New Jersey from Newark Airport, call **Olympic Limousine** (☎ 800/822-9797 or 908/938-4300) for Ocean and Monmouth counties; the **Airporter** (☎ 800/385-4000 or 609/587-6600; www.goairporter.com) to Middlesex and Mercer counties; or **State Shuttle** (☎ 800/427-3207 or 973/729-0030) for other Jersey destinations.

I've had the best luck with **Carmel** (☎ 800/922-7635 or 212/666-6666) and **Legends** (☎ 888/LEGENDS or 718/788-1234); **Allstate** (☎ 800/453-4099 or 212/741-7440) and **Tel-Aviv** (☎ 800/222-9888 or 212/777-7777) are also reliable bets.

## BY TRAIN

**Amtrak** (☎ 800/USA-RAIL; www.amtrak.com) runs frequent service to New York City's **Penn Station,** on Seventh Avenue between 31st and 33rd streets, where you can easily pick up a taxi, subway, or bus to your hotel.

If you're traveling to New York from a city along Amtrak's Northeast Corridor—such as Boston, Philadelphia, Baltimore, or Washington, D.C—Amtrak might be your best travel bet now that they've rolled out their new high-speed Acela trains, which will have replaced all the old Metroliners by the time you read this. The Acela Express trains cut travel time from D.C. down to $2^{1}/_{2}$ hours, and travel time from Boston to a lightning-quick 3 hours, and are often cheaper than airline fares. Trains can also be less of a hassle, because they take you right into Manhattan (thereby avoiding complicated, time-consuming, and expensive airport transfers).

To get the best rates, book early (as much as 6 months in advance) and travel on weekends. See "60 Money-Saving Tips," above, for more wallet-friendly advice, and check Amtrak's Web site for special discounted fares.

## BY BUS

Buses arrive at the **Port Authority Terminal,** on Eighth Avenue between 40th and 42nd streets, where you can easily transfer to your hotel by taxi, subway, or bus. Buses are slow and uncomfortable, but fares are usually much lower than train and airline fares. For complete schedule and fare information, contact **Greyhound Bus Lines** (☎ 800/231-2222 or 402/330-8552; www.greyhound.com). You'll find a complete list of their special fares and discounts on their Web page; be sure to ask about special deals if you call.

Although the bus is likely to be the cheapest option, don't just assume. Always compare fares; sometimes, a full-fare bus ticket is no cheaper than the train. If you get lucky, you might even catch an airline fare sale that will make flying the most prudent option.

## BY CAR

From the **New Jersey Turnpike** (I-95) and points west, there are three Hudson River crossings into the city's west side: the **Holland Tunnel** (lower Manhattan), the **Lincoln Tunnel** (Midtown), and the **George Washington Bridge** (upper Manhattan).

From **upstate New York,** take the **New York State Thruway** (I-87), which crosses the Hudson on the Tappan Zee Bridge and becomes the **Major Deegan Expressway** (I-87) through the Bronx. For the east side, continue to the Triborough Bridge and then down the FDR Drive. For the west side, take the Cross Bronx Expressway (I-95) to the Henry Hudson Parkway or the Taconic State Parkway to the Saw Mill River Parkway to the Henry Hudson Parkway south.

From **New England,** the **New England Thruway** (I-95) connects with the **Bruckner Expressway** (I-278), which leads to the Triborough Bridge and the FDR on the east side. For the west side, take the Bruckner to the Cross Bronx Expressway (I-95) to the Henry Hudson Parkway south.

Note that you'll have to pay tolls along some of these roads and at most crossings.

Once you arrive in Manhattan, park your car in a garage (expect to pay at least $20 to $35 per day) and leave it there. Don't use your car for traveling within the city. Public transportation, taxis, and walking will easily get you where you want to go without the headaches of parking, gridlock, and dodging crazy cabbies. For tips on parking, see "Deals for Visitors with Wheels: Cheap Parking Tips" in chapter 4.

# Planning Your Trip: An Online Directory

**D**ay by day, the Internet becomes more integrated into our lives—including the way we plan and book our travel. By early 2000, one in every ten trips was being booked online, a trend that's sure to accelerate.

The Internet not only provides a wealth of destination information, but also it gives you the chance to compare experiences with fellow travelers, ask experts for pre-trip advice, seek out discounted fares once only accessible to travel industry insiders, and stay in touch via e-mail while you're away.

This Online Directory will help you take better advantage of the travel-planning information available online, and it's best used in conjunction with this book. Part 1 lists general Internet resources that can make any trip easier, such as sites for obtaining the best possible prices on airline tickets. In Part 2 you'll find some top online guides for New York City, organized by category.

Please keep in mind that this is not a comprehensive list, but rather a discriminating selection to get you started. Recognition is given to sites based on their content value and ease of use and are not paid for—unlike some Web-site rankings, which are based on payment. Finally, remember this is a press-time snapshot of leading Web sites; some undoubtedly will have evolved, changed, or moved by the time you read this.

## 1 Top Travel-Planning Web Sites

*by Lynne Bairstow*

Although the Internet was once a conglomerate of sites for researching places to visit, several key companies have emerged that offer comprehensive travel planning and booking. In addition to Frommer's Online (see box), we list the other top online travel agencies below, along with some more specialized services.

### WHY BOOK ONLINE?

Online agencies have come a long way over the past few years, now providing tips for finding the best fare and giving you suggested dates or times to travel that yield the lowest price if your plans are at all flexible. Other sites even allow you to establish the price you're willing to pay, and they check the airlines' willingness to accept it. However, in some cases, these sites might not always yield the best price. Unlike a

# Editor's Note: What You'll Find
## at the Frommer's Site

We highly recommend **Arthur Frommer's Budget Travel Online** (**www.frommers.com**) as an excellent travel-planning resource. Of course, we're a little biased, but you'll find indispensable travel tips, reviews, monthly vacation giveaways, and online booking. Among the most popular features of this site is the regular "Ask the Expert" bulletin boards, which feature one of the Frommer's authors answering your questions via online postings.

Subscribe to Arthur Frommer's Daily Newsletter (**www.frommers.com/ newsletters**) to receive the latest travel bargains and inside travel secrets via e-mail every day. You'll read daily headlines and articles from the dean of travel himself, highlighting last-minute deals on airfares, accommodations, cruises, and package vacations. You'll also find great travel advice by checking our Tip of the Day or Hot Spot of the Month.

Search our Destinations archive (**www.frommers.com/destinations**) of more than 200 domestic and international destinations for great places to stay, tips for traveling there, and what to do while you're there. Once you've researched your trip, the online reservation system (**www. frommers.com/booktravelnow**) takes you to Frommer's favorite sites for booking your vacation at affordable prices.

travel agent, for example, they might not have access to charter flights offered by wholesalers.

Online booking sites aren't the only places to reserve airline tickets; all major airlines have their own Web sites and often offer incentives—such as bonus frequent-flyer miles or net-only discounts—when you buy online or buy an e-ticket.

The new trend is toward conglomerated booking sites. By mid-2000, a consortium of U.S. and European-based airlines is planning to launch an as-yet-unnamed Web site that will offer fares lower than those available through travel agents. United, Delta, Northwest, and Continental have initiated this effort, based on their success at selling airline seats at their own online sites.

The best of the travel-planning sites are now highly personalized; they store your seating preferences, meal preferences, tentative itineraries, and credit-card information, allowing you to quickly plan trips or check agendas.

In many cases, booking your trip online can be better than working with a travel agent. It gives you the widest variety of choices, control, and the 24-hour convenience of planning your trip when you choose. All you need is some time—and often a little patience—and you're likely to find the fun of online travel research will greatly enhance your trip.

## WHO SHOULD BOOK ONLINE?

Online booking is best for travelers who want to know as much as possible about their travel options, those who have flexibility in their travel dates and are looking for the best price, and bargain hunters driven by a good value, who are open-minded about where they travel.

One of the biggest successes in online travel for both passengers and airlines is the offer of last-minute specials, such as American Airlines' weekend deals

More people still look online than book online, partly due to fear of putting their credit-card numbers out on the Net. Secure encryption, and increasing experience buying online, has removed this fear for most travelers. In some cases, however, it's simply easier to buy from a local travel agent who can deliver your tickets to your door (especially if your travel is last-minute or if you have special requests). You can find a flight online and then book it by calling a toll-free number or contacting your travel agent, although this is somewhat less efficient. To be sure you're in secure mode when you book online, look for an icon of a key (in Netscape) or a padlock (in Internet Explorer) at the bottom of your Web browser.

or other Internet-only fares that must be purchased online. Another advantage is that you can cash in on incentives for booking online, such as rebates or bonus frequent-flyer miles.

Business and other frequent travelers also have found numerous benefits in online booking, as the advances in mobile technology provide them with the ability to check flight status, change plans, or get specific directions from handheld computing devices, mobile phones, and pagers. Some sites even e-mail or page a passenger if the flight is delayed.

Online booking is increasingly able to accommodate complex itineraries, even for international travel. The pace of evolution on the Net is rapid, so you'll probably find additional features and advancements by the time you visit these sites. What the future holds for online travelers is ever-increasing personalization and customization, Web sites reaching out to you.

## TRAVEL PLANNING & BOOKING SITES

Below are listings for the top sites for planning and booking travel. The following sites offer domestic and international flight, hotel, and rental car bookings, plus news, destination information, and deals on cruises and vacation packages. Free (one-time) registration is required for booking.

○ **Travelocity (incorporates Preview Travel). www.travelocity.com; www.previewtravel.com; www.frommers.travelocity.com**

Travelocity is Frommer's online travel-planning and booking partner. Travelocity uses the SABRE system to offer reservations and tickets for more than 400 airlines, plus reservations and purchase capabilities for more than 45,000 hotels and 50 car-rental companies. An exclusive feature of the SABRE system is its **Low Fare Search Engine,** which automatically searches for the three lowest-priced itineraries based on a traveler's criteria. Last-minute deals and consolidator fares are included in the search. If you book with Travelocity, you can select specific seats for your flights with online seat maps, and also view diagrams of the most popular commercial aircraft. Its hotel finder provides street-level location maps and photos of selected hotels. With the **Fare Watcher** e-mail feature, you can select up to five routes and receive e-mail notices when the fare changes by $25 or more.

Travelocity's **Destination Guide** includes updated information on some 260 destinations worldwide—supplied by Frommer's.

*Note to AOL Users:* You can book flights, hotels, rental cars, and cruises on AOL at keyword: Travel. The booking software is provided by Travelocity/Preview Travel and is similar to the Internet site. Use the AOL "Travelers Advantage" program to earn a 5% rebate on flights, hotel rooms, and car rentals.

**Online Directory**

# Airline Web Sites

Below are the Web sites for the major airlines. These sites offer schedules and flight booking, and most have pages where you can sign up for e-mail alerts for weekend deals and other late-breaking bargains.

**Aer Lingus.** www.aerlingus.ie
**Air France.** www.airfrance.com
**Alitalia.** www.alitalia.it
**America West.** www.americawest.com
**American Airlines.** www.aa.com
**British Airways.** www.british-airways.com
**Canadian Airlines.** www.cdnair.ca
**Continental Airlines.** www.continental.com
**Delta.** www.delta-air.com
**Iberia.** www.iberia.com
**Lufthansa.** www.lufthansa.com
**Northwest Airlines.** www.nwa.com
**Southwest.** www.southwest.com
**TWA.** www.twa.com
**United Airlines.** www.ual.com
**USAirways.** www.usairways.com
**Virgin Atlantic.** www.virgin-atlantic.com

**Online Directory**

○ **Expedia. expedia.com**
Expedia is Travelocity's major competitor. It offers several ways of obtaining the best possible fares: **Flight Price Matcher** service allows your preferred airline to match an available fare with a competitor; a comprehensive **Fare Compare** area shows the differences in fare categories and airlines; and **Fare Calendar** helps you plan your trip around the best possible fares. Its main limitation is that like many online databases, Expedia focuses on the major airlines and hotel chains, so don't expect to find too many budget airlines or one-of-a-kind B&Bs here.

**TRIP.com. www.trip.com**
TRIP.com began as a site geared for business travelers, but its innovative features and highly personalized approach have broadened its appeal to leisure travelers as well. It is the leading travel site for those using mobile devices to access Internet travel information.

TRIP.com includes a trip-planning function that provides the average and lowest fare for the route requested, in addition to the current available fare. An on-site "newsstand" features breaking news on airfare sales and other travel specials. Among its most popular features are Flight TRACKER and intelliTRIP. **Flight TRACKER** allows users to track any commercial flight en route to its destination anywhere in the U.S., while accessing real-time FAA-based flight monitoring data. **intelliTRIP** is a travel search tool that allows users to identify the best airline, hotel, and rental car fares in less than 90 seconds. In addition, it offers e-mail notification of flight delays, plus city resource guides, currency converters, and a weekly e-mail newsletter of fare updates, travel tips, and traveler forums.

**Yahoo Travel. www.travel.yahoo.com**

Yahoo is currently the most popular of the Internet information portals, and its travel site is a comprehensive mix of online booking, daily travel news, and destination information. The **Best Fares** area offers what it promises and provides feedback on refining your search if you have flexibility in travel dates or times. There is also an active section of message boards for discussions on travel in general and to specific destinations.

## SPECIALTY TRAVEL SITES

Although the sites listed above provide the most comprehensive services, some travelers have specialized needs that are best met by a site that caters specifically to them.

For travelers who prefer unique accommodations, **InnSite** (**www.innsite.com**) offers listings for inns and B&Bs in all 50 U.S. states and dozens of countries around the globe. Find an inn at your destination, take a look at images of the rooms, check prices and availability, and then send e-mail to the innkeeper if you have further questions. This is an extensive directory of bed and breakfast inns but only includes a listing if the proprietor submitted one (*Note:* It's free to get an inn listed.) The descriptions are written by the innkeepers and many listings link to the inn's own Web sites, where you can find more information and images.

"Have Kids, Still Travel!" is the motto of the **Family Travel Forum** (FTF; **www.familytravelforum.com**), a site dedicated to the ideals, promotion, and support of travel with children. FTF is supported by memberships, which are available in flexible prices ranging from a $2.95 monthly fee to a heftier, annual fee for more comprehensive services. Because no advertising is accepted, FTF provides its members with honest, unbiased information, informed advice, and practical tips designed to make traveling with children a healthier, safer, hassle-free experience, not to mention a better value.

## TOP VACATION PACKAGE SITES

Both **Expedia** and **Travelocity** (see above) offer excellent selections and searches for complete vacation packages. Travelers can search by destination and desired dates coupled with how much they are willing to spend. Travel wholesalers, such as **Apple Vacations** (**www.applevacations.com**) and **Funjet** (**www.funjet.com**) are also good starting points but still require that the final booking be handled through a travel agent.

As travel agents tend to be more expert at sorting through the values in vacation packages, you might find **Vacation.com** (**www.vacation.com**) helpful in previewing packages and finding an appropriate agent to help you book the deal. This site represents a nationwide network of 9,800 local travel agencies that specialize in finding the best values in cruises, vacation packages, tours, and other leisure travel services. To find a Vacation.com member

---

**Big Apple Trip Planning**

You can buy a complete vacation—including hotel stay, theater tickets, and more—from **New York City Vacations**, a Big Apple–dedicated online travel agency, endorsed by the New York Convention and Visitors Bureau. It'll even handle your travel arrangements if you choose. Packages always include a few admission freebies and dining discounts. Find them at **www.nycvp.com**.

---

agency, enter your ZIP code and the Vacation.com Agency Finder will locate a nearby office.

## LAST-MINUTE DEALS AND OTHER ONLINE BARGAINS

There's nothing airlines hate more than flying with a lot of empty seats. The Net has enabled airlines to offer last-minute bargains to entice travelers to fill those seats. Most of these are announced on Tuesday or Wednesday and are valid for travel the following weekend, but some can be booked weeks or months in advance. You can sign up for weekly e-mail alerts at airlines' sites (for Web sites of airlines, see "Airline Web Sites," above) or check sites that compile lists of these bargains, such as **Smarter Living** or **WebFlyer** (see below). To make it easier, visit a site that will round up all the deals and send them in one convenient weekly e-mail. But last-minute deals aren't the only online bargains; other sites can help you find value even if you haven't waited until the eleventh hour. Increasingly popular are services that let you name the price you're willing to pay for a airline seat or vacation package and travel auction sites.

**Cheap Tickets. www.cheaptickets.com**
Cheap Tickets has exclusive deals that aren't available through more main-stream channels. One caveat about the Cheap Tickets site is that it will offer fare quotes for a route and later show this fare is not valid for your dates of travel; most other Web sites, such as Expedia, consider your dates of travel before showing what fares are available. Despite its problems, Cheap Tickets can be worth the effort because its fares can be lower than those offered by its competitors.

✪ **1travel.com. www.1travel.com**
Here you'll find deals on domestic and international flights, cruises, hotels, and all-inclusive resorts such as Club Med. 1travel.com's **Saving Alert** compiles last-minute air deals so you don't have to scroll through multiple e-mail alerts. A feature called "Drive a little using low-fare airlines" helps map out strategies for using alternate airports to find lower fares. And **Farebeater** searches a database that includes published fares, consolidator bargains, and special deals exclusive to 1travel.com. *Note:* The travel agencies listed by 1travel.com have paid for placement.

**Bid for Travel. www.bidfortravel.com**
Bid for Travel is another of the travel auction sites, similar to Priceline (see below), which are growing in popularity. In addition to checking airfares, Internet users can place a bid for vacation packages and hotels.

**LastMinuteTravel.com. www.lastminutetravel.com**
Suppliers with excess inventory come to this online agency to distribute unsold airline seats, hotel rooms, cruises, and vacation packages. It's got great deals, but you have to put up with an excess of advertisements and slow-loading graphics.

✪ **Priceline.com. travel.priceline.com**
Even people who aren't familiar with many Web sites have heard about Priceline.com. Launched in 1998 with a $10 million ad campaign featuring William Shatner, Priceline lets you "name your price" for domestic and international airline tickets and hotel rooms. In other words, you select a route and dates, guarantee with a credit card, and make a bid for what you're willing to pay. If one of the airlines in Priceline's database has a fare lower than your bid, your credit card will automatically be charged for a ticket.

Online Directory

Although most people learn about last-minute weekend deals from e-mail dispatches, it can be best to find out precisely when these deals become available. Because these deals are limited, they can vanish within hours—sometimes even minutes—so it pays to log on as soon as they're available. Check the pages devoted to these deals on airlines' Web pages to get the info. An example: Southwest's specials are posted at 12:01am Tuesdays (Central time). So if you're looking for a cheap flight, stay up late and check Southwest's site to grab the best new deals.

You can't say when you want to fly; you have to accept any flight leaving between 6 a.m. and 10 p.m. on the dates you selected, and you might have to make a stopover. No frequent-flyer miles are awarded, and tickets are nonrefundable and can't be exchanged for another flight. So if your plans change, you're out of luck. Priceline can be good for travelers who have to take off on short notice (and who are thus unable to qualify for advance-purchase discounts). But be sure to shop around first, because if you overbid, you'll be required to purchase the ticket—and Priceline will pocket the difference between what it paid for the ticket and what you bid.

Priceline says that more than 35% of all reasonable offers for domestic flights are being filled on the first try, with much higher fill rates on popular routes (New York to San Francisco, for example). They define "reasonable" as not more than 30% below the lowest generally available advance-purchase fare for the same route.

### Smarter Living. www.smarterliving.com

Best known for its e-mail dispatch of weekend deals on 20 airlines, Smarter Living also keeps you posted about last-minute bargains on everything from Windjammer Cruises to flights to Iceland.

### SkyAuction.com. www.skyauction.com

An auction site with categories for airfare, travel deals, hotels, and much more.

### Travelzoo.com. www.travelzoo.com

At this Internet portal, more than 150 travel companies post special deals. It features a Top 20 list of the best deals on the site, selected by its editorial staff each Wednesday night. This list is also available via an e-mail list, free to those who sign up.

### WebFlyer. www.webflyer.com

WebFlyer is a comprehensive online resource for frequent flyers and also has an excellent listing of last-minute air deals. Click on DEAL WATCH for a round-up of weekend deals on flights, hotels, and rental cars from domestic and international suppliers.

## ONLINE TRAVELER'S TOOLBOX

Veteran travelers usually carry some essential items to make their trips easier. Following is a selection of online tools to smooth your journey.

### Visa ATM Locator. www.visa.com/pd/atm/

### MasterCard ATM Locator. www.mastercard.com/atm

Find ATMs in hundreds of cities in the United States and around the world. Both include maps for some locations and both list airport ATM locations, some with maps. *Tip:* You'll usually get a better exchange rate using ATMs

**Online Directory**

One of the best sources of travel information is word-of-mouth from someone who has just been there. Internet discussion groups are offering an unprecedented way for travelers around the globe to connect and share experiences. The **Frommer's Online** site (www.frommers.com) offers these message boards and also areas where you can pose questions to the guidebook writers themselves, in the section, "Ask the Expert." **Yahoo Travel, Expedia,** and **Travelocity** are other good sources of online travel discussion groups.

The granddaddy of specialized discussions on particular topics is **Usenet,** a collection of more than 50,000 newsgroups. You'll find a comprehensive list at **Deja News (www.dejanews.com/usenet)** or at **www.liszt.com.**

than exchanging traveler's checks at banks, but check in advance to see what kind of fees your bank will assess for using an overseas ATM.

**Intellicast. www.intellicast.com**
Weather forecasts for all 50 states and cities around the world. Note that temperatures are in Celsius for many international destinations, so don't think you'll need that winter coat for your next trip to Athens.

**✪ Mapquest. www.mapquest.com**
The best of the mapping sites that lets you choose a specific address or destination, and in seconds, it will return back a map and detailed directions. It really is easier than calling, asking, and writing down directions. The site also links to special travel deals and helpful sites.

**Net Café Guide. www.netcafeguide.com/mapindex.htm**
Locate Internet cafes at hundreds of locations around the globe. Catch up on your e-mail, log onto the Web, and stay in touch with the home front, usually for just a few dollars per hour.

**The Travelite FAQ. www.travelite.org**
Tips on packing light, choosing luggage, and selecting appropriate travel wear—helpful if you always tend to pack too much or are a compulsive list-maker.

**Universal Currency Converter. www.xe.net/currency**
See what your dollar or pound is worth in more than a hundred other countries.

**U.S. Customs Service Traveler Information. www.customs.ustreas.gov/ travel/index.htm**
Wondering what you're allowed to bring into the United States? Check at this thorough site, which includes maximum allowance and duty fees.

**Web Travel Secrets. www.web-travel-secrets.com**
If this list leaves you yearning for more travel-oriented sites, Web Travel Secrets offers one of the best compilations around. One section offers advice and tips on how to find the lowest prices for airlines, hotels, and cruises. The other section provides a comprehensive listing of Web travel links for airfare deals, airlines, booking engines, cars, cruise lines, discount travel and best deals, general travel resources, hotels and hotel discounters, search engines, and travel magazines and newsletters.

**Online Directory**

# 2 The Top Web Sites for New York City

*by Cheryl Farr Leas*

## CITY GUIDES

The **New York Convention and Visitor Bureau**'s **www.nycvisit.com** is a terrific online resource offering tons of information on the city, from trip-planning basics to tips on where to take the kids; you can even book a hotel right online.

But there's much more to be learned about New York in cyberspace than the official line. Sure, there's a lot of junk out there—but the Net boasts some

## Check Your E-Mail While You're on the Road

You don't have to be out of touch just because you don't carry a laptop while you travel. Web browser–based free e-mail programs make it much easier to stay in e-touch.

Just open a freemail account at a browser-based provider, such as **MSN Hotmail** (**hotmail.com**) or **Yahoo! Mail** (**mail.yahoo.com**). Be sure to give your freemail address to the family members, friends, and colleagues with whom you'd like to stay in touch while you're in New York. All you need to check your freemail account while you're away from home is a Web connection, easily available at Net cafes, copy shops, and cash- and credit-card Internet-access machines (often available in hotel lobbies or business centers) throughout the Big Apple. After logging on, point the browser to **www.hotmail.com** or **www.yahoo.com** and enter your username and password, and you'll have access to your mail, both for receiving and sending messages to friends and family back home, for just a few dollars an hour.

The **Times Square Visitors Center,** 1560 Broadway, between 46th and 47th streets (☎ **212/768-1560**), has computer terminals that you can use to send e-mails courtesy of Yahoo; you can even send an electronic postcard with a photo of yourself home to Mom. The **Internet Cafe,** 82 E. 3rd St., between First and Second avenues in the East Village (☎ **212/614-0747;** www.bigmagic.com), offers direct Internet access at $2.50 per 15 minutes. **Cybercafe** (www.cyber-cafe.com), in SoHo at 273 Lafayette St., at Prince Street (☎ **212/334-5140**), and in Times Square at 250 W. 49th St., between Broadway and Eighth Avenue (☎ **212/ 333-4109**), is more expensive at $6.40 per half hour, with a half-hour minimum (you're billed $3.20 for every subsequent 15 minutes). But their T1 connectivity gives you much speedier access, and they offer a full range of other cyber and copy services; there are even Macs on hand, and AOL users can access their accounts. **Kinko's** (www.kinkos.com) charges 20¢ per minute ($12 per hour) and has four downtown locations, all open 24 hours: 100 Wall St., at Water Street (☎ **212/269-0024**); near City Hall at 105 Duane St., between Broadway and Church streets (☎ **212/406-1220**); 250 E. Houston St., between avenues A and B (☎ **212/253-9020**); and 21 Astor Place, at Lafayette Street (☎ **212/ 228-9511**).

terrific sites on the city, which can supply up-to-the minute news and events information; recommendations for those of you with a special interest, whether it be shopping or club-hopping; or just another point of view. These are the city's best general information sites.

### About.com—New York City for Visitors. www.gonyc.about.com

This network of sites has a very useful New York page, hosted by an insightful and opinionated local expert. The site is most notable for its extensive list of links to museums, attractions, guided-tour operators, and the like. Those looking for a more extensive list of bed-and-breakfasts than I could include in this book will find some helpful links under "Accommodations."

### ✪ CitySearch. www.newyork.citysearch.com

Done in cooperation with the *Daily News* and *Time Out New York* magazine—hands down the best weekly magazine source for what's going on in the city—CitySearch is the city's hippest and most comprehensive general-information site, with reviews and listings for restaurants, shopping, hotels and inns, attractions, and nightlife. (The only other site that gives CitySearch a run for its money is New York Today, below.) It's all over current happenings, from the latest museum and gallery shows to the newest restaurants to what's happening on the club scene. CitySearch does take paid advertising and hosts Web sites for advertisers, but the text is always clearly labeled (links say "editorial profile" or "advertiser's Web site"). I've never noted any bias; you'll notice, however, that advertisers' Web sites will pop up first if you do a general search.

### Digital City New York. www.digitalcity.com/newyork

Much like CitySearch, but not quite as comprehensive or quick on the uptake. Still, it's good for an alternative view.

### New York City Reference. www.panix.com/clay/nyc

Commonly referred to as New York City Reference, this handy site is a virtual hyperlink index of New York–related sites. It's regularly updated, and at press time there were about 2,000 links covering every subject area from "The Best Public Toilets" (**www.besttoilets.com,** if you want to bypass the middleman) to "Webcams: Live Pictures of New York City."

### New York Magazine. www.newyorkmag.com

Insightful features on the city. But it doesn't give it all away; some articles are available only in the print magazine. Especially useful are the critics and columnists archives and the "Marketplace" section for shoppers.

### The New York Times Online. www.nytimes.com

The authoritative scoop from the paper of record: news, sports, arts, and much more.

### ✪ New York Today. www.nytoday.com

*The New York Times* created this site as a gift to those of us who want access to the *Times'* cultural coverage without having to wade through the main site (above), which requires you to register and pay archiving fees on past articles. Set up in an easy-access daily calendar format, the site is an expanded version of the paper's cultural coverage. You'll find even more events listings and critics' reviews in this electronic version, including museum schedules and sports events, plus the *Times'* definitive restaurant reviews.

### Paper. www.papermag.com

The online version of the glossy alterna-monthly *Paper* serves as good prep for those of you who want to experience the hipper side of the city. There's opinionated coverage on clubs and bars (including extensive gay-scene coverage)—virtually all downtown, of course.

✪ **The Village Voice. www.villagevoice.com**
Features, columns, and reviews from New York's legendary left-leaning alternative weekly. The up-to-date cultural and entertainment calendar couldn't be more extensive, and it's much easier to search on this user-friendly site than in the rather unwieldy paper. This site is especially good for live music coverage.

## WEATHER FORECASTS

**CNN Interactive. www.cnn.com**

**New York 1 News. www.ny1.com**

**The Weather Channel. www.weather.com**

## GETTING AROUND

**MetroCard.com. www.citysearch.metrocard.com**
The only official outlet for online advance purchases of MetroCard subway and bus fare cards.

✪ **Metropolitan Transportation Authority (MTA). www.mta.nyc.ny.us**
The official site for transportation information. Here you'll find comprehensive information on the MTA subway and bus systems, plus the Long Island Rail Road, Long Island Bus, Metro-North Railroad, and the city's bridges and tunnels.

**New York Transportation. www.newyorktransportation.com**
A private guide to the city's buses, subway, taxis, and car services. You'll also find parking-garage locations throughout the city, towing and auto-repair companies, and other transportation-related stuff.

✪ **The Port Authority of New York & New Jersey. www.panynj.gov**
This terrific official site will tell you everything you need to know about area airports—JFK, LaGuardia, and Newark—including transportation information, the latest terminal construction advisories, and more. You'll also find information on the city's bridges and tunnels (including toll and EZ Pass info), the Port Authority Bus Terminal, the PATH trains that link Manhattan and New Jersey, and ferry services.

## DINING

Don't forget to also check out **New York Today** and **CitySearch,** which have the best and most up-to-date online coverage of the city's dining scene (see "City Guides," above).

**CuisineNet. www.cuisinenet.com**
Listings and reviews for New York and other U.S. cities. Each restaurant has a capsule review compiled by CuisineNet and numeric ratings based on survey responses from site users. For many restaurants, only two or three people have bothered to submit ratings, so they might not be statistically significant. However, comments can be instructive and fun to browse for restaurant buffs.

**Zagat Survey. www.zagat.com**
Reviews of top restaurants for New York and other worldwide cities. Zagat has made a name for itself as the people's choice, as its listings are based on extensive surveys.

**Online Directory**

## SHOPPING

Also check out **CitySearch,** which is beginning to improve its shopping coverage, and *New York* **Magazine** (see "City Guides," above).

**InShop. www.inshop.com**

**NYSale. www.nysale.com**

**Style Shop. www.styleshop.com**

These free registration sites let you in on unadvertised sales taking place throughout the city. InShop is best for detailed information on retail sales, and NYSale and Style Shop are particularly useful for letting you in on unadvertised designer sample sales (in addition to retail sales).

## ARTS & ENTERTAINMENT

In addition to these specific sites, don't forget to check out those listed under "City Guides" above.

### THE PERFORMING ARTS

**CultureFinder. www.culturefinder.com**

An excellent site for all things arts and entertainment in New York City, with an emphasis on museum shows, theater, and classical music. Direct links to ticket sellers, plus exclusive discount ticket offers.

**Broadway.com. www.broadway.com**

✪ **Playbill Online. www.playbill.com or www.playbillclub.com**

**TheaterMania. www.theatermania.com**

✪ **Theatre.com. www.theatre.com**

Each of these competing commercial sites offers complete online information to Broadway and off-Broadway shows, with links to the ticket-buying agencies once you've selected your show. I like the user-friendliness of Theatre.com best, but they all serve fundamentally the same function.

Each offers an **online theater club** that's free to join and can yield substantial savings—from 20 to 50%—on advance-purchase theater tickets for select Broadway and off-Broadway shows. All you have to do is register, and you'll have access to discounts that can range from a few dollars to as much as 50% off regular ticket prices. You can sign up to be notified by e-mail as offers change. (TheaterMania's club only provides information this way, which I consider a downside; both Playbill and Theatre.com allow members to access offers on their sites at any time.) I like the Playbill Club best; it was the first of the bunch and its discounts are wide-ranging, often including the best Broadway and off-Broadway shows. It also offers members excellent deals at city hotels as well as dining discounts on occasion. (Theatre.com offers hotel discounts too, in a more limited fashion).

Broadway.com had not launched at press time, but it's expected to offer a similar sign-up service.

**CurtainUp. www.curtainup.com**

**New York Theatre Wire. www.nytheatre-wire.com**

These sites provide news and reviews of what's playing on the city's stages. In addition to theater, Theatre Wire also includes dance and performance art among its reviews and has a strong alternative bent; good for those looking for something different.

**Live Broadway. www.broadway.org**
The Live Broadway site is run by the League of American Theaters and Producers and offers information and links to official Web sites for Broadway shows exclusively.

**NYC/Onstage. www.tdf.org**
Run by the Theatre Development Fund (the same people behind the TKTS discount ticket booth in Times Square). Click on NYC/ONSTAGE under "The TDF Story." The bias is toward Broadway and off-Broadway plays, but NYC/Onstage is also a good source for chamber and orchestral music (including all Lincoln Center events), dance, opera, cabaret, and family entertainment, too. Once you've chosen an option, you can link to the appropriate ticket-selling outlet, which can be TicketMaster or TeleCharge, or you'll be provided with contact information for the theater's box office.

## LIVE MUSIC & CLUB LISTINGS

**Local Music.com. www.localmusic.com**

**Metropolitan Concert Hotline. www.concerthotline.com**

**Gigmania. www.gigmania.com**
The sources for live music schedules and news. Local Music and Gigmania cover all genres and venues, ranging from tiny downtown clubs to Madison Square Garden, but Metropolitan concentrates on midsize and larger venues. Gigmania has the most comprehensive day-by-day jazz and rock club listings online.

**PromoNY.com. www.promony.com**
This club resource site is most useful for its online guest lists, which can supply you with access and discounted admission to select clubs.

## TICKET SOURCES

**TicketMaster. www.ticketmaster.com**
This national outlet sells tickets for sports, most concerts, and some Broadway shows—all with a hefty service charge.

**TeleCharge. www.telecharge.com**
TeleCharge handles most Broadway and off-Broadway shows and some concerts; expect a surcharge to be added to each purchase.

**TicketWeb. www.ticketweb.com**
TicketWeb also sells theater and concert tickets, generally at smaller venues like Bowery Ballroom and the Knitting Factory. Service charges are usually substantially lower than what TicketMaster tacks on.

**Theatre Direct International (TDI). www.theatredirect.com**

**Keith Prowse & Co. www.keithprowse.com**

**Ticket Depot. www.ticketdepot.com**
These reliable ticket brokers sell tickets at a premium to sold-out shows. The first two brokers specialize in theater tickets, but Ticket Depot handles all kinds of events.

# For Foreign Visitors  3

You've seen it all already—the high-rises, the bustling crowds, the glittering nightlife and shopping. New York's global media profile might make it appear familiar, but movies and TV, music videos, and news images all distort as much as they reflect. The gap between image and reality can make certain situations puzzling for foreign—or even domestic—visitors. This chapter will help prepare you for the more common issues or problems that you might encounter.

## 1 Preparing for Your Trip

### ENTRY REQUIREMENTS

Immigration laws are a hot political issue in the United States these days, and the following requirements may have changed somewhat by the time you plan your trip. Check at any U.S. embassy or consulate for current information and requirements, or plug into the U.S. State Department's Web site at **travel.state.gov**. Click on VISA SERVICES for the latest entry requirements; LINKS TO FOREIGN EMBASSIES will provide you with contact information for U.S. embassies and consulates worldwide.

**VISAS** The U.S. State Department has a **Visa Waiver Pilot Program** allowing citizens of certain countries to enter the United States without a visa for stays of up to 90 days. At press time, this visa waiver program applied to citizens of these countries: Andorra, Argentina, Australia, Austria, Belgium, Brunei, Denmark, Finland, France, Germany, Iceland, Ireland, Italy, Japan, Liechtenstein, Luxembourg, Monaco, the Netherlands, New Zealand, Norway, Portugal, San Marino, Singapore, Slovenia, Spain, Sweden, Switzerland, the United Kingdom, and Uruguay.

Citizens of these countries need only a valid passport and a round-trip air or cruise ticket in their possession upon arrival. (Greece has been preliminarily approved, but at press time, visas were still required.) If they first enter the United States, they can also visit Mexico, Canada, Bermuda, and/or the Caribbean islands and return to the United States without a visa. Further information is available from any U.S. embassy or consulate.

Canadian citizens may enter the United States without visas; they need only proof of residence.

Citizens of all other countries must have: (1) a valid passport that expires at least six months later than the scheduled end of their visit to the United States and (2) a tourist visa, which can be obtained without charge from any U.S. consulate.

**OBTAINING A VISA**    To obtain a visa, you must submit a completed application form (either in person or by mail) with a 1½-inch-square photo and must demonstrate binding ties to a residence abroad. Usually you can obtain a visa at once or within 24 hours, but it might take longer during the summer rush from June through August. If you cannot go in person, contact the nearest U.S. embassy or consulate for directions on applying by mail. Your travel agent or airline office might also be able to provide you with visa applications and instructions. The U.S. consulate or embassy that issues your visa will determine whether you will be issued a multiple- or single-entry visa and any restrictions regarding the length of your stay.

Inquiries about visa cases and the application process can be made by calling ☎ 202/663-1225.

**IMMIGRATION QUESTIONS**    Automated information and live operator assistance regarding U.S. immigration policies and laws is available from the **Immigration and Naturalization Service's Customer Information Center** (☎ 800/375-5283; www.ins.usdoj.gov).

**MEDICAL REQUIREMENTS**    Unless you're arriving from an area known to be suffering from an epidemic (particularly cholera or yellow fever), inoculations or vaccinations are not required for entry into the United States. If you have a disease that requires treatment with narcotics or syringe-administered medications, carry a valid signed prescription from your physician to allay any suspicions that you might be smuggling narcotics (a serious offense that carries severe penalties in the United States).

For HIV-positive visitors, requirements for entering the United States are somewhat vague and change frequently. If an HIV-positive noncitizen applying for a non-immigrant visa knows that HIV is a communicable disease of public health significance but checks "no" on the question about communicable diseases, INS might deny the visa because it thinks the applicant committed fraud. If a non-immigrant visa applicant checks "yes," or if INS suspects the person is HIV positive, it will deny the visa unless the applicant asks for a special waiver for visitors. This waiver is for people visiting the United States for a short time, to attend a conference, for instance, to visit close relatives, or to receive medical treatment.

For up-to-the-minute information concerning HIV-positive travelers, contact the **HIV/AIDS Treatment Information Service** (☎ 800/HIV-0440 or 301/519-0459; www.hivatis.org), the Centers for Disease Control and Prevention's **National AIDS Hotline** (☎ 800/342-2437, or 800/344-7432 in Spanish; www.cdc.org), or the **Gay Men's Health Crisis** (☎ 800/AIDS-NYC or 212/807-6655; www.gmhc.org).

**DRIVER'S LICENSES**    Foreign driver's licenses are mostly recognized in the U.S., although you might want to get an international driver's license if your home license is not written in English.

## PASSPORT INFORMATION

Safeguard your passport in an inconspicuous, inaccessible place like a money belt. If you lose this, visit the nearest consulate of your native country as soon as possible for a replacement (a list of major consulates can be found in "Fast Facts" at the end of this chapter). Passport applications are downloadable from the Internet sites listed below.

**FOR RESIDENTS OF CANADA**    You can pick up a passport application at one of 28 regional passport offices or most travel agencies. A passport is valid for five years (check Web site or call for fee schedule). Children under 16 may be included on a parent's passport, but they will need their own passport to travel if unaccompanied by the parent. Applications, which must be accompanied by two identical passport-size photographs and proof of Canadian citizenship, are available at travel agencies throughout Canada or from the central **Passport Office, Department of Foreign Affairs and International Trade,** Ottawa, K1A 0G3 (☎ **800/567-6868;** www. dfait-maeci.gc.ca/passport). Processing takes 5 days if you apply in person, about 10 days upon receipt if you apply by mail.

**FOR RESIDENTS OF THE UNITED KINGDOM**   To pick up an application for a regular 10-year passport, visit your nearest passport office, major post office, or travel agency, or contact the **UK Passport Agency** (☎ **0870/521-0410;** www.ukpa.gov.uk).

**FOR RESIDENTS OF IRELAND**   Passport applications are available at all Garda stations, at post offices with Passport Express Service, and from the Passport Offices at Setanta Centre, Molesworth Street, Dublin 2 (☎ **353-1/671-1633**), or at 1a South Mall, Cork (☎ **353-21/272-525** or 353-21/276-964). For additional information, visit the Department of Foreign Affairs Web site at **www.irlgov.ie/iveagh** and click on TRAVELING ABROAD.

**FOR RESIDENTS OF AUSTRALIA**   Apply at your State Passports Office (you can also apply at most local post offices). For further information, see the government's Foreign Affairs and Trade Office Web site at **www.dfat.gov.au/passports**.

**FOR RESIDENTS OF NEW ZEALAND**   Complete information and download-able applications can be found online at **www.passports.govt.nz**, or call the Passport Office at ☎ **0800/22-50-50.**

# CUSTOMS
## WHAT YOU CAN BRING IN
Every visitor over 21 years of age may bring in, free of duty, the following: (1) one liter of wine or hard liquor; (2) 200 cigarettes, 100 cigars (but not from Cuba), or three pounds of smoking tobacco; and (3) $100 worth of gifts. These exemptions are offered to travelers who spend at least 72 hours in the United States and who have not claimed them within the preceding six months. It is altogether forbidden to bring into the country foodstuffs (particularly fruit, cooked meats, and canned goods) and plants (vegetables, seeds, tropical plants, and the like). Foreign tourists may bring in or take out up to $10,000 in U.S. or foreign currency with no formalities; larger sums must be declared to U.S. Customs upon entering or leaving, which includes filing form CM 4790. For more specific information regarding U.S. Customs, contact your nearest U.S. embassy or consulate or the **U.S. Customs** office (☎ **202/927-1770;** www.customs.ustreas.gov).

## WHAT YOU CAN BRING HOME
Check with your country's customs or foreign affairs department for the latest guidelines—including items that are not allowed to be brought in to your home country—just before you leave home.

   **U.K. citizens** should contact **HM Customs & Excise Passenger Enquiries** (☎ **0181/910-3744**) or visit **www.open.gov.uk**.

   For a clear summary of **Canadian** rules, visit the comprehensive Web site of the **Canada Customs and Revenue Agency** at **www.ccra-adrc.gc.ca**.

   Citizens of **Australia** should request the helpful Australian Customs brochure *Know Before You Go*, available by calling ☎ **1-300/363-263** from within Australia, or 61-2/6275-6666 from abroad. For additional information, go online to **www. dfat.gov.au** and click on HINTS FOR AUSTRALIAN TRAVELERS.

For **New Zealand** customs information, contact the **New Zealand Customs Service** at ☎ 09/359-6655, or go online to **www.customs.govt.nz.**

## INSURANCE

Although it's not required of travelers, health insurance is highly recommended. Unlike many European countries, the United States does not usually offer free or low-cost medical care to its citizens or visitors. Doctors and hospitals are expensive and in most cases will require advance payment or proof of coverage before they render their services. Travel insurance policies can cover everything from the loss or theft of your baggage and trip cancellation to the guarantee of bail in case you're arrested. Good policies will also cover the costs of an accident, repatriation, or death. See "Health & Insurance" in chapter 2 for more information. Packages such as **Europ Assistance** in Europe are sold by automobile clubs and travel agencies at attractive rates. **Worldwide Assistance Services, Inc.** (☎ 800/777-8710, ext. 409, or 703/204-1897; www.worldwideassistance.com) is the agent for Europ Assistance in the United States.

Although lack of health insurance might prevent you from being admitted to a hospital in nonemergencies, don't worry about being left on a street corner to die: The American way is to fix you now and bill the living daylights out of you later.

**FOR BRITISH TRAVELERS**   Most big travel agents offer their own insurance and will probably try to sell you their package when you book a holiday. Think before you sign. Britain's Consumers' Association recommends that you insist on seeing the policy and reading the fine print before buying travel insurance. **The Association of British Insurers** (☎ 0171/600-3333) gives advice by phone and publishes the free *Holiday Insurance*, a guide to policy provisions and prices. You might also shop around for better deals: Try **Columbus Direct** (☎ 0171/375-0011; www.columbusdirect.co.uk).

**FOR CANADIAN TRAVELERS**   Canadians should check with their provincial health plan offices or call **HealthCanada** (☎ 613/957-2991) to find out the extent of their coverage and what documentation and receipts they must take home in case they are treated in the United States.

## MONEY

**CURRENCY**   The U.S. monetary system is painfully simple: The most common bills (all ugly, all green) are the $1 (colloquially, a "buck"), $5, $10, and $20 denominations. There are also $2 bills (seldom encountered), $50 bills, and $100 bills (the last two are usually not welcome as payment for small purchases). Note that a newly redesigned $100 and $50 bill were introduced in 1996, and a redesigned $20 bill in 1998, but the old-style bills are still legal tender. Expect to see redesigned $10 and $5 notes by the time you arrive.

There are six denominations of coins: 1¢ (1 cent, or a penny); 5¢ (5 cents, or a nickel); 10¢ (10 cents, or a dime); 25¢ (25 cents, or a quarter); 50¢ (50 cents, or a half dollar); and, prized by collectors, the rare $1 piece (the older, large silver dollar and the newer, small Susan B. Anthony coin).

The "foreign-exchange bureaus" so common in Europe are rare even at airports in the United States and nonexistent outside major cities. You'll find them in New York's prime tourist areas such as Times Square, but expect to get extorted on the exchange rate. **American Express** (☎ 800/AXP-TRIP; www.americanexpress.com) has many offices throughout the city, including at the New York Hilton, 1335 Sixth Ave., at 53rd Street (☎ 212/664-7798); the New York Marriott Marquis, 1535 Broadway, in the 8th floor lobby (☎ 212/575-6580); on the mezzanine level at Macy's Herald Square, 34th Street and Broadway (☎ 212/695-8075); and 65 Broadway, between

Exchange Place and Rector Street (☎ 212/493-6500). **Thomas Cook Currency Services** (☎ **800/223-9920;** www.thomascook.com) has locations throughout the city, including JFK Airport and 41 E. 42nd St. (☎ 212/883-0400). Call for additional locations.

It's best not to expect to change foreign money (or traveler's checks denominated in a currency other than U.S. dollars) at a bank branch in New York. In fact, it's best to just leave any currency other than U.S. dollars at home; it might prove a greater nuisance to you than it's worth.

**TRAVELER'S CHECKS**   Although traveler's checks are widely accepted, make sure that they're denominated in U.S. dollars, as foreign-currency checks are often difficult to exchange. The three traveler's checks that are most widely recognized—and least likely to be denied—are **Visa, American Express,** and **Thomas Cook/MasterCard.** Be sure to record the numbers of the checks, and keep that information separate in case they get lost or stolen. Most businesses are pretty good about taking traveler's checks, but you're better off cashing them in at a bank (in small amounts, of course) and paying in cash. Remember: You'll need identification, such as a driver's license or passport, to change a traveler's check.

**CREDIT CARDS & ATMS**   Credit cards are the most widely used form of payment in the United States: **Visa** (BarclayCard in Britain), **MasterCard** (Eurocard in Europe, Access in Britain, Chargex in Canada), **American Express, Diners Club, Discover,** and **Carte Blanche;** you'll also find that New York vendors might also accept international cards such as **enRoute, Eurocard,** and **JCB,** but not as universally as AmEx, MasterCard, or Visa. There are, however, a handful of stores and restaurants that do not take credit cards, so be sure to ask in advance. Most businesses display a sticker near their entrance to let you know which cards they accept. And be aware that often businesses require a minimum purchase price, usually around $10 or $15, to use a credit card.

It is strongly recommended that you bring at least one major credit card. Hotels, car-rental companies, and airlines usually require a credit-card imprint as a deposit against expenses, and in an emergency a credit card can be priceless.

You'll find automated teller machines (ATMs) on just about every block in Manhattan. Some ATMs will allow you to draw U.S. currency against your bank and credit cards. Check with your bank before leaving home, and remember that you will need your personal identification number (PIN) to do so. Most accept Visa, MasterCard, and American Express, as well as ATM cards from other U.S. banks. Expect to be charged up to $3 per transaction, however, if you're not using your own bank's ATM.

## SAFETY

Tourist areas in Manhattan are generally safe, and the city has experienced a dramatic drop in its crime rate in recent years. Still, crime is a national problem, and U.S. urban areas tend to be less safe than those in Europe or Japan. You should always stay alert, use common sense, and trust your instincts. If you feel you're in an unsafe area or situation, you probably are and should leave as quickly as possible.

For more about personal security, see "Playing It Safe" in chapter 4.

**Travel Tip**

Be sure to keep a copy of all your travel papers separate from your wallet or purse, and leave a copy with someone at home should you need it faxed in an emergency.

**DRIVING**   An inviolable rule of thumb for New York: Don't even think of driving within the city. Like many cities, New York has its own arcane rules of the road, confusing one-way streets, incomprehensible street-parking signs, and outrageously expensive parking garages. Public transport—whether buses, subways, or taxis—will get you anywhere you want to go quickly and easily, and that's where you'll be most comfortable.

If you drive to New York in a rental car, return it as soon as you arrive and rent another when you're ready to leave the city. Always keep your car doors locked. Never leave any packages or valuables in sight, because thieves will break car windows. If someone attempts to rob you or steal your car, don't resist. Report the incident to the police department immediately.

## 2  Getting to the United States

In addition to the domestic airlines listed in chapter 2, many international carriers serve John F. Kennedy International and Newark airports. **British Airways** (☎ **0345/ 222-111** in the U.K., 800/AIRWAYS in the U.S.; www.british-airways.com) has daily service from London as well as direct flights from Manchester and Glasgow. **Virgin Atlantic** (☎ **01293/747-747** in the U.K., 800/862-8621 in the U.S.; www. virgin-atlantic.com) flies from London's Heathrow to New York.

Canadian readers might book flights on **Air Canada** (☎ **888/247-2262;** www. aircanada.ca), which offers direct service from Toronto, Montréal, Ottawa, and other cities, and **Canadian Airlines** (☎ **800/426-7000;** www.cdnair.ca).

**Aer Lingus** flies from Ireland to New York (☎ **01/886-8888** in Dublin, 800/IRISH-AIR in the U.S.; www.aerlingus.ie). The following U.S. airlines fly to New York from most major European cities: **Continental** (☎ **01293/776-464** in the U.K., 800/525-0280 in the U.S.; www.continental.com); **TWA** (☎ **0181/815-0707** in the U.K., 800/221-2000 in the U.S.; www.twa.com); **United** (☎ **0845/8-444-777** in the U.K., 800/538-2929 in the U.S.; www.ual.com); **American** (☎ **0181/572-5555** in the U.K., 800/433-7300 in the U.S.; www.americanair.com); and **Delta** (☎ **0800/ 414-767** in the U.K., 800/221-1212 in the U.S.; www.delta-air.com).

**Qantas** (☎ **13-13-13** in Australia, 800/227-4500 in the U.S.; www.qantas.com.au) and **Air New Zealand** (☎ **0800/737-000** in New Zealand, 800/262-1234 in the U.S.; www.airnewzealand.co.nz) fly to the West Coast and will book you straight through to New York City on a partner airline.

**IMMIGRATION & CUSTOMS CLEARANCE**   Visitors arriving by air, no matter what the port of entry, should cultivate patience and resignation before setting foot on U.S. soil. Getting through immigration control might take as long as 2 hours on some days, especially on summer weekends. Add the time it takes to clear Customs, and you'll see that you should make a 2- to 3-hour allowance for delays when you plan your connections between international and domestic flights.

In contrast, for the traveler arriving by car or rail from Canada, the border-crossing formalities have been streamlined to the vanishing point. People traveling by air from Canada, Bermuda, and some places in the Caribbean can sometimes clear Customs and Immigration at the point of departure, which is much quicker.

## 3  If You're Traveling Beyond New York City

**BY PLANE**   Some major American carriers—including Delta and Continental— offer travelers on their transatlantic or transpacific flights special low-price tickets on U.S. continental flights under the **Discover America** program (sometimes called **Visit USA,** depending on the airline). Offering one-way travel between U.S. destinations at

# How to Save on International Airfares

The idea of traveling abroad on a budget is something of an oxymoron, especially when pricey New York is your destination, but you can reduce the price of a plane ticket by several hundred dollars if you take the time to shop around.

If you're on a tight budget and you're coming from Europe, you might want to consider traveling to New York between January and March. That's when airlines such as British Airways and Virgin Atlantic pull out all the stops to fill their post-holiday flights, and fares plummet. Hotels are also suffering the after-Christmas blues, and rooms often go for a relative song.

If you're coming from anywhere overseas, you can take advantage of the APEX (Advance Purchase Excursion) reductions offered by all major U.S. and European carriers. These usually require 7 to 21 days advance booking, cannot be canceled, and might come with significant change fees, but they'll save you hundreds of dollars over full-fare rates. For the best rates, compare fares by calling a number of airlines that serve your departure city and be flexible with your dates and times of travel.

Operated by the European Travel Network, **www.discount-tickets.com** is a great online source for regular and discounted airfares to New York and other destinations around the world. You can also use this site to compare rates and book accommodations, car rentals, and tours. Click on SPECIAL OFFERS for the latest package deals. Students should also try **Campus Travel** (☎ **0171/730-2101;** www.usitcampus.co.uk).

For more money-saving airline advice, see "60 Money-Saving Tips" in chapter 2.

---

significantly reduced prices, this coupon-based airfare program is the best and easiest way to tour the United States at low cost.

These discounted fare coupons are not available in the United States and must be purchased abroad in conjunction with your international ticket. You should ask your travel agent or the airline reservations agent about this program well in advance of your departure date—preferably when you buy your international ticket—because the regulations might govern your trip planning, and conditions can change without notice.

**BY TRAIN**   If you're making a short hop to another East Coast city, such as Boston, Philadelphia, or Washington, D.C., rail is the best way to go. **Amtrak** (☎ **800/USA-RAIL;** www.amtrak.com) trains leave from New York's Pennsylvania Station, at Seventh Avenue and 34th Street.

If you're visiting more than one city, you might want to consider buying a **USA Rail Pass,** which can really save you money over purchasing individual tickets. It's available to international visitors only and good for 15 or 30 days of unlimited travel on Amtrak. The pass is available through many foreign travel agents; with a foreign passport, you can also buy passes at some Amtrak offices in the United States. Your best bet is to call for details or visit the Web site to order the informational brochure as far in advance as possible.

## Fast Facts: For the Foreign Traveler

Also see "Fast Facts" in chapter 4 for city-specific information.

**Automobile Organizations**   The **American Automobile Association (AAA)** is the major auto club in the United States. If you belong to an auto club in your home country, inquire about AAA reciprocity before you leave. You might be able to join AAA even if you're not a member of a reciprocal club; to inquire, call ☎ **800/222-4357,** or visit **www.aaa.com.** AAA is actually an organization of regional auto clubs, so look under "AAA Automobile Club" in the White Pages of the telephone directory. AAA has a nationwide emergency road service telephone number (☎ **800/AAA-HELP).**

**Automobile Rentals**   To rent a car, you need a valid driver's license, a passport, and a major credit card. The minimum age is usually 25, but some companies will rent to younger people and add a surcharge. It's a good idea to buy maximum insurance coverage unless you're positive your own auto or credit-card insurance is sufficient. All major car-rental agencies have branches in Manhattan; try **Hertz** (☎ **800/654-3131;** www.hertz.com), **National** (☎ **800/227-7368;** www.nationalcar.com), or **Avis** (☎ **800/230-4898;** www.avis.com).

**Currency & Currency Exchange**   See "Money" under "Preparing for Your Trip," earlier in this chapter. For the latest market conversion rates, go online to **www.cnn.com/travel/currency**.

**Drinking Laws**   The legal age for purchase and consumption of alcoholic beverages is 21; proof of age is required and often requested at bars, nightclubs, and restaurants, so it's always a good idea to bring ID when you go out. Liquor stores, the only retail outlets for wine as well as hard liquor in New York, are closed on Sundays, holidays, and election days while the polls are open. Beer can be purchased in grocery stores and delis all day Monday to Saturday and Sunday after noon.

Do not carry open containers of alcohol in your car or any public area that isn't zoned for alcohol consumption. The police can, and probably will, fine you on the spot. And nothing will ruin your trip faster than getting a citation for DUI ("driving under the influence"), so don't even think about driving while intoxicated.

**Electricity**   The United States uses 110 to 120 volts AC (60 cycles), compared to 220 to 240 volts AC (50 cycles) in most of Europe, Australia, and New Zealand. If your small appliances use 220 to 240 volts, you'll need a 110-volt transformer and a plug adapter with two flat parallel pins to operate them here. Downward converters that change 220–240 volts to 110–120 volts are difficult to find here, so bring one with you.

**Embassies/Consulates**   All embassies are in Washington, DC Some countries have consulates general in major U.S. cities, and most have a mission to the United Nations in New York City. If your country isn't listed below, call for directory information in Washington, DC (☎ **202/555-1212**) or go online to **www. embassy.org/embassies** for the location and phone number of your national embassy.

**Australia:** Embassy, 1601 Massachusetts Ave. NW, Washington, D.C. 20036 (☎ 202/797-3000; www.austemb.org). Consulate General, 150 E. 42nd St., New York, NY 10117 (☎ 212/351-6500). **Canada:** Embassy, 501 Pennsylvania Ave. NW, Washington, DC 20001 (☎ 202/682-1740; www.cdnemb-washdc.org). Consulate General, 1251 Ave. of the Americas, New York, NY 10020 (☎ 212/ 596-1628; www.canada-ny.com). **Ireland:** Embassy, 2234 Massachusetts Ave. NW, Washington, DC 20008 (☎ 202/462-3939; www.irelandemb.org). Consulate General, 345 Park Ave., New York, NY 10154-0037 (☎ 212/319-2555). **Japan:** Embassy, 2520 Massachusetts Ave. NW, Washington, DC 20008 (☎ 202/ 238-6700; www.embjapan.org). **New Zealand:** Embassy, 37 Observatory Circle,

Washington, DC 20008 (☎ 202/328-4800; www.emb.com/nzemb). Consulate General, 780 Third Ave., New York, NY, 10017 (☎ 212/832-4038). **United Kingdom:** Embassy, 3100 Massachusetts Ave. NW, Washington, DC 20008 (☎ 202/588-6500; www.britainusa.com/bis/embassy/embassy/htm). Consulate General, 845 Third Ave., New York, NY 10022 (☎ 212/745-0200; www.britainusa.com/bis/consular/ny/ny.stm).

**Emergencies**    Call ☎ **911** to report a fire, call the police, or get an ambulance anywhere in the United States. This is a toll-free call (no coins are required at public telephones).

If you have a medical emergency that doesn't require an ambulance, you can walk into a hospital's 24-hour emergency room (usually a separate entrance). For a list of hospitals, see "Fast Facts: New York City" in chapter 4. Because emergency rooms are often crowded and waits are long, one of the walk-in medical centers listed under "Finding a Doctor" under "Health & Insurance" in chapter 2 might be a better option. Otherwise, call ☎ **212/737-2333,** a referral service available 8am to midnight, for doctors who make house calls. Don't be surprised if the first question you are asked is, "Do you have medical insurance?"

**Gasoline (Petrol)**    Petrol is known as gasoline (or simply "gas") in the United States, and petrol stations are known as both gas stations and service stations. Gasoline costs about half as much here as it does in Europe, and taxes are already included in the printed price. One U.S. gallon equals 3.8 liters or .85 Imperial gallons.

**Holidays**    Banks, government offices, post offices, and many stores, restaurants, and museums are closed on the following legal national holidays: January 1 (New Year's Day), the third Monday in January (Martin Luther King, Jr. Day), the third Monday in February (Presidents' Day, Washington's Birthday), the last Monday in May (Memorial Day), July 4 (Independence Day), the first Monday in September (Labor Day), the second Monday in October (Columbus Day), November 11 (Veterans' Day/Armistice Day), the fourth Thursday in November (Thanksgiving Day), and December 25 (Christmas). Also, the Tuesday following the first Monday in November is Election Day and is a federal government holiday in presidential-election years (held every four years, in 2000 and next in 2004).

**Legal Aid**    You will probably never become involved with the American legal system. If you are stopped for a minor infraction (for example, of the highway code, such as speeding), never attempt to pay the fine directly to a police officer; this could be construed as attempted bribery, a much more serious crime. If it's a traffic infraction, do not get out of the car; stay seated and with your hands on the steering wheel until the officer approaches you. Pay fines by mail or directly into the hands of the clerk of the court. If accused of a more serious offense, say and do nothing before consulting a lawyer. Here the burden is on the state to prove a person's guilt beyond a reasonable doubt, and everyone has the right to remain silent, whether he or she is suspected of a crime or actually arrested. Once arrested, a person can make one telephone call to a party of his or her choice. Call your embassy or consulate.

**Mail**    Generally found at intersections, mailboxes are blue with a white eagle logo and carry the inscription U.S. MAIL. If your mail is addressed to a U.S. destination, don't forget to add the five-digit postal code (or ZIP code), after the two-letter abbreviation of the state to which the mail is addressed.

At press time, domestic postage rates are 20¢ for a postcard and 33¢ for a letter. For international mail, a first-class letter of up to one-half ounce costs 60¢ (46¢ to Canada and 40¢ to Mexico); a first-class postcard costs 50¢ (40¢ to Canada and 35¢ Mexico); and a preprinted postal aerogramme costs 50¢. Visit **www.usps.gov** for complete U.S. postal information, or see "Post Offices" under "Fast Facts: New York City" in chapter 4.

**Newspapers/Magazines**    In addition to *The New York Times* and other city papers, many newsstands in New York City carry a selection of international newspapers and magazines. For nearly all major newspapers and magazines from around the world, head to **Universal News & Magazines,** 977 Eighth Ave., at 57th Street (☎ **212/459-0932**), or **Hotalings News Agency,** 142 W. 42nd St., between Broadway and Sixth Avenue (☎ **212/840-1868**).

**Taxes**    There is no value-added tax (VAT) or other indirect tax at the national level, but every state, county, and city has the right to levy its own local tax on all purchases, including hotel and restaurant checks, airline tickets, and so on. Sales tax is usually not included in the price tags on merchandise but is added at the cash register. These taxes aren't refundable. In New York City, the **sales tax** is 8.25%, but there is no sales tax on individual clothing items costing less than $110. The **hotel tax** is 13.25% plus $2 per room per night. The **parking garage tax** is 18.25%.

**Telephone, Telegraph, & Fax**    The telephone system in the United States is run by private corporations, so rates, especially for long-distance service and operator-assisted calls, can vary widely. Generally, hotel surcharges on long-distance and local calls are astronomical, so you're usually better off using a **public pay telephone,** which you'll find clearly marked in most public buildings and private establishments as well as in hotel lobbies and on the street. Many convenience stores and newsstands sell **prepaid calling cards** in denominations up to $50; these can be the least expensive way to call home. Some public phones now accept American Express, MasterCard, and Visa credit cards. **Local calls** made from public pay phones usually cost 25¢ for the first 5 minutes, but sometimes it's 35¢. Pay phones do not accept pennies, and few will take anything larger than a quarter.

Most long-distance and international calls can be dialed directly from any phone. **For calls within the United States and to Canada,** dial 1 followed by the area code and the seven-digit number. **For other international calls,** dial 011 followed by the country code, city code, and the telephone number of the person you are calling. Some country and city codes are as follows: **Australia** 61, Melbourne 3, Sydney 2; **Ireland** 353, Dublin 1; **New Zealand** 64, Auckland 9, Wellington 4; **United Kingdom** 44, Belfast 232, Birmingham 21, Glasgow 41, London 71 or 81. If you're calling the **United States** from another country, the country code is 01.

For **reversed-charge, collect, operator-assisted,** and **person-to-person calls,** dial 0 (the number zero) followed by the area code and number you want; an operator will then come on the line, and you should specify that you are calling collect, or person-to-person, or both. If your operator-assisted call is international, ask for the overseas operator.

For local and national directory assistance ("information"), dial ☎ **411.**

**Telegraph services** are provided primarily by **Western Union.** You can bring your telegram into the nearest Western Union office (there are hundreds across the country) or dictate it over the phone (☎ **800/325-6000;** www. westernunion.com). You can also telegraph money or have it telegraphed to you very quickly, but this service can cost as much as 15% to 20% of the amount sent.

Most hotels have **fax machines** available for guest use (be sure to ask about the charge to use it). Receiving faxes is usually free (always ask first if it matters, though), but a less expensive way to send faxes may be at stores such as **Mail Boxes Etc.,** a national chain of packing service shops (look in the Yellow Pages under "Packing Services").

There are two kinds of telephone directories in the United States. The **White Pages** list private households and business subscribers in alphabetical order. The inside front cover lists emergency numbers for police, fire, ambulance, the poison-control center, crime-victims hot line, and so on. The first few pages will tell you how to make long-distance and international calls, complete with country codes and area codes. Government numbers are usually printed on blue paper within the White Pages. Printed on yellow paper, the **Yellow Pages** list all local services, businesses, industries, and houses of worship according to activity with an index at the front or back. The Yellow Pages also include city plans or detailed area maps, postal ZIP codes, and public transportation routes. A useful online "yellow pages" for finding phone numbers and addresses in New York and other U.S. cities is **www.yp.ameritech.net.**

**Time** The continental United States is divided into **four time zones:** eastern standard time (EST), the time zone New York is in, which is five hours behind Greenwich Mean Time (GMT); central standard time (CST); mountain standard time (MST); and Pacific standard time (PST). Alaska and Hawaii have their own zones. For example, noon in New York City (EST) is 11am in Chicago (CST), 10am in Denver (MST), 9am in Los Angeles (PST), 8am in Anchorage (AST), and 7am in Honolulu (HST).

**Daylight saving time** moves the clock one hour ahead of standard time and is in effect from 1am on the first Sunday in April through 1am the last Sunday in October. When daylight saving time is in effect, New York is only four hours behind Greenwich Mean Time.

For the correct local time, dial ☎ **212/976-1616.**

**Tipping** Tips are a very important part of certain workers' salaries and aren't automatically added to restaurant and hotel bills, so it's necessary to leave appropriate gratuities. **In restaurants,** a tip to the waitperson of 15% to 20% of the total check is customary (in New York City, just double the 8.25% tax to figure the appropriate tip.

**Other tipping guidelines:** 15 to 20% of the fare to taxi drivers, 10% to 15% of the tab to bartenders, $1 to $2 per bag to bellhops, $1 per day to hotel maids, $1 per item to checkroom attendants, $1 to valet parking attendants, and 15%

---

**Money-Saving Calling Tip**

Calls to area codes **800, 888,** and **877** are toll-free. However, calls to numbers in area codes **700** and **900** (chat lines, "dating" services, and so on) can be very expensive— usually 95¢ to $3 or more per minute, and they sometimes have minimum charges that can run as high as $15 or more.

to 20% to hairdressers. Tipping theater ushers, gas station attendants, and cafeteria and fast-food restaurant employees isn't expected.

**Toilets**    In general, you won't find public toilets or "rest rooms" on the streets in New York, but they can be found in hotel lobbies, bars, restaurants, museums, or department stores. See "Rest Rooms" under "Fast Facts: New York City" in chapter 4.

**Traveler's Assistance**    See "Fast Facts: New York City" in chapter 4.

# Getting to Know New York City

## 4

This chapter gives you an insider's take on Manhattan's most distinctive neighborhoods and streets, tells you how to get around town, and serves as a handy reference to everything from personal safety to libraries and liquor laws.

## 1 Orientation

### VISITOR INFORMATION

**INFORMATION OFFICES**  ☼ **The Times Square Visitors Center,** 1560 Broadway, between 46th and 47th streets (where Broadway meets Seventh Avenue), across from the TKTS booth (☎ **212/ 768-1560;** www.timessquarebid.org), is the city's top info stop. This pleasant and attractive center features a helpful information desk offering loads of citywide information. There's also a tour desk selling tickets for Gray Line bus tours and Circle Line boat tours; a Metropolitan Transportation Authority (MTA) desk staffed to sell MetroCard fare cards, provide public transit maps, and answer all of your questions on the transit system; a Broadway Ticket Center providing show information and selling full-price show tickets; ATMs and currency exchange machines; a worldwide newsstand; computer terminals with free Internet access courtesy of Yahoo; an international newsstand; and more. It's open daily from 8am to 8pm.

The New York Convention and Visitors Bureau runs the **NYCVB Visitor Information Center** at 810 Seventh Ave., between 52nd and 53rd streets. In addition to loads of information on citywide attractions and a multilingual information counselor on hand to answer questions, the center also has interactive terminals that provide free touch-screen access to visitor information via CitySearch and sell advance tickets to major attractions (which can save you from standing in long ticket lines once you arrive). There's also an ATM, a gift shop, and a bank of phones that connect you directly with American Express card member services. The center is open Monday through Friday from 8:30am to 6pm, Saturday and Sunday from 9am to 5pm. For over-the-phone assistance, call ☎ **212/484-1222.**

**Grand Central Partnership** runs a staffed information window on the main concourse of Grand Central Terminal, East 42nd Street at the corner of Vanderbilt Avenue (☎ **212/883-2420;** www. grandcentralterminal.com). It's open daily from 9am to 6pm.

**34th Street Partnership,** operates a visitor information kiosk in Penn Station, Seventh Avenue between 31st and 33rd streets (☎ **212/868-0521**), that's well stocked with brochures and staffed Monday through Friday from 8:30am to 5:30pm and Saturday and Sunday from 9am to 6pm.

The **Lower East Side Business Improvement District** operates a neighborhood visitor center at 261 Broome St., between Orchard and Allen streets (☎ **888/ VALUES-4-U** or 212/226-9010), that's open Sunday through Friday from 10am to 4pm (sometimes later). Stop in for an Orchard Street Bargain District shopping guide (which they can also send you in advance), plus other information on this historic, yet newly hip, 'hood.

**PUBLICATIONS**    For comprehensive listings of films, concerts, performances, sporting events, museum and gallery exhibits, street fairs, and special events, the following local publications are your best bets:

*The New York Times* (**www.nytimes.com** or **www.nytoday.com**) features terrific arts and entertainment coverage, particularly in the two-part Friday "Weekend" section and the Sunday "Arts & Leisure" section. Both days boast full guides to the latest happenings in Broadway and off-Broadway theater, classical music, dance, pop and jazz, film, and the art world. Friday is particularly good for cabaret, family fun, and general-interest recreational and sightseeing events.

*Time Out New York* (**www.timeoutny.com**) is my favorite weekly magazine. Dedicated to weekly goings-on, it's attractive, well organized, and easy to use. *TONY* features excellent coverage in all categories, from live music, theater, and clubs (gay and straight) to museum shows, dance events, book and poetry readings, and kids' stuff. The regular "Check Out" section, unequaled in any other listings magazine, will fill you in on upcoming sample and closeout sales, crafts and antiques shows, and other shopping-related scoop. A new issue hits newsstands every Thursday.

The free weekly *Village Voice* (**www.villagevoice.com**), the city's legendary alterna-paper, is available late Tuesday downtown and early Wednesday in the rest of the city. From classical music to clubs, the arts and entertainment coverage couldn't be more extensive, and just about every live music venue advertises its shows here. But I find the paper a bit unwieldy to navigate, and the exposé tone of its features can be tiresome.

Other useful weekly rags include the glossy *New York* magazine (**www.newyorkmag. com**), whose "Cue" section is a selective guide to city arts and entertainment, and *The New Yorker,* which features an artsy "Goings On About Town" section at the front of the magazine. Monthly **Paper** (**www.papermag.com**) is a glossy alterna-mag that serves as good prep for those of you who want to experience the hipper side of the city.

## CITY LAYOUT

Open the sheet map that comes free with this book and you'll see the city consists of five boroughs: **Manhattan,** where most of the visitor action is; the **Bronx,** the only borough connected to the mainland United States; **Queens,** where Kennedy and LaGuardia airports are located and which borders the Atlantic Ocean and occupies part of Long Island; **Brooklyn,** south of Queens, which is also on Long Island and is famed for its attitude, accent, and Atlantic-front Coney Island; and **Staten Island,** the least populous borough, bordering Upper New York Bay on one side and the Atlantic Ocean on the other.

But it is Manhattan, the long finger-shaped island pointing southwest off the mainland—surrounded by the Harlem River to the north, the Hudson River to the west, the East River (really an estuary) to the east, and the fabulous expanse of Upper New York Bay to the south—that most visitors think of when they envision New York.

Despite the fact that it's the city's smallest borough (13$^1$/$_2$ miles long, 2$^1$/$_2$ miles wide, 22 square miles), Manhattan contains the city's most famous attractions, buildings, and cultural institutions. For that reason, all of the accommodations and most of the restaurants suggested in this book are in Manhattan.

In most of Manhattan, finding your way around is a snap because of the logical, well-executed grid system by which the streets are numbered. If you can discern Uptown and Downtown, and East Side and West Side, you can find your way around pretty easily. In real terms, **Uptown** means north of where you happen to be and **Downtown** means south, although sometimes these labels have vague psychographical meanings (generally speaking, "Uptown" chic versus "Downtown" bohemianism).

**Avenues** run north and south (uptown and downtown). Most are numbered. **Fifth Avenue** divides the East Side from the West Side of town and serves as the eastern border of Central Park north of 59th Street. **First Avenue** is all the way east and **Twelfth Avenue** is all the way west. The three most important unnumbered avenues on the East Side you should know are between Third and Fifth Avenues: **Madison** (east of Fifth), **Park** (east of Madison), and **Lexington** (east of Park, just west of Third). Important unnumbered avenues on the West Side are **Avenue of the Americas,** which all New Yorkers call Sixth Avenue; **Central Park West,** which is what Eighth Avenue north of 59th Street is called as it borders Central Park on the west (hence the name); **Columbus Avenue,** which is what Ninth Avenue is called north of 59th Street; and **Amsterdam Avenue,** or Tenth Avenue north of 59th.

**Broadway** is the exception to the rule—the only major avenue that doesn't run uptown–downtown. It cuts a diagonal path across the island, from the northwest tip down to the southeast corner. As it crosses most major avenues, it creates **squares** (Times Square, Herald Square, Madison Square, and Union Square, for example).

**Streets** run east–west (crosstown) and are numbered consecutively as they proceed uptown from Houston (HOUSE-ton) Street. So to go uptown, simply walk north of, or to a higher-numbered street than, where you are. Downtown is south of (or a lower-numbered street than) your current location. If you can see a major landmark like the Empire State Building or the World Trade Center, it's easy to determine uptown from downtown if you know what street you are on and remember that the former is on 34th Street and the latter near the southern tip of the island.

As I've already mentioned, Fifth Avenue is the dividing line between the **East Side** and **West Side** of town (except below Washington Square, where Broadway serves that function). On the East Side of Fifth Avenue, streets are numbered with the distinction "East," on the West Side of that avenue they are numbered "West." East 51st Street, for example, begins at Fifth Avenue and runs east to the East River, and West 51st Street begins at Fifth Avenue and runs west to the Hudson River.

**If you're looking for a particular address,** remember that even-numbered street addresses are on the south side of streets and odd-numbered addresses are on the north. Street addresses increase by about 50 per block starting at Fifth Avenue. For example, nos. 1 to 50 East are just about between Fifth and Madison avenues, while nos. 1 to 50 West are just about between Fifth and Sixth avenues. Traffic generally runs east on even-numbered streets and west on odd-numbered streets, with a few exceptions, such as the major east–west thoroughfares—**14th, 23rd, 34th, 42nd, 57th, 72nd, 79th, 86th,** and so on—which have two-way traffic. Therefore 28 W. 23rd St., is a short walk west of Fifth Avenue; 325 E. 35th Street would be a few blocks east of Fifth.

Avenue addresses are irregular. For example, 994 Second Avenue is at East 51st Street, but so is 320 Park Avenue. Thus, it's important to know a building's cross street to find it easily.

## Orientation Tips

I've indicated the cross streets for all destinations in this book, but be sure to ask for the cross street (or avenue) if you're ever calling for an address.

When you give a taxi driver an address, always specify the cross streets. New Yorkers, even most cab drivers, probably wouldn't know where to find 284 E. 81st St., but they do know where to find 81st and Second. If you're heading to the Afghan Kebab House, for example, tell them that it's on Ninth Avenue between 51st and 52nd. The exact number (in this case, 764) is given only as a further precision.

If you have only the numbered address on an avenue and need to figure out the cross street, put new batteries in your calculator and refer to the address locator in the front of the Yellow Pages.

---

Unfortunately, these rules don't apply to neighborhoods in Lower Manhattan, south of 14th Street—such as Wall Street, Chinatown, SoHo, TriBeCa, and the Village—because they sprang up before engineers devised this brilliant grid scheme. A good map is essential when exploring these areas.

**STREET MAPS** You'll find a useful pull-out map of Manhattan at the back of this book. There's also a decent one available for free as part of the **Official NYC Visitor Kit** (see "Visitor Information" in chapter 2); you can also pick it up for free at most of the visitor centers listed above.

Even with all these freebies at hand, I suggest investing in a map with more features if you really want to zip around the city like a pro. **Hagstrom** maps are my favorites, because they feature block-by-block street numbering—so instead of trying to guess what the cross street for 125 Prince Street is, you can see right on your map that it's Greene Street. Stephen Van Dam's **New York City Unfolds,** a pop-up map that unfolds and refolds like an origami flower, is a good idea because it's easy to handle on the run and pack away into a purse or pocket; it can also be read discreetly, which is a major deterrent to crime. These and other visitor-friendly maps are available at just about any good bookstore, including the Barnes & Noble and Borders Books & Music branches around town; see chapter 8 for locations.

# Manhattan's Neighborhoods in Brief

Because they grew up over the course of hundreds of years, all of Manhattan neighborhoods have multiple, splintered personalities and fluid boundaries. Still, it's relatively easy to agree upon what they stand for in general terms—so if you stop a New Yorker on the street and ask them to point you to, say, the Upper West Side or the Flatiron District, they'll know where you want to go. From south to north, here is how I've defined Manhattan's neighborhoods for use throughout this book. It's a good idea to refer to the fold-out map in the back of this book as you review this section to get your bearings.

### Downtown

**Lower Manhattan: South Street Seaport & the Financial District** At one time, this was New York. Originally established by the Dutch in 1625 (hence the city's original name, Nieuw Amsterdam), the first settlements sprung up here, on the southern tip of Manhattan island, and everything uptown was farm country and wilderness. Although all that's changed, this is still the best place in the city to search for the past. (The Wall Street and Financial District walking tour in chapter 7 can guide you.)

# Manhattan Neighborhoods

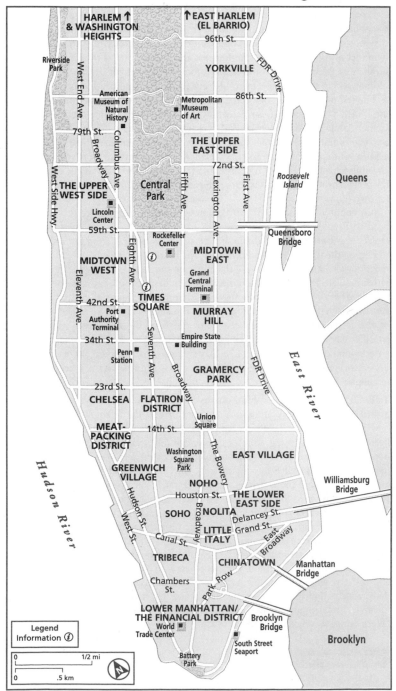

HARLEM ↑
& WASHINGTON
HEIGHTS

↑EAST HARLEM
(EL BARRIO)

96th St.

Riverside
Park

YORKVILLE

86th St.

FDR Drive

West End Ave.

American
Museum of
Natural
History

Metropolitan
Museum
of Art

79th St.

Columbus Ave.

THE UPPER
EAST SIDE

72nd St.

West Side Hwy.

THE UPPER
WEST SIDE

Broadway

Central
Park

Fifth Ave.

Lexington Ave.

First Ave.

Roosevelt
Island

Queens

Lincoln
Center

59th St.

Rockefeller
Center

Queensboro
Bridge

MIDTOWN
WEST

Eighth Ave.

ⓘ

MIDTOWN
EAST

Eleventh Ave.

ⓘ

TIMES
SQUARE

Grand
Central
Terminal

42nd St.
Port
Authority
Terminal

MURRAY
HILL

34th St.

Empire State
Building

Penn
Station

Seventh Ave.

Broadway

GRAMERCY
PARK

FDR Drive

East River

23rd St.

CHELSEA

FLATIRON
DISTRICT

Union
Square

MEAT-
PACKING
DISTRICT

14th St.

Washington
Square
Park

The Bowery

EAST VILLAGE

GREENWICH
VILLAGE

NOHO

Williamsburg
Bridge

Houston St.

THE LOWER
EAST SIDE

SOHO

Hudson St.

NOLITA

Broadway

Delancey St.

LITTLE
ITALY

Grand St.

West St.

Canal St.

East Broadway

TRIBECA

CHINATOWN

Manhattan
Bridge

Park Row

Chambers
St.

Hudson River

LOWER MANHATTAN/
THE FINANCIAL DISTRICT

Brooklyn
Bridge

Legend
Information ⓘ

World
Trade Center

South Street
Seaport

Brooklyn

Battery
Park

0                1/2 mi

0        .5 km

Lower Manhattan constitutes everything south of Chambers Street. Battery Park, the point of departure for the Statue of Liberty, Ellis Island, and Staten Island, is on the very south tip of the island. The South Street Seaport, now touristy but still a reminder of times past when shipping was the raison d'etre of the city, lies a bit north on the east coast; it's just south of the Brooklyn Bridge, which stands proudly as the ultimate engineering achievement of New York's 19th-century Industrial Age.

The rest of the area is considered the Financial District. It's anchored by the towering World Trade Center (also known as the Twin Towers), with the World Financial Center complex and residential Battery Park City to the west, and Wall Street—now a state of mind much grander than the actual narrow street itself—running crosstown a little south and to the east. City Hall is at the northern border of the district, abutting Chambers Street (look for City Hall Park on the map). Most of the streets of this neighborhood are narrow concrete canyons, with Broadway serving as the main uptown–downtown artery.

Just about all of the major subway lines congregate here before they either end or head to Brooklyn (the Sixth Avenue B, D, F, Q line being the chief exception—it crosses into Brooklyn from the Lower East Side, over the Manhattan Bridge).

During the week this neighborhood is the heart of capitalism and city politics, and the sidewalks are crowded with the business-suit set. The neighborhood still feels rather desolate after work and on the weekends, despite the fact that some office buildings have been redeveloped into high-end apartments. This might sound like the most romantic time to explore the area, but it's actually more fun to be here at the height of the hustle and bustle, between 8am and 6pm on weekdays. Still, you might consider staying down here on the weekend or during the holidays, when you can find an accommodations bargain in the luxury hotels that business travelers have abandoned for home; see "Getting the Most for Your Money, Part I: Weekend Packages" in chapter 5.

**TriBeCa**    Bordered by the Hudson River to the west, the area north of Chambers Street, west of Broadway, and south of Canal Street is the *Tri*angle *Be*low *Ca*nal Street, or TriBeCa. Since the 1980s, as SoHo became saturated with chic, the spillover has been quietly transforming TriBeCa into one of the city's hippest residential neighborhoods, where celebrities and families quietly coexist in cast-iron warehouses converted into spacious, expensive loft apartments. Artists' lofts and galleries as well as hip antiques and design shops pepper the area, as do as some of the city's best restaurants. Robert DeNiro gave the neighborhood a tremendous boost when he established the Tribeca Film Center, and Miramax headquarters gave the area further capitalist-chic cachet. Still, historic streets such as White (especially the Federal-style building at no. 2) and Harrison (the complete stretch west from Greenwich Street) evoke a bygone, more human-scaled New York, as do a few hold-out businesses and old-world pubs. I love this neighborhood, because it seems to have brought together the old city and the new without bastardizing either. And because retail spaces are usually a few doors apart rather than right on top of one another, it also manages to be more peaceful than similarly popular neighborhoods. It also happens to be home to one of my favorite budget hotels in the city (see chapter 5).

**Impressions**

*Can we actually "know" the universe? It's hard enough finding your way around Chinatown.*

—Woody Allen

The main uptown–downtown drag is West Broadway (two blocks to the west of Broadway), and the main subway line is the 1/9, which stops at Franklin in the heart of the 'hood. Take your map; the streets are a maze.

**Chinatown**   New York City's most famous ethnic enclave is bursting past its traditional boundaries and encroaching on Little Italy, much to the chagrin of civic fathers there. The former marshlands northeast of City Hall and below Canal Street, from Broadway to the Bowery, are where Chinese immigrants arriving from San Francisco were forced in the 1870s. This booming neighborhood is now a conglomeration of Asian populations. As such, it offers tasty cheap eats in kaleidoscopic cuisines from Szechuan to Hunan to Cantonese to Vietnamese to Thai. Exotic shops offer strange foods, herbs, and souvenirs, and bargains on clothing and leather are plenty. The area is also home to sweatshops, however, and doesn't have quite the quaint character you'd find in San Francisco; although it does feel more authentic. And walking down Canal Street, peering into the myriad electronics and luggage stores and watching crabs cut loose from their handlers at the exotic fish markets, is some of the city's best free entertainment.

The Grand Street (B, D, Q) and Canal Street (J, M, Z, N, R, 6) street stations will get you to the heart of the action. The streets are crowded during the day and empty out after around 9pm; they remain quite safe, but the neighborhood is more enjoyable during the bustle.

**Little Italy**   Nearby is Little Italy, just as ethnic if not quite so vibrant and compelling for its own culinary treats. Traditionally the area east of Broadway between Houston and Canal streets, the community is shrinking today, due to the encroachment of thriving Chinatown. It's now limited mainly to Mulberry Street, where you'll find most restaurants. With rents going up in the increasingly trendy Lower East Side, a few chic spots are moving in, further intruding upon the old-world landscape. To reach Little Italy, your best bet is to walk up Mulberry Street from the Grand Street station or east from the Spring Street station on the no. 6 line. September is a great time to visit, when Mulberry Street comes alive during the **Feast of San Gennaro.**

**The Lower East Side**   Of all the successive waves of immigrants and refugees who passed through this densely populated tenement neighborhood from the mid-19th century to the 1920s, it was the Eastern European Jews who left the most lasting impression here.

Drugs and crime ultimately supplanted the Jewish communities that first popped up between Houston and Canal streets, east of the Bowery, dragging the Lower East Side into the gutter—until recently, that is. The neighborhood has experienced quite a renaissance over the last few years; lots of hip Generation Y–targeted bars, clubs, and boutiques have sprung up, prompting complaints from old-time residents who seem to have preferred the desolation and crime of the old days. Still, the area can still be a tad grungy.

There are some remnants of what was once the largest Jewish population in America along Orchard Street, where you'll find great bargain hunting in its many old-world fabric and clothing stores still thriving between the club-clothes boutiques and trendy lounges. There's a good visitor center, where you can get your bearings and pick up a shopping guide, just around the corner at 261 Broome St. Keep in mind that the old-world shops (and the visitor center) close early on Friday afternoon and all day on Saturday (the Jewish Sabbath). The trendy set can be found mostly along **Orchard and Ludlow streets** south of Houston and north of Delancey, with more new shops, bars, and restaurants popping up in the blocks to the east every day.

**Impressions**

*Nobody's going to come from the boondocks anymore and live in SoHo and be an artist. You can't afford to park there, let alone live there.*

—Pete Hamill

This area is not well served by the subway system (one cause for its years of decline), so your best bet is to take the F train to Second Avenue and walk east on Houston; when you see Katz's Deli, you'll know you've arrived.

**SoHo & NoLiTa**    No relation to the London neighborhood of the same name, SoHo is an abbreviation of "South of Houston Street" (pronounced HOUSE-ton). This super-fashionable neighborhood extends down to Canal Street, between Sixth Avenue to the west and Lafayette Street (one block east of Broadway) to the east.

An industrial zone during the 19th century, SoHo retains the impressive cast-iron architecture of the era, and in many places, cobblestone peeks out from beneath the street's asphalt. In the early 1960s, cutting-edge artists began occupying the drab and deteriorating buildings, soon turning it into the trendiest neighborhood in the city. SoHo is now a prime example of urban gentrification and a major New York attraction thanks to its impeccably restored buildings, influential arts scene, fashionable restaurants, and stylish boutiques. On weekends, the cobbled streets and narrow sidewalks are crowded with gallery goers and shoppers, with the prime action being between Broadway and Sullivan Street north of Grand Street.

Some critics claim that SoHo is becoming a victim of its own popularity—witness the recent departure of several imaginative galleries and independent boutiques to TriBeCa and Chelsea as well as the unfortunate influx of suburban mall-style stores such as J. Crew and Victoria's Secret. However, SoHo is still one of the best shopping neighborhoods in the city, and few are more fun to browse. High-end street peddlers set up along the boutique-lined sidewalks. At night, the neighborhood is transformed into a terrific, albeit pricey, dining and bar-hopping neighborhood (although I recommend some appealing affordable options, too; see chapter 6). It's easily accessible by subway: Take the B, D, F, or Q train to the Broadway–Lafayette stop; the N, R to the Prince Street Station; or the C, E to Spring Street.

In recent years SoHo has been crawling its way east, taking over Mott and Mulberry streets—and white-hot Elizabeth Street in particular—north of Kenmare Street, an area now known as **NoLiTa** for its *No*rth of *Li*ttle *Ita*ly location. NoLiTa is becoming increasingly well known for its hot shopping prospects. Some of the city's most promising young clothing designers have taken up residence here, but don't expect bargains. Good, affordable restaurants abound, though, making the neighborhood well worth a browse. Taking the 6 to Spring Street will get you closest by subway, but it's just a short walk east from SoHo proper.

**The East Village & NoHo**    The **East Village,** which extends between 14th Street and Houston Street, from Broadway east to First Avenue and beyond to Alphabet City—avenues A, B, C, and D—is where the city's real Bohemia has gone. Once, flower children tripped along St. Mark's Place and listened to music at the Fillmore East. Now the East Village is a fascinating mix of some of the city's best wallet-friendly restaurants; upstart clothing designers and kitschy boutiques offering affordable, one-of-a-kind fashions and souvenirs; punk-rock clubs (yep, still) and folk cafes; plus a half-dozen or so off-Broadway theaters—all of which give the neighborhood a youthful vibe and a low-budget appeal for both visitors and locals with limited resources.

The gentrification that has swept the city has made a huge impact on the East Village, but there's still a seedy element that some of you won't find appealing. Now yuppies and other ladder-climbing types make their homes alongside old-world Russian immigrants who have lived in the neighborhood forever and the cross-dressers and squatters who settled here in between. The neighborhood still embraces great ethnic diversity, with strong elements of its Ukrainian and Irish heritage, and more recent immigrants have taken over Sixth Street between First and Second avenues, turning it into a haven of cheap eats known as Little India.

The East Village isn't very accessible by subway; unless you're traveling along 14th Street (the L Line will drop you off at Third and First avenues), your best bet is to take the N, R to 8th Street or the 6 to Astor Place and walk east.

Until 1998 or so, Alphabet City resisted gentrification and remained a haven of drug dealers and other unsavory types. No more. Bolstered by a major real-estate boom, this way-east area of the East Village has blossomed, especially among New York's young Internet-industry techies, who have a few bucks to spend. French bistros and smart shops are popping up on every corner. Nevertheless, the neighborhood can get deserted late at night because it's generally the province of locals and so far off the subway line, so know where you're going if you venture out here.

The southwestern section of the East Village, around Broadway and Lafayette between Bleecker and 4th streets, is called **NoHo** (for *No*rth of *Ho*uston), and has a completely different character. As you might have guessed from its name, this area has developed much more like its neighbor to the south, SoHo. Here you'll find a crop of trendy lounges, stylish restaurants, cutting-edge designers, and upscale antiques shops. NoHo is wonderful fun to browse; the Bleecker Street stop on the no. 6 line will land you right in the heart of it, and the Broadway/Lafayette stop on B, D, F, Q lines will drop you right at its edge.

**Greenwich Village**   Tree-lined streets crisscross and wind, following ancient streams and cow paths. Each block reveals yet another row of Greek Revival town houses, a well-preserved Federal-style house, or a peaceful courtyard or square. This is "the Village," from Broadway west to the Hudson River, bordered by Houston Street to the south and 14th Street to the north. It defies Manhattan's orderly grid system with streets that predate it, virtually every one choc-a-block with activity, and unless you live here it might be impossible to master the lay of the land—so be sure to have a map on hand as you explore. The Seventh Avenue line (1, 2, 3, 9) is the area's main subway artery, and the West 4th Street stop (where the A, C, E lines meet the B, D, F, Q lines) serves as its central hub.

Nineteenth-century artists such as Mark Twain, Edgar Allan Poe, Henry James, and Winslow Homer first gave the Village its reputation for embracing the unconventional. Groundbreaking artists such as Edward Hopper and Jackson Pollack were drawn in, as were writers like Eugene O'Neill, e.e. cummings, and Dylan Thomas. Radical thinkers from John Reed to Upton Sinclair basked in the neighborhood's liberal ethos, and beatniks Allen Ginsberg, Jack Kerouac, and William Burroughs dug the free-swinging atmosphere. Now it's the roost of choice for the young celebrity set, with the likes of Gwyneth Paltrow, the Beastie Boys, and Matthew Broderick and Sarah Jessica Parker drawn by its historic, low-rise, laid-back charms. Gentrification and escalating real-estate values conspire to push out the artistic element, but culture and counter-culture still rub shoulders in cafes, internationally renowned jazz clubs, neighborhood bars, off-Broadway theaters, and an endless variety of tiny shops and restaurants. With a few charming and affordable hotels on hand (see chapter 5), the Village makes a great base for independent-minded visitors who prefer to avoid more touristy areas in favor of a quirkier, more residential view of the city.

The Village is probably the most chameleon-like of Manhattan's neighborhoods. Some of the highest-priced real estate in the city runs along lower Fifth Avenue, which dead-ends at Washington Square Park. Serpentine Bleecker Street stretches through most of the neighborhood and is emblematic of the area's historical bent. The tolerant, anything-goes attitude in the Village has fostered a large gay community, which is still largely in evidence around Christopher Street and Sheridan Square. The West Village, west of Seventh Avenue, boasts a more relaxed vibe and some of the city's most charming and historic brownstones. Three colleges—New York University, Parsons School of Design, and the New School for Social Research—keep the area thinking young—hence the popularity of Eighth Street, lined with shops selling cheap, hip clothes to bridge-and-tunnel kids and the college crowd. Streets are often crowded with weekend warriors and teenagers, especially on Bleecker, West 4th, 8th, and surrounding streets, so keep an eye on your wallet when navigating the weekend throngs.

## Midtown

**Chelsea & the Meat-Packing District**   Chelsea has come on strong of late as a hip address, especially for the gay community. A low-rise composite of town houses, tenements, lofts, and factories, the neighborhood comprises roughly the area west of Sixth Avenue from 14th to 30th streets. (Sixth Avenue itself below 23rd Street is actually considered part of the Flatiron District; see below.) Chelsea has also turned into one of the city's best-value accommodations neighborhoods for budget-minded travelers looking for something that's special as well as affordable (see chapter 5). Its main arteries are Seventh and Eighth avenues, and it's primarily served by the C, E and 1, 9 subway lines.

The Chelsea Piers sports complex to the far west and a host of shops, well-priced bistros, and thriving bars along the main drags have contributed to the area's rebirth. Even the Hotel Chelsea—the neighborhood's most famous architectural and literary landmark, where Thomas Wolfe and Arthur Miller wrote, Bob Dylan composed "Sad-Eyed Lady of the Low Land," Viva and Edie Sedgwick of Andy Warhol fame lived, and Sid Vicious killed screechy girlfriend Nancy Spungen—has undergone a renovation (be sure to pop into the lobby if you're a pop-culture buff). You'll find a number of popular flea markets set up in parking lots along Sixth Avenue, between 24th and 27th streets, on the weekends.

One of the most influential trends in Chelsea has been the establishment of far **West Chelsea** (from Ninth Avenue west) and the adjacent **Meat-Packing District** (south of West Chelsea, roughly from 17th Street to Little West 12th Street) as the style-setting neighborhoods for the 21st century. What SoHo was in the '60s, this industrial westworld (dubbed "the Lower West Side" by *New York* magazine) is today. New restaurants, cutting-edge shopping, and super-hot nightspots pop up daily in the still-beefy Meat-Packing District, and the area from West 22nd to West 29th Street between Tenth and Eleventh avenues is home to the cutting edge of today's New York art scene, with West 26th serving as the unofficial "gallery row." The power of art can also be found at the Joyce Theater, New York's principal modern-dance venue. This area is still seriously industrial and in the early stages of transition, however, and not for everyone. With galleries and bars tucked away in converted warehouses and former meat lockers, browsing can be frustrating and the sometimes-desolate streets a tad intimidating. Your best bet is to have a specific destination (and an exact address) in mind, be it a restaurant, gallery, boutique, or nightclub, before you come.

**The Flatiron District, Union Square & Gramercy Park**   These adjoining and, at places, overlapping neighborhoods are some of the city's most appealing. Their streets have been rediscovered by New Yorkers and visitors alike thanks to great shopping and dining opportunities, and an impressive new hotel has been added to the mix this year. The commercial spaces are often large loftlike expanses with witty designs and graceful columns.

The **Flatiron District** lies south of 23rd Street to 14th Street, between Broadway and Sixth Avenue and centers around the historic Flatiron Building on 23rd (so named for its triangular shape) and Park Avenue South, which has become a sophisticated (and pricey) new Restaurant Row. Below 23rd Street along Sixth Avenue, mass-market discounters such as Filene's Basement, Bed, Bath & Beyond, Old Navy, and others have moved in. The shopping gets classier on Fifth Avenue, where you'll find a mix of national names (including Kenneth Cole, Banana Republic, and trendy Restoration Hardware) and hip boutiques. Lined with Oriental-carpet dealers and high-end fixture stores, Broadway is becoming the city's home-furnishings alley; its crowning jewel is the gargantuan, and justifiably famous, ABC Carpet & Home.

**Union Square** is the hub of the entire area; the N, R, 4, 5, 6, and L trains stop here, making it easy to reach from most other city neighborhoods. Long in the shadows of the more bustling (Times and Herald) and high-toned (Washington) city squares, Union Square has experienced a major renaissance in the last decade. Local businesses joined forces with the city to rid the park of drug dealers a few years back, and now it's a delightful place to spend an afternoon. Union Square is best known as the setting for New York's premier greenmarket every Monday, Wednesday, Friday, and Saturday. Musical acts often play the small pavilion at the north end of the park, and in-line skaters take over the market space in the after-work hours. A number of hip restaurants rim the square, as do superstores such as Toys 'R' Us, the city's best Barnes & Noble superstore, and a Virgin Megastore.

From about 16th to 23rd streets, east from Park Avenue South to about Second Avenue, is the leafy, largely residential district known as **Gramercy Park.** The pity of the Gramercy Park district is that so few can enjoy the park of the same name: Built by Samuel Ruggles in the 1830s to attract buyers to his property in the area, it is the only private park in the city and is locked to all but those who live on its perimeter (the rule is that your windows have to look over the park for you to have a key). Located at the southern endpoint of Lexington Avenue (at 21st Street), it is one of the most peaceful spots in the city. If you know someone who has a magic key, go there.

At the northern edge of the area, fronting the Flatiron Building on 23rd Street and Fifth Avenue, is another of Manhattan's lovely little parks, **Madison Square.** Across from its northeastern corner once stood Stanford White's original Madison Square Garden (in whose roof garden White was murdered in 1906 by possibly deranged, but definitely jealous, millionaire Harry K. Thaw). It's now majestically presided over by the massive New York Life Insurance building, the masterful New York State Supreme Court, and the Metropolitan Life Insurance Company, whose tower in 1909 was the tallest building in the world at 700 feet.

**Times Square & Midtown West**    Midtown West, the vast area from 34th to 59th streets west of Fifth Avenue to the Hudson River, encompasses several famous names: Madison Square Garden, the Garment District, Rockefeller Center, the Theater District, and Times Square. This is New York's tourism central, where you'll find the bright lights and bustle that draws people from all over the world. As such, this is the city's biggest hotel neighborhood, with a lot of budget and midpriced choices amidst the famous-name luxury hotels.

The 1, 2, 3, 9 subway line serves the massive neon station at the heart of Times Square, at 42nd Street between Broadway and Seventh Avenue, and the B, D, F, Q line runs up Sixth Avenue to Rockefeller Center. The N, R line cuts diagonally across the neighborhood, following the path of Broadway before heading up Seventh Avenue at 42nd Street. The A, C, E line serves the west side, running along Eighth Avenue.

If you know New York but haven't been here in a few years, you'll be quite surprised by the "new" **Times Square.** Longtime New Yorkers like to kvetch nostalgic about the glory days of the old peep-show-and-porn-shop Times Square that this cleaned-up, Disney-fied one supplanted, but the truth is that it's a hugely successful regentrification. Grand old theaters have come back to life as Broadway and children's playhouses, and scores of new family-friendly restaurants and shops have opened (including the terrific Virgin Megastore on Broadway). Plenty of businesses have moved in; MTV studios overlook Times Square at 1515 Broadway, and, taking a key note from the far more successful *Today* show, *Good Morning America* now has its own street-facing studio at Broadway and 44th Street. The neon lights have never been brighter, and Middle America has never been more welcome. (See the box called "What's New in Times Square" in chapter 7.)

Most of the great Broadway theaters light up the streets just off Times Square, in the West 40s just east and west of Broadway. At the heart of the **Theater District,** where Broadway meets Seventh Avenue, is the TKTS booth, where crowds line up daily to buy discount tickets for tonight's shows.

Unlike neighboring Times Square, gorgeous **Rockefeller Center** has needed no renovation. Situated between 46th and 50th streets from Sixth Avenue east to Fifth, this art deco complex contains some of the city's great architectural gems, which house hundreds of offices, a number of NBC studios (including *Saturday Night Live, Late Night with Conan O'Brien,* and the famous glass-walled *Today* show studio at 48th Street), and some pleasing upscale boutiques. Holiday time is a great time to be here, as ice skaters take over the central plaza and the huge Christmas tree twinkles against the night sky.

Along Seventh Avenue south of 42nd Street is the **Garment District,** of little interest to most visitors except for its sample sales, where some great new fashions are sold off cheap to serious bargain hunters willing to scour the racks (see chapter 8 for details). Other than that, it's a pretty grim commercial area. Between Seventh and Eighth avenues and 31st and 33rd streets, Penn Station sits beneath Madison Square Garden, where the Rangers and the Knicks play. Taking up all of 34th Street between Sixth and Seventh Avenues is Macy's, the world's largest department store; exit Macy's at the southeast corner and you'll find more famous-label shopping around **Herald Square.**

Farther north, despite the presence of grand dame Carnegie Hall, West 57th Street has become a theme-restaurant bonanza, with Planet Hollywood (for now, anyway; it might move to Times Square), the Harley-Davidson Cafe, Brooklyn Diner USA, and the venerable Hard Rock in residence. There are a good number of hotels in all price categories in this area, and their convenience to Central Park (which starts at 59th Street) is an extra plus.

If you're looking for something a little more culture-rich than an over-priced burger and a logo T-shirt, Midtown West is also home to the Museum of Modern Art, Radio City Music Hall, and the *Intrepid* Sea-Air-Space Museum.

**Midtown East & Murray Hill**   **Midtown East,** the area including Fifth Avenue and everything east from 34th to 59th streets, is the more upscale side of the Midtown map. This side of town is short of subway trains, served primarily by the Lexington Avenue 4, 5, 6 line.

Midtown East is where you'll find the city's finest collection of grand hotels, mostly along Lexington Avenue and near the park at the top of Fifth, with a handful of affordable choices dotting the luxury landscape (although far fewer than you'll find in Midtown West). The stretch of Fifth Avenue from Saks at 49th Street to FAO Schwarz at 59th is home to the city's most high-profile haute shopping, including Tiffany & Co. and Bergdorf Goodman, but a few midpriced names such as Banana Republic and Liz Claiborne have moved in their superstores of late. The stretch of 57th Street between Fifth and Lexington avenues is also known for high-fashion boutiques (Chanel, Hermès) and high-ticket galleries, but change is underway since Warner Bros. (at the intersection with Fifth), Levi's, Niketown, and the NBA Store squeezed in. You'll find plenty of spillover along Madison Avenue, a great strip for shoe shopping in particular, some of it actually priced for real people.

Magnificent architectural highlights include the recently repolished Chrysler Building, with its stylized gargoyles glaring down on passersby; the beaux arts tour de force that is Grand Central Terminal; magnificent St. Patrick's Cathedral; and the glorious Empire State Building.

Far east, swank Sutton and Beekman places are enclaves of beautiful town houses, luxury living, and postage stamp–sized parks that look out over the East River. Along the river is the United Nations, which isn't officially in New York City, or even the United States, but is on a parcel of international land belonging to member nations.

Claiming the territory east from Madison Avenue, **Murray Hill** begins somewhere north of 23rd Street (the line between it and Gramercy Park is fuzzy) and is most clearly recognizable north of 30th Street to 42nd Street. This brownstone-lined quarter is largely a quiet residential neighborhood, most notable for its handful of good budget and midpriced hotels.

## Uptown

**The Upper West Side**   North of 59th Street and encompassing everything west of Central Park, the Upper West Side contains Lincoln Center, arguably the world's premier performing-arts venue; the American Museum of Natural History, whose new Rose Center for Earth and Space is drawing record crowds; and a number of midpriced hotels whose larger-than-Midtown rooms and nice residential location make them some of the best values in the entire city. Unlike the more stratified Upper East Side, the Upper West Side is home to an egalitarian mix of middle-class yuppiedom, laid-back wealth (lots of celebs and monied media types call the grand apartments along Central Park West home), and ethnic families who were here before the gentrification.

The neighborhood runs all the way up to Harlem, around 125th Street, and encompasses Morningside Heights, where you'll find Columbia University and the perennial construction project known as the Cathedral of St. John the Divine. North of 59th Street is where Eighth Avenue becomes Central Park West, the eastern border of the neighborhood (and the western border of Central Park); Ninth Avenue becomes Columbus Avenue, lined with attractive boutiques and cafes; and Tenth Avenue becomes Amsterdam Avenue, less charming than Columbus to the east and less trafficked than bustling Broadway (whose highlights are the gourmet mega-marts Zabar's and Fairway) to the west. Still, Amsterdam has blossomed into quite a happening restaurant and bar strip over the last couple of years. You'll find Lincoln Center in the mid-60s, where Broadway crosscuts Amsterdam.

Two major subway lines service the area: The 1, 2, 3, 9 line runs up Broadway, and the B and C trains run up glamorous Central Park West, stopping right at the historic Dakota apartment building (where John Lennon was shot and Yoko still lives, albeit without an all-grown-up Sean) at 72nd Street and at the Museum of Natural History at 81st Street.

**The Upper East Side**    North of 59th Street and east of Central Park is some of the city's most expensive residential real estate. This is New York at its most gentrified: Walk along Fifth and Park avenues, especially between 60th and 80th streets, and you're sure to encounter some of the wizened WASPs and Chanel-suited socialites that make up the most rarefied of the city's population. Madison Avenue to 79th Street is the monied crowd's main shopping strip, recently vaunting ahead of Hong Kong's Causeway Bay to become to most expensive retail real estate *in the world*. This is an area for browsing only, unless you book a room or attend a program at the 92nd Street Y, one of the city's best arts and cultural institutions, particularly for culture vultures with limited budgets (see chapters 5 and 9 for details).

The main attraction of this neighborhood is Museum Mile, the stretch of Fifth Avenue fronting Central Park that's home to no fewer than 10 terrific cultural institutions, including Frank Lloyd Wright's Guggenheim, and anchored by the mind-boggling Metropolitan Museum of Art. But the elegant rows of landmark townhouses are worth a look alone: East 70th Street, from Madison east to Lexington, is one of the world's most charming residential streets. If you want to see where real people live, move east to Third Avenue and beyond; that's where affordable restaurants and active street life start popping up.

A second subway line is in the works, but it's still no more than an architect's blueprint. For now, the Upper East Side is served solely by the Lexington Avenue line (4, 5, 6 trains), so wear your walking shoes (or bring taxi fare).

**Harlem**    Harlem is really two areas. Harlem proper stretches from river to river, beginning at 125th Street on the West Side and 96th Street on the East Side. East of Fifth Avenue, Spanish Harlem (El Barrio) runs between East 100th and East 125th streets.

Parts of Harlem are benefiting from the revitalization that has swept so much of the city, with national-brand retailers moving in and visitors arriving to tour historic sites related to the Golden Age of African-American culture, when great bands such as the Count Basie and Duke Ellington orchestras played the Cotton Club and Sugar Cane Club, and literary giants such as Langston Hughes and James Baldwin soaked up the scene. Some houses date back to a time when the area was something of a country retreat and represent some of the best brownstone mansions in the city, most notably on Sugar Hill and Strivers Row. For cultural visits, there's the Morris-Jumel Mansion, the Schomburg Center, the Studio Museum, and the Apollo Theatre.

By all means, come see Harlem; it's one of the city's most vital and historic neighborhoods. But for most visitors, the best bet is to take a guided tour (see chapter 7). Sights tend to be far apart, and neighborhoods change quickly. Don't wander thoughtlessly through Harlem, especially at night.

**Washington Heights & Inwood**    Located at the northern tip of Manhattan, Washington Heights (the area from 155th Street to Dyckman Street, with adjacent Inwood running to the tip) is home to a large segment of Manhattan's Latino community. Fort Tryon Park and the Cloisters are the two big reasons to come up this way. The Cloisters houses the Metropolitan Museum of Art's stunning medieval collection in a building perched atop a hill, with excellent views across the Hudson to the Palisades. Committed off-the-beaten-path sightseers might also want to visit the Dyckman

Farmhouse, a historic jewel built in 1783 and the only remaining Dutch Colonial structure in Manhattan.

## 2 Getting Around

Frankly, Manhattan's transportation systems are a marvel. It's simply miraculous that so many people can gather on this little island and move around it. For the most part, you can get where you're going pretty quickly and easily using some combination of subways and buses, with maybe a pricier cab ride here and there if you're traveling in a group or late at night. This section tells you how to use the city's public systems with the confidence and skill of a native New Yorker.

But between traffic gridlock and subway delays, sometimes you just can't get there from here—unless you walk. Walking can be the fastest way to navigate the island. During rush hours, you'll easily beat car traffic while on foot, as taxis and buses stop and groan at gridlocked corners (don't even *try* going crosstown in a cab or bus in Midtown at midday). You'll also see a whole lot more by walking than you will if you ride beneath the street in the subway or fly by in a cab. So pack your most comfortable shoes and hit the pavement; it's the best, cheapest, and most appealing way to experience the city.

### BY SUBWAY

The much-maligned subway system is actually the best way to travel around New York, especially during rush hours. Some $3^{1}/_{2}$ million people a day seem to agree with me, as it's their primary mode of transportation. The subway is quick, inexpensive, relatively safe, and pretty efficient, as well as a genuine New York experience that you really shouldn't miss.

The subway runs 24 hours a day, 7 days a week (although the rules can change during off-peak hours: pay attention to posted signs that announce station and line closings). The rush-hour crushes are roughly from 8am to 9:30am and from 5pm to 6:30pm on weekdays; the rest of the time the trains are relatively uncrowded.

**PAYING YOUR WAY**   The subway fare is $1.50 (half-price for seniors and those with disabilities), and children under 44 inches tall ride free (up to three per adult). **Tokens** still exist (although they might be phased out altogether), but most people pay

### On the Sidewalks

What's the primary means New Yorkers use for getting around town? The subway? Buses? Taxis? Nope. Walking. They stride across wide, crowded pavements without any regard for the light, weaving through crowds at high speeds, dodging taxis and buses whose drivers are forced to interrupt the normal flow of traffic to avoid flattening them. **Never take your walking cues from the locals.** Wait for walk signals, and always use crosswalks; don't cross in the middle of the block. Do otherwise, and you could quickly end up with a jaywalking ticket—or as a flattened statistic.

**Always pay attention to the traffic flow.** Walk as if you're driving, staying to the right. Pay attention to what's happening in the street, even if you have the right of way. At intersections, keep an eye out for drivers who don't yield, turn without looking, or think a yellow traffic light means "Hurry up!" as you cross. Unfortunately, most bicyclists seem to think that the traffic laws don't apply to them; they'll often blithely fly through red lights and dash the wrong way on one-way streets, so be on your guard.

fares with the **MetroCard,** a magnetically encoded card that debits the fare when swiped through the turnstile or the farebox on any city bus. Once you're in the system, you can transfer freely to any subway line that you can reach without exiting your station. MetroCards—not tokens—also allow you **free transfers** between the bus and subway within a two-hour period.

The MetroCard can be purchased in a few different configurations:

**Pay-Per-Ride MetroCards,** which can be used for up to four people by swiping up to four times (bring the whole family). You can put any amount from $3 (two rides) to $80 on your card. Every time you put $15 on your Pay-Per-Ride MetroCard, it's automatically credited 10% that's one free ride for every $15. You can buy Pay-Per-Ride MetroCards in any denomination at any subway stations; an increasing number of stations now have automated MetroCard vending machines, which allow you to buy MetroCards using your major credit card. MetroCards are also available from shops and newsstands around town in $15 and $30 values. You can refill your card at any time until the expiration date on the card, usually about a year from the date of purchase, at any subway station.

**Unlimited-Use MetroCards,** which can't be used for more than one person at a time or more frequently than 18-minute intervals, are available in four values: the **daily Fun Pass,** which allows you a day's worth of unlimited subway and bus rides for $4; the **7-Day MetroCard,** for $17; and the **30-Day MetroCard,** for $63. Seven-and 30-day Unlimited-Use MetroCards can be purchased at any subway station or a MetroCard merchant. Fun Passes, however, cannot be purchased at token booths; you can only buy them from a MetroCard merchant such as most Rite Aid drugstores; at the MTA information desk in the Times Square Visitor Center, 1560 Broadway, between 46th and 47th streets; at a station that has a MetroCard vending machine; or by ordering them online at **www.metrocard.citysearch.com** (more on this below). Unlimited-Use MetroCards go into effect not at the time you buy them, but the first time you use them—so if you buy a card on Monday and don't begin to use it until Wednesday, Wednesday is when the clock starts ticking on your MetroCard. A Fun Pass is good from the first time you use it until 3am the next day, but 7- and 30-day MetroCards run out at midnight on the last day. These MetroCards cannot be refilled; you throw it out once it's been used and buy a new one.

**Tips for using your MetroCard:** The MetroCard-swiping mechanism at turnstiles is the source of much grousing among subway riders. If you swipe too fast or too slow, the turnstile will ask you to swipe again. If this happens, *do not move to a different turnstile,* or you may end up paying twice. If you've tried a bunch of times and really can't make your MetroCard work, tell the token booth clerk; chances are good, though, that you'll get the movement down after a couple of uses.

If you're not sure how much money you have left on your MetroCard, or what day it expires, use the station's MetroCard Reader, usually located near the station entrance or the token booth (on buses, the fare box will also provide you with this information).

To locate the nearest MetroCard merchant, or for any other MetroCard questions, call ☎ **800/METROCARD** or 212/METROCARD (638-7622), or go online to **www.mta.nyc.ny.us/metrocard**. MetroCards in any denomination can be ordered online at **www.metrocard.citysearch.com**. There is no additional charge or shipping fee, but be sure to place your order more than a week before your departure date so the post office has time to get it to you.

**USING THE SYSTEM**　　As you can see from the full-color subway map on the inside front cover of this book, the subway system basically mimics the lay of the land above ground, with most lines in Manhattan running north and south, like the avenues, and a few lines east and west, like the streets.

To go up and down the east side of Manhattan (and to the Bronx and Brooklyn), take the 4, 5, or 6 train.

To travel up and down the west side (and also to the Bronx and Brooklyn), take the 1, 2, 3, or 9 line; the A, C, E, or F line; or the B or D line.

The N and R lines first cut diagonally across town from east to west and then snake under Seventh Avenue before shooting out to Queens.

The crosstown S line runs back and forth between Times Square and Grand Central Terminal. Farther downtown, across 14th Street, the L line works its own crosstown magic.

**Lines** have assigned colors on subway maps and trains—red for the 1, 2, 3, 9 line; green for 4, 5, 6 trains; and so on—but nobody ever refers to them by color. Always refer to them by number or letter when asking questions. Within Manhattan, the distinction between different numbered trains that share the same line is usually that some are express and others local. **Express trains** often skip about three stops for each one that they make; express stops are indicated on subway maps with a white (rather than solid) circle. Local stops usually come about nine blocks apart.

**Directions** are almost always indicated using "Uptown" (northbound) and "Downtown" (southbound), so be sure to know what direction you want to head in. The outsides of some subway entrances are marked UPTOWN ONLY or DOWNTOWN ONLY; read carefully, as it's easy to head in the wrong direction. Once you're on the platform, check the signs overhead to make sure that the train you're waiting for will be traveling in the right direction. If you do make a mistake, it's a good idea to wait for an express station, like 14th Street or 42nd Street, so you can get off and change for the other direction without paying again.

The days of graffiti-covered cars are gone, but the stations—and an increasing number of trains—are not nearly as clean as they could be. Trains are air-conditioned (move to the next car if yours isn't), although during the dog days of summer, the platforms can be sweltering. In theory, all subway cars have PA systems to allow you to hear the conductor's announcements, but they don't always work well. It's a good idea to move to a car with a working PA system in case any sudden service changes are announced that you'll want to know about.

For **subway safety tips,** see "Playing It Safe" later in this chapter.

## For More Bus & Subway Information

For additional transit information, call the **MTA/New York City Transit's Travel Information Center** at ☎ **718/330-1234.** Extensive automated information is available at this number 24 hours a day, and travel agents are on hand to answer your questions and provide directions daily from 6am to 9pm. For online information, point your Web browser to **www.mta.nyc.ny.us.**

To request system maps, call the **Customer Assistance Line** at ☎ **718/330-3322** (Mon–Fri 9am–5pm). Disabled riders should direct inquires to ☎ **718/596-8585** (recorded information 24/7; staffed daily 6am–9pm). For MetroCard information, call ☎ 212/638-7622 (or 800/638-7622 outside of New York), or go online to **www.mta.nyc.ny.us/metrocard** or **www.metrocard.citysearch.com.**

You can get bus and subway maps and additional transit information at most tourist information centers (see "Visitor Information" earlier in this chapter); there's a particularly helpful MTA transit information desk at the Times Square Visitor Center, 1560 Broadway, between 46th and 47th streets, where you can also buy MetroCards. Maps are sometimes available in subway stations (ask at the token booth), but rarely on buses.

**Money-Saving Transit Tips: Free Transfers**

If you pay your subway or bus fare with a **MetroCard,** you can freely transfer to another bus or to the subway (or from the subway to a bus) for up to 2 hours. You don't need to do anything special: Just swipe your card at the token box or turnstile, and the automated system keeps track.

If you use a token or coins to board a bus and you expect to transfer to another line, you must request a free **transfer slip** that allows you to change to an intersecting bus route only (legal transfer points are listed on the transfer paper) within 1 hour of issue. Transfer slips cannot be used to enter the subway.

## BY BUS

Less expensive than taxis and more pleasant than subways (they provide a mobile sightseeing window on Manhattan), buses are a good transportation option. Their very big drawback: They can get stuck in traffic, sometimes making it quicker to walk. They also stop every couple of blocks, rather than the eight or nine blocks that local subway traverse between stops. So for long distances, the subway is your best bet; but for short distances or traveling crosstown, try the bus.

**PAYING YOUR WAY**   Like the subway fare, the **bus fare** is $1.50, half-price for seniors and riders with disabilities, free for children under 44 inches (up to three per adult). The fare is payable with a **MetroCard, token** (for now, anyway), or **exact change.** Bus drivers don't make change, and fare boxes don't accept dollar bills or pennies. You can't purchase MetroCards or tokens on the bus, so you'll have to have them before you board; for details, see "Paying Your Way" under "By Subway" above.

**USING THE SYSTEM**   You can't flag down a city bus; you have to meet it at a bus stop. **Bus stops** are located every two or three blocks on the right-side corner of the street (facing the direction of traffic flow). They're marked by a curb painted yellow and a blue-and-white sign with a bus emblem and the route number or numbers. Guide-A-Ride boxes at most stops display a route map and a hysterically optimistic schedule.

Almost every major avenue has its own **bus route.** They run either north or south: downtown on Fifth, uptown on Madison, downtown on Lexington, uptown on Third, and so on. There are **crosstown buses** at strategic locations all around town: 8th Street (eastbound); 9th (westbound); 14th, 23rd, 34th, and 42nd (east- and westbound); 49th (eastbound); 50th (westbound); 57th (east- and westbound); 65th (eastbound across the West Side, through the park, and then north on Madison, continuing east on 68th to York Avenue); 67th (westbound on the East Side to Fifth Avenue and then south on Fifth, continuing west on 66th Street through the park and across the West Side to West End Avenue); and 79th, 86th, 96th, 116th, and 125th (east- and westbound). Some bus routes, however, are erratic: The M104, for example, starts at the East River and then turns at Eighth Avenue and goes up Broadway. The buses of the Fifth Avenue line go up Madison or Sixth and follow various routes around the city. Most routes operate 24 hours a day, but service is infrequent at night. Some say that New York buses have a herding instinct: They come only in groups. During rush hour, main routes have "limited" buses, identifiable by the red card in the front window; they stop only at major cross streets.

To make sure the bus you're boarding goes where you're going, check the maps on the bus signs, get your hands on a route map (see "For More Bus & Subway Information," above), or **just ask.** The drivers are helpful, as long as you don't hold up the line too long.

While traveling, look out the window, not only to take in the sights but also to keep track of cross streets so you know when to get off. Signal for a stop by pressing the tape strip above and beside the windows and along the metal straps, about two blocks before you want to stop. Exit through the pneumatic back doors (not the front door) by pushing on the yellow tape strip; the doors open automatically (pushing on the handles is useless unless you're as buffed as Hercules). Most city buses are equipped with wheelchair lifts, making buses the preferable mode of public transportation for wheelchair-bound travelers; for more on this topic, see "Tips for Travelers with Special Needs" in chapter 2. Buses also "kneel," lowering down to the curb to make boarding easier.

## BY TAXI

If you don't want to deal with the hustle and bustle of public transportation, find an address that might be a few blocks from the subway station, or share your ride with 3½ million other people, then take a taxi. The biggest advantages are that cabs can be hailed on any street (providing you find an empty one—often simple, yet at other times nearly impossible) and will take you right to your destination.

**Official New York City taxis,** licensed by the Taxi and Limousine Commission, are yellow, with the rates printed on the door and a light with a medallion number on the roof. You can hail a taxi on any street. *Never* accept a ride from any other car except an official city yellow cab (private livery cars are not allowed to pick up fares on the street).

If you're planning to take extensive advantage of taxis, be prepared to pay. The **base fare** on entering the cab is $2. The cost is 30¢ for every ¹/₅ mile or 20¢ per minute in stopped or very slow-moving traffic (or for waiting time). There's no extra charge for each passenger or for luggage. However, you must pay bridge or tunnel tolls (sometimes the driver will front the toll and add it to your bill at the end; most times, however, you pay the driver before the toll). You'll also pay a 50¢ night surcharge after 8pm and before 6am. A 15 to 20% tip is customary.

Because it's going to cost you at least $2 just to get in the car, taxis are far more expensive than other forms of public transportation and can really jack up your expenses quickly. Visitors on a limited travel budget are generally better off relying on subways and buses to get around town, using taxis only late at night (after 11pm or midnight, when buses and subway trains start getting fewer and farther between and standing at a bus stop or on a lonely platform might seem a little daunting) or to reach an out-of-the-way destination (maybe a bar or restaurant on the Lower East Side or the far East Village, neighborhoods not well served by the subway). You'll also get your money's worth out of a taxi at night, when there's little traffic to keep them from speeding you to your destination.

Although taxis are generally far more expensive than taking the subway or a bus, consider taking cabs for short hauls if there's three or four in your group. A taxi might

---

### Taxi-Hailing Tips

- When you're waiting on the street for an available taxi, look at the medallion light on the top of the coming cabs. If the light is out, the taxi is in use. When the center part (the number) is lit, the taxi is available; this is when you raise your hand to flag the cab. If all the lights are on, the driver is off duty.
- A taxi can't take more than four people, so expect to split up if your group is larger.

not actually save you money, but you'll get door-to-door service for about the same price: It costs four people $6 to take the subway, which is no less than you'd pay for a short taxi ride from Times Square to the West Village, say, or from Carnegie Hall to your Murray Hill hotel. Skip taxis entirely at rush hour, though, when it's more convenient and cheaper to take the subway, because you don't want to end up stuck in traffic, delayed and paying for unnecessary wait time.

Forget about hopping into the back seat and having some double-chinned, cigar-chomping, all-knowing driver slowly turn and ask nonchalantly, "Where to, Mac?" Nowadays most taxi drivers speak only an approximation of English and drive in engagingly exotic ways. Always wear your seat belt; taxis are required to provide them.

The TLC has posted a **Taxi Rider's Bill of Rights** sticker in every cab. Drivers are required by law to take you anywhere in the five boroughs, to Nassau or Westchester counties, or to Newark Airport. They are supposed to know how to get you to any address in Manhattan and all major points in the outer boroughs. They are also required to provide air conditioning and turn off the radio on demand, and they cannot smoke while you're in the cab. They are also required to be polite.

You are allowed to dictate the route that is taken. It's a good idea to look at a map before you get in a taxi. Taxi drivers have been known to jack up the fare on visitors who don't know better by taking a circuitous route between point A and point B. Know enough about where you're going to know that something's wrong if you hop in a cab at Sixth Avenue and 57th Street to go to the Empire State Building (Fifth Avenue and 34th Street), say, and you suddenly find yourself on Ninth Avenue.

On the other hand, listen to drivers who propose an alternate route. These guys spend 8 or 10 hours a day on these streets, and they know them well—where the worst midday traffic is, where Con Ed has dug up an intersection that should be avoided. A knowledgeable driver will know how to get you to your destination quickly and efficiently.

Another important tip: **Always make sure the meter is turned on at the start of the ride.** You'll see the red LED read-out register the initial $2 and start calculating the fare as you go. I've witnessed a good number of unscrupulous drivers buzzing unsuspecting visitors around the city with the meter off and then overcharging them at drop-off time.

**Always ask for the receipt;** it comes in handy if you need to make a complaint or have left something in a cab. In fact, it's a good idea to make a mental note of the driver's four-digit medallion number (usually posted on the divider between the front and back seats) just in case you need it later. You probably won't, but it's a good idea to play it safe.

For driver complaints and lost property, call the 24-hour Consumer Hotline at ☎ 212/NYC-TAXI. For details on getting to and from the local airports by taxi, see "By Plane" under "Getting There" in chapter 2. For further taxi information—including a complete rundown of your rights as a taxi rider—go online to **www.ci. nyc.ny.us/taxi**.

## BY CAR

Forget driving yourself around the city. It's not worth the headache. Traffic is horrendous, the streets have all the civility of the Wild West, and street parking is nearly impossible (not to mention the security risks).

---

**Impressions** ─────────────────────────────────

*Traffic signals in New York are just rough guidelines.*

—David Letterman

---

# Deals for Visitors with Wheels: Cheap Parking Tips

If you're driving into the city and have to find somewhere to put your car, don't despair. Even under the best of circumstances, you'll probably pay more for parking in New York than you would in other cities, but it doesn't have to break the bank.

When planning your trip, your best bet is to pick a hotel that has a favorable parking agreement with a nearby garage. This is common practice with city hotels, and the rate that management has negotiated will always be much better than the full rate you would pay on your own. Many hotels are able to negotiate daily rates between $15 and $25 in neighborhoods where the going rate is anywhere from $25 to $40. In chapter 5, "Accommodations You Can Afford," you'll see estimated parking rates in each of the listings, most based on existing agreements with nearby garages. There are even two hotels, **Travel Inn** and the **Skyline Hotel,** that provide garage parking to guests for free.

If you have to find your own parking, your best bet is to choose a lot on the far west or far east fringes of Midtown, near the West Side Highway to the west or the FDR Drive to the east. You won't have easy access to your wheels, but you'll pay a much lower daily rate—probably $15 or $20 as opposed to a minimum of $25 or $30—than in prime Midtown.

If you'd rather have your car closer at hand, Midtown west of Seventh Avenue is always cheaper than more eastern Midtown areas (around $25 or $30 as opposed to $45 or $50, which is what you'll pay near Fifth or Sixth avenues). Residential Murray Hill is also cheaper than more commercial Midtown East. If you're staying on the Upper West Side, you might be able to save a few dollars by garaging your car north of 96th Street, where garage parking is significantly cheaper than in the ritzy residential area between 59th and 86th streets.

If you drive into the city, garage your car for the duration of your stay and use it again only when you're ready to leave the city. Most city garages do not provide in-and-out privileges, so expect to pay twice the daily rate, or a much higher hourly rate, if you plan to use your car and return it later that same day.

Also remember that a steep **parking garage tax** of 18.25% is added to every parking bill, so be sure to factor that in to your calculations. See why I recommend that you just leave your car at home?

One last note: Despite the fact that a few crazy New Yorkers risk it every day, don't try street parking. You don't know the arcane alternate-side-of-the-street parking regulations (in fact, precious few New Yorkers do). You don't want to find out the monstrous price of parking violations or the Kafkaesque tragedy of liberating a vehicle from the tow pound. And your car is sure to come home with a new dent or two (at minimum) if you leave it on the street for a few days. As expensive as garaging it may be, trust me; it's cheaper in the long run.

If you do arrive in New York City by car, park it in a garage (expect to pay in the neighborhood of $20 to $35 per day) and leave it there for the duration of your stay. If you drive a rental car in, return it as soon as you arrive and rent another on the day you leave. Just about all of the major car-rental companies, including **National** (☎ 800/227-7368; www.nationalcar.com), **Hertz** (☎ 800/654-3131; www.hertz. com), and **Avis** (☎ 800/230-4898; www.avis.com), have Manhattan locations.

## FROM THE CITY TO THE SUBURBS

The **PATH** (☎ 800/234-7284; www.panynj.gov/path) system connects urban communities in New Jersey, including Hoboken and Newark, to Manhattan by subway-style trains. Stops in Manhattan are at the World Trade Center, Christopher and 9th streets, and along Sixth Avenue at 14th, 23rd, and 33rd streets. The fare is $1.

**New Jersey Transit** (☎ 973/762-5100; www.njtransit.state.nj.us) operates commuter trains from Penn Station, and buses from the Port Authority at Eighth Avenue and 42nd Street, to points throughout New Jersey.

The **Long Island Rail Road** (☎ 718/217-5477; www.mta.nyc.ny.us/lirr) runs from Penn Station, at Seventh Avenue between 31st and 33rd streets, to Queens (ocean beaches, Shea Stadium, Belmont Park) and points beyond on Long Island, to even better beaches and summer hot spots such as Fire Island and the Hamptons.

**Metro North** (☎ 800/638-7646 or 212/532-4900; www.mta.nyc.ny.us/mnr) departs from Grand Central Terminal, at 42nd Street and Lexington Avenue, for areas north of the city, including Westchester County, the lovely Hudson Valley, and Connecticut.

## 3  Playing It Safe

Sure, there's crime in New York City, but millions of people spend their lives here without being robbed and assaulted. In fact, New York is safer than any other big American city and is listed by the FBI as somewhere around 150th in the nation for total crimes. Although that's quite encouraging for all of us, it's still important to take precautions. Visitors especially should remain vigilant, as swindlers and criminals are expert at spotting newcomers who appear disoriented or vulnerable.

Men should carry their wallets in their front pockets and women should keep constant hold of their purse straps. Cross camera and purse straps over one shoulder, across your front, and under the other arm. Never hang a purse on the back of a chair or on a hook in a bathroom stall; keep it in your lap or between your feet with one foot through a strap and up against the purse itself. Avoid carrying large amounts of cash. You might carry your money in several pockets so that if one is picked, the others might escape. Skip the flashy jewelry and keep valuables out of sight when you're on the street.

Panhandlers are seldom dangerous but should be ignored (more aggressive pleas should firmly be answered, "Not today"). I hate to be cynical, but experience teaches that if a stranger walks up to you on the street with a long sob story ("I live in the suburbs and was just attacked and don't have the money to get home") it should be ignored; it's a scam. If someone approaches you with any kind of elaborate tale, it's most definitely a confidence game. Walk away and don't feel bad. Be wary of an individual who "accidentally" falls in front of you or causes some other commotion, because he or she might be working with someone else who will take your wallet when you try to help. And remember: You *will* lose if you place a bet on a sidewalk card game or shell game.

Certain areas should be avoided late at night. I don't recommend going to the Lower East Side, Alphabet City in the far East Village, or the Meat-Packing District

### Impressions

*I like it here in New York. I like the idea of having to keep eyes in the back of your head all the time.*

—John Cale

## The Top Safety Tips

Trust your instincts, because they're usually right. You'll rarely be hassled, but it's always best to walk with a sense of purpose and self-confidence, and don't stop in the middle of the sidewalk to pull out and peruse your map. Anywhere in the city, if you find yourself on a deserted street that feels unsafe, it probably is; leave as quickly as possible. If you do find yourself accosted by someone with or without a weapon, remember to keep your anger in check and that the most reasonable response (maddening though it may be) is not to resist.

unless you know where you're going; head straight for your destination and don't wander onto side streets. The areas above 96th Street aren't the best, either. Times Square has been cleaned up, and there'll be crowds around until midnight, when theater- and moviegoers leave the area. Still, stick to the main streets, such as Broadway. The areas west and south of Times Square are best avoided after dark. Take a cab or bus when visiting the Jacob Javits Center on 34th Street and the Hudson River. Don't go wandering the parks after dark, unless you're going to a performance; if that's the case, stick with the crowd.

If you plan on visiting the outer boroughs, go only during the daylight hours. If the subway doesn't go directly to your destination (such as the Bronx Zoo or the Brooklyn Museum of Art), your best bet is to take a taxi. Don't wander the side streets; many areas in the outer boroughs are absolutely safe, but neighborhoods change quickly, and it's easy to get lost.

All this said, don't panic. Remember that New York has experienced a dramatic drop in crime and is generally safe these days, especially in the neighborhoods visitors are prone to frequent. There's a good police presence on the street, so don't be afraid to stop an officer, or even a friendly looking New Yorker (trust me—you can tell), if you need help getting your bearings.

**SUBWAY SAFETY TIPS**    In general, the subways are safe, especially in Manhattan. There are panhandlers and questionable characters as anywhere else in the city, but subway crime has gone down to 1960s levels. Still, stay alert and trust your instincts. Always keep a hand on your personal belongings.

When using the subway, don't wait for trains near the edge of the platform or on extreme ends of a station. During non-rush hours, wait for the train in view of the token booth clerk or under the yellow DURING OFF HOURS TRAINS STOP HERE signs, and ride in the train operator's or conductor's car (usually in the center of the train; you'll see his or her head stick out of the window when the doors open). Choose crowded cars over empty ones; there's safety in numbers.

Avoid subways late at night, and splurge on a cab after about 10 or 11pm; it's money well spent to avoid a long wait on a deserted platform. Or take the bus.

## Fast Facts: New York City

**Ambulance & Emergencies**    Dial ☎ **911.**

**American Express**    Travel service offices are at many Manhattan locations, including the New York Hilton, 1335 Sixth Ave., at 54th Street (☎ 212/664-7798); the New York Marriott Marquis, 1535 Broadway, in the 8th floor lobby (☎ 212/575-6580); on the balcony level at Macy's Herald Square, 34th Street and Broadway (☎ 212/695-8075); and 65 Broadway, between Exchange

Place and Rector Street (☎ 212/493-6500). Call ☎ **800/AXP-TRIP** or go online to **www.americanexpress.com** for other city locations or general information.

**Area Codes**    There are four area codes in the city: two in Manhattan, the original **212** and new **646,** and two in the outer boroughs, the original **718** and new **347.** Also common is the **917** area code, which is assigned to cell phones, pagers, and the like. All calls between these area codes are local calls, but you'll have to dial 1 + the area code + the 7 digits if the number you're calling is not within your area code.

**Business Hours**    In general (although this varies according to neighborhood), **retail stores** are open Monday to Saturday from 10am to 6pm or 7pm, Thursday from 10am to 8:30 or 9pm, and Sunday from noon to 5pm (see chapter 8). **Banks** tend to be open Monday to Friday from 9am to 3pm and sometimes Saturday mornings.

**Dentists**    See "Health & Insurance" in chapter 2.

**Doctors**    For medical emergencies requiring immediate attention, head to the nearest emergency room (see "Hospitals" below). For less urgent health problems, see "Health & Insurance" in chapter 2 for walk-in medical centers and doctor referral services.

**Embassies/Consulates**    See "Fast Facts: For the Foreign Traveler" in chapter 3.

**Emergencies**    Dial ☎ **911** for fire, police, and ambulance. The **Poison Control Center** is at ☎ **212/764-7667** or 212/340-4494.

**Fire**    Dial ☎ **911.**

**Hospitals**    **Downtown: New York Downtown Hospital,** 170 William St., between Beekman and Spruce streets (☎ 212/312-5063); **St. Vincent's Hospital,** 153 W. 11th St., at Seventh Avenue (☎ 212/604-7000); and **Beth Israel Medical Center,** First Avenue and 16th Street (☎ 212/420-2000). **Midtown: Bellevue Hospital Center,** 462 First Ave., at 27th Street (☎ 212/562-4141); **New York University Medical Center,** 560 First Ave., at 33rd Street (☎ 212/263-7300); and **Roosevelt Hospital,** 425 W. 59th St., between Ninth and Tenth avenues (☎ 212/523-4000 or 212/523-6800). **Upper West Side: St. Luke's Hospital Center,** Amsterdam Avenue and 113th Street (☎ 212/523-4000 or 212/523-3335); and **Columbia Presbyterian Medical Center,** 622 W. 168th St., at Broadway (☎ 212/305-2500). **Upper East Side: New York Presbyterian Hospital's Emergency Center,** 525 E. 68th St., at York Avenue (☎ 212/746-5050); **Lenox Hill Hospital,** 100 E. 77th St., between Park and Lexington avenues (☎ 212/434-2000); and **Mount Sinai Hospital,** Madison Avenue between 100th and 101st (☎ 212/241-6500). Don't forget your insurance card.

**Hot Lines**    The 24-hour **Crime Victims Hot Line** is ☎ **212/577-7777.** You can reach **Alcoholics Anonymous** at ☎ **212/870-3400** (general office) or 212/647-1680 (intergroup, for alcoholics who need immediate counseling from a sober recovering alcoholic). Other useful numbers include **Sex Crimes Report Line** ☎ 212/267-7273; **Crisis Help Line** ☎ 212/532-2400; **Samaritans' Suicide Prevention Line** ☎ 212/673-3000; local **police precincts** ☎ 212/374-5000; **Department of Consumer Affairs** ☎ 212/487-4444; **Taxi complaints** ☎ 212/NYC-TAXI.

**Internet Centers**   See "Check Your E-Mail While You're on the Road" in the Frommer's Online Directory.

**Libraries**   The **New York Public Library** is on Fifth Avenue at 42nd Street (☎ 212/930-0830). This beaux arts beauty houses more than 38 million volumes, and the beautiful reading rooms have been restored to their former glory. More efficient and modern, if less charming, is the mid-Manhattan branch at 455 Fifth Ave., at 40th Street, across the street from the main library (☎ 212/340-0833). There are other branches in almost every neighborhood; you can find a list online at **www.nypl.org**.

**Liquor Laws**   The minimum legal age to purchase and consume alcoholic beverages in New York is 21. Liquor and wine are sold only in licensed stores, which are closed on Sundays, holidays, and election days while the polls are open. Beer can be purchased in grocery stores and delis 24 hours a day, except Sundays before noon.

**Newspapers/Magazines**   There are three major daily newspapers: *The New York Times*, the *Daily News*, and the *New York Post*. For details on where to find arts and entertainment listings, see "Orientation" earlier in this chapter.

In addition to the dailies, many newsstands carry a selection of newspapers and magazines. If you want to find your hometown paper, try **Universal News & Magazines,** 977 Eighth Ave., between 57th and 58th streets (☎ 212/459-0932), or **Hotalings News Agency,** inside the Times Square Visitor Center at 1560 Broadway, between 46th and 47th streets (☎ 212/840-1868). Both have huge selections of international and domestic newspapers and magazines.

**Pharmacies**   **Duane Reade** has 24-hour pharmacies in Midtown at 224 W. 57th St., at Broadway (☎ 212/541-9708), and on the Upper East Side at 1279 Third Ave., at 74th Street (☎ 212/744-2668).

**Police**   Dial ☎ 911 in an emergency; otherwise, call ☎ 212/374-5000 for the number of the nearest precinct.

**Post Office**   The main post office is at the monumental James A. Farley Building, 421 Eighth Ave., between 31st and 33rd streets (☎ 212/967-8585); it's open 24 hours, although services are limited after regular hours. There's a second branch with extended hours (Mon–Fri 7am–midnight, Sat 9am–5pm) north of the World Trade Center at 90 Church St., between Barclay and Vesey streets (☎ 212/330-5313). There are branches and drop boxes throughout the city; call ☎ 800/275-8777 to locate the branch nearest you. Most are open Monday to Friday from 8am to 5 or 6pm, Saturday from 9am to 3pm.

**Rest Rooms**   Public rest rooms are available at the visitors centers in Midtown (1560 Broadway, between 46th and 47th streets; and 810 Seventh Ave., between 52nd and 53rd streets). Grand Central Terminal, at 42nd Street between Park and Lexington avenues, also has clean rest rooms. Your best bet on the street is Starbucks. You can't walk more than a few blocks without seeing one, and I've found that the only good thing the evil empire has brought to the city is a plethora of clean bathrooms. I've always gotten away with using them without a purchase. (Ditto at Timothy's and New World Coffee, other city java chains.) The big chain bookstores are good for this, too (in addition to bedtime reading material). You can also head to hotel lobbies (especially the big Midtown ones) and department stores such as Macy's and Bloomingdale's. On the Lower East

Side, stop into the Lower East Side BID visitor center, 261 Broome St., between Orchard and Allen streets (open Sunday to Friday 10am to 4pm, sometimes later).

**Smoking**    Smoking is prohibited on all public transportation, in the lobbies of hotels and office buildings, in taxis, and in most shops. Smoking also might be restricted or not permitted in restaurants; for more on this, see chapter 6.

**Taxes**    **Sales tax** is 8.25% on meals, most goods, and some services, although as of March 1, 2000, sales tax was eliminated on clothing and footwear items under $110. **Hotel tax** is 13.25% plus $2 per room per night (including sales tax). **Parking garage tax** is 18.25%.

**Transit Information**    For information on getting to and from the airport, see "Getting There" in chapter 2 or call **Air-Ride** at ☎ **800/247-7433.** For information on subways and buses, see "Getting Around" earlier in this chapter.

**Traveler's Assistance**    **Travelers Aid** helps distressed travelers with all kinds of problems, including accidents, sickness, and lost or stolen luggage. There is an office on the second floor of the International Arrivals Building at JFK Airport (☎ **718/656-4870**) and one in Newark Airport's Terminal B (☎ **973/623-5052**).

**Telephone Information**    Dial ☎ **411,** or the area code of the area you want to reach plus 555-1212.

**Time**    For the correct time, dial ☎ **212/976-1616.**

**Weather**    For the current temperature and next day's forecast, look in the upper-right corner of the *New York Times* or call ☎ **212/976-1212.** If you want to know how to pack before you arrive, visit **www.cnn.com/weather** or **www.weather.com** for the four- or five-day forecast.

# Accommodations You Can Afford

## 5

**A**s you're probably well aware, New York is more popular than it has been in decades. On one hand, that's terrific: This popularity makes the city feel vital and self-assured; you can practically feel the excitement and energy as you walk down the street. From a more practical standpoint, it has also made the city safer and more visitor-friendly than ever.

Now the downside: With increased demand comes higher prices—Econ 101. Average room rates are now hovering perilously close to $200, higher than ever before in the city's history and out of reach of many budget travelers. But don't get discouraged yet; there are still a few remarkable bargains to be had if you know where to look. In the pages that follow, I tell you about some truly wonderful places to stay that won't break your bank account.

Nevertheless, this is the land of $200-a-night Holiday Inns and HoJos—so forget about calling up one of the chains and booking a reliable $75 motel room as you could in any other U.S. city. To stay in New York, you must carefully weigh what you're willing to afford versus what you're willing to put up with. If you only want to spend 100 or so bucks a night—a very budget-basic rate in this city—you're going to have to live with some inconveniences.

First and foremost, be aware that many of New York's budget hotels have **shared bathrooms.** There are a few exceptions to the rule, but in general don't count on scoring a double room with a private bathroom for less than $100 a night.

Even if you're willing to spend a bit more, don't expect much in the way of **space.** Space is New York's most coveted commodity, its most precious resource, and most of it doesn't go to visitors on tight budgets. Don't be surprised if your hotel room isn't much bigger than the bed that's in it, the closet is just a rack screwed to the wall, and the bathroom is the smallest you've ever seen. Pack light.

Also, you might have to stay in a residential district rather than your first-choice neighborhood. In general, it's more expensive to stay in the heart of the Theater District than in Chelsea, Murray Hill, or the Upper West Side. But this can be a good thing, especially if you like peace and quiet. Staying in a residential area will also give you better access to affordable restaurants where locals eat rather than places in tourist-heavy neighborhoods, which tend to jack up their prices. For more help in choosing a location, take a close look at "Manhattan's Neighborhoods in Brief" in chapter 4 before you delve into the hotel listings.

For an easy-to-scan introduction to the best of what the city has to offer, take a moment to check out "Best Low-Cost Hotel Bets" in chapter 1, if you haven't already.

## HOW TO SAVE ON YOUR HOTEL ROOM

The **rates** quoted in the listings below are the rack rates—the maximum rates that a hotel charges for rooms. But rack rates are only guidelines, and there are often ways around them. Before you even start calling, be sure to review the "60 Money-Saving Tips" in chapter 2, including the box called "Homestay Sweet Homestay," where you'll find terrific time-tested advice on how to get the most for your accommodations dollar.

The hotels listed below have provided us with their best rate estimates for 2001, and all quoted rates were correct at press time. Be aware, however, that **rates can change at any time.** Rates are always subject to availability, seasonal fluctuations, and plain old increases—especially with demand for hotel rooms being what it is in New York City. All bets are off at Christmas; expect everyone to be charging over their rack rates.

## 1 TriBeCa

✪ **Cosmopolitan Hotel–Tribeca.** 95 W. Broadway (at Chambers St.), New York, NY, 10007. ☎ **888/895-9400** or 212/566-1900. Fax 212/566-6909. www.cosmohotel.com. 104 units. A/C TV TEL. $99–$149 double. AE, CB, DC, EC, JCB, MC, V. Parking $20, 1 block away. Subway 1, 2, 3, 9, to Chambers St.

Hiding behind a plain-vanilla TriBeCa awning is the best hotel deal in Manhattan for budget travelers who don't want to sacrifice the luxury of a private bathroom. Every room comes with its own small but spotless bathroom, telephone with dataport, air-conditioning, satellite TV, alarm, and ceiling fan. Everything is strictly budget, but nice: The modern IKEA-ish furniture includes an armoire (a few rooms have a dresser and hanging rack instead) and a work desk; for a few extra bucks, you can have a loveseat, too. Beds are comfy, and sheets and towels are better quality than in many more expensive hotels. Rooms are small but make the most of the limited space, and the whole place is pristine. The two-level mini-lofts have lots of character, but expect to duck on the second level: Downstairs is the bathroom, TV, closet, desk, and club chair, and upstairs is a low-ceilinged bedroom with a second TV and phone. The neighborhood is safe, hip, and subway-convenient; the Financial District is just a walk away. There's no room service, but a range of great restaurants, from budget to deluxe, will deliver. All services are kept at a bare minimum to keep costs down, so you must be a low-maintenance guest to be happy here. If you are, this place is a smokin' deal.

## 2 The Lower East Side

**Off SoHo Suites.** 11 Rivington St. (btw. Chrystie St. and the Bowery), New York, NY 10002. ☎ **800/OFF-SOHO** or 212/979-9808. Fax 212/979-9801. www.offsoho.com. 38 units (28 with bathroom). A/C TV TEL. $102–$125 economy suite (2 people maximum); $188–$251 deluxe suite (4 people maximum). AE, EC, JCB, MC, V. Parking $14, 3 blocks away. Subway: F to Second Ave.; B, D, Q to Grand St. Pets allowed.

Used to be that to enjoy the bargain that is Off SoHo Suites—a hotel with clean, welcoming rooms with full kitchen facilities at surprisingly low prices—you had to put up with a desolate, industrial edge-of-Chinatown neighborhood. No more. The neighborhood is getting better by the minute, and it's just a stone's throw from the city's coolest dining, shopping, and nightlife; NoLiTa's trendy Elizabeth Street is just 2 blocks west, and the Lower East Side's super-hot Orchard and Ludlow streets are just a half-dozen blocks east, not to mention Chinatown's nearby cheap eats. The spaces

# Downtown Accommodations

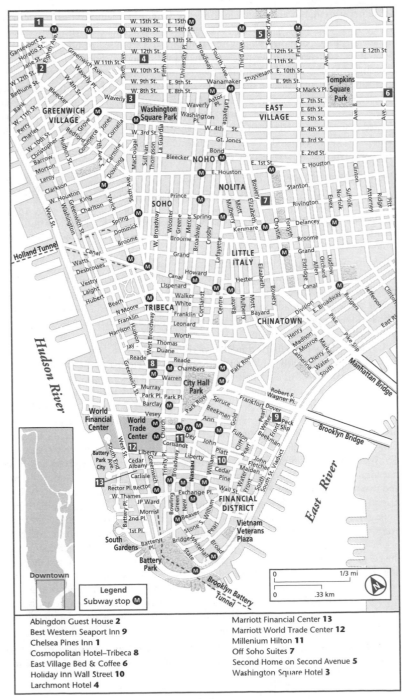

Abingdon Guest House **2**
Best Western Seaport Inn **9**
Chelsea Pines Inn **1**
Cosmopolitan Hotel–Tribeca **8**
East Village Bed & Coffee **6**
Holiday Inn Wall Street **10**
Larchmont Hotel **4**

Marriott Financial Center **13**
Marriott World Trade Center **12**
Millenium Hilton **11**
Off Soho Suites **7**
Second Home on Second Avenue **5**
Washington Square Hotel **3**

are rather spartan, but you'll get a lot for your dough: The deluxe suites have a living and dining area with a pullout sofa, fully outfitted kitchen (with coffeemaker, microwave, fridge, and dishes), private bathroom, and separate bedroom. In the economy suites, a kitchen and bathroom are shared with another room; if four of you are traveling together, you can combine two economy suites into a sizable apartment. Everything is pretty basic and the beds are a bit harder than I like, but the whole place is well kept. Telephones have voice mail and dataport, a hair dryer is in the bathroom, a self-service laundromat and a workout room are on premises, and there's even limited room service from the on-site cafe (open for breakfast and lunch). The neighborhood isn't for everyone, however; if you're not going to like the youth-oriented, still-gentrifying scene, stay elsewhere.

## 3 The East Village

**East Village Bed & Coffee.** 110 Ave. C (btw. 7th and 8th sts.), New York, NY 10009. ☎ and fax **212/533-4175.** www.eastvillagebed.citysearch.com. 6 rooms (all with shared bathroom). A/C. $50 single, $75 double; rates include tax. AE, MC, V. Nearby street parking. Subway: L to First Ave.; 6 to Astor Place.

Fair warning: This funny little guest house isn't for everyone. If you're turned off by the idea of staying behind a graffiti-covered facade in a space that's still a work in progress, set in a scruffy neighborhood that's also an ongoing project, skip this one. But if you're a young, adventurous, easygoing traveler who likes a communal vibe, who's willing to put up with a few eccentricities and an off-the-beaten-path location for a rock-bottom deal, read on.

Committed to providing affordable accommodations to budget travelers from around the globe, friendly innkeeper Carlos Delfin has created a series of private guest rooms on two floors. All are small, basic, and hostel-like, with little more than a bed and a loose "theme" that you might miss if you don't look carefully. Best is the sunlit French room, with queen bed and a chest of drawers. Also on the second floor are some very petite rooms, including the cute Mexican room (painted in a pretty South-of-the-Border palette), plus a common kitchen, living room with TV, and bathroom. Downstairs is a large loftlike space with Carlos's workroom up front; a living area with TV, stereo, and VCR; an office space where you can send and receive faxes and make free local calls; another kitchen with a big farmstead dining table; a second bathroom; and two more Japanese-style bedrooms (with low ceilings and low platform beds) built as enclosed lofts over the main space. These are for heavy sleepers only, as they're subject to noise from above and below. Furnishings are a hodge-podge collection; everything I saw was well worn but clean, and a wonderful ethnic art collection brightens the mix. Every room got a new high-quality mattress and other upgrades in the fall of 1999, including new curtains and its own work desk. Carlos lives in the space as well (with his shepherd Fang, whose fierce name belies her sweet disposition), so he's on hand to answer questions; he even cooks dinner for guests from time to time. The Alphabet City neighborhood has improved dramatically in the last few years, but it's still the hinterlands as far as most visitors are concerned. Subways are a significant walk away, so use the money you save on your room to take cabs back late at night.

**Second Home on Second Avenue.** 221 Second Ave. (btw. E. 13th and 14th sts.), New York, NY 10003. ☎ and fax **212/677-3161.** www.secondhome.citysearch.com. 7 units (2 with bathroom). A/C TV TEL. $70–$90 single with shared bathroom, $110 double with shared bathroom, $135 double with private bathroom, $165 suite. Extra person $20. 2-night minimum stay required. AE, MC, V. Parking about $20 nearby. Subway: L to 3rd Ave.; N, R, 4, 5, 6 to Union Square.

Here's another guest house run by Carlos Delfin, this one a big step up in quality, location, and price from his East Village Bed & Coffee, above. It's a nice guest house for young, independent-minded travelers who'd prefer the restaurant- and club-heavy East Village over more tourist-heavy neighborhoods. The rooms are large and decently, if eclectically, furnished, with some surprisingly nice touches here and there. Each is outfitted with two full beds, good closet space, and a large TV with VCR and a CD player in every room (otherwise unheard of in this price category). If there's more than two of you, the suite, which has a separate living room with a nice leather sofa that pulls out into a queen bed and a big private bathroom, is a good bet. Bathrooms are older but clean. One of the features that makes this a recommendable choice is the fully outfitted common kitchen, with full stove and fridge, toaster oven, coffeemaker, and dishwasher, plus free coffee and tea on hand at all times.

A few words of caution, though: Don't expect lots in the way of service; friendly innkeeper Carlos Delfin lives off-site, so you're really on your own here. Rooms are on the third and fourth floors, so this isn't the place for visitors with mobility issues. And the guest house is popular with European travelers, who like to smoke, so stay elsewhere if the odor bothers you.

## 4 Greenwich Village

**✪ Abingdon Guest House.** 13 Eighth Ave. (btw. W. 12th and Jane sts.), New York, NY 10014. ☎ **212/243-5384.** Fax 212/807-7473. www.abingdonguesthouse.com. 9 units (7 with private bathroom). A/C TV TEL. High season (April–June and Sept–Jan 15) $120–$145 double with shared bathroom, $165–$220 double with private bathroom; low season (Jan 16–March and July–Aug) $105–$130 double with shared bathroom, $145–$185 with private bathroom. $15 less for single travelers. Extra person $25. 4-night minimum on weekends, 2-night minimum on weekdays. AE, DC, DISC, MC, V. Parking $20 nearby. Subway: A, C, E to 14th St.; 1, 2, 3, 9 to 14th St.

Steve Austin, who has a hotel management degree, and his partner, Zachary Stass, educated in interior design, now run this lovely guest house (and its downstairs coffee bar, Brewbar) in a wonderful West Village neighborhood. Both men have an eye for style and take the guest-house business seriously, and their commitment shows; the Abingdon is beautifully outfitted and professionally run. All the rooms are done in bold colors and outfitted with well-chosen art and furnishings; each can be previewed on their Web site, so your best bet is to choose the one that best fits your personal style and budget. I suggest opting for one with a new bathroom (they're large and well done). But no matter which one you choose, you'll get a superior-quality mattress and linens (better than at most hotels that cost more), hair dryer, soft polyfleece bathrobes, alarm, a small TV, and telephone with your own answering machine (a splitter can be provided for your laptop); five rooms also have ceiling fans.

The neighborhood is terrific, especially for those who want to be close to good restaurants and boutiques, but it's a bit off the beaten path if you're planning on lots of Midtown sightseeing. And the Abingdon is best for mature, independent-minded travelers because there's no regular staff on site. No smoking.

**✪ Larchmont Hotel.** 27 W. 11th St. (btw. Fifth and Sixth aves.), New York, NY 10011. ☎ **212/989-9333.** Fax 212/989-9496. www.larchmonthotel.citysearch.com. 57 units (none with private bathroom). A/C TV TEL. $70–$80 single, $85–$109 double. Rates include continental breakfast. Children under 13 stay free in parents' room. AE, CB, DC, DISC, MC, V. Parking $18 nearby. Subway: 4, 5, 6, N, R, L to Union Square; A, C, E, B, D, F, Q to West 4th St. (use 8th St. exit); F to 14th St.

Supremely located on a beautiful tree-lined block in a quiet residential part of the Village, this European-style hotel is simply a gem. If you're willing to put up with the

# Dealmaking with the Chains

As you consider hotels, keep in mind that most—particularly those with recognizable names, such as Comfort Inn, Holiday Inn, and Best Western—are highly market-sensitive, in both directions. Because they hate to see rooms sit empty, they'll often negotiate astounding rates at the last minute and in slow seasons.

The chains are also where you're able to pull out all the stops for discounts, from auto club membership to senior status. AAA or AARP membership is well worth the annual fee for the 10% off it will garner you at most of the chains. And you might be able to take advantage of corporate rates or highly discounted weekend stays. Most chain hotels let the kids stay with mom and dad for free. Always ask for every possible kind of discount; if you find that you get an unhelpful reservation agent at the main number, dial back and you're likely to get a more helpful one. And it's worth calling the hotel direct, where the front-desk staff will wheel and deal to keep their occupancy rate (the badge of honor among city hotels these days) high.

Of course, there's no guarantee what you'll be offered. Even if you're traveling in the off-season, you could stumble on a big convention or some other event that drives rates up. Your chances of getting a deal aren't great if you're visiting in a busy season. But if you're willing to make a few extra calls, or spend some time surfing online reservations systems—which might net you a 10 percent discount for just booking in cyberspace—you might find that you can get a lot for your money at some very comfortable hotels that would otherwise be out of your price range.

**Best Western** (☎ 800/528-1234; www.bestwestern.com) is one of the most reliable hotel chains in the nation, but the rack rates for their Big Apple hotels are higher than you'd expect. At the **Best Western Seaport Inn,** 33 Peck Slip at South Street Seaport (☎ 800/HOTEL-NY or 212/766-6600), doubles go for $169 to $209 but can drop to $149 with corporate, family, weekend, and seasonal discounts. Because rates include continental breakfast, that's a great deal on a very comfortable and well-kept hotel. At Midtown's beautifully renovated and located **Best Western Woodward,** 210 W. 55th St. (☎ 800/336-4110 or 212/247-2000; www.bestnyhotels.com or www.bestwestern.com), rack rates go well into the $200s, but I've found rates as low as $119 double ($107 to seniors and AAA members) in slower periods. Ditto for other hotels handled by Hampshire Hotels & Suites, the company that manages this and great mid-priced chain hotels such as the **Comfort Inn—Central Park West** (p. 121), the **Best Western President** (p. 112), and the **Quality Hotel on Broadway** (p. 126), where rooms can go as low as $89 on occasion.

At these and other franchised hotels—such as the ones run by Apple Core Hotels, a small management company that handles the **Comfort Inn Midtown** (p. 113) and the **Quality Hotel Eastside** (p. 120), as well as the **Best Western Manhattan,** 17 W. 32nd St. (☎ 212/736-1600), and Manhattan's first **Red Roof Inn,** on 32nd Street just west of Fifth Avenue (☎ 800/RED-ROOF)—if you're not quoted a good advance-booking rate directly or through the management company's online reservations system, check with the franchiser (Comfort

inconvenience of shared bathrooms, you can't do better for the money. The entire place has a wonderful air of warmth and sophistication; the butter-yellow lobby even *smells* good. Each bright guest room is tastefully done in rattan and outfitted with a

Inn, Best Western, and so on) next. I find that the global 800 and online reservations systems for these franchisers will often garner you a better rate, which might include a franchise-wide promotion—or, at minimum, an "Internet User's Rate" that's 10% lower than the standard. A good source for one-stop shopping is **Choice Hotels** (☎ 800/4-CHOICE; www.hotelchoice.com), which oversees Comfort Inn, Quality Hotel, and Clarion Hotel chains, all of which have terrific Manhattan branches. If you can snare a low rate at the otherwise-beyond-budget **Clarion Hotel Fifth Avenue,** 3 E. 40th St. (☎ **800/252-7466**), don't pass it up; you won't be disappointed. But if it's a last-minute deal you seek, you might be able to do better by talking directly to the hotel; I've heard the desk clerks at Apple Core Hotels, where rack rates generally range from $109 to $249, negotiate rates as low as $79 more than once, which is a smokin' deal.

**Comfort Inn Manhattan,** 42 W. 35th St. (☎ **800/228-5150** or 212/947-0200; www.comfortinnmanhattan.com), can also offer some great deals on comfortable rooms. The best time to stay here is between January and July, when standard rates run $129 to $234 double (including a substantial continental breakfast), and you might be able to do better with discounts and a little negotiation. Again, **www.comfortinn.com** is your best bet, if only for a 10% online booking discount.

Another chain hotel worth trying is the **Days Hotel Midtown,** centrally located in the Theater District at 790 Eighth Ave. (☎ 800/544-8313 or 212/581-7000; www.daysinn.com). The motel-like rooms aren't worth the upper end of the $120 to $180 rack rates—but they are worth the $98 to $120 rate you might be able to snare in slower seasons.

You might be able to save big by staying in the Financial District, where hotels are abandoned for the weekend by their regular tenants, business travelers. At the downright luxurious **Millenium Hilton,** across from the World Trade Center at 55 Church St. (☎ 800/835-2220 or 212/693-2001; www.hilton.com), rooms that go for a whopping $289 to $509 during the week drop to $149 to $199 on weekends, depending on the season. Ditto for the **Marriott Financial Center,** 85 West St. (☎ 800/242-8685 or 212/385-4900), and the **Marriott World Trade Center,** 3 World Trade Center (☎ 800/228-9290 or 212/938-9100), both excellent outposts, and the **Best Western Seaport Inn** (see above). But the first Financial District hotel that budget travelers should try for deals is the **Holiday Inn Wall Street,** 15 Gold St. (☎ 800/HOLIDAY or 212/232-7700; www.holidayinnwsd.com), whose comfortable, business-minded rooms come with Internet-access TV, Nintendo, and a CD player; standard rates run $169 to $345 and go as low as $139 for weekenders.

If you're intrigued by the notion of weekend discounts but prefer a Midtown location, check with **Crowne Plaza at the United Nations,** 304 E. 42nd St. (☎ 800/879-8836; www.crowneplaza-un.com or www.crowneplaza.com), where weekend rates on *very* nice rooms that usually run $229 to $379 can sometimes be had for just $169.

writing desk, a wash basin, a mini-library of books, an alarm clock, and a few extras that you normally have to pay a lot more for, such as cotton bathrobes and ceiling fans. Every floor has two shared bathrooms (with hair dryers) and a small, simple kitchen.

The management is constantly renovating, so everything feels clean and fresh. Free continental breakfast, including fresh-baked goods every morning, is the crowning touch that makes the Larchmont an unbeatable deal. And with some of the city's best shopping, dining, and sightseeing, plus your choice of subway lines, just a walk away, you couldn't be better situated. Book *well* in advance (the management suggests 6 to 7 weeks' lead time).

**Washington Square Hotel.** 103 Waverly Place (btw. Fifth and Sixth aves.), New York, NY 10011. ☎ **800/222-0418** or 212/777-9515. Fax 212/979-8373. www.wshotel.com. 180 units. A/C TV TEL. $110–$125 single, $135–$165 double, $165–$180 quad. Rates include continental breakfast. AE, MC, JCB, V. Parking $27 nearby. Subway: A, B, C, D, E, F, Q to West 4th St.

The best thing about this hotel is its great location, right in the heart of Greenwich Village overlooking Washington Square Park. The pretty facade and marble-and-brass lobby come as quite a surprise—not exactly what you expect from a budget hotel.

The tiny, plain rooms are a decent value. Each comes with a private bathroom, a deposit-activated phone with voice mail and dataport, and a small closet with a pint-sized safe; irons and hair dryers are available from the front desk. Beds are firm but the pillows are flat, and a little more elbow grease could go into the detailing of some of the petite bathrooms. Still, for the money, you could do worse. It's worth paying a few extra dollars for a south-facing room on a high floor, because others can be a bit dark. There's a basic gym and a very good restaurant, CIII, that even draws locals with its well-priced bistro fare, friendly staff, two-for-one happy hours (Monday through Friday 4 to 7pm), and Sunday jazz brunch that Zagat's calls "marvelous." However, the hotel staff has been terse on occasion, so be on your guard and let me know if you have any problems.

# 5 Chelsea

✪ **Chelsea Lodge.** 318 W. 20th St. (btw. Eighth and Ninth aves.), New York, NY 10011. ☎ **800/373-1116** or 212/243-4499. Fax 212/342-7852. www.chelsealodge.com. 22 units (all with semi-private bathroom). A/C TV. $70–$90 single, $85–$105 double. AE, DC, DISC, EC, MC, V. Parking about $20 nearby. Subway: C, E to 23rd St.

Put down this book right *now* and go book a room at Chelsea Lodge, before every other budget-minded traveler looking for the city's best new bargain gets here first. Housed in a lovely brownstone on a landmarked block, this small hotel is brand-new, utterly charming, and a terrific value. The young, friendly husband-and-wife owners have put in an incredible effort: Impeccable renovations have restored original wood-work to mint condition and created a homey, country-in-the-city vibe with beautiful wallpapers and wainscotting, smartly refinished vintage furniture, and lovely little touches like Hershey's Kisses on the fluffy pillows. The beds are the finest and best outfitted I've seen in this price category. The only place with a similar grown-up sensibility for the same money is Greenwich Village's Larchmont (above), but all bath-room facilities are shared there; at Chelsea Lodge, each room has its own sink and in-room shower stall, so you only have to share a cute toilet room with your neigh-bors. I won't kid you; rooms are petite, the open closets are small, and beds are merely full-size. But considering the stylishness, the amenities—which include TV (not common in this price category), a ceiling fan, a small desk, and an alarm clock—and the great neighborhood, you'd be hard-pressed to do better for the money. Best for couples rather than shares. *Tip:* Try to book 2A, which is bigger than most, or one of the first-floor rooms, whose high ceilings make them feel more spacious.

**Chelsea Pines Inn.** 317 W. 14th St. (btw. Eighth and Ninth aves.), New York, NY 10014. ☎ **212/929-1023.** Fax 212/620-5646. www.q-net.com/chelseapines. 23 units (8 with semi-private bathrooms). A/C TV TEL. $89–$139 double with semi-private bathroom, $119–$169 with private bathroom. Rates include continental breakfast. Extra person $20. 3-night minimum stay on weekends. AE, DC, DISC, MC, V. Parking $20–$25 nearby. Subway: A, C, E to 14th St. Inappropriate for children.

This very charming inn caters largely to gay travelers, but all adult travelers are welcome as long as they'll be comfortable in a gay-oriented atmosphere. The location couldn't be better: The inn straddles the border between the West Village, the traditional heart of New York's gay community, and Chelsea, the latest hip address for the same-sex scene. The impeccably kept rooms have comfortable furnishings, cozy floral-print textiles, and a terrific collection of vintage movie posters that adds the appropriate touch of fabulousness. Each room is dedicated to a Golden-Age-of-Hollywood star; the Paul Newman room, for instance, boasts original posters from movies such as *Hud* and *The Drowning Pool*. Rooms aren't big, but they are well outfitted and thoughtfully arranged. All have minifridges, free HBO, a clock radio, an answering machine, and an iron and mini-board in the closet; most have queen beds and comfy daybeds for extra seating, and a half-dozen have breakfast areas with cafe tables and microwaves. Private bathrooms are all bright and new. The cheapest (semi-private) rooms have in-room showers and sinks, so you just have to share a hall toilet. There's a payoff if you're willing to stay at the top of the five-story walkup, which is where you'll find the nicest rooms: The Rock Hudson comfortably sleeps four and has a terrific green-and-white bathroom with a skylight. The front desk is manned around the clock by the friendly staff, and continental breakfast is served in a cute breakfast room. There's a greenhouse-like enclosed patio, and the small backyard garden is open on nice days.

○ **Chelsea Savoy Hotel.** 204 W. 23rd St. (at Seventh Ave.), New York, NY 10011. ☎ **212/929-9353.** Fax 212/741-6309. www.chelseasavoy.qpg.com. 90 units. A/C TV TEL. $99–$115 single, $125–$165 double, $155–$195 quad. Rates include continental breakfast. Children stay free in parents' room. AE, JCB, MC, V. Parking $18 nearby. Subway: 1, 9 to 23rd St.

This three-year-old hotel has been a welcome addition to Chelsea, a neighborhood abloom with art galleries, restaurants, and weekend flea markets but formerly devoid of nice, affordable hotels. The six-story Savoy was built from the ground up, so it isn't subject to the eccentricities of the mostly older hotels in this price range: The hallways are attractive and wide, the elevators are swift and silent, and the generic but cheery rooms are good-sized and have big closets and roomy, immaculate bathrooms with tons of counter space. Creature comforts abound: The rooms boast mattresses, furniture, textiles, and linens of high quality, plus the kinds of amenities you usually have to pay more for, such as hair dryers, minifridges, alarm clocks, irons and ironing boards, in-room safes, and toiletries. Most rooms are street-facing and sunny; corner rooms tend to be brightest and noisiest. Ask for a darker, back-facing room if you crave total silence. There's a plain but pleasant sitting room off the lobby where you can relax and enjoy your morning coffee over a selection of newspapers and magazines. The staff is young and helpful, and the increasingly hip neighborhood makes a good base for exploring both Midtown and Downtown.

○ **Chelsea Star Hotel.** 300 W. 30th St. (at Eighth Ave.), New York, NY 10001. ☎ **877/827-6969** or 212/244-7827. Fax 212/279-9018. www.chelseastarhotel.citysearch.com or www.starhotelny.com. 25 rooms (none with private bathrooms), 5 apartments, 30 dorm beds. A/C. $59–$79 single, $79–$99 double, $99–$109 triple or quad; $149–$169 apartment (sleeps up to 4), $820–$980 weekly, $2,800 monthly; $35 per person in dorm (tax included). Extra person $10. AE, DISC, MC, V. Parking about $20 nearby. Subway: A, C, E to 34th St./Penn Station. Guests must be at least 18 years old.

It's hard to argue with the prices at this brand-new Generation Y–targeted place, especially considering the fresh feel and central-to-everything location. Industrial-chic hallways lead to private rooms that are miniscule and bare-bones basic—more hostel than hotel-like, with nothing more than a firm bed and an open closet. But they're spotless, the mattresses and linens are good quality, and designer Rob Graf has infused them with enough style that they don't feel dour as do most super-cheap sleeps. They're individually dressed in cheeky themes ranging from the Disco Room (graced by a *Fever*-era Travolta in all his white-suited glory) to the Asian mod Madame Butterfly Room (tiny, but lovely) to the glow-in-the-dark cosmos of the Orbit Room (complete with blacklight). Most popular—and the one to grab if you can snare it— is the Madonna Room, a relatively spacious quad where the Material Girl actually lived for a year just before she hit it big. Shoestring travelers who don't mind snoozing with strangers can opt for a single bunk in one of the charm-free but perfectly serviceable dorms. The shared hallway bathrooms have showers only, but they're smart, clean, and new.

For a bit more money, you can even have your own pad: a stylishly retro-modern, fully loaded apartment with an equipped kitchen, private bathroom, and TV in the furnished living room. These babies are quite a deal, so book way ahead. *Tip:* The courtyard-facing apartments are quietest. The front desk is professionally staffed from 8am to midnight. Pay phones are available, as is a cash- and credit-activated Internet PC. The neighborhood—at the brink of Penn Station, more Midtown than Chelsea— might not be New York's finest, but it's cleaner and safer than ever, and cheap eateries and Irish pubs abound.

The Chelsea Star is a great addition to the budget hotel scene, but a word of warning: It is decidedly youth-oriented; mature travelers looking for standard amenities might be disappointed.

**Colonial House Inn.** 318 W. 22nd St. (btw. Eighth and Ninth aves.), New York, NY 10011. ☎ **800/689-3779** or 212/243-9669. Fax 212/633-1612. www.colonialhouseinn.com. 20 rooms (12 with shared bathroom). A/C TV TEL. $80–$99 single or double with shared bathroom; $125–$140 with private bathroom. Rates include expanded continental breakfast. 2-night minimum on weekends. Extra person $15. Weekly rates available. MC, V. Parking $20 nearby. Subway: C, E to 23rd St.

This charming 1850 brownstone, on a pretty residential block in the heart of gay-friendly Chelsea, was the first permanent home of the Gay Men's Health Crisis. The four-story walk-up caters to a largely gay and lesbian clientele, but the friendly staff welcomes everybody equally, and straight couples are a common sight. The whole place is beautifully maintained and professionally run. Rooms are small and basic but clean; all have radios and hair dryers, and those that share a hall bathroom (at a ratio of about three rooms per bathroom) have in-room sinks. Deluxe rooms—those with private bathrooms—also have minifridges, and a few have fireplaces that accommodate Duraflame logs. Both private and shared bathrooms are basic but nice. A terrific, mostly abstract art collection brightens the public spaces. At parlor level is a cute breakfast room where a continental spread is put out from 8am to noon daily, and coffee and tea is available all day. There's a nice roof deck split by a privacy fence; the area behind the fence is clothing-optional. The neighborhood is chock-full of great restaurants and shopping and offers easy access to the rest of the city. Book at least a month in advance for weekend stays, as the inn regularly sells out.

## SUPER-CHEAP SLEEPS

Also consider the dorm beds ($35) at the **Chelsea Star Hotel,** above.

**Chelsea International Hostel.** 251 W. 20th St. (btw. Seventh and Eighth aves.), New York, NY 10011. ☎ **212/647-0010.** Fax 212/727-7289. www.chelseahostel.com. 223 dorm beds, 57 private units (all with shared bathroom). $25 dorm bed, $60 double. AE, MC, V. Subway: 1, 9 to 18th St.

As hostels go, this is a good one. The only other private hostel in this league, both in terms of cleanliness and location, is the Big Apple Hostel (see "Times Square & Midtown West" below). The well-managed and well-maintained Chelsea International consists of a warren of low-rise buildings organized around a central courtyard, much like a cottage complex. True to its name, it's hugely popular with young international travelers. Accommodations and shared bathrooms are older and plain but fine; the shared rooms come with nice extras such as wall hooks, sinks, and in-room lockers big enough for most backpacks (BYO combination lock and towels). The miniscule private rooms have little more than a double bed and some shelf units for your stuff, but you can call one your own for a mere 60 bucks. Some rooms have air-conditioning, so request one if it matters to you. The two fully equipped common kitchens (with microwaves) are the best I've seen in a hostel, and free coffee, tea, sugar, and cream is on hand. The private courtyard has picnic tables and barbecues. There are also dining and lounge areas with TV, Internet access machines, self-service laundry, and soda machines. Free luggage storage is another plus. The neighborhood is great, the desk is attended 24 hours, and maintenance is on hand around the clock. There's even a police precinct on the same block, so it would be harder to choose a safer location.

## WORTH A SPLURGE

**The Inn on 23rd.** 131 W. 23rd St. (btw. Sixth and Seventh aves.), New York, NY 10011. ☎ **877/387-2323** or 212/463-0330. Fax 212/463-0302. www.bbonline.com/ny/innon23rd. 11 units. A/C TV TEL. $150–$250 double, $350 suite. Rates include generous continental breakfast. Extra person $20; children under 12 stay free in parents' room. AE, JCB, MC, V. Parking about $20 nearby. Subway: 1, 9, F to 23rd St.

Once the kids were grown, friendly folks Annette and Barry Fisherman decided to abandon their historic Long Island home in favor of city living. After five years of house-hunting and renovations, they've launched one of Manhattan's few—and one of its finest—full-service bed-and-breakfast inns.

The building was gutted and laid out afresh, so all guest rooms are spacious. Each has a king or queen bed outfitted with a supremely comfy pillowtop mattress and top-quality linens; satellite TV; a new private bathroom with hair dryer and thick Turkish terry towels; phone with dataport on the desk; iron and board in the roomy closet; and a wonderfully homey vibe. The gorgeous mix of antiques, family heirlooms, and contemporary art is the product of Annette's impeccable eye. A number of rooms are at the lower end of the price range, less than $180, and they're well worth the money. I love the coolly sophisticated Rosewood room, with gorgeous 60s built-ins; the Bamboo room, peacefully quiet and elegantly Asian; and the 40s room, a Heywood-Wakefield lover's dream come true.

Welcoming public spaces include a cozy library with a stereo and VCR. An elevator means you don't have to cart your luggage up multiple flights of stairs, and a number of rooms have pull-out sofas or Murphy beds to accommodate more than two travelers. A real winner!

## 6  The Flatiron District & Gramercy Park

**Chelsea Inn.** 46 W. 17th St. (btw. Fifth and Sixth aves.), New York, NY 10011. ☎ **212/ 640-6469.** Fax 212/645-8989. www.chelseainn.com. 25 units (17 with bathroom). A/C TV TEL. $99–$129 double with shared bathroom, $139–$159 double with private bathroom, $179–$259 suite (for up to 4). Check Web site for available specials. AE, DISC, MC, V. Parking $20 nearby. Subway: 4, 5, 6, N, R to 14th St./Union Sq.

The name may say Chelsea, but the east-of-Sixth-Avenue address is really Flatiron. It's a great location no matter how you see it, what with Union Square just a stone's throw in one direction and Chelsea in the other (great for shoppers and club-hoppers).

The inn is housed in two 19th-century landmark brownstones, but don't expect too much. Staying here is sort of like living in your own New York City tenement for a few days: The rooms feature an eclectic mix of well-worn thrift-store furniture; the beds in the twin rooms are little more than rollaways, and the quality of the mattresses throughout is a crapshoot. Everything's faded, but the place is clean and well-kept. More on the upside: Closets are big, bathrooms are fine, and all rooms feature a hot plate, minifridge, coffeemaker, a cheap set of cups and utensils, a safe, voice mail, and free coffee; those without private bathroom have their own sink, too. Shared bathrooms are livened with cheerful murals, and you'll only have to split yours with one other room. If there's more than two of you, you can pair up two doubles that share a bathroom, creating a family-sized unit, and usually negotiate a discount on it. Groups of three or four will also like no. 102, a good-value suite with lots of space, a private bathroom, and a good dining table and kitchenette. Deals are often available, and rates can go as low as $79 in winter, $89 in summer. Not my favorite place in town, but just fine. The staff is accommodating, and a new lobby (under renovation at press time) should cheer things up quite a bit.

✪ **Gershwin Hotel.** 7 E. 27th St. (btw. Fifth and Madison aves.), New York, NY 10016. ☎ **212/545-8000.** Fax 212/684-5546. www.gershwinhotel.com. 94 doubles, 31 4-person dorms. A/C TV TEL (in private rooms only). $109–$139 double, $125–$149 triple, $139–$159 quad; $35 per person in dorm (tax included). Check Web site for seasonal deals. Extra person $10. AE, CB, EC, MC, V. Valet parking $20. Subway: N, R, 6 to 28th St.

If you see glowing horns protruding from a lipstick-red facade, you're in the right place. This budget-conscious, youth-oriented hotel caters to up-and-coming artistic types with its bold modern art collection and wild style. The lobby is a colorful, postmodern cartoon of kitschy furniture and pop art by Lichtenstein, Warhol, de Koonig, and lesser names. The standard rooms are clean and saved from the budget doldrums by bright colors, Picasso-style wall murals, Starck-ish takes on motel furnishings, and more modern art. All have dataports on the phones and private bathrooms with hair dryers; none of the bathrooms are bad, but try to nab yourself one of the cute, colorful new ones. The cheapest accommodations are four- and eight-bedded dorms: just basic rooms with IKEA bunk beds sharing a bathroom, but better than a hostel, especially if you're traveling with a group and can claim one as your own.

One of the best things about the Gershwin is its great, Factory-esque vibe, sort of like an artsy frat or sorority house. The hotel is more service-oriented than most at this price level—concierge and dry-cleaning/laundry service are even available—and there's always something going on, whether it's live comedy or jazz in the "Living Room" or Red Room Bar, a film screening or barbecue on the rooftop garden, or an opening at the hotel's own art gallery. An Internet-accessible computer is available for guests' use if you don't bring your own.

**Gramercy Park Hotel.** 2 Lexington Ave. (btw. 21st and 22nd sts.), New York, NY 10010. ☎ **800/221-4083** or 212/475-4320. Fax 212/505-0535. 360 units. A/C TV TEL. $165–$170 single, $180 double, from $210 suite. Extra person $10. Children under 12 stay free in parents' room. AE, CB, DC, DISC, EC, JCB, MC, V. Parking $28 nearby. Subway: 6 to 23rd St. Pets accepted.

Opened in 1924, this Old World hotel has one of the best settings in the city. It's in one of New York's loveliest neighborhoods, ideally located on the edge of the private park—restricted to just a few area residents and to hotel guests, who can also get a key—that gives Gramercy Park the air of a quiet London square. The hotel has been plagued by claims of neglect in recent years, but management is responding well, and the old place is looking good these days. You'll still have to overlook the finer details—expect chipped paint here and there, Brady Bunch–era shag carpeting in some halls, mix-and-match bathrooms that have been updated haphazardly, and ancient TVs. But rooms are big by city standards, decently furnished, and comfortable, and the hotel has a surprisingly appealing old New York vibe. Standard doubles have a king bed or two doubles, and some suites have pullout sofas that make them large enough to sleep six; all have big closets, minifridges, and hair dryers and fluffy towels in the roomy bathrooms. Best of all is the old-style pricing scheme: Request a park-facing room, which costs no more but features a great view and a small kitchenette. Off the bustling knotty pine-paneled lobby is a continental restaurant and a smokey, divey lounge with nightly entertainment that's drawing a young, retro-obsessed crowd with its old school appeal; there's also a beauty salon and newsstand. Valet service and morning room service (7:30am to 11am) are available.

**Hotel 17.** 225 E. 17th St. (btw. Second and Third aves.), New York, NY 10003. ☎ **212/475-2845.** Fax 212/677-8178. www.hotel17.citysearch.com. 160 units (none with private bathroom). A/C TEL. $90 single, $121–$138 double, $200 3-person suite. All prices include tax. No credit cards. Parking $16–$20 nearby. Subway: 4, 5, 6 to 14th St.; L to Third Ave. Children under 18 not accepted.

In the last couple of years, Hotel 17 has managed to garner a reputation as the hippest budget hotel in Manhattan, no doubt thanks (at least in part) to the fact that Madonna, David Bowie, and Maxwell have all been photographed in the eclectic, eccentric rooms. But it's not all hype. Hotel 17 has a lot to recommend it: The neighborhood is great, the block peaceful, and the individually decorated rooms surprisingly attractive. Look beyond the stylish veneer, though, and you'll find rooms that are small, dark, and basic—definitely not for travelers looking for creature comforts. Each has its own sink; the shared bathrooms are older but kept very clean. Recent renovation has softened the edge, adding air-conditioning, hair dryers, and alarm clocks to all rooms (TVs are in all but singles). The lobby has a funky streamline moderne feel to it, but the security glass separating you from the front-desk staff detracts from the ambience. There's a roof garden and self-service laundry. All in all, a good deal for the money, especially if you're the sort who requires some individuality in your lodgings. Expect lots of younger and international travelers, who don't mind the inconveniences.

## SUPER-CHEAP SLEEPS
Travelers on a shoestring budget should consider the dorm beds ($35) at the **Gershwin Hotel,** above.

# Midtown Accommodations

Americana Inn **20**
Best Western Manhattan **24**
Best Western–President Hotel **13**
Best Western Woodward **2**
Big Apple Hostel **9**
Broadway Inn **17**
Carlton Arms **33**
Chelsea Inn **36**
Chelsea International Hostel **39**
Chelsea Lodge **41**
Chelsea Pines Inn **42**
Chelsea Savoy Hotel **38**
Chelsea Star Hotel **23**
Clarion Hotel Fifth Avenue **19**
Colonial House Inn **40**
Comfort Inn Manhattan **21**
Comfort Inn Midtown **11**
Crowne Plaza
  at the United Nations **8**
Days Hotel Midtown **14**
Gershwin Hotel **32**
Gramercy Park Hotel **34**
Habitat Hotel **5**
Herald Square Hotel **26**
Hotel Edison **12**
Hotel Grand Union **28**
Hotel Metro **22**
Hotel 17 **35**
Hotel 31 **29**
Hotel Wolcott **27**
The Inn on 23rd **37**
Murray Hill Inn **31**
Park Savoy Hotel **3**
Pickwick Arms Hotel **6**
Quality Hotel Eastside **30**
Red Roof Inn **25**
Skyline Hotel **16**
Travel Inn **18**
Vanderbilt YMCA **7**
Washington Jefferson Hotel **15**
West Side YMCA **1**
The Wyndham **4**

## 7  Times Square & Midtown West

**Americana Inn.** 69 W. 38th St. (at Sixth Ave.), New York, NY 10018. ☎ **888/HOTEL58** or 212/840-2019. Fax 212/840-1830. www.newyorkhotel.com. 50 units (all with shared bathroom). A/C TV TEL. $75–$105 double. Extra person $10. AE, MC, V. Parking $27 nearby. Subway: B, D, F, Q to 42nd St.; N,R to 34th St.

The cheapest hotel from the Empire Hotel Group—the people behind the Newton among other top-notch, pricier properties—is a winner in the budget-basic category. Linoleum floors give the rooms an unfortunate institutional quality, but the hotel is professionally run and immaculately kept. Rooms are mostly spacious, with good-size closets and private sinks, and the beds are the most comfortable I've found at this price. Rooms come with a double bed or two twins; a few can accommodate three guests in two twin beds and a pullout sofa. There's one hall bathroom for every three rooms or so, and all are spacious and spotless. Every floor has a common kitchenette with microwave, stove, and fridge (BYO cooking tools and utensils, or go plastic). The five-story building has an elevator, and four rooms are handicap accessible. The Garment District location couldn't be more convenient for Midtown sightseeing and shopping. Ask for a back-facing room away from the street noise.

**Best Western—President Hotel.** 234 W. 48th St. (btw. Broadway and Eighth Ave.), New York, NY 10036. ☎ **800/826-4667** or 212/632-9000. Fax 212/974-3922. www. bestnyhotels.com or www.bestwesternhotels.com. 400 units. A/C TV TEL. $129–$229 double, $229–$499 suite. Children under 12 stay free in parents' room. AE, DC, DISC, JCB, MC, V. Parking about $25 nearby. Subway: 1, 9 to 50th St.

It's hard to go wrong at this nice, well-managed chain hotel. Rooms are slightly more expensive than at other budget hotels, but the decor is fresh and pleasant, beds are especially comfortable, and the heart-of-the–Theater District location is great. Best of all, rates have been known to drop to $89 in the lower seasons, most notably winter and midsummer, and you might be able to do even better if you qualify for senior or AAA rates. Dataport on the phone, concierge service, limited room service, dry cleaning and laundry service, free newspaper delivery, express checkout, and an on-site restaurant, cafe, and lounge add to the better-than-budget comforts. You'll be perfectly happy at this hotel; it's just great in a nondescript, reliable way.

❂ **Broadway Inn.** 264 W. 46th St. (at Eighth Ave.), New York, NY 10036. ☎ **800/ 826-6300** or 212/997-9200. Fax 212/768-2807. www.broadwayinn.com. 40 units. A/C TV TEL. $95–$105 single, $125–$180 double, $205 suite. Rates include continental breakfast. Extra person $10; children under 12 stay free in parents' room. AE, DC, DISC, JCB, MC, V. Parking $18 3 blocks away. Subway: 1, 2, 3, 7, 9, S to 42nd St./Times Square; A, C, E to 42nd St.; N, R to 49th St.

More like a San Francisco B&B than a Theater District hotel, this lovely, welcoming inn is a real charmer. The second-floor lobby sets the homey, easygoing tone with stocked bookcases, cushy seating, and cafe tables where breakfast is served. The rooms are basic but comfy, outfitted in an appealing neo-deco style with firm beds, good-quality linens and textiles, and hair dryers in the nice bathrooms. The whole place is impeccably kept; neatniks won't have a quibble. Two rooms have king beds and Jacuzzi tubs, but the standard doubles are just fine for two if you're looking to save some dough. If there's more than two of you, or you're looking to stay awhile, the suites— with pullout sofa, microwave, minifridge, dataports on the phones, and lots of closet space—are a great deal. The location can be noisy, but double-paned windows keep the rooms surprisingly peaceful; still, ask for a back-facing one if you're extra-sensitive.

The inn's biggest asset is its staff, who go above and beyond to make guests happy and at home in New York; service doesn't get any better in this price range. And this corner of the Theater District is now porn-free and gentrifying beautifully; it makes a great home base, especially for theatergoers. The inn has inspired a loyal following, so reserve early. However, there's no elevator in the four-story building, so overpackers and travelers with limited mobility should book elsewhere.

**Comfort Inn Midtown.** 129 W. 46th St. (btw. Sixth Ave. and Broadway), New York, NY 10036. ☎ **800/567-7720** or 212/221-2600. Fax 212/790-2760. www.applecorehotels.com. 79 units. A/C TV TEL. $89–$219 double, depending on season. Rates include continental breakfast. Extra person $10; children under 14 stay free in parents' room. Ask about senior, AAA, corporate, and promotional discounts; check www.comfortinn.com for online booking discounts. AE, DC, DISC, MC, V. Parking $24 nearby. Subway: 1, 2, 3, 9 to 42nd St./ Times Square; N,R to 49th St.; B, D, F, Q to 47–50th sts./Rockefeller Center.

A major 1998 renovation has turned the formerly dour Hotel Remington into a pleasingly value-minded member of the Comfort Inn chain. Rates can climb higher than they should in autumn or at Christmastime, but low-season rates often make the rooms one of Midtown's best bargains. A attractive mahogany-and-marble lobby leads to the petite but nicely outfitted guest rooms, which boast nice floral patterns, neo-Shaker furnishings, and good marble and tile bathrooms (a few have showers only, so be sure to request a tub if it matters). Everything's fresh and comfortable. In-room extras include hair dryers, coffeemakers (oddly situated in the bathroom), blackout drapes, pay movies, in-room safes, and phones with voice mail and dataport. Don't expect much in the way of personal service, but on-site amenities such as a small but satisfying fitness room (Stairmaster, treadmill, and bike) and a business center (with PC, fax, and copier) pick up the slack. The location is excellent, steps from Times Square, Rockefeller Center, and the Theater District.

**Herald Square Hotel.** 19 W. 31st St. (btw. Fifth Ave. and Broadway), New York, NY 10001. ☎ **800/727-1888** or 212/279-4017. Fax 212/643-9208. www.heraldsquarehotel.com. 123 units (112 with private bathroom). A/C TV TEL. $60–$115 single, $115–$130 double. Extra person $10; children under 12 stay free in parents' room. AE, DISC, JCB, MC, V. Parking $21. Subway: N, R to 28th St.; B, D, F, Q, N, R to 34th St.

Presiding regally over the entrance, Philip Martiny's gilded sculpture *Winged Life* is certainly emblematic of the new life the Puchall family has breathed into this older Manhattan hotel. They took the Carrère & Hastings beaux-arts building that was once home to *Life* magazine and reinvented it as a budget hotel with a sense of history. *Life* covers decorate the lobby, hallways, and some of the rooms. The rooms themselves are small and basic, with cheap laminated furniture, florescent lighting, and good-size but older bathrooms; some rooms I saw were worn looking and in need of a fresh paint job, but voice mail and in-room safes soften the blow. Still, if you're looking for a great location on a shoestring, this is a good bet (although I'd try booking in at the Portland Square, the Herald Square's sister hotel, first; see below). The friendly staff can arrange bus tours and airport transportation. The hotel is popular with Europeans and other visitors who love the nearby shopping (Macy's, Lord & Taylor, the Manhattan Mall) and sightseeing (the Empire State Building).

✪ **Hotel Edison.** 228 W. 47th St. (btw. Broadway and Eighth Ave.), New York, NY 10036. ☎ **800/637-7070** or 212/840-5000. Fax 212/596-6850. www.edisonhotelnyc.com. 869 units. A/C TV TEL. $130 single, $150 double, $175 quad, $210 suite. Extra person $15. AE, CB, DC, DISC, MC, V. Valet parking $22. Subway: N, R to 49th St.; 1, 9 to 50th St.

There's no doubt about it—the Edison is one of the Theater District's best hotel bargains, if not the best. No other area hotel is so consistently value-priced. The recently renovated rooms are much nicer than what you'd get for just about the same money at the nearby Ramada Inn Milford Plaza (which ain't exactly the "Lullabuy of Broadway!" these days). Don't expect much more than the basics, but you will find a firm bed (flat pillows, though), motel decor that's more attractive than most I've seen in this category, a phone with dataport, and a clean, perfectly adequate tile bathroom. Most double rooms feature two twins or a full bed, but there are some queens; request one at booking and show up early in the day for your best chance at one. Quad rooms are larger, with two doubles.

Off the attractive deco-style lobby is Cafe Edison, an old-style Polish deli that's a favorite among ladder-climbing theater types and downmarket ladies who lunch; Sofia's, an Italian restaurant; a tavern with live entertainment most nights; and a gift shop. Services are kept at a bare minimum to keep rates down, but dry-cleaning/laundry service and express checkout is available; there is also a beauty salon as well as a guest services desk where you can arrange tours, theater tickets, and transportation. The hotel fills up with tour groups from the world over, but because it has nearly 1,000 rooms, you can carve out some space if you call early enough.

**Hotel Wolcott.** 4 W. 31st St. (at Fifth Ave.), New York, NY 10001. ☎ **212/268-2900.** Fax 212/563-0096. www.wolcott.com. 250 units. A/C TV TEL. $120 double, $140 triple, $170 suite. Discounted AAA, AARP, and promotional rates may be available. Extra person $20. AE, JCB, MC, V. Parking $17 next door. Subway: B, D, F, Q, N, R to 34th St.

The Wolcott was one of the grande dames of Manhattan hotels at the start of the 20th century. Somewhat less than that now, it has been reinvented as a good-value option for bargain-hunting travelers. Only the lobby hints at the hotel's former grandeur; these days, the rooms are motel-standard, but they're well kept and quite serviceable. Plusses include spacious bathrooms and phones with dataports and voice mail, plus minifridges in most rooms. On the downside, some of the mattresses aren't as firm as I might like, and the closets tend to be on the small side. And some of the triples are poorly configured—the front door to one I saw hit up right against a bed—but they're plenty big enough for three, and come with two TVs to avoid before-bedtime conflicts (as do the suites). All in all, you get your money's worth here. One of the hotel's most recommendable features is its basement coin-op laundry, a rarity for Manhattan. There's also a tour desk, plus a decent fitness center, meeting rooms, and a business center that you can use without additional charge.

**Park Savoy Hotel.** 158 W. 58th St. (btw. Sixth and Seventh aves.), New York, NY 10019. ☎ **212/245-5755.** Fax 212/765-0668. 70 units. A/C TV TEL. $95–$145 single, $105–$185 double. All rates include tax. AE, MC, V. Parking $20 next door. Subway: A, B, C, D, 1, 9 to 59th St./Columbus Circle; N, R to 57th St.

The Park Savoy isn't quite as nice as its sister hotel, the Chelsea Savoy (see "Chelsea" earlier in this chapter), but the lower prices reflect the quality difference, making it a good deal nonetheless. The hotel has been recently renovated so that all rooms have nice new black-and-white–tiled private bathrooms, which are petite (with showers only) but attractive and clean. If your budget is tight, two of you can make do in the smallest rooms; the biggest ones can accommodate three or four in two double beds. Rooms are basic, and a few I saw were in need of a fresh coat of paint, but they do the job. All have voice mail and alarm clocks, most have walk-in closets, and a few have minifridges. Services are kept to a minimum to keep rates low, but there's a good Pasta Lovers restaurant in the building that gives guests 10% off and will deliver to your room. Best of all is the attractive and convenient location—a block from Central Park and a stone's throw from Carnegie Hall, Lincoln Center, and the Columbus Circle subway lines, which give you easy access to the rest of the city.

**Portland Square Hotel.** 132 W. 47th St. (btw. Sixth and Seventh aves.), New York, NY 10036. ☎ **800/388-8988** or 212/382-0600. Fax 212/382-0684. www.portlandsquarehotel. com. 145 units (115 with private bathroom). A/C TV TEL. $60–$70 single with shared bathroom, $99 single with private bathroom, $115–$125 double with private bathroom, $135–$145 triple or quad (2 double beds) with private bathroom. Extra person $10. AE, JCB, MC, V. Parking $24. Subway: B, D, F, Q to 47th–50th sts./Rockefeller Center.

Another Puchall family project (see the Herald Square Hotel, above), the Portland Square is a good Theater District bet for budget travelers. I like this hotel slightly better than the Herald Square: The public spaces have been nicely renovated, and everything seems to be in pretty good shape. The rooms are small, simple, and cheaply furnished (think laminated furniture, fluorescent lighting), but clean. Ask for one with an extra-large bathroom; some are almost as big as the bedroom. Avoid the shared bathroom singles if you can: The ratio is a high four rooms to a bathroom, the hall bathrooms I saw were on the crusty side, and most of the shared bathrooms I visited had a smoky odor. But the private bathrooms are a decent deal if money's tight. Every room has its own safe, voice mail on the phone, and air-conditioning year-round (many hotels take window units out in the winter). The staff is friendly and cooperative, but don't expect much in the way of service (that's one way they keep rates low). Luggage lockers are available.

**Skyline Hotel.** 725 Tenth Ave. (at 49th St.), New York, NY 10019. ☎ **800/433-1982** or 212/586-3400. Fax 212/582-4604. www.skylinehotelny.com. 230 units. A/C TV TEL. $149–$179 double, $171–$219 junior or full suite. Extra person $15; children 14 and under stay free in parents' room. AE, CB, DISC, MC, V. Free storage parking (charge for in/out privileges). Subway: A, C, E to 50th St. Pets accepted with $200 deposit.

This nice, newly renovated motor hotel offers predictable comforts and some uncommon extras—free storage parking (easily worth $25 or more a day) and a lovely indoor pool—that make it an excellent value. A pleasant wood-paneled lobby leads to motel-standard rooms that are a far cry from stylish, but so what? They're bigger than most in this price range and boast double-paned windows that open to let fresh air in and shut out a surprising amount of street noise when closed; decent-sized closets; and small work desks. Some rooms have brand-new bathrooms, but the older bathrooms are still fine. Everything is very well kept, and lots of freshening was in progress during my last visit. The suites have pullout sofas, making them a great deal for families. (The junior suites are basically one large room, while the full suites have the sitting area and an extra TV in a separate room.) On the downside, some closets are open to the room, there are no bedside alarm clocks or dataports (dataports are scheduled), and hair dryers and irons must be requested from housekeeping.

On site is a pleasing restaurant with a full bar; a Gray Line tour desk; a gift shop; a big, nice ballroom; and a bright rooftop meeting room. Room service is offered from 7am to 11pm, and laundry service is available. The pool has a nicely tiled deck and plush deck chairs, but it's only open in the evenings Monday through Friday (all day Saturday and Sunday), so don't count on an early-morning swim.

**Travel Inn.** 515 W. 42nd St. (just west of Tenth Ave.), New York, NY 10036. ☎ **888/ HOTEL58,** 800/869-4630, or 212/695-7171. Fax 212/268-3542. www.newyorkhotel.com. 160 units. A/C TV TEL. $150–$200 double; $250 executive suite. Extra person $15; children under 16 stay free in parents' room. AAA discounts available; check Web site for special Internet deals. AE, DC, DISC, MC, V. Free self-parking. Subway: A, C, E to 42nd St.–Port Authority Bus Terminal.

Extras such as a huge outdoor pool and sundeck, an up-to-date fitness room, and free parking (with in and out privileges!) make Travel Inn another terrific deal, similar to the one offered by the Skyline Hotel (directly above). Like the Skyline, Travel Inn might not be loaded with personality, but it does offer the clean, bright regularity of a good chain hotel—an attractive trait in a city where "quirky" is the catchword at most affordable hotels. Rooms are oversized and comfortably furnished, with extra-firm beds, a work desk, alarm clock, full-length mirrors, iron and board, and hair dryers in the bathrooms. (Phones have voice mail but no dataports yet.) A total renovation had just been completed at press time, and everything feels new and fresh, even the nicely tiled bathrooms. Even the smallest double is sizable and has a roomy bathroom. There's an on-site coffee shop, a gift shop run by Gray Line that can book tours and airport transfers, a well-equipped conference room, a nice fitness room, and, in season, a lifeguard on duty at that terrific pool. The neighborhood has gentrified nicely and isn't as far-flung as you might think: Off-Broadway theaters and great affordable restaurants are at hand, and it's just a 10-minute walk to the Theater District. A good bet even if you don't have a car.

**Washington Jefferson Hotel.** 318 W. 51st St. (just west of Eighth Ave.), New York, NY 10019. ☎ **888/567-7550** or 212/246-7550. Fax 212/246-7622. www.washingtonjeff. citysearch.com. 150 units (35 with private bathroom). A/C (in summer) TV TEL. $68–$99 double with shared bathroom; $109–$149 double with private bathroom; $129–$169 suite, depending on season. Ask about special deals. AE, MC, V. Parking $15–$20 nearby. Subway: C, E to 50th St. Pets accepted.

Here's a good choice in gentrifying Hell's Kitchen, just west of the Theater District. The lobby is warm and welcoming, the old-time staff service oriented, and the leafy, bistro-lined block one of the nicest in the neighborhood. The no-frills, mix-and-match rooms aren't anything special—expect small and K-Mart quality and you won't be disappointed—but they do the job. The private bathrooms have tiny tiled bathrooms with shower stalls, and the shared bathrooms have older but larger in-hall bathrooms at a room-to-bathroom ratio of about 3 to 1. All rooms have clock radios and dataports on the telephones, and shared bathrooms have private sinks. Minifridges, microwaves, hair dryers, irons, and coffee-makers are available on request. The clientele comprises largely young travelers and up-and-coming actors who like the proximity to Broadway and the affordable restaurants that line Eighth and Ninth avenues.

**☻ The Wyndham.** 42 W. 58th St. (btw. Fifth and Sixth aves.), New York, NY 10019. ☎ **800/257-1111** or 212/753-3500. Fax 212/754-5638. 212 units. AC TV TEL. $160 double, $190–$230 1-bedroom suite, $330–$375 2-bedroom suite (up to 4 guests included in rate). AE, DC, MC, V. Parking $45 next door. Subway: N, R to Fifth Ave.; B, Q to 57th St.

This family-owned charmer is one of Midtown's best hotel deals—and it's perfectly located to boot, on a great block steps away from Fifth Avenue shopping and Central Park. The quirky Wyndham is stuck in the 70s on all fronts, but its guest rooms are enormous by city standards, comfortable, and loaded with character. The entire hotel features a wild collection of wallpaper, from candy stripes to crushed velvets, so some rooms definitely cross the ticky-tacky line. But others are downright lovely, with such details as rich oriental carpets and well-worn libraries, and the eclectic art collection that lines the walls boasts some real gems. If you're put in a room that's not to your taste, just ask politely to see another one; the staff is usually happy to accommodate.

Most important, you get a lot for your money: The rooms are universally large, and all feature huge walk-in closets (the biggest I've ever seen). The surprisingly affordable suites also have full-fledged living rooms, dressing areas, and cold kitchenettes (fridge only). You'll need a two-bedroom suite if you're bringing the kids (only two guests are allowed in standard rooms or one-bedroom suites), but the rate is a steal considering the space you get. Valet service is available, as is limited room service (the restaurant should be in full swing by the time you arrive). They tell me that the phones have dataports now, but don't expect an alarm clock, a hair dryer, luxury toiletries, or other modern amenities. But so what? At these prices, you can afford to invest in travel sizes.

## SUPER-CHEAP SLEEPS

**✪ Big Apple Hostel.** 119 W. 45th St. (btw. Sixth and Seventh aves.), New York, NY 10036. ☎ **212/302-2603.** Fax 212/302-2605. www.bigapplehostel.com. 112 dorm beds, 11 private units. TV TEL. $28–$33 dorm bed, $80–$85 double. MC, V. Subway: N, R, S, 1, 2, 3, 7, 9 to Times Sq./42nd St.

This is the nicest hostel in Midtown, if not the nicest in all of Manhattan. It's not fancy, mind you, but it's exceptionally well run, spotlessly clean, and ideally located in the heart of the Theater District; many luxury hotels wish they had it so good. All dorm rooms are four-bedded; they're well spaced and very well kept, with metal bunks and good mattresses (if flat pillows). Only guests in private rooms are provided with towels, so bunkers should bring their own. Private rooms are extremely basic but better than most in hostels; all have phones, and some have a cafe table and chairs. The shared bathrooms are definitely better than average. There's a stocked kitchen with microwave, a small furnished backyard patio with barbecue, and a cafe and coffee bar that's ideal for the morning caffeine fix or lunch. Very popular with young Japanese and other international travelers who like the central location. All in all, it doesn't get much better at bargain-basement prices—much better than the more well-known Aladdin Hostel farther west on 45th Street.

## WORTH A SPLURGE

**Hotel Metro.** 45 W. 35th St. (btw. Fifth and Sixth aves.), New York, NY 10001. ☎ **800/ 356-3870** or 212/947-2500. Fax 212/279-1310. www.hotelmetronyc.com. 174 units. A/C TV TEL. $150–$225 standard double, $165–$325 deluxe double/quad, $205–$400 suite. Rates include continental breakfast. Extra person $25; children under 13 stay free in parents' room. Check with airlines and other package operators for package deals. AE, DC, MC, V. Parking $18 nearby. Subway: B, D, F, Q, N, R to 34th St.

The Metro is the hands-down best choice in Midtown for those who don't want to sacrifice either style or comfort for affordability. This lovely art deco-style jewel has larger rooms than you'd expect for the price. They're outfitted with smart retro furnishings, playful textiles, and extras such as voice mail and dataport on the phone, hair dryers and huge mirrors in the smallish but well-appointed marble bathrooms, alarm clocks, and irons and boards in the closets. Only about half the bathrooms have tubs, but the others have shower stalls big enough for two (executive rooms have Jacuzzi tubs). The neo-deco design gives the whole place an air of New York glamour that I've not otherwise seen in this price range.

One of the really nice things about this hotel is its welcoming public spaces: The comfy, firelit library/lounge area off the lobby, where buffet breakfast is laid out and the coffeepot's on all day, is a popular hangout, and the well-furnished rooftop terrace boasts one of the most breathtaking views of the Empire State Building I've ever seen (a great place to order up room service from the stylish Metro Grill). Valet service, a sizable fitness room, and complimentary breakfast add to the great value. One of my all-time favorites—highly recommendable.

# 8 Midtown East & Murray Hill

In addition to the choices below, there's also **Hotel 31,** 120 E. 31st St., between Park and Lexington avenues (☎ 212/685-3060; www.hotel31.citysearch.com). This sister hotel to Hotel 17 (see "The Flatiron District & Gramercy Park" above) is very similar in style, quality, comforts, and price ($100–$130 double).

**Carlton Arms.** 160 E. 25th St. (btw. Lexington and Third aves.), New York, NY 10010. ☎ **212/679-0680** (reservations) or 212/684-8337 (guests). www.carltonarms.com. 54 units

(20 with private bathroom). $63–$105 single–quad with shared bathroom, $75–$117 single–triple with private bathroom. Discounts for students and foreign visitors. 10% discount on 7-night stays paid upon arrival. MC, V. Parking about $20 nearby. Subway: 6 to 23rd St.

The motto at the Carlton Arms is THIS AIN'T NO HOLIDAY INN—and boy, ain't that the truth. The true spirit of bohemianism and artistic freedom reigns in this back-packer's delight of a hotel, where every room is a work of art executed by an edgy artist given full license to go hog wild. Some spaces are sublime, such as Robin Banks' Cartoon Room (#5B), Thias Charbonet's Underwater Room (#1A), the ocean-blue lobby (complete with fish in the TV), and the stunning first-floor mosaic bathroom; others are simply bizarre. Whether you end up with a mermaid mural or a wall of teddy bears, you'll see why this is one of the most extraordinary hotels in the city.

But if you're looking for creature comforts and modern conveniences, this is *not* the place for you. The cramped rooms are basic—*very* basic. The beds are lumpy, there's no air-conditioning, and everything's on the stale side. Each room has a sink, but you'll most likely end up sharing a hallway bathroom with your fellow travelers: mainly students, foreign travelers, and fellow existentialists. The place is kept clean, but there's no maid service during your stay. Still, I'd try the Chelsea Star first (earlier in this chapter). On the upside, the staff is super-friendly, and they'll be happy to take phone messages for you in the office (there's a pay phone in the lobby for outgoing calls). Reserve 1 to 2 months in advance, because despite the inconveniences, this place is almost always full.

**Habitat Hotel.** 130 E. 57th St. (at Lexington Ave.), New York, NY 10022. ☎ **800/ 255-0482** or 212/753-8841. Fax 212/829-9605. www.habitatny.com or www.stayinny.com. 300 units (about 40 with private bathroom). A/C TV TEL. $95–$135 single or double with shared bathroom; $135–$185 single or double with private bathroom; $190–$270 for 2 single/double rooms sharing a bathroom; $285–$350 penthouse deluxe double (with private bathroom). Rates include continental breakfast. Check Web site for student rates and seasonal specials as low as $75 double. AE, CB, DC, DISC, JCB, MC, V. Parking $25. Subway: 4, 5, 6 to 59th St.; E, F to Lexington Ave.

This new-in-1999 hotel is marketed as "upscale budget," with rooms dressed to appeal to travelers who are short on funds but big on style. They're well designed in a natural palette accented with black-and-white photos. Everything is better quality and more attractive than I usually see in this price range, from the firm mattresses to the plush towels to the pedestal sinks in every room. (All rooms have voice mail and dataports on the phones, too.) The bathrooms—shared (one for every three to four rooms), semi-private (two rooms sharing a adjacent bathroom), and private—are all brand-new.

The only downside—and it might be a big one for romance-seeking couples—are the sleeping accommodations. A few queens are available (with private bathrooms), but most of the double rooms consist of a twin bed with a pullout trundle, which when open takes up most of the width of the narrow room. The prices are high on the pri-vate bathrooms considering the setup and downright exorbitant on the four penthouse deluxe rooms, which have queen beds, private bathrooms, microwaves, and mini-fridges. Rates are very attractive for the shared bathrooms, however, especially consid-ering the *Metropolitan Home* mindset and the A-1 location. Two single travelers or couples traveling together can book two rooms that share one private bathroom (the semi-private situation) for a very good rate. The neighborhood is safe, chic, and super-convenient—especially for shoppers, because Bloomingdale's is just 2 blocks away.

The public spaces were under renovation when I visited, but you should find a glass-enclosed veranda with great views down Lexington Avenue, a bar, and a library lounge.

- clams
- Bacon
- clam juice
- half & half
- ~~tarragon~~ thyme
- flour
- onion

**Hotel Grand Union.** 34 E. 32nd St. (btw. Madison and Park aves.), New York, NY 10016. ☎ **212/683-5890.** Fax 212/689-7397. 95 units. A/C TV TEL. $110–$120 double, $125–$138 twin or triple, $150–$165 quad. Rates increase during the holiday season. AE, DC, DISC, JCB, MC, V. Parking $21 nearby. Subway: 6 to 33rd St.

This centrally located hotel is big with budget-minded international travelers. A pleasant white-on-white lobby leads to rooms that are spacious and clean and come with nice extras such as voice mail and dataport on the telephone, minifridge, and free HBO. But bad florescent overhead lighting, ugly colonial-style furniture, and an utter lack of natural light dampen the mood. Still, considering the roominess and low rates, the Grand Union is a pretty good deal. No. 309 is a nicely configured quad with two twins and a queen in a separate alcove; priced at around $150, it's a great value, too. Most bathrooms have been freshly outfitted in granite or tile; ask for a newly renovated one to get the most for your money. The staff is helpful, there's a pleasant sitting room off the lobby, and an adjacent coffee shop is convenient for morning coffee or a quickie burger at lunch.

**Murray Hill Inn.** 143 E. 30th St. (btw. Lexington and Third aves.), New York, NY 10016. ☎ **888/996-6376** or 212/683-6900. Fax 212/545-0103. www.murrayhillinn.com. 50 units (39 with shared bathroom). A/C TV TEL. $65–$75 single with shared bathroom, $85–$95 double with shared bathroom; $125–$145 double with private bathroom. Extra person $20; children under 12 stay free in parents' room. Ask about discounts and packages. No credit cards. Parking $25 nearby. Subway: 6 to 28th St.

Housed in a renovated five-story walk-up, the Murray Hill Inn (like its Upper West Side sibling, the Amsterdam Inn) is a bit high priced for what you get. Still, there's no arguing with the cleanliness, which is key when judging budget accommodations. Rooms are tiny and no-frills, with not much more than basic bedding (two twins or a full size) with flat pillows, motel-standard bedspread and furnishings, a wall rack, and a small TV. On the upside, most rooms with shared bathrooms have private sinks (request one when booking), bathrooms are new and spotless, and the residential neighborhood is quiet and nice. Some doubles also have an alcove that can accommodate nicely enough a third traveler on a cot, if you're on an extra-tight budget. The Euro-style rooms share the in-hall bathrooms at a ratio of about 8 rooms to 3 bathrooms—not bad, but not great, either. Rooms with private bathrooms are definitely the nicest; they're spacious, with new bathrooms, and most have pullout sofas. The public spaces are freshly redone, the staff is personable, and there's a pleasant (if tiny) lobby, plus a plain downstairs sitting area and luggage storage area.

**Pickwick Arms Hotel.** 230 E. 51st St. (btw. Second and Third aves.), New York, NY 10022. ☎ **800/PICKWIK** in the U.S., 800/874-0074 in Canada, or 212/355-0300. Fax 212/755-5029. 320 units (200 with private bathroom). A/C TV TEL. $70–$100 single, $125–$145 double or twin, $140–$175 double studio (with sofa), $150–$160 triple. AE, CB, DC, MC, V. Parking $25 1 block away. Subway: 6 to 51st St.

What keeps the Pickwick booked up well in advance is its prices; for a Midtown hotel on the East Side, this is like entering an economic time warp. The location, in one of the city's most prestigious neighborhoods, couldn't be better. The older, sometimes astoundingly small rooms are spare (think monk's cell), but they're well kept, and the entire place is safe and well run. There are a few doubles and twins with private bathrooms (the larger deluxe twins can accommodate a rollaway for a third person), but the majority of rooms are singles with private, semi-private, or shared hall bathrooms. Two friends traveling together can take advantage of the semi-private situation: Two singles—each with their own sink, TV, desk, small closet, and telephone—that share a bathroom can be had for the same price as a twin room. All of the bathrooms are worn looking and have showers only, but they're clean. A renovation has spiffed up the halls and some rooms a bit. Still, don't expect anything more than the basics—but if you want a great location and you're on a tight budget, this is a good choice. On site is a rooftop patio with skyline views; there's also a Continental restaurant and lounge for dinner and drinks and a cafe serving breakfast and lunch.

**Quality Hotel Eastside.** 161 Lexington Ave. (at 30th St.), New York, NY 10016. ☎ **800/ 567-7720** or 212/545-1800. Fax 212/790-2760. www.applecorehotels.com. 95 units (59 with private bathroom). A/C TV TEL. $89–$209 double, depending on season. Rates include continental breakfast. Extra person $12; children under 14 stay free in parents' room. Ask about senior, AAA, corporate, and promotional discounts; check www.hotelchoice.com for online booking discounts. AE, DISC, MC, V. Parking $20 nearby. Subway: 6 to 33rd St.

This hotel is nothing special—just some small, standard rooms done in a vaguely early-American style with older bathrooms. Its recommendable features are the location, in Murray Hill, a nice, quiet residential neighborhood; the amenities, which include a business center (with copy and fax machines, plus Internet access), and a fitness room (with treadmill, lifecycle, and Nordic Track); and the great low-season rates. In-room extras include coffeemaker, iron and board, alarm clock, hair dryer, and dataport and voice mail on the phone; free local phone calls are another plus. There's a meeting room on premises and an affordable pasta restaurant next door. Don't expect much in the way of service or anything in the style department—but considering how expensive an average room has become in this city, this hotel is a pretty good value, particularly when rooms go for as little as $79. Don't bother if rates are higher than $159, as you'll probably find more for your money elsewhere (unless it's holidaytime, of course). And skip the shared bathrooms altogether.

**Vanderbilt YMCA.** 224 E. 47th St. (btw. Second and Third aves.), New York, NY 10017. ☎ **212/756-9600.** Fax 212/752-0210. www.ymcanyc.org. 377 units (7 with private bathroom). A/C TV. $72–$86 single, $86–$106 twin, $138 suite. AE, MC, V. Parking $20–$25 nearby. Subway: S, 4, 5, 6, 7 to 42nd St./Grand Central.

This YMCA boasts a friendly, youthful atmosphere and a fashionable East Side location that's also convenient: It's within walking distance of the United Nations, Rockefeller Center, and Grand Central Terminal, as well as lots of good shopping and restaurants. The rooms are spartan and tiny—I repeat, tiny—but the beds do somehow fit, as do the TVs, dressers, and desks. The more expensive rooms have sinks, and the suites have private bathrooms. The communal bathrooms and showers are well kept. The sports facilities and reasonably priced meals at the on-site cafe alone make the Y an excellent choice for wallet-watchers. There's a state-of-the-art fitness center— with two pools, a sauna, and sundeck, and a full calendar of fitness classes—plus room service from the cafe, luggage storage, safe-deposit boxes, tour and transportation assistance, and a self-service laundromat. The rooms are booked far in advance, so call well ahead.

## 9 The Upper West Side

**Amsterdam Inn.** 340 Amsterdam Ave. (at 76th St.), New York, NY 10023. ☎ **212/ 579-7500.** Fax 212/579-6127. www.amsterdaminn.com. 25 units (12 with private bathroom). A/C TV TEL. $75–$95 single or double with shared bathroom, $115–$135 single or double with private bathroom. Extra person $10. Packages and group discounts might be available; ask about weekly rates on shared bathrooms. No credit cards. Parking $20–$25 nearby. Subway: 1, 9 to 79th St.

Housed on the top three floors of a newly renovated five-story walk-up, the Amsterdam Inn offers very basic accommodations. The private bathrooms are better at the sibling Murray Hill Inn (earlier in this chapter)—mainly because they're bigger—but I'd opt

# Get Away For Less.

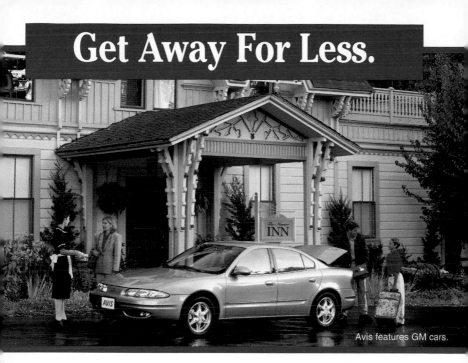

Avis features GM cars.

With great offers and services from Avis, you'll get more out of your vacation! And now you can **save $20 on a weekly rental**. All the information you need is on the coupon below. Plus most rentals come with free unlimited mileage to save you even more.

As an added touch you can count on our famous "We try harder." service for a fast, hassle-free rental. Because speed and personal service is what everyone at Avis is dedicated to delivering.

For more information and reservations, call your travel agent or Avis toll free at **1-800-831-8000**.

**AVIS**®

We try harder.® For You.

## Save $20 On A Weekly Rental

Reserve an Avis Intermediate through Full Size 4-Door car for a minimum of five consecutive days. At time of rental, present this coupon at the Avis counter and you can save $20. **An advance reservation is required.** Subject to complete Terms and Conditions below. Rental must begin by 06/30/01.

For reservations and information, call your travel consultant or Avis toll free at **1-800-831-8000**.

**Terms and Conditions**: Coupon valid on an Intermediate (Group C) through a Full Size 4-Door (Group E) car. Dollars off applies to the cost of the total rental with a minimum of 5 days. A Saturday night overstay is required. Coupon must be surrendered at time of rental; one per rental. Coupon valid at Avis participating locations in the U.S. An advance reservation is required. Cars subject to availability. Taxes, local government surcharges, vehicle licensing and an airport recruitment fee at some locations, optional items such as LDW, additional driver fee and refueling fee are extra. Renter must meet Avis driver and credit requirements. Minimum age is 25 but may vary by location. Rental must begin by 6/30/01.

Coupon #: **MUNA002**

| Rental Sales Agent Instructions |
| --- |
| *At checkout:* |
| In AWD, enter AWD number. |
| In CPN, enter **MUNA002**. |
| Complete this information: |
| RA # _____ |
| Rental location _____ |
| Attach to COUPON tape. |

**AVIS**®

©1999 Avis Rent A Car System, Inc.          **www.avis.com**          11/99  DTPP

# It's a Whole New World with

# Frommer's

for the Amsterdam if I were going to share a bathroom. The inn's biggest assets are its prime Upper West Side location, its newness, and its consistent cleanliness. Accommodations are no-frills: The building is a walk-up, and rooms are small and narrow, with not much more than a bed, a wall rack to hang your clothes on, a cheap set of drawers with a TV on top, a side table with a lamp and a phone that requires a deposit to activate, and a sink if there's no private bathroom. The Euro-style rooms share the in-hall bathrooms at a ratio of about 2¹/₂-to-1. All the bathrooms are brand new but have showers only. Frankly, I think the rates are a bit too high, but the friendly management seems willing to negotiate, so try to talk them down if you can. If you book a double, make sure it's a *real* double, with a double bed. The singles with trundles can (theoretically) accommodate two, but don't expect to have (any) space left over.

**Belleclaire Hotel.** 250 W. 77th St. (at Broadway), New York, NY 10024. ☎ **HOTEL-BC** or 212/362-7700. Fax 212/362-1004. www.belleclaire.com. 189 units (39 with shared bathroom). AAA, corporate, and government discounts might be available. A/C TV TEL. $79–$119 double with shared bathroom, $129–$169 double with private bathroom, $199 family suite. Parking $25 nearby. Subway: 1, 9 to 79th St.

This beaux-arts hotel boasts a great Upper West Side location and newly renovated guestrooms that are larger than most (225 square feet and up) but could use a little more attention to detail. I saw a few minor stains, marks, and unfinished final touches here and there. Still, the accommodations do the job, and the management seems intent on pleasing guests. The rooms are dressed in peach paint with contemporary gray accents and have small, freshly tiled hunter-green bathrooms. Cushioned headboards, small TVs, phones with dataport, and alarm clocks are the biggest luxuries; otherwise, they're pretty basic. Closets are small. The shared bathrooms are exactly the same but have in-room sinks and share hall bathrooms at a ratio of 3 to 1. The family suite features two attached, semi-private bedrooms with one bathroom, a minifridge, and a big walk-in closet. Not my first choice—you'll save on a private bathroom or get more for your money at the Milburn, just around the corner; the Comfort Inn— Central Park West in less busy seasons; and the Ellington, if you're willing to go 30 more blocks uptown (an additional 5 minutes on the subway to Midtown). Nevertheless, a decent back-up choice.

**♻ Comfort Inn—Central Park West.** 31 W. 71st St. (btw. Columbus Ave. and Central Park West), New York, NY 10023. ☎ **800/228-5150** (worldwide reservations), 877/727-5236 (hotel direct), or 212/721-4770. Fax 212/579-8544. www.bestnyhotels.com. 96 units. A/C TV TEL. $119–$259 standard double, $149–$299 executive double. Rates include extended continental breakfast. Ask about senior, AAA, corporate, and promotional discounts; check www.hotelchoice.com for online booking discounts (rooms as low as $98 at press time). Extra person $15; children 12 and under stay free in parents' room. AE, DC, DISC, MC, V. Parking $25–$35 nearby. Subway: B, C to 72nd St.

This very nice, newly renovated chain hotel is a great place to stay if you can snag a good rate. It's fabulously located, in the Upper West Side's best residential territory just steps from the finest areas of Central Park. Everything is fresh, new, spotlessly kept, and professionally done. Rooms aren't huge or exactly stylish, but there's no arguing with the quality. Layout is smart; bedding, textiles, and window treatments are good; and blackout drapes let you sleep 'til noon if you so choose. Closets are on the small side, but you'll have an alarm clock, voice mail and dataport, and a new tiled bathroom, some with a hair dryer (can otherwise be provided upon request). Most rooms have work desks, too. Executive rooms are a little more modern-smart, with nice mahogany built-ins and individual climate controls.

Amenities really up the value-for-dollar ratio. An extended continental breakfast— cereals, fresh fruit, donuts, and more—is served in the charming breakfast room,

# Uptown Accommodations

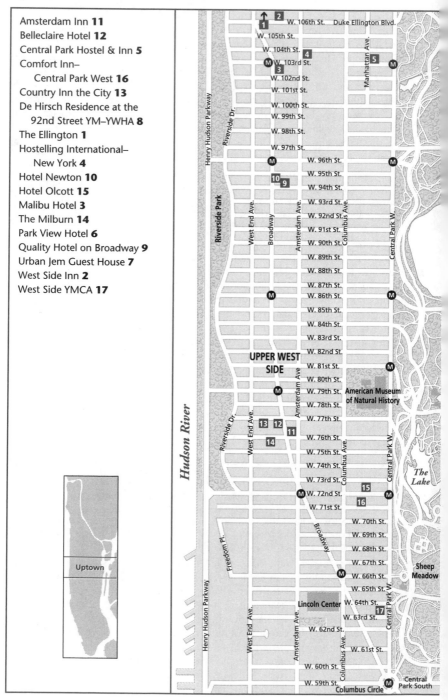

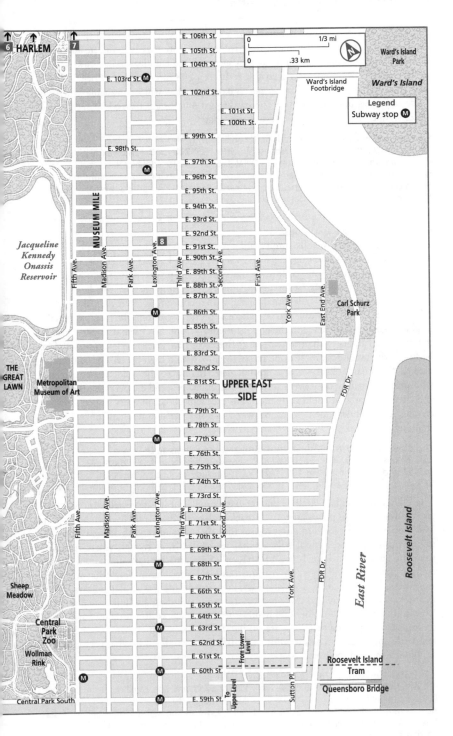

where free newspapers are on hand. There's a business center with Internet access machines and a fax/printer. A small fitness room has a stationary bike and treadmill, and soda and snack machines are on hand. Dry cleaning and laundry service is available.

Rates are seasonal, but I was even able to book a $98 room for early April 2000 and over the Fourth of July holiday. I can't guarantee what will be available when you book, of course, but it isn't usually too hard to get one for less than $170 in the busier seasons, especially if you can be flexible with dates.

✪ **Country Inn the City.** W. 77th St. (btw. Broadway and West End Ave.), New York, NY 10024. (Exact address omitted by request of owner.) ☎ 212/580-4183. Fax 212/874-3981. www.countryinnthecity.com. 4 units. A/C TV TEL. $150–$195 double. Rates include continental breakfast. No sales tax added for stays of 7 nights or more. 3-night minimum. Maximum 2 guests per apartment. No credit cards. Parking $25 nearby. Subway: 1, 9 to 79th St. No children under 12.

If this marvelous gem fits your budget, book now; it's well worth every penny and then some. This charming townhouse features four beautifully outfitted guest rooms that are rich with original details, impeccable Americana-style decor, and more homey comforts than you'll find anywhere else for the price. Each is actually a full studio apartment, with a cozy sofa, table and chairs for two, a private phone with answering machine, and a gorgeous, supremely comfortable queen bed in the large, high-ceilinged bedroom; a big galley kitchenette with a coffeemaker and everything you'll need to prepare a full meal; and a spacious, pretty bathroom. The whole place is bright, elegant, and homey, and the appointments—from the Oriental carpets covering the hardwood floors to the (nonworking) fireplaces that grace every room—couldn't be finer. My favorite is no. 4, done in soft yellow with a high poster bed and white-washed floorboards. Everything is immaculate, thanks to the resident housekeeper, who provides maid service every other day. A quiet, peaceful air pervades the house, and the neighborhood couldn't be nicer. An excellent choice in every respect; best for travelers of the independent sort, however, because there's no resident innkeeper. No smoking is allowed.

**The Ellington.** 610 W. 111th St. (btw. Broadway and Riverside Dr.), New York, NY 10025. ☎ 212/864-7500. Fax 212/749-5852. www.nycityhotels.net. 85 units. A/C TV TEL. $65–$160 double (most often $99–$120). Rates include continental breakfast. Extra person $15. AE, DC, MC, V. Parking $20 3 blocks away. Subway: 1, 9 to 110th St./Cathedral Pkwy.

The Ellington is fundamentally a budget-basic hotel, but it's appreciably more attractive than most in this price category. A black-and-white marble lobby with Streamline Moderne furnishings leads to guest rooms that are smart and stylish, done in a soothing cream, beige, and natural pallette that feels upscale, as though you're spending more money than you actually are. Ditto for the smart marble bathrooms, with decent counter space and hair dryer. Each room has black metal furnishings that include a work desk, an alarm clock, a small closet, and firm bedding with flat pillows. A few maintenance issues here and there prevent me from awarding the Ellington a star, but I saw nothing major. Continental breakfast features juice, coffee, tea, and bagels with cream cheese, and soda machines are on hand. The block is pretty and the neighborhood safe and nice, with lots of affordable dining on hand. All in all, a very good bet for budget-minded travelers.

✪ **Hotel Newton.** 2528 Broadway (btw. 94th and 95th sts.), New York, NY 10025. ☎ 888/HOTEL58 or 212/678-6500. Fax 212/678-6758. www.newyorkhotel.com. 110 units (10 with shared bathroom). A/C TV TEL. $95 double with shared bathroom, $99–$140 double with private bathroom, $170 junior suite. Extra person $20; children under 15 stay free. AAA discounts available; check Web site for special Internet deals. AE, DC, DISC, MC, V. Parking $17 nearby. Subway: 1, 2, 3, 9 to 96th St.

Finally—an inexpensive hotel that's actually *nice*. Unlike many of its peers, the Newton doesn't scream "budget!" at every turn or require you to have the carefree attitude of a college student to put up with it. As you enter the pretty lobby, you're greeted by a uniformed staff that's attentive and professional. The rooms are generally large, with good, firm beds, a work desk, and a sizable new bathroom with hair dryer, plus roomy closets in most (a few of the cheapest have wall racks only). (Sorry, no voice or dataports, though.) Some are big enough to accommodate families with two doubles or two queen beds. The suites feature two queen beds in the bedroom, a sofa in the sitting room, plus niceties such as a microwave, minifridge, and iron and board, making them well worth the few extra dollars. The bigger rooms and suites have been upgraded with cherry-wood furnishings, but even the older laminated furniture is much nicer than I usually see in this price range. The AAA-approved hotel is impeccably kept, and there was lots of sprucing up going on—new drapes here, fresh paint there—during my last visit. The nice neighborhood boasts lots of affordable restaurants, and a cute diner in the same block provides room service from 6am to 2am. The 96th Street express subway stop is just a block away, providing convenient access to the rest of the city. A great bet all the way around.

**Hotel Olcott.** 27 W. 72nd St. (btw. Columbus Ave. and Central Park West), New York, NY 10023. ☎ **212/877-4200.** 212/877-4600. 200 units. A/C TV TEL. $125 studio double ($805 weekly), $150 suite ($945 weekly). Extra person $15. MC, V. Parking $18 next door. Subway: B, C to 72nd St.

Even as the residential real estate around it soars into the stratosphere, this old dowager remains one of New York's best budget bargains. About half of this residential hotel houses permanent and long-term residents (including a fair number of doctor's offices), but the rest is open to out-of-towners. The studios and suites are an excellent deal for short-term stays and a downright steal if you take advantage of the weekly rates.

The apartments are about as stylish as Aunt Edna's house—circa 1970, no less—but they're maintained with care and even the studios are bigger than most NYC apartments (the suites are enormous). If only I had this much closet space! The discount furnishings are not pretty, but perfectly comfortable. Every apartment has a big bathroom and a kitchenette with minifridge, hotplate with kettle, toaster, and basic dishes and utensils; studios generally have a dining table for two, and suites have a four-top. Phones have voice mail and dataports. Suites have TV only in the living room and sofas don't pull out, but the friendly management will lend you a cot (or even an additional bed) if you're bringing the family or sharing with friends. Ask for a renovated room when you book; most of the suites and about half of the studios have brandnew, bright-white kitchenettes and freshly laid tile in the bathroom.

The Olcott is steps from Central Park on one of Manhattan's most high-class blocks (the famed Dakota apartment building is just doors way). Nearby Columbus Avenue bustles with boutiques and restaurants. Just off the surprisingly sophisticated lobby is Dallas BBQ for decent cheap eats and bathtub-size cocktails.

**☉ The Milburn.** 242 W. 76th St. (btw. Broadway and West End Ave.), New York, NY 10023. ☎ **800/833-9622** or 212/362-1006. Fax 212/721-5476. www.milburnhotel.com. 112 units. A/C TV TEL. $129–$159 studio double, $149–$180 junior suite, $159–$195 1-bedroom suite. Extra person $10; children 12 and under stay free in parents' room. AE, CB, DC, MC, V. Self-parking $20. Subway: 1, 9 to 79th St.

The Milburn offers studios and suites with equipped kitchenettes in a first-rate neighborhood for less than you'd pay for many standard hotel rooms. It is a great value for your dollar, especially in the less busy seasons, when a double studio goes for just $129. Every room is rife with amenities: dining area, VCR, safe, iron and ironing board, two-line phone with dataport, alarm, nice newish bathroom with hair dryer, and kitchenette with minifridge, microwave, coffeemaker (with free coffee!), and all the necessary equipment. The one-bedroom suites also boast a pullout queen sofa, an extra TV, and a work desk. Don't expect much from the decor, and the laminated furniture is clearly a cheap grade, but everything is attractive and in good shape. In fact, the whole place is spotless. But what makes the Milburn a real find is that it's more service-oriented than most hotels in this price range. The friendly staff will do everything from providing free copy, fax, and e-mail services to picking up your laundry at the dry cleaners next door. Additional amenities include a self-serve Laundro-mat, a new fitness room, free videos, Sony Playstation on request, newspaper delivery, wheelchair-accessible rooms, and a conference room. All in all, a great choice for bargain-hunters.

**Quality Hotel on Broadway.** 215 W. 94th St. (at Broadway), New York, NY 10025. ☎ **800/228-5151** (worldwide reservations), 800/834-2972 (hotel direct), or 212/866-6400. Fax 212/866-1357. www.bestnyhotels.com. 350 units. A/C TV TEL. $109–$270 double, $129–$339 suite. Ask about senior, AAA, corporate, and promotional discounts; check www.hotelchoice.com for online booking discounts (rooms as low as $89 at press time). Extra person $15; children under 18 stay free in parents' room. AE, DC, DISC, MC, V. Parking $18 nearby. Subway: 1, 2, 3, 9 to 96th St.

This freshly renovated chain hotel is yet another great low-season bargain bet from Hampshire Hotels & Suites, the terrific management team behind the Theater District's Best Western President and the Comfort Inn—Central Park West. The Comfort Inn is a bit smarter, but stay here if you like lots of space; some rooms are large enough for two doubles or a king bed. Rooms feature dark-wood, hotel-standard furnishings that include a nice work desk with a good ergonomic chair; an armoire holds the TV and good drawer space. All rooms have a coffeemaker, an alarm clock, voice mail and dataport, an extra phone, a make-up mirror, and a hair dryer in the bathroom. Some also have a minifridge or a kitchenette; request one when you book. Most bathrooms have spacious granite countertops. A nice library-style sitting room is off the lobby. There's no on-site room service, but management has arranged for a special full-breakfast rate ($8.50 at press time) for guests at a diner around the corner, which will also deliver into the wee hours.

**West Side YMCA.** 5 W. 63rd St. (btw. Broadway and Central Park West), New York, NY 10023. ☎ **212/875-4100.** Fax 212/875-1334. www.ymcanyc.org. 550 units (30 with pri-vate bathroom). A/C TV. $65–$120 single or double. Children under 10 stay free in parents' room. AE, MC, V. Parking about $25 next door. Subway: A, B, C, D, 1, 9 to Columbus Circle.

Another Y with a stellar location (see the Vanderbilt YMCA, above, and the 92nd Street Y, below), this one is housed in a National Historic Landmark building just steps from Lincoln Center and Central Park. A multimillion-dollar renovation of the public areas and guest rooms has made it more attractive and modern than the typical Y. The rooms are small and most share bathrooms down the hall, but they're well kept and outfitted like a real hotel room. Frankly, the Y is no cheaper than staying at a private hotel, but what makes it worth the money are the new state-of-the-art health and fitness facilities, which include two pools, gyms, an indoor running track, handball and racquetball courts, exercise classes, steam room, sauna, massage therapy, and much more. Other great-value amenities include room service, tour and transportation services, a self-service laundromat, an on-site cafe, luggage storage, and use of safe-deposit boxes. (Only some rooms have telephones, however, so request one in advance if it matters.) Although not the equal of the 92nd Street Y, the West Side Y does offer a busy slate of arts and cultural programs. It's also a good bet for older travelers because the fitness center gives exercise and aqua-therapy classes for seniors and hosts an extensive Elderhostel Program from September through May. The location and price keep the Y filled to capacity virtually every night, so book well in advance.

**West Side Inn.** 237 W. 107th St. (btw. Broadway and Amsterdam Ave.), New York, NY 10025. ☎ **212/866-0061.** Fax 212/866-0062. www.westsideinn.com. A/C TV. 102 units. $59–$99 double, triple, or quad; $18 dorm bed. Discounts available on long-term stays. Parking about $25 nearby. Subway: 1, 9 to 103rd St.

It's clean enough—okay for young travelers who don't mind, not for anyone who's going to subject it to a white-glove test. Rooms are spartan but painted in cheery primary colors. Plastic mattress liners are a tad institutional, but in-room TV, alarm, radio, and minifridge are nice plusses. Some rooms have sinks, too. There's a basic kitchenette on each floor, and an elevator means you don't have to haul your luggage up multiple flights as you have to at so many budget-basic hotels. Pay phones and a cash- and credit-activated Internet access machine is available in the pleasant lobby. The front desk is attended around the clock, and management takes pride in the property. Frankly, at these prices—and in such a good location, no less—you can't expect much more. Strictly for those on the super-cheap who don't want to do without a private room or TV.

## SUPER-CHEAP SLEEPS

**Central Park Hostel & Inn.** 19 W. 103rd St. (between Central Park West and Manhattan Ave.), New York, NY 10025. ☎ **877/PARK-BED** or 212/678-0491. Fax 212/678-0453. www.centralparkhostel.com. 150 dorm beds. A/C. $26–$36 dorm bed, $65–$85 private twin. No credit cards. Subway: B, C to 103rd St.

There's really no inn here—just hostel. Run by the people behind the Amsterdam Inn and the Murray Hill Inn, its best points are its newness and cleanliness. Everything is fresh and of decent quality; mattresses, pillows, and linens are better than in most hostels, and towels are provided. Rooms are painted a soothing cornflower blue or green, and the shared bathrooms are brand-new (shared at a ratio of about 10 beds to a bathroom). Each floor has a locker area, and the front desk is staffed around the clock. The building is generally bright and sunny. A basement rec room and lounge is in the planning stages. Now, the downside: Most dorm rooms have one too many bunk-bed sets in it; there's barely any floor space for luggage. And the location is poor. Columbia University is helping matters by building student housing throughout the area, but it's still sketchy, and I don't care for the isolation: It's separated from virtually all commercial activity (along Broadway and Amsterdam Avenue) by a major housing project. Luckily, the B and C subway stop is at the end of the block. I'd try to stay at another city hostel first—the Big Apple and Chelsea International are just as clean, much better located, and can be cheaper—and book here only if you must.

**Hostelling International–New York.** 891 Amsterdam Ave. (at 103rd St.), New York, NY 10025. ☎ **800/909-4776, code 01** or 212/932-2300. Fax 212/932-2574. www.hinewyork.org. 624 beds, 4 units with private bathroom. A/C. $22–$24 AYH members, $3 extra nonmembers; private rooms $100 for up to 4 guests. Stays limited to 7 days (length of stay can be negotiable). Individual travelers must be 18 or older. JCB, MC, V. Subway: 1, 9 to 103rd St.

This landmark building is home to American Youth Hostels' largest hostel. Staying here is like going back to college—a very international college, with clocks set for six different time zones behind the front desk and a young, backpack-toting clientele from around the globe. Beds are incredibly cheap, but expect to bunk it (upper or lower?)

## ⓘ  Affordable Family-Friendly Hotels

The best way for families on a budget to save is to bunk together in a larger room with two double or queen beds. However, some hotels have wallet-friendly suite deals that allow the kids to sleep on a pullout sofa, thus giving everybody a little well-deserved privacy.

**Chelsea Savoy Hotel** *(p. 105)*   This newish Chelsea hotel boasts attractive, affordable rooms that are large and comfy enough to accommodate four. Big closets and roomy, immaculate bathrooms with tons of counter space make sharing even easier. Children stay free, and continental breakfast is included.

**Hotel Edison** *(p. 113)*   The freshly renovated Edison is one of the Theater District's best hotel bargains. Quads can accommodate four in two double beds, and value-priced suites with pullout sofas offer even more space to spread out. The nearly 1,000-room hotel bustles around the clock with families and tour groups from around the world, so you can feel comfortable allowing the kids to act like kids here. Services are kept to a minimum to keep rates low, but there's a guest-services desk, plus a coffee shop/deli that serves wallet-friendly meals.

**Hotel Olcott** *(p. 125)*   Families looking for cheap digs will be happy as clams here. Every big one-bedroom apartment has a stocked kitchenette, a dining table for four, and space to spread out. On the downside, there's TV only in the living room and sofas don't pull out, but the bedroom usually has two queens, and the friendly management will lend you a cot or an extra bed for the living room if you prefer. Central Park is just steps away, and there's even a barbecue joint in the building for affordable family meals.

**The Milburn** *(p. 125)*   This budget-minded Upper West Sider is a real suite deal for any visitor, but their kids-under-12-stay-free policy make it a particularly stellar choice for families. Every room has a fully outfitted kitchenette (with microwave!) and a comfortable dining area, which can really save you money on meals. The one-bedroom suites are a bargain, and a pullout queen sofa in the living room makes them plenty comfortable for families. The terrific residential neighborhood is extremely kid friendly, and Central Park is an easy walk away.

**Skyline Hotel** and **Travel Inn** *(p. 115)*   Hauling the kids to town in the minivan? You can take advantage of the free parking—which saves you a minimum of $25 a day (probably more)—at these two nice, newly renovated motor hotels. Even if you're not sporting your own wheels, you'll like the family-sized rooms, and the kids will love the pools at playtime (a rarity in affordable hotels). Yet another plus: Children stay free (under 14 at the Skyline, under 16 at the Travel Inn).

with people you don't know in rooms of 4, 6, 8, or 12. Everything is extremely basic, but the mattresses are firm and the shared bathrooms are nicely kept. There are also four rooms with one double and two bunk beds that have private bathrooms. The well-managed hostel feels like a student union, with bulletin boards and listings of events posted; a coffee bar with an ample menu and pleasant seating; two TV rooms; a sundries shop; a game room; and a smoky library with bill- and credit-card–operated computers with Internet access. (An ATM and electronic luggage lockers were to be added during the renovation of the public spaces, which was ongoing at press time.) There's also a common kitchen, vending machines on each floor, a nice coin-op laundry, a terrace, and a pleasant, big yard with picnic tables and barbecues in summer. The neighborhood has improved over the years, but it's still a little sketchy; 1 block over is much nicer Broadway, lined with affordable restaurants and shops.

## 10  The Upper East Side

**De Hirsch Residence at the 92nd Street YM–YWHA.** 1395 Lexington Ave. (at 92nd St.), New York, NY 10128. ☎ **888/699-6884,** or 212/415-5650. Fax 212/415-5578. www. 92ndsty.org. 300 units (none with private bathroom). A/C. $79 single, $98 double; long-term stays (2 months or more) $895/month single, $1,190–$1,450/month double. AE, MC, V. Parking $20 nearby. Subway: 4, 5, 6 to 86th St.; 6 to 96th St. Guests must be at least 18 and no older than 30 for long-term stays.

Travelers on a tight budget should contact the 92nd Street Y well in advance. The de Hirsch Residence offers basic but comfortable rooms, each with either one or two single beds, a dresser, and bookshelves. Each floor has a large communal bathroom, a fully equipped kitchen/dining room with microwave, and laundry facilities. The building is rather institutional looking, but it's well kept and secure, the staff is friendly, and the location is terrific. This Upper East Side neighborhood is just blocks from Central Park and Museum Mile, and there's plenty of cheap eats and places to pick up meal fixings within a few blocks. Daily maid service and use of the Y's state-of-the-art fitness facility (pool, Jacuzzi, weights, racquetball, aerobics) are included in the daily rates, making this a stellar deal. This is a great bet for lone travelers in particular, because the 92nd Street Y is a community center in a true sense of the word, offering a real sense of kinship and a mind-boggling slate of top-rated cultural happenings (see chapter 9).

## 11  Harlem

**Urban Jem Guest House.** 2005 Fifth Ave. (btw. 124th and 125th sts.). ☎ **877/476-4914** or 212/831-6029. Fax 212/831-6940. www.urbanjem.com. 4 units (2 with shared bathroom that can be combined into a suite). A/C TV TEL. $105 double with shared bathroom, $120 double with private bathroom, $200 suite. Rates include continental breakfast upon request. Extra person $15. 2-night minimum on weekends or holidays. 10% off 7–13 nights, 15% off 14 days or more. AE, MC, V. Parking $15 nearby. Subway: 2, 3 or 4, 5, 6 to 125th St.

This B&B is Harlem's best place to stay. It's run by Jane Alex Mendelson, a refugee from the corporate world who has successfully reinvented herself as an innkeeper. Located in the Mount Morris Historic District, her renovated 1878 brownstone is graced with fine woodwork and beautiful original (nonworking) fireplaces. The house is a work in progress, so don't expect perfection; there's still plenty to be done, and the furnishings are largely an odds-and-ends mix. But the accommodations offer good value. The second floor has two guest rooms with firm queen beds, new private bathrooms, and spacious kitchenettes with stove, minifridge, microwave, and the basic tools for preparing and serving a meal. On the third floor are two nice rooms that share a hall bathroom and fully equipped kitchen: one a pretty bedroom with a queen bed, the other a spacious room with two foldout futon sofabeds. They can also be combined into a two-bedroom suite, which gives you a whole floor to yourself.

You can pay an extra $7.50 for daily maid service (the trash is taken out daily); otherwise, sheets and towels are changed weekly. There's also a washer and dryer for use ($3). Jane is friendly and helpful and can provide lots of neighborhood information. The neighborhood isn't a regular base for tourists, but the bustling urban neighborhood has welcomed the inn, and it makes a good starting point for exploring jazz-, gospel-, and history-rich Harlem. Midtown is about a half-hour subway ride away, but Jane recommends taking a cab back after 11pm or so.

## SUPER-CHEAP SLEEPS

**Park View Hotel.** 55 Central Park North (110th St. at Lenox Ave.), New York, NY 10025. ☎ **212/369-3340.** Fax 212/369-3046. E-mail ParkViewNYC@aol.com. 40 private units, 140 dorm beds (all with shared bathroom). $20 dorm bed (tax included); $50–$60 double or twin, $70–$80 triple or quad, $80–$90 family room. Extra person $10. AE, DISC, MC, V. Subway: 2, 3 to 110th St./Central Park North.

Sleeps don't get cheaper than the dorm beds at this brand-new hostel (from the same team behind the Ellington and the West Side Inn), which is actually quite nice. The large lobby has been done in a terrific retro-60s, pop-modern style, with a comfy lounge, a TV, cash- and credit card–activated Internet access machine and pay phones, an international fax/phone machine, vending machines, and a friendly front desk. An elevator (not common in hostels) leads to guest floors that have been completely renovated—new windows, new metal firedoors, even re-sheetrocked walls for a nice finished look—in a bold, welcoming IKEA-ish palette. The dorm rooms (coed or all female) are basic, with nothing more than metal bunks outfitted with new plastic-lined mattresses, but the two- to six-bunk rooms are more spacious than most. You'll have plenty of floor space for your stuff, and groups of friends traveling together can have a room to themselves. Most rooms are bright and have park views. The new shared bathrooms are just fine, and there's one for every five rooms or so. (Private rooms have towels, but BYO if you're reserving a dorm bed.)

The Harlem location is a bit out of the way, but the hostel is on a busy, well-lit, decently gentrified corner across from Central Park. A market and other shops are on hand. Across the street is the 2, 3 subway stop, which can whisk you right to Times Square or the Village. Management is big on safety; they have a closed-circuit security system installed, and both entrances are manned 24 hours a day. Look for a rooftop terrace and lounge to offer spectacular views by the time you arrive.

# Great Deals on Dining 6

**A**ttention foodies: Welcome to Mecca. Without a doubt, New York is the best restaurant town in the country, perhaps tops in the world. Other cities might have particular specialties—Paris has better bistros, of course, Hong Kong better Chinese, Los Angeles better Mexican, Austin better barbecue—but no culinary capital spans the globe so successfully as the Big Apple.

The sheer variety of eating places is astounding. That's due in part to New York's vibrant immigrant mix. Let a newcomer arrive and see that his or her native foods aren't being served and *zap!*—there's a new restaurant, cafe, or grocery to fill the void. Yet we New Yorkers can be fickle: One moment a restaurant is hot; the next it's passé. So restaurants close with a frequency we wish applied to the arrival of subway trains. Always call ahead.

But there's one thing we all have to face sooner or later: Eating in New York just ain't cheap. The primary cause? The high cost of real estate, which is reflected in what you're charged. Wherever you're from, particularly if you're from the reasonably priced American heartland, New York's restaurants will seem *expensive*. Yet as you peruse the chapter that follows, you'll see that good values abound—especially if you're willing to eat ethnic and venture beyond tourist zones into the neighborhoods where budget-challenged real New Yorkers eat, such as Chinatown, the Upper West Side, and the East Village, which is particularly good for getting a lot of bang for your buck. But even if you have no intention of venturing beyond Times Square, don't worry: I've included inexpensive restaurants in every neighborhood in the list below—including some of the city's best-kept secrets.

For the absolute best of what the city has to offer, check out "Best Low-Cost Dining Bets" in chapter 1, if you haven't already. Also take a quick look at the dining section in chapter 2's "60 Money-Saving Tips" for general advice on how to save while you're in the city.

**RESERVATIONS** Reservations are always a good idea in New York and a virtual necessity if your party is bigger than two. Do yourself a favor and make them so you won't be disappointed. If you're booking dinner on a weekend night, it's a good idea to call a few days to a week in advance if you can. In some cases—you want to score a bargain prix-fixe lunch, say, or dinner at TV chef Mario Batali's perennial hotspot P6—calling a month ahead isn't too soon. Your best bets for snaring a tough-to-get table is to try to book a weeknight dinner (the earlier in the week the better) or early (before 7pm) or late (after 9pm) in the evening.

**But What If They Don't *Take* Reservations?**    Lots of city restaurants, especially at the affordable end of the price continuum, don't take reservations at all. One of the ways they're able to keep prices down is by packing people in as quickly as possible. This means that the best cheap and midpriced restaurants often have a wait. Again, your best bet is to go early or late. Often, you can get in more quickly on a weeknight. Or just go knowing that you'll have to wait if you head to a popular spot such as Boca Chica. There are worse things than sipping a margarita at the festive bar.

**THE LOWDOWN ON SMOKING**    Following the national trend, New York City enacted strict no-smoking laws a few years back that made the majority of the city's dining rooms blessedly smoke-free. However, that doesn't mean that smokers are completely prohibited from lighting up. Here's the deal: Restaurants with more than 35 seats cannot allow smoking in their dining rooms. They can, however, allow smoking in their bar or lounge areas, and most do.

Restaurants with fewer than 35 seats—and there are more of those in the city than you'd think, especially in the budget category—can allow or prohibit smoking as they see fit. This ruling has turned some of the city's restaurants (like NoLiTa's Cafe Gitane, for instance) into particularly smoker-friendly establishments, which might be a turnoff for nonsmokers.

Whether you're a smoker or nonsmoker, your best bet is to call ahead and ask if it matters to you. If you're hell-bent on enjoying an after-dinner cigarette indoors, make sure that the restaurant has a bar or lounge that allows smoking. Some restaurants even offer dinner tables in their bar areas, such as Bar Pitti, where you can puff away during the meal if you so choose. And smoking is usually allowed in alfresco dining areas, but never assume; always ask. If you're a nonsmoker who doesn't want to be bothered by second-hand smoke, make sure your seat is well away from the bar.

**TIPPING**    Tipping is easy in New York. The way to do it: Double the 8¹/₄% sales tax and voilà! Happy waitperson.

If you check your coat, leave a dollar per item, no matter how small, for the checkroom attendant.

## 1  Restaurants by Cuisine

### AMERICAN

Bendix Diner (p. 159)
Big Nick's Burger Joint (p. 179)
Bubby's (p. 138)
Chat 'n' Chew (p. 162)
Coffee Shop (p. 162)
Corner Bistro (p. 154)
The Dish (p. 159)
EJ's Luncheonette (p. 156)
Empire Diner (p. 160)
ESPN Zone (p. 174)
Fanelli's Cafe (p. 145)
Gray's Papaya (p. 158)
Hamburger Harry's (p. 165)
Hard Rock Cafe (p. 174)
Harley-Davidson Cafe (p. 174)

Jackson Hole (p. 185)
Joe Allen (p. 168)
Kitchenette (p. 138)
Manhattan Chili Co. (p. 170)
Mars 2112 (p. 174)
Old Town Bar & Restaurant (p. 162)
Official All-Star Cafe (p. 174)
Papaya King (p. 173)
Planet Hollywood (p. 174)
Popover Cafe (p. 183)
Prime Burger (p. 176)
Serendipity 3 (p. 186)
66 Cafe (p. 172)
Tom's Restaurant (p. 184)
Walker's (p. 139)
WWF New York (p. 174)

**Key to Abbreviations:** *VE* = Very Expensive;  *E* = Expensive;  *M* = Moderate;  *I* = Inexpensive

## ASIAN FUSION/PAN-ASIAN

Junno's (p. 156)
Republic (p. 163)
Zen Palate (p. 163)

## BELGIAN

B. Frites (p. 173)

## BRAZILIAN/SOUTH AMERICAN

Boca Chica (p. 147)
Coffee Shop (p. 162)
Rice 'n' Beans (p. 171)

## BRITISH

The British Open (p. 175)
North Star Pub (p. 135)
Tea & Sympathy (p. 158)

## CHINESE

Grand Sichuan Restaurant
   (p. 160)
Hunan Park (p. 182)
Joe's Shanghai (p. 140)
New York Noodletown (p. 140)
Sweet-n-Tart Cafe (p. 141)
Sweet-n-Tart Restaurant (p. 141)

## CONTEMPORARY AMERICAN

Bouley Bakery (p. 139)
Sarabeth's Kitchen (p. 184)
The Tavern Room at Gramercy
   Tavern (p. 164)
Time Cafe (p. 151)

## ETHIOPIAN

Meskerem (p. 170)

## FRENCH

Cafe Gitane (p. 144)
Florent (p. 160)
Franklin Station Cafe (p. 138)
La Bonne Soupe (p. 169)
La Crêpe de Bretagne (p. 169)
Le Pere Pinard (p. 144)
Pastis (p. 161)
Payard Pâtisserie & Bistro (p. 187)
Tartine (p. 158)

## GOURMET SANDWICHES/ CAFE/TAKEOUT

Amy's Bread (p. 161)
Bagel & Bean (p. 173)
Bouley Bakery (p. 139)

Bruno the King of Ravioli (p. 185)
Cafe Balducci (p. 158)
Canova Market (p. 172)
Dean & Deluca (p. 158)
Devon & Blakely (p. 136)
Ecce Panis (p. 136)
Emerald Planet (p. 153)
Ess-A-Bagel (p. 175)
Ferrara (p. 142)
H&H Bagel (p. 173)
Housing Works Used Books Cafe
   (p. 146)
Island Burgers & Shakes (p. 165)
Little Pie Company (p. 161)
Mangia (p. 134)
Soup Kitchen International (p. 173)
Yura & Company (p. 186)

## GREEK

Niko's Mediterranean Grill & Bistro
   (p. 183)

## INDIAN

Bombay Dining (p. 148)
Gandhi (p. 148)
Haveli (p. 148)
Mitali East (p. 148)
New Madras Palace (p. 176)
Passage to India (p. 148)
Pongal (p. 176)
Salaam Bombay (p. 139)

## ITALIAN

Bar Pitti (p. 154)
Bruno the King of Ravioli (p. 185)
Carmine's (p. 175)
Ferrara (p. 142)
Frank (p. 148)
Lupa (p. 156)
Pietrasanta (p. 171)
Pó (p. 157)
Umberto's Clam House (p. 142)

## JAPANESE

Katsu-Hama (p. 176)
Menchenko-Tei (p. 136)
Sandobe Sushi (p. 150)
Sapporo (p 171)
Shabu Tatsu (p. 150)
Soba-Ya (p. 150)
Village Yokocho (p. 151)

## JEWISH

Barney Greengrass, the Sturgeon King
(p. 179)
Carnegie Deli (p. 168)
Fine & Shapiro (p. 136)
Katz's Delicatessen (p. 144)
Stage Deli (p. 168)

## KOREAN

Village Yokocho (p. 151)

## LATIN AMERICAN

Cafe Habana (p. 145)
La Caridad 78 (p. 182)
La Rosita Restaurant (p. 183)
La Taza de Oro (p. 161)

## MALAYSIAN

Franklin Station Cafe (p. 138)

## MIDDLE EASTERN

Afghan Kebab House (p. 165)
Bereket (p. 142)
Lemon Tree Cafe (p. 169)
Moustache (p. 157)
Sam's Falafel (p. 136)

## MEXICAN/TEX-MEX

Burritoville (p. 136)
Gabriela's (p. 179)
Los Dos Rancheros Mexicanos
(p. 170)
Manhattan Chili Co. (p. 170)
Nacho Mama (p. 183)
Taco & Tortilla King (p. 177)
Tajin Restaurant (p. 135)

## PIZZA

California Pizza Oven (p. 164)
Grimaldi's Pizzeria (p. 188)
John's Pizzeria (p. 168)
Lombardi's (p. 145)
Pintaile's Pizza (p. 187)
Totonno's Pizzeria Napolitano (p. 187)
Two Boots to Go (p. 159)
V&T Pizzeria (p. 185)

## SCANDINAVIAN

Good World Bar & Grill (p. 142)

## SEAFOOD

Oyster Bar & Restaurant (p. 178)
Pisces (p. 149)

## SOUL FOOD

Sylvia's (p. 187)

## SOUTHERN/BARBECUE

Acme Bar & Grill (p. 147)
Virgil's Real BBQ (p. 172)

## SPANISH

La Paella (p. 149)
La Rosita Restaurant (p. 183)

## SWISS

Roetelle A.G. (p. 149)

## THAI

Chanpen (p. 165)
Siam Inn Too (p. 172)
Thailand Restaurant (p. 141)

## TIBETAN

Tsampa (p. 151)

## UKRAINIAN

Veselka (p. 151)

## VEGETARIAN/HEALTH-CONSCIOUS

Angelica Kitchen (p. 147)
Josie's Restaurant & Juice Bar
(p. 182)
Pongal (p. 176)
The Pump (p. 178)
Spring Street Natural Restaurant
(p. 146)
Tsampa (p. 151)
Zen Palate (p. 163)

## VIETNAMESE

Nha Trang (p. 141)

# 2 South Street Seaport & the Financial District

**Mangia.** 40 Wall St. (btw. Nassau and William sts.). ☎ **212/425-4040.** Main courses $6–$11. AE, CB, DISC, DC, MC, V. Mon–Fri 7am–6pm (delivery 6–10pm). Subway: 4, 5 to Wall St.; J, M, Z to Broad St. GOURMET DELI.

This big, bustling gourmet cafeteria is an ideal place to take a break during your day of Financial District sightseeing. Between the giant salad and soup bars, the sandwich and hot entree counters, and an expansive cappuccino-and-pastry counter at the front of the cavernous room, even the most finicky eater will have a hard time deciding what to eat. Everything is freshly prepared and beautifully presented. The soups and stews are particularly good (there are always a number of daily choices), and a cup goes well with a fresh-baked pizzette (a mini-pizza). Pay-by-the-pound salad bars don't get any better than this, hot meal choices (grilled mahi-mahi, cumin-marinated lamb kabob) are cooked to order, and sandwiches are assembled as you watch. This place is packed with Wall Streeters between noon and 2pm, but things move quickly and there's enough seating so usually no one has to wait. Come in for a late breakfast or an afternoon snack, and you'll virtually have the place to yourself.

Mangia also has two cafeteria-style cafes in Midtown that offer similar, if not such expansive, menus: at 50 W. 57th St., between Fifth and Sixth avenues (☎ 212/582-5882); and at 16 E. 48th St., just east of Fifth Avenue (☎ 212/754-7600).

**North Star Pub.** At South Street Seaport, 93 South St. (at Fulton St.). ☎ **212/509-6757.** www.northstarpub.com. Main courses $7.50–$13. AE, CB, DC, EC, MC, V. Daily 11:30am–10:30pm (bar open later). Subway: 2, 3, 4, 5 to Fulton St. BRITISH.

This friendly place is a refreshing bit of authenticity in the mallified, almost theme park–like Seaport. It's the spitting image of a British pub, down to the chalkboard menus boasting daily specials such as kidney pie and strictly British and Irish ales on tap. I love the ale-battered fish 'n' chips, deep-fried-just-right (not too greasy) fish; the excellent golden-browned shepherd's pie; the bangers 'n' mash, made with grilled Cumberland sausage; and the traditional Ploughman's, including very good pâté, a sizable hunk of cheddar or stilton, fresh bread, and all the accompaniments (even Branston pickle!). All in all, a fun, relaxing place to hang out and eat and drink heartily (and cheaply). Look for an expansion and redecoration by the time you arrive, plus an expanded menu featuring influences from the former British Empire.

**Tajin Restaurant.** 85 Greenwich St. (south of Rector St.). ☎ **212/509-5017.** Reservations not accepted. Main courses 65¢–$6 at breakfast, $5–$10 at lunch and dinner. AE, MC, V. Mon–Fri 7am–9pm, Sat 9am–5pm. Subway: 1, 9 to Rector St. MEXICAN.

This Mexican luncheonette is a favorite among savvy Wall Streeters who love the bullish portions of authentic South-of-the-Border cooking at low, low prices. Tostadas might be the best budget deal: crisp tortillas come piled with traditional fillings, including your choice of chicken and beef, for just $2.95 as a starter. The enchiladas are fresh made and saucy; I love the spinach and mushroom version, topped with cheese and salsa verde. There's always something interesting on the "specials" board, and it seldom disappoints. Excellent guacamole, too. Come early, before you begin your lower Manhattan sightseeing, to launch your day with huevos rancheros, huevos con chorizo, or a generous breakfast burrito stuffed with scrambled eggs, potatoes, green pepper, onions, and a touch of jalapeño. The small dining room is spare but not unpleasant. Food comes, oddly enough, on real plates but with plastic forks. Service can be a tad gruff on occasion, but it's generally fine. There may be a short line for a table at the height of the lunch hour (between noon and 1:30pm), but it moves very quickly.

## QUICK BITES

The Twin Towers and environs abound with places to nosh. After all, those on-the-go bankers and traders have to eat lunch, don't they? But with so many options at hand, the trick is knowing where to go.

On the main concourse of the World Trade Center (WTC) is **Sbarro Pizza, Menchenko-Tei** for authentic Japanese, and **Fine & Shapiro**, right in a row between Borders and the center of the concourse (where the escalators to the PATH trains are). Menchenko-Tei is actually two restaurants in one: In front they sell Japanese bento box lunches with teriyakis and relatively cheap sushi, which are perfect for taking outdoors in warm weather; in the back are steam tables with Chinese food as well as a counter where you can order hearty udon and soba noodle bowls, which you can dine on at tables in back and upstairs. Fine & Shapiro has two entrances, one for full table service and one for the "only-to-go" deli.

Across the hall from those three is **Ecce Panis,** an excellent bakery with a small selection of sandwiches, focaccias, breakfast and sweet treats, two daily soups, and tons of variations on the staff of life, including an amazing little creation: the ham and cheese brioche, a sort of filled popover.

Just outside the WTC, between the north concourse entrance and Borders Books & Music, is **Devon & Blakely.** This appealing gourmet shop features lots of yuppie sandwiches (ham and camembert; smoked chicken with roasted tomatoes, spinach, and Caesar dressing), a few daily soups, a good chili with fixins and cornbread, British candy bars, pastries, and an espresso bar. The wide sidewalk just out front is lined with tables when the weather's nice.

Last but not least, there's **Sam's Falafel,** the best falafel cart in these parts, at the southwest corner of Broadway and Liberty Street. Sam's is well known, so the line can be long at lunchtime, but it always moves quickly. Nearby Liberty Plaza or Trinity Churchyard, two blocks south at Wall Street, both make great spots to enjoy your pita-wrapped lunch on a lovely day.

Once you're done, head over to **Krispy Kreme Doughnuts,** at 5 WTC, for a sweet, light-as-air treat (the entrance is outside on the plaza next to Borders, near Church and Vesey streets).

**Burritoville.** 36 Water St. (at Broad St.). ☎ **212/747-1100.** Main courses $4.50–$9. AE, DISC, MC, V. Daily 11am–midnight. Subway: 2, 3 to Wall St.; 1, 9 to South Ferry. TEX-MEX.

For a quick, healthy, and inexpensive lunch in the Seaport area, Burritoville fits the bill. These storefront taco shops serve up forward-thinking Mexican fare, all prepared with the freshest and healthiest ingredients, using no lard, preservatives, or canned goods; even the tortillas are pressed every day. Options range from well-stuffed taco and burrito standards to only-at-Burritoville creations such as a spicy white chicken chili with cumin and a number of choice veggie wraps. As you might expect, there are lots of choices for vegetarians as well as anyone looking for a quick bite on the go.

In addition to a second lower Manhattan location in the Wall Street area at 20 John St., between Broadway and Nassau (☎ 212/766-2020), there are 10 more Burritovilles throughout the city, a number of them quite pleasantly renovated with comfortable

---

### You Want Fries with That?

Wall Street's famous **McDonald's,** 160 Broadway, between Maiden Lane and Liberty Street (☎ 212/385-2063), elevates the Happy Meal to a whole new level. Ever been to another McDonald's where a doorman in tails greets you, a hostess finds you a table and sets it with place mats, and a tux-clad pianist twinkles the ivories at a candelabra-topped baby grand? But lest you fear that Ronald has abandoned his winning formula, don't worry: Everything else, from the quarter pounders to the ice-milk shakes, is comfortingly familiar.

# Lower Manhattan, TriBeCa & Chinatown Dining

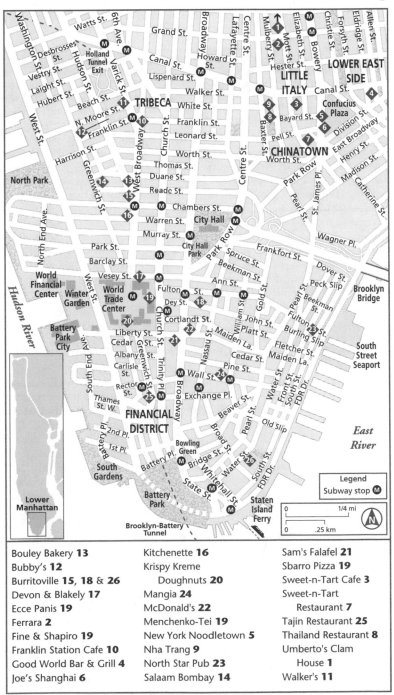

LOWER EAST SIDE

LITTLE ITALY

TRIBECA

CHINATOWN

Confucius Plaza

North Park

Hudson River

World Financial Center

Winter Garden

World Trade Center

Battery Park City

City Hall

City Hall Park

Brooklyn Bridge

South Street Seaport

FINANCIAL DISTRICT

Bowling Green

South Gardens

Battery Park

East River

Staten Island Ferry

Brooklyn-Battery Tunnel

Legend
Subway stop Ⓜ

0     1/4 mi
0    .25 km

Lower Manhattan

| | | |
|---|---|---|
| Bouley Bakery **13** | Kitchenette **16** | Sam's Falafel **21** |
| Bubby's **12** | Krispy Kreme | Sbarro Pizza **19** |
| Burritoville **15**, **18** & **26** | Doughnuts **20** | Sweet-n-Tart Cafe **3** |
| Devon & Blakely **17** | Mangia **24** | Sweet-n-Tart |
| Ecce Panis **19** | McDonald's **22** | Restaurant **7** |
| Ferrara **2** | Menchenko-Tei **19** | Tajin Restaurant **25** |
| Fine & Shapiro **19** | New York Noodletown **5** | Thailand Restaurant **8** |
| Franklin Station Cafe **10** | Nha Trang **9** | Umberto's Clam |
| Good World Bar & Grill **4** | North Star Pub **23** | House **1** |
| Joe's Shanghai **6** | Salaam Bombay **14** | Walker's **11** |

seating. See "Quick Bites" under each neighborhood section below to see whether there's one near you.

## 3 TriBeCa

○ **Bubby's.** 120 Hudson St. (at N. Moore St.). ☎ **212/219-0666.** www.bubbys.com. Reservations recommended for dinner. Main course $2–$16 at breakfast, brunch, and lunch; $10–$22 at dinner. AE, DC, DISC, MC, V. Mon–Thurs 8am–11pm, Fri 8am–midnight, Sat 9am–midnight, Sun 9am–10pm. Subway: 1, 9 to Franklin St. AMERICAN.

How do I love Bubby's? Let me count the ways. I love Bubby's for the sublime macaroni and cheese, for the divine garlic burger and fries (accompanied by Bubby's own "wup-ass" ketchup), for the homemade meat loaf with warm cider gravy and garlic mashies—better than Ma used to make. I love Bubby's for the roasted rosemary chicken and chipotle-crusted Black Angus steak and the classic cocktail the bartender will make for me when I'm in the mood. I love Bubby's generous portions, fresh-from-the-field greens, and big homestyle breakfasts. I love Bubby's coziness: The high-ceilinged, brick-walled loftlike space is very homey—very TriBeCa—and I love the candlelight that adds a touch of romance to the evening. I love the friendly waitstaff that doesn't neglect me, even when Harvey Keitel is sitting two tables over. Best of all, I love Bubby's pies: the core of Bubby's business, baked fresh daily, a half-dozen to choose from (along with another half-dozen homemade cakes) and topped with fresh-made whipped cream (pumpkin's my favorite). See for yourself.

**Franklin Station Cafe.** 222 W. Broadway (at Franklin St.). ☎ **212/274-8525.** Reservations not usually accepted. Breakfast $4.50–$7.50, sandwiches and noodle bowls $6–$9, house specials $10.50–$16.50. AE, DC, MC, V. Daily 8am–11pm. Subway: 1, 9 to Franklin St. FRENCH-MALAYSIAN.

This charming brick-walled cafe is a winner for affordable Malaysian noodle and curry bowls and French-inspired sandwiches. All the dishes on the cute-as-a-button, handwritten-and-illustrated menu are prepared by the health-minded kitchen with all-natural ingredients. Sandwiches are simple but satisfying creations such as home-baked ham with honey mustard, lettuce, and tomato; fresh mozzarella with leafy basil, vine-ripened tomato, and extra-virgin olive oil; smoked salmon with mascarpone and chives; and old-fashioned tuna salad with jalapeno. For warm and cozy, you can't do better than one of Franklin Station's flavorful noodle bowls, such as tom yum shrimp, with sprouts, pineapple, and cucumber in a pleasingly hot-and-sour broth; or seafood udon, with generous helpings of squid, shrimp, and salmon in a milder vegetable broth. For a more substantial meal, check the blackboard for such specials as Chilean sea bass in cardamom sauce or French- and Malaysian-style mussels. Service is friendly and efficient, wine and beer is available, and the desserts (a scrumptious fresh-baked tart, crème caramel, and home-baked banana or carrot-raisin cake are usually among the choices) are well priced and pleasing. Omelets dominate the morning menu.

**Kitchenette.** 80 W. Broadway (at Warren St.). ☎ **212/267-6740.** www.kitchenettenyc. com. Main courses $3.75–$6.50 at breakfast; $4–$8 at lunch and brunch, $9–$16 at dinner. AE ($20 minimum). Mon–Fri 7:30am–10pm, Sat–Sun 9am–10pm. Subway: 1, 2, 3, 9 to Chambers St. AMERICAN HOME COOKING.

This unpretentious TriBeCa luncheonette has become a prime contender on the comfort-food circuit, thanks to Hungry Man–sized breakfasts and just-like-home cooking. The little room has the feel of a New England country diner, with rough-edged folk art on the walls and mismatched country-rustic chairs at the tables. Expect high-cholesterol farmhouse breakfasts and hearty salads and sandwiches during the day. Weekly lunchtime blue-plate specials include excellent shepherd's pie with mashed potato crust on Tuesday and gooey and delicious four-cheese mac and cheese on Friday (specials are always subject to change). In addition to salads and burgers, the nighttime menu features more sophisticated entrees such as chicken pot pie with a cheddar biscuit crust, pot roast with pan potatoes and carrots, grilled pork chops (with Kitchenette's secret herb rub), and roast turkey with cornbread stuffing and sweet potato mashies. Everything is well prepared and filling (skip the prepackaged sandwiches at lunch, though). Service is sit down at breakfast and dinner, but lunch is more cafeteria style, with orders taken at the counter. No wine or beer is served, but you're welcome to BYOB.

✪ **Salaam Bombay.** 317 Greenwich St. (btw. Duane and Reade sts.). ☎ **212/226-9400.** www.salaambombay.com. Main courses $9–$18; daily all-you-can-eat buffet lunch $10.95. AE, DC, DISC, MC, V. Sun–Thurs 11:30am–3pm and 5–10:30pm, Fri 11:30am–3pm and 5–11pm, Sat 5–11pm. Subway: 1, 2, 3, 9 to Chambers St. PAN-INDIAN.

This Indian restaurant is much more attractive than most curry houses, and the pan-Indian cuisine is a cut above the standard fare. The kitchen roams the subcontinental map, from Punjabi tandooris to Goan spicy fish and back again; all the dishes are confidently prepared with quality ingredients. The $10.95 all-you-can-eat lunch, offered every day except Saturday, is an extraordinary bargain. I know the notion can be a turnoff (buffet? yuck!), but this is a freshly prepared, top-quality spread; you'll watch the tandoori chef pulling fresh-baked naan from the clay oven as you fill your plate. There's a dozen or so fresh-made meat and vegetarian dishes to choose from, as well as all the traditional accompaniments. Dinnertime is a real treat: The room is low-lit and formally outfitted, and service is professional and attentive; my husband and I even celebrated Valentine's Day here a few years back. The tandoori specialties are succulent and the sauces generous and delicately spiced. In addition to your familiar favorites, consider trying some of the lesser-known regional specialties, such as *gosht dum pasanda,* a Kashmiri lamb specialty; marinated in yogurt and cooked in a sealed pot, the meat emerges tender and succulent. Terrific!

**Walker's.** 16 No. Moore St. (at Varick St.). ☎ **212/941-0142.** Reservations accepted for dinner. Main courses $7.75–13.75 at dinner. AE, CB, DC, DISC, MC, V. Daily 11:45am–4am (food served until 1am). Subway: 1, 9 to Franklin St. AMERICAN.

Down-to-earth as ever, Walker's is an old holdout from pre-fabulous TriBeCa. I love this pub and restaurant; prices are low across the board, and the space is quite charming, with a tin ceiling, a long wooden bar, oldies on the sound system, friendly bartenders, and cozy tables where you can dine on affordable—and surprisingly good—meat and potatoes fare. There's a terrific 8-ounce sirloin burger, a yummy grilled ribeye, and well-roasted organic chicken with mashies among the pretty extensive list of entrees and nightly specials, plus crisp, fresh salads for lighter tastes. The fried oysters with Cajun aioli make a great starter. Low lighting sets a nice dinnertime mood, and service is friendly and attentive enough, as long as you're not in a hurry.

## QUICK BITES

There's also **Burritoville** (p. 136) at 144 Chambers St., at Hudson Street (☎ 212/964-5048).

✪ **Bouley Bakery.** 120 W. Broadway (btw. Duane and Reade sts.). ☎ **212/964-2525.** www.bouley.net. Menu items $1.75–$10. AE, DC, MC, V. Mon–Fri 7am–7pm, Sat–Sun 8am–7pm. Subway: 1, 2, 3, 9 to Chambers St. GOURMET CONTEMPORARY AMERICAN TAKEOUT.

Here's a terrific opportunity to sample the bounty of one of New York's best chefs, the masterful David Bouley, at wallet-friendly prices. You'll pay $75 to $100 per person to dine in Bouley Bakery's *New York Times* four-star-winning dining room, but you can assemble a stellar lunch from the takeout menu at the adjoining bakery for just a few dollars. This is yummy stuff: inventive soups made fresh daily, such as Maine mussels in saffron broth with fingerling potatoes or white bean with smoked ham and duck confit; hearty country sandwiches such as house-cured roast beef dressed with swiss, horseradish mayo, cornichons, lettuce, and tomato on bold pepper bread or roasted red pepper with fresh mozzarella, basil, tomato, and balsamic glaze on super-soft, powdery ciabatta. Salads and bite-size pizzas are available, as is a roasted all-natural whole chicken ($10) that's ideal for building a sophisticated take-home dinner around. The fresh-baked breads and pastries are some of the finest in the city; this is a perfect place to start your morning or celebrate midday with a latte and brioche or another sweet treat. The counter staff is held to the same standard as their dining-room compatriots, so expect four-star service, too.

## 4 Chinatown & Little Italy

**♻ Joe's Shanghai.** 9 Pell St. (btw. Bowery and Mott sts.). ☎ 212/233-8888. www. joesshanghai.com. Reservations recommended for 10 or more. Main courses $4.25–$13. No credit cards. Daily 11am–11:15pm. Subway: N, R, 6 to Canal St; B, D, Q to Grand St. SHANGHAI CHINESE.

Tucked away on a little elbow of a side street just off the Bowery is this Chinatown institution, which serves up authentic cuisine to enthusiastic crowds nightly. The stars of the huge menu are the signature soup dumplings, quivering steamed pockets filled with hot broth and your choice of pork or crab, accompanied by a side of seasoned soy. Listed on the menu as "steamed buns" (item numbers 1 and 2), these culinary marvels never disappoint. Neither does the rest of the authentic Shanghai-inspired menu, which boasts such main courses as whole yellowfish bathed in spicy sauce; excellent "mock duck," a saucy bean-curd dish similar to Japanese yuba that's a hit with vegetarians and carnivores alike; and lots of well-prepared staples. The room is set mostly with round tables of 10 or so, and you'll be asked whether you're willing to share. I encourage you to do so; it's a great way to watch and learn from your neighbors (many of whom are Chinese), who are usually happy to tell you what they're eating. If you want a private table, expect a wait.

Joe's Shanghai now has a second Manhattan location, in Midtown at 24 W. 56th St., between Fifth and Sixth avenues (☎ 212/333-3868).

**♻ New York Noodletown.** 28¹/₂ Bowery (at Bayard St.). ☎ 212/349-0923. Reservations accepted. Main courses $4–$12. No credit cards. Daily 9am–4am. Subway: N, R, 6 to Canal St. SEAFOOD/CHINESE.

This just might be the best Chinese food in New York City. Among its fans are Ruth Reichl, former restaurant critic for *The New York Times* and now editor-in-chief of *Gourmet* magazine, who constantly puts it at the top of the heap. So what if the room is reminiscent of a school cafeteria? The food is fabulous. The mushroom soup is a lunch in itself, thick with earthy chunks of shiitakes, vegetables, and thin noodles. Another appetizer that can serve as a meal is the hacked roast duck in noodle soup. The kitchen excels at seafood preparations, so be sure to try at least one: Looking like a snow-dusted plate of meaty fish, the salt-baked squid is sublime. The quick-woked Chinese broccoli or the crisp sautéed baby bok choy make great accompaniments. Other special dishes are various sandy pot casseroles, hearty, flavorful affairs slow-simmered in clay vessels. Unlike most of its neighbors, New York Noodletown keeps very long hours, which makes it the best late-night bet in the neighborhood, too.

**Nha Trang.** 87 Baxter St. (btw. Canal and Bayard sts.). ☎ **212/233-5948.** Reservations accepted. Main courses $4–$12.50. No credit cards. Daily 10:30am–9:30pm. Subway: N, R, 6 to Canal St. VIETNAMESE.

The decor might be standard-issue, no-atmosphere Chinatown (glass-topped tables, linoleum floors, mirrored walls), but this friendly, bustling place serves up the best Vietnamese in Chinatown. A plate of crispy, finger-sized spring rolls is a nice way to start; the slightly spicy pork-and-shrimp filling is nicely offset by the wrapping of lettuce, cucumber, and mint. The pho noodle soup comes in a quart-sized bowl brimming with bright vegetables and various meats and seafood. But my favorite dish is the simple barbecued pork chops—sliced paper-thin, soaked in a soy/sugar-cane marinade, and grilled to utter perfection. Everything is well prepared, and your waiter will be glad to help you design a meal to suit your tastes. If there's a line, stick around; it won't take long to get a table.

**Sweet-n-Tart Cafe.** 76 Mott St. (just south of Canal St.). ☎ **212/334-8088.** Reservations not accepted. Main courses $2–$10. No credit cards. Daily 9am–midnight. Subway: N, R, 6 to Canal St. CHINESE.

Here's Chinatown's best super-cheap cuisine. There's only one dish over $6—and, considering the bargain-basement prices, the quality is stellar. Rarely is Chinese food described as airy and light, but this cuisine is, especially the excellent noodle soups. The scallion pancake is a beautifully seasoned sleeper, and the Taiwan-style salt-baked chicken, served on broth-soaked rice, is a don't-miss. There are plenty of familiar dishes to satisfy finicky eaters—fried rice, lo mein, pan-fried dumplings, and the like—but this is also a good bet for adventurous diners who'd like to try something new, be it shredded jellyfish, chicken with sea cucumber, or broiled frog. Sweet-n-Tart's specialty is tong shui, a broth or gelatin made with herbal, nut, or fruit essences. Served cold or hot, they're taken as invigorating medicinal tonics. You can have yours brought at any time during the meal, but I've found them to offer a clean, fresh finish to the meal; consider the quail eggs with lotus seed in a light, peppery broth. There's zero ambiance in the small, fluorescent-lit dining room, but it's pleasant enough, and the service is some of the best I've experienced in Chinatown. No alcohol is served, but the servers keep your glass filled with warm Chinese tea, and a juicer blends thick, sweet papaya and other fresh-fruit shakes.

If you'd like beer or wine with your meal, head a couple of blocks south to **Sweet-n-Tart Restaurant,** 20 Mott St., between Park Row and Pell Street (☎ 212/964-0380), which has a semblance of decor and a wider-ranging menu ($3 to $19).

**Thailand Restaurant.** 106 Bayard St. (at Baxter St.). ☎ **212/349-3132.** Reservations recommended. Main courses $5–$13; weekday lunch special (11:30am–4pm) $4.25–$6. AE. Daily 11:30am–11pm. Subway: N, R, 6 to Canal St. THAI.

This kitchen turns out first-rate Thai dishes—aromatic, searing, full of zest and colors. The sliced charcoal steak with onions, hot pepper, lemon juice, and mint is a fabulously fiery, flavorful appetizer. The tasty green curry with coconut milk, eggplant, bamboo shoots, and green chiles comes with your choice of chicken, beef, pork, lamb, or shrimp. Sautéed rice noodles are a good choice to offset the tangier dishes. The whole fish, especially sea bass, are delicately crispy outside, moist and flaky inside. Mean it if you say spicy, because your tongue will sizzle like a Midtown sidewalk in August. The coconut milk dessert, with slices of ice cubes, is the perfect cool finish.

**Umberto's Clam House.** 386 Broome St. (btw. Mulberry and Mott sts.). ☎ **212/431-7545.** www.umbertosclamhouse.com. Reservations accepted (recommended for Friday and Saturday dinner). Pastas $8.50–$16.50, main courses $6–$21.50 (most less than $16). AE. Daily 11am–4am. Subway: N, R to Prince St.; 6 to Spring St. ITALIAN SEAFOOD.

Umberto's has true-crime cachet. It was at the original Mulberry Street location, in 1973, that "reputed" mafioso Joey Gallo was assassinated while savoring a plate of scungilli. Umberto's moved to this spot a few years back, leaving those famed bullet holes behind, but it still brims with classic Little Italy ambiance.

The traditional, seafood-heavy menu is genuinely pleasing. I found the scungilli to be a bit tough but the baked clams were divine. You can also expect first-rate raw cherry-stones on the half-shell; perfectly *al dente* linguine with a generous helping of fresh shelled clams in red sauce or extra-virgin olive oil; and excellent lobster ravioli stuffed with whole chunks of lobster (a steal at $10.95). Plenty of meat and pasta dishes are on hand for non-seafood eaters. The wine list is decent and affordable. The atmosphere is unpretentious, vaguely (and a tad cheesily) nautical, with comfortably spaced tables and a small outdoor patio. Autographed pictures line the walls (of course) and run the gamut from Sinatra to never-beens with big dreams. The restaurant is staffed with career waiters who are friendly and attentive. All in all, a very good bet.

## QUICK BITES

America's first espresso bar was **Ferrara,** 195 Grand St., between Mott and Mulberry streets (☎ **212/226-6150**), founded in 1892. This pleasant *pasticceria* is still the place to go for yummy Italian treats such as cannoli, pastiacotti (Italian cream puffs), sfogliatelle (a flaky shell stuffed with baked ricotta and a Sopranos favorite), Napoleans, pignolis, macaroons, and more.

## 5 The Lower East Side

In addition to the choices below, the **Good World Bar & Grill,** 3 Orchard St., between Division and Canal streets (☎ **212/925-9975**), serves up affordable Scandinavian eats ($9 to $16), including excellent herring and gravlax plates, Swedish meatballs, and grated potato pancakes, to a hip, young bar crowd. A good bet for intrepid budget travelers; see "Bars & Cocktail Lounges" in chapter 9 for more info.

**Bereket.** 187 Houston St. (at Orchard St.). ☎ **212/475-7700.** Reservations not accepted. Main courses $4–$10. No credit cards. Open 24 hours. Subway: F to Second Ave. TURKISH.

This popular Turkish kebab house is little more than a hole in the wall, but there's no arguing with the excellent quality of their grilled meats. Order at the counter, where you'll see the freshly skewered kebabs displayed behind glass, just waiting to hit the grill, and then try to snare one of the few tables as your plate is being prepared. The kofte, ground lamb mixed with spices, is a favorite, but you won't go wrong with any of the choices. Complete dinners—two skewers of your choice, rice, and salad—are a steal at $8, or $10 for the mixed grill, which features chicken, shish (beef), and doner (lamb) kebabs. Vegetarians have a lot to choose from as well, including excellently herbed hummus, falafel, great piyaz (white bean salad with chopped onions and parsley), and babaganoush. The counter staff is friendly and accommodating. No alcohol is served, but Turkish coffee should provide the necessary jolt. (Or consider getting your order to go and walking a couple of blocks up to dba, on First Avenue between 2nd and 3rd streets, where you can match your takeout meal with any number of fine brews; see chapter 9).

# East Village & SoHo Area Dining

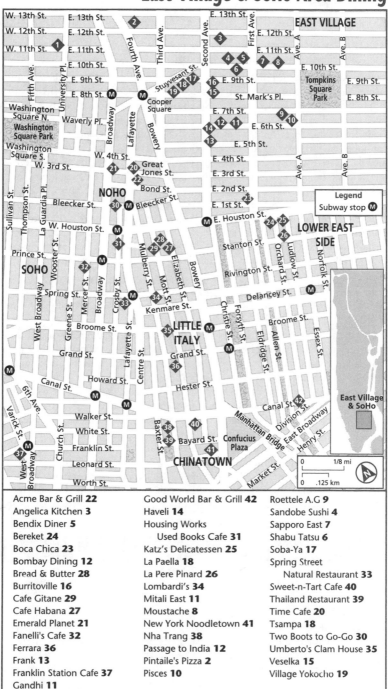

| | | |
|---|---|---|
| Acme Bar & Grill **22** | Good World Bar & Grill **42** | Roettele A.G **9** |
| Angelica Kitchen **3** | Haveli **14** | Sandobe Sushi **4** |
| Bendix Diner **5** | Housing Works | Sapporo East **7** |
| Bereket **24** | Used Books Cafe **31** | Shabu Tatsu **6** |
| Boca Chica **23** | Katz's Delicatessen **25** | Soba-Ya **17** |
| Bombay Dining **12** | La Paella **18** | Spring Street |
| Bread & Butter **28** | La Pere Pinard **26** | Natural Restaurant **33** |
| Burritoville **16** | Lombardi's **34** | Sweet-n-Tart Cafe **40** |
| Cafe Gitane **29** | Mitali East **11** | Thailand Restaurant **39** |
| Cafe Habana **27** | Moustache **8** | Time Cafe **20** |
| Emerald Planet **21** | New York Noodletown **41** | Tsampa **18** |
| Fanelli's Cafe **32** | Nha Trang **38** | Two Boots to Go-Go **30** |
| Ferrara **36** | Passage to India **12** | Umberto's Clam House **35** |
| Frank **13** | Pintaile's Pizza **2** | Veselka **15** |
| Franklin Station Cafe **37** | Pisces **10** | Village Yokocho **19** |
| Gandhi **11** | | |

143

⊙ **Katz's Delicatessen.** 205 E. Houston St. (at Ludlow St.). ☎ **212/254-2246.** www.katzdeli.com. Reservations not accepted. Sandwiches $2.15–$10, other main courses $5–$17.45. AE, MC, V ($20 minimum). Sun–Tues 8am–10pm, Wed–Thurs 8am–11pm, Fri–Sat 8am–3am. Subway: F to Second Ave. JEWISH DELI.

Here's the city's best Jewish deli for budget diners. The motto is, "There's Nothing More New York than Katz's," and it's spot-on. Founded in 1888, this cavernous, brightly lit place is suitably pre-IPO Noo Yawk, with dill pickles, Dr. Brown's cream soda, and old-world attitude to spare. This Lower East Side institution draws everybody from New Jersey housewives in for a day of bargain shopping to pierced and tattooed clubgoers looking for a few nutrients. Half of the space is dedicated to traditional cafeteria-style counter service—perfect for budget travelers who'd rather save on tip money—but the other half offers waiter service. All of Katz's traditional eats are first-rate—from the matzo ball and chicken noodle soups to the potato latkes to the cheese blintzes to the egg creams—and particularly the beloved all-beef hot dogs. There's no faulting the pastrami, smoked to perfection, or the dry-cured roast beef, and the well-stuffed sandwiches are substantially cheaper than you'll find at any other deli in town. What's more, Katz's is the only deli cool enough to let you split one with your travel partner without adding a bogus $2 to $3 "sharing" charge.

⊙ **Le Père Pinard.** 175 Ludlow St. (south of Houston St.). ☎ **212/777-4917.** Reservations recommended. Main courses $3.50–$14 at lunch (2-course lunch special $9.50), $11.50–$19.50 at dinner. AE. Sun–Thurs 10am–midnight, Fri–Sat 10am–1am. Subway: F to Delancey St. FRENCH WINE BAR.

Here's my favorite spot on the Lower East Side's burgeoning dining scene. This little-known French wine bar and bistro is authentic and charming, with high ceilings, burnished brick walls, well-spaced tables with mix-and-match chairs, and an authentic come-as-you-are air. The kitchen specializes in the Gallic version of comfort food: steak frites, shell steak with roquefort sauce, a delectable shepherd's pie with a pleasingly cheesy crust, a good brandade, and a generous charcuterie and cheese plate—the perfect match for the sublime crusty-on-the-outside, soft-in-the-middle bread that accompanies every meal. Greens are fresh and well prepared; even a simple mesculun salad wears a just-right viniagrette. There are lots of wine choices by both the bottle and glass; I like the restaurant's protocol, which allows you to taste first even if you're just ordering by the glass. Excellent kir royales, too. Service is attentive, but in a casual, easygoing way. Smoking is allowed in the front (bar) room, but the back room is dedicated to nonsmokers. There's also a pleasant garden in warm weather. The lunch special is a bargain.

# 6  SoHo & NoLiTa

**Cafe Gitane.** 242 Mott St. (at Prince St.). ☎ **212/334-9552.** Reservations not accepted. Main courses $4.50–$6 at breakfast, $7.50–$9.25 at lunch and dinner. No credit cards. Daily 9am–midnight. Subway: B, D, F, Q to Broadway–Lafayette St.; 6 to Spring St. FRENCH CAFE.

This NoLiTa cafe feels as if it came straight out of the Latin Quarter, complete with lithe French-accented waiters, black-clad bohemian hipsters, and clouds of imported cigarette smoke. It's quite an affected place, alright, but somehow the attitude is the appeal—not to mention the good, cheap eats. The short, internationally accented menu mainly consists of sandwiches and noodle bowls. Appealing choices include baked eggs with baguette; noodles with shrimp and white beans in curried coconut milk; smoked salmon with red onions, capers, and lemon wasabi on sourdough; and—my favorite—roasted chicken with chipotle mayo, fresh Parmesan, and anchovies on a toasted baguette. In true French style, all the breads are admirable and ultra-fresh. Meals are well worth the money but on the small side; big appetites will have plenty of room for dessert. Beverage choices include strong coffee drinks and French wines by the glass or bottle. The servers might not have found their true calling yet, but they're perfectly polite. Don't miss the petite bathroom, which boasts gorgeous mosaic work. There's outside seating in warm weather.

**✪ Cafe Habana.** 17 Prince St. (at Elizabeth St.). ☎ **212/625-2001.** Reservations not accepted. Main courses $5–$13. AE, MC, V. Daily 9am–midnight. Subway: B, D, F, Q to Broadway/ Lafayette St.; 6 to Spring St. CUBAN/LATIN AMERICAN.

I just love this sleek update on a typical Latin American luncheonette. It manages to be hip without being the least bit pretentious, and what the food might lack in authenticity it more than makes up for in quality and flavor: Shrimps are big and hearty, pork is moist and flavorful, and cilantro and other spices are fresh and aromatic. Winning starters include *pozole*, hominy corn stew with shredded chicken or pork in a clear broth that you season to taste with oregano, chile, and lime; and the hugely popular Mexican corn on the cob, which is skewered, coated with lime juice and grated cheese, sprinkled with chile powder, and grilled into a messy but sweet popcorny treat. Main courses include the ultra-moist roast pork (perfect with a squeeze of lime) and *camarones al Ajillo*, shrimp in spicy garlic sauce. Most everything comes with your choice of red or black beans and rice; go with the yellow rice, as the white tends to be a tad anemic. Wine and Mexican beers are served, but I love the not-too-sweet red Hibiscus tea. The room is narrow and tables are petite (especially those for two), but a middle aisle keeps the place from feeling too crowded, and service is easygoing and friendly. Don't be surprised if there's a wait for a table.

There's also a second location, at 11 Abingdon Square (on Eighth Avenue between West 12th and Bleecker streets) in the West Village (☎ **212/989-6883**) that tends to be less buzzy and crowded.

**Fanelli's Cafe.** 94 Prince St. (at Mercer St.). ☎ **212/226-9412.** Reservations not accepted. Main courses $5–$12. AE, MC, V. Mon–Wed 10am–2am, Thurs–Sat 10am–4am; Sun noon–2am. Subway: N, R to Prince St. AMERICAN.

Once upon a time, SoHo consisted of a few daring galleries, a gaggle of artists living illegally in loft space that no one wanted, a few Italian bakeries, and Fanelli's. Matters couldn't be more different now: The galleries have given way to Banana Republic, the bakeries have moved over for Balthazar, and people pay millions for those lofts. Thankfully, Fanelli's remains the same. This place is classic New York pub: The long bar is propped up by regulars, and its corner door and pressed-tin ceiling have locked in the 1847 atmosphere (this is the second-oldest continuously operating establishment in the city). If smoke bothers you, ask to be seated in the back. There's not much point in getting fancy with your order: The giant burgers are great, the pastas fresh, the beer served in pint glasses. The daring will give the mussels a shot. Wine? House red. No kidding. If you're coming for dinner, especially on a weekend, your best bet is to arrive before 7pm, when the noise level really starts to escalate.

**✪ Lombardi's.** 32 Spring St. (btw. Mott and Mulberry sts.). ☎ **212/941-7994.** Reservations accepted for parties of 6 or more. Small pies (6 slices) $10.50–$16, large pies (6 slices) $12.50–$20; extra charge for additional toppings. No credit cards. Mon–Thurs 11:30am–11pm, Fri–Sat 11:30am–midnight, Sun 11:30am–10pm. Subway: 6 to Spring St.; N, R to Prince St. PIZZA.

Lombardi's is a living gem in the annals of the city's culinary history. First opened in 1905, "America's first licensed pizzeria" cooks Manhattan's best pizza in its original coal brick oven. The wonderfully smoky crust (a generations-old family recipe that Gennaro Lombardi hand-carried from Naples at the turn of the century) is topped with fresh mozzarella, basil, Pecorino romano, and San Marzano tomato sauce. From there, the choice is yours. Topping options are suitably old-world (Citterio pancetta, calamata olives, Esposito sweet Italian sausage, homemade meatballs, beefsteak tomatoes, and the like), but Lombardi's specialty is the fresh clam pie, with hand-shucked clams, oregano, fresh garlic, romano, extra-virgin olive oil, and fresh-ground pepper (no sauce). The main dining room is narrow but very pleasant, with the usual checkered tablecloths and exposed brick walls. A big draw is the garden out back; walk past the kitchen and up a flight of stairs to reach this lovely second-floor deck, where tables sport Cinzano umbrellas and a flowering tree shoots up through the concrete. Another plus: In a city where rudeness is a badge of honor, Lombardi's wait staff is extremely affable.

**Spring Street Natural Restaurant.** 62 Spring St. (at Lafayette St.) ☎ **212/966-0290.** Reservations accepted for parties of 8 or more only. Main courses $8–$16. AE, DC, MC, V. Sun–Thurs 11:30am–midnight, Fri–Sat 11:30am–1am. Subway: 6 to Spring St. HEALTH-CONSCIOUS.

This 28-year-old spot is as comfortable and easygoing as your old college hangout—and just about as affordable, too. The expansive brick-walled room is filled with leafy greenery and anchored by an old oak bar. This is the kind of place where you can set yourself down at a table and camp out for a while, poring over a good book while you nosh on a farm-fresh entree-sized salad or a terrific tempeh burger; the staff will happily refill your coffee mug as you relax. But although the food is fresh, all-natural, unprocessed, and prepared with good health in mind, it's not strictly vegetarian: There's lots of fresh-off-the-boat seafood to choose from, plus free-range chicken and turkey. And the menu isn't restricted to soups, sandwiches, and salads, as at many other health-minded restaurants. You can come for a full meal, dining on such entrees as broiled New England bluefish with shiitake mushrooms, roasted chicken with pommery mustard glaze, or any number of pastas and stir-frys. Everything is well prepared and satisfying. The kitchen can also satisfy sugar, dairy, and other dietary restrictions. There's pleasant outdoor seating along Lafayette Street in good weather.

## QUICK BITES

If you need a coffee break, skip Starbucks and head instead to ✪ **Housing Works Used Books Cafe,** 126 Crosby St. (one block east of Broadway), just south of Houston Street (☎ **212/334-3324; www.housingworksubc.com).** This attractive and airy used-book shop (whose proceeds support AIDS charities) has an appealing cafe in back that serves up coffee and tea, sandwiches, sweets, and other light bites. There are plenty of tables where you can pull up a chair, and you're welcome to read while you nosh. Beer and wine is served, and such events as literary readings and wine tastings are common in the evenings, especially Wednesdays and Thursdays (look for an expanded calendar when the downstairs performance space is complete).

## 7 The East Village & NoHo

In addition to the choices below, also consider the East Village branch of **Bendix Diner** (p. 159), 167 First Ave., between 10th and 11th streets (☎ 212/260-4220) for homestyle favorites. A great choice for wallet-friendly Middle Eastern fare is **Moustache** (p. 157), at 265 E. 10th St., between First Avenue and Avenue A (☎ 212/ 228-2022). There's also an East Village branch of **Sapporo** (p. 171) at 245 E. 10th St., at First Avenue (☎ 212/260-1330), for cheap Japanese eats.

**Acme Bar & Grill.** 9 Great Jones St. (at Lafayette St.). ☎ **212/420-1934.** Reservations not accepted. Main courses $6–$14 at lunch, $7–$16 at dinner. DC, DISC, MC, V. Sun–Thurs 11am–11pm, Fri–Sat 11am–midnight. Subway: 6 to Bleecker St.; B, D, F, Q to Broadway/ Lafayette St. SOUTHERN/BARBECUE.

Acme's motto is AN OKAY PLACE TO EAT—a witty bit of clear-eyed candor in this best-obsessed town. This easygoing NoHo joint is divey in a pleasing way, with a good-natured staff, a Louisiana roadhouse theme, and the comfortable vibe of a well-worn neighborhood favorite. Acme serves up heaping platters of Southern home cooking and barbecue: po-boys, jambalaya, seafood gumbo, thick-cut pork chops, chicken-fried steak, baby-back ribs—not gourmet grub, but good, cheap, filling eats. The restaurant is a hot-sauce lover's delight, with dozens of bottles lining the walls so you can douse your dish with the perfect measure of heat. Yummy fresh-baked cornbread starts the meal, and a range of beers are available. Downstairs is **Acme Underground,** a small, low-cover, live music venue that books a broad range of hopeful rock and blues acts.

**Angelica Kitchen.** 300 E. 12th St. (just east of Second Ave.). ☎ **212/228-2909.** Reservations accepted for 6 or more Mon–Thurs. Main courses $6–$14.25; lunch deal (Mon–Fri 11:30am–5pm) $6.75. No credit cards. Daily 11:30am–10:30pm. Subway: L, N, R, 4, 5, 6, to 14th St./Union Sq. ORGANIC VEGETARIAN.

This cheerful restaurant is serious about vegan cuisine. The kitchen prepares everything fresh daily; they guarantee that at least 95% of all ingredients are organically grown, with sustainable agriculture and responsible business practices additionally required before food can cross the kitchen's threshold. But good-for-you (and good-for-the-environment) doesn't have to mean boring; this is flavorful, beautifully prepared cuisine served in a lovely country kitchen–style setting. Salads spill over with sprouts and all kinds of crisp veggies and are crowned with homemade dressings. The Dragon Bowls, a specialty, are heaping portions of rice, beans, tofu, and steamed vegetables. The daily seasonal specials feature the best of what's fresh and in season in such dishes as fiery three-bean chili, slow-simmered with sundried tomatoes and a blend of chile peppers; baked tempeh nestled in a sourdough baguette and dressed in mushroom gravy; and lemon-herb baked tofu layered with roasted vegetables and fresh pesto on mixed-grain bread. Breads and desserts are fresh baked and similarly wholesome (and made without eggs, of course).

**Boca Chica.** 13 First Ave. (at 1st St.). ☎ **212/473-0108.** Reservations accepted for parties of 6 or more Sun–Wed only. Main dishes $7.50–$20 (most less than $13). AE, MC, V. Mon–Thurs 5:30–11pm, Fri–Sat 5:30pm–midnight, Sun noon–4pm and 5:30–11pm. Subway: F to Second Ave. SOUTH AMERICAN.

This lively and colorful joint is always packed with a gleefully mixed crowd working its way through a round of margaritas or a few pitchers of beer. The cuisine is a down-market version of the pan-Latino favorites that have captivated palates farther uptown, most notably at Patina and Calle Ocho. The food at Boca Chica is a little closer to its hearty South American roots: well-prepared pork, beef, fish, and vegetarian dishes, most pleasingly heavy on the sauce and spice, accompanied by plantains, rice, and beans. There's also a bevy of interesting appetizers, including black bean soup well seasoned with lime juice and terrific coconut-fried shrimp. Although this approach to cooking now tends to be well out of reach of the under-$25 crowd, Boca Chica keeps things affordable, much to the delight of those of us without bottomless wallets. *Be forewarned:* Getting in on weekends in about as hard as sneaking into Havana.

## Dining Zone: Little India

The stretch of East 6th Street between First and Second avenues in the East Village is known as "Little India," thanks to the dozen or more Indian restaurants that line the block (Subway: F to Second Avenue). Dining here isn't exactly high style, but Little India's restaurants do offer decent Indian food at discount prices, sometimes accompanied by live sitar music. It's loads of fun to grab a bottle of wine or a six-pack from one of the corner stores on Second Avenue (many of Little India's restaurants don't serve alcohol, but even those who do will often let you bring in your own) and cruise the strip, deciding which one most appeals to you. In the warm weather, each usually stations a hawker out front to help convince you that theirs is *so* much better than the competition.

Some people speculate that there's one big kitchen in the alley behind East 6th, but a few of Little India's restaurants deserve special attention. **Bombay Dining,** at 320 E. 6th St. (☎ 212/260-8229), is a standout, serving excellent *samosa* (crisp vegetable-and-meat patties), *pakora* (banana fritters), and *papadum* (crispy bean wafers with coarse peppercorns). Also satisfying is **Gandhi,** 345 E. 6th St. (☎ 212/614-9718), for a touch of low-light romance; **Mitali East,** 334 E. 6th St. (☎ 212/533-2508), the king of curry; and **Passage to India,** 308 E. 6th St. (☎ 212/529-5770), for North Indian tandoori. The Phyllis Diller of Little India, Christmas-light-bedecked **Rose of India,** 308 E. 6th St. (☎ 212/533-5011), used to be a kitschy favorite, but the food has been disappointing of late.

Around the corner—and a giant step up in quality—from Little India is ✪ **Haveli,** 100 Second Ave. (☎ 212/982-0533), where the authentically prepared dishes, setting, and service are far superior. Prices are steeper—$8.50 to $19—but the Haveli experience is worth the extra dough if you can afford the tab.

---

✪ **Frank.** 88 Second Ave. (btw. 5th and 6th sts.). ☎ **212/420-0202.** Reservations not accepted. Main courses $9–$14. No credit cards. Mon–Thurs 10:30am–4pm and 5pm–1am, Fri–Sat 10:30am–4pm and 5pm–2am, Sun 10:30am–midnight. Subway: 6 to Astor Place. ITALIAN.

These days, the first thought that pops into my mind when I try a new Italian restaurant is, "What would Tony Soprano think?" T would definitely give Frank the big thumbs up. This homestyle restaurant serves no-nonsense, straight-from-the-boot cuisine that's everything it should be. The menu is small but satisfying, focusing on what the kitchen knows they do well: Rigatoni al ragu wears a hearty meat-and-tomato "gravy" that's been slow-cooked to perfection. It appears again on the house specialty, the polpettone—literally "the big meatball"—a moist, beautifully seasoned mound of beef accompanied by a cheesy potato-and-pancetta gratin that's better than dessert in my book. The spaghetti with garlic and extra-virgin olive oil is a simple dish, but the pasta is ideally *al dente* and tossed to perfection with just the right bit of finely grated cheese; anchovy lovers (I know there must be more of you out there!) should go with the fishy version for supreme pleasure. There's always homemade gnocchi and ravioli, plus spiced meat loaf and a couple of fish dishes. The wine list is huge and well priced, with a good selection by the glass. The young waitstaff is easygoing and earnest, and the brick-walled room is dimly lit and attractive in a cozy, homey way. On the downside, the tables are so close together that you can't help but overhear your neighbors' conversation; the open kitchen can make the dining room rather smoky at times; and there's often a wait (although adjacent Vera, Frank's bar, now offers a place to while away the time with a glass of wine). But these minor inconveniences are well worth putting up with for the marvelous payoff that is Frank fare.

**La Paella.** 214 E. 9th St. (at Second Ave.). ☎ **212/598-4321.** Reservations accepted for 6 or more. Tapas $4.50–$9; paella for 2 $22–$36. MC, V. Sun–Thurs 5–11pm, Fri–Sat 5– 12:30pm. Subway: 6 to Astor Place. BASQUE/SPANISH.

La Paella's tapas are the best in town, and the paella can hardly be outdone. This is fun eating, the kind of place where patrons return again and again to wash down fish cro-quettes, chorizos, and green olives with bottles of chilled Negro Modela, a dark Mex-ican brew that goes well with the flavorful menu of (primarily) grilled delights, or the terrific sangria, served in generous pitchers by the frisky waitstaff, many of whom seem as though they just blew in from Madrid. Tapas here are more generously apportioned than at many other places; the grilled calamari is a perfectly sized appetizer without being overwhelming. Everything is well priced, but it's easy to run up a tab in the fes-tive setting, which tends to attract large parties after 8pm. There are two dining rooms: Upstairs is baroque-lite, with walls glazed to a gentle, earthen tone; a funkier, moodier, and more masculine vibe rules downstairs.

✪ **Pisces.** 95 Ave. A (at 6th St.). ☎ **212/260-6660.** Reservations recommended. Main courses $9–$20; 2-course prix-fixe dinner (Mon–Thurs 5:30–7pm, Fri–Sun 5:30–6:30pm) $15. AE, CB, DC, MC, V. Mon–Thurs 5:30–11:30pm, Fri 5:30pm–1am, Sat 11:30am–3:30pm and 5:30pm–1am, Sun 11:30am–3:30pm and 5:30–11:30pm. Subway: 6 to Astor Place; F to Sec-ond Ave. SEAFOOD.

This excellent fish house serves up the best inexpensive seafood in the city. All fish is top-quality and fresh daily, and all smoked items are prepared in the restaurant's own smoker. But it's the creative kitchen, which shows surprising skill with vegetables as well as fish, that makes Pisces a real winner. The mesquite-smoked whole trout in sherry oyster sauce is sublime, better than trout I've had for twice the price; start with the phyllo-fried shrimp or the tuna ceviche with curried potato chips and roasted pepper coulis, and the world is yours. Other winning dishes include flaky pan-fried skate in a burgundy reduction with garlicky mashed potatoes and roasted pearl onions. There are daily specials in addition to the menu; last time we dined here, I feasted on an excellent grilled mako shark with chard in a cockle stew. The wine list is appealing and very well priced, the decor suitably nautical without being kitschy, and the service friendly and attentive. For wallet-watchers, the early-bird prix-fixe makes an already terrific value even better. The Alphabet City locale gives Pisces serious hip, but it's laid-back enough that even Grandma will be comfortable here. Tables spill out onto the sidewalk on warm evenings, giving you a ringside seat for the funky East Village show.

**Roettele A.G.** 126 E. 7th St. (btw. First Ave. and Ave. A). ☎ **212/674-4140.** Reservations recommended, especially on weekends. Main courses $8–$17; fondue for 2 $32–$36. AE, DC, DISC, MC, V. Tues–Thurs 5:30–10:30pm, Fri 5:30–11:30pm, Sat noon–3pm and 5:30–11:30pm, Sun noon–3pm and 5:30–10pm. Subway: L to First Ave.; 6 to Astor Place. SWISS.

This snug Swiss chalet hideaway is a winner. The cheese fondue, a hearty dinner for two, is smooth and beautifully presented with crusty bread and fresh vegetables. Build your meal around it by supplementing with other Alpine and house specialties, such as air-dried beef, classic raclette and wienerschnitzl, duck liver mousse, and terrific sautéed wild mushrooms over fresh herbs and polenta—plus spaetzle on the side, of course. They stock Swiss and German wines and beers, plus a few French bottles; try the medium-bodied Spatenlager to help wash down all that melted cheese. In keeping with the theme, a wide selection of tempting French and German pastries are available. The only downside used to be harried service, but everything was perfect on my last visit. A real treat!

**Sandobe Sushi.** 330 E. 11th St. (btw. First and Second aves.). ☎ 212/780-0328. Reservations not accepted. À la carte sushi (2 pieces per order) $3.30–$5.50, sushi rolls $3.50–$6.75, sushi combos $9.75–$17.75. No credit cards. Mon–Sat 5pm–12:30am, Sun 5pm–midnight. Subway: 6 to Astor Place; L to First Ave. SUSHI.

This plain-Jane sushi joint offers the best price-to-quality ratio for bargain-hunting sushi lovers. It's almost always packed, but the efficient servers turn the tables over quickly, and the payoff is worth the wait. Take it from this sushi hound: You'll pay significantly more—and wait no less time—for sushi of this consistently high quality anywhere else in town. The fresh-off-the-boat fish is generously and expertly cut. The sushi combos are a good-value starting point; supplement with some sea-salty *edamame* (soy been pods) and a few of your favorites individual sushi pieces, or one or two of the creative house-special rolls, such as the Hawaiian (ruby-red tuna and real crabmeat). All in all, a stellar value.

**۞ Shabu Tatsu.** 216 E. 10th St. (btw. First and Second aves.). ☎ 212/477-2972. Reservations accepted for parties of 4 or more. Full shabu-shabu dinners for two $28–$39. AE, DC, DISC, MC, V. Daily 5pm–12:30am. Subway: L to First Ave., 6 to Astor Place. JAPANESE SHABU-SHABU.

This casual place features shabu-shabu, a dish you prepare yourself in the hotpot of boiling water built into the center of your table. The interactive excitement begins when the waiter brings a plate piled high with raw beef (turkey is also available), tofu, and vegetables and gives an introductory lesson on how to make "shabu." It's lots of fun poking into the pot with your chopsticks, watching your meat and veggies cook to your satisfaction, then dipping them in one of two sauces, one peanuty and the other a tart vinegar, soy, and scallion sauce. After you're done, noodles are piled in and the broth is turned into a yummy after-dinner soup. The food is fresh, high-quality, and appealing even to those who otherwise don't care for Japanese food. The pure entertainment value makes this a great place to take kids or a group and completely impractical for single diners. Duos can snare a table, but because you can't reserve ahead, don't be surprised if there's a wait; the restaurant is always busy, so it's best to go early or late.

Also on the Upper East Side at 1414 York Ave., at 75th Street (☎ 212/472-3322).

**۞ Soba-Ya.** 229 E. 9th St. (btw. Second and Third aves.). ☎ 212/533-6966. Reservations not accepted. Main courses $6.50–$14. AE, DC, DISC, JCB, MC, V. Daily noon–4pm and 5:30–10:30pm. Subway: 6 to Astor Place. JAPANESE NOODLES.

Shhh—don't tell anybody else about Soba-Ya. It has a loyal following, but the masses haven't discovered it yet. Good! That makes it easy to walk in and sit down to an affordable, healthful Japanese meal without a wait (the constant bane of Big Apple budget diners). Start with one of the special starters, which might be grilled shiitakes or luscious *toro* (tuna belly) sashimi, and then move on to one of the house specialties: generous, steaming noodle bowls. They come with *soba* (thin buckwheat) or udon (my favorite, a very thick noodle much like pasta) and in a number of combinations. A menu with descriptions and pictures makes it easy for noodle novices to order. I love the nabeyaki, an udon bowl with shrimp tempura, and the excellent-quality una-don, broiled eel over rice (even better than the one at Village Yokocho, below). Cold soba dishes topped with your choice of ingredients are also available. Everything is beautifully presented on delicate Japanese dishware, and there's a lengthy list of sakes to choose from. The lovely blond-wood dining room is blessed with a soothing, Zen-like vibe and the kind of attentive service that you usually have to pay more for.

**Time Cafe.** 380 Lafayette St. (at Great Jones St.). ☎ **212/533-7000.** www.feznyc.com. Reservations recommended on weekends. Main courses $4–$13.50 at breakfast and brunch, $7.50–$14 at lunch, $8–$22 at dinner; 2- to 3-course prix-fixe $16.50–$19.50 at lunch, $27.50–$47.50 at dinner. AE, MC, V. Mon–Thurs 8am–midnight, Fri 8am–1am, Sat 10:30am–1am, Sun 10:30am–midnight. Subway: 6 to Bleecker St.; B, D, F, Q to Broadway–Lafayette St. CONTEMPORARY AMERICAN.

This easygoing, attractive, and affordable spot can provide a night's entertainment or the ideal brunch. The menu features a large selection of contemporary fare with a healthy bent, such as a very good grilled rare tuna sandwich with organic daikon sprouts and sesame wasabi on seven-grain bread; herb-roasted free-range chicken with roasted garlic hominy grits and sauteed spinach; and a host of creative thin-crust pizzas. The food isn't the best in town but it's perfectly satisfying, and I like the health-minded preparations and the casual, laid-back vibe. I've spotted Michael Stipe here more than once. This branch has a wonderful Moroccan lounge and basement performance space called Fez (see chapter 9).

In addition to this one, there's also the Upper West Side variation, **Time Cafe North,** at 2330 Broadway, at 85th St. (☎ **212/579-5100**), which also has a Fez lounge for cocktails.

**Tsampa.** 212 E. 9th St. (btw. Second and Third aves.). ☎ **212/614-3226.** Reservations accepted. Main courses $9–$16 (most less than $13). AE, MC, V. Daily 5pm–11pm. Subway: 6 to Astor Place. TIBETAN.

Here's something you're unlikely to stumble across in your hometown: Tibetan food. It's light, wholesome, and vegetarian-friendly, prepared with filtered water and mostly organic produce, but not strictly vegetarian. Some of the dishes are a bit on the bland side (skip the boring curry, which doesn't deserve to be in the same room with a real one), but most are flavorfully spiced. Start with an order of momo, Tibet's signature dish, beautifully done here. Momo are steamed or fried dumplings stuffed with your choice of ingredients—from chicken and veggies to tofu and chives—and served with a pair of wonderfully spicy red and green hot sauces. A baked udon noodle dish makes a pleasing follow-up, as does the seasoned whole grilled fish and the *sherpa khala,* baby potatoes sauteed with chicken, fresh greens, garlic, and ginger and served with Tibetian bread. A relaxing, candlelit ambiance, and mature service makes Tsampa a good bet for budget-friendly romance.

**Veselka.** 144 Second Ave. (at 9th St.). ☎ **212/228-9682.** Reservations not accepted. Main courses $5–$13. AE, MC, V. Daily 24 hours. Subway: 6 to Astor Place. UKRAINIAN DINER.

Whenever the craving hits for hearty Eastern European fare at old-world prices, Veselka fits the bill with *pierogi* (small doughy envelopes filled with potatoes, cheese, or sauerkraut), *kasha varnishkes* (cracked buckwheat and noodles with mushroom sauce), stuffed cabbage, grilled polish kielbasa, freshly made potato pancakes, and classic soups such as a sublime scarlet borscht, voted best in the city by *The New York Times* and *New York* magazine. Try the buckwheat pancakes for a perfect breakfast or brunch. Despite the authentic fare, the diner is comfortable and appealing, with an artsy slant. Thanks to Veselka's we-never-close policy, it's a favorite after-hours hangout with club kids and other night owls.

**Village Yokocho.** 8 Stuyvesant St. (at Third Ave. and E. 9th St.), 2nd floor. ☎ **212/598-3041.** Reservations not accepted. Main courses $4–$12. AE, MC, V. Sun–Wed 5pm–2:40am; Thurs–Sat 5pm–3:40am. Subway: 6 to Astor Place. JAPANESE/KOREAN BBQ.

## Bargain Alert—Prix-Fixe Meal Deals

New York has one of the finest—and most expensive—dining scenes on the planet. Despite the fact that so many restaurants will think nothing of charging you upwards of $35 or $40 an entrée, these restaurants are not entirely off limits to budget travelers. If you want to dine in high style on a low-volume wallet, you just have to be a little creative about it. And the best time to be creative is at lunch.

**Restaurant Week**   Many of New York's best restaurants offer special prix-fixe lunches for a full week in late June (exact dates vary from year to year) at a cost mimicking the year (a flat $20 in 2000, probably $20.01 in—you guessed it—2001). It's an exceptional value, especially considering that lunch alone at some of these places can run upwards of $50 per person. Participating restaurants shift from year to year, but past participants have included **Jean Georges** (☎ 212/299-3900), **Union Square Cafe** (☎ 212/243-4020), **Aureole** (☎ 212/319-1660), **Le Cirque 2000** (☎ 212/303-7788), **Daniel** (☎ 212/288-0033), **Nobu** (☎ 212/219-0500), **Le Bernardin** (☎ 212/489-1515), and other *New York Times* 3- and 4-star winners.

There are catches, of course. The offer applies only for lunch, and most restaurants limit your selection to three choices per course. At some restaurants, you must eat at the bar or in a subsidiary room. Wine, tip, and tax are extra; occasionally you'll have to dine at a late hour, such as after 2pm.

If you think you might be visiting during Restaurant Week, be on the lookout for this year's schedule as early as mid-April. There's always a full spread in *The New York Times,* as well as announcements on the restaurant pages of online sources such as **www.newyork.citysearch.com**. If you catch the announcement, start dialing immediately, because many restaurants—particularly the most popular ones—book up instantly. Or just start calling the restaurants you're interested in and ask; many will even start taking reservations before the official announcement. (A good source for which pricey restaurants to call is Zagat's, online at **www.zagat.com**.)

A new winter version of this favorite summer event was instituted in 2000; look for another one in late January or early February of 2001.

Village Yokocho is about as authentic as Japanese restaurants get. Entering this casual second-floor spot feels just like stepping into a Tokyo yakitori bar, complete with a hip, young clientele that's a mix of Japanese and in-the-know Americans. Between the regular menu and the many handwritten sheets taped to the wall advertising the current specials, the choices are vast. Dishes run the gamut from familiar dumplings and yakisoba noodles to exotica such as deep-fried squid eggs. The generous broiled eel bowl is finer quality than eel you'll get at many sushi restaurants and a deal at $8. The barbecued yakitori skewers, both meat and veggie choices grilled over an open flame just behind the counter, are excellent. Korean dishes include flavorful oxtail soup and *bibinbop,* a hearty rice bowl topped with veggies, ground beef, and a fried egg. The specials change depending on what's in season and available, but you might find softshell crab in ponzu sauce, broiled yellowtail with teriyaki sauce, and any number of sashimi appetizers. There's a big, affordable sake menu as well as a choice of beers. At press time, late-nighters benefited from 50% off Korean barbecue Sunday through

**But What If I'm Going to Miss Restaurant Week?**    A number of superb restaurants maintain their Restaurant Week deal all summer long or offer a wallet-friendly lunchtime prix-fixe year-round. Four-star **Chanterelle** (☎ 212/966-6960; www.chanterellenyc.com) offers two daily prix-fixe lunches, one $20 and the other $35. **Gramercy Tavern** (☎ 212/477-0777) always offers a 3-course prix-fixe lunch for $36. **Gotham Bar & Grill** (☎ 212/620-4020) has been offering a hugely successful $20 prix-fixe lunch for years. The midday deal is just $29 at the legendary **"21" Club** (☎ 212/582-7200) and $22 at the legendary caviar house **Petrossian** (☎ 212/245-2214), where you'll pay a still-bargain-basement $39 if you want caviar. Upscale tavern **Molyvos** (☎ 212/582-7500) has a stellar 3-course meal for $22.50 that includes their wonderful baklava. Celebrity chef Jean-Georges Vongerichten's celebrated cuisine can be had for just $28 midday at French/Thai fusion stalwart **Vong** (☎ 212/486-9592).

If you're willing to slum it in the lounge, you can even enjoy a prix-fixe lunch at **Le Cirque 2000** (☎ 212/303-7788) for just $25 or **Daniel** (☎ 212/288-0033) for $36 (same-day reservations only).

**What About Dinner?**    Three of Midtown's best restaurants also offer three of its best pre-theater values. At elegant **San Domenico** (☎ 212/265-5959), the room is swanky, the service impeccable, and the Bolognese-inspired Italian some of the best in the city. The pre-theater prix fixe is just $32.50. Dazzling Greek seafooder **Estiatorio Milos** (☎ 212/245-7400) offers pre- and post-theater prix-fixe meals for just $32. For classic New York ambiance, there's no better place to dine than the aforementioned **"21" Club** (☎ 212/582-7200), favored dining room for the city's old-school business and celebrity power set, where the pre-theater prix-fixe is just $33.

So for foodies whose palettes are broader than their bank accounts, the lesson is this: Get on the horn and start calling, preferably before you come to town. Always ask when you're booking what the details of the prix fixe are; deals can change at any time, and you don't want any unpleasant surprises when you're already ensconced at your table. And if it's a pre-theater deal you're booking, specify when you book (if you're seated too late, you'll miss out).

Wednesday between midnight and 3am; call to see whether this or any other after-hours specials are on while you're in town.

## QUICK BITES

There's also **Burritoville** (p. 136), at 141 Second Ave., between St. Mark's Place and 9th Street (☎ 212/260-3300).

**Emerald Planet.** 2 Great Jones St. (at Broadway). ☎ 212/353-9727. www.emeraldplanet. citysearch.com. Wraps $4–$8. AE, MC, V. Mon–Fri 9am–10pm, Sat noon–10pm, Sun noon–8pm. Subway: 6 to Bleecker St.; N, R to 8th St. INTERNATIONAL.

This San Francisco import has lead the charge to bury the sandwich and replace it with the wrap, a phenomenon that has reached every mall in America by now. The Emerald Planet ideology is simple: You can eat wraps at every meal, from bacon and eggs (the Omaha) in the AM to fresh grilled veggies with goat cheese (the Sonoma) at noon to Jerk chicken, mango salsa, and jasmine rice (the Kingston) at dinner. The tortilla-like wrapping changes depending on the ingredients, from flour to whole wheat to tomato to spinach. All ingredients are fresh, and the emphasis is on healthy. Supplement your wrap with one of the champion smoothies. Or opt for a margarita, fresh-brewed iced tea, a latte from the espresso bar, fresh sangria, or one of the international bottled beers on offer. The decor is haute NoHo—wee dangling halogen lights, clean woody surfaces, rain forest–green walls—but don't be put off. This is one of Downtown's best stops for quick, quality chow; just ask Madonna, an Emerald Planet regular.

Look for a second location in Rockefeller Center, on the concourse at 30 Rockefeller Plaza (☎ 212/218-1133), by the time you arrive.

## 8  Greenwich Village

**Cafe Habana** (p. 145) has a second location at 11 Abingdon Square, on Eighth Avenue between West 12th and Bleecker streets (☎ 212/989-6883).

**Aggie's.** 146 W. Houston St. (at MacDougal St.). ☎ **212/673-8994.** Main courses $7–$13. MC, V. Mon–Thurs 8am–10pm, Fri 8am–11pm, Sat 10am–4pm and 6–11pm, Sun 10am–4pm. Subway: A, B, C, D, E, F, Q to W. 4th St. ECLECTIC.

This funky diner on the southern outskirts of the Village dishes up sandwiches, pastas, and simple American comfort food with a healthful gourmet bent—crab cakes, meat loaf, grilled portabellos, and duck stroganoff with black pepper sauce are favorites. Some complain that portions are not as generous as they were before Aggie's became hip, but they're still plenty big. The hearty breakfasts are especially pleasing; go early or expect a line on weekends.

✪ **Bar Pitti.** 268 Sixth Ave. (btw. Bleecker and Houston sts.). ☎ **212/982-3300.** Reservations only accepted for 4 or more. Main courses $6–$15 (some specials might be higher). No credit cards. Daily noon–midnight. Subway: A, B, C, D, E, F, Q to W. 4th St. (use 3rd St. exit). TUSCAN ITALIAN.

This indoor/outdoor Tuscan-style trattoria is a perennially hip sidewalk scene and one of Downtown's best dining bargains. Waiting for a table can be a chore (the wait list never seems very organized), but all is forgiven once you take a seat, thanks to authentic, affordably priced cuisine and some of the friendliest waiters in town. Despite the tightly packed seating, Bar Pitti wins you over with its rustic Italian charm; it's the kind of place where the waiter brings over the list of daily specials to your table on a well-worn blackboard, and if you want more cheese, a block of Parmesan and a grater suddenly appears. Peruse the laminated menu, but don't get your heart set on anything until you see the board, which boasts the best of what the kitchen has to offer; the last time we dined here, they wowed us with a fabulous veal meatball special. Winners off the regular menu, which focuses heavily on pastas and panini, include excellent rare beef carpaccio; grilled country bread with prosciutto, garlic, and olive oil; and spinach and ricotta ravioli in a creamy sage and Parmesan sauce. The all-Italian wine list is high-priced compared to the menu, but you'll find a few good value choices.

✪ **Corner Bistro.** 331 W. 4th St. (at Jane St., near Eighth Ave.). ☎ **212/242-9502.** Reservations not accepted. Burgers and sandwiches $2.50–$5. No credit cards. Mon–Sat 11am–4am, Sun noon–4am. Subway: A, C, E to 14th St. (go 2 blocks south on Eighth Ave.). BURGERS.

This unpretentious, old-time neighborhood bar serves up what some people (including Jon Stewart) consider the best burger in the city. The Corner Bistro's well-charred, beefy burgers are deservedly famous—and you'd be hard-pressed to dine so well for so

# Greenwich Village Dining

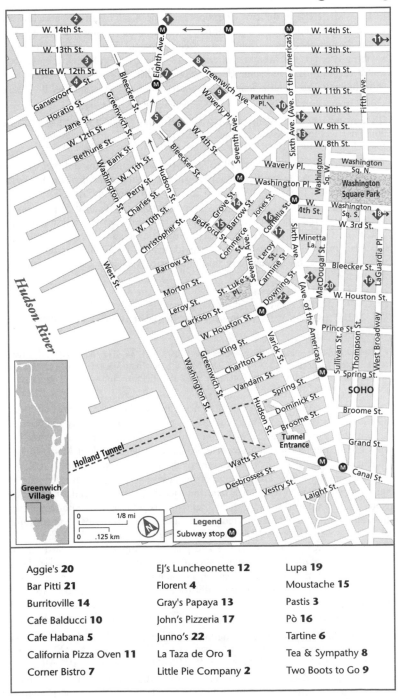

Aggie's **20**

Bar Pitti **21**

Burritoville **14**

Cafe Balducci **10**

Cafe Habana **5**

California Pizza Oven **11**

Corner Bistro **7**

EJ's Luncheonette **12**

Florent **4**

Gray's Papaya **13**

John's Pizzeria **17**

Junno's **22**

La Taza de Oro **1**

Little Pie Company **2**

Lupa **19**

Moustache **15**

Pastis **3**

Pò **16**

Tartine **6**

Tea & Sympathy **8**

Two Boots to Go **9**

little anywhere else in the city. The top of the line is the bistro burger, with bacon, cheese, lettuce, and tomato, for all of five bucks. The thin, crispy fries, served up on a crimped paper plate, are an appropriate accompaniment. Head elsewhere if you want anything else, because the other offerings are limited to a grilled chicken sandwich, grilled cheese, a BLT, and some chunky chili—all half-hearted at best, except for the chili. Beers on tap include Sam Adams, local McSorley's, and good ol' Bud. Service can be slow, but who's ever in a rush at a neighborhood local like this?

**EJ's Luncheonette.** 432 Sixth Ave. (btw. 9th and 10th sts.). ☎ **212/473-5555.** Reservations not accepted. Main courses $4–$12. AE. Sun–Thurs 10am–11pm, Fri–Sat 10am–11:30pm, Sun 10am–10:30pm. Subway: 6 to 77th St. AMERICAN DINER.

This retro diner is popular with all Village types, including yups and their kids, who come for hearty American fare in a 1950s setting—turquoise vinyl booths, Formica tabletops, a soda fountain, and a lunch counter with stools that spin. The menu features a large selection of breakfasts so good you won't be ashamed of indulging in a stack of banana-pecan pancakes for dinner. There's also a terrific selection of burgers (including a great veggie version), well-stuffed sandwiches, hearty green salads, and blue-plate main dishes such as meat loaf with mashed potatoes. Everything is better than you'd expect from a joint like this, and service is friendly. Don't miss the amazing sweet potato fries.

Also on the Upper West Side at 447 Amsterdam Ave., between 81st and 82nd streets (☎ **212/873-3444**), and on the Upper East Side, 1271 Third Ave., at 73rd (☎ **212/472-0660**). Weekend brunch is a big deal at all three locations, but expect a wait.

**✪ Junno's.** 64 Downing St. (btw. Bedford and Varick sts.). ☎ **212/627-7995.** Reservations not accepted. Main courses $8–$14. AE, DC, MC, V. Mon–Thurs 5:30pm–2am (kitchen closes at 11:30pm), Fri–Sat 5:30pm–4am (kitchen closes at midnight). Subway: 1, 9 to Houston St. JAPANESE FUSION.

Junno's is my second-favorite affordable newcomer of the year (behind Lupa, below). The sophisticated industrial-moderne space is painted a soothing gray and warmed by retro leather banquettes and a marvelous blue bar. Following the current trend, start with one of the inventive house cocktails, such as the Schoolgirl Martini (Absolut Kurant and Japanese plum wine, shaken) or the Tokyo (Maker's Mark, a dash of bitters, Sapporo dry draft). The Japanese fusion cuisine is very good, especially for those (like me) who favor creative Asian fare, and shockingly cheap considering the quality. Korea and France lend the most prominent accents. Among the standout starters are tuna tataki with fennel and gingered ponzu sauce and scrumptious sweet-shrimp ravioli in miso-mustard sauce. Mains of note include miso-marinated Spanish mackerel, served napoleon style with shiso rice and pickled cucumbers, and grilled marinated short ribs, served off the bone with a slightly tart sesame and scallion salad. Portions aren't stingy, but they're not huge, either, so you might want to order a starter and an entree even if that's not your normal habit (or three starters between the two of you if it is). Ginger crème brûlée is the best among the so-so desserts. Come early if you want to enjoy a quiet dinner, later in the evening if you want to revel in the party scene.

**✪ Lupa.** 170 Thompson St. (btw. Houston and Bleecker sts.). ☎ **212/982-5089.** Reservations recommended. Pastas $9–$12, main courses $11–$15. AE, DC, MC, V. Tues–Sun noon–3pm and 5:30–11:30pm. Subway: 1, 9 to Houston St. NORTHERN ITALIAN.

God bless Mario Batali, the one big-name chef in the city who thinks you shouldn't have to spend a fortune to eat like a king. *Molto Mario* on TV's Food Network and the man behind Babbo (above) launched this trattoria for regular folks in late 1999, and it's a winner. Reservations are taken for the back room only, and I strongly advise you to arrange for them if you can, because it's quieter and more civilized. The front room is reserved for walk-ins (to avoid the perpetual inaccessibility of Batali's always-packed first restaurant, Pó). It's loud and cramped and you'll probably have to wait for a table unless you come early, but so what? The food is worth it.

Don't be scared off by the all-Italian menu, as were a few folks on our first visit; the helpful, butcher-coated waiter will steer you through the language and preparations. It's a short list, but one that boasts lots of treats. As always with Mario, pastas, in particular, excel: The *bucatini all'Amatriciana,* a classic Italian tube pasta in a smoky tomato sauce made from hog jowl (bacon), is divine, as is the creamy ricotta gnocchi with Italian sausage and fennel. Lupa is also a *salumeria,* so don't miss an opportunity to start with the prosciutto di carpegna with roasted figs, an ideal marriage of salt and sweet. Among the mains, the classic saltimbocca was a disappointment, but the oven-roasted littleneck clams with sweet soppresata were a joy. Another delight: The wine list is massive and super-affordable.

**Moustache.** 90 Bedford St. (btw. Barrow and Grove sts.). ☎ **212/229-2220.** Reservations not accepted. Main dishes $5–$12. No credit cards. Daily noon–midnight (kitchen closes at 11:30pm). Subway: 1, 9 to Christopher St. MIDDLE EASTERN.

Moustache (pronounced moo-STAH-sh) is the sort of exotic neighborhood spot that's just right. On a quiet side street in the West Village, this charming hole-in-the-wall boasts a cozy Middle Eastern vibe and authentic fare that's both palate-pleasing and wallet-friendly. Delicately seasoned dishes bear little resemblance to the food at your average falafel joint. Expect subtly flavored hummus, tabbouleh, and spinach-chickpea-tomato salad (or a large plate of all three); excellent oven-roasted "pitzas," thin, matzoh-like pita crusts topped with spicy minced lamb and other savory ingredients; and—best of all—fluffy, hot-from-the-oven homemade pita bread, which puts any of those store-bought Frisbees to shame. Moustache is hugely and justifiably popular, so don't be surprised if there's a line—but it's well worth the wait.

A second Manhattan location is in the East Village at 265 E. 10th St., between First Avenue and Avenue A (☎ **212/228-2022**).

✪ **Pó.** 31 Cornelia St. (btw. Bleecker and W. 4th sts.). ☎ **212/645-2189.** Reservations highly recommended well in advance. Main courses $8–$10 at lunch, $12–$15 at dinner; tasting menu $21 at lunch, $35 at dinner. Tues 5:30–11pm, Wed–Thurs 11:30am–2:15pm and 5:30–11pm, Fri–Sat 11:30am–2:15pm and 5:30–11:30pm, Sun 11:30am–2:15pm and 5:30–10pm. AE. Subway: A, B, C, D, E, F, Q to W. 4th St. (use 3rd St. exit). ITALIAN.

Chef Mario Batali's zesty Italian food has attracted a lot of attention since he began appearing on TV's Food Network. Well, kudos to Mario for keeping Pó, his original outpost, real despite his burgeoning fame; it's well priced and justifiably popular. One of the nice things about Pó is that it's the kind of place where you'd enjoy celebrating a special occasion, yet you can still keep things affordable. Batali's pastas are unparalleled; even a simple white-bean ravioli in balsamic vinegar and browned butter takes on new, remarkable life in his kitchen. Other winning entrees include cavatelli with sage and three mushrooms (including stellar porcinis) and beautifully tender veal picatta with baby artichokes. The wine list is surprisingly affordable, and the service appealingly old world despite the hip address. The only downsides are that the pretty, narrow room is too tightly packed and smoking is allowed at the bar (a little too close to some dining tables in my view). Still, Pó is more romantic and quintessentially Greenwich Village in personality than the newer Lupa (see above). Call well ahead—a month to the day if you can—because Pó is perpetually booked.

**Tartine.** 253 W. 11th St. (at W. 4th St.). ☎ **212/229-2611.** Reservations not accepted. Main courses $8–$16. No credit cards. Tues–Sun 8:30am–10:30pm. Subway: 1, 2, 3, 9 to 14th St. FRENCH BISTRO.

Tucked away on a leafy corner in the West Village, this authentic French bistro and BYOB stalwart (no corkage fee) has been cooking up first-rate chicken pot pies and croque monsieurs for a friendly crowd for more than a decade. Packed at lunch, and then packed again from 7pm until closing, Tartine is famous for its mignonettes of beef, served with a mountain of delectable golden frites. The food (including made-on-the-premises bread and baked goods) is so good that crowds are willing to put up with long lines and harried service. The only way to avoid the wait is to arrive early; otherwise, be prepared to hang around for an hour, but the line can actually be enjoyable on nice evenings.

**Tea & Sympathy.** 108 Greenwich Ave. (btw. 12th and 13th sts.). ☎ **212/807-8329.** Reservations not accepted. Main courses $5.50–$12 at lunch and brunch, $10.50–$17 at dinner; full afternoon tea $18 ($32 for 2). No credit cards. Mon–Fri 11:30am–10pm, Sat–Sun 10am–10pm. Subway: A, C, E, 1, 2, 3, 9 to 14th St. BRITISH.

When Londoner Nicky Perry moved to New York, she was disappointed to find no proper British tearoom where she could get a decent cup, so she opened her own in the heart of the West Village. Tea & Sympathy seems as if it was transplanted wholesale from Greenwich or Highgate, complete with oddball collection of creamers and teapots, snappy British waitstaff, and plenty of old-time charm. Elbow room is at a minimum, but it's worth the squeeze for the full afternoon tea, which comes on a tiered tray with trimmed-crust finger sandwiches such as hearty chicken salad and egg and 'cress, scones with jam and Devonshire cream, and cakes and cookies for a sugary finish. The menu also features such traditional British comforts as shepherd's pie, bangers and mash, and a savory chicken and leek pie. Anglophiles line up for the Sunday dinner—roast beef and Yorkshire pudding, of course. For dessert, try the treacle pudding, warm ginger cake, or the yummy sherry trifle. Next door is a cute shop selling Cadbury Flake bars, Hob Nob biscuits, and other imported English groceries and trinkets.

## QUICK BITES

Ask any New Yorker—one of the cheapest, most satisfying meals to be had in the city is the $1.95 two-dogs-and-drink deal from ✪ **Gray's Papaya,** 402 Sixth Ave., at 8th Street (☎ **212/260-3532**). This legendary storefront hot-dog stand hawks nothing but all-beef dogs, crispy thin fries, and your choice of tropical-flavored fruit drinks ranging from piña colada to Orange Julius–style OJ. The permanent "Recession Special" is $1.95 for two dogs and a drink—a bargain in any economic climate. Best of all, you can indulge in a Gray's frank and juice at any hour, because they never close.

Gourmet grocer **Dean & Deluca** has a cafe at 11th Street and University Place (☎ **212/473-1908**), which makes a great stop for a well-made sandwich or afternoon cafe au lait and pastry.

There's a nice branch of **Burritoville** (p. 136) at 298 Bleecker St., at Seventh Avenue (☎ **212/633-9249**).

**Cafe Balducci.** 445–447 Sixth Ave. (at 10th St.). ☎ **212/673-6369.** Reservations not accepted. Breakfast $4.75–$7, salads and sandwiches $4.50–$11. AE, DISC, MC, V. Mon–Fri 7:30am–8:30pm, Sat–Sun 11:30am–8:30pm. Subway: A, B, C, D, E, F, Q to W. 4th St. (use 8th St. exit). GOURMET DELI.

Manhattan's best gourmet grocer, Balducci's (see chapter 8) also operates this gourmet cafeteria-style cafe, which allows you to enjoy the market's bounty without forcing you

## Pizza! Pizza!

In the mood for a slice or two . . . or three? The Village is the perfect place to be. The original location of **John's Pizzeria** (p. 168), 278 Bleecker St. between Sixth and Seventh avenues (☎ 212/243-1680), is a New York original and still one of the city's best. The pies are thin-crusted, properly sauced, and fresh and served up piping hot in an authentic old-world setting. Sorry, no slices.

For something more funky, head to **Two Boots to Go,** 201 W. 11th St., at Seventh Avenue (☎ 212/633-9096), or **Two Boots to Go-Go,** 74 Bleecker St., at Broadway (☎ 212/777-1033), where creative variations on the traditional pie are precisely the point: Consider the Larry Tate, a "bewitching" blend (not my joke) of spinach, garlic, and fresh tomatoes on a white pie; or the Bayou Beast, with BBQ shrimp, andouille sausage, crawfish, and jalepeños. Both are predominately takeout and delivery locations, but there are a few tiny tables for in-house eaters.

---

to go the takeout route. You can order from the extensive and first-rate selection of prepared foods (including a great selection of soups) and hearty made-to-order sandwiches and salads, and enjoy your meal right at one of the pleasant tables. Fresh-from-the-oven pastries, breakfast paninis, and egg dishes make this a terrific spot to pore over the morning paper or sketch out your day's activities.

# 9  Chelsea & the Meat-Packing District

**Bendix Diner.** 219 Eighth Ave. (at 21st St.). ☎ 212/366-0560. Main courses $4.50–$15 (most less than $10). AE, MC, V. Tues–Sat 8am–1am, Sun–Mon 8am–11pm. Subway: C, E to 23rd St. AMERICAN DINER/THAI.

For the same reason that it's just plain wrong to order healthy at Bob's Big Boy when you're on a road trip, it's nutty to go for the gentler side of the menu at this funky Chelsea stalwart. Ignore the bizarro Thai dishes (head to a real Thai restaurant for pad thai and curries) and indulge in the big, patriotic, all-American grub. The burgers are served deluxe with a heap of French fries, the chili con carne (over rice with onions, peppers, and cheese) is heavy with beef and beans, and the meat loaf and mashed potatoes are better than Ma used to make. I love the chicken noodle soup, with its richer-than-usual broth (no bouillon cubes here, brother). Breakfast is available any time of day, and it's as hearty and wholesome as you'd expect. Sunday brunch gets alarmingly crowded, so bring a chunk of the *Times* to tide you over.

Also in the East Village at 167 First Avenue, between 10th and 11th streets (☎ 212/260-4220).

**The Dish.** 201 Eighth Ave. (btw. 20th and 21st sts.). ☎ 212/352-9800. Reservations not accepted. Breakfast $3.50–$9.25, sandwiches $3.50–$20.25, $7.25–$19 at dinner. AE, DC, DISC, MC, V. Daily 8am–2am. Subway: C, E to 23rd St. AMERICAN.

When the brunch lines are out the door at high-profile Bendix or Empire, do what savvy locals do: Skirt over to the Dish, a nice neighborhood diner/restaurant that's more pleasingly reliable than eternally hip. The room is spacious and nice, with high ceilings and brick walls adorned with black-and-white cityscapes. There's a sophisticated side to the menu, but it's easy to keep it cheap with generous omelets, french toast, and fresh-baked muffins to start the day or burgers, gourmet sandwiches, homemade chili and soups, and good hearty salads at lunch and dinner.

**Empire Diner.** 210 Tenth Ave. (at 22nd St.). ☎ **212/243-2736.** Reservations not accepted. Main courses $9–$18. AE, CB, DC, DISC, MC, V. Daily 24 hours. Subway: C, E to 23rd St. AMERICAN DINER.

Used to be that the Empire was the only thing doing this far west in Chelsea, but the emergence of the gallery and club scene in this area has raised the neighborhood's profile a few notches. Not that it matters in this throwback shrine to the slicked-up all-American diner, which looks suspiciously like an Airstream camper plunked down on the corner. The food is basic diner fare: eggs, omelets, burgers, overstuffed sandwiches, and a very nice turkey platter. Frankly, I think the Empire Diner is overrated—you'll find better breakfast fare elsewhere—but there's no denying its permanent status as a hot-spot fixture on the late-night scene. If you want an eyeful, 1 to 3am offers the best people-watching, when Prada and Gucci meld with Phat Farm and Levi's. There's live music courtesy of a pianist regularly. When the weather's warm, a pleasing sidewalk cafe appears, and the limited traffic this far over—mostly aiming for the Lincoln Tunnel—keeps the soot-and-fumes factor down.

**✪ Florent.** 69 Gansevoort St. (2 blocks south of 14th St. and 1 block west of Ninth Ave., btw. Greenwich and Washington sts.). ☎ **212/989-5779.** Reservations recommended for dinner. Main courses $4–$14.50 at brunch and lunch, $8–$19.50 at dinner; 2-course lunch prix-fixe $7.25–$11, 3-course dinner prix-fixe $17.50 before 7:30pm, $19.50 7:30pm–midnight. No credit cards. Mon–Fri 9am–5am, Sat–Sun 24 hours. Subway: A, C, E, L to 14th St. FRENCH BISTRO/DINER.

So you get a craving at 3am for homemade rillettes, boudin noir, or steak frites and can't decide whether you'd like to eat with club kids, partying celebrities, cross-dressed revelers, truckers from Jersey, or the odd stockbroker? Then get thee down to Florent, the nearly 24-hour French bistro dressed up as a 50s-style diner, where you can have it all. Located in the Meat-Packing District, Florent is a perennial hotspot no matter what the time of day; a kid's menu makes this the perfect place to bring the tykes for lunch or early dinner. But it's after the clubs close that the joint really jumps. Tables are tightly packed, almost uncomfortably so in some cases, but it's all part of the late-night festivities. This place has a real sense of humor (check out the menu boards above the bar) and a CD catalog that adds to the hipster fun. The food's good, too: The grilled chicken with herbs and mustard sauce is a winner, moist and flavorful, as is the french onion soup crowned with melted gruyere. There are always diner faves such as burgers and chili in addition to Gallic standards such as moules frites, and comfort food specialties such as chicken pot pie make regular appearances. Try not to miss the fries, which are light, crispy, and addictive.

**✪ Grand Sichuan Restaurant.** 229 Ninth Ave. (at 24th St.). ☎ **212/620-5200.** Reservations accepted for parties of more than 2. Main courses $3.25–$14; lunch special $4.50, dinner special $6.25. AE, DC, MC, V. Daily 11:30am–11pm. Subway: C, E to 23rd St. SZECHUAN CHINESE.

There's no need to head to Chinatown; Grand Sichuan serves up the real thing right here in Chelsea. This comfortable spot has garnered rave reviews from restaurant reviewers galore for its authentic Szechuan cuisine. Spicy-food lovers will be particularly thrilled, as the kitchen excels at dishes that are intensely spiced without being palate numbing—a brilliant culinary balance that few Chinatown kitchens can achieve. The flavors are complex and strong, especially in such top choices as Szechuan wontons in red oil, Chairman Mao's pork with chestnuts, and my favorite, boneless whole fish with pinenuts in a modified sweet-and-sour sauce. The house bean curd in spicy sauce is another winner, but only for those with a high tolerance for hot. Other terrific surprises include the sauteed loofah, a squashlike vegetable served in a variation on an oyster sauce—excellent. If some in your party shy away from hot and spicy, never fear: The staff will be more than happy to recommend milder dishes.

**La Taza de Oro.** 96 Eighth Ave. (btw. 14th and 15th sts.). ☎ **212/243-9946.** Main courses $5–$11. No credit cards. Mon–Sat 6am–11pm. Subway: A, C, E to 14th St. PUERTO RICAN.

This brightly lit luncheonette serves up some of the best and most authentic Latin American food in the city. Tuned-in locals know you won't find better, or better-priced, *chutelas fritas* (fried pork chops—and say yes to the garlic). *Mondongo* is a delicious rendering of traditional tripe soup. If that's just a bit too adventurous for you, try the beef stew (*carne guisada*), which is slow-cooked until meltingly tender. The squid and shrimp dishes are always supple, never rubbery, and the chicken is perfectly roasted. All the dishes are super flavorful without being overwhelming. Portions are huge, and most come with huge portions of red beans and yellow rice. Service is exuberant and efficient. The desserts are limited and there's no beer, just soda; the cafe con leche is great. *¡Que bien!*

## QUICK BITES

At Chelsea Market, 75 Ninth Ave., between 15th and 16th streets, a second branch of **Amy's Bread** (p. 173) has cafe tables where you can enjoy a light bite for breakfast or lunch. **Burritoville** (p. 136) is at 264 W. 23rd St., between Seventh and Eighth avenues (☎ 212/367-9844).

There's also the wonderful **Little Pie Company** at 407 W. 14th Street, just west of Ninth Avenue (☎ 212/414-2324), where you can enjoy a slice of one of the classic pies and cakes, which many consider New York's best, at a cafe table and counter stool.

## WORTH A SPLURGE

**Pastis.** 9 Ninth Ave. (at Little W. 12th St.). ☎ **212/929-4844.** Reservations accepted for 6–7pm seatings. Salads and sandwiches $9–$14, main courses $12–$18. AE, MC, V. Mon–Thurs 9am–5pm and 6pm–2am, Fri 9am–5pm and 6pm–3am, Sat 9am–4pm and 6pm–3am, Sun 9am–4pm and 6pm–2am. Subway: A, C, E to 14th St. FRENCH BISTRO.

Pastis is a spitting image of big sister hotspot Balthazar—complete with straight-from-the–Left Bank decor, classic bistro fare, ridiculously close tables, and the noise level of a Metallica show. Still, I like Pastis a lot better; frankly, the wallet-friendlier prices make the annoyances much easier to put up with. The food is terrific. The *rillettes fermière,* a thick-cut rabbit pate served with greens and toasts, makes a hearty starter, and the nicely seasoned grilled octopus with white beans is a great choice for lighter tastes. On my last visit, the plat du jour was *poulet a la crème*—a comforting Gallic TV dinner in a crock pot, complete with super-moist roast chicken, veggies, and rice. The steak frites with rich bearnaise is a classic, as it should be in a place like this. Plenty of good, affordable wines are available by the carafe (don't make the mistake we did and order a half-carafe, which was only $4 less than the full). The crepes Suzette are a delightful finish.

Your best bet is to dine early, when you can make a reservation (accepted for 6, 6:30, and 7pm seatings). Or come for weekday breakfast or lunch, when things are quieter and cheaper. Otherwise, expect to pony up to the bar and wait awhile; the fashionable crowd makes for great people-watching.

## 10  The Flatiron District, Union Square & Gramercy Park

**Chat 'n' Chew.** 10 E. 16th St. (btw. Fifth Ave. and Union Sq. W.). ☎ **212/243-1616.** Reservations not accepted. Sandwiches $6–$11, main courses $7–$13. AE, MC, V. Mon–Thurs 11:30am–11pm, Fri 11:30am–11:30pm, Sat 10am–11:30pm, Sun 10am–10pm. Subway: L, N, R, 4, 5, 6 to 14th St./Union Sq. AMERICAN.

Looking for a decent place to get an honest square meal that won't break the bank or leave you hungry? Then head to Chat 'n' Chew, a cute little hole in the wall that excels at down-home American cooking. In fact, the space is so down-homey that it's on the brink of becoming a theme restaurant, but the chow's the real thing. Look for honey-dipped fried chicken, roast turkey with all the fixins, BBQ pork chops with skin-on mashed potatoes, and mac 'n' cheese that's as crispy on the outside and gooey on the inside as it should be. There are a few unnecessary nods to contemporary tastes—if you're looking for grilled tuna, you don't belong here!—but the only real misstep I can see is the meat loaf, which was a bready disappointment. Weekend brunch sees such standards as hot oatmeal with brown sugar and hearty three-egg omelets with honey-baked ham on the side. Portions are all Hungry Man–sized, service is snappy, and beer's available to wash it all down. Desserts are of the Duncan Hines layer-cake variety (just like Ma used to make!), and the soda fountain serves up everything from egg creams to Haagen Dazs shakes. The crowd mainly consists of the very young and hip (the kind that can afford to throw caution to the wind when it comes to calories), but everyone will feel perfectly welcome.

**Coffee Shop.** 29 Union Sq. W. (at 16th St.). ☎ **212/243-7969.** Reservations accepted for 6 or more. Main courses $8–$17. AE, MC, V. Mon 7am–2am, Tues–Fri 7am–5am, Sat 8am–5:30am, Sun 8am–2am. Subway: L, N, R, 4, 5, 6 to 14th St./Union Sq. AMERICAN/ BRAZILIAN.

There are worse ways to spend a sunny afternoon than sitting at a sidewalk table at the Coffee Shop, watching the world go by while chowing down on a Brazilian *feijoada* (pork and bean stew), a *churrasquino carioca* (steak sandwich topped with peppers and onions), a Sonia Braga sandwich (chicken salad in a flour tortilla with papaya and cashews), or a good old burger (beef, turkey, or veggie—your choice) with a side of excellently crisped fries. The barbecued chicken sandwich with nonfat cilantro-lime mayonnaise will keep you trim and satisfied. The food isn't anything special, but it's not hard to see why this spirited perch, situated just across the street from Union Square Park, is a magnet for models, club kids, and scores of celebrities. Of course, its own celebrity can make it hard to get a seat here on a balmy summer day. But the inside space is pleasant as well, with funky 1950s lamps and sleek chrome touches. The service can be a roll of the dice, so come with a nonchalant attitude and just enjoy the affordable food and the pretty scene. Also inside is the World Room, which serves up exotic cocktails and a party scene into the wee hours.

**✪ Old Town Bar & Restaurant.** 45 E. 18th St. (btw. Broadway and Park Ave. South). ☎ **212/529-6732.** Reservations unnecessary. Main courses $6–$15. AE, MC, V. Mon–Sat 11:30am–1am (kitchen closes at 11:30pm), Sun 11:30am–10:30pm. Subway: 4, 5, 6, L, N, R to 14th St./Union Sq. AMERICAN.

If you've watched TV at all over the last couple of decades, this place should look familiar: It was featured nightly in the old *Late Night with David Letterman* intro, starred as Riff's Bar in *Mad About You,* and appeared in too many commercials to count, as well as in such movies as *The Devil's Own* and Woody Allen's *Bullets Over*

*Broadway.* But this is no stage set; it's a genuine tin-ceilinged 19th-century bar serving up good pub grub, lots of beers on tap, and a real sense of New York history. Sure, there are healthy salads on the menu, but everybody comes for the burgers. Whether you go low-fat turkey or bacon-chili-cheddar, they're perfect every time. You have your choice of sides, but go with the shoestring fries; what else in a traditional place like this? Other good choices include spicy Buffalo wings with bleu cheese, fiery bowls of chili sprinkled with cheddar cheese and dollopped with sour cream, and a Herculean Caesar salad slathered with mayo and topped with anchovies. Food comes up from the basement kitchen courtesy of ancient dumbwaiters behind the bar, where equally crusty bartenders would rather *not* make you a Cosmopolitan, thank you very much. If you want to escape the cigarettes and the predatory singles scene that pulls in on weekends, head upstairs to the blissfully smoke-free dining room.

**Republic.** 37 Union Sq. West (btw. 16th and 17th sts.). ☎ **212/627-7172.** Reservations accepted only for parties of 10 or more. Main courses $6–$9. AE, MC, V. Sun–Wed noon–11pm, Thurs–Sat noon–midnight. Subway: L, N, R, 4, 5, 6 to 14th St./Union Sq. PAN-ASIAN NOODLES.

Proving once and for all that you don't have to sacrifice high style for wallet-friendly prices, this ultra-chic noodle joint serves up affordable fast food in an area where it's getting harder and harder to find a deal. Cushionless, backless benches pulled up to pine-and-steel refectory tables don't encourage lingering, but that's precisely the point: This is the kind of place that knows how to make you feel hip and happy and get you out the door efficiently. The Chinese-, Vietnamese-, and Thai-inspired noodle menu attracts a steady stream of impossibly chic on-the-go customers. For a one-bowl meal, try the spicy coconut chicken (chicken slices in coconut milk, lime juice, lemongrass, and galangal) or spicy beef (rare beef with wheat noodles in spiced with chiles, garlic, and lemongrass). The long curving bar is perfect for solitary diners.

**Zen Palate.** 34 Union Square East (at 16th St.). ☎ **212/614-9345.** www.zenpalate.com. Reservations recommended. Main courses $7–$17; lunch specials $6–$9. AE, DC, MC, V. Mon–Thurs 11am–11pm, Fri–Sat 11am–midnight, Sun noon–10:30pm. Subway: L, N, R, 4, 5, 6 to 14th St./Union Sq. PAN-ASIAN VEGETARIAN.

The hallmark of Asian dining has long been the health factor, particularly with so many vegetarian dishes (MSG notwithstanding). This might not be true of old-school Chinese, with its viscous sauces, but it certainly is of Zen Palate, which has adopted the less-is-more approach to Asian cuisine. Each location shares the same Japanese-influenced postmodern decor, with teak and patinaed copper governing the aesthetic; the Union Square flagship is a standout, with a long counter downstairs for on-the-run eaters and a warren of spare but attractive dining rooms upstairs, including some with Japanese-style seating. Tofu is king here, but you're not limited to it. Stars on the wide-ranging menu include taro spring rolls and basil moo-shu rolls for something creative, as well as steamed veggie dumplings and buns for a more traditional Asian choice. Despite the good-for-you approach, main courses such as Rose Petals (home-made soy pasta in a sweet rice ginger sauce with garden vegetables) and Curry Supreme (with tofu, potatoes, and carrots) are very flavorful, and some will particularly appeal to spicy food lovers. All in all, a good bet for health-minded diners. Lest it all sound too good for you, you're welcome to BYOB with no corkage fee in the upstairs dining room.

Also at 663 Ninth Ave., at 46th Street in midtown (☎ **212/582-1669**), and Uptown at 2170 Broadway, between 76th and 77th streets (☎ **212/501-7768**).

## Pizza! Pizza!

**Pintaile's Pizza,** 124 Fourth Ave., between 12th and 13th streets (☎ 212/475-4977; www.pintailespizza.com), dresses their daintily crisp organic crusts with layers of plum tomatoes, extra virgin olive oil, and other fabulously fresh ingredients. This new branch of the Upper East Side favorite even has lots of seating for in-house eating.

Also in the Union Square neighborhood is **California Pizza Oven,** at 122 University Place, between 13th and 14th streets (☎ 212/989-4225), which cooks their thin-crust brick-oven pizzas over hickory and cherry wood, imbuing them with a rich, smoky flavor and topping them with everything from pepperoni and Italian sausage to goat cheese and baby eggplant. A line of tables near the hearth make a cozy spot to enjoy a quick slice.

## QUICK BITES

A great choice for a sinful pastry (I just love the tea cake) or a well-made salad or sandwich is **Eureka Joe,** 168 Fifth Ave., at 22nd Street (☎ 212/741-7500). One of my favorite coffeehouses in the city, Eureka Joe boasts comfy sofa nooks and a loungey, stay-as-long-as you want vibe, plus a wine and beer bar and live music or readings in the evenings.

## WORTH A SPLURGE

**The Tavern Room at Gramercy Tavern.** 42 E. 20th St. (btw. Broadway and Park Ave. South). ☎ **212/477-0777.** Reservations not accepted. Starters $6–$9.50, main courses $12.50–$18. AE, DC, MC, V. Mon–Thurs and Sun noon–11pm; Fri–Sat noon–midnight. Subway: 6, N, R to 23rd St. CONTEMPORARY AMERICAN.

Unquestionably, Gramercy Tavern's main dining room is one of New York's finest. However, dining there requires reservations weeks in advance and deep, deep pockets. Not so in the front Tavern Room, a friendly, informal bistro-style alternative where you can decide to eat at the last minute and still dine on some of the best food in town—without breaking the bank in the process. The compact but immensely appealing menu offers a lighter, more casual take on Chef Tom Colicchio's excellent, creative American fare. I love the perfectly roasted baby chicken with butternut squash succotash; nobody in town does chicken better. And where else are you going to get a filet mignon this good for less than $20? There's a good selection of salads, a terrific tomato garlic-bread soup, and a handful of fish dishes and sandwiches for lighter eaters, plus the restaurant's signature selection of cheeses and desserts. The room is very comfortable, with well-spaced tables and a pleasant energy that still allows for conversation; owner Danny Meyer's blanket no-smoking policy prevents any second-hand smoke from interfering with your meal. Service is top-notch, too. All in all, one of the best dining values in town.

## 11 Times Square & Midtown West

Even uninitiated palates will appreciate the Asian-nouvelle vegetarian cuisine at stylish **Zen Palate** (p. 163), at 663 Ninth Ave., at 46th Street (☎ 212/582-1669). **Joe's Shanghai** (p. 140) has a Midtown branch at 24 W. 56th St., just west of Fifth Avenue (☎ 212/333-3868), but expect to pay a bit more here than you would at the Chinatown location.

**Afghan Kebab House.** 764 Ninth Ave. (btw. 51st and 52nd sts.). ☎ **212/307-1612** or 212/307-1629. Reservations accepted. Main courses $7–$12. No credit cards. Mon–Sat 11am–11pm. Subway: C, E to 50th St. MIDDLE EASTERN.

Bring your own bottle of wine or six-pack (there's a liquor store just across the street) and dig into heaping plates of first-rate Indian-accented Middle Eastern fare. Kebabs are the first order of business: All are pleasing, but my favorite is the sultani, chunks and ground lamb marinated in aromatic spices and broiled over wood charcoal with green peppers and tomatoes. The tikka kebabs—lamb and beef—are also impressive, as is the chicken korma, slow-cooked with fresh onions, tomatoes, peppers, and fresh herbs. All plates come with brown Indian basmati rice and flat Afghan bread. The veggie dishes make great sides. The room is simple and well worn but evocative, with Oriental carpets serving as table runners, and service is attentive. A wallet-friendly winner!

**Chanpen.** 761 Ninth Ave. (at 51st St.). ☎ **212/586-6808.** Reservations accepted for dinner Sun–Thurs. Main courses $8–$15; lunch special (Mon–Fri 11:30am–3pm) $7–$8. AE, MC, V. Sun–Thurs 11:30am–10:30pm, Fri–Sat 11:30am–11:30pm. Subway: C, E to 50th St. THAI.

This charming restaurant serves bold Thai food at Chinatown prices. It's a tad cheaper than nearby Siam Inn Too (see below), especially at lunch, when Siam Inn caters to a middle-management crowd; Chanpen's lunch specials are remarkable values that draw savvy worker bees from throughout the neighborhood. In addition to the wallet-friendly prices, you'll be pleased by the bright dining room, the pleasant and attentive service, and the classic preparations of all the familiar Thai favorites.

**Hamburger Harry's.** 145 W. 45th St. (btw. Sixth and Seventh aves.). ☎ **212/840-0566.** Reservations recommended for large groups. Burgers, sandwiches, and burritos $7.50–$10; other main courses $11.50–$16. AE, CB, DC, DISC, MC, V. Mon–Thurs 11:30am–11pm, Fri–Sat 11:30am–11:30pm, Sun noon–7pm. Subway: N, R, S, 1, 2, 3, 7, 9 to 42nd St./Times Sq. AMERICAN/BURGERS.

Harry's is the perfect stop for everyday refueling at the right price. The casual, pleasant restaurant has distinguished itself by turning out delicious 7-ounce mesquite-grilled burgers that are the best in Times Square. Served with curlicue fries, homemade potato salad, or Harry's coleslaw, burger platters are a belly-busting bargain. They come in a range of varieties, from plain and simple to the Ha Ha Burger, topped with Texas chili, cheddar cheese, onion, guacamole, and pico de gallo. There are turkey and veggie versions for waist-watchers, too, as well as chicken breast sandwiches, fajitas, southwest-style burritos, Cajun catfish, and New York steak. A great place to take the kids; you can even finish off with an old-fashioned hot fudge sundae. Grown-up wallet-watchers might want to belly up to the bar weekdays between 4 and 7pm, when you can nosh on chicken wings, mozzarella sticks, and onion rings, and other politically incorrect munchies for half-price.

✪ **Island Burgers & Shakes.** 766 Ninth Ave. (btw. 51st and 52nd sts.). ☎ **212/307-7934.** www.island.citysearch.com. Reservations not accepted. Sandwiches and salads $5.25–$9. No credit cards. Sat–Thurs noon–10:30pm, Fri noon–11pm. Subway: C, E to 50th St. GOURMET BURGERS/SANDWICHES.

This excellent aisle-sized diner glows with the wild colors of a California surf shop. A small selection of sandwiches and salads are on hand, but as the name implies, folks come here for the Goliath-sized burgers—either beef hamburgers or, the house specialty, *churascos* (flattened grilled chicken breasts). Innovation strikes with the more than 40 topping combinations, from the horseradish, sour cream, and black pepper burger to the Hobie's (with black pepper sauce, bleu cheese, onion, and bacon).

# Midtown Dining

Afghan Kebab House **19**
Amy's Bread **39** & **71**
Bagel & Bean **11**
Bendix Diner **66**
B. Frites **23**
The British Open **3**
Burritoville **44, 46** & **65**
California Pizza Oven **58**
Canova Market **24**
Carmine's **49**
Carnegie Deli **12**
Chanpen **20**
Chat 'n' Chew **60**
Coffee Shop **59**
Dean & Deluca **30** & **37**
The Dish **67**
Empire Diner **65**
ESPN Zone **33**
Ess-A-Bagel **26** & **56**
Eureka Joe **64**
Grand Sichuan Restaurant **68**
H&H Bagel **42**
Hamburger Harry's **32**
Hard Rock Cafe **14**
Harley-Davidson Cafe **10**
Island Burgers & Shakes **19**
Jackson Hole **51**
Joe Allen **38**
Joe's Shanghai **5**
John's Pizzeria **1, 2** & **48**
Katsu-Hama **28**
La Bonne Soupe **7**
La Crepe de Bretagne **8**
La Taza de Oro **72**
Lemon Tree Cafe **20**
Little Pie Company **69**
Los Dos Rancheros Mexicanos **45**
Mangia **9** & **29**
Manhattan Chili Co. **17** & **34**
Mars 2112 **22**
Meskerem **40**
New Madras Palace **54**
Official All-Star Cafe **36**
Old Town Bar & Restaurant **62**
Oyster Bar & Restaurant **27**
Papaya King **47**
Pastis **70**
Pietrasanta **41**
Planet Hollywood **13**
Pongal **53**
Prime Burger **25**
The Pump **6** & **52**
Republic **61**
Rice 'n' Beans **21**
Sapporo **31**
Serendipity 3 **4**
Siam Inn Too **18**
66 Cafe **16**
Soup Kitchen International **15**
Stage Deli **11**
Taco & Tortilla King **55**
The Tavern Room at Gramercy Tavern **63**
Virgil's Real BBQ **35**
WWF New York **50**
Zen Palate **43** & **57**

166

## The Midtown Deli News

If you're in Midtown and looking for one of the Big Apple's quintessential Jewish delis, head to the **Stage Deli,** 834 Seventh Ave., between 53rd and 54th streets (☎ 212/245-7850; www.stagedeli.com), known for its jaw-distending celebrity sandwiches, from the Joe DiMaggio (corned beef, pastrami, chopped liver, and Bermuda onion) to the Julia Roberts (chicken salad, hard-boiled egg, lettuce, and tomato); or the **Carnegie Deli,** 854 Seventh Ave., at 55th Street (☎ 212/757-2245; www.carnegiedeli.com), for first-rate pastrami, corned beef, and cheesecake. But know that these landmarks specialize in tourist-target pricing, with sandwiches coming in between $12 to $20. You get your money's worth—they come so stuffed with meat that they're more than most average mortals can consume in one sitting—but beware: You'll be charged a ridiculous $2 to $3 sharing charge to split one with your travel partner. Head downtown to Katz's (p. 144) or uptown to Barney Greengrass (p. 129) for less touristy, and less expensive, deli experiences.

Choose your own bread from a wide selection, ranging from soft sourdough to crusty ciabatta. Although Island Burgers serves fries now, you're meant to eat these fellows with their tasty dirty potato chips. Terrifically thick shakes and cookies are also available to satisfy your sweet tooth.

## MIDTOWN DINING

○ **Joe Allen.** 326 W. 46th St. (btw. Eighth and Ninth aves.). ☎ **212/581-6464.** Reservations recommended (a must for pre-theater dining). Main courses $9–$21 (most less than $17). MC, V. Sun–Tues and Thurs–Fri noon–midnight, Wed and Sat 11:30am–midnight. Subway: A, C, E to 42nd St./Port Authority. AMERICAN PUB.

This upscale Restaurant Row pub is a glorious throwback to the old days of Broadway, when theater types went to places like Sardi's and Lüchow's—and yep, Joe Allen—to toss back a few after the curtain went down. The good news is that Joe Allen is still going strong; in fact, don't be surprised if you spot a stage star or two among the clientele. The uncomplicated American pub food is reliable and well priced and served at big, comfortable tables (the kind that restaurant managers don't order anymore because they take up too much real estate) covered with red-checked cloths. The meat loaf, in particular, is terrific, but you can't go wrong with the chili, the decent Greek salad, the great burgers, or anything that comes with mashed potatoes. More than 30 beers are available and some good wines by the glass. You'll thoroughly enjoy perusing the walls, which are covered with posters and other memorabilia from legendary Broadway flops.

○ **John's Pizzeria.** 260 W. 44th St. (btw. Broadway and Eighth Ave.). ☎ **212/391-7560.** Reservations accepted for 10 or more. Pizzas $10–$13.50 (plus toppings), pastas $6.50–$11. AE, MC, V. Daily 11:30am–11:30pm. Subway: A, C, E to 42nd St./Port Authority; 1, 2, 3, 9, N, R, S, 7 to 42nd St./Times Square. PIZZA.

Thin-crusted, properly sauced, and fresh, the pizza at John's has long been one of New York's best; some even consider these *the* best pies New York has to offer. Housed in the century-old Gospel Tabernacle Church, the split-level dining room is vast and pretty, featuring a gorgeous stained-glass ceiling and chefs working at classic brick ovens right in the room. More importantly, it's big enough to hold pre-theater crowds, so there's never too long of a wait despite the place's popularity. Unlike most pizzerias, at John's, you order a whole made-to-order pie rather than by the slice, so come with friends or family. There's also a good selection of traditional pastas to choose from, such as baked ziti, and well-stuffed calzones.

This Theater District location is my favorite, but the original Village location, at 278 Bleecker St., between Sixth and Seventh avenues (☎ 212/243-1680), is loaded with old-world atmosphere. The ones near Lincoln Center, 48 W. 65th St., between Broadway and Central Park West (☎ 212/721-7001), and on the Upper East Side, 408 E. 64th St., between First and York avenues (☎ 212/935-2895), are also worth checking out.

**La Bonne Soupe.** 48 W. 55th St. (btw. Fifth and Sixth aves.). ☎ **212/586-7650.** www. labonnesoupe.com. Reservations recommended for parties of more than 2. Main courses $9–$20 (most less than $15); "les bonnes soupes" prix-fixe $14; 3-course prix-fixe $20 at lunch and dinner. AE, DC, MC, V. Mon–Sat 11:30am–midnight, Sun 11:30am–11pm. Subway: E, F to Fifth Ave.; B, Q to 57th St. FRENCH BISTRO.

This little slice of Paris has been around forever; I remember discovering the magic of fondue here on a high school French Club field trip that took place more years ago than I care to think about. For gourmet at good prices, it's still hard to best this authentic bistro, where you'll even see French natives seated elbow-to-elbow in the newly renovated dining room. "Les bonnes soupes" are satisfying noontime meals of salad, bread, a big bowl of soup (mushroom and barley with lamb is a favorite), dessert (chocolate mousse, crème caramel, or ice cream), and wine or coffee—a great bargain at just $12.95. The menu also features entree-sized salads (including a good niçoise), high-quality steak burgers, and traditional bistro fare such as omelets, quiche Lorraine, croque monsieur, and fancier fare such as steak frites and filet mignon au poivre. Rounding out the menu are those very French fondues: emmethal cheese, beef, and yummy, creamy chocolate to finish off the meal in perfect style. Bon appétit!

**La Crepe de Bretagne.** 46 W. 56th St. (btw. Fifth and Sixth aves.). ☎ **212/245-4565.** Reservations accepted. Crepes $4–$7, main courses $11–$22; lunch prix-fixe (before 12:30pm) $9.95, 3-course pre-theater prix fixe $15.95. AE, DC, MC, V. Sun–Mon 11:30am–9pm, Tues–Thurs 11:30am–10pm, Fri–Sat 11:30am–11pm. Subway: B, Q to 57th St. FRENCH CREPES.

The classic main courses can get a tad pricey at the lovely, wood paneled French bistro, but the reason to come is for the super-affordable crepes. There's a huge list from which to choose, divided into savory—the main course, with such ingredients as ham and sauteed mushrooms or smoked salmon with bearnaise—and sweet, which serve as delectable desserts. Two average eaters can lunch on one savory crepe each and one sweet crepe to share and walk away sated and charmed for about 20 bucks. If you'd rather diverge from the crepes as main courses, take advantage of the value-minded early-bird lunch or dinner prix-fixes, which feature such bistro favorites as croque monsieur and quiche lorraine at lunch, chicken forestière and moules marinières at dinner. Finish up with any crepe featuring chocolate and bananas, and you'll be in heaven. Hugely popular with the local lunch crowd, so weekday reservations aren't a bad idea.

**Lemon Tree Cafe.** 769 Ninth Ave. (btw. 51st and 52nd sts.). ☎ **212/245-0818.** Reservations not accepted. Main courses $5–$9.50. MC, V ($20 minimum). Daily 11am–11pm. Subway: C, E to 50th St. MIDDLE EASTERN.

Lemon Tree is bare-bones decor-wise, with institutional furnishings and just a few posters of Egypt or Syria distracting you from the fake wood paneling and worn linoleum floor. But the food is fresh, tasty, and more than plentiful. Skip those Midtown falafel carts; readers of *New York Press* voted Lemon Tree's crispy, savory falafel sandwich best in the city. All pita sandwiches come overstuffed with lettuce, tomato, cabbage, onion, and tahini sauce. Veggie platters are light and delicious, particularly the lemony hummus, babaganoush, and tabouli. The grilled meat platters (served with salad and rice) could feed an army. Service can be slow and quirky (one day I was in, a 10-year-old girl served us), but it's worth putting up with for the great meal deal.

**Los Dos Rancheros Mexicanos.** 507 Ninth Ave. (at 38th St.). ☎ **212/868-7780.** Reservations not accepted. Tacos $2–$3, burritos and sandwiches $4–$7, platters $7–$12. No credit cards. Daily 11am–11pm. Subway: A, C, E to 42nd St./Port Authority. MEXICAN.

This big, bright place is probably the most authentic Mexican restaurant in New York City. The decor is no-frills on every front—expect fluorescent lighting, tables with paper menus beneath the glass, plastic cups, and cheap dishes—but mural paintings and a neon-bright Wurlitzer jukebox pumping out Latin pop add genuine charm. The hearty Pueblo-style food isn't for the faint of heart: The justifiably famous moles are extra-rich; the housemade salsas are hot, hot, hot; and barbecued goat, tripe soup, and tongue tacos are among the specialties. But even the less adventurous will dig into the enchiladas (don't pass up the beef), burritos with your choice of fillings, and other, more familiar choices with gusto. Everything is extremely affordable and excellently prepared, and warm, soft, freshly made corn tortillas are served with just about every dish. Service is attentive, and Mexican beers are available. Check the wall behind the open kitchen for the specials. A few blocks south of the most gentrified stretch of Ninth Avenue, the neighborhood can be desolate at night, so I suggest going earlier rather than later.

**Manhattan Chili Co.** 1500 Broadway (entrance on 43rd St.). ☎ **212/730-8666.** www.manhattanchili.com. Reservations accepted. Main courses $8–$15. AE, DISC, MC, V. Sun–Mon 11:30am–11pm, Tues–Sat 11:30am–midnight. Subway: N, R, S, 1, 2, 3, 7, 9 to 42nd St./Times Sq. AMERICAN SOUTHWESTERN.

This fun, cartoonish Theater District restaurant is a great choice if you have the kids in tow. The big, hearty chili bowls are geared to young palates, which tend to be suspicious of anything unfamiliar. The extensive list of chili choices is clearly marked by spice level, from the traditional Abilene with ground beef, tomatoes, basil, and red wine (mild enough for tenderfeet), to the Texas Chain Gang, which adds jalapenos to the mix for those who prefer hot. In addition, expect familiar favorites such as nachos, chicken wings, big salads, and generous burritos and burgers. It's really hard to go wrong here; even vegetarians have lots to choose from.

A second location is next to Dave Letterman's Ed Sullivan Theatre at 1697 Broadway, between 53rd and 54th streets (☎ **212/246-6555**), where the expanded menu includes seafood and there's live music, ranging from salsa to reggae to jazz, after 10pm.

**Meskerem.** 468 W. 47th St. (btw. Ninth and Tenth aves.). ☎ **212/664-0520.** Reservations recommended. Main courses $7–$12. DISC, MC, V. Daily 11:30am–11:30pm. Subway: C, E to 50th St. ETHIOPIAN.

Here's an exotic and affordable Theater District choice. Ignore the plain-Jane surroundings, get over the lack of silverware (you eat this African cuisine with your hands), and you'll enjoy a great dining experience here. Ethiopian stews of beef, lamb, chicken, and vegetables are served on communal platters and sopped up with spongy *injera* bread, made from fermented *tef,* an Ethiopian grain. The flavorful dishes range from the mild *doro alecha* (chicken seasoned with onions, garlic, and ginger in a butter sauce) to the spicy ribs dishes, simmered in a spicy berber sauce. The house specialty, *kitfo,* is Ethiopian-style steak tartare; less-adventurous eaters can ask for the beef rare instead of raw. For a little bit of everything, order a combination plate; two combos will easily feed three.

**Pietrasanta.** 683 Ninth Ave. (at 47th St.). ☎ **212/265-9471.** Reservations recommended. Main courses $8–$19. AE, MC, V. Sun–Mon noon–10:30pm, Tues and Thurs noon–11pm, Wed 11am–11pm, Fri noon–midnight, Sat 11:30am–midnight. Subway: C, E to 50th St. TUSCAN ITALIAN.

This charming trattoria is an excellent choice for an affordable pre-theater meal. The well-priced pastas are far superior to what you'll get for the same money—or even more—at countless other pasta houses around town. The chef has a deft hand and a fondness for bold flavors, so the dishes are at once refined and appealingly robust. Look for such winning starters as grilled calamari seasoned with fresh basil, white wine, and the perfect squirt of lemon juice; asparagus spears wrapped in imported prosciutto and dressed in a divine lemon-butter sauce; and *fagioli con pancetta,* an unassuming white-bean dish that springs to life with the first bite thanks to flavorful pancetta, rosemary, and lemon. Pasta mains worth seeking out include *agnolotti di Angello,* hand-formed half-moon pasta filled with hearty lamb in a rosemary, basil, and red-wine sauce; and *trenette con calamari,* a simple but gorgeous tri-color dish of black squid-ink pasta, white calamari rings, and roasted red peppers. The kitchen also has an excellent reputation for its time-honored fish, chicken, veal, and pasta preparations. The efficient staff is well known for keeping an eye on curtain time.

**Rice 'n' Beans.** 744 Ninth Ave. (btw. 50th and 51st sts.) ☎ **212/265-4444.** Reservations not accepted. Full plates $6–$15. MC, V. Sun–Thurs 11am–10pm, Fri–Sat 11am–10:30pm. Subway: C, E to 50th St. BRAZILIAN.

This cool, dark, hallway-sized restaurant dishes up kick-ass, stick-to-your-ribs fare. Between the bold flavors and the bargain-basement prices, you'll want to stand up and samba. Among the Brazilian specialties they whip up here are *feijoada*—the national dish of Brazil—a hearty, brackish-looking stew of black beans, pork ribs, and linguiça (Portuguese sausage); and a lovely roasted chicken seasoned with tomato and cilantro. By far the best bargain is the eponymous dish: For less than $10 you get a large oval plate mounded with rice, beans, mixed vegetables, collard greens, and sweet plantains—a vegetarian's delight. Portions are monstrous across the board. The weekday lunch specials—full meals with rice, beans, plantains, and your choice of roasted or sauteed chicken, beef stew, thin-cut sauteed pork chops, or the day's fried fish—are a steal at less than $9. Service can be slow at times and don't expect much in the way of ambiance—but at these prices, who cares?

✪ **Sapporo.** 152 W. 49th St. (btw. Sixth and Seventh aves.). ☎ **212/869-8972.** Reservations not accepted. Main courses $6–$9. No credit cards. Mon–Sat 11am–11pm, Sun 11am–10pm. Subway: N, R to 49th St. JAPANESE.

In my world, comfort food doesn't get any better than a big ramen or fried rice bowl from Sapporo. This bustling, no-frills restaurant serves up good and cheap Japanese eats, and the mostly Japanese crowd is testimony to the food's authenticity. Sapporo is famous for their excellent *gyoza,* pork-filled dumplings that are pan fried and served with a soy, rice vinegar, and chili oil dipping sauce. Other winning choices include *chahan,* lightly fried Japanese rice with veggies, egg, fish cake, and your choice of pork or chicken; appealingly sweet beef and tofu sukiyaki; cleanly fried pork cutlets; and any of the gargantuan noodle bowls. Frankly, you can't really go wrong with anything; I've eaten here more times than I can count, and I've never been disappointed by a dish. Some of the servers speak little English, so feel free to just point to your choice, and don't hesitate to ask for silverware if you prefer it to chopsticks. Beer and sake are served in addition to soft drinks.

In the East Village, you'll find **Sapporo East** at 245 E. 10th St., at First Avenue (☎ 212/260-1330).

**Siam Inn Too.** 854 Eighth Ave. (btw. 51st and 52nd sts.). ☎ **212/757-4006.** Reservations accepted. Main courses $7–$16. AE, DC, MC, V. Mon–Fri noon–11:30pm, Sat 4–11:30pm, Sun 4–11pm. Subway: C, E to 50th St. THAI.

Situated on an unremarkable stretch of Eighth Avenue, Siam Inn is an attractive outpost of very good Thai food. All of your Thai favorites are here, well prepared and served by a brightly attired and courteous waitstaff. Tom kah gai soup (with chicken, mushrooms, and coconut milk), chicken satay with yummy peanut sauce, and light, flaky curry puffs all make good starters. Among noteworthy entrees are the masaman and red curries (the former rich and peanuty, the latter quite spicy), spicy sautéed squid with fresh basil and chiles, and perfect pad thai. And unlike many of the drab restaurants in this neighborhood, the decor is pretty and pleasing—black deco tables and chairs, cushy rugs underfoot, and soft lighting.

**66 Cafe.** 858 Ninth Ave. (btw. 55th and 56th sts.). ☎ **212/977-7600.** Reservations not accepted. Breakfast $3.50–$7, sandwiches $4–$9.50, dinner entrees $9–$15.50. AE, DC, DISC, MC, V. Daily 7am–midnight. Subway: A, B, C, D, 1, 9 to 59th St./Columbus Circle. AMERICAN DINER.

Here's a good bet for straightforward American eats. The brick-walled room is light, bright, and spacious, a nice place to enjoy a casual and affordable meal. Expect a huge menu brimming with decently prepared diner standards, from morning waffles, eggs, and lox-crowned bagels to burgers, salads, triple-decker sandwiches, meat loaf, and pastas for afternoon and evening. The food is nothing special, but it satisfies and isn't overpriced as is most Theater District fare. A fresh-fruit and juice bar adds a nice, healthy twist.

**Virgil's Real BBQ.** 152 W. 44th St. (btw. Sixth and Seventh aves.). ☎ **212/921-9494.** Reservations recommended. Main courses and barbecue platters $6–$25. AE, DC, MC, V. Sun–Mon 11am–11pm, Tues–Sat 11:30am–midnight. Subway: 1, 2, 3, 7, 9, N, R to 42nd St./Times Sq. SOUTHERN/BARBECUE.

Virgil's might look like a comfy theme-park version of a down-home barbecue joint, but this place takes its barbecue seriously. The meat is house-smoked with a blend of hickory, oak, and fruitwood chips, and most every regional school is represented, from Carolina pulled pork to Texas beef brisket to Memphis ribs. You might not consider this contest-winning chow if you're from barbecue country, but we less-savvy Yankees are thrilled to have Virgil's in the 'hood. I love to start with the barbecued shrimp, accompanied by mustard slaw, and a plate of buttermilk onion rings with bleu cheese for dipping. The ribs are lip-smackin' good, but the chicken is moist and tender; go for a combo if you just can't choose. Burgers, sandwiches, and other entrees (chicken-fried steak, anyone?) are also available if you can't face up to all that meat 'n' sauce. And cast that cornbread aside for a full order of buttermilk biscuits, which come with maple butter so good it's like dessert. So hunker down, pig out, and don't worry about making a mess; when you're through eating, you get a hot towel for washing up. The bar offers a huge selection of on-tap and bottled brews.

## QUICK BITES

**Canova Market,** 134 W. 51st St., between Sixth and Seventh avenues (☎ 212/969-9200), is a sprawling gourmet deli where your choices are only limited by your imagination (or your stomach). There's a fresh salad bar, an expansive deli counter, a soup bar, a sushi bar, and—my favorite—a pay-per-pound Mongolian grill, where you assemble your own concoction of fresh veggies, meats, seafood, rice, noodles, and seasonings to be grilled and then watch the chefs do their stuff ($4.99 per pound). There's a large dining area in the back where you can eat once you've paid. This place really bustles at lunch, but lines move fast. Canova Market is open around the clock, but don't expect all facilities (such as the Mongolian barbecue grill) to be going at all hours.

**Amy's Bread,** 672 Ninth Ave., between 46th and 47th streets (☎ 212/977-2670; www.amysbread.com), makes a great daytime stop. The cute, brick-walled bakery/cafe serves up fresh-baked breakfast pastries, quiches, sandwiches made on some of the city's best homemade bread, and excellent sweets as well as cappuccino. Pastries are $1 to $3.75, sandwiches $2.50 to $5.50. A few tables are on hand in addition to the takeout counter.

Friendly ✪ **Bagel & Bean,** 828 Seventh Ave., at 53rd Street (☎ 212/262-6340), is a great stop for lunchtime bagel sandwiches. The fresh-baked bagels are first-rate, and top-quality fillings range from cream cheese to terrific whitefish salad to an excellent veggie burger. There's no table seating, but it's easy to park yourself on a corporate plaza in this area, and Central Park is just a half-dozen blocks to the north.

Little more than a jazzy, neon-lit storefront, **B. Frites,** 1657 Broadway, between 51st and 52nd streets (☎ 212/767-0858), is a purveyor of authentic Belgian fries. They dole out their golden, thick-cut, perfectly crisped and salted potatoes in hand-held cones, ideal for munching on the go. You can choose from at least a dozen sauces, ranging from traditional mayo to herb-seasoned tomato purée.

**Papaya King** (p. 186) has a new location at 255 W. 43rd St., just off Eighth Ave. (☎ 212/944-4590). The two-all-beef-franks-and-an-all-natural-fruit-drink combo is a bargain at $3.99.

Healthy eaters will enjoy the all-natural eats at **The Pump** (p. 178), 40 W. 55th St., between Fifth and Sixth avenues (☎ 212/246-6844).

Cafeteria-style **Mangia** (p. 134) is at 50 W. 57th St., between Fifth and Sixth avenues (☎ 212/582-5882). And gourmet grocer **Dean & Deluca** has two cafes in the neighborhood: a roomy branch at 9 Rockefeller Center, across from the *Today* show studio (☎ 212/664-1363); and in the Theater District at 235 W. 46th St., between Broadway and Eighth Avenue (☎ 212/869-6890).

If you're over by the *Intrepid,* stop into **H&H Bagel,** 639 W. 46th St., at Twelfth Avenue (☎ 212/595-8000), to sample the best bagel in town.

Lastly, two nice new branches of **Burritoville** (p. 136) have popped up at 352 W. 39th St., at Ninth Avenue (☎ 212/563-9088), and 625 Ninth Ave., near 44th Street (☎ 212/333-5352).

**Soup Kitchen International.** 259A W. 55th St. (at Eighth Ave.). ☎ **212/757-7730.** Soup $6–$25. Oct–June, Mon–Fri noon–6pm. Closed summer. Subway: C, E to 50th St. GOURMET SOUP.

It's not hard to find Al Yeganeh, the famously dour soup vendor parodied on *Seinfeld;* just head for 55th Street, and walk to the end of the very long line. Many wait for the novelty and even hope to be yelled at. (The real-life Kramer once posted a billboard next to the store with "behavior tips," but Yeganeh painted over the sign in red shortly after it appeared.) Here's the deal: It's ridiculously expensive for takeout soup, but it's really that good. Yeganeh labors fiercely, coddling the Hungarian goulash, mushroom barley, and mulligatawny, all subtly spiced and sublime. The seafood bisque gets deserved kudos; I once found an entire lobster claw in mine. The 12 or so soups offered change daily, but don't call because he'll hang up on you. "Whatever soup you want, I have!" he snaps. So come after 2pm to minimize waiting; yes, have your money ready; and no, don't ask to take his picture, because he finds that insulting.

# Theme Restaurant Thrills!

The theme-restaurant biz might be on the wane, but the World Wrestling Federation is always happy to buck the trend. Their brand-new **WWF New York** is drawing massive crowds of rabid wrestling fans to 1501 Broadway, at 43rd Street (☎ 212/398-2563). Don't expect WWF stars such as The Rock, Ivory, or Stone Cold Steve Austin to be in residence, but you'll find plenty of memorabilia, high-tech (and low-brow) interactive video exhibits, and perfectly acceptable burger-and-ribs fare—not to mention the WWF's signature raucous atmosphere. There's also a temporary tattoo parlor and plenty to spend your loot on at the WWF store.

Also new on the scene is ✪ **ESPN Zone,** 1472 Broadway, at 42nd Street (☎ 212/921-3776). The mammoth 42,000-square-foot space houses the Studio Grill, with nonstop ESPN programming; the Screening Room, with 2 giant screens surrounded by a dozen 36-inchers, customized audio and video touch screens, and reclining leather chairs with built-in speakers (ideal for watching the game); and the Sports Arena, a full floor of sports-related arcade games; set replicas from ESPN's hit shows (including *Sportscenter* and *NBA 2night*); and much more. A sports fan's dream come true.

Always the perennial favorite, New York's ✪ **Hard Rock Cafe,** 221 W. 57th St., between Broadway and Seventh Avenue (☎ 212/459-9320), is one of the originals of the chain and a terrific realization of the concept. The memorabilia collection is terrific, with lots of great Lennon collectibles. The menu boasts all the Hard Rock standards, and the comfortable bar mixes up great cocktails.

**Harley-Davidson Cafe,** 1370 Sixth Ave., at 56th Street (☎ 212/245-6000), brings out the Hell's Angel in all of us. The just-fine munchies do the trick, and memorabilia documents 90 years of Hog history.

The subterranean red planet-themed **Mars 2112,** 1633 Broadway, at 51st Street (☎ 212/582-2112), is a hoot, from the simulated red-rock rooms to the Martian-costumed waitstaff to the silly "Man Eats on Mars!" newspaper-style menu. The eclectic food is better than you might expect, but skip the Star Tours–style simulated spacecraft ride at the entrance if you don't want to lose your appetite before you get to your table. The kids won't mind, though; they'll love it, along with the video arcade.

At the **Official All-Star Cafe,** 1540 Broadway, at 45th Street (☎ 212/840-8326), center court has a full-size scoreboard, booths shaped like baseball mitts crowd the sidelines, and video monitors guarantee that the great plays in sports history live forever. The food is straight from the ballpark—hot dogs, St. Louis ribs, Philly cheese steak sandwiches. The All-Star is now facing tough competition from the impressive ESPN Zone, however, and rumors are that Planet Hollywood might move from its 57th Street perch to this space sometime in 2000. Call ahead to avoid disappointment.

The celebrity orbit has dimmed a bit since Ah-nuld left the fold and plans for a Times Square hotel went bust in early 2000, but, at press time, **Planet Hollywood** was still going strong at 140 W. 57th St., between Sixth and Seventh avenues (☎ 212/333-7827). Frankly, the movie memorabilia doesn't hold the same excitement as the genuine rock 'n' roll goods over at the Hard Rock (didn't I see the R2D2 and C3PO robots at three *other* PHs?), but it's still plenty of fun for Hollywood buffs nonetheless. A move to Times Square might be in the offing, so call before you go.

## WORTH A SPLURGE

**Carmine's.** 200 W. 44th St. (btw. Broadway and Eighth Ave.). ☎ **212/221-3800.** Reservations recommended before 6pm, after 6pm accepted only for 6 or more. Family-style main courses $9–$11.50 at lunch, $15–$47 at dinner (most less than $22). AE, DC, MC, V. Tues–Sat 11:30am–midnight, Sun–Mon 11:30am–11pm. Subway: N, R, S, 1, 2, 3, 7, 9 to 42nd St./Times Square. SOUTHERN ITALIAN FAMILY STYLE.

Everything is done B-I-G at this rollicking, family-style Times Square mainstay. The dining room is vast enough to deserve a map, massive platters of pasta hold Brady Bunch–size portions, and large groups wait to join in the rambunctious atmosphere at this sibling of the original Upper West Sider. This is a value-priced restaurant where the bang for your buck increases for every person you add to your party—but so does the wait, so come early or late to avoid the crowds. Caesar salad and a mound of fried calamari are a perfect beginning, followed by heaping portions of pasta topped with red or white clam sauce, mixed seafood, zesty marinara, and meatballs. The meat entrees include veal parmigiana, chicken marsala, and shrimp scampi. The tiramisù is pie-size, thick and creamy, bathed in Kahlúa and marsala. Order half of what you think you'll need.

The original Carmine's at 2450 Broadway, between 90th and 91st streets (☎ **212/362-2200**) is the same—but even B-I-G-G-E-R.

## 12  Midtown East & Murray Hill

There's also **Jackson Hole** (p. 185), 521 Third Ave., at 35th Street (☎ 212/679-3264), for burgers and other affordable diner fare.

**The British Open.** 320 E. 59th St. (btw. First and Second aves.). ☎ **212/355-8467.** www.britishopen.citysearch.com. Reservations accepted. Main courses $9–$20 (most less than $15). AE, DC, DISC, MC, V. Mon–Sat noon–2am (kitchen closes at midnight), Sun noon–1am (kitchen closes at 11pm). Subway: 4, 5, 6 to 59th St. BRITISH.

Here's the perfect pub for golf lovers or anybody who pines for a pint and some good English grub. This charmer of an alehouse is more sophisticated than most, with a mahogany bar polished to a high sheen, a pretty dining room in back, and friendly, attentive service. Tartan carpet heightens the theme (aye, the Scots would be proud) and little blue lights create a romantic glow. This isn't a copy of a Brit pub; it's the real thing, transplanted from the other side of the Atlantic wholesale, bartender, malt vinegar, and all. The North Star at South Street Seaport is equally genuine, but it's more after-work local than Sunday dinner, if you know what I mean. The extensive menu serves well-prepared versions of the pub staples, plus steaks, chops, and the like. But go for the standards: light, well-battered fish with crispy chips; excellent cottage pie with veggies and mash; plus steak and kidney pie, bangers and mash, and so on. You'll find Guinness, Bass, Fullers ESB, and other British imports on tap and golf and other sports on the telly at any hour.

✪ **Ess-A-Bagel.** 831 Third Ave. (at 51st St.). ☎ **212/980-1010.** www.ess-a-bagel.com. Reservations not taken. Sandwiches $1.35–$8.35. AE, DC, DISC, MC, V. Mon–Fri 6:30am–10pm, Sat–Sun 8am–5pm. Subway: 6 to 51st St.; E, F to Lexington Ave. BAGEL SANDWICHES.

Ess-A-Bagel turns out the city's best bagel, edging out rival H&H, who won't make you a sandwich. Baked daily on-site, the giant hand-rolled delicacies come in 12 flavors—plain, sesame, poppy, onion, garlic, salt, whole wheat, pumpernickel, pumpernickel raisin, cinnamon raisin, oat bran, and everything. They're so plump, chewy, and satisfying it's hard to believe they contain no fat, cholesterol, or preservatives. Head to the back counter for a baker's dozen or line up for a sandwich overstuffed with scrumptious salads and spreads. Fillings can range from a generous schmear of cream cheese to smoked Nova salmon or chopped herring salad (both have received national acclaim) to sun-dried tomato tofu spread. There are also lots of deli-style meats to choose from, plus a wide range of cheeses and salads (egg, chicken, light tuna, and so on) and an expanded selection of vegetarian items in 1999. The cheerful dining room has plenty of bistro-style tables.

A second, smaller location is at 359 First Ave., at 21st Street (☎ **212/260-2252**).

**Katsu-Hama.** 11 E. 47th St. (btw. Fifth and Madison aves.). ☎ **212/758-5909.** www. katsuhama.com. Reservations accepted. Main courses and complete dinners $7–$16. AE, DC, DISC, JCB, MC, V. Mon–Thurs 11:30am–3pm and 5–10:30pm, Fri 11:30am–10:30pm, Sat–Sun 11:30am–9:30pm. Subway: B, D, F, Q to 47th–50th sts./Rockefeller Center. JAPANESE KATSU.

Even if you have never dined on Japanese before, give this appealing restaurant a try. It specializes in katsu, which is breaded and cleanly fried cutlets, usually pork, and very American-palate friendly. Katsu-Hama also katsus good-quality chicken, prawns, and potatoes ("cream croquettes") in addition to moist pork tenderloin. Complete dinners start at $8.95 and come with as much rice, miso, and cabbage salad as you can eat. Japanese curries and skewers (yakitori) are also on hand, and there's a kid's menu if you have tykes in tow. The pretty butter-yellow room features attractive modern art and comfy seating. Service is welcoming, knowledgeable, and generous with seconds. Beer and a short but good sake selection are on hand. An excellent value offering a much more pleasing all-around dining experience than most in this price range.

✪ **Pongal.** 110 Lexington Ave. (btw. 27th and 28th sts.). ☎ **212/696-9458.** Reservations recommended. Main courses $5–$10. DC, DISC, MC, V. Mon–Fri noon–3pm and 5–10pm, Sat–Sun noon–10pm. Subway: 6 to 28th St. VEGETARIAN INDIAN.

Pongal is a real standout on Curry Hill, the stretch of Lexington in the high 20s that's home to a number of Indian restaurants. It specializes in the vegetarian cuisine of southern India and also happens to be kosher (only in New York!). Trust me—you don't have to be a vegetarian to love this place. The hearty dishes are always freshly prepared to order by the conscientious kitchen (no vats of saag paneer sitting around this joint). Ingredients are always top-quality, vegetables and legume dishes are never overcooked, and the well-spiced sauces are particularly divine. The specialty of the house is *dosai,* a large golden crepe filled with onions, potatoes, and other goodies, accompanied by coconut chutney and flavorful sauce. The food is very cheap, but that doesn't mean you have to put up with a crusty cafeteria to get such a bargain: The restaurant is low-lit and attractive, with professional service and a pleasing ambiance, making it a nice choice for a special night on the town.

If Pongal is too crowded, head across the street to **New Madras Palace,** 101 Lexington Ave. (☎ **212/889-3477**), which is almost as good and a smidgen cheaper.

**Prime Burger.** 5 E. 51st St. (btw. Fifth and Madison aves.). ☎ **212/759-4729.** Reservations not accepted. Burgers and main courses $3.25–$8.50. No credit cards. Mon–Fri 6am–7pm, Sat 6am–5pm. Subway: 6 to 51st St. AMERICAN/HAMBURGERS.

Just across the street from St. Patrick's Cathedral, this no-frills coffee shop is a heavenly find. The burgers and sandwiches are tasty, the fries crispy and generous. The front seats, which might remind you (if you're old enough) of old wooden grammar-school desks, are great fun—especially when business-suited New Yorkers quietly take their places at these oddities. A great quickie stop during a day of Fifth Avenue shopping.

## ⓕ Affordable Family-Friendly Restaurants

Although it's always a smart move to call ahead to make sure the restaurant you're interested in can accommodate kids with such amenities as kids' menus and high chairs, you can always count on the following restaurants.

**Carmine's** *(p. 175)*   This rollicking Italian restaurant was created with kids in mind. Expect family-size portions of all the favorites, including pasta topped with zesty marinara and little fist-sized meatballs. The bigger the group, the better the bargain.

**EJ's Luncheonette** *(p. 156)*   These pleasing retro-1950s diners do what they're supposed to do best: serve up great burgers, fries, and blue plate specials. There's even a kids' menu featuring peanut butter–and-jelly sandwiches along with downsized versions of the classics. Order your kids a milk shake and they'll be in hog heaven.

**John's Pizzeria** *(p. 168)*   What kid doesn't love pizza? The Times Square location is particularly well located and kid-friendly, with family-sized tables, chefs cooking up pies in brick ovens right in the cavernous room, and a bustling atmosphere where kids are welcome to be kids.

**Manhattan Chili Co.** *(p. 170)*   This fun, cartoonish Theater District restaurant is geared for all-American tastes and palates. Expect kid-friendly nachos, chicken wings, not-too-hot bowls of thick and meaty chili, and other faves such as burritos and burgers. It's really hard to go wrong here.

**Nacho Mama** *(p. 183)*—Here's more kid-friendly Tex-Mex fare, ideal for families taking advantage of one of the Upper West Side's many good hotel values. Everybody will appreciate the kids menu: the young'uns for its not-too-spicy fare and mom and dad for its wallet-friendly pricing ($4 to $5).

**Popover Cafe** *(p. 183)*   This country-cozy cafe is especially welcoming for breakfast and lunch, when the hearty home cooking is at its best. Even cute-o-phobes will warm to the teddies that line the banquettes—and everybody loves the baskets of warm, fluffy popovers, which come with delectable strawberry butter.

**Serendipity 3** *(p. 186)*   Little ones love this whimsical restaurant and ice cream shop, which serves up a huge menu of American favorites, followed up by colossal ice-cream treats. This irony-free charmer even makes grown-ups feel like kids again.

**Virgil's Real BBQ** *(p. 172)*   This pleasing Times Square barbecue joint welcomes kids with open arms—and Junior will be more than happy, I'm sure, to be *allowed* to eat with his hands.

And what would kid-friendly dining in the Big Apple be without visiting at least one of the city's many theme restaurants? Check out the "Theme Restaurant Thrills!" box earlier in this chapter.

---

**Taco & Tortilla King.** 285 Third Ave. (btw. 22nd and 23rd sts.). ☎ **212/679-8882.** Tacos, burritos, and sandwiches $1–$7, fajitas $13–$15. AE, MC, V ($10 minimum). Daily 11am–11pm. Subway: 6 to 23rd St. MEXICAN.

This low-profile sleeper is little more than a lunch counter with a few tables and chairs, but the authentic Mexican food can't be beat. Sit down to a couple of tacos and you'll think you've been temporarily transported to one of those super-cheap, gourmet

Mexican joints your friends in southern California keep raving about. The kitchen won me over with the basics: Chunky fresh-made guacamole infused with lime and flour tortillas made from scratch and baked on the premises. All the Mexican staples, from well-stuffed burritos to sizzling fajitas, are authentically prepared, hearty, and satisfying; a good portion of the offerings can be prepared meatless for vegetarians. An all-around winner for a fast meal at an unbeatable price.

## QUICK BITES

In addition to the listings below, there's also a cafeteria-style branch of gourmet **Mangia** (p. 134) at 16 E. 48th St., just east of Fifth Avenue (☎ 212/754-7600).

**The Pump.** 113 E. 31st St. (btw. Park and Lexington aves.). ☎ **212/213-5733.** Breakfast $2.50–$7, sandwiches and salads $3–$7, full plates $6.50–$12. All prices include tax. AE, MC, V. Mon–Thurs 9:30am–9:30pm, Fri 9:30am–8pm, Sat 11am–6:30pm. Subway: 6 to 33rd St. HEALTH-CONSCIOUS.

Here's a terrific stop for diners who are watching their figures as well as their wallets. An appealing mix of retro-cute and future-chic, with just a counter in back and a few high tables with stools, the Pump espouses a philosophy that eating right doesn't have to mean boring. Everything on the menu is low in fat and high in protein but doesn't sacrifice flavor for healthfulness. This is casual food made with all-natural ingredients that's easy to enjoy as a quick meal: salads, sandwiches, "supercharged" combo platters, fresh juices, high-protein and health shakes. Although they serve up a great nature burger (a pleasing blend of brown rice, sunflower seeds, herbs, and veggies), the Pump isn't a vegetarian restaurant; lean beef, turkey, and chicken are served. And because they cater to a big workout crowd that needs energy, portions are substantial. Salad dressings are fat-free creations, such as tahini and honey mustard, and guilt-free pizzas are prepared with non-fat mozzarella, low sodium tomato sauce, and whole wheat crust. At breakfast, eggs, pancakes, and potatoes are baked, never fried—which is precisely why you can indulge in the steak and eggs sandwich (served on a whole wheat pita) and feel not the least bit sinful.

There's now a second location in Midtown West, at 40 W. 55th St., between Fifth and Sixth avenues (☎ **212/246-6844**).

## WORTH A SPLURGE

✪ **Oyster Bar & Restaurant.** In Grand Central Terminal (lower level), 23 Vanderbilt Ave. (at 42nd St.). ☎ **212/490-6650.** Reservations recommended. Main courses $10–$35. AE, DC, MC, V. Mon–Fri 11:30am–9:30pm (last seating), Sat 5:30–9:30pm. Subway: 4, 5, 6, 7, S to 42nd St./Grand Central. SEAFOOD.

Here's one New York institution housed within another: the city's most famous seafood joint in the world's greatest train station, beautifully renovated Grand Central Terminal. The restaurant is looking spiffy, too, with a main dining room sitting under an impressive curved and tiled ceiling, a more casual luncheonette-style section for walk-ins, and a wood-paneled saloon-style room for smokers. If you love seafood, don't miss this place. A new menu is prepared every day, because only the freshest fish is served. Most dinners go for between $20 and $25, and the list of daily catches, which can range from Arctic char to mako shark to ono (Hawaiian wahoo), is impressive. But it's just as easy to keep the tab down by sticking with hearty fare such as one of the excellent stews and panroasts (from about $10 for oyster stew to $20 for a combo panroast rich with oysters, clams, shrimp, lobster, and scallops) or by pairing the New England clam chowder (at $5, an unbeatable lunch) with a smoked starter to make a great meal.

## 13  The Upper West Side

For fun, family-style Italian, there's **Carmine's** (p. 175) at 2450 Broadway, between 90th and 91st streets (☎ 212/362-2200).

**Time Cafe North** (p. 151), 2330 Broadway, at 85th St. (☎ 212/579-5100), has casual, healthy eats and a cool Moroccan-themed lounge for cocktails. For good burgers and diner fare, head to **EJ's Luncheonette** (p. 156), 447 Amsterdam Ave., between 81st and 82nd streets (☎ 212/873-3444), or **Jackson Hole** (p. 185), 517 Columbus Ave., at 85th St. (☎ 212/362-5177).

You'll find healthful **Zen Palate** (p. 163) at 2170 Broadway, between 76th and 77th streets (☎ 212/501-7768).

**Barney Greengrass, the Sturgeon King.** 541 Amsterdam Ave. (btw. 86th and 87th sts.). ☎ 212/724-4707. Reservations not accepted. Breakfast $3.50–$14, sandwiches $2.50–$15.75 (most less than $10), smoked fish platters $16–$36 (most less than $22). No credit cards. Tues–Fri 8:30am–4pm, Sat–Sun 8:30am–5pm. Subway: 1, 9 to 86th St. JEWISH DELI.

It's hard to get more authentic than Barney Greengrass. This unassuming, daytime-only deli, going strong since 1908, is different from other local Jewish delis; it's small and rather quiet, with an emphasis on smoked fish and service that's friendly rather than attitude laden. It's legend for its high-quality salmon (sable, gravlax, Nova Scotia, kippered, lox, pastrami—you choose), whitefish, and sturgeon (of course). But meat-lovers won't be disappointed, either: The triple-deckers are terrific (and substantially cheaper than at Midtown's delis, it's worth noting), and the chicken liver inspired nothing less than a raging, months-long debate among restaurant critics a few years back. Great for morning eggs and omelets, too; the bagels are fresh from H&H. Purists will be in heaven.

**Big Nick's Burger Joint.** 2175 Broadway (at 77th St.). ☎ 212/362-9238. Reservations not necessary. Main courses $3.50–$15. MC, V. Daily 24 hours. Subway: 1, 9 to 79th St. AMERICAN.

A neighborhood legend since 1962, Big Nick's is one of the best spots in the city for a midnight snack. Nick offers a full menu 24 hours a day, which includes everything from killer french toast and pancakes to Nick's infamous gourmet beefburgers. The classic charbroiled burgers come in a host of varieties, from your all-American cheeseburger to the Mediterranean, stuffed with herbs, spices, and onions and topped with anchovies, feta, and tomato. Or how 'bout a Texasburger, with an egg on top for "eggstra" energy (Nick's joke, not mine)? There's also a good selection of Big Nick–style pizzas, such as the Gyromania, topped with well-seasoned gyro meat and onions. As the name suggests, Nick's is a real joint, specializing in homegrown Noo Yawk fare; however, the kitchen gets kudos for developing a dietwatchers menu, with such specialties as pizzas prepared with skim cheese and lean-ground veal and turkey burgers. There really is something for everyone here; in 1999, the menu grew to more than 1,000 items when Nick added steaks to his repertoire. The atmosphere is suitably lively, with waiters and buspeople scrambling about, cooks calling out orders, and crowded tables full of diners happily chowing down.

**✪ Gabriela's.** 311 Amsterdam Ave. (at 75th St.). ☎ 212/875-8532. Reservations accepted for parties of 6 or more. Main courses $7–$13. AE, MC, V. Mon–Thurs noon–11pm, Fri–Sat noon–midnight, Sun noon–10pm. Subway: 1, 2, 3, 9 to 96th St. MEXICAN.

If you love roast chicken, trust me: Gabriela's bird is the best. A blend of Yucatan spices and a slow-roasting rotisserie results in some of the tenderest, juiciest chicken in town—and at $6.95 for a half-chicken with two sides (plenty for all but the biggest

# Uptown Dining

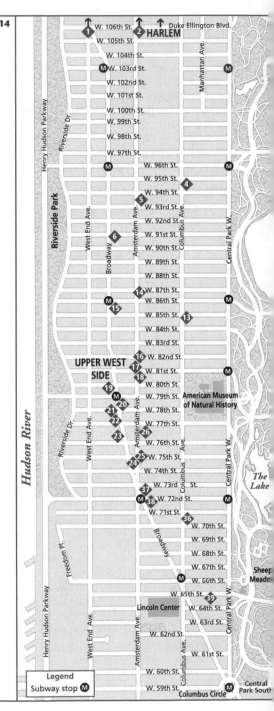

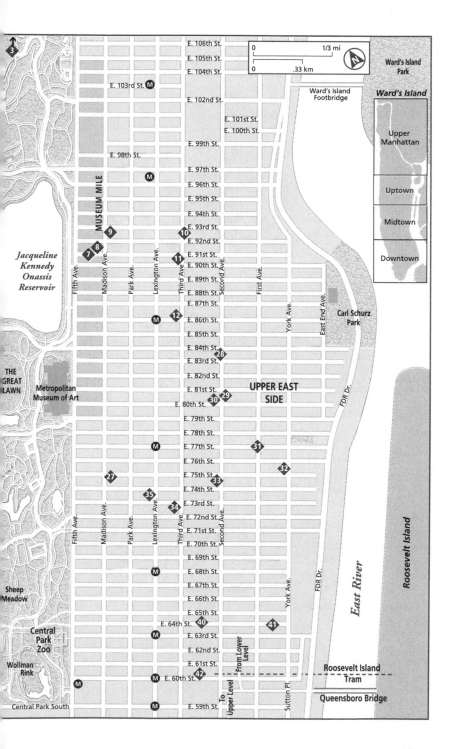

eaters) and $12.95 for a whole, it's one of the city's best bargains, too. All of the Mexican specialties on the extensive menu are well prepared, generously portioned, and satisfying, from the monster tacos to the well-sauced enchiladas. The fresh, chunky, perfectly limed guacamole should please even Southwest natives. The dining room is large, bright, and pretty, with a pleasing South-of-the-Border flair, and the service is quick and attentive. Mexican beers and wine are available, but you might want to consider pairing your meal with one of Gabriela's refreshing fruit shakes (both mango and papaya are good bets) or tall agua frescas (fresh fruit drinks), which come in a variety of tropical flavors. Terrific!

Gabriela's original location, 685 Amsterdam Ave., at 93rd Street (☎ 212/961-0574), is still going strong, too.

**Hunan Park.** 235 Columbus Ave. (btw. 70th and 71st St.). ☎ **212/724-4411.** members.aol.com/hunanpark/hunan.htm. Reservations accepted for groups of 5 or more. Main courses $5.25–$13 (most less than $10; Peking duck $24); lunch special (daily 11:30am–4pm) $4.50–$6.50. AE, MC, V. Sun–Tues noon–midnight, Wed–Sat noon–12:30am. Subway: B, C, 1, 2, 3, 9 to 72nd St. HUNAN CHINESE.

This casual place has been earning broad-sweeping kudos for years from Zagat's to *New York* magazine to Alan Alda for its well-prepared, inexpensive Chinese standards. Everything about it—quality, service, decor—is a cut above the standard. Expect all the familiar favorites, plus satisfying specialties such as ginger chicken, spicy four-flavor beef, and crispy sea bass in a rich Hunan sauce. Service is friendly and efficient.

There's a second location farther uptown at 721 Columbus Ave., at 95th St. (☎ 212/222-6511).

**Josie's Restaurant & Juice Bar.** 300 Amsterdam Ave. (at 74th St.). ☎ **212/769-1212.** www.josiesnyc.com. Reservations recommended. Main courses $9–$17. AE, DC, MC, V. Mon–Fri noon–midnight, Sat 11:30am–midnight, Sun 11:30am–11pm. Subway: 1, 2, 3, 9 to 72nd St. HEALTH-CONSCIOUS.

You have to admire the sincerity of an organic restaurant that uses chemical-free milk paint on its walls. Chef/owner Louis Lanza doesn't stop there: His adventurous menu shuns dairy, preservatives, and concentrated fats. Free-range and farm-raised meats and poultry augment vegetarian choices such as baked sweet potato with tamari brown rice, broccoli, roasted beets, and tahini sauce; eggless Caesar salad; and a great three-grain vegetable burger with homemade ketchup and caramelized onions. The yellowfin tuna wasabi burger with pickled ginger is another signature. Everything is made with organic grains, beans, and flour as well as organic produce when possible. You don't have to be a health nut to enjoy Josie's; Lanza's eclectic cuisine really satisfies. And nobody's gonna actually make you do without: If wheat grass isn't your thing, a full wine and beer list is served in this pleasing modern space, which boasts enough *Jetsons*-style touches to give the room a playful, relaxed feel.

**La Caridad 78.** 2199 Broadway (at 78th St.). ☎ **212/874-2780.** Reservations not accepted. Main courses $6–$11.25. No credit cards. Mon–Sat 11:30–1am, Sun 11:30am–10:30pm. Subway: 1, 9 to 78th St. LATIN AMERICAN/CHINESE.

This neighborhood stalwart is the best of a string of uniquely New York institutions: the Chinese-Latin hybrid restaurant (supposedly the result of cultural inter-marrying between Chinese and Hispanic immigrants). The cuisine isn't a cross; rather, the menu features both Latino and Chinese sections, so you could conceivably start with an egg roll, move on to Cuban-style fried pork with black beans and yellow rice, and follow up with moo goo gai pan if you were still hungry. Atmosphere is not the point, so ignore the bare-bones interior and fluorescent lighting. Instead, line up with the rest of the crowd for the huge portions of good, cheap eats. The lemon pork chops, shrimp in tomato sauce, and stir-fried chicken are all recommendable choices. No beer or wine is served. If you're staying in the neighborhood, they'll deliver (until 11pm Monday through Saturday, until 10pm on Sunday).

**La Rosita Restaurant.** 2809 Broadway (btw. 108th and 109th sts.). ☎ **212/663-7804** or 212/663-9806. Reservations not accepted. Main courses $3.25–$20.75 (most less than $12). AE, DC, DISC, MC, V. Daily 7am–1am. Subway: 1, 9 to 110th St./Cathedral Pkwy. CUBAN/SPANISH.

Traveling up Broadway on the way to Columbia University, you'll pass through the neighborhoods that Oscar Hijuelos lovingly evoked in his book *The Mambo Kings Play Songs of Love*. They're brimming with yuppies now, but pre-gentrification La Rosita stays, defiantly, the same as ever. This plain, unassuming diner is hugely popular with expat Cubanos for the authentic taste of the old country it offers. Navigate your way past the crowded entrance, where folks stop in for to-go orders of *cafe con leche* and *cubano* sandwiches (a savory jumble of meats, cheese, and lettuce on skinny cuban bread, grilled flat on a sandwich press). Sidle up to the counter or grab a table to enjoy an appetizer of crispy *tostones*, fried green plantains seasoned with garlic and salt, or the hearty white-bean soup, studded with ham, greens, and potato. Entrees range from a fluffy *tortilla*, an omelet stuffed with chorizo, onions, and peppers, to a substantial slab of roast pork, served with rice and beans. The succulent roast chicken is another first-rate fave. Portions are on the giant side of generous. An excellent value.

**Nacho Mama.** 2893 Broadway (btw. 112th and 113th sts.). ☎ **212/665-2800.** Reservations accepted. Main courses $5–$14 (most less than $10). MC, V. Daily 11:30am–midnight (bar until 4am). Subway: 1, 9 to 110th St./Cathedral Pkwy. TEX-MEX.

I really like this earnest and attractive restaurant and bar, which caters to a Columbia U. crowd with value-minded Tex-Mex fare that's more Tex than Mex but won me over with its fresh preparations and neat creative twists. The loftlike space is airy and attractive, with the burnished brick, wood, and terra-cotta look of an upscale southwestern cantina. Everything is simply and generously prepared. I was surprised at how much I enjoyed the enchiladas filled with sweetly spiced, slow-braised pork. You can order it in a giant burrito if you prefer or opt for one of the many other fillings: wild mushrooms (crimini, white, and portobello, lightly sauteed in tomato and chiles); white-hominy pozole with red pepper, onion, and a light touch of cilantro; steak, chicken, or grilled shrimp; and a few others. The salsa is fresh and on the mild side, not too heavy on the cilantro, and the guacamole is chunky and pleasing. Tex-Mex-style salads, sandwiches, and chicken wings are also available, plus a few more sophisticated entrees at dinner. A terrific bar serves up monster real-lime margaritas and martinis for just $5 to $6, plus good drafts and an extensive bottled beer list that roams the globe.

**Niko's Mediterranean Grill & Bistro.** 2161 Broadway (at 76th St.). ☎ **212/873-7000.** Reservations accepted for parties of more than 5. www.nikosgrill.com. Main courses $5.50–$8.50 at lunch, $5–$19 at dinner; daily brunch special (11am–4pm) $8.95. AE, DC, DISC, MC, V. Sun–Thurs 11am–11:45pm, Fri–Sat 11am–12:45am. Subway: 1, 9 to 79th St. GREEK.

If you're in a feta-and-phyllo mood, head to Niko's, where the Greek Isles get the Big Nick treatment (see above). The menu is huge, prices are low, and all the standards are up to snuff. Don't pass on the flaming saganaki, even if you're only stopping in for lunch. Killer falafel, too.

**Popover Cafe.** 551 Amsterdam Ave. (btw. 86th and 87th sts.). ☎ **212/595-8555.** Reservations not accepted. Main courses $5.75–$15.50 at breakfast and lunch, $12.50–$22 at dinner. AE, MC, V. Mon–Thurs 8am–10pm, Fri–Sat 8am–11pm, Sun 9am–10pm. Subway: 1, 9 to 86th St. AMERICAN.

The first thing people usually call Popover's is kid-friendly. Not that it isn't—there's the child-size burger, PBJ sandwiches, and cutesy decor chock-a-block with teddy bears—but grownups will like it just as much. Everybody gets addicted to the name-sake item: big, fluffy popovers served with strawberry butter or preserves. The full dinner entrees are too pricey, but Popover's real forte is the kind of comfort food that makes hearty and affordable breakfasts and lunches: three-egg omelets and scrambles, savory home-style chili and soups, and generous salads and sandwiches. A bowl of one of the day's hearty homemade soups (vegetarian three-bean and split pea are two of my favorites) accompanied by a popover makes a more-than-satisfying lunch. Service is appropriately warm and welcoming. In fact, eating here feels like stepping into some-body's big old, hospitable New England home. Well worth a stop. Beware brunch, however, which can ruin the mood.

**Sarabeth's Kitchen.** 423 Amsterdam Ave. (btw. 80th and 81st sts.). ☎ **212/496-6280.** Reservations accepted for dinner only. Main courses $5–$10 breakfast, $10.50–$15 at lunch, $12–$26 at dinner. AE, CB, DC, DISC, JCB, MC, V. Mon–Sat 8am–11pm, Sun 8am–9:30pm. Subway: 1, 9 to 79th St. CONTEMPORARY AMERICAN.

Its 200-year-old family recipe for orange-apricot marmalade rooted Sarabeth's Kitchen into New York's consciousness, and now its fresh-baked goods, award-winning pre-serves, and creative American cooking with a European touch keep a loyal following. This charming country restaurant with a distinct Hamptons feel is best known for its breakfast and weekend brunch, when the menu features such treats as porridge with wheatberries, fresh cream, butter, and brown sugar; pumpkin waffle topped with sour cream, raisins, pumpkin seeds, and honey (a sweet tooth's delight); and a whole host of farm-fresh omelets. But midday is just as good and a lot less crowded. Lunch might be a generous Caesar with aged Parmesan, brioche croutons, and a tangy anchovy dressing, accompanied by velvety cream of tomato soup; a beautifully built country-style sandwich; or a good old-fashioned chicken pot pie. Dinner is more sophis-ticated and splurge-priced, with specialties such as hazelnut-crusted halibut and oven-roasted lamb crusted in black mushrooms. Leave room for the luscious desserts no matter what time you come—or stop by just for dessert!

There's another full-service location at 1295 Madison Ave., at 92nd Street (☎ **212/410-7335**); a cafe inside the Whitney Museum, 945 Madison Ave., at 75th Street (☎ **212/606-0218**); and a bakery at Chelsea Market, 75 Ninth Ave., between 15th and 16th streets (☎ **212/989-2424**).

**Tom's Restaurant.** 2880 Broadway (at 112th St.). ☎ **212/864-6137.** Reservations not accepted. Main courses $3–$10. No credit cards. Sun–Wed 6am–1:30am; Thurs–Sat 24 hours. Subway: 1, 9 to 110th St./Cathedral Pkwy. AMERICAN.

Tom's would be just any other diner if it weren't for its famous connections: This is the restaurant that served as the exterior for Monk's on *Seinfeld* and inspired a young Suzanne Vega to write "Tom's Diner." It's worth a pilgrimage if you're a diehard Jerry fan or worth a stop if you're in the neighborhood. Tom's is hugely popular with Columbia students, thanks to its long hours and super-cheap coffee-shop fare. Expect all the standards, from three-egg omelets to burgers to Virginia ham dinners with applesauce. The circa-'72 waitstaff emits the requisite attitude and won't think twice of rushing you when it's crowded.

## QUICK BITES

For one of the cheapest, most satisfying meal deals in New York, head to the Uptown branch of **Gray's Papaya** (p. 158), 2090 Broadway, at 72nd Street (☎ **212/799-0243**), where first-rate all-beef dogs are just 50¢ each around the clock. Pair your franks with some crispy fries and a tropical juice drink.

## Pizza! Pizza!

The Upper West Side does not lack for good pizza. Near Lincoln Center, **John's Pizzeria** (p. 168), 48 W. 65th St., between Broadway and Central Park West (☎ 212/721-7001), serves up one of the city's best pies in a nice brick-walled dining room.

Farther uptown, the place to go for real Noo Yawk pie is **V&T Pizzeria**, 1024 Amsterdam Ave., between 110th and 111th streets (☎ 212/666-8051 or 212/663-1708). This is a sit-down (or carry-out) restaurant with red-checked tablecloths, old-world service, and traditional pies with rich red sauce and a yummy chewy crust. And because V&T caters to a Columbia University crowd, prices stay low—so how can you *not* splurge on one of the delectable mascarpone-filled cannolis for dessert, right?

---

And what would the Upper West Side be without its own **Burritoville** (p. 136)—or two? There's one at 166 W. 72nd St., at Amsterdam Avenue (☎ 212/580-7700), and a second at 451 Amsterdam Ave., at 81st Street (☎ 212/787-8181).

**Bruno the King of Ravioli**, 2204 Broadway, between 78th and 79th streets (☎ 212/580-8150), is a takeout storefront specializing mostly in fresh pastas, but it also makes a terrific stop for really nice pre-prepared and made-to-order Italian heros, salads, and the like ($5 to $7).

**H&H Bagel**, 2239 Broadway, at 80th Street (☎ 212/595-8003), is the king of New York bagel makers. Stop in to this bare-bones, we-never-close takeout shop for a piping-hot bagel, which is so good it needs no accompaniment. Traditional toppings—cream cheese, lox, and the like—are sold in the refrigerator cases.

If you're stationed farther uptown, the lovely, worn **Hungarian Pastry Shop**, 1030 Amsterdam Ave., between 110th and 111th streets (☎ 212/866-4230), makes an ideal stop for morning coffee and pastry or a late-night plateful of crumbly, buttery cookies. Open Monday through Saturday from 8am to 11:30pm, Sunday to 10:30pm.

# 14 The Upper East Side

Also consider the local branch of **Shabu Tatsu** (p. 150), at 114 York Ave., at 75th Street (☎ 212/472-3322), which is well worth the trip to the far east side of town. There's a branch of **EJ's Luncheonette** (p. 156), the retro all-American diner, at 1271 Third Ave., at 73rd Street (☎ 212/472-0600). Or head to **Sarabeth's Kitchen** (p. 184), which has two eastside locations for top-notch breakfasts or sweet treats: a full-service outpost at 1295 Madison Ave., at 92nd (☎ 212/410-7335), and inside the Whitney Museum, 945 Madison Ave., at 75th (☎ 212/606-0218).

**Jackson Hole.** 232 E. 64th St. (btw. Second and Third aves.). ☎ 212/371-7187. Reservations not accepted. Sandwiches and main courses $3–$11. AE. Daily 10:30am–1am. Subway: 6 to 68th St. AMERICAN.

The "home of the 7 oz. burger" serves satisfying all-American diner food at super-low prices. There's no faulting the juicy burger, which comes in more than 30 topping combos, all piled high on a hefty beef or turkey patty, or a marinated and grilled chicken breast. The Eastsider—a bacon-cheese version topped with ham, mushrooms, tomatoes, and fried onions—is actually trademarked. Hearty salads, blue-plate specials, and stuffed baked potatoes are also on hand, and eggs, omelets, and fluffy pancakes are served all day. This one has garden dining; you'll find other locations at

521 Third Ave., at 35th Street (☎ **212/679-3264**); 1611 Second Ave., between 83rd and 84th (☎ **212/737-8788**); 1270 Madison Ave., at 91st (☎ **212/427-2820**); and on the Upper West Side at 517 Columbus Ave., at 85th St. (☎ **212/362-5177**).

**Pamir.** 1437 Second Ave. (btw. 74th and 75th sts.). ☎ **212/734-3791.** Reservations recommended. Main courses $11.50–$16.50 (salad, rice, and Afghan bread included). MC, V. Tues–Sun 5–11pm. Subway: 6 to 77th St. AFGHAN.

Pamir might not be the sexiest place in town, but it's a good place to sample full-flavored Afghan cuisine. Afghanistan's position astride the main western land route to India through the famed Khyber Pass has resulted in a culinary tradition marked by Middle Eastern and Indian influences. Peruse the menu while sipping *doodh*, a refreshing mix of yogurt, club soda, mint, and a touch of salt. You might start with the combination appetizer, one of which should be *bulanee kachalou*, a tasty turnover stuffed with mildly spiced potatoes and onions, with a tangy yogurt sauce (much like an Indian samosa). If there's an appealing-sounding fish special available, go for it; this is what Pamir does best. Other main-course favorites include *korma-e-murgh*, a hearty stew of delicately seasoned chicken with tomatoes, onions, garlic, and Afghan spices. The kebabs are particularly tasty; try the Pamir Kebab sampler for a taste of beef, chicken, and lamb. Afghan pudding with almonds and pistachios is the perfect finish.

**Serendipity 3.** 225 E. 60th St. (btw. Second and Third aves.). ☎ **212/838-3531.** www. serendipity3.com. Reservations recommended for dinner. Main courses $6–$18, sweets and sundaes $4.50–$10. AE, DC, DISC, MC, V. Sun–Thurs 11:30am–midnight, Fri 11:30am–1am, Sat 11:30am–2am. Subway: 4, 5, 6 to 59th St.; N, R to Lexington Ave. AMERICAN.

You'd never guess that this whimsical place was once a top stop on Andy Warhol's agenda. Wonders never cease—and neither does the confection at this delightful restaurant and sweet shop, tucked into a cozy brownstone a few steps from Bloomingdale's. Remember Farrell's? This is the better version (complete with candy to tempt the kids on the way out), and it's still going strong. Happy people gather at marble-topped ice-cream parlor tables for burgers and foot-long hot dogs, country meat loaf with mashed potatoes and gravy, and salads and sandwiches with cute names such as "The Catcher in the Rye" (their own twist on the BLT, with chicken and Russian dressing—on rye, of course). The food isn't great, but the main courses aren't the point; as at Farrell's, they're just an excuse to get to the desserts. The restaurant's signature is Frozen Hot Chocolate, a slushie version of everybody's cold weather favorite, but other crowd pleasers include dark double devil mousse, celestial carrot cake, lemon ice-box pie, and anything with hot fudge. So cast that willpower aside and come on in; Serendipity is an irony-free charmer to be appreciated by adults and kids alike.

## QUICK BITES

**Papaya King,** 179 E. 86th St., at Third Avenue (☎ **212/369-0648;** www.papayaking. com), is the originator of the two-franks-and-a-fruit-drink combo that Gray's Papaya (p. 158) has popularized in other 'hoods. Papaya King isn't quite so inexpensive as Gray's—the combo is $3.99 here—but the quality is high (exclusive all-beef dogs, all-natural drinks). Open weekdays from 8:30am to midnight, to 1am on Friday and Saturday.

For more refined tastes, there's **Yura & Company,** 6045 Third Ave., at 92nd Street (☎ **212/860-8060**), one of the Upper East Side's best-kept secrets. This quaint gourmet bakery/cafe serves good coffee, superlative scones and muffins, and a nice selection of prepared gourmet foods that are perfect for a Central Park picnic (the 90th Street pedestrian entrance is just a few blocks away). Or you can opt for table service

---

**Pizza! Pizza!**

**Pintaile's Pizza**, at 26 E. 91st St., between Fifth and Madison avenues (☎ 212/722-1967; www.pintailespizza.com), dresses their daintily crisp organic crusts with layers of plum tomatoes, extra-virgin olive oil, and other fabulously fresh ingredients.
For something more traditional, head to **Totonno's Pizzeria Napolitano,** 1544 Second Ave., between 80th and 81st streets (☎ 212/327-2800), for killer coal-oven pies. Some naysayers consider this a pale comparison to the Coney Island original, but I think they're just hung up on the fancier digs. At 408 E. 64th St. between First and York avenues, is a branch of **John's Pizzeria** (☎ 212/935-2895) that's worth checking out (p. 168).

---

in the country-style dining room, a cute spot for a quick breakfast or well-made sandwich. Good angel-food cake, too. There's a second, takeout-only location at Madison Avenue and 92nd Street.

**H&H Bagel** (p. 185), has an outlet at 1551 Second Ave., between 80th and 81st streets (☎ 212/734-7441), where you can stop in around the clock to sample the king of Noo Yawk bagels.

**Burritoville** (p. 136) is at 1489 First Ave., at 77th Street (☎ 212/472-8800), and 1606 Third Ave., between 90th and 91st (☎ 212/410-2255).

## WORTH A SPLURGE

**Payard Pâtisserie & Bistro.** 1032 Lexington Ave. (at 73rd St.). ☎ 212/717-5252. www.payard.com. Reservations not accepted in patisserie. Main courses $11–$24 at lunch, $23–$28 at dinner; prix-fixe lunch $28; dinner tasting menu $56. AE, DC, MC, V. Patisserie open daily 7am–11pm. Subway: 6 to 77th St. FRENCH BISTRO/DESSERT.

It's well worth the trip to this grand turn-of-the-century, Parisian-style cafe for New York's best sweets. There's no need to splurge on pricey lunch or dinner; feel free to pop in just for afternoon tea or dessert if the entree prices are too rich for your wallet. The biggest problem with Payard? Choosing among the fabulous, beautifully presented sweets. Elegant cakes, pastries, and handmade chocolates fill glass cases up front, and mirrors, mahogany, and straightforward bistro fare entice patrons to the cafe in back. Everything is house-made, from the signature cakes, breads, and pastries to the delicate candies. Whether you go with the classic crème brûlée or something more decadent (anything chocolate is to die for), you're sure to be wowed. The rest of the menu is unabashedly classic, with homemade duck confit, thick slabs of foie gras terrine, sublime steak frites, and fragrant bouillabaisse.

## 15  Harlem

**Sylvia's.** 328 Lenox Ave. (btw. 126th and 127th sts.). ☎ 212/996-0660. Reservations accepted for 10 or more. Main courses $8–$16; Sunday gospel brunch $17. AE, DISC, MC, V. Mon–Thurs 8am–10:30pm, Fri–Sat 7:30am–10:30pm, Sun 11am–8pm. Subway: 2, 3 to 125th St. SOUL FOOD.

South Carolina–born Sylvia Woods is the last word in New York soul food. The place is so popular with both locals and visiting celebs that the dining room has spilled into the building next door. Since 1962, her Harlem institution has dished up the southern-fried goods: turkey with down-home stuffing; smothered chicken and pork chops; fried chicken and baked ham; collard greens and candied yams; and cavity-inducing sweet tea. And then of course there's "Sylvia's World Famous, Talked About, Bar-B-Que Ribs

Special"; the sauce is sweet, with a potent afterburn. This Harlem landmark is still presided over by 72-year-old Sylvia, who's likely to greet you at the door herself. Some naysayers say that Sylvia's just isn't what it used to be, but chowing down here is still a one-of-a-kind New York experience. Sunday gospel brunch is a joyous time to go.

## QUICK BITES

**Papaya King** (p. 173) has another location at 121 W. 125th St., between Lenox Avenue and Adam Clayton Powell Boulevard (☎ **212/665-5732** or 212/665-5755). The two-all-beef-franks-and-an-all-natural-fruit-drink combo is a bargain at $3.99.

## 16  Brooklyn

✪ **Grimaldi's Pizzeria.** 19 Old Fulton St. (btw. Front and Water sts.), Brooklyn Heights. ☎ **718/858-4300.** Reservations not accepted. Pies $14 and up, depending on toppings. No credit cards. Mon–Thurs 11:30am–11pm, Fri 11:30am–midnight, Sat–Sun noon–11pm. Subway: 2, 3 to Clark St (use Henry St. exit); A, C to High St. Walk downslope, toward the water; it will be on your right in the last block, across from the Eagle Warehouse. PIZZA.

Here's New York's best pizza. You don't have to take it from me; just check Zagat's, which gives this Brooklyn classic a whopping 26 (out of 30) for food, a rating usually reserved for the likes of Le Cirque. Thin coal-oven crust is topped with perfectly seasoned red sauce, leafy basil, and only the freshest, whitest mozzarella. Crown this perfect pie with your choice of traditional toppings, including meaty pepperoni and house-roasted red peppers. And you don't have to suffer a greasy pizza joint to enjoy this sublime pizza: Grimaldi's is a surprisingly pleasant place, with red-checked tablecloths, photos of Sinatra covering the walls, and the Chairman of the Board himself crooning from the jukebox. Patsy Grimaldi is likely to greet you himself, warmly, with stogie in hand (despite the no smoking signs). Otherwise, the service can be gruff, but that's how you'll know you've arrived—in Brooklyn, that is. The best time to come is in summer, when the restaurant sets up tables on the wide sidewalk outside, where you'll have the kind of spectacular views of the Brooklyn Bridge and twinkling lower Manhattan that usually only big money buys.

# Exploring New York City 7

**F**ace facts, newcomers: It will be impossible to take in the entire city on your first visit. Because New York is almost unfathomably big and constantly changing, you could live your whole life here and still make fascinating daily discoveries; we New Yorkers do. This chapter is designed to give you an overview of what's available in this multifaceted place so you can narrow your choices to an itinerary that's digestible for the amount of time you'll be here—be it a day, a week, or something in between.

So don't try to tame New York; you can't. Decide on a few must-see attractions, and then let the city take you on its own ride. Inevitably, as you schlep around the city you'll be blown off course by unplanned diversions that are just as alluring as what you meant to see. After all, the true New York is in the details, which are free for everyone to enjoy. Take time to admire a lovely cornice on a pre-war building, linger over a cup of coffee at a sidewalk cafe, or just idle away a few minutes on a bench watching New Yorkers parade through their daily lives.

Before you start planning your time and money, be sure to review the sightseeing advice under "60 Money-Saving Tips" in chapter 2.

**LET'S GET LOST**    One of the best ways to experience New York is to pick a neighborhood and just stroll it. Bring a map for reference, but put it in your pocket; let yourself get lost. Walk the prime thoroughfares, poke your head into shops, park yourself on a bench or at an outdoor cafe, and just watch the world go by. For tips on where to go, how to get there, and what highlights to be on the lookout for, see the "Manhattan's Neighborhoods in Brief" in chapter 4.

If getting lost isn't your style—or even if it is—you might consider taking an organized tour. That doesn't have to mean a big bus with an out-of-work-actor pointing out the Empire State Building (although general introductory tours are available, too). Many wonderful walking tours are offered throughout the city. Walking tours are cheap, they're fun, and there's no better way to get to know a neighborhood than with an expert at the helm. For a complete rundown of operators and the kinds of tours they offer, see "Affordable Sightseeing Tours" later in this chapter.

# 1 Sights & Attractions by Neighborhood

## MANHATTAN

### CHELSEA

Chelsea Piers Sports & Entertainment Complex (p. 250)

### EAST VILLAGE & NOHO

Merchant's House Museum (p. 221)

### THE FINANCIAL DISTRICT

Battery Park (p. 206)
Bowling Green Park (p. 206)
Brooklyn Bridge (p. 194)
City Hall & City Hall Park (p. 212)
Cunard Building (p. 208)
Ellis Island (p. 193)
Federal Hall National Memorial (p. 209)
Fraunces Tavern Museum (p. 208)
*Group of Four Trees* (p. 210)
Kalikow Building (p. 211)
Liberty Plaza (p. 210)
The Municipal Building (p. 213)
Museum of American Financial History (p. 209)
Museum of Jewish Heritage (p. 226)
National Museum of the American Indian (p. 227)
New York Stock Exchange (p. 208)
*The Red Cube* (p. 210)
South Street Seaport & Museum (p. 197)
Staten Island Ferry (p. 193)
Statue of Liberty (p. 192)
St. Paul's Chapel (p. 211)
Surrogate's Court (The Hall of Records) (p. 213)
Trinity Church (p. 209)
Tweed Courthouse (p. 212)
U.S. Customs House (p. 206)
Wall Street (p. 209)

Woolworth Building (p. 211)
World Trade Center (p. 210)

### THE FLATIRON DISTRICT

Flatiron Building (p. 237)
Union Square Park (p. 248)

### GREENWICH VILLAGE

Forbes Magazine Galleries (p. 222)
Washington Square Park (p. 249)

### LOWER EAST SIDE

Lower East Side Tenement Museum (p. 225)

### HARLEM & UPPER MANHATTAN

Astor Row Houses (p. 256)
The Cloisters (p. 220)
Dyckman Farmhouse Museum (p. 221)
Morris-Jumel Mansion (p. 221)
Schomburg Center for Research in Black Culture (p. 230)
Strivers' Row (p. 256)
Sugar Hill (p. 257)
Studio Museum in Harlem (p. 230)

### MIDTOWN EAST

Bryant Park (p. 248)
Dahesh Museum (p. 222)
Chrysler Building (p. 231)
Empire State Building (p. 232)
Grand Central Terminal (p. 232)
Japan Society (p. 224)
Morgan Library (p. 225)
Newseum/NY (p. 230)
New York Public Library (p. 233)
Sony Wonder Technology Lab (p. 220)
St. Patrick's Cathedral (p. 238)
United Nations (p. 235)
Whitney Museum of American Art at Philip Morris (p. 231)

## MIDTOWN WEST

International Center of Photography
(p. 223)
*Intrepid* Sea-Air-Space Museum (p. 224)
Lever House (p. 235)
Madison Square Garden (p. 262)
Museum of Modern Art (p. 215)
Museum of Television and Radio
(p. 227)
Rockefeller Center (p. 234)
Seagram Building (p. 235)
Sony Building (p. 235)
Times Square (p. 236)

## SoHo

Children's Museum of the Arts (p. 254)
Guggenheim Museum SoHo (p. 223)
Museum for African Art (p. 226)
New Museum of Contemporary Art
(p. 229)

## TRIBECA

New York City Fire Museum (p. 254)

## UPPER EAST SIDE

Abigail Adams Smith Museum &
Gardens (p. 220)
Asia Society (p. 220)
Central Park (p. 242)
Central Park Wildlife Center/Tisch
Children's Zoo (p. 246)
Cooper-Hewitt National Design
Museum (p. 222)
El Museo del Barrio (p. 222)
The Frick Collection (p. 223)
Gracie Mansion (p. 221)
The Jewish Museum (p. 224)
Metropolitan Museum of Art (p. 214)
Museum of the City of New York
(p. 226)
National Academy of Design (p. 227)
Neue Gallerie New York (p. 228)
Solomon R. Guggenheim Museum
(p. 218)
Temple Emanu-El (p. 238)
Whitney Museum of American Art
(p. 218)

## UPPER WEST SIDE

American Museum of Natural
History (p. 213)
The Ansonia (p. 236)
Cathedral of St. John the Divine
(p. 236)
Central Park (p. 242)
Children's Museum of Manhattan
(p. 254)
The Dakota (p. 236)
Museum of American Folk Art
(p. 226)
New-York Historical Society (p. 230)
Rockefeller Center (p. 234)

# OUTER BOROUGHS
## THE BRONX

Bronx Zoo Wildlife Conservation
Park (p. 257)
Edgar Allen Poe Cottage (p. 221)
New York Botanical Garden
(p. 258)
Yankee Stadium (p. 262)

## BROOKLYN

Brooklyn Botanic Garden (p. 259)
Brooklyn Heights Historic District
(p. 196)
Brooklyn Museum of Art (p. 259)
Coney Island (p. 260)
New York Aquarium (p. 260)
Prospect Park (p. 260)

## QUEENS

American Museum of the Moving
Image (p. 261)
Flushing Meadows–Corona Park
(p. 255)
Isamu Noguchi Garden Museum
(p. 219)
New York Hall of Science (p. 254)
P.S. 1 Contemporary Art Center
(p. 261)
Queens Museum of Art (p. 262)
Shea Stadium (p. 262)

## 2 In New York Harbor: The Statue of Liberty, Ellis Island & the Staten Island Ferry

Budget a full day for the Statue of Liberty and Ellis Island if you intend to explore both attractions thoroughly.

**✪ Statue of Liberty.** On Liberty Island in New York Harbor. ☎ **212/363-3200** (general info) or 212/269-5755 (ticket/ferry info). www.nps.gov/stli. Ferry ticket/admission to Statue of Liberty and Ellis Island $7 adults, $6 seniors, $3 children under 17. Daily 9am–5pm (last ferry departs around 3:30pm); extended hours in summer. Subway: 4, 5 to Bowling Green; N, R to Whitehall St./South Ferry; 1, 9 to South Ferry (the platform at this station is shorter than the train, so ride in the first 5 cars). Walk south through Battery Park to Castle Clinton; the fort houses the ferry ticket booth.

For the millions who first came by ship to America in the last century—either as privileged tourists or needy, hopeful immigrants—Lady Liberty, standing in the Upper Bay, was their first glimpse of America. No monument so embodies the nation's, and the world's, notion of political freedom and economic potential. Even if you don't make it out to Liberty Island, you can get a spine-tingling glimpse from Battery Park, from the New Jersey side of the bay, or during a free ride on the Staten Island Ferry (see below). It's always reassuring to see her torch lighting the way.

Proposed by French statesman Edouard de Laboulaye as a gift from France to the United States commemorating the two nations' friendship and joint notions of liberty, the statue was designed by sculptor Frédéric-Auguste Bartholdi with the engineering help of Alexandre-Gustave Eiffel (responsible for the famed Paris tower), and unveiled on October 28, 1886. Despite the fact that Joseph Pulitzer had to make a mighty effort to attract donations on this side of the Atlantic for her pedestal (designed by American Richard Morris Hunt), more than a million people watched as the French tricolor veil was pulled away. After nearly 100 years of wind, rain, and exposure to the harsh sea air, Lady Liberty received a resoundingly successful $150-million face-lift (including the relandscaping of Liberty Island and the replacement of the torch's flame) in time for its centennial celebration on July 4, 1986. Feted in fireworks, Miss Liberty became more of a city icon than ever before.

**Touring Tips:** Ferries leave daily every half-hour to 45 minutes from 9am to about 3:30pm (their clock), with more frequent ferries in the morning and extended hours in summer. Try to go early on a weekday to avoid the crowds that swarm in the afternoon, on weekends, and on holidays. Be sure to arrive by noon if your heart's set on experiencing everything; go later and you might not have time to make it to the crown (summer visitors should see "Attention: Crown Climbers" below for details on possible restrictions). A stop at Ellis Island (below) is included in the fare, but if you catch the last ferry, you can only visit the statue or Ellis Island, not both.

The ferry ride takes about 20 minutes. Once on Liberty Island, you'll start to get an idea of the statue's immensity: She weighs 225 tons and measures 152 feet from foot to flame. Her nose alone is 4$^1$/2 feet long, and her index finger is 8 feet long. You might have to wait as long as 3 hours to walk up into the crown (the torch is not open to visitors). If it's summer, or if you're just not in shape for it, you might want to skip it: It's a grueling 354 steps (the equivalent of 22 stories) to the crown, or you can cheat and take the elevator the first 10 stories up (an act I wholeheartedly endorse). But even if you take this shortcut, the interior is stifling once the temperature starts to climb. However, you don't have to go all the way up to the crown; there are a number of **observation decks** at different levels, including one at the top of the pedestal reachable by elevator. Even if you don't go inside, a stroll around the base is an extraordinary experience, and the views of the Manhattan skyline are stellar.

## Attention: Crown Climbers

At press time, the park had instituted a special "crown" policy during the peak **summer** season: Visitors who want to walk up to the crown must be on one of the **first two ferries of the day** in order to do so. This policy is subject to change at any time, of course, so your best bet is to call ahead to learn the current policy before you plan your day.

At other times of year, you must be on line to climb to the crown by 2pm; otherwise, you will not be allowed up.

---

○ **Ellis Island.** Located in New York Harbor. ☎ **212/363-3200** (general info) or 212/269-5755 (ticket/ferry info). www.ellisisland.org. For subway, hours, and ferry ticket details, see the Statue of Liberty, directly above (ferry trip includes stops at both sights).

One of New York's most moving sights, the restored Ellis Island opened in 1990, slightly north of Liberty Island. Roughly 40% of Americans (me included) can trace their heritage back to an ancestor who came through here. For the 62 years when it was America's main entry point for immigrants (from 1892 to 1954), Ellis Island processed some 12 million people. The greeting was often brusque—especially in the early years of the century, until 1924, when as many as 12,000 came through in a single day. The statistics and their meaning can be overwhelming, but the **Immigration Museum** skillfully relates the story of Ellis Island and immigration in America by placing the emphasis on personal experience.

Today you enter the Main Building's baggage room, just as the immigrants did, and then climb the stairs to the **Registry Room,** with its dramatic vaulted tiled ceiling, where millions waited anxiously for medical and legal processing. A step-by-step account of the immigrants' voyage is detailed in the exhibit, with haunting photos and touching oral histories. What might be the most poignant exhibit is **"Treasures from Home,"** 1,000 objects and photos donated by descendants of immigrants, including family heirlooms, religious articles, and rare clothing and jewelry. Outside, the **American Immigrant Wall of Honor** commemorates the names of more than 500,000 immigrants and their families, from Myles Standish to Jay Leno. You can even research your own family's history at the interactive **American Family Immigration History Center.** You might also make time to see the award-winning short film **"Trail of Hope, Trail of Tears,"** which plays on a continuous loop in two theaters. Additionally, the museum now stages a 30-minute play five times daily from 10:30am to 3:30pm called **"Ellis Island Stories,"** based on stories from the Ellis Island Oral History Archive ($3 adults, $2.50 seniors and kids 4–17). Whether you make time for this live performance or not, it's difficult to leave the museum unmoved.

**Touring Tips:** Ferries run daily to Ellis Island and Liberty Island from Battery Park and Liberty State Park at frequent intervals; see the Statue of Liberty listing (directly above) for details.

**Staten Island Ferry.** Departs from the Whitehall Ferry Terminal at the southern tip of Manhattan. ☎ **718/815-BOAT.** www.SI-Web.com/transportation/dot.htm. Free ($3 for car transport on select ferries). 24 hours; every 20–30 min weekdays, less frequently on off-peak and weekend hours. Subway: 1, 9 to South Ferry (ride in the first 5 cars); N, R to Whitehall St./South Ferry; 4, 5 to Bowling Green.

Here's New York's best freebie—especially if you just want to glimpse the Statue of Liberty and not climb her steps. You get an enthralling hour-long excursion (round-trip) into the world's biggest harbor. This is not strictly a sightseeing ride, but commuter

# Cheap Thrills: What to See & Do for Free

I won't kid you—New York can be an expensive city. But the good news is that it doesn't have to be. The Big Apple offers more freebies than you might think:

- **Ride the Staten Island Ferry.** This iconic ride into the world's biggest harbor has many charms, not the least of which is that it's absolutely free. The hour-long excursion offers the same brilliant Lower Manhattan skyline views as private harbor cruises with high price tags. And if you want to see the Statue of Liberty from the water but prefer to skip the tourist crowds, the ferry will take you gliding right by Lady Liberty.

- **Promenade Across the Brooklyn Bridge.** This is one of my favorite activities in the entire city. The easy walk from end to end offers a remarkable, up-close perspective of the marvelous Gothic-inspired stone pylons and intricate steel-cable webs that established the first physical connection between Brooklyn and Manhattan in 1883. Start at the Brooklyn end for the best views.

- **Take a Walking Tour.** The best way to get to know New York is to pick one or two of its distinctive neighborhoods and meet them on a human scale. I recommend a number of very good guides that offer affordable walks later in this chapter, but there's no need to spend a dime on one if you don't want to. A self-guided walking tour of historic Lower Manhattan is included in this chapter—or, if you'd rather go with a guide, consider one of the freebies offered by a local business improvement district, or arrange in advance to take a walk through the neighborhood of your choice with Big Apple Greeter (see "Show Me, Show Me, Show Me: Free Walking Tours" later in this chapter). Or just take out a map and chart a route for yourself.

- **Visit Museums.** Many museums are charging upwards of 10 bucks to get in the door these days—but the culture vulture who plans ahead can enjoy a whole vacation's worth of museum-going for absolutely free. Every week many of the city's top museums and lesser-known gems set aside an afternoon, evening, or even an entire day when you can donate what you like or explore at no charge. Some are even free every day. See the "Free Culture at Big Apple Museums" box below.

- **Ogle the City's Architecture.** New York boasts such a wealth of architectural treasures that this one could easily keep you busy for a full day or more. It doesn't cost a penny to admire such works of art and engineering as the neo-Gothic Woolworth Building; Rockefeller Center, an art-deco delight; regal Uptown apartment buildings such as the legendary Dakota; paragons of the International Style such as the Lever House; and majestic Grand Central Terminal, recently restored to its original glory. See "Skyscrapers & Other Architectural Marvels," below.

- **Spend Saturday Afternoon Gallery Hopping.** You don't have to be carting a big fat checkbook to peruse New York's world-class art galleries. Virtually all

transportation to Staten Island (remember Melanie Griffith, in big hair and sneakers, heading to the office in *Working Girl?*). As a result, during business hours, you'll share the boat with working stiffs reading papers and drinking coffee inside, blissfully unaware of the sights outside.

You, however, should go on deck and enjoy the busy harbor traffic. The old orange-and-green boats usually have open decks along the sides or at the bow and stern; try to catch one of these boats if you can because the newer white boats don't are open free to the public—and most people who come through the door don't buy, so nobody will be expecting you to whip out the gold card, either. Consider going on Saturday afternoon, a particularly popular time for gallery hopping. See "Art for Art's Sake: The Gallery Scene."

- **Go to the Park.** Lots of travelers don't bother with Central Park—and they're making a huge mistake. An urban miracle, this massive verdant playground forms the backbone of the city, both physically and socially. This is where New Yorkers come year-round to relax, play, commune with nature, and get to know one another. Don't skip the chance to enjoy its many wonders. Or, if you like things on a smaller scale, head to one of the city's other green spaces, each of which has its own winning personality, from memorial-heavy Battery Park to the pleasing social scene at Union Square.

- **Attend a TV Show Taping.** With some advance planning—or just the right amount of luck on tape day—you can be an audience member at your favorite morning gabfest, network sitcom, or late-night talk show for absolutely free. I can't guarantee that you'll score tickets to Dave, Rosie, or Regis for the date of your choice (Montel, Sally, or Ricki are much surer bets), but who knows? For tips on getting tix, see "Talk of the Town: Free TV Tapings."

- **Celebrate Sunday Morning in Harlem.** In a mixed blessing for local congregations, Sunday-morning gospel services have become so popular that tour groups sometimes outnumber parishioners at Abyssinian Baptist Church; see "Attractions in Upper Manhattan."

- **Hear Some Classical Music.** Juilliard is one of New York's greatest cultural bargains. The nation's premier music school sponsors excellent-quality performances, ranging from classical concerts to opera to drama to dance, throughout the year—and most are free. The best way to learn about the wide array of productions is to call (☎ 212/769-7406) or visit the schools' Web site (www.juilliard.edu). Watch for master classes and discussions open to the public featuring celebrity guest teachers. For further details, see chapter 9.

- **Take Advantage of Summer's Outdoor Events.** New York's parks overflow with freebies in the warm months. The city's most famous freebie is **Shakespeare in the Park,** a quintessential New York activity that can feature such names as Patrick Stewart and Andre Braugher taking on the Bard under the stars. Central Park also hosts a full slate of concerts at **SummerStage** that can range from James Brown to Verdi opera, as well as the **Metropolitan Opera** and **New York Philharmonic** beneath the stars. See "Park It! Shakespeare & Other Free Fun" in chapter 9 for details on these and other free events.

have decks. Grab a seat on the right side of the boat for the best view. On the way out of Manhattan, you'll pass the Statue of Liberty (the boat comes closest to Lady Liberty on the way to Staten Island), Ellis Island, and from the left side of the boat, Governor's Island; you'll see the Verranzano Narrows bridge spanning the distance from Brooklyn to Staten Island in the distance.

When the boat arrives at St. George, Staten Island, everyone must disembark. Follow the boat loading sign on your right as you get off; you'll circle around to the next loading dock, where there's usually another boat waiting to depart for Manhattan. The skyline views are simply awesome on the return trip. Well worth the time spent—and the fare simply can't be beat.

## 3  Historic Lower Manhattan's Top Attractions

✪ **Brooklyn Bridge.** Subway: 4, 5, 6 to Brooklyn Bridge/City Hall; A, C to High St.

Its Gothic-inspired stone pylons and intricate steel-cable webs have moved poets such as Walt Whitman and Hart Crane to sing the praises of this great span, the first to cross the East River and connect Manhattan to Brooklyn. Begun in 1867 and ultimately completed in 1883, the beautiful Brooklyn Bridge is now the city's best-known symbol of the age of growth that seized the city during the late 19th century. Walk across the bridge, and imagine the awe that New Yorkers of that age felt at seeing two boroughs joined by this monumental span. It's still astounding.

Designed by John Roebling, this massive engineering feat was plagued by death and disaster at its birth. Roebling was fatally injured in 1869 when a ferry rammed a waterfront piling on which he stood. His son, Washington, who was subsequently put in charge, contracted the bends in 1872 while working underwater to construct the bridge's towers and oversaw the rest of the construction with a telescope from his bed at the edge of the East River in Brooklyn Heights (his wife relayed his instructions to the workers). Washington refused to attend the 1883 opening ceremonies, having had a bitter disagreement with the company that financed the construction. Although it was declared the "eighth wonder of the world" upon its completion, the bridge's troubles were not over: Twelve pedestrians were killed in a stampede when panic about its eminent collapse spread like wildfire on the day it opened to the public. Things are usually calmer now.

**Walking the Bridge:** Walking the Brooklyn Bridge is one of my all-time favorite New York activities. A wide wood-plank pedestrian walkway is elevated above the traffic, making it a relatively peaceful, and popular, walk. It provides a great vantage point from which to contemplate the New York skyline and the East River.

There's a sidewalk entrance on Park Row, just across from City Hall Park (take the 4, 5, or 6 train to Brooklyn Bridge/City Hall). But why do this walk *away* from Manhattan, toward the far less impressive Brooklyn skyline? For gorgeous Manhattan skyline views, take an A or C train to High Street, one stop into Brooklyn. From there, you'll be on the bridge in no time: Come above ground, walk through the little park to Cadman Plaza East, and head downslope (left) to the stairwell that will take you up to the footpath. (Following Prospect Place under the bridge, turning right onto Cadman Plaza East, will also take you directly to the stairwell.) It's a 20- to 40-minute stroll over the bridge to Manhattan, depending on your pace, the amount of foot traffic, and the number of stops you make to contemplate the spectacular views (there are benches along the way). The footpath will deposit you right at City Hall Park.

**New York Stock Exchange.** 20 Broad St. (between Wall St. and Exchange Place). ☎ **212/ 656-5165.** www.nyse.com. Free admission. Mon–Fri 9am–4:30pm (ticket booth opens at 8:45am). Subway: 2, 3, 4, 5 to Wall St.; J, M, Z to Broad St.

Wall Street—it's an iconic name and ground zero for bulls and bears everywhere. This narrow 18th-century lane (you'll be surprised at how little it is) is appropriately monumental, lined with neoclassical towers that reach as far skyward as the dreams and greed of investors who built it into the world's most famous financial market. At the heart of the action is the New York Stock Exchange, the world's largest securities trader, where you can watch the billions change hands and get a fleeting idea of how the money merchants work.

Although the NYSE is on Wall Street, the ticket kiosk is around the corner at 20 Broad St., where you'll be issued a ticket with a time on it; you must enter during the 45-minute window of opportunity specified on your ticket. The staff starts handing out tickets at 8:45am, but get in line early if you want to be inside to see all hell break loose at the 9:30am opening bell. The 3,000 tickets issued per day are usually gone by noon; plan on having to return unless you're one of the first in line. Despite the number of visitors, things move pretty quickly.

Don't expect to come out with a full understanding of the market; if you didn't have one going in, you won't leave any more enlightened. Still, it's fun watching the action on the trading floor from the glass-lined, mezzanine-level **observation gallery** (look to the right, and you'll see the Bloomberg people sending their live reports back to the newsroom). You can stay as long as you like, but it doesn't really take more than 20 minutes or so to peruse the other jingoistic exhibits ("NYSE—our hero!"), which include a rather oblique explanation of the floor activities, interactive exhibits, and a short film presentation of the Exchange's history and present-day operations.

**South Street Seaport & Museum.** At Water and South sts.; museum is at 12–14 Fulton St. ☎ 212/748-8600 or 212/SEA-PORT. www.southstseaport.org or www.southstreetseaport. com. Museum admission $6 adults, $5 seniors, $3 children. Museum: May–Sept, Fri–Wed 10am–6pm, Thurs 10am–8pm; Oct–Apr, Wed–Mon 10am–5pm. Subway: 2, 3, 4, 5 to Fulton St. (walk east, or downslope, on Fulton St. to Water St.).

This landmark district on the East River encompasses 11 square blocks of historic buildings, a maritime museum, several piers, shops, and restaurants (including the authentically old-world North Star Pub; see chapter 6), and even a Best Western hotel (see chapter 5).

You can explore most of the seaport on your own. It's an odd place. The 18th- and 19th-century buildings lining the cobbled streets and alleyways are beautifully restored but nevertheless have a theme-park air about them, no doubt due to the J. Crews, Brookstones, and Body Shops housed within. The height of the cheesiness is **Pier 17,** a historic barge converted into a mall, complete with food court and cheap jewelry kiosks.

Despite its rampant commercialism, the seaport is worth a look. There's a good amount of history to be discovered here, most of it around the **South Street Seaport Museum,** a fitting tribute to the sea commerce that once thrived here.

Including the galleries—which house paintings and prints, ship models, scrimshaw, and nautical designs, as well as frequently changing exhibitions—there are a number of historic ships berthed at the pier to explore, including the 1911 four-masted *Peking* and the 1893 Gloucester fishing schooner *Lettie G. Howard.* A few of the boats are living museums and restoration works in progress; others are available for private charters. You can actually hit the high seas on the 1885 cargo schooner *Pioneer* (☎ 212/ 748-8786), which offers 2-hour public sails daily from early May through September. Tickets are $20 for adults, $15 for seniors and students, and $12 for children. Advance reservations are recommended; always call ahead to confirm sailing times.

Even **Pier 17** has its merits. Head up to the third-level deck overlooking the East River, where the long wooden chairs will have you thinking about what it was like to cross the Atlantic on the *Normandie.* From this level you can see south to the Statue of Liberty and north to the Gothic majesty of the Brooklyn Bridge and Brooklyn Heights on the opposite shore.

# Downtown Attractions

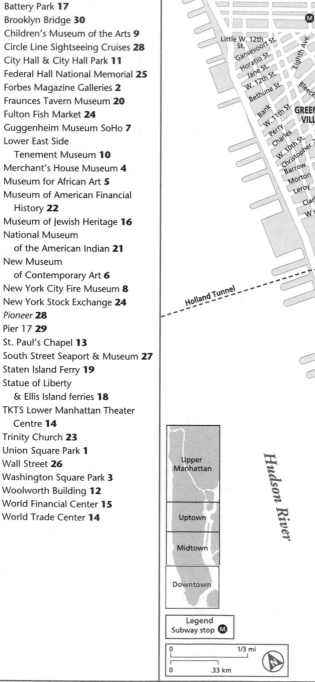

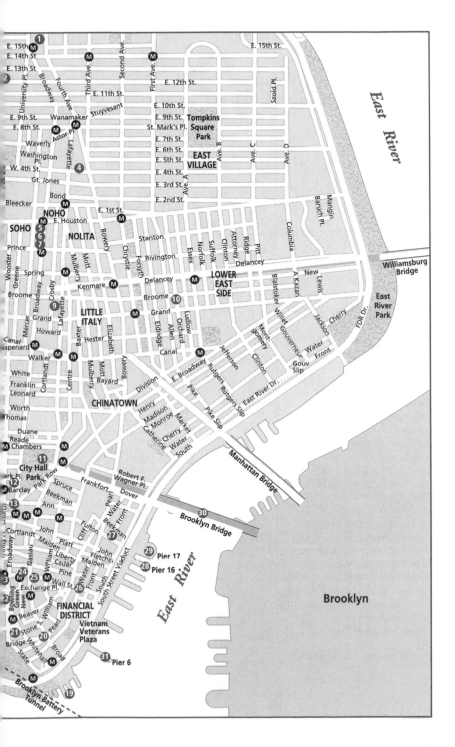

# Midtown Attractions

# Uptown Attractions

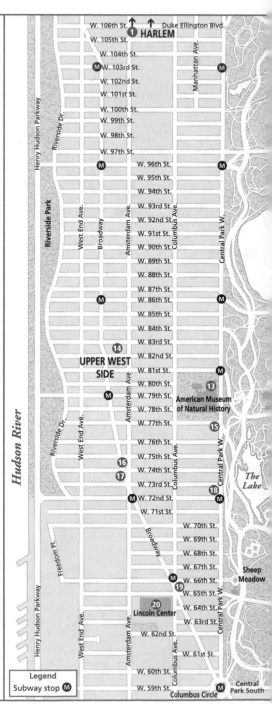

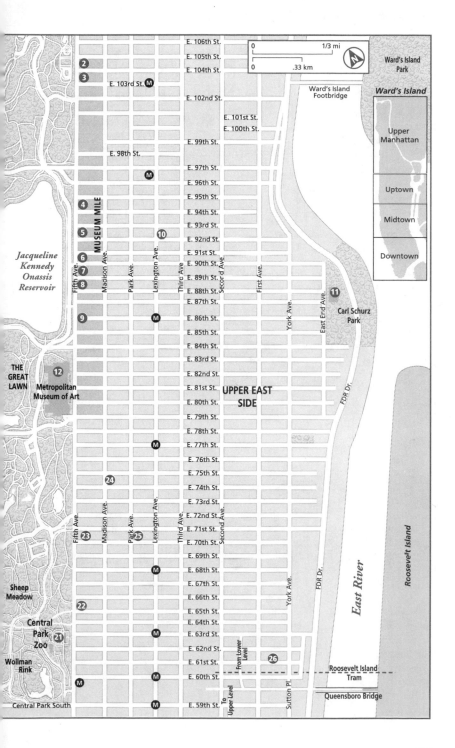

# Upper Manhattan Attractions

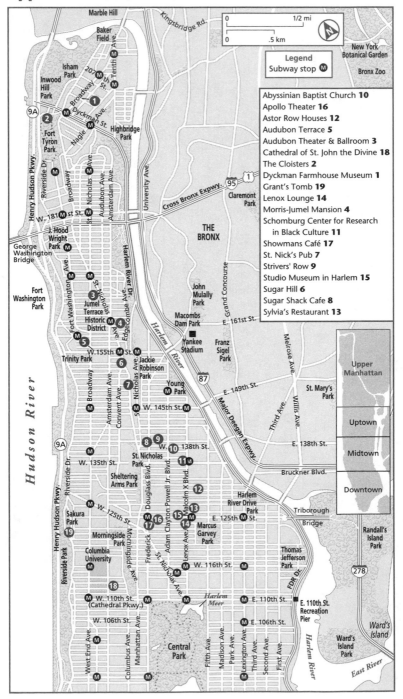

Abyssinian Baptist Church **10**
Apollo Theater **16**
Astor Row Houses **12**
Audubon Terrace **5**
Audubon Theater & Ballroom **3**
Cathedral of St. John the Divine **18**
The Cloisters **2**
Dyckman Farmhouse Museum **1**
Grant's Tomb **19**
Lenox Lounge **14**
Morris-Jumel Mansion **4**
Schomburg Center for Research
  in Black Culture **11**
Showmans Café **17**
St. Nick's Pub **7**
Strivers' Row **9**
Studio Museum in Harlem **15**
Sugar Hill **6**
Sugar Shack Cafe **8**
Sylvia's Restaurant **13**

Just to the north of Pier 17 is the famous **Fulton Fish Market,** on Fulton Street at the East River, the nation's largest wholesale fish market. If you're willing to come back down here at 4am, you can watch the catch of the day from all over the globe being tossed, traded, and sold the old-fashioned way. The city's great chefs and wholesale buyers from all over the country gather here daily to snap up untold pounds of fish.

At the gateway to the Seaport, at Fulton and Water streets, is the *Titanic* **Memorial Lighthouse,** a monument to those who lost their lives when the ocean liner sank on April 15, 1912. It was erected overlooking the East River in 1913 and moved to this spot in 1968, just after the historic district was so designated.

A variety of events takes place year-round, ranging from street performers to concerts to fireworks; check the Web site or dial ☎ **212/SEA-PORT.**

**World Trade Center.** Bounded by Church, Vesey, Liberty, and West sts. ☎ **212/ 323-2340.** Admission to observation deck $13 adults, $9.50 seniors, $11 students 13–17, $6.50 children 6–12. Observation deck: Sept–May, daily 9:30am–9:30pm; June–Aug, daily 9:30am–11:30pm. Subway: C, E to World Trade Center; 1, 9, N, R to Cortlandt St.

Nowhere near as romantic as the Empire State Building (see "Skyscrapers & Other Architectural Marvels" later in this chapter), the World Trade Center is nevertheless just as heroic, having withstood a bombing in its basement garage in 1993 without so much as a flinch. Built in 1970, the center is actually an immense complex of seven buildings on 16 acres housing offices, restaurants, a hotel, an underground shopping mall, and an outdoor plaza with fountains, sculpture, and summer concerts and performances. But the parts you'll be interested in are the Twin Towers, which usurped the Empire State to become New York's tallest structures.

The box-like buildings are so nondescript that the local Channel 11 once used them to represent that number in their commercials. Each is 110 stories and 1,350 feet high. The **Top of the World** observation deck is high atop 2 World Trade Center, to the south. On the 107th floor, it's like a cheesy mini theme park, offering (besides the views, of course) a 6-minute simulated helicopter tour over Manhattan that's so low-grade it looks like it was filmed in 1978; high-tech kiosks pointing out the sights in every direction; a food court; and a gift shop.

But the reason to come is for those incredible views. The enclosed top floor offers incredible panoramas on all sides, with windows reaching right down to the floor. Go ahead, walk right up to one, and look down—*scaaary.*

If you're lucky and the weather is good, you'll be able to go out on the **rooftop promenade,** the world's highest open-air observation deck. (It's only open under perfect conditions; I've only been able to go out once in a lifetime of visits.) You thought inside was incredible? Wait 'til you see this. While you're up here, look straight down and wonder what Frenchman Philippe Petit could've been thinking when in 1974 he shot a rope across to tower no. 1, grabbed his balancing pole, and walked gingerly across, stopping to lie down for a moment in the center.

You can have a similar view in more convivial conditions by going to the top of 1 World Trade Center, where you can linger over a drink and munchies—or put on some dancing shoes and hit the floor—at the Greatest Bar on Earth (see chapter 9).

# Walking Tour: Wall Street & the Financial District

**Start:** Battery Park/U.S. Customs House.
**Subway:** Take the 4 or 5 to Bowling Green, the 1 or 9 to South Ferry, or the N or R to Whitehall St./South Ferry.
**Finish:** The Municipal Building.

**Time:** Approximately 3 hours.

**Best Time:** Any weekday, when the wheels of finance are spinning and lower Manhattan is a maelstrom of frantic activity.

**Worst Time:** Weekends, when most buildings and all the financial markets are closed.

The narrow winding streets of the Financial District occupy the earliest-settled area of Manhattan, where the Dutch established the colony of Nieuw Amsterdam in the early 17th century. Before their arrival, downtown was part of a vast forest, a lush hunting ground for the Native Americans, inhabited by mountain lions, bobcats, beavers, white-tailed deer, and wild turkeys. A hunting path—which later evolved into Broadway—extended from the Battery to the present City Hall Park.

Today this section of the city, much like Nieuw Amsterdam, centers on commerce. Wall Street is America's most cogent symbol of money and power; bulls and bears have replaced the wild beasts of the forest, and conservatively attired lawyers, stockbrokers, bankers, and businesspeople have supplanted the Native Americans and Dutchmen who once traded otter skins and beaver pelts on these very streets.

A highlight of this tour is the Financial District's architecture, in which the neighborhood's modern manifestations and grand historical structures are dramatically juxtaposed: Colonial, 18th-century Georgian/Federal, and 19th-century neoclassical buildings stand in the shadow of colossal skyscrapers.

The subways all exit in or near **Battery Park,** an expanse of green at Manhattan's tip resting entirely upon landfill—an old strategy of the Dutch to expand their settlement farther into the bay. The original tip of Manhattan ran somewhere right along Battery Place, which borders the north side of the park. State Street flanks the park's east side, and stretched along it, filling the space below Bowling Green, squats the beaux arts bulk of the old:

1. **Alexander Hamilton U.S. Customs House,** housing the Smithsonian's George Gustav Haye Center of the National Museum of the American Indian (☎ 212/ 668-6624; www.si.edu/nmai) until the museum's new home in Washington, DC, is completed in 2002. The giant statues lining the front of this granite 1907 structure personify *Asia* (pondering philosophically), *America* (bright-eyed and bushy-tailed), *Europe* (decadent, whose time has passed), and *Africa* (sleeping) and were carved by Daniel Chester French of Lincoln Memorial fame. The most interesting, if unintentional, sculptural statement—keeping in mind the building's current purpose—is the giant seated woman to the left of the entrance representing America. The young, upstart America is surrounded by references to Native America: Mayan pictographs adorning her throne, Quetzalcoatl under her foot, a shock of corn in her lap, and the generic plains Indian scouting out from over her shoulder. Look behind her throne for the stylized crow figure—an important animal in many native cultures, usually playing a trickster character in myths, which is probably why he's hiding back here.

    The airy oval rotunda inside was frescoed by Reginald Marsh to glorify the shipping industry (and, by extension, the customs office once here). The museum is free; for more information, see "More Manhattan Museums," later in this chapter.

    As you exit the building, directly in front of you sits the pretty little oasis of:

2. **Bowling Green Park.** This is probably the spot, or at least near enough, where in 1626 Dutchman Peter Minuit gave glass beads and other trinkets worth about 60 Guilders ($24) to a group of Indians and then claimed he had thereby bought Manhattan. Now the local Indians didn't consider that they owned this island—

# Walking Tour: Wall Street & the Financial District

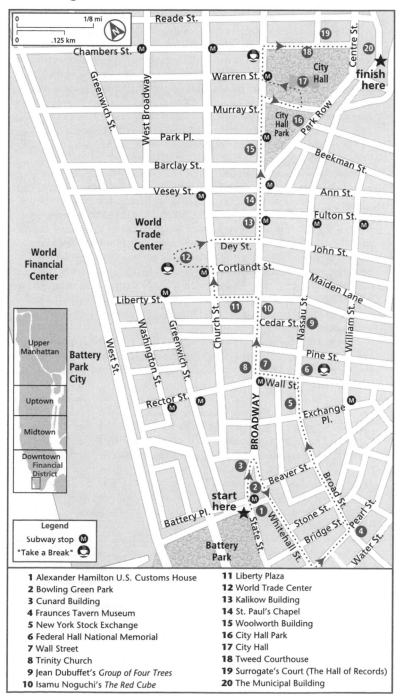

**Legend**
- Subway stop Ⓜ
- "Take a Break" 🍴

1 Alexander Hamilton U.S. Customs House
2 Bowling Green Park
3 Cunard Building
4 Fraunces Tavern Museum
5 New York Stock Exchange
6 Federal Hall National Memorial
7 Wall Street
8 Trinity Church
9 Jean Dubuffet's *Group of Four Trees*
10 Isamu Noguchi's *The Red Cube*
11 Liberty Plaza
12 World Trade Center
13 Kalikow Building
14 St. Paul's Chapel
15 Woolworth Building
16 City Hall Park
17 City Hall
18 Tweed Courthouse
19 Surrogate's Court (The Hall of Records)
20 The Municipal Building

not because they didn't believe in property (that's a colonial myth), as they did have their own territories nearby. But Manhattan (which in local language means "hilly island") was considered communal hunting ground, shared by several different groups. So it isn't clear what the Indians thought the trinkets meant. Either (a) they just thought the exchange was a formal way, one to which they were accustomed, of closing an agreement to extend the shared hunting use of the island to this funny-looking group of pale people with yellow beards; or (b) they were knowingly selling land that they didn't own in the first place, thus performing the first shrewd real-estate deal of the Financial District.

The park also marks the start of Broadway. Walk up the left side of Broadway; at no. 25 is the:

3. **Cunard Building,** now a post office but in 1921 the ticketing room for Cunard, one of the world's most glamorous shipping and cruise lines and proprietors of the *QEII*. Cunard established the first passenger steamship between Europe and the Americas, and in this still-impressive Great Hall, you once could book passage on any one of their famous fantastically unfortunate ships, from the *Lusitania* (blown up by the Germans) to the *Titanic* (well, you know the story).

As you exit the building, cross to the traffic island to pat the enormous bronze **bull,** symbol of a strong stock market, ready to charge up Broadway. This instant icon began as a practical joke by Italian sculptor Arturo DiModica, who originally stuck it in front of the New York Stock Exchange building in the middle of the night. The unamused brokers had it promptly removed, and it eventually got placed here.

Now you're going to backtrack a bit. Head south on Whitehall Street (around the left side of the U.S. Customs House) and turn left onto Pearl Street. Just past Broad Street stretches a historic block lined with (partially rebuilt) 18th- and 19th-century buildings, including:

4. **Fraunces Tavern,** 54 Pearl St. The restaurant on the main floor is now closed, but the two upper stories still house the **Fraunces Tavern Museum (☎ 212/425-1778),** where you can see the Long Room, in which George Washington made his historic farewell to his soldiers at the end of the American Revolution, and other American history exhibits, including "Fraunces Tavern & World War I" and "A Flash of Color," chronicling early American flags and standards. Admission is $2.50 for adults, $1 for seniors and students. Open Monday through Friday from 10am to 4:45pm, Saturday from noon to 4pm.

From Fraunces Tavern, head straight up Broad Street. At no. 20, on the left, is the visitor's entrance to the:

5. **New York Stock Exchange (☎ 212/656-5165),** which came into being in 1792, when merchants met daily under a nearby buttonwood tree to try and pass off to each other the U.S. bonds that had been sold to fund the Revolutionary War. By 1903, they were trading stocks of publicly held companies in this Corinthian-columned beaux arts "temple" designed by George Post. More than 3,000 companies are listed on the exchange, trading nearly 281 billion shares valued at more than $12 trillion. The observation platform has been glassed in since the 1960s, when Abbie Hoffman and Jerry Rubin created chaos by tossing dollar bills onto the exchange floor. Admission is free; for more information, see "Historic Lower Manhattan's Top Attractions" directly above.

Continue north (left) up Broad Street. At the end of the block you'll see the Parthenon-inspired:

## The Money Museum

Real money buffs (and who among us isn't?) might want to make a brief stop at the **Museum of American Financial History,** 28 Broadway, just north of Bowling Green Park (☎ **212/908-4110** or 212/908-4519; www.financialhistory.org). Exhibits housed in this little museum include numismatic and vintage ticker-tape displays; murals and photos depicting historic Wall Street scenes; and interactive financial news terminals, in partnership with CNNfn, so little bulls and bears can learn how to keep up with the market. Open Tuesday through Saturday from 10am to 4pm; the suggested donation is $2.

**6. Federal Hall National Memorial.** 26 Wall St., at Nassau Street (☎ **212/825-6888;** www.nps.gov/feha). Fronted by 32-foot fluted marble Doric columns, this imposing 1842 neoclassical temple is most famous for the history of the old British City Hall building, later called Federal Hall, that once stood here. Peter Zenger, publisher of the outspoken *Weekly Journal,* stood trial in 1735 for "seditious libel" against Royal Gov. William Cosby. Defended brilliantly by Alexander Hamilton, Zenger's eventual acquittal (based on the grounds that anything you printed that was true, even if it wasn't very nice, couldn't be construed as libel) set the precedent for freedom of the press, later guaranteed in the Bill of Rights, which was drafted and signed inside this building.

New York's first major rebellion against British authority occurred here when the Stamp Act Congress met in 1765 to protest King George III's policy of "taxation without representation." J.Q.A. Ward's 1883 statue of George Washington on the steps commemorates the spot of the first presidential inauguration, in 1789. Congress met here after the revolution, when New York was briefly the nation's capital.

Exhibits within (open Monday through Friday 9am to 5pm, daily in July and August) elucidate these events along with other aspects of American history. Admission is free; call ahead if you'd like to hook up with one of the 20- to 30-minute guided tours, which usually take place between 12:30 and 3:30pm.

☕ **TAKE A BREAK**   If you're ready to rest your weary toes for a few minutes, turn left out of Federal Hall and proceed to **Mangia,** at 40 Wall St., between Nassau and William streets (☎ **212/425-4040**). This big, bustling gourmet cafeteria is the ideal place to relax over a mid-morning snack or a full lunch. Open weekdays from 7am to 6pm; for more information, see chapter 6.

From Federal Hall, or Mangia, turn right up the road that has become the symbol of high finance the world over:

**7. Wall Street.** It is narrow, just a few short blocks long, and started out as a service road that ran along the fortified wall the Dutch erected in 1653 to defend against Indian attack. (Gov. Peter Stuyvesant's settlers had at first played tribes off against each other in order to trick them into more and more land cessation, but the native groups quickly realized that their real enemies were the Dutch.)

Wall Street hits Broadway across the street from:

**8. Trinity Church** (☎ **212/602-0800;** www.trinitywallstreet.org). This Wall Street house of worship—with neo-Gothic flying buttresses, beautiful stained-glass windows, and vaulted ceilings—was designed by Richard Upjohn and consecrated in 1846. At that time its 280-foot spire dominated the skyline. Its main doors, embellished with biblical scenes, were inspired in part by Ghiberti's famed doors on Florence's Baptistery.

The first church on this site went up in 1697 and burned down in 1776. The church runs a brief tour daily at 2pm. There's a small museum at the end of the left aisle displaying documents (including the 1697 church charter from King William III), photographs, replicas of the Hamilton-Burr duel pistols, and other items. Alexander Hamilton is buried in the churchyard (against the south fence, next to steamboat inventor Robert Fulton), where the oldest grave dates from 1681. Lined with benches, this makes a wonderful picnic spot on warm days.

The church is open to the public weekdays 7am to 6pm, Saturday 8am to 4pm, and Sunday 7am to 4pm. Services are held weekdays at 8:15am and 12:05 and 5:15pm, Saturday at 9am, and Sunday at 9 and 11:15am. Trinity holds its Noonday Concert series of chamber music and orchestral concerts Thursdays at 1pm; a $2 contribution is requested. Call ☎ 212/602-0747 or visit the Web site for details.

Take a left as you leave the church and walk two short blocks up Broadway. As you pass Cedar Street, look (don't walk) to your right, across Broadway, and at the end of the street you'll see:

**9. Jean Dubuffet's** *Group of Four Trees,* installed in 1972 in the artist's patented style: amorphous mushroomlike white shapes traced with undulating black lines. Closer at hand, in front of the tall black HSBC building on Broadway between Cedar and Liberty streets, is:

**10. Isamu Noguchi's 1967** *The Red Cube,* another famed outdoor sculpture (some of you might recognize it from Beck's "Devil's Haircut" video). Noguchi fancied that this rhomboid "cube"—balancing on its corner and shot through with a cylinder of empty space—represented chance, like the "rolling of the dice." It is appropriately located in the gilt-edged gambling den that is the Financial District.

As you're looking at the Cube across Broadway, behind you is the tiny square called:

**11. Liberty Plaza,** a block off Liberty Street with some benches and shade for lunching CEOs. Turn left and walk through the park, heading east toward Trinity Place. Mingling among the flesh-and-blood office workers seated here is one in bronze, called *Double Check* (1982), by realist American sculptor J. Seward Johnson, Jr.

At Trinity Place, take a right. A short block up on the left will open the grand plaza of the:

**12. World Trade Center (WTC),** bounded by Vesey, West, Liberty, and Church streets and best known for its famous 110-story twin towers. The WTC is an immense complex. Its 12 million square feet of rentable office space houses more than 350 firms and organizations. About 50,000 people work in its precincts, and some 70,000 others (tourists and businesspeople) visit them each day. The complex occupies 16 acres and includes, in addition to the towers, a 22-story Marriott hotel, a plaza the size of four football fields, an underground shopping mall, and several restaurants.

The plaza, like much of downtown, is rich in outdoor sculpture, including the polished black granite miniature mountains (as you enter) crafted by Japanese artist Masayuki Nagare (1972). Fritz Keonig's 25-foot-high bronze morphing sphere (1971) forms the centerpiece of the plaza's wide fountain. Hang a right here between two of the squat black glass buildings to get a glance of Alexander

Calder's *Three Wings*. Take particular notice of the curving, metal, winglike flanges, riveted together and painted red.

Do an about-face to return to the central plaza. The left-hand of the twin towers is 2 World Trade Center. As you enter on the mezzanine level, to your left, you'll see a 1974 tapestry by Spanish artist Joan Miró and a TKTS booth if you want to pick up half-price tickets to one of tonight's Broadway or off-Broadway shows (for details, see chapter 9). The real thing to do, of course, is head around the elevator banks to the right to buy tickets and whiz up to the 107th-floor **Top of the World** Observation Deck, where you're treated to a 1,377-foot-high perspective of the city and New York Harbor. If it's open, be sure to ascend to the 110th-floor rooftop promenade, the world's highest open-air viewing platform, for even more magnificent views. For more information, see "Historic Lower Manhattan's Top Attractions," above.

☕ **TAKE A BREAK** There's a snack bar on the **107th-floor observation deck of WTC2,** but you'll dine better at one of the number of casual choices on the main (street-level) concourse, including **Sbarro Pizza; Menchenko-Tei** for Japanese bento-box lunches; **Fine & Shapiro** for deli; **Ecce Panis,** an excellent bakery; and **Krispy Kreme Doughnuts,** on the plaza at 5 WTC, for a sweet treat. See chapter 6 for further details.

Walk out the front side of WTC plaza again the way you came in, cross Church Street, and head straight down Dey Street, which is in front of you, back to Broadway. Take a left, and on your left is the:

13. **Kalikow Building,** at 195 Broadway. This 1915–22 neoclassic tower, formerly AT&T headquarters, has more exterior columns than any other building in the world. The 25-story structure rests on a Doric colonnade, with Ionic colonnades above. The lobby evokes a Greek temple with a forest of massive fluted columns. The building's tower crown is modeled on the Mausoleum of Halicarnassus, the great Greek monument of antiquity. The bronze panels over the entranceway by Paul Manship (sculptor of Rockefeller Center's *Prometheus*) symbolize wind, air, fire, and earth.

Continue south on Broadway. The next block contains the small:

14. **St. Paul's Chapel,** between Vesey and Fulton streets, New York's only surviving pre-Revolutionary church and now a transition shelter for homeless men. Built by Thomas McBean, with a templelike portico and fluted Ionic columns supporting a massive pediment, the chapel resembles London's St. Martin-in-the-Fields. Under the east portico is a 1789 monument to Gen. Richard Montgomery, one of the first revolutionary patriots to die in battle. During the two years that New York was the nation's capital, George Washington worshiped at this Georgian chapel belonging to Trinity Church and dating from 1766. Explore the small **graveyard** where 18th- and early 19th-century notables rest in peace and modern businesspeople sit for lunch; it's open Monday through Friday 9am to 3pm, Sunday 7am to 3pm. Trinity's Noonday Concert series is held here on Mondays at noon; the suggested donation is $2. Call the concert hotline at ☎ **212/ 602-0747,** or visit **www.trinitywallstreet.org**.

Continue up Broadway, crossing Vesey and Barclay streets, and at 233 Broadway is the:

15. **Woolworth Building.** This soaring "Cathedral of Commerce" cost Frank W. Woolworth $13.5 million worth of nickels and dimes in 1913. Designed by Cass Gilbert, it was the world's tallest edifice until 1930, when it was surpassed by the

Chrysler Building. At its opening, Pres. Woodrow Wilson pressed a button from the White House that illuminated the building's 80,000 electric lightbulbs. The neo-Gothic architecture is rife with spires, gargoyles, flying buttresses, vaulted ceilings, 16th-century–style stone-as-lace traceries, castlelike turrets, and a churchlike interior.

Step into the lofty marble entrance arcade to view the gleaming mosaic, Byzantine-style ceiling and gold-leafed, neo-Gothic cornices. The corbels (carved figures under the crossbeams) in the lobby include whimsical portraits of the building's engineer Gunwald Aus measuring a girder (above the staircase to the left of the main door), Gilbert holding a miniature model of the building, and Woolworth counting coins (both above the left-hand corridor of elevators). Stand near the security guard's central podium and crane your neck for a glimpse at Paul Jennewein's murals of *Commerce* and *Labor,* half hidden up on the mezzanine.

To get an overview of the Woolworth's architecture, cross Broadway. On this side of the street, you'll find scurrying city officials and greenery that together make up:

**16. City Hall Park,** a 250-year-old green surrounded by landmark buildings. A Frederick MacMonnies statue near the southwest corner of the park depicts Nathan Hale at age 21, having just uttered his famous words before execution: "I only regret that I have but one life to lose for my country." Northeast of City Hall in the park is a statue of Horace Greeley (seated with newspaper in hand) by J.Q.A. Ward. This small park has been a burial ground for paupers and the site of public executions, parades, and protests. It is the setting for:

**17. City Hall,** the seat of municipal government, housing the offices of the mayor and his staff, the city council, and other city agencies. City Hall combines Georgian and French Renaissance styles, designed by Joseph F. Mangin and John McComb Jr. in 1803–11. Later additions include the clock and 6,000-pound bell in the cupola tower. The cupola itself is crowned with a stately, white-painted copper statue of *Justice* (anonymously produced in a workshop).

☕ **TAKE A BREAK**   Grab an oven-fresh pastry or a diner lunch at **Ellen's Cafe and Bake Shop,** 270 Broadway, at Chambers Street (☎ **212/962-1257**). Owner Ellen Hart won the Miss Subways beauty pageant in 1959, and the restaurant walls are lined with her own and other winners' posters, plus photographs of the many politicians who have eaten here, including Al D'Amato, Rudy Giuliani, Bella Abzug, Mario Cuomo, and Geraldine Ferraro. Open weekdays 6am to 7pm, Saturday 8am to 4:30pm.

Along the north edge of City Hall Park, on Chambers Street, sits the:

**18. Tweed Courthouse** (New York County Courthouse, 52 Chambers St.). This 1872 Italianate courthouse was built during the tenure of William Marcy "Boss" Tweed, who, in his post on the board of supervisors, stole millions in construction funds. Originally budgeted as a $250,000 job in 1861, the courthouse project escalated to the staggering sum of $14 million. Bills were padded to an unprecedented extent; Andrew Garvey, who was to become known as the "Prince of Plasterers," was paid $45,966.89 for a single day's work! The ensuing scandal (Tweed and his cronies, it came out, had pocketed at least $10 million) wrecked Tweed's career; he died penniless in jail.

Across Chambers Street and to the right, at the corner of Elk Street, lies the turn-of-the-century:

**19. Surrogate's Court (The Hall of Records),** 31 Chambers St. Housed in this sumptuous beaux-arts structure are all the legal records relating to Manhattan real-estate deeds and court cases, some dating from the mid-1600s. Heroic statues of distinguished New Yorkers (Peter Stuyvesant, De Witt Clinton, and others) front the mansard roof, and the doorways, surmounted by arched pediments, are flanked by Philip Martiny's sculptural groups portraying *New York in Revolutionary Times* (to your left) and *New York in Its Infancy* (to your right). Above the entrance is a three-story Corinthian colonnade. Step inside to see the vestibule's beautiful barrel-vaulted mosaic ceiling; the ornate staircase in back was adapted from the foyer of the Grand Opera House in Paris.

Exiting from the front door, you'll see to your left, at the end of the block, that Chambers Street disappears under:

**20. The Municipal Building,** a grand civic edifice built between 1909 and 1914 to augment City Hall's government office space. It was designed by the famed architectural firm of McKim, Mead, and White (as in Stanford White), who used Greek and Roman design elements such as a massive Corinthian colonnade, ornately embellished vaults and cornices, and allegorical statuary. A triumphal arch, its barrel-vaulted ceiling adorned with relief panels, forms a magnificent arcade over Chambers Street; it has been called the "gate of the city." The heroic hammered-copper statue of *Civic Fame,* Manhattan's largest statue, tops the structure 582 feet above the street and holds a crown whose five turrets represent New York's five boroughs.

See many lovey-dovey couples walking in and out? The city's marriage license bureau is on the second floor, and a wedding takes place about every 20 minutes.

## 4 The Top Museums

✪ **American Museum of Natural History.** Central Park West (btw. 77th and 81st sts.) ☎ **212/769-5100** for information, or 212/769-5200 for tickets (tickets can also be ordered online). www.amnh.org. Suggested admission $9.50 adults, $7.50 seniors and students, $6 children 2–12. Combination packages available that include IMAX films, audio tours, and/or special exhibitions. Space Show tickets (museum admission included) $19 adults, $14 seniors and students, $11.50 children under 12. Sun–Thurs 10am–5:45pm, Fri–Sat 10am–8:45pm. Subway: B, C to 81st St.; 1, 9 to 79th St.

This is the hottest ticket in town as of February 2000, thanks to the grand opening of the new $210-million ✪ **Rose Center for Earth and Space,** home to the brand-new **Hayden Planetarium.** The planetarium's 4-story-tall sphere hosts the Tom Hanks–narrated Space Show, the most technologically advanced sky show on the planet; *New York* magazine has called it "the world's largest, most powerful virtual-reality simulator." Prepare to be blown away. The Rose Center is a cutting-edge scientific wonderland that also houses the Big Bang Theater, which recreates the theoretical birth of the universe; halls chronicling the evolution and history of the cosmos; its own $15\frac{1}{2}$-ton meteorite; and much more.

The rest of the four-square-block museum is nothing to sneeze at, either. It houses the world's greatest natural science collection in a group of buildings made of towers and turrets, pink granite and red brick—a mishmash of architectural styles, but overflowing with neo-Gothic charm. The diversity of the holdings is astounding: some 36 million specimens ranging from microscopic organisms to the world's largest cut gem, the Brazilian Princess Topaz (21,005 carats). It would take all day to see the entire museum, and then you still wouldn't get to everything. If you don't have a lot of time, you can see the best of the best on free **highlights tours** offered daily every hour at

15 minutes after the hour from 10:15am to 3:15pm. Free daily **spotlights tours,** thematic tours that change monthly, are also offered; stop by an information desk for the day's schedule. **Audio Expeditions,** high-tech audio tours that allow you to access narration in the order you choose, are also available to help you make sense of it all.

If you only see one exhibit, see the ✪ **dinosaurs,** which take up the entire fourth floor. Start in the **Orientation Room,** where a short video gives an overview of the 500 million years of evolutionary history that led to you. Continue to the **Vertebrate Origins Room,** where huge models of ancient fish and turtles hang overhead, with plenty of interactive exhibits and kid-level displays on hand to keep young minds fascinated. Next come the great **dinosaur halls,** with mammoth, spectacularly reconstructed skeletons and more interactive displays. **Mammals and Their Extinct Relatives** bring what you've learned in the previous halls home, showing how yesterday's prehistoric monsters have evolved into today's modern animals. Simply marvelous—you could spend hours in these halls alone.

Many other areas of the museum pale in comparison. The **animal habitat dioramas** and **halls of peoples** seem dated but still have something to teach, especially the Native American halls. Other than peeking in to see the giant whale (viewable from the cafe below) skip the **ocean life** room altogether; let's hope this is next on the restoration agenda, because the current exhibit makes Disneyland's submarine ride look high-tech. The new **Hall of Biodiversity** is an impressive multimedia exhibit, but the doom-and-gloom story it tells about the future of rainforests and other natural habitats might be too much for the little ones. Kids 5 and older should head to the **Discovery Room,** with lots of hands-on exhibits and experiments. (Be prepared, Mom and Dad; there seems to be a gift shop overflowing with fuzzy stuffed animals at every turn.)

The museum excels at **special exhibitions,** so I recommend checking to see what will be on while you're in town in case any advance planning is required. Highlights of the past year have included the magical Butterfly Conservatory, a walk-in enclosure housing nearly 500 free-flying tropical butterflies.

In addition, an **IMAX Theater** shows neat films such as *Everest* and *Africa's Elephant Kingdom* on a four-story screen that puts you right in the heart of the action.

**Getting Planetarium Tickets:** Admission to the Rose Center is included in museum admission, but separate tickets are required to view the planetarium's 30-minute Space Show; don't show up without advance tickets, or you're likely to come away disappointed. At press time, tickets were sold out six weeks in advance; demand might slow down by the time you arrive, but placing your order before you leave home is a good idea so you have your choice of dates and showtimes. IMAX tickets can also be ordered in advance.

✪ **Metropolitan Museum of Art.** Fifth Ave. at 82nd St. ☎ **212/535-7710.** www. metmuseum.org. Suggested admission (includes same-day entrance to the Cloisters) $10 adults, $5 seniors and students, free for children under 12 when accompanied by an adult. Sun and Tues–Thurs 9:30am–5:30pm, Fri–Sat 9:30am–9pm. No strollers allowed Sun (back carriers available at 81st St. entrance coat-check area). Subway: 4, 5, 6 to 86th St.

Home of blockbuster after blockbuster exhibition, the Metropolitan Museum of Art attracts some 5 million people a year, more than any other spot in New York City. And it's no wonder; this place is magnificent. At 1.6 million square feet, this is the largest museum in the Western Hemisphere. Nearly all the world's cultures are on display through the ages—from Egyptian mummies to ancient Greek statuary to Islamic carvings to Renaissance paintings to Native American masks to 20th-century decorative arts—and masterpieces are the rule. You could go once a week for a lifetime and still find something new on each visit.

So unless you plan on spending your entire vacation in the museum (some people do), you cannot see the entire collection. My recommendation is to give it a good day—or better yet, two half days so you don't burn out. One good way to get an overview is to take advantage of the little-known **Museum Highlights Tour.** Even some New Yorkers who've spent many hours in the museum could profit from this once-over. Call ☎ **212/570-3711** (Mon–Fri 9am–5pm) or visit the museum's Web site for a schedule of this and subject-specific walking tours (Old Master Paintings, American Period Rooms, Arts of China, and so on); you can also get a schedule of the day's tours at the Visitor Services desk when you arrive.

The least overwhelming way to see the Met on your own is to pick up a map at the round desk in the entry hall and choose to concentrate on what you like, whether it's 17th-century paintings, American furniture, or the art of the South Pacific. Highlights include the American Wing's **Garden Court,** with its 19th-century sculpture, the lower-level **Costume Hall,** and the **Frank Lloyd Wright room.** The beautifully renovated **Roman and Greek galleries** are overwhelming, but in a marvelous way, as is the collection of later **Chinese art.** The setting of the **Temple of Dendur** is dramatic, in a specially built glass-walled gallery with Central Park views. But it all depends on what your interests are. Don't forget the marvelous **special exhibitions,** which can range from "Jade in Ancient Costa Rica" to "Cubism and Fashion." If you'd like to plan your visit ahead of time, the museum's Web site is a useful tool; there's also a list of current exhibitions in the Friday and Sunday editions of *The New York Times.*

Special programs abound. To purchase tickets for concerts and lectures, call ☎ **212/570-3949** (Monday through Saturday 9:30am to 5pm). The museum contains several dining facilities, including a **full-service restaurant** serving continental cuisine (☎ **212/570-3964** for reservations). The roof garden is worth visiting if you're here from spring to autumn, offering peaceful views over Central Park and the city.

On **Friday and Saturday evenings,** the Met remains open late not only for art viewing but also for cocktails in the Great Hall Balcony Bar (4 to 8:30pm) and classical music from a string quintet or trio. A slate of after-hours programs (gallery talks, walking tours, family programs) changes by the week; call for this week's schedule. The restaurant stays open until 10pm (last reservation at 8:30pm), and dinner is usually accompanied by piano music.

The Met's medieval collections are housed in Upper Manhattan at the **Cloisters;** see "More Manhattan Museums" below.

✪ **Museum of Modern Art.** 11 W. 53rd St. (btw. Fifth and Sixth aves.). ☎ **212/ 708-9400.** www.moma.org. Admission $10 adults ($14 with audio tour), $6.50 seniors and students ($10.50 with audio tour), free for children under 16 accompanied by an adult; pay what you wish Fri 4:30–8:15pm. Sat–Tues and Thurs 10:30am–5:45pm, Fri 10:30am–8:15pm. Subway: E, F to Fifth Ave.; B, D, F, Q to 47–50th sts./Rockefeller Center.

The Museum of Modern Art (or MoMA, as it's usually called) boasts the world's greatest collection of painting and sculpture ranging from the late 19th century to the present, including everything from van Gogh's *Starry Night*, Picasso's early *Les Demoiselles*

## A Tip for Avoiding the Crowds

Many of the city's top museums—including the Natural History Museum, the Met, and MoMA—have late hours on Friday and/or Saturday nights. Take advantage of them. Most visitors run out of steam by dinnertime, so even on jam-packed weekends you'll largely have the place to yourself by 5 or 6pm—which, in most cases, leaves you hours left to explore, unfettered by crowds or screaming kids.

# Free Culture at Big Apple Museums

New York's gargantuan stash of museums, galleries, and attractions makes this city one of the cultural capitals of the world. But the cost of absorbing all this culture can be pretty high, especially because many museums are now asking around $10 to get in the door. But don't get discouraged; as you'll see from the list below, there are plenty of ways around these steep admission fees.

Some city attractions are free all the time. Some set aside an afternoon, evening, or even an entire day during the week when you can explore at no charge. Others offer "pay what you wish" times, which allow you to determine what contribution you make upon entering, be it $1 or the full admission price.

Most museums keep pretty solid schedules, but it's always a good idea to call ahead and confirm free and "pay what you wish" times—because these, like everything else, are always subject to change.

**Always Free**

- **Dahesh Museum** (p. 222)
- **Federal Hall National Memorial** (p. 209)
- **Forbes Magazine Galleries** (p. 222)
- **Guggenheim Museum SoHo** (p. 223)
- **Museum of American Folk Art** ($3 voluntary donation requested; p. 226)
- **National Museum of the American Indian** (p. 227)
- **Newseum/NY** (p. 230)
- **Exhibitions at the New York Public Library** (p. 233)
- **New York Stock Exchange** (p. 208)
- **Exhibitions at the Schomburg Center for Research in Black Culture** (p. 257)
- **Sony Wonder Technology Lab** (p. 255)
- **St. Patrick's Cathedral** (p. 238)
- **The Bernard Museum at Temple Emanu-El** (p. 238)
- **Whitney Museum of American Art at Phillip Morris** (p. 231)

**Sometimes Free (or Pay What You Wish)**

- **American Craft Museum:** Thursday from 6 to 8pm; regular admission $5 (p. 220)
- **Asia Society:** Thursday from 6 to 8pm; regular admission $4 (p. 220)

*d'Avignon,* Monet's *Water Lilies,* and Klimt's *The Kiss* to later masterworks by Frida Kahlo, Edward Hopper, Andy Warhol, Robert Rauschenberg, and many others. Top that off with an extensive collection of modern drawings, photography, architectural models and furniture (including the Mies van der Rohe collection), iconic design objects ranging from tableware to sports cars, and film and video (including the world's largest collection of D.W. Griffith films), and you have quite a museum. If you're into modernism, this is the place to be.

Although not quite Met-sized, MoMA is probably still more than you can see in a day. In true modern style, the museum is efficient and well organized, so it's easy to focus on your primary interests; just grab a museum map after you pay your admission.

- **Bronx Zoo Wildlife Conservation Park:** All day Wednesday; regular admission $7.75 (p. 257)
- **Brooklyn Botanic Garden:** All day Tuesday through Friday from mid-November to mid-March and year-round Saturday from 10am to noon; regular admission $3 (p. 259)
- **Brooklyn Museum of Art:** First Saturday of the month from 5 to 11pm; regular admission $4 (p. 259)
- **Children's Museum of the Arts:** Wednesday from 5 to 7pm; regular admission $5 (p. 254)
- **Cooper-Hewitt National Design Museum:** Tuesday from 5pm to 9pm; regular admission $8 (p. 222)
- **International Center of Photography:** Tuesday from 5 to 8pm; regular admission $6 (p. 223)
- **The Jewish Museum:** Tuesday from 5 to 8pm; regular admission $8 (p. 224)
- **Museum of Modern Art:** Friday from 4:30 to 8:15pm; regular admission $10 (p. 215)
- **New Museum of Contemporary Art:** Thursday from 6 to 8pm; regular admission $6 (p. 229)
- **New York Hall of Science:** Thursday and Friday from 2pm to 5pm; regular admission $7.50 (p. 254)
- **Solomon R. Guggenheim Museum:** Friday from 6 to 8pm; regular admission $12 (p. 218)
- **Studio Museum in Harlem:** First Saturday of the month; regular admission $5 (p. 257)
- **Whitney Museum of American Art:** Thursday from 6 to 8pm; regular admission $10 (p. 218)

**Almost Free (admission of $2.50 or less)**
- **Cathedral of St. John the Divine: $2** (p. 236)
- **Fraunces Tavern Museum: $2.50** (p. 208)
- **Museum of American Financial History: $2** (p. 209)
- **Prospect Park Wildlife Conservation Center: $2.50** (p. 260)

For an overview, take the **self-guided tour** that stops at the collection's highlights, chosen by the different departments' curators. The **sculpture garden**—an island of trees and fountains in which to enjoy the works of Calder, Moore, and Rodin—is of particular note. In addition, there's usually at least one beautifully mounted **special exhibition** in house that's worth a special trip, whether it be the works of Finnish master architect Alvar Aalto, Julia Margaret Cameron's remarkable 19th-century photographs of women, or a celebration of sight gags in contemporary art.

Even if you've been to MoMA before, you might want to take another look, especially if your visit falls before March 2001. Conceived as a preliminary experiment in reinstallation (practice for the museum's expansion project, overseen by Japanese architect Yoshio Taniguchi and set to be complete in 2004), **MoMA 2000** sets the museum's old order on end. Organized in three consecutive exhibition cycles—you're likely to encounter *Open Ends,* focusing on 1960 to the present, running from mid-September 2000—the show is installed throughout the entire museum and juxtaposed with works from other periods to illustrate the relationship between various historical movements. (Note that certain works of art that are part of the permanent collection will not be on display during this exhibition, so call ahead if you're coming to see a particular work.) After March 2001, the museum restores its regular exhibition arrangement.

MoMA also boasts a good number of special programs. There's live jazz Thursday and Saturday evenings at **Sette MoMA** (☎ 212/708-9710), the museum's notable Italian restaurant overlooking the sculpture garden, and Friday evening at the more casual (and cheaper) **Garden Cafe.** A full slate of symposiums, gallery talks by contemporary artists, interactive family programs, and brown-bag lunch lectures are always on offer; call ☎ 212/708-9781 or visit the museum's Web site to see what's on while you're in town. Additionally, there's always a multifaceted film and video program on the schedule; call the main number to see what's on. Films are included in the price of admission, but arrive early to make sure you get a seat.

**Solomon R. Guggenheim Museum.** 1071 Fifth Ave. (at 88th St.). ☎ 212/423-3500. www.guggenheim.org. Admission $12 adults, $7 seniors, children under 12 free; pay what you wish Fri 6–8pm. Sun–Wed 9am–6pm, Fri–Sat 9am–8pm. Subway: 4, 5, 6 to 86th St.

It has been called a bun, a snail, a concrete tornado, and even a giant wedding cake; bring your kids, and they'll probably see it as New York's coolest opportunity for skateboarding or in-line skating. Whatever descriptive you choose to apply, Frank Lloyd Wright's only New York building, completed in 1959, is best summed up as a brilliant work of architecture—so consistently brilliant that it competes with the art for your attention. If you're looking for the city's best modern art, head to MoMA or the Whitney first; come to the Guggenheim to see the house.

It's easy to see the bulk of what's on display in two to four hours. Inside, a spiraling rotunda circles over a slowly inclined ramp that leads you past changing exhibits. Scheduled for late 2000 through early 2001 are "Amazons of the Avant Garde," focusing on six Russian women who made significant contributions to modern art in the early 20th century, and a Giorgio Armani career retrospective. Usually the progression is counterintuitive: from the first floor up, rather than from the sixth floor down. If you're not sure, ask a guard before you begin. Permanent exhibits of 19th- and 20th-century art, including strong holdings of Kandinsky, Klee, Picasso, and French impressionists, occupy a stark annex called the **Tower Galleries,** an addition accessible at every level that some critics claimed made the original look like a toilet bowl backed by a water tank (judge for yourself—I think there may be something to that view).

The Guggenheim runs some interesting special programs, including free docent tours (there's a one-hour highlights tour daily at noon), a limited schedule of lectures, free family films along the lines of *The Red Balloon* and *Babar: The Movie,* avant-garde screenings for grown-ups, and the World Beat Jazz Series, which resounds through the rotunda on Friday and Saturday evenings from 5 to 8pm.

For details on the **Guggenheim Museum SoHo,** the museum's Downtown annex, see "More Manhattan Museums," below.

✪ **Whitney Museum of American Art.** 945 Madison Ave. (at 75th St.). ☎ 877/WHITNEY or 212/570-3676. www.whitney.org. Admission $10 adults, $8 seniors and students, free for children under 12; pay what you wish Thurs 6–8pm. Tues–Wed and Fri–Sun 11am–6pm, Thurs 1pm–8pm. Subway: 6 to 77th St.

What is arguably the finest collection of 20th-century American art in the world belongs to the Whitney, thanks to the efforts of Gertrude Vanderbilt Whitney. A sculptor herself, she organized exhibitions by American artists shunned by traditional academies, assembled a sizable personal collection, and founded the museum in 1930 in Greenwich Village.

Today's museum is an imposing presence on Madison Avenue—an inverted three-tiered pyramid of concrete and gray granite with seven seemingly random windows designed by Marcel Breuer, a leader of the Bauhaus movement. The rotating permanent collection consists of an intelligent selection of major works by Edward Hopper, George Bellows, Georgia O'Keeffe, Roy Lichtenstein, Jasper Johns, and other significant artists. A pleasing fifth-floor exhibit space, the museum's first devoted exclusively to works from its permanent collection from 1900 to 1950, opened in 1998.

There are usually several simultaneous shows, generally all well curated and edgier than what you'd see at the MoMA or the Guggenheim. Topics range from topical surveys, such as "American Art in the Age of Technology" and "The Warhol Look: Glamour Style Fashion" to in-depth retrospectives of famous or lesser-known movements (such as Fluxus, the movement that spawned Yoko Ono, among others) and artists (Mark Rothko, Keith Haring, Duane Hanson, and Bob Thompson). The next Whitney Biennial is scheduled for spring 2002. A major event on the national museum calendar, the Biennials serve as the premier launching pad for new American artists working on the vanguard in every media.

The Whitney is also notable for having the best museum restaurant in town: **Sarabeth's at the Whitney** (☎ **212/606-0218**), worth a visit in its own right (see chapter 6).

Free **gallery tours** are offered daily; call for the current schedule, or check at the Information desk when you arrive.

For details on the **Whitney Museum of American Art at Philip Morris,** the petite Midtown annex, see "More Manhattan Museums," below.

# 5  More Manhattan Museums

In 1978, New York's finest cultural institutions located on Fifth Avenue from 82nd to 104th streets formed a consortium called **Museum Mile,** the name New York City officially gave to the stretch several years later. The "mile" begins at the **Metropolitan Museum of Art** (see "The Top Museums" above) and moves north to **El Museo del Barrio.** However, even the smallest museums along this stretch require some time, so don't plan on just popping into a few as you stroll along, or you'll be sorely disappointed by what you're able to see. Your best bet is to head directly to the museum that's tops on your list first and then proceed to your second choice along the mile if you have time. If you're heading to the Metropolitan, forget trying to squeeze in anything else; as it is, you'll only see a portion of the collection there in a full day.

For details on **Federal Hall National Memorial** and **Fraunces Tavern Museum,** see the walking tour earlier in this chapter. For the **Brooklyn Museum of Art,** the **American Museum of the Moving Image,** the **Queens Museum of Art,** the **Isamu Noguchi Garden Museum,** and the **P.S. 1 Contemporary Art Center,** see "Highlights of the Outer Boroughs" later in this chapter.

If you're traveling with the kids, also consider the museums listed under "Especially for Kids" later in this chapter, which include the **Children's Museum of Manhattan,** the **Sony Wonder Technology Lab,** the **New York Hall of Science,** and the **New York City Fire Museum.**

Also, don't forget to see what's on at the monumental **New York Public Library,** which regularly holds excellent exhibitions; see "Skyscrapers & Other Architectural Marvels" later in this chapter.

**Abigail Adams Smith Museum & Gardens.** 421 E. 61st St. (btw. First and York aves.). ☎ 212/838-6878. Admission $4 adults, $3 seniors, children under 12 free. Tues–Sun 11am–4pm, Tues to 9pm in June and July; closed Aug. Subway: 4, 5, 6 to 59th St.; N, R to Lexington Ave.

It's a shock, a very pleasant one, to find such a little-known jewel on this otherwise thoroughly modern block. This rare survivor from the early American republic was built as a carriage house for Abigail Adams Smith, daughter of President John Adams, and her husband, William Stephens Smith, in 1799. It's been painstakingly restored by the Colonial Dames of America to its early-19th-century condition, when the house served as the Mount Vernon Hotel—a country hotel for bucolic overnights away from the city, if you can believe it. You can explore nine period rooms, outfitted in authentic Federal style, as well as the grounds, planted as a late 18th-century garden would be. By the time you arrive, the new orientation center, offering a scale model of the building as it looked in 1799 and a video on New York City in the early 19th century, will also be open for perusal.

**American Craft Museum.** 40 W. 53rd St. (btw. Fifth and Sixth aves.). ☎ 212/956-3535. $5 adults, $2.50 students and seniors, free for children under 12; pay what you wish Thurs 6–8pm. Tues–Sun 10am–6pm (Thurs to 8pm). Subway: E, F to Fifth Ave.

This small but aesthetically pleasing museum is the nation's top showcase for contemporary crafts. The collection focuses on objects that are prime examples of form and function, ranging from jewelry to baskets to vessels to furniture. You'll see a strong emphasis on material as well as craft, whether it be fiber, ceramics, or metal. Special exhibitions can range from hand-blown glass works to fine bookbinding. Stop into the gorgeous shop even if you don't make it into the museum, especially if you have some gift buying to do—but once you do, don't be surprised if you're tempted to peruse the permanent collection.

**Asia Society.** 725 Park Ave. (at 70th St.). ☎ 212/517-ASIA. www.asiasociety.org. Gallery admission $4 adults, $2 seniors, children under 13 free; free Thurs 6–8pm. Tues–Sat 11am–6pm (to 8pm Thurs), Sun noon–5pm. Subway: 6 to 68th St./Hunter College.

The Asia Society was founded in 1956 by John D. Rockefeller III with the goal of increasing understanding between Americans and Asians through art exhibits, lectures, films, performances, and international conferences. The society is a leader in presenting contemporary Asian and Asian-American art. Recent exhibits have included "Bamboo Masterworks," and "Monks and Merchants at the Gateway: Silk Road Art from Northwest China, 4th to 7th Centuries C.E.," is on the schedule for fall 2001. The core collection, comprised of Rockefeller's pan-Asian acquisitions dating from 2000 B.C. to the 19th century, is also worth a peek.

✪ **The Cloisters.** At the north end of Fort Tryon Park. ☎ 212/923-3700. www.metmuseum. org. Suggested admission (includes same-day entrance to the Metropolitan Museum of Art) $10 adults, $5 seniors and students, free for children under 12. Nov–Feb, Tues–Sun 9:30am–4:45pm; Mar–Oct, Tues–Sun 9:30am–5:15pm. Subway: A to 190th St., then a 10-minute walk north along Margaret Corgan Dr., or pick up the M4 bus at the station (one stop to Cloisters). Bus: M4 Madison Ave. (FORT TRYON PARK–THE CLOISTERS).

# In Search of Historic Homes

New York's voracious appetite for change often means that older residential archi-tecture is torn down so that money-earning high-rises can go up in its place. Sur-prisingly, however, the city maintains a truly fine collection of often-overlooked historic houses that are more than a tale of architecture; they're the stories of the people who passed their ordinary or extraordinary lives in buildings that range from humble to magnificent.

The **Historic House Trust of New York City** preserves 19 houses, located in city parks in all five boroughs. Those particularly worth seeking out include the **Morris-Jumel Mansion,** in Upper Manhattan at 65 Jumel Terrace (at 160th Street, east of St. Nicholas Avenue; ☎ 212/923-8008), built circa 1765 and Manhattan's oldest surviving house. The **Dyckman Farmhouse Museum,** far-ther uptown at 4881 Broadway (at 204th Street; ☎ 212/304-9422), is the only Dutch Colonial farmhouse remaining in Manhattan, stoically and stylishly sur-viving the urban development that grew up around it.

The **Edgar Allan Poe Cottage,** 2460 Grand Concourse, at East Kingsbridge Road in the Bronx (☎ 718/881-8900), was the last home of the brilliant but troubled poet and author, who moved his wife here because he thought the "country air" would be good for her tuberculosis. And the ✪ **Merchant's House Museum,** 29 E. 4th St. between Lafayette Street and Bowery in the East Village (☎ 212/777-1089), is a rare jewel: a perfectly preserved 19th-century home, complete with intact interiors, whose last resident is said to be the inspiration for Catherine Sloper in Henry James's *Washington Square.*

Built in 1809, Federal-style **Gracie Mansion,** in Carl Schurz Park, at 89th Street and East End Avenue on the Upper East Side (☎ 212/570-4751), is now the official residence of "Hizzoner," the mayor of New York. It's open for guided tours on Wednesdays only from late March through mid-November; call for reservations.

Each of the 14 others also has its own fascinating story to tell. A brochure list-ing the locations and touring details of all 19 of the historic homes is available by calling ☎ 212/360-8282; recorded information is available at ☎ 212/360-3448. You'll also find complete information online at **www.ci.nyc.ny.us/html/dpr/html/nav.html**; click on HISTORIC HOUSES.

If it weren't for this branch of the Metropolitan Museum of Art, many New Yorkers would never get to this northernmost point in Manhattan. This remote yet lovely spot is devoted to the art and architecture of medieval Europe. Atop a magnificent cliff overlooking the Hudson River, you'll find a 12th-century chapter house, parts of five cloisters from medieval monasteries, a Romanesque chapel, and a 12th-century Span-ish apse brought intact from Europe. Surrounded by peaceful gardens, this is the one place on the island that can even approximate the kind of solitude suitable to such a collection. Inside you'll find extraordinary works that include the famed Unicorn tapestries, sculpture, illuminated manuscripts, stained glass, ivory, and precious metal-work. Despite its remoteness, the Cloisters are extremely popular, especially in fine weather, so try to schedule your visit during the week rather than on a crowded week-end afternoon. A free guided tour is offered Tuesday through Friday at 3pm and Sun-day at noon.

⊙ **Cooper-Hewitt National Design Museum.** 2 E. 91st St. (at Fifth Ave.). ☎ **212/ 849-8300.** www.si.edu/ndm. Admission $8 adults, $5 seniors and students, free for children under 12; free to all Tues 5–9pm. Tues 10am–9pm, Wed–Sat 10am–5pm, Sun noon–5pm. Subway: 4, 5, 6 to 86th St.

Part of the Smithsonian Institution, the Cooper-Hewitt is housed in the Carnegie Mansion, built by steel magnate Andrew Carnegie in 1901. The museum underwent an ambitious $20-million renovation in 1996 that gave the building a long-overdue refreshening. Some 11,000 square feet of gallery space is devoted to changing exhibits that are invariably well conceived, engaging, and educational. Shows are both historic and contemporary in nature, and topics range from "The Work of Charles and Ray Eames: A Legacy of Invention" to "The Architecture of Reassurance: Designing the Disney Theme Parks." Many installations are drawn from the museum's own vast collection of industrial design, drawings, textiles, wall coverings, books, and prints. Exhibitions scheduled for 2001 include a retrospective on the modernist glass design of Venetian artist Paolo Venini, and a look at the use of landscape images in wall coverings in the 19th century.

On your way in, note the fabulous art nouveau–style copper-and-glass canopy above the entrance. And be sure to visit the garden, ringed with Central Park benches from various eras.

**Dahesh Museum.** 601 Fifth Ave. (at 48th St.). ☎ **212/759-0606.** www.daheshmuseum. org. Free admission. Tues–Sat 11am–6pm. Subway: B, D, F, Q to 47–50th sts./Rockefeller Center.

If you consider yourself a classicist, this small museum is for you. It's dedicated to 19th- and early 20th-century European academic art, a continuation of Renaissance, Baroque, and Rococo traditions that were overshadowed by the arrival of Impressionism on the art scene. If you're not familiar with the academic school, expect lots of painstaking renditions of historical subjects and pastoral life. Artists represented include Jean-Léon Gérôme, Lord Leighton, and Edwin Long, whose *Love's Labour Lost* is a cornerstone of the permanent collection.

**El Museo del Barrio.** 1230 Fifth Ave. (at 104th St.). ☎ **212/831-7272.** www.elmuseo.org. Suggested admission $4 adults, $2 seniors and students, children under 12 free. Wed–Sun 11am–5pm. Subway: 6 to 103rd St.

What started in 1969 with a small display in a local school classroom in East Harlem is today the only museum in America dedicated to Puerto Rican, Caribbean, and Latin American art. The northernmost Museum Mile institution has a permanent exhibit ranging from pre-Columbian artifacts to photographic art and video. The display of *santos de palo*, wood-carved religious figurines, is especially worth noting. The well-curated changing exhibitions tend to focus on 20th-century artists and contemporary subjects.

**Forbes Magazine Galleries.** 62 Fifth Ave. (at 12th St.). ☎ **212/206-5548.** Free admission. Tues, Wed, Fri, Sat 10am–4pm. Subway: L, N, R, 4, 5, 6 to 14th St./Union Sq.

The late publishing magnate Malcolm Forbes may have been a self-described "capitalist tool," but he had esoteric, almost childish, tastes. He also had the altruism to share what he collected with the public for free. With its model boats, toy soldiers, old Monopoly game sets, quirky collection of trophies, miniature rooms, presidential papers and memorabilia, and jewel-encrusted Fabergé eggs, this is a great museum for both you and the kids. Personal anecdotes explain why certain objects attracted Forbes's attention and turn the collection into an oddly interesting biographical portrait.

**✪ The Frick Collection.** 1 E. 70th St. (at Fifth Ave.). ☎ **212/288-0700.** www.frick.org. Admission $7 adults, $5 seniors and students. Children under 10 not admitted; children under 16 must be accompanied by an adult. Tues–Sat 10am–6pm, Sun 1–6pm (closed all major holidays). Subway: 6 to 68th St./Hunter College.

Henry Clay Frick could afford to be an avid collector of European art after amassing a fortune as a pioneer in the coke and steel industries at the turn of the century. To house his treasures and himself, he hired architects Carrère & Hastings to build this 18th-century-French–style mansion (1914), one of the most beautiful remaining on Fifth Avenue.

Most appealing about the Frick is its intimate size and setting. This is a living testament to New York's vanished Gilded Age: The interior still feels like a private home (albeit a really, really rich guy's home) graced with beautiful paintings, rather than a museum. Come here to see the classics, by some of the world's most famous painters: Titian, Bellini, Rembrandt, Turner, Vermeer, El Greco, and Goya, to name only a few. A highlight of the collection is the **Fragonard Room,** graced with the sensual Rococo series *The Progress of Love*. The portrait of Montesquieu by Whistler is also stunning. Sculpture, furniture, Chinese vases, and French enamels complement the paintings and round out the collection. Included in the price of admission, the AcousticGuide audio tour is particularly useful, because it allows you to follow your own path rather than a proscribed route. A free video presentation is screened every half-hour; starting with this helps to set the tone for what you'll see.

In addition to the permanent collection, the Frick regularly mounts small, well-focused temporary exhibitions. Look for "A Brush with Nature: The Gere Collection of Landscape Oil Sketches" and "The Draftsman's Art: Master Drawings from the National Gallery of Scotland" in late 2000 and early 2001.

Free **chamber music concerts** are held twice a month, generally every other Sunday at 5pm; call or visit the Web site for the current schedule and ticket information.

**Guggenheim Museum SoHo.** 575 Broadway, at Prince St. ☎ **212/423-3500.** Free admission. Thurs–Mon 11am–6pm. Subway: N, R to Prince St.

Reopened after a lengthy closing, this annex to the Solomon R. Guggenheim Museum (see "The Top Museums," above) now has a considerably lower profile than in past years, but it's worth checking out what's on if you consider yourself a post-modern enthusiast. (And it's easy to pair a stop with a visit to the New Museum of Contemporary Art and/or the Museum of African Art; see below.) The space generally houses temporary installations of high-tech multimedia works. On an open-ended schedule at press time was Andy Warhol's swansong, *The Last Supper* (1986), his monumental final cycle, comprising more than 60 silkscreens, paintings, and works on paper.

**International Center of Photography.** 1133 Sixth Ave. (at 43rd St.). ☎ **212/768-4680** or 212/860-1777. www.icp.org. Admission $6 adults, $4 seniors, $1 children under 13; Tues 5–8pm pay what you wish. Tues–Thurs 10am–5pm, Fri 10am–8pm, Sat and Sun 10am–6pm. Subway: B, D, F, Q to 42nd St.

In September 2000, the ICP—one of the world's premier educators, collectors, and exhibitors of photographic art—is scheduled to relocate its museum galleries from its original Museum Mile location (1130 Fifth Ave., at 94th Street) to this expanded Midtown facility. The new space is the work of the top-flight architectural firm Gwathmey Siegel & Associates (the people behind the Guggenheim's expansion a few years back), so expect it to be state-of-the-art gallery space—ideal for viewing rotating exhibitions of the museum's 50,000-plus prints as well as visiting shows. The emphasis is on contemporary photographic works, but historically important photographers aren't ignored. A must on any photography buff's list. Do call ahead or visit the Web site, though, to check current exhibitions and make sure the move is complete by the time you arrive, as anything can happen to delay a project of this magnitude. Don't be surprised if you find a change in hours and admission fees, too; policies for the new facility were not yet set at press time. Additionally, a limited schedule of exhibitions is set to show at the Museum Mile headquarters through September 2001.

**Intrepid Sea-Air-Space Museum.** Pier 86 (W. 46th St. at Twelfth Ave.). ☎ 212/245-0072 or 212/957-7055. www.intrepidmuseum.org. Admission $12 adults; $9 veterans, seniors, and students; $6 children 6–11; $2 children 2–5. Apr–Sept, Mon–Fri 10am–5pm, Sat–Sun 10am–6pm; Oct–Mar, Tues–Sun 10am–5pm. Last admission 1 hour before closing. Subway: A, C, E to 42nd St./Port Authority. Bus: M42 crosstown.

The most astonishing thing about the aircraft carrier USS *Intrepid* is how it can be simultaneously so big and so small. It's a few football fields long, weighs 40,000 tons, holds 40 aircraft, and sometimes doubles as a ballroom for society functions. But stand there and think about landing an A-12 jet on the deck and suddenly, it's minuscule. Furthermore, in the narrow passageways below, you'll find it isn't quite the roomiest of vessels. Now a National Historic Landmark, the entire exhibit also includes the naval destroyer USS *Edson,* and the submarine USS *Growler,* the only intact strategic missile submarine open to the public anywhere in the world, as well as a collection of vintage and modern aircraft, including the A-12 Blackbird, the world's fastest spy plane. Kids just love this place. New in 2000 are exhibits on defense technology and space exploration in the 21st century, and a grand $5.5-million visitor center, which will be open by the time you arrive. At least one Saturday a month is dedicated to families as part of the "Seaworthy Saturdays" program; look for such events as "Undersea Exploration," in which kids meet the Intrepid Dive Team and examine recovered treasures. But think twice about going in winter; it's almost impossible to heat an aircraft carrier.

**Japan Society.** 333 E. 47th St. (btw. First and Second aves.). ☎ 212/832-1155. www.japansociety.org. Admission $5 adults, $3 seniors and students. Gallery hours: Tues–Fri 11am–6pm, Sat–Sun 11am–5pm. Subway: 6 to 51st St.; E, F to Lexington Ave.

In a striking modern building by Junzo Yoshimuro (1971), the U.S. headquarters of the Japan Society mounts highly regarded exhibits of Japanese art in a suitably serene gallery. Changing displays have included "Japanese Theater in the World" and "Treasures of Japanese Art from the San Francisco Art Museum." The society also hosts a wide variety of lectures, gallery talks, films, and classes throughout the year; you'll also find a list of other Japan-related events and exhibits taking place throughout the city on the Web site.

**The Jewish Museum.** 1109 Fifth Ave. (at 92nd St.). ☎ 212/423-3200. www.jewishmuseum. org. Admission $8 adults, $5.50 seniors and students, free for children under 12; pay what you wish Tues 5–8pm. Check Web site for special online admission discounts (50% off at press time). Sun, Mon, Wed, Thurs 11am–5:45pm, Tues 11am–8pm. Subway: 4, 5 to 86th St.; 6 to 96th St.

Housed in a Gothic-style mansion renovated in 1993 by AIA Gold Medal–winner Kevin Roche, this wonderful museum now has the world-class space it deserves to showcase its remarkable collections, which chronicle 4,000 years of the Jewish experience. The two-floor permanent exhibit, "Culture and Continuity: The Jewish Journey," tells the story of the Jewish experience from ancient times through today and is the museum's centerpiece. Artifacts include daily objects that might have served the authors of the books of Genesis, Psalms, and Job and a great assemblage of intricate

Torahs. A wonderful collection of classic TV and radio programs is available for viewing through the Goodkind Resource Center (as any fan of television's Golden Age knows, its finest comic moments were Jewish comedy). The scope of the exhibit is phenomenal and its story an enlightening—and intense—one. In addition, there's a rotating calendar of special exhibitions, plus a gift shop and an adjacent design store showcasing contemporary Jewish crafts.

✪ **Lower East Side Tenement Museum.** Visitors' Center at 90 Orchard St. (at Broome St.). ☎ **212/431-0233.** www.tenement.org or www.wnet.org/tenement. $8 adults, $6 seniors and students for tenement tour. Multiple tours available on weekends: $14 adults, $10 seniors and students for any 2 tours; $20 adults, $14 seniors and students for all 3 tours. Tenement tours depart Tues–Fri every half-hour 1pm–4pm and Thurs at 6 and 7pm, Sat–Sun every half-hour 11am–4:30pm. Neighborhood Heritage Tour Apr–Dec, Sat–Sun 1:30 and 2:30pm. Confino Apartment living history program Sat–Sun hourly noon–3pm. Subway: F to Delancey St.; B, D, Q to Grand St.

This museum is the first-ever National Trust for Historic Preservation site that was not the home of someone rich or famous. It's something quite different: A five-story tenement that 10,000 people from 25 countries called home between 1863 and 1935—people who had come to the United States looking for the American dream and made 97 Orchard St. their first stop. The Tenement Museum tells the story of the great immigration boom of the late 19th and early 20th centuries, when the Lower East Side was considered the "Gateway to America." A visit here makes a good follow-up to an Ellis Island trip; what happened to all the people who passed through that famous waystation?

The only way to see the museum is by guided tour. The primary tenement tour, held on all open days, offers a satisfying exploration of the museum. A knowledgeable guide leads you into the dingy urban time capsule, where several apartments have been faithfully restored to their exact lived-in condition, and recounts the real-life stories of the families who occupied them in fascinating detail. It's not really for kids, however, who won't enjoy the serious tone and "don't touch" policy. Much better for them is the weekends-only Confino Apartment tour, an interactive living history program geared to families, which allows kids to converse with a interpreter who plays teenage immigrant Victoria Confino circa 1916; kids can also handle whatever they like in the apartment and even try on period clothes. A weekend neighborhood heritage walking tour is also offered on weekends.

All tours are limited in number, so it pays to reserve ahead. The Visitors' Center has several small exhibits, including photos, videos, and a model tenement.

✪ **Morgan Library.** 29 E. 36th St. (at Madison Ave.). ☎ **212/685-0008.** www. morganlibrary.org. Admission $7 adults, $5 seniors, children under 12 free. Tues–Thurs 10:30am–5pm, Fri 10:30am–8pm, Sat 10:30am–6pm, Sun noon–6pm. Subway: 6 to 33rd St.

Here's an undiscovered New York treasure, boasting one of the world's most important collections of original manuscripts, rare books and bindings, master drawings, and personal writings. Among the remarkable artifacts on display under glass are stunning illuminated manuscripts (including Gutenberg bibles), a working draft of the U.S. Constitution bearing copious handwritten notes, Voltaire's personal household account books, and handwritten scores by the likes of Beethoven, Mozart, and Puccini. The collection of mostly 19th-century drawings—by Seurat, Degas, Rubens, and other great masters—have an excitement of immediacy about them that the artists' more well-known paintings often lack. This rich repository originated as the private collection of turn-of-the-century financier J. Pierpont Morgan and is housed in a landmark Renaissance-style palazzo building (1906) he commissioned from

McKim, Mead & White to hold his masterpieces. Morgan's library and study are pre-served virtually intact and worth a look unto themselves for their landmarked archi-tecture (particularly the rotunda) and richly detailed fittings. The special exhibitions are particularly well chosen and curated; subjects can range from medieval bookbind-ing techniques to the literary genesis of the mystery novel and pulp fiction to a display of treasures from the royal tombs of Ur. A reading room is available by appointment.

**Museum for African Art.** 593 Broadway (btw. Houston and Prince sts.). ☎ **212/ 966-1313.** www.africanart.org. Admission $5 adults, $2.50 seniors, students, and children. Tues–Fri 10:30am–5:30pm, Sat–Sun noon–6pm. Subway: N, R to Prince St.

This captivating museum (whose interior was designed by architect Maya Lin, best known for her Vietnam Veterans Memorial in Washington, D.C.) is a leading orga-nizer of temporary exhibits dedicated to historic and contemporary African art and culture. Exhibitions on the calendar for 2001 include "Caravans: Nomads and Traders in Northern Africa," examining the evolution of art through time through immigra-tion, emigration, and diaspora; and "Controlling Power: Gender Roles in African Art," focusing on gender issues as they relate to African masks and statuary. An excel-lent museum shop showcases contemporary African crafts.

**Museum of American Folk Art.** 2 Lincoln Sq. (Columbus Ave. between 65th and 66th sts., across from Lincoln Center). ☎ **212/977-7298** or 212/595-9533. www.folkartmuseum.org. Free admission; $3 voluntary donation requested. Tues–Sun 11:30am–7:30pm. Subway: 1, 9 to 66th St.

This museum displays a wide range of works from the 18th century to the present, reflecting the breadth and vitality of the American folk-art tradition. The textiles col-lection is the museum's most popular, highlighted by a splendid variety of quilts. The gift shop is filled with one-of-a-kind objects.

**Relocation note:** In late spring 2001, the museum is scheduled to move to new digs at 45 W. 53rd St., just down the block from the Museum of Modern Art. The new building will quadruple the existing exhibit space.

**Museum of Jewish Heritage—A Living Memorial to the Holocaust.** 18 First Place (at Battery Place), Battery Park City. ☎ **212/509-6130.** www.mjhnyc.org. Admission $7 adults, $5 seniors and students, children under 5 free. Sun–Wed 9am–5pm, Thurs 9am–8pm, Fri and eves of Jewish holidays 9am–3pm. Last admission 1 hour before closing. Subway: 1, 9 to South Ferry; 4, 5 to Bowling Green.

Located in the south end of Battery Park City, this museum occupies a strikingly spare six-sided building designed by award-winning architect Kevin Roche, with a six-tier roof alluding to the Star of David and the 6 million murdered in the Holocaust. The permanent exhibits—"Jewish Life a Century Ago," "The War Against the Jews," and "Jewish Renewal"—recount the daily pre-war lives, the unforgettable horror that destroyed them, and the tenacious renewal experienced by European and immigrant Jews in the years from the late 19th century to the present. Its power derives from the way it tells that story: through the objects, photographs, documents, and, most poignantly, through the videotaped testimonies of Holocaust victims, survivors, and their families, all chronicled by Steven Spielberg's Survivors of the Shoah Visual His-tory Foundation.

Advance tickets are recommended to guarantee admission and can be purchased by calling ☎ **212/945-0039** or TicketMaster (☎ **800/307-4007** or 212/307-4007; www.ticketmaster.com).

**Museum of the City of New York.** 1220 Fifth Ave. (at 103rd St.). ☎ **212/534-1672.** www.mcny.org. Suggested admission $5 adults, $4 seniors, students and children, $10 fami-lies. Wed–Sat 10am–5pm, Sun noon–5pm. Subway: 6 to 103rd St.

A wide variety of objects—costumes, photographs, prints, maps, dioramas, and memorabilia—traces the history of New York City from its beginnings as a humble Dutch colony in the 16th century to its present-day prominence. Two outstanding permanent exhibits are the re-creation of John D. Rockefeller's master bedroom and dressing room and the space devoted to "Broadway!", a history of New York theater. The permanent "Furniture of Distinction, 1790–1890" displays 33 elegant pieces representing New York's central role in American cabinetmaking that will have you eyeing your IKEA with new contempt. Kids will love "New York Toy Stories," a permanent exhibit showcasing toys and dolls owned and adored by centuries of New York children. Look for *"Guys and Dolls,"* a tribute to the 50th anniversary of the celebrated musical showcasing costumes and ephemera, from November 2000 to June 2001.

**Museum of Television & Radio.** 25 W. 52nd St. (btw. Fifth and Sixth aves.). ☎ **212/ 621-6800** or 212/621-6600. www.mtr.org. Admission $6 adults, $4 seniors and students, $3 children under 13. Tues–Sun noon–6pm (Thurs to 8pm, Fri theater programs to 9pm). Subway: B, D, F, Q to 47–50th sts./Rockefeller Center; N, R to 49th St.

If you can resist the allure of this museum, I'd wager you've spent the last 70 years in a bubble. You can watch and hear all the great personalities of TV and radio—from Uncle Miltie to Johnny Carson to Jerry Seinfeld—at a private console (available for 2 hours). And amazingly, you can also conduct computer searches to pick out the great moments of history, viewing almost anything that made its way onto the airwaves, from the Beatles' first appearance on *The Ed Sullivan Show* to the crumbling of the Berlin Wall (the collection consists of 75,000 programs and commercials). The museum was founded by former CBS head William Paley, in a building designed by Philip Johnson. Selected programs are also presented in two theaters and two screening rooms, which can range from "Barbra Streisand: The Television Performances" to little-seen Monty Python episodes; check to see what's on while you're in town.

**National Academy of Design.** 1083 Fifth Ave. (at 89th St.). ☎ **212/369-4880.** www. nationalacademy.org. Admission $8 adults, $5 seniors and students. Wed–Sun 11:45am–5pm (extended Fri hours during annual exhibition). Subway: 4, 5, 6, to 86th St.

Founded in 1825, the National Academy is one of the oldest art institutions in the country and dedicated to preserving the academic tradition. There are three components: a fine arts school, an honorary professional association of artists, and a museum, which mounts regular exhibits drawn from its large collection on such themes as "Art in the Age of Queen Victoria" and "The Watercolors of Charles Hawthorne." The annual Open Annual Exhibition is the nation's oldest continuing juried show; look for the 176th edition to be held in February and March.

**National Museum of the American Indian, George Gustav Heye Center.** 1 Bowling Green (btw. State and Whitehall sts.). ☎ **212/668-6624.** www.si.edu/nmai. Free admission. Daily 10am–5pm (Thurs to 8pm). Subway: 1, 9 to South Ferry; 4, 5 to Bowling Green.

Part of the Smithsonian Institution, this collection is the oldest of its kind in the country. It's housed in the beautiful 1907 beaux-arts U.S. Customs House (a National Historic Landmark that's worth a look in its own right), but only until its new home is completed on the Mall in Washington, D.C., in 2002. Until then, enjoy items spanning more than 10,000 years of native heritage, collected mainly by New York banking millionaire George Gustav Heye a century ago. About 70% of the collection is dedicated to the native peoples of the United States and Canada; the rest represents the cultures of Mexico and south and central Americas. There's a the wealth of material here, but it's rather poorly organized. The museum also hosts interpretive programs

# Art for Art's Sake: The Gallery Scene

Art galleries are open free to the public, generally Tuesday through Saturday from 10am to 6pm. Saturday-afternoon gallery hopping, in particular, is a favorite pastime. Nobody will expect you to buy, so don't worry; it's all about looking.

The best way to choose where to go is by perusing the Art Guide in the Friday Weekend section of *The New York Times,* or the back of the Sunday Arts & Leisure section; the Art section in the weekly *Time Out New York;* the "Cue" section at the back of the weekly *New York* magazine; or the *New Yorker's* weekly "Goings on About Town" section. You can also find the latest exhibition listings online at **www.newyork.citysearch.com** (click on ARTS & ENTERTAINMENT), **www.artnet.com**, and **www.galleryguideonline.com**. An excellent source—more for practicals on the galleries and the artists and genres they represent rather than current shows—is the comprehensive **www.artincontext.org**. The *Gallery Guide* is available at most galleries around town.

I suggest picking a gallery or a show in the major gallery neighborhood that seems to suit your taste and just start browsing from there. I've listed a few good starting points below. This list doesn't even begin to scratch the surface; there are many, many more galleries in each neighborhood, as well as smaller concentrations of galleries in areas like the East Village, TriBeCa, and Brooklyn (www.artincontext.org is a good way to locate them). Keep in mind that Uptown galleries tend to be more traditional, Downtown galleries more contemporary, and far-west Chelsea galleries the most cutting edge. But you'll find that there are constant surprises in all neighborhoods.

**UPTOWN**　Uptown galleries are clustered in and around the glamorous crossroads of Fifth Avenue and 57th Street as well as on and off stylish Madison Avenue in the 60s, 70s, and 80s. Unlike their upstart Chelsea and SoHo counterparts, these blue-chip galleries maintain their quiet white-glove demeanor. If you feel uncomfortable browsing anywhere, it will be here. Galleries include **Hirschl & Adler,** 21 E. 70th St. (☎ 212/535-8810; www.hirschlandadler.com), for 18th- to 20th-century European and American painting and decorative arts; art-world powerhouses **Gagosian,** 980 Madison Ave. (☎ 212/744-2313; www.gagosian.com), and **PaceWildenstein,** 32 E. 57th St. (☎ 212/421-3292; www.pacewildenstein.com); **Knoedler & Company,** 19 E. 70th St. (☎ 212/ 794-0550), representing such artists as Helen Frankenthaler, Nancy Graves, and Frank Stella; **Mary Boone,** 745 Fifth Ave. (☎ 212/752-2929), known for

plus free storytelling, music, and dance presentations; call for a current calendar, call ☎ **212/514-3888.**

**Neue Gallerie New York.** 1048 Fifth Ave. (at 86th St.). ☎ **212/628-6200.** www. neuegallerie.org. Admission $10. Fri–Mon 11am–7pm. Subway: 4, 5, 6 to 86th St.

Scheduled to open in fall 2000 is this new museum dedicated to German and Austrian art, with a focus on the early 20th century. The emphasis will be works on paper, but the collection will also include decorative arts, painting, and other media. Expect works from such artists as Klimt, Kokoschka, and leaders of the Wiener Werkstätte and Bauhaus movements. Once occupied by Mrs. Cornelius Vanderbilt III, the landmark-designated 1914 Carrèrre & Hastings building is currently being restored success with such artists as Ross Bleckner and Eric Fischl; and **Wildenstein,** the classical big brother of PaceWildenstein, 19 E. 64th St. (☎ 212/879-0500; www. wildenstein.com), specializing in big-ticket works: old masters, Impressionism, and Renaissance paintings and drawings.

**CHELSEA**   The area in the West 20s between Tenth and Eleventh avenues is home to the avant garde of today's New York art scene, with West 26th serving as the unofficial "gallery row." Most galleries are not in storefronts but in the large spaces of multi-story former garages and warehouses. Those worth seeking out include **Paula Cooper,** 534 W. 21st St. (☎ 212/255-1105), offering a wide range of well-known artists and specializing in conceptual and minimal art; **George Billis,** 526 W. 26th St., 9F (☎ 212/645-2621; www.georgebillis.com), who shows works by talented emerging artists (I saw a marvelous Tom Gregg show here last fall); **Barbara Gladstone,** 515 W. 24th St. (☎ 212/206-9300; www.gladstonegallery.com); powerhouse **Gagosian,** 555 W. 24th St. (☎ 212/ 228-2828; www.gagosian.com), which shows such major artists as Richard Serra; **Cheim & Read,** 521 W. 23rd St. (☎ 212/242-7727), which often shows works by such high-profile pop artists as Diane Arbus, Larry Clark, and Nan Goldin; **DCA Gallery,** 525 W. 22nd St. (☎ 212/255-5511; www.dcagallery.com), specializing in contemporary Danish artists; and **Alexander & Bonin,** 132 Tenth Ave. (☎ **212/367-7474;** www.alexanderandbonin.com), which mounts excellent solo exhibitions by select artists from the Americas and Europe.

**SOHO**   SoHo remains colorful, if less edgy than it used to be, with the action centered around West Broadway and encroaching onto the edge of Chinatown of late. Start with **Bronwyn Keenan,** 3 Crosby St. (☎ 212/431-5083), who's known for keen eye for spotting emerging talent; **O.K. Harris,** 383 W. Broadway (☎ 212/431-3600; www.okharris.com), which shows contemporary painting, sculpture, and photography; **P.P.O.W,** 476 Broome St. (☎ 212/941-8642), known for the high quality of their emerging American artists; **Louis K. Meisel,** 141 Prince St. (☎ 212/677-1340; www.meiselgallery.com), specializing in photorealism and American pin-up art (yep, Petty and Vargas girls); and **Holly Solomon,** 172 Mercer St. (☎ 212/941-5777), representing such heavyweights as William Wegman and Nam June Paik as well as talented up-and-comers.

and should be worth a look in itself, as will the bookshop, specializing in related art, architecture, and literature topics. Call before you go to guard against unforeseen delays in opening.

**New Museum of Contemporary Art.** 583 Broadway (btw. Houston and Prince sts.). ☎ **212/219-1222.** www.newmuseum.org. Admission $6; $3 for artists, students, and seniors; free for visitors 18 and under; free to all Thurs 6–8pm. Sun and Wed noon–6pm, Thurs–Sat noon–8pm. Subway: N, R to Prince St.; B, D, F, Q to Broadway–Lafayette St.

With 33,000 square feet of space and the former curator of contemporary art at the Whitney as its brand-new director, the New Museum is now a prime contender on the museum scene. This contemporary arts museum has moved closer to the mainstream in recent years, but it's only a safety margin in from the edge as far as most of us are concerned. Expect adventurous and well-curated exhibitions. Subject matter on the schedule for late 2000–2001 includes "Pierre et Gilles," a survey of the French team's photo-paintings, including their superlative celebrity portraits; and a exhibition of Los Angeles-based artist Paul McCarthy's multimedia architectural installations.

**Newseum/NY.** 580 Madison Ave. (btw. 56th and 57th sts.). ☎ **212/317-7503.** www.newseum.org/newseumny. Free admission. Mon–Sat 10am–5:30pm. Subway: 4, 5, 6 to 59th St.

An adjunct to the main Newseum in Arlington, VA, Newseum/NY is a photojournalism gallery dedicated to broadening the public's understanding of the press's role and First Amendment issues. It's run by the Freedom Forum (www.freedomforum. org), a nonpartisan foundation dedicated to the support of free speech and free press around the world. This multimedia gallery is only a fraction of the size of the big Newseum, but it's worth checking out nonetheless. You can easily explore it in a half-hour or so.

In addition to the rotating mounted exhibit, Newseum/NY hosts a regular free program of evening gallery talks, films, and lectures, such as "Coverage of Poverty in the U.S." and "School Violence: A Figment of the Media's Imagination?" Call or visit the Web site to check the current schedule.

**New-York Historical Society.** 2 W. 77th St. (at Central Park West). ☎ **212/873-3400.** www.nyhistory.org. Admission $5 adults, $3 seniors and students, free for children 12 and under. Tues–Sun 11am–5pm. Subway: B, C to 81st St.; 1, 9 to 79th St.

Launched in 1804, the New-York Historical Society is a major repository of American history, culture, and art, with a special focus on New York and its broader cultural significance. The grand neoclassical edifice near the Museum of Natural History is finally undergoing major renovations. By fall 2000, the fourth floor will be transformed into the new Henry Luce III Center for the Study of American Culture, a state-of-the-art study facility and gallery, and 65% of the society's phenomenal collection will be on permanent display. For the first time, museumgoers will be able to view many large objects stored offsite for decades, including paintings, decorative arts collections, and carriages. Already on display is a small but notable selection of Tiffany lamps and paintings from Hudson River School artists Thomas Cole, Asher Durand, and Frederic Church, including Cole's five-part masterpiece, *The Course of Empire*. Also of note are the society's wide-ranging temporary exhibits; call or check the Web site to see what's on while you're in town.

**Schomburg Center for Research in Black Culture.** 515 Malcolm X Blvd. (Lenox Ave., btw. 135th and 136th sts.). ☎ **212/491-2200,** or 212/491-2265 for program and exhibition information. www.nypl.org. Free admission. Gallery hours: Mon–Sat 10am–6pm, Sun 1–5pm. Subway: 2, 3 to 135th St.

Arturo Alfonso Schomburg, a Puerto Rican black, set himself to accumulating materials about blacks in America, and his massive collection is now housed and preserved at this research branch of the New York Public Library. The Exhibition Hall and Latimer/Edison Gallery host changing exhibits related to black culture, such as "Black New York Artists of the 20th Century" and "Black New Yorkers/Black New York: 400 Years of African-American History." A rich calendar of talks and performing arts events is also part of the continuing program. Make an appointment—it'll be worth your while—to see the 1930s murals by Harlem Renaissance artist Aaron Douglas. Academics and others interested in a more complete look at the center's holding can preview what's available online.

**Studio Museum in Harlem.** 144 W. 125th St., btw. Malcolm X Blvd. (Lenox Ave.) and Adam Clayton Powell Jr. Blvd. ☎ **212/864-4500.** www.studiomuseuminharlem.org.

Admission $5 adults, $3 seniors and students, $1 children under 12. Free to all first Sat of the month. Wed–Fri 10am–5pm, Sat–Sun 1–6pm. Subway: 2, 3 to 125th St.

The small but excellent museum is devoted to presenting 19th- and 20th-century African-American art as well as 20th-century African and Caribbean art and traditional African art and artifacts. Rotating exhibitions are a big part of the museum's focus, such as "Explorations in the City of Light: African-American Artists in Paris, 1945–1965," and an annual exhibition of works by emerging artists as part of its Artists-in-Residence program. There's also a small sculpture garden, a good gift shop, and a full calendar of special events that includes gallery talks, artist interviews, and workshops. With a new director and deputy director on board—from the Metropolitan Museum and the Whitney, respectively—look for exciting changes and improvements in the coming year.

**Whitney Museum of American Art at Philip Morris.** 120 Park Ave. (at 42nd St., opposite Grand Central Terminal). ☎ **917/663-2453.** www.whitney.org. Free admission. Gallery: Mon–Wed and Fri 11am–6pm, Thurs 11am–7:30pm. Sculpture Court: Mon–Sat 7:30am–9:30pm, Sun 11am–7pm. Subway: 4, 5, 6, 7, S to 42nd St./Grand Central.

This Midtown branch of the Whitney Museum of American Art (see "The Top Museums" earlier in this chapter) features an airy sculpture court and a petite gallery that hosts changing exhibits, usually the works of living contemporary artists. Well worth peeking into if you're in the neighborhood; I popped in recently and found a wonderful exhibition that juxtaposed the organic-inspired sculptures and drawings of Isamu Noguchi and Ellsworth Kelly. Go to the Web site and click on INFORMATION and then BRANCH MUSEUMS if you want to see what's on in advance. Free hour-long gallery tours are offered Wednesday and Friday at 1pm.

## 6  Skyscrapers & Other Architectural Marvels

### THE TOP STRUCTURES

For details on the **World Trade Center,** see p. 210, and the **Brooklyn Bridge,** see p. 194; the **Woolworth Building** is discussed on p. 211.

**Chrysler Building.** 405 Lexington Ave. (at 42nd St.). Subway: 4, 5, 6, 7, S to 42nd St./Grand Central.

Built as Chrysler Corporation headquarters in 1930 (they moved out decades ago), this is perhaps the 20th century's most romantic architectural achievement, especially at night, when the lights in its triangular openings play off its steely crown. As you admire its facade, be sure to note the gargoyles reaching out from the upper floors, looking for all the world like streamline-Gothic hood ornaments.

There's a fascinating tale behind this building. While it was under construction, its architect, William Van Alen, hid his final plans for the spire that now tops it. Working at a furious pace in the last days of construction, the workers assembled in secrecy the elegant pointy top—and then they raised it right through what people had assumed was going to be the roof, and for a brief moment it was the world's tallest building (a distinction stolen by the Empire State Building only a few months later). Its exterior chrome sculptures are magnificent and spooky. The observation deck closed long ago, but you can visit its lavish ground-floor interior, which is art deco to the max. The ceiling mural depicting airplanes and other early marvels of the first decades of the 20th century evince the bright promise of technology. The elevators are works of art, masterfully covered in exotic woods (especially note the lotus-shaped marquetry on the doors).

## Empire State Ticket-Buying Tip

Lines can be frightfully long at the concourse-level ticket booth, so be prepared to wait—or consider purchasing **advance tickets** online using a credit card at **www. esbnyc.org**. You'll pay a $3 service charge for the privilege, but it's well worth it, especially if you're visiting during a busy season, when the line can be shockingly long. You're not required to choose a time or date for your tickets in advance; they can be used on any regular open day. However, order them well before you leave home, because they're sent only by regular mail. Expect them to take 7 to 10 days to reach you (longer if you live out of the country). With tickets in hand, you're allowed to proceed directly to the second floor—past everyone who didn't plan as well as you did!

✪ **Empire State Building.** 350 Fifth Ave. (at 34th St.). ☎ **212/736-3100.** www. esbnyc.com. Observatory admission $7 adults, $4 seniors and children 6–12, free for children under 5. Daily 9:30am–midnight (tickets sold until 11:30pm). Subway: B, D, F, Q, N, R to 34th St.; 6 to 33rd St.

King Kong climbed it in 1933. A plane slammed into it in 1945. The World Trade Center superseded it in 1970 as the island's tallest building. And in 1997, a gunman ascended it to stage a deadly shooting. But through it all, the Empire State Building has remained one of the city's favorite landmarks and its signature high-rise. Completed in 1931, it climbs 102 stories (1,454 feet) and now harbors the offices of fashion firms and, in its upper reaches, a jumble of high-tech broadcast equipment.

Always a conversation piece, the Empire State Building glows every night, bathed in colored floodlights to commemorate events of significance (red, white, and blue for Independence Day; green for St. Patrick's Day; red, black, and green for MLK Day; blue and white for Chanukah; even lavender and white for Gay Pride Day). The familiar silver spire can be seen from all over the city. My favorite view of the building is from 23rd Street, where Fifth Avenue and Broadway converge. On a lovely day, stand at the base of the Flatiron Building (see below) and gaze up Fifth; the crisp, gleaming deco tower jumps out, soaring above the sooty office buildings that surround it.

But the views that keep nearly 3 million visitors coming every year are the ones from the 86th- and 102nd-floor **observatories.** The lower one is best; you can walk out on a windy deck and look through coin-operated viewers (bring quarters!) over what, on a clear day, can be as much as an 80-mile visible radius. The citywide panorama is magnificent. One surprise is the flurry of rooftop activity, an aspect of city life that thrives unnoticed from our everyday sidewalk vantage point. The higher observation deck is glass-enclosed and cramped.

Light fog can create an admirably moody effect, but it goes without saying that a clear day is best. Dusk brings the most remarkable views and the biggest crowds. Consider going in the morning, when the light is still low on the horizon, keeping glare to a minimum. Starry nights are pure magic.

In your haste to go up, don't rush through the beautiful three-story-high marble **lobby** without pausing to admire its features.

✪ **Grand Central Terminal.** 42nd St. at Park Ave. www.grandcentralterminal.com. Subway: 4, 5, 6, 7, S to 42nd St./Grand Central.

After more than two years and $175 million, this 1913 landmark (originally designed by Warren & Wetmore with Reed & Stem) was reborn in 1998 as one of the most magnificent public spaces in the country. The restoration, by the New York firm of Beyer Blinder Belle, is an utter triumph. Their work has reanimated the genius of the station's original intent: to inspire those who pass through this urban meeting point with lofty feelings of civic pride and appreciation for Western architectural traditions. In short, they've put the "grand" back into Grand Central.

By all means, come and visit, even if you're not catching one of the subway lines or Metro North commuter trains that rumble through the bowels of this great place. And even if you arrive and leave by subway, be sure to exit the station, walk a couple of blocks south to about 40th Street, and turn around to admire Jules-Alexis Coutan's neo-classical sculpture *Transportation* hovering over the south entrance, with a majestically buff Mercury, the Roman god of commerce and travel, as its central figure.

The greatest visual impact comes when you enter the vast **main concourse.** Cleaned of decades of grime and cheesy advertisements, it boasts renewed majesty. The high windows once again allow sunlight light to penetrate the space, glinting off the half-acre Tennessee marble floor. The brass clock over the central kiosk gleams, as do the gold- and nickel-plated chandeliers piercing the side archways. The masterful **sky ceiling,** again a brilliant greenish blue, depicts the constellations of the winter sky above New York. They're lit with 59 stars, surrounded by dazzling 24-karat-gold and emitting light fed through fiber-optic cables, their intensities roughly replicating the magnitude of the actual stars as seen from Earth. Look carefully, and you'll see a patch near one corner left unrestored as a useful reminder of the neglect once visited on this splendid overhead masterpiece. On the east end of the main concourse is a grand **marble staircase** where there had never been one before, but as the original plans had always intended.

This dramatic beaux-arts splendor serves as a hub of social activity as well. New retail shops and restaurants have taken over the mezzanine and lower levels. The highlights of the west mezzanine are **Michael Jordan's—The Steak House,** a gorgeous art deco space; stop into the welcoming, comfortable bar, where you can enjoy the marvelous views for the price of a drink. You'll eat substantially cheaper on the **lower concourse,** which houses newsstands, a food court offering everything from deli sandwiches to the famous **Oyster Bar & Restaurant,** also restored to its original old-world glory (see chapter 6). Off the main concourse at street level, there's a nice mix of specialty shops and national retailers, plus the grand new **Grand Central Market** for gourmet foodstuffs (see chapter 8). The **Transit Museum Store,** in the shuttle passage, is worth a look for transit buffs.

**New York Public Library.** Fifth Ave. and 42nd St. ☎ **212/869-8089** (exhibits and events) or 212/661-7220 (library hours). www.nypl.org. Free admission to all exhibitions. Rose Main Reading Room and exhibition halls, Mon and Thurs–Sat 10am–6pm, Tues–Wed 11am–7:30pm. Subway: B, D, F, Q to 42nd St.; 4, 5, 6, 7, S to Grand Central/42nd St.

The New York Public Library, adjacent to Bryant Park (see "Central Park & Other Places to Play" below) and designed by Carrére & Hastings (1911), is one of the country's finest examples of beaux-arts architecture, a majestic structure of white Vermont marble with Corinthian columns and allegorical statues. Before climbing the broad flight of steps to the Fifth Avenue entrance, take note of the famous lion sculptures— *Fortitude* on the right and *Patience* on the left—so dubbed by whip-smart former mayor Fiorello LaGuardia. At Christmastime they don natty wreaths to keep warm.

This library is actually the **Humanities and Social Sciences Library,** only one of the research libraries in the New York Public Library system. The interior is one of the finest in the city and features **Astor Hall,** with high arched marble ceilings and grand staircases. The stupendous **Main Reading Rooms** have undergone a massive restoration and modernization that both brought them back to their stately glory and moved them into the computer age (goodbye, card catalogs!).

Even if you don't stop in to peruse the periodicals, you might want to check out one of the excellent rotating **exhibitions,** which can range from "The Drawings of Charles Addams" to "Utopia: The Search for the Ideal Society in the Western World" (through January 27, 2001). There's also a full calendar of **lecture programs,** with past speakers ranging from Tom Stoppard to Cokie Roberts; popular speakers often sell out, so it's a good idea to purchase tickets in advance.

**☉ Rockefeller Center.** Between 48th and 50th sts., from Fifth to Sixth aves. ☎ **212/ 632-3975.** Subway: B, D, F, Q to 47th–50th sts./Rockefeller Center.

A streamline modern masterpiece, Rockefeller Center is one of New York's central gathering spots for visitors and New Yorkers alike. A prime example of the city's sky-scraper spirit and historic sense of optimism, it was erected mainly in the 1930s, when the city was deep in a depression as well as its most passionate art deco phase. Desig-nated a National Historic Landmark in 1988, it's now the world's largest privately owned business-and-entertainment center, with 18 buildings on 21 acres.

For a dramatic approach to the entire complex, start at Fifth Avenue between 49th and 50th streets. The builders purposely created the gentle slope of the Promenade, known here as the **Channel Gardens** because it's flanked to the south by La Maison Française and to the north by the British Building (the Channel, get it?). You'll also find a number of attractive shops along here, including a big branch of the **Metro-politan Museum of Art Store,** a good stop for elegant gifts. The Promenade leads to the **Lower Plaza,** home to the famous ice-skating rink in winter (see next paragraph) and alfresco dining in summer in the shadow of Paul Manship's gilded bronze statue *Prometheus,* more notable for its setting than its magnificence as an artwork. All around the flags of the United Nations' member countries flap in the breeze. Just behind *Prometheus,* in December and early January, towers the city's official and majes-tic Christmas tree.

The **Rink at Rockefeller Plaza** (☎ 212/332-7654) is tiny but positively roman-tic, especially during the holidays, when the giant Christmas tree's multicolored lights twinkle from above. It's open from mid-October to mid-March, and you'll skate under the magnificent tree for the month of December.

The focal point of this "city within a city" is the **GE Building,** at 30 Rockefeller Plaza, a 70-story showpiece towering over the plaza. It's still one of the city's most impressive buildings; walk through for a look at the granite marble lobby, lined with monumental sepia-toned murals by José Maria Sert. You can pick up a walking-tour brochure highlighting the center's art and architecture at the main information desk in this building.

**NBC** television maintains studios throughout the complex. *Saturday Night Live,* the *Rosie O'Donnell Show,* and *Late Night with Conan O'Brien* originate in the GE Build-ing (see "Talk of the Town: TV Tapings" later in this chapter for tips on getting tick-ets). If you're a fan of NBC's Today Show, the glass-enclosed studio from which the show is broadcast live weekdays from 7 to 9am is on the southwest corner of 49th Street and Rockefeller Plaza; come early if you want a visible spot, and bring your HI MOM! sign. Who knows? You might even get to chat with Al, Katie, or Matt in a seg-ment. Other notable buildings throughout the complex include the **International Building,** on Fifth Avenue between 50th and 51st streets, worth a look for its Atlas statue out front; and the **McGraw-Hill Building,** on Sixth Avenue between 48th and 49th streets, with its 50-foot sun triangle on the plaza.

The newly restored **Radio City Music Hall,** 1260 Sixth Ave., at 50th Street (☎ 212/247-4777; www.radiocity.com), is perhaps the most impressive architectural

feat of the complex. Designed by Donald Deskey, it's one of the largest indoor theaters, with 6,200 seats. But its true grandeur derives from its magnificent art deco
appointments. The crowning touch is the stage's great proscenium arch, which from
the distant seats, evokes a faraway sun setting on the horizon of the sea. The men's and
women's lounges are also splendid. The theater hosts the annual **Christmas Spectacular,** starring the Rockettes. The one-hour **Stage Door Tour** is offered Monday
through Saturday from 10am to 5pm, Sunday from 11am to 5pm; tickets are $15 for
adults, $9 for children under 12.

**United Nations.** At First Ave. and 46th St. ☎ **212/963-TOUR (8687).** www.un.org. Guided
tours $7.50 adults, $6 seniors, $5 students, $4 children (those under 5 not permitted). Daily
tours every half-hour 9:15am–4:45pm; closed weekends Jan–Feb. Subway: 4, 5, 6, 7, S to
42nd St./Grand Central.

In the midst of what some consider the world's most cynical city is this working monument to world peace. The U.N. headquarters occupies 18 acres of international
territory—neither New York City nor the United States has jurisdiction here—along
the East River from 42nd to 48th streets. Designed by an international team of architects (led by American Wallace K. Harrison and including Le Corbusier) and finished
in 1952, the complex weds the 39-story glass slab Secretariat with the free-form General Assembly on beautifully landscaped grounds donated by John D. Rockefeller, Jr.,
along the East River. One hundred eighty nations use the facilities to arbitrate worldwide disputes.

    **Guided one-hour tours** take you to the General Assembly Hall and the Security
Council Chamber and introduce the history and activities of the United Nations and
its related organizations. Along the tour, you'll see donated objects and artwork,
including charred artifacts that survived the atomic bombs at Hiroshima and Nagasaki,
stained-glass windows by Chagall, a replica of the first *Sputnik,* and a colorful mosaic
called *The Golden Rule,* based on a Norman Rockwell drawing, which was a gift from
the United States in 1985.

    If you take the time to wander the beautifully landscaped **grounds,** you'll be
rewarded with lovely views and some surprises. The mammoth monument *Good
Defeats Evil,* donated by the Soviet Union in 1990, uses parts of a Russian ballistic
missile and an American Pershing missile to fashion a contemporary St. George slay-
ing a dragon.

    The **Delegates' Dining Room** (☎ 212/963-7625), which affords great views of
the East River, is open to the public on weekdays for lunch 11:30am to 2:30pm
(reserve in advance). The **gift shop** sells flags and unusual handcrafted items from all
over the world, and the **post office** sells unique United Nations stamps that can be
purchased and posted only here.

## OTHER NOTABLE STRUCTURES

In addition to the landmarks below, architecture buffs might also want to seek out
these notable buildings: The **Lever House,** built in 1952 at 390 Park Ave., between 53rd
and 54th streets, and the neighboring **Seagram Building** (1958), at 375 Park Ave.,
which are the city's best examples of the form-follows-function, glass-and-steel International style, with the latter designed by master architect Mies van der Rohe himself. Also
in Midtown East is the **Sony Building,** at 550 Madison Ave., designed in 1984 by
Philip Johnson with a pretty rose-granite facade and a playful Chippendale-style top that
puts it a cut above the rest on the block.

    The Upper West Side is home to two of the city's prime examples of residential
architecture. On Broadway, taking up the block between 73rd and 74th streets, is the

# What's New in Times Square

The writer, O. Henry—most famous for his own open-ended stories, it's worth noting—once observed that "New York City will be a great place if they ever finish it." Indeed, no other city is so darn good at, and so continually committed to, reinventing itself. This quirky, century-transcending preoccupation is best illustrated in the "new" Times Square. The dust is finally settling on the epic renewal of the crossroads where Broadway meets 42nd Street, and what was once the city's gritty heart is now the hub of its tourism-friendly rebirth.

The neon lights of Broadway are more dazzling than ever, now that ABC's *Good Morning America* has set up a street-facing studio at Broadway and 44th Street (just across from MTV), and **Nasdaq**'s 8-story, 90-by-120-foot billboard—the world's largest video screen, at Broadway and 43rd, and probably the most expensive, costing $37 million—have joined the landscape. **WWF New York** and **ESPN Zone** both landed on Broadway in 1999, reinvigorating the whole notion of themed dining (see "Theme Restaurant Thrills!" in chapter 6). Corporate America has even moved in; among the big-name headquarters that have relocated to prime Times Square real estate in '99 and 2000 are Morgan Stanley and Reuters.

In February 2000, the city chose a winning design that will give the **TKTS** discount theater tickets booth at the neighborhood's bustling heart—a bargain beacon for budget-minded visitors and New Yorkers alike—its own brand-new look. The current modified ramshackle trailer will be replaced by a grand red 16-foot staircase, with the new booth tucked underneath. After making your ticket purchase, you'll be able to take a seat on the steps and watch the real-life theater of the absurd taking place around you. Extra ticket windows are set to be added, too, which should speed up the lines. Construction is set to begin in late 2000.

The biggest news for 2000 is 42nd Street. This former porn peddler's paradise is being rebuilt from scratch as a family-oriented amusement mecca—a couple of 'em, in fact. By the end of 2000, the south side of 42nd between Seventh and Eighth avenues will be reinvented as the Forest City Ratner entertainment complex (bound to be christened with a sexier name by the time you arrive). It will include **Madame Tussaud's New York,** a 6-floor, fully interactive New World version of London's famous wax museum; a 26-screen movie complex; and plenty of mall-familiar shopping, including a Disney Store and HMV Records. But wait, there's more: Across the street will be E-Walk, where the multi-level **Broadway City** video arcade will be joined in late 2000 by **B.B. King's Blues Room** (☎ 212/997-4144), a 550-seat music club and restaurant that promises to be a slice of authenticity among the tourist schlock (the legendary Blue Note jazz club is behind the development), plus 13 extra movie screens and more shopping and dining straight from the mall back home. To quote the great Bart Simpson: Ay carumba!

**Ansonia,** looking for all the world like a flamboyant architectural wedding cake. This splendid beaux arts building has been home to the likes of Stravinsky, Toscanini, and Caruso, thanks to its virtually soundproof apartments; it was also featured prominently as the thrill-a-minute residence of Bridget Fonda and Jennifer Jason Leigh in

*Single White Female.* Even more notable is the **Dakota,** at 72nd Street and Central Park West. Legend has it that the angular 1884 apartment house—accented with gables, dormers, and oriel windows that give it a brooding appeal—earned its name when its forward-thinking developer, Edward S. Clark, was teased by friends that he was building so far north of the city that he might he might as well be building in the Dakotas. The building's most famous resident, John Lennon, was gunned down outside the 72nd Street entrance on December 8, 1980; Yoko Ono still lives inside, but the all-grown-up Sean has since relocated to a downtown loft.

For **City Hall,** see the walking tour under "Historic Lower Manhattan's Top Attractions" earlier in this chapter.

**✪ Cathedral of St. John the Divine.** 1047 Amsterdam Ave. (at 112th St.). ☎ **212/ 316-7540** for general information, 212/932-7347 for tour information and reservations, 212/662-2133 for event information and tickets. www.stjohndivine.org. Suggested admission $2; tour $3; tower tour $10. Mon–Sat 8am–6pm, Sun 7am–7:30pm. Tours offered Tues–Sat 11am, Sun 1pm; tower tours 1st and 3rd Sat of the month at noon and 2pm. Services Mon–Sat 8am and 12:15 and 5:30pm; Sun 8, 9, and 11am and 7pm. Subway: 1, 9, B, C to Cathedral Pkwy.

The world's largest Gothic cathedral, St. John the Divine has been a work in progress since 1892. Its sheer size is amazing enough—a nave that stretches two football fields and a seating capacity of 5,000—but keep in mind that there is no steel structural support. The church is being built using traditional Gothic engineering; blocks of granite and limestone are carved out by master masons and their apprentices (some from the surrounding Harlem neighborhood). Perhaps that's why the construction is still going on, more than 100 years after it began, with no end in sight. But what makes this place so wonderful is that finishing isn't necessarily the point.

Although the seat of the Episcopal Diocese of New York, St. John's embraces an interfaith tradition. Internationalism is a theme found throughout the cathedral's iconography; each chapel is dedicated to a different national or ethnic group. You can explore it on the **Public Tour,** offered six days a week, or on the twice-monthly **Vertical Tour,** which takes you on a hike up the 11-flight circular staircase to the top, for spectacular views. The cathedral is known for presenting outstanding musical events and important speakers. The free **New Year's Eve concert** draws thousands of New Yorkers; so, too, does its annual **Blessing of the Animals,** held in early October (see the "Calendar of Events" in chapter 2).

If you need a snack after your tour, stop into the lovely, worn **Hungarian Pastry Shop,** 1030 Amsterdam Ave., between 110th and 111th streets (☎ 212/866-4230), a favorite among Columbia University students. Order a plateful of crumbly, buttery cookies from the display case up front, and then set up camp; this is another place you won't be rushed out of.

**Flatiron Building.** 175 Fifth Ave. (at 23rd St.). Subway: R to 23rd St.

This triangular masterpiece was one of the first skyscrapers. Its knife-blade wedge shape is the only way the building could fill the triangular property created by the intersection of Fifth Avenue and Broadway, and that happy coincidence created one of the city's most distinctive buildings. Built in 1902 and fronted with limestone and terra cotta (not iron), the Flatiron measures only 6 feet across at its narrow end. So called for its resemblance to the laundry appliance, it was originally named the Fuller Building, then later "Burnham's Folly" (because folks were certain that architect

Daniel Burnham's 21-story structure would fall down). It didn't. There's no observation deck, and the building mainly houses publishing offices, but a few shops do grace the ground floor. The building's existence has served to name the neighborhood around it—the Flatiron District (see "Manhattan's Neighborhoods in Brief" in chapter 4).

**St. Patrick's Cathedral.** Fifth Ave. (btw. 50th and 51st sts.) ☎ **212/753-2261.** www.stpatrickscathedral.org. Free admission. Mon–Fri and Sun 7am–8:30pm, Sat 8am–8:30pm. Mass Mon–Fri 7, 7:30, 8, and 8:30am, noon, and 12:30, 1, and 5:30pm; Sat 8 and 8:30am, noon, and 12:30 and 5:30pm; Sun 7, 8, 9, and 10:15am, noon, and 1, 4, and 5:30pm. Subway: B, D, F, Q to 47–50th sts./Rockefeller Center.

The largest Catholic cathedral in the United States is also the seat of the Archdiocese of New York. Designed by James Renwick, begun in 1859, and consecrated in 1879, St. Patrick's wasn't completed until 1906. Strangely, Irish Catholics picked one of the city's WASPiest neighborhoods for this Gothic church, constructed of white marble and stone. Look for Mother Elizabeth Seton, the first American-born saint, among the statues in the nave.

**Temple Emanu-El.** 1 E. 65th St. (at Fifth Ave.). ☎ **212/744-1400.** www.emanuelnyc.org. Free admission. Museum hours: Sun–Thurs 10am–4:30pm, Fri–Sat 1–4pm. Services Sun–Thurs 5:30pm, Fri 5:15pm, Sat 10:30am. Subway: 6 to 68th St.; N, R to Fifth Ave.

Many of New York's most prominent and wealthy families are members of this Reform congregation, housed in the city's most famous synagogue. The largest house of Jewish worship in the world is a blend of Moorish and Romanesque styles, symbolizing the mingling of Eastern and Western cultures. The **Herbert and Eileen Bernard Museum** houses a small but remarkable collection of Judaica, including a collection of Hanukkah lamps with examples ranging from the 14th to the 20th centuries.

## 7 Affordable Sightseeing Tours

Reservations are required on some of the tours listed below, but even if they're not it's always best to call ahead to confirm prices, times, and meeting places.

### DOUBLE-DECKER BUS TOURS

Taking a narrated sightseeing tour is one of the best ways to see and learn quickly about New York's major sights and neighborhoods. However, keep in mind that the commentary is only as good as the guide, who is seldom an expert. Tour guides tend toward hyperbole and might get a few of the facts wrong. *The New York Times* recently found tour-bus guides spouting the following inaccuracies: 65 people were killed in the World Trade Center blast (it was 6); New York has the oldest subway system in the world (third, behind London's—41 years before New York—and Boston's, the first in the U.S.); Frank Sinatra was born in Jersey City (it was Hoboken); and Herald Square was named after the founder of the *New York Herald Tribune* (there was no Mr. Herald). But the idea is to see the highlights, not write a dissertation from this stuff. So enjoy the ride—and take the "facts" you hear along the way with a grain of salt.

**Gray Line New York Tours.** In the Port Authority Bus Terminal, Eighth Ave. and 42nd St.; also at Times Square Visitors Center, 1560 Broadway (btw. 46th and 47th sts.). Tours depart from four additional Manhattan locations. ☎ **212/397-2600.** www.graylinenewyork.com. Hop-on, hop-off bus tours from $25 adults, $16 children 5–11; hop-on, hop-off full-city tour $35 adults, $23 children.

Gray Line offers just about every sightseeing tour option and combination you could want. There are bus tours by day and by night that run uptown, downtown, and all around the town, as well as bus combos with Circle Line cruises, helicopter flights, museum entrances, and guided visits of sights. Two-day options are available, as are some out-of-town day trips (even a full day at Woodbury Commons, if you can't resist an opportunity for outlet shopping).

There's no real point to purchasing some combination tours—you don't need a guide to take you to the top of the World Trade Center or to the Statue of Liberty, and you don't save any money on admission by buying the combo ticket—but others, such as the Sunday Harlem Gospel tour, which features a tour of Harlem's top sights and a gospel service, is worth the $33 price tag ($24 for kids 5–11). I've found Gray Line to put a higher premium on accuracy than the other big tour-bus operators, so this is your best bet among the biggies.

## HARBOR CRUISES

If you'd like to sail the New York Harbor aboard the 1885 cargo schooner *Pioneer,* see the listing for South Street Seaport & Museum earlier in this chapter, under "Historic Lower Manhattan's Top Attractions."

✪ **Circle Line Sightseeing Cruises.** Departing from Pier 83, at W. 42nd St. and Twelfth Ave. and Pier 16 at South Street Seaport. Also departing from Pier 16 at South Street Seaport, 207 Front St. Sales desk at Times Square Visitors Center, 1560 Broadway (btw. 46th and 47th sts.). ☎ **212/563-3200.** www.circleline.com. Cruises $12–$22 adults, $10–$19 seniors, $6–$12 children 12 and under. Subway to Pier 83: A, C, E to 42nd St. Subway to Pier 16: J, M, Z, 2, 3, 4, 5 to Fulton Street.

Circle Line is the only tour company that circumnavigates the entire 35 miles around Manhattan, and I love this ride. The **Full Island** cruise takes three hours and passes by the World Trade Center, the Statue of Liberty, Ellis Island, the Brooklyn Bridge, the United Nations, Yankee Stadium, the George Washington Bridge, and more, including Manhattan's wild northern tip. The panorama is riveting, and the commentary isn't bad. The big boats are basic but fine, with lots of deck room for everybody to enjoy the view. Snacks, soft drinks, coffee, and beer are available on board for purchase.

If three hours is more than you or the kids can handle, go for either the $1\frac{1}{2}$-hour **Semi-Circle** or **Sunset/Harbor Lights** cruise, both of which show you the highlights of the skyline. There's also a 1-hour **Seaport Liberty** version that sticks close to the south end of the island. But of all the tours, the kids might like **The Beast** best, a thrill-a-minute speedboat ride offered in summer only.

In addition, a number of adults-only **Live Music & DJ Cruises** sail regularly from the seaport from May through September ($20 to $40 per person). Depending on the night of the week, you can groove to the sounds of jazz, Latin, gospel, dance tunes, or blues as you sail along the skyline.

## SPECIALTY TOURS
### MUSEUMS & CULTURAL ORGANIZATIONS

The **Municipal Art Society** (☎ **212/935-3960;** www.mas.org) offers excellent historical and architectural walking tours aimed at intelligent, individualistic travelers, not the mass market. Each is led by a highly qualified guide who gives insights into the significance of buildings, neighborhoods, and history. Topics range from the urban history of Greenwich Village to "Money Matters: The Interiors of Wall Street." Weekday walking tours are $10, $8 for seniors and students; weekend tours are $15, $12 for seniors and students. Reservations may be required depending on the tour, so it's always best to call ahead. A full schedule of upcoming tours is available online.

The ✪ **92nd Street Y** (☎ **212/996-1100;** www.92ndsty.org) offers a wonderful variety of **walking tours,** many featuring funky themes or behind-the-scenes visits. Subjects can range from "Diplomat for a Day at the UN" to "Secrets of the Chelsea Hotel" to "Artists of the Meat-Packing District" to "Jewish Harlem." Prices range from $15 to $40, but many include ferry rides, afternoon tea, dinner, or whatever suits the program. Guides are well-chosen experts on their subjects, ranging from highly respected historians to an East Village poet, mystic, and art critic (for "Allen Ginsberg's New York" and "East Village Night Spots"), and many routes travel into the outer boroughs. Advance registration is required for all walking tours. Schedules are planned out a few months in advance, so check the Web site for tours that might interest you.

The **New-York Historical Society** (☎ **212/873-3400;** www.nyhistory.org), offers walking tours of various Manhattan neighborhoods on Wednesdays and Saturdays throughout the year, usually led by an expert guide with special insight into a given area. At press time, author Edward Hayman (*Signs and Wonders: The Spectacular Marketing of America*) was leading guided walks through Times Square, with special emphasis on its neon history. Call or check the Web site to see what's on when you're in town. Tours are generally $12 for adults, $10 for students and seniors.

## INDEPENDENT OPERATORS

One of the most highly praised sightseeing organizations in New York is ✪ **Big Onion Walking Tours** (☎ **212/439-1090;** www.bigonion.com). Enthusiastic Big Onion guides (all hold an advanced degree in American history from Columbia or New York universities) peel back the layers of history to reveal the city's inner secrets. The 2-hour tours are offered mostly on weekends, and subjects include the "The Bowery," "Presidential New York," "Irish New York," "Central Park," "Greenwich Village in Twilight," "Historic Harlem," and numerous historic takes on Lower Manhattan. One of the most popular programs is the "Multi-Ethnic Eating Tour" of the Lower East Side, where you munch on everything from dim sum and dill pickles to fresh mozzarella. Big Onion also conducts exclusive visits to Ellis Island and Roosevelt Island. Tour prices range from $10 to $16 for adults, $8 to $14 for students and seniors. Reservations aren't taken, but Big Onion strongly recommends that you call to verify schedules.

All tours offered by ✪ **Joyce Gold History Tours of New York** (☎ **212/ 242-5762;** www.nyctours.com) are offered by Joyce Gold herself, an instructor of Manhattan history at New York University and the New School for Social Research, who has been conducting history walks around New York since 1975. Her tours can really cut to the core of this town; Joyce is full of fascinating stories about Manhattan and its people. Tours are arranged around themes such as "The Colonial Settlers of Wall Street," "The Genius and Elegance of Gramercy Park," "Downtown Graveyards," "The Old Jewish Lower East Side," "Historic Harlem," and "TriBeCa: The Creative Explosion." Tours are offered most weekends March to December and last from 2 to 4 hours, and the price is $12 per person; no reservations are required. Private tours can be arranged.

Alfred Pommer has conducted **New York City Cultural Walking Tours** (☎ **212/ 979-2388;** www.nycwalk.com) in nearly every Manhattan neighborhood for more than 15 years. He focuses on history and architecture, making the past come alive via photographs and stories. A number of his tours focus on specific subjects, such as "Gargoyles in Manhattan" and "Rockefeller Center's Public Art." His 2- to 2¹/₂-hour tours take place every Sunday from March through September and often Thursdays in winter. The charge is $10 per person, and no reservation is needed; you just need to

# Show Me, Show Me, Show Me: Free Walking Tours

A number of neighborhood organizations and business improvement districts (BIDs) offer free guided walks to highlight the new developments and hidden joys of their neighborhoods. For travelers on a budget, these introductory freebies are well worth taking advantage of:

The **Times Square Exposé Tour,** sponsored by the Times Square Visitors Center, 1560 Broadway, between 46th and 47th streets (☎ **212/768-1560;** www.timessquarebid.org), offers a fun and enlightening behind-the-scenes look at the Theater District's architecture, history, and current trends. Tours meet at the center Friday at noon.

The **Orchard Street Bargain District Tour,** sponsored by the Lower East Side Business Improvement District (☎ **888/VALUES-4-U** or 212/226-9010), explores the general history and long-standing retail culture of this historic neighborhood. This is a particularly good bet for bargain-hunters, who will learn all about the famous Old World shops and newer outlet stores in this discount shopping destination. The free tours are offered Sundays at 11am from April to December, rain or shine, and no reservation is required. Meet up with the guide in front of Katz's Delicatessen, 205 E. Houston St., at Ludlow Street.

On Wednesdays at 12:30pm, the Municipal Art Society (☎ **212/935-3960;** www.mas.org) sponsors a free tour of **Grand Central Terminal** (although donations are accepted). It's a real joy now that Grand Central has been so beautifully restored. Call to confirm the schedule and meeting spot.

If you're looking to tour a specific neighborhood with an expert guide, call **Big Apple Greeter** (☎ **212/669-8159;** www.bigapplegreeter.org). This non-profit organization consists of specially trained New Yorkers who volunteer to take visitors around town for a free 2- to 4-hour tour of a particular neighborhood. Reservations must be made in advance, preferably at least 1 week ahead of your arrival. Big Apple Greeter is also well suited to accommodating disabled travelers; see "Tips for Travelers with Special Needs" in chapter 2 for details.

show up at the assigned spot. Private tours are available at $15 per hour for one to three people or $25 per hour for four or more.

A landscape designer by trade, Patricia Olmstead offers **Urban Explorations** walking tours (☎ **718/721-5254**). One of her best tours is "Hidden Gardens of New York," but her knowledge of art, architecture, history, and trivia makes each one engaging. Most tours are $12, $10 for students, seniors, and repeat customers.

Behind the scenes is the focus of **Adventure on a Shoestring** (☎ **212/265-2663**), a membership organization that offers 90-minute public walking tours on weekends year-round for just $5. One of the earliest entrants in the now-burgeoning walking tour market, Howard Goldberg has provided unique views of New York since 1963, exploring Manhattan's neighborhoods with a breezy, man-of-the-people style. Past tours have featured more offbeat adventures such as backstage tours of Broadway shows, visits to handwriting analysts, and lessons in flamenco dancing. If you're going to be in the city for awhile, you might want to pay the $40 membership fee for access to some of the more unusual activities. Call for reservations.

Self-proclaimed "radical historian" Bruce Kayton leads unconventional **Radical Walking Tours** (☎ **718/492-0069;** www.he.net/~radtours) to conventional tourist sights. A tour of Harlem covers the Black Panthers, the Communist Party, and Malcolm X in addition to the Apollo Theater and the Schomburg Center, and a visit to the Lower East Side focuses on radical Jews such as Abraham Cahan (founder of the influential newspaper *Jewish Daily Forward* in 1897) and the Rosenbergs. Two Greenwich Village tours are offered, of course. Tour prices are $10, and tours last 3 to 4$^1$/$_2$ hours; no reservations are required.

**Harlem Spirituals** (☎ 212/391-0900; www.harlemspirituals.com) specializes in gospel and jazz tours of Harlem that can be combined with a traditional soul food meal. A variety of options is available, including a tour of Harlem sights with gospel service, and soul food lunch (brunch on Sunday) as an add-on ($35 adults, $27 children 12 and under; $65 adults, $55 children with lunch or brunch) that's offered both Wednesdays and Sundays. Bronx, Queens, and Brooklyn tours are also offered for those who want a taste of the outer boroughs. All tours leave from Harlem Spirituals' Midtown office (690 Eighth Ave., between 43rd and 44th), and all transportation is included.

## 8  Central Park & Other Places to Play

### ✪ CENTRAL PARK

Without this miracle of civic planning, Manhattan would be a virtual unbroken block of buildings. Instead, smack in the middle of Gotham, an 843-acre natural retreat provides a daily escape valve and tranquilizer for millions of New Yorkers.

While you're in the city, be sure to take advantage of the park's many charms—not the least of which is its sublime layout. Frederick Law Olmsted and Calvert Vaux won a competition with a plan that marries flowing paths with sinewy bridges, integrating them into the natural rolling landscape with its rocky outcroppings, man-made lakes, and wooded pockets. The park's construction, between 1859 and 1870, provided much-needed employment during an economic depression and drew the city's population into the upper reaches of the island, which at that time were still quite rural. Nevertheless, designers predicted the hustle and bustle to come and tactfully hid traffic from the eyes and ears of parkgoers by building roads that are largely hidden from the bucolic view.

On just about any day, Central Park is crowded with New Yorkers and visitors alike. On nice days, especially weekend days, it's the city's party central. Families come to play in the snow or the sun, depending on the season; in-line skaters come to fly through the crisp air and twirl in front of the bandshell; couples come to stroll or paddle the lake; dog people come to hike and throw frisbees to Bowser; and just about everybody comes to sunbathe at the first sign of summer. On beautiful days, the crowds are part of the appeal; everybody's come here to peel off their urban armor and relax, and the common goal puts a general feeling of camaraderie in the air. On these days, the people watching is more compelling than anywhere else in the city. But one of Central Park's great appeals is that even on the most crowded days, there's always somewhere to get away from it all, if you just want a little peace and quiet and a moment to commune with nature.

**ORIENTATION & GETTING THERE**    Look at your map; that great green swath in the center of Manhattan is Central Park. It runs from 59th Street (also known as Central Park South) at the south end to 110th Street at the north end and from Fifth Avenue on the east side to Central Park West (the equivalent of Eighth Avenue) on the west side. A 6-mile rolling road, **Central Park Drive,** circles the park and has a lane set aside for bikers, joggers, and in-line skaters. A number of **transverse** (crosstown)

**roads** cross the park at major points—at 65th, 79th, 86th, and 97th streets—but they're built down a level, largely out of view, to minimize intrusion on the bucolic nature of the park.

A number of subway stops and lines serve the park, and which one you take depends on where you want to go. To reach the southernmost entrance on the west side, take an A, B, C, D, 1, or 9 to 59th St./Columbus Circle. To reach the southeast corner entrance, take the N, R to Fifth Avenue; from this stop, it's an easy walk into the park to the Information Center in the **Dairy** (☎ **212/794-6564;** open Tues–Sun 10am–5pm), midpark at about 65th Street. Here you can ask questions, pick up park information, and purchase a good park map.

If your time for exploring is limited, I suggest entering the park at 72nd or 79th streets for maximum exposure (subway: B, C to 72nd St. or 81st St./Museum of Natural History). From here, you can pick up park information at the visitor center at **Belvedere Castle** (☎ **212/772-0210;** open Wed–Mon 11am–4pm), midpark at 79th Street. There's also a third Visitor Center at the **Charles A. Dana Discovery Center** (☎ **212/860-1370;** open daily 11am–5pm, to 4pm in winter), at the northeast corner of the park at Harlem Meer, at 110th Street between Fifth and Lenox avenues (subway: 2, 3 to Central Park North/110th St.). The Dana Center is also an environmental education center hosting workshops, exhibits, music programs, and park tours and lends fishing poles for fishing in Harlem Meer (park policy is catch-and-release).

Food carts and vendors are set up at all of the park's main gathering points, selling hot dogs, pretzels, and ice cream, so finding a bite to eat is never a problem. You'll also find a fixed food counter at the **Conservatory,** on the east side of the park north of the 72nd Street entrance, and both casual snacks and more sophisticated dining at **Park View at the Boathouse.**

**GUIDED TOURS    Trolley tours** of the park are offered weekdays from May through November. Tours last 90 minutes and depart from Grand Army Plaza at Fifth Avenue and 59th Street; call ☎ **212/397-3809** for details.

The Dana Center hosts ranger-guided tours on occasion (☎ **212/860-1370**). Also consider a private walking tour; many of the companies listed under "Organized Sightseeing Tours" earlier in this chapter offer guided tours.

**FOR FURTHER INFORMATION**    Call the main number at ☎ **212/360-3444** for recorded information. Call ☎ **212/360-3456** for special events information. The park also has a comprehensive Web site that's worth checking out before you go at **www.centralpark.org**. If you have an **emergency** in the park, dial ☎ **800/ 201-PARK.**

**SAFETY TIP**    Even though the park has the lowest crime rate of any of the city's precincts, be wary, especially in the more remote northern end. It's a good idea to avoid the park entirely after dark, unless you're heading to one of the restaurants for dinner or to a Summerstage or Shakespeare at the Park event (see chapter 9), when you should stick with the crowds. For more safety tips, see "Playing It Safe" in chapter 4.

### EXPLORING THE PARK

The best way to see Central Park is to wander along the park's 58 miles of winding pedestrian paths, keeping in mind the following highlights.

Before starting your stroll, stop by the **Information Center** in the Dairy, midpark in a 19th-century–style building overlooking Wollman Rink at about 65th Street, to get a good park map and other information on sights and events and to peruse the kid-friendly exhibit on the park's history and design.

**Where's Balto?**

The people at Central Park say that the question they're asked almost more than any other these days is "Where is the statue of Balto?" The heroic dog is just northwest of the zoo, midpark at about 66th Street.

The southern part of Central Park is more formally designed and heavily visited than the relatively rugged and remote northern end. Not far from the Dairy is the **carousel** with 58 hand-carved horses (open daily 10:30am–6pm, to 5pm in winter; rides are 90¢); the zoo (see "Central Park Wildlife Center" below); and the Wollman Rink for roller- or ice-skating (see "Activities" below).

The **Mall,** a long formal walkway lined with elms shading benches and sculptures of sometimes forgotten writers, leads to the focal point of Central Park, **Bethesda Fountain** (along the 72nd Street transverse road). **Bethesda Terrace** and its grandly sculpted entryway border a large **lake** where dogs fetch sticks, rowboaters glide by, and dedicated early-morning anglers try their luck at catching carp, perch, catfish, and bass. You can rent a rowboat at or take a gondola ride from **Loeb Boathouse,** on the eastern end of the lake (see "Activities" below). Boats of another kind are at **Conservatory Water** (on the east side at 73rd Street), a stone-walled pond flanked by statues of both **Hans Christian Andersen** and **Alice in Wonderland.** On Saturdays at 10am, die-hard yachtsmen race remote-controlled sailboats in fierce competitions, following Olympic regulations. (Sorry, model boats aren't for rent.)

If the action there is too intense, **Sheep Meadow** on the southwestern side of the park is a designated quiet zone, where Frisbee throwing and kite flying are as energetic as things get. Another respite is **Strawberry Fields,** at 72nd Street on the West Side. This memorial to John Lennon, who was murdered across the street at the Dakota apartment building (72nd Street and Central Park West, northwest corner), is a gorgeous garden centered around an Italian mosaic bearing the title of the lead Beatle's most famous solo song, and his lifelong message: imagine. In keeping with its goal of promoting world peace, the garden has 161 varieties of plants, donated by each of the 161 nations in existence when it was designed in 1985. This is a wonderful place for peaceful contemplation.

**Bow Bridge,** a graceful lacework of cast-iron designed by Calvert Vaux, crosses over the lake and leads to the most bucolic area of Central Park, the **Ramble.** This dense 38-acre woodland with spiraling paths, rocky outcroppings, and a stream is the best spot for bird watching and feeling as if you've discovered an unimaginably leafy forest right in the middle of the city.

North of the Ramble, **Belvedere Castle** is home to the **Henry Luce Nature Observatory** (☎ 212/772-0210), worth a visit if you're with children. From the castle, set on Vista Rock (the park's highest point at 135 feet), you can look down on the **Great Lawn,** which has emerged lush and green from renovations, and the **Delacorte Theater,** home to Shakespeare in the Park (see chapter 9). The small **Shakespeare Garden** south of the theater is scruffy, but it does have plants, herbs, trees, and other bits of greenery mentioned by the playwright. Behind the Belvedere Castle is the **Swedish Cottage Marionette Theatre** (☎ 212/988-9093), hosting various marionette plays for children throughout the year; call to see what's on.

Continue north along the east side of the Great Lawn, parallel to East Drive. Near the glass-enclosed back of the **Metropolitan Museum of Art** (see "The Top Museums" earlier in this chapter) is **Cleopatra's Needle,** a 69-food obelisk originally erected in Heliopolis around 1475 B.C. It was given to the city as a gift from the khedive of

# Central Park

Alice in Wonderland Statue **14**
Balto Statue **20**
The Bandshell **18**
Belvedere Castle **6**
Bethesda Terrace
& Bethesda Fountain **16**
Bow Bridge **8**
Carousel **26**
Central Park Wildlife Center **23**
Charles A. Dana
Discovery Center **1**
Cleopatra's Needle
(The Obelisk) **9**
Conservatory **13**
Conservatory Garden **1**
The Dairy Information Center **25**
Delacorte Clock **22**
Delacorte Theater **7**
Diana Ross Playground **4**
Hans Christian Andersen
Statue **12**
Harlem Meer **1**
Hecksher Playground **28**
Henry Luce
Nature Observatory **6**
*Imagine* Mosaic **17**
Jacqueline Kennedy Onassis
Reservoir **2**
Loeb Boathouse **15**
The Mall **19**
Pat Hoffman Friedman
Playground **10**
Park View at the Boathouse **11**
Rustic Playground **21**
Shakespeare Garden **8**
Spector Playground **3**
Swedish Cottage
Marionette Theatre **5**
Tavern on the Green **27**
Tisch Children's Zoo **23**
Wollman Rink **24**

Legend
Information (*i*)
Subway stop (M)

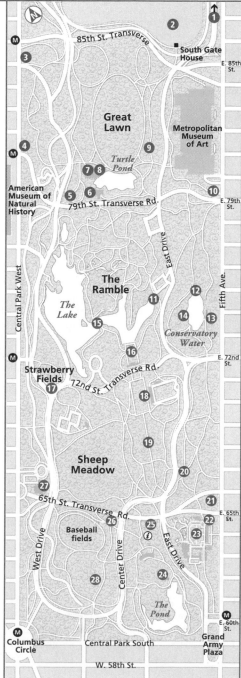

Egypt in 1880. (The khedive bestowed a similar obelisk to the city of London, which now sits on the Embankment of the Thames.)

North of the 86th Street Transverse Road is the **Jacqueline Kennedy Onassis Reservoir,** so named after the death of the beloved first lady, who lived nearby and often enjoyed a run along the 1¹/₂-mile jogging track that circles the reservoir.

At the northeast end of the park is the **Conservatory Garden** (at 105th Street and Fifth Avenue), Central Park's only formal garden, with a magnificent display of flowers and trees reflected in calm pools of water. (The gates to the garden once fronted the Fifth Avenue mansion of Cornelius Vanderbilt II.) **Harlem Meer** and its boathouse were recently renovated and look beautiful. The boathouse now berths the **Dana Discovery Center** (☎ 212/860-1370), where children learn about the environment and borrow fishing poles at no charge; see "Orientation & Getting There" under "Central Park & Other Places to Play" earlier in this chapter for further details.

## GOING TO THE ZOO

**Central Park Wildlife Center/Tisch Children's Zoo.** At Fifth Ave. and 64th St. ☎ 212/861-6030. www.wcs.org/zoos. Admission $3.50 adults, $1.25 seniors, 50¢ children 3–12, under 3 free. Apr–Oct, Mon–Fri 10am–5pm, Sat–Sun 10:30am–5:30pm; Nov–Mar, daily 10am–4:30pm. Subway: N, R to Fifth Ave.

It has been nearly a decade since the zoo in Central Park was renovated, making it in the process both more human and more humane. Lithe sea lions frolic in the central pool area with beguiling style. The gigantic but graceful polar bears (one of whom, by the way, made himself a true New Yorker when he began regular visits with a shrink) glide back and forth across a watery pool that has glass walls through which you can observe very large paws doing very smooth strokes. The monkeys seem to regard those on the other side of the fence with knowing disdain. In the hot and humid Tropic Zone, large colorful birds swoop around in freedom, sometimes landing next to non-plussed visitors.

Because of its small size, the zoo is at its best with its displays of smaller animals. The indoor, multi-level Tropic Zone is a real highlight, its steamy rainforest home to everything from black-and-white Colobus monkeys to Emerald tree boa constrictors to a leaf-cutter ant farm. So is the large penguin enclosure in the Polar Circle, which is better than the one at San Diego's Sea World. In the Temperate Territory, look for the Asian red pandas (cousins to the big black-and-white ones), which look like the world's most beautiful raccoons. Despite their pool and piles of ice, however, the polar bears still look sad.

The entire zoo is good for short attention spans; you can cover the whole thing in 1¹/₂ to 3 hours, depending on the size of the crowds and how long you like to linger. It's also very kid-friendly, with lots of well-written and -illustrated placards that older kids can understand. For the littlest ones, there's the $6-million **Tisch Children's Zoo.** With pigs, llamas, potbellied pigs, and more, this new (in fall 1997) petting zoo and playground is a real blast for the five-and-under set.

## ACTIVITIES

The 6-mile rolling road circling the park, **Central Park Drive,** has a lane set aside for bikers, joggers, and in-line skaters. The best time to use it is when the park is closed to traffic: Monday to Friday 10am to 3pm (except Thanksgiving to New Year's) and 7 to 10pm. It's also closed from 7pm Friday to 6am Monday, but when the weather is nice, the crowds can be hellish.

**BIKING**   Off-road mountain biking isn't permitted; stay on Central Park Drive or your bike might be confiscated by park police.

You can rent 3- and 10-speed bikes as well as tandems in Central Park at the **Loeb Boathouse,** midpark near 72nd Street and East Drive (☎ 212/517-3623), for $8 to $12 a day; at **Metro Bicycles,** 1311 Lexington Ave., at 88th Street (☎ 212/427-4450), for $35 a day; at **Pedal Pushers,** 1306 Second Ave., between 68th and 69th streets (☎ 212/288-5592), for about $18 a day; and at **Toga Bike Shop,** 110 West End Ave., at 64th Street (☎ 212/799-9625), for $25 a day.

**BOATING**   From spring to fall, gondola rides and canoe rentals are available at the **Loeb Boathouse,** midpark near 74th Street and East Drive (☎ 212/517-3623). Rentals are $10 for the first hour, $2.50 every 15 minutes thereafter, and a $30 deposit is required.

**HORSE-DRAWN CARRIAGE RIDES**   At the entrance to the park at 59th Street and Central Park South, you'll see a line of **horse-drawn carriages** waiting to take passengers on a ride through the park or along certain of the city's streets. Horses belong on city streets as much as chamber pots belong in our homes. You won't need me to tell you how forlorn most of these horses look; if you insist, a ride is about $50 for two for a half-hour, but I suggest skipping it.

**IN-LINE SKATING**   Central Park is the city's most popular place for blading. See the top of this section for details on Central Park Drive, main drag for skaters. On weekends, head to West Drive at 67th Street, behind Tavern on the Green, where you'll find trick skaters weaving through an NYRSA slalom course at full speed, or the Mall in front of the bandshell (above Bethesda Fountain) for twirling to tunes. In summer, **Wollman Rink** converts to a hot-shot roller rink, with half-pipes and lessons available (see "Ice Skating" below).

You can rent skates for $16 a day weekdays and $27 a day weekends from **Blades Board and Skate,** 120 W. 72nd St., between Broadway and Columbus Avenue (☎ 212/787-3911). Wollman Rink also rents in-line skates for park use at similar rates (directly below).

**ICE SKATING**   Central Park's **Wollman Rink,** at 59th Street and Sixth Avenue (☎ 212/396-1010), is the city's best outdoor skating spot. It's open for skating generally from mid-October to mid-April, depending on the weather. Rates are $7 for adults, $3.50 for seniors and kids under 12, and skate rental is $3.50; lockers are available (locks are $6.75).

**PLAYGROUNDS**   Nineteen Adventure Playgrounds are scattered throughout the park, perfect for jumping, sliding, tottering, swinging, and digging. At Central Park West and 81st Street is the **Diana Ross Playground,** voted the city's best by *New York* magazine. Also on the west side is the **Spector Playground,** at 85th Street and Central Park West, and, a little farther north, the **Wild West Playground** at 93rd Street. On the east side is the **Rustic Playground,** at 67th Street and Fifth Avenue, a delightfully landscaped space rife with islands, bridges, and big slides; and the **Pat Hoffman Friedman Playground,** right behind the Metropolitan Museum of Art at East 79th Street, is geared towards older toddlers.

**RUNNING**   Marathoners and wannabes regularly run in Central Park along the 6-mile **Central Park Drive,** which circles the park (run toward traffic to avoid being mowed down by wayward cyclists and in-line skaters). For a shorter loop, try the midpark 1.58-mile track around the **Jacqueline Kennedy Onassis Reservoir** (keep your eyes ready for spotting Madonna and other famous bodies). It's safest to jog only during daylight hours and where everybody else does. Avoid the small walks in the Ramble and at the north end of the park.

## OTHER PARKS

For parks in Brooklyn and Queens, see "Highlights of the Outer Boroughs" later in this chapter. For more information on these and other city parks, go online to **www.ci.nyc.ny.us/html/dpr**.

✪ **Battery Park.** From State Street to New York Harbor. Subway: N, R to Whitehall St.; 1, 9 to South Ferry; 4, 5 to Bowling Green.

As you traverse Manhattan's concrete canyons, it's sometimes easy to forget you're actually on an island. But here, at Manhattan's southernmost tip, you get the very real sense that just out past Liberty, Ellis, and Staten islands is the vast Atlantic Ocean.

The 21-acre park is named for the cannons built to defend residents after the American Revolution. **Castle Clinton National Monument** (the place to purchase tickets for the Statue of Liberty and Ellis Island ferry; see section 2 earlier in this chapter) was built as a fort before the War of 1812, although it was never used as such. You'll most likely recognize Battery Park for the prominent role it played in *Desperately Seeking Susan*, Madonna's first movie. Besides the requisite T-shirt vendors and hot-dog carts, you'll find several statues and memorials scattered throughout the park. This is quite the civilized park, with lots of STAY OFF THE GRASS! signs and Wall Streeters eating deli sandwiches on the many park benches. Pull up your own bench for a good view out across the harbor.

**Bryant Park.** Behind the New York Public Library, at Sixth Ave. between 40th and 42nd sts. Subway: B, D, F, Q to 42nd St.; 7 to Fifth Ave.

Another success story in the push for urban redevelopment, Bryant Park is the latest incarnation of a 4-acre site that was, at various times in its history, a graveyard and a reservoir. Named for poet and *New York Evening Post* editor William Cullen Bryant (look for his statue on the east end), the park actually rests atop the New York Public Library's many miles of underground stacks. Another statue is also notable: a squat and evocative stone portrait of Gertrude Stein, one of the few outdoor sculptures of women in the city.

This simple green swath, just east of Times Square, is welcome relief from Midtown's concrete, taxi-choked jungle, and good weather attracts brownbaggers from neighboring office buildings. Just behind the library is **Bryant Park Grill** (☎ 212/840-6500), an airy bistro with New American food and service that doesn't live up to its fine setting (or high prices). Still, the casual outdoor cafe is quite affordable.

The park plays host to New York's invitation-only **Seventh on Sixth** fashion shows, set up in billowy white tents (open to the trade only) in the spring and fall.

**Union Square Park.** From 14th to 17th sts., btw. Park Ave. South and Broadway. Subway: L, N, R, 4, 5, 6 to 14th St./Union Sq.

Here's a delightful place to spend an afternoon. Reclaimed from drug dealers and abject ruin in the late '80s, Union Square Park is now one of the city's best assets. The seemingly endless subway work should no longer be disturbing the peace by the time you're here. This patch of green remains, with or without the construction, the focal point of the newly fashionable Flatiron and Gramercy Park neighborhoods. Don't miss the grand equestrian statue of George Washington at the south end or the bronze statue (by Bartholdi, the sculptor of the Statue of Liberty) of the marquis de Lafayette at the eastern end, gracefully glancing toward France.

This charming square is now best known as the site of New York's premier **Greenmarket.** Every Monday, Wednesday, Friday, and Saturday, vendors come down from upstate, Long Island, and as far away as Pennsylvania to hawk fresh veggies and fruits, organic baked goods, cider, wine, and even fresh fish and lobsters in booths that flank

## We Can Work It Out

So your hotel doesn't have a gym, and walking around New York just isn't enough of a workout for you? Never fear: The city has a number of health clubs that are open to out-of-towners on a day-to-day basis.

Because many of the city's private gyms charge upwards of 40 bucks for day passes, the best bet for wallet-watching visitors is **Crunch Fitness** (www.crunch.com), 404 Lafayette St., between West 4th Street and Astor Place in NoHo (☎ 212/ 614-0120); in the Union Square area at 54 E. 13th St., between University Place and Broadway (☎ 212/475-2018); 144 W. 38th St., between Broadway and Seventh Avenue (☎ 212/869-7788); 162 W. 83rd St., between Columbus and Amsterdam avenues on the Upper West Side (☎ 212/875-1902), and at other locations throughout Manhattan (check the Web site or Yellow Pages). Crunch charges a more reasonable per-day drop-in fee of $22, and the Lafayette Street location is open 24 hours on weekdays (8am to 9pm on weekends).

Two favorites of Midtown office workers are the **Midtown YWCA,** 610 Lexington Ave., at 53rd Street (☎ 212/755-2700; $12 day-pass fee), and the **Vanderbilt YMCA,** 224 E. 47 St. (☎ 212/756-9600; $25 day-pass fee), both with pools. The **West Side YMCA,** 5 W. 63rd St., between Broadway and Central Park West (☎ 212/875-4100), has two pools and a day-pass fee of $15. It's always a good idea to bring your driver's license or other ID to show that you're from out of town when using a Y for the day. The **92nd Street YM–YWHA,** on the Upper East Side at 1395 Lexington Ave., at 92nd Street (☎ 212/415-5729), has some of the best state-of-the-art facilities in town (including a pool and Jacuzzi) and charges $20 for a day pass.

---

the north and west sides of the square. Fresh-cut flowers and plants are also for sale, as are books and postcards. During summer and fall, you can graze the bazaar and easily assemble a cheap and healthy lunch to munch under the trees, or at the picnic tables at the park's north end. Musical acts regularly play the small pavilion at the north end of the park, and in-line skaters take over the market space in the after-work hours. At the north end of the park, a small cafe called **Luna Park** (☎ 212/ 475-8464) is open in warm weather. A number of superstores and affordable restaurants rim the small park—so on a nice day, pop in to **Barnes & Noble** superstore for a book or a magazine, stop into the **Virgin Megastore** for some new tunes for your Walkman, pick a bench in the park, and you'll be happy as a clam for a few hours.

**Washington Square Park.** At the southern end of Fifth Ave. (where it intersects Waverly Place btw. MacDougal and Wooster sts.). Subway: A, B, C, D, E, F, Q to West 4th St./ Washington Sq.

You'll be hard-pressed to find much "park" in this mainly concrete square—once a burial ground in the late 18th century—but it's undeniably the focal point of Greenwich Village. Chess players, skateboarders, street musicians, New York University students, gay and straight couples, the occasional film crew, and not a few homeless people compete for attention throughout the day and most of the night. (If anyone issues a friendly challenge to play you in the ancient and complex Chinese game of Go, don't take any of them up on it; you'll lose money.)

The lively scene belies a macabre past. Once marshland traversed by Minetta Brook, it became in 1797 a potter's field (most green and fertile downtown parks were originally graveyards), and the remains of some 10,000 bodies are buried here. In the early

1800s the square, or more specifically the infamous Hanging Elm in the northwest corner where MacDougal Street meets the park, was used for public executions. It wasn't until the 1830s that the elegant Greek Revival town houses on Washington Square North known as "The Row" (note especially nos. 21–26) attracted the elite. Stanford White designed Washington Arch (1891–92) to commemorate the centenary of George Washington's inauguration as first president. While in the neighborhood, peek down charming MacDougal Alley and Washington Mews, both lined with delightful old carriage houses.

Despite a city cleanup and increased police presence, it's a good idea to stay out of the park after dark.

## CHELSEA PIERS

One of the city's biggest—and most successful—private urban development projects of the last few years has been the 30-acre **Chelsea Piers Sports and Entertainment Complex** (☎ 212/336-6666; www.chelseapiers.com). Jutting out into the Hudson River on four huge piers between 17th and 23rd streets, it's a terrific multi-functional recreational facility.

The ✪ **Sports Center** (☎ 212/336-6000), a three-football-fields-long mega-facility, does health clubs one better. In addition to the usual cardiovascular training, weights, and aerobics, it boasts a four-lane, quarter-mile indoor running track; a boxing ring; basketball courts; a sand volleyball court; a gorgeous 25-yard indoor pool with a whirlpool and sundeck; and the world's most challenging rock-climbing wall, plus a bouldering wall. Day passes are $40 for nonmembers—worth it for hardcore exercisers looking for the best.

The **Golf Club** (☎ 212/336-6400), has 52 all-weather, fully automated hitting stalls on four levels and a 200-yard net-enclosed artificial-turf fairway jutting out over the water, making it the best place in the city to hit a few. Pre-paid ball cards start at $15 for 65 balls, and club rentals are available.

The **Sky Rink** (☎ 212/336-6100), the city's latest ice spot, has twin around-the-clock indoor rinks for recreational skating and pickup hockey games with Hudson River views. General skating is $11 for adults, $8 for seniors and kids; skate rental is $5.

If wheels are your thing, there are two outdoor **Roller Rinks** (☎ 212/336-6200) for in-line skating and roller hockey games. Expect to pay $6 for adults, $5 for kids for general skating; skate rentals are available (adult $15, child $10).

The **Field House** (☎ 212/336-6500) is mainly for team sports, but young rock climbers will enjoy the 30-foot indoor **climbing wall,** designed to be suitable for kids as well as grown-ups. Open climbs are $17, and children's lessons are available. **Batting cages** are also available ($1 per 10 pitches).

Feeling like a little 10-pin tonight? State-of-the-art **AMF Chelsea Piers Bowl** (☎ 212/835-BOWL) offers 40 lanes of fun. Games are $6.25 per person, and shoe rental is $4.

Beyond its athletics, the complex is a destination in and of itself. The 1.2-mile **esplanade** has benches and picnic tables with terrific river views. For waterfront dining there's New York's largest microbrewery/restaurant, the **Chelsea Brewing Company** (☎ 212/336-6440), on Pier 61, serving up very good brews and okay food on a terrific waterfront terrace.

**Getting There:** Chelsea Piers is accessible by taxi and the M23 or M14 crosstown buses. The nearest subway is the C and E at 23rd Street and Eighth Avenue; then pick up the M23 and walk 4 long blocks west. Another option is to take the A, C, E to 14th Street or the L train to Eighth Avenue, walk to the river, and then follow the walking/riding/running path along the river north.

# 9 Talk of the Town: Free TV Tapings

The trick to getting tickets for TV tapings in this city is to be from out of town. You visitors have a much better chance than we New Yorkers; producers are gun-shy about filling their audiences with obnoxious locals and see everybody who's not from New York as being from the heartland—and therefore their target TV audience. Whatever. This means good news for you, as long as you don't live in the city. If you do, my best advice is to use Uncle Phil's address in Boise when you send in your postcard for tickets.

If your heart's set on getting tickets to a show, be sure to request them as early as possible; six months ahead isn't too early, and even earlier is better for the most popular shows. You're usually asked to send a postcard. Always include the number of tickets you want, your preferred dates of attendance (be as flexible as you can with this one), and your address *and* phone number. Tickets are always free. The shows tend to be pretty good about trying to meet your specific date requests, but don't be surprised if Queen Latifah is far more responsive than, say, Dave. And even if you send in your response extra-early, don't be surprised if tickets don't show up at your house until one or two weeks before tape date.

If you come to town without any tickets, all hope is not lost. Because they know that every ticket holder won't make it, many studios give out a limited number of standby tickets on the day of taping. If you can just get up a little early and don't mind standing in line for a couple (or a few) hours, you have a good chance of getting one. Now, the bad news: Only one standby ticket per person is allowed, so everybody who wants to get in has to get up at the crack of dawn and stand in line. And even if you get your hands on a standby ticket, it doesn't guarantee admission; they usually only start seating standbys after the regular ticketholders are in. Still, chances are good.

For additional information on getting tickets to tapings, call ☎ 212/484-1222, the New York Convention and Visitors Bureau's 24-hour hot line. And remember— you don't need a ticket to be on the *Today* show. *Good Morning America* also has a street-facing studio now, in Times Square on Broadway between 43rd and 44th streets, but it's on the second floor (just like the MTV studios across the street, at 1515 Broadway), so you won't be able to peer directly in.

If you do attend a taping, be sure to bring a sweater, even in winter. As anybody who watches Letterman knows, it's an icebox in those studios. And bring ID, as proof of age might be required.

***The Daily Show with Jon Stewart*** Comedy Central's boldly irreverent, often hilariously funny mock newscast tapes every Monday through Thursday at 5:45pm, at 513 W. 54th St. Make your advance ticket requests by phone at ☎ 212/586-2477, or check with them for any cancellation tickets for the upcoming week.

***Late Night with Conan O'Brien*** Conan tix might not quite have the cachet of a Dave ticket, but they're a hot commodity nevertheless—so start planning now. Tapings are Tuesday through Friday at 5:30pm (plan on arriving by 4:45pm if you have tickets), and you must be 16 or older to attend. You can keep trying to get through on the operator line to arrange for tickets by phone, or send your postcard to NBC Studios/*Late Night*, 30 Rockefeller Plaza, New York, NY 10112 (☎ **212/664-3056** or 212/664-3057). Standby tickets are distributed Tuesday through Friday at 9am outside 30 Rockefeller Plaza, on 49th Street side of the building, on a first-come, first-served basis (read: come early if you actually want to get one).

*The Late Show with David Letterman*   Here's the most in-demand TV ticket in town—so planning nine months ahead isn't too soon. Tapings are Monday through Thursday at 5:30pm (arrive by 4:15pm), with a second taping Thursday at 8pm (arrive by 6:45pm). You must be 16 or older to attend. Send your postcard at least six months early (two tickets max; one request only or all will be disregarded), to *Late Show* Tickets, Ed Sullivan Theater, 1697 Broadway, New York, NY 10019 (☎ 212/975-5853). On tape days, call ☎ **212/247-6497** at 11am for standby tickets (no in-line standbys anymore); start dialing early, because the machine will kick in as soon as all standbys are gone.

*Later Today*   Tickets for this post–*Today Show* hour starring Florence Henderson can be requested by calling (☎ **212/664-3056** or 212/664-3057). Standby tickets are available in the main lobby of NBC Studios, 30 Rockefeller Plaza, at 7:30am on a first-come, first-served basis.

*Live! with Regis and Kathie Lee*   Even once Kathie Lee has flown the coop (her replacement had not yet been named at press time), expect this to remain the *other* hottest ticket in town. Tapings of this popular couple are Monday to Friday at 9am at the ABC Studios at 7 Lincoln Square (Columbus Avenue and West 67th Street) on the Upper West Side. You must be 10 or older to attend (under 18s must be accompanied by a parent). Send your postcard (four tickets max) at least a *full year* in advance to *Live!* Tickets, Ansonia Station, P.O. Box 777, New York, NY 10023-0777 (☎ **212/456-3054**). Standby tickets are sometimes available. Arrive at the studio no later than 7am and request a standby number; they're handed out on a first-come, first-served basis, so earlier is better. You might also have a chance at last-minute tickets by calling ☎ **212/456-2410** or 212/456-3055, but this is a longer shot than standby.

*The Montel Williams Show*   Order tickets by calling ☎ **212/989-8101.** You must be 18 or older to attend.

*The Ricki Lake Show*   Tickets can be requested by calling ☎ **800/GO-RICKI**. You can also use this line to volunteer yourself as a guest for shows as "I'll Give You My Virginity for a Price" or "I Want to Tell My Girl I Slept with Her Mom." You must be 18 or older to attend.

*Queen Latifah Show*   Requests for tickets can be made by calling ☎ **877/485-7144,** by filling out the online request form at **www.latifahshow.com**, or by sending a self-addressed, stamped envelope to *Queen Latifah Tickets,* P.O. Box 2656, G.P.O., New York, NY 10199. You must be 16 or older to attend, and quantities are limited to six per request.

*The Rosie O'Donnell Show*   Rosie is so popular that she's one of the toughest tickets in town right now. The schedule varies, but in general Rosie tapings are Monday through Thursday at 10am, and Thursday again at 2pm. No children under 5 are allowed, and under 18s must be accompanied by an adult. Send your postcard as far in advance as possible to NBC Studios/*The Rosie O'Donnell Show,* 30 Rockefeller Plaza, Suite 800E, New York, NY 10112 (☎ **212/506-3288** or 212/664-3056). Call before you send, because demand is so great that requests are sometimes suspended or limited to certain months of the year. Standby tickets, if available, are distributed Monday through Thursday at 7:30am outside 30 Rockefeller Plaza, on 49th Street side of the building; it's a random lottery system, so it doesn't help to show up too early.

*The Sally Show*   Call ☎ **800/411-7941** or 212/244-3595 for tickets to Sally Jesse Raphaël's talkfest. You must be 18 or older to attend.

*Saturday Night Live*   Everything about the show might change, but one thing remains the same—SNL's enduring popularity. This is another extremely hard ticket to come by. Tapings are Saturday at 11:30pm (arrival time 10pm); there's also a full dress rehearsal (arrival time 7pm). You must be 16 or older to attend. Send your postcard to arrive *in the month of August only* to NBC Studios/*Saturday Night Live*, 30 Rockefeller Plaza, New York, NY 10112 (☎ **212/664-4000**); at press time, postcards were being accepted in the month of August only. Lotteries for pairs of tickets are held during the season; if you're a winner, you'll be notified with only one to two weeks' advance notice. Standby tickets might be a better bet: They're available at 9:15am on tape day at the 49th Street entrance to 30 Rockefeller Plaza.

*The Today Show*   As most of you know, anybody can be on TV with Katie, Matt, and cuddly weatherman Al Roker. All you have to do is show up outside the *Today* show's glass-walled studio at Rockefeller Center, on the southwest corner of 49th Street and Rockefeller Plaza, with your very own HI, MOM! sign. Tapings are Monday through Friday at 7am sharp, but come at the crack of dawn if your heart's set on being in front. Who knows? If it's a nice day, you might even get to chat with Katie, Matt, or Al in a segment.

*Total Request Live*   The countdown show that made Carson Daly a household name is broadcast live from MTV's second-floor glass-walled studio at 1515 Broadway, at 44th Street in Times Square, weekdays at 3:30pm. Crowds start gathering down below at all hours, depending on the drawing power of the day's guest. Arrive by 2pm at the latest if you want to have a prayer of making it into the in-studio audience (a very long shot). And don't forget to make your WE LOVE YOU, BRITNEY! and MARRY ME, CARSON! signs large enough to be captured on camera.

*The View*   ABC's girl power gabfest tapes live Monday through Friday at 11am (ticketholders must arrive by 10am). Requests, which should be send 12 to 16 weeks in advance, can be submitted online (**www.abc.go.com/theview**) or via postcard to Tickets, *The View*, 320 W. 66th St., New York, NY 10023. Because date requests are not usually accommodated, try standby: Arrive at the studio before 10am and put your name on the standby list; earlier is better, because tickets are handed out on a first-come, first-served basis.

*Who Wants to Be a Millionaire?*   This Regis Philbin–hosted phenomenon is filmed at ABC's Upper West Side studios. To request tickets to be an audience member, send a postcard to *Who Wants to Be a Millionaire?*, Columbia University Station, P.O. Box 250225, New York, NY 10025. Ticket requests are limited to four, and you must be 18 or older to attend. If your request can be met, tickets will be sent approximately two weeks prior to showtime.

## 10  Especially for Kids

This section is dedicated to those Big Apple attractions designed specifically with kids in mind. But many of the attractions discussed in the rest of this chapter are terrific for kids as well as adults; I've also included cross-references to the best of them below.

Probably the best place of all to entertain the kids is in ✪ **Central Park,** which has kid-friendly diversions galore; see section 8 earlier in this chapter.

For general tips and other resources for visiting the city with the kids, see "For Families" under "Tips for Travelers with Special Needs" in chapter 2.

## MUSEUMS

In addition to the museums designed specifically for kids below, also consider the following, discussed elsewhere in this chapter: The **American Museum of Natural History** (p. 213), whose dinosaur displays are guaranteed to wow both you and the kids; the *Intrepid* **Sea-Air-Space Museum** (p. 224), on a real battleship with an amazing collection of vintage and high-tech airplanes; the **Forbes Magazine Galleries** (p. 222), whose wacky collection includes a number of vintage toys and games; the **Museum of Television & Radio** (p. 227), where you and the kids can pull up episodes of *Sesame Street* and other classic kids' TV shows to watch; the **American Museum of the Moving Image** (p. 261), where you and the kids can learn how movies are actually made; the **Lower East Side Tenement Museum** (p. 225), whose weekend living-history program really intrigues school-age kids; and the **South Street Seaport & Museum** (p. 197), which little ones will love for its theme park–like atmosphere and old boats bobbing in the harbor.

**Children's Museum of the Arts.** 182 Lafayette St. (btw. Broome and Grand sts.). ☎ **212/941-9198** or 212/274-0986. Admission $5 for everyone 1–65; pay what you wish Wed 5–7pm. Wed noon–7pm, Thurs–Sun noon–5pm. Subway: 6 to Spring St.

Interactive workshop programs for children ages 1 to 12 and their families are the attraction here. Kids dabble in puppet making and computer drawing or join in singalongs and live performances. Call for the current schedule.

✪ **Children's Museum of Manhattan.** 212 W. 83rd St. (btw. Broadway and Amsterdam Ave.). ☎ **212/721-1234.** www.cmom.org. Admission $6 children and adults, $3 seniors. Wed–Sun 10am–5pm. Subway: 1, 9 to 86th St.

Here's a great place to take the kids when they're tired of being told not to touch. Designed for kids 2 to 12, this museum is strictly hands-on. Interactive exhibits and activity centers encourage self-discovery—and a recent expansion means that there's now more than ever before to keep the kids busy and learning. The Time Warner Media Center takes children through the world of animation and helps them produce their own videos. The Body Odyssey is a zany, scientific journey through the human body (just like Will Robinson on *Lost in Space* or *Sabrina the Teenage Witch*, depending what TV generation you belong to). This isn't just a museum for the five-and-up set; there are exhibits especially designed for babies and toddlers, too. The busy schedule also includes daily art classes and storytellers and a full slate of entertainment on weekends.

**New York City Fire Museum.** 278 Spring St. (btw. Varick and Hudson sts.). ☎ **212/691-1303.** www.nyfd.com/museum.html. Admission $4 adults, $2 seniors and students, $1 children under 12. Tues–Sun 10am–4pm. Subway: C, E to Spring St.; 1, 9 to Houston St.

What's better than fire trucks when you're a little kid? Not much. Housed in a real three-story 1904 firehouse, this museum displays include vintage fire trucks and equipment all the way back to the horse-drawn days (including the last-known example of a 1921 pumper). Look for the leather hoses, fire boats, poles, bells, Currier & Ives prints, and even a stuffed firehouse dog. Tours with an emphasis on fire safety are available for small groups by calling ahead.

✪ **New York Hall of Science.** 4701 111th St., in Flushing Meadows–Corona Park, Queens. ☎ **718/699-0005.** www.nyhallsci.org. Admission $7.50 adults, $5 children and seniors; free Thurs–Fri 2–5pm. Mon–Wed 9:30am–2pm (Tues–Wed to 5pm in summer), Thurs–Sun 9:30am–5pm. Subway: 7 to 111th St.

Children of all ages will love this huge, hands-on museum, which bills itself as New York's only Science Playground. This place is amazing for school-age kids; it's just like Beakman's World come to life. Exhibits let them be engulfed by a giant soap bubble, float on air in an antigravity mirror, compose music by dancing in front of light beams, and explore the more-than-miniature world of microbes. There are even video machines that kids can use to retrieve astronomical images, including pictures taken by the *Galileo* in orbit around Jupiter. There's a Preschool Discovery Place for the really little ones. But probably best of all is the summertime Outdoor Science Playground for kids six and older—ostensibly lessons in physics, but really just a great excuse to laugh, jump, and play on jungle gyms, slides, seesaws, spinners, and more.

The museum is located in **Flushing Meadows–Corona Park,** where kids can enjoy even more fun beyond the Hall of Science. Not only are there more than 1,200 acres of park and playgrounds, but there's also a zoo, a carousel, an indoor ice-skating rink, an outdoor pool, and bike and boat rentals. Kids and grown-ups alike will love getting an up-close look at the Unisphere steel globe, which was not really destroyed in *Men in Black.* The park is also home to the **Queens Museum of Art** (see "Highlights of the Outer Boroughs," below) as well as Shea Stadium and the U.S. Open Tennis Center.

**Sony Wonder Technology Lab.** Sony Plaza, 550 Madison Ave. (at 56th St.). ☎ **212/ 833-8100.** www.sonywondertechlab.com. Free admission. Tues–Sat 10am–6pm (Thurs to 8pm), Sun noon–6pm (last entrance 30 minutes before closing). Subway: 4, 5, 6 to 59th St.; E, F, to Fifth Ave.

Not as much of an infomercial as you'd expect. Both kids and adults love this four-level high-tech science and technology center, which explores communications and information technology. You can experiment with robotics, explore the human body through medical imaging, edit a music video, mix a hit song, design a video game, and save the day at an environmental command center. The lab also features the first high-definition interactive theater in the United States.

## THEATER FOR KIDS

The theater scene for kids is flourishing. There's so much going on that it's best to check *New York* magazine, *Time Out New York,* or the Friday *New York Times* for current listings. Besides larger-than-life Broadway shows, the following are some dependable entertainment options.

The ✪ **New Victory Theater,** 209 W. 42nd St. (☎ 212/382-4020; www.newvictory. org), reopened a few years back as the city's first full-time family-oriented performing-arts center and has hosted companies ranging from the Trinity Irish Dance Company to the astounding Flaming Idiots, who juggle everything from fire and swords to bean-bag chairs.

The **Paper Bag Players,** called "the best children's theater in the country" by *Newsweek,* perform funny tales for children 4 to 9 in a set made from bags and boxes, in winter only, at Hunter College's Sylvia and Danny Kaye Playhouse, 68th Street between Park and Lexington avenues (☎ 212/772-4448). If you can't make it to the Kaye, call the players at ☎ 212/362-0431 to inquire whether they'll be staging other performances about town.

**TADA!,** 120 W. 28th St. (☎ 212/627-1732; www.tadatheater.com), is a terrific youth ensemble that performs musicals and plays with a multi-ethnic perspective for kids and their families.

The **Swedish Cottage Marionette Theatre** (☎ 212/988-9093; www.centralpark. org) puts on marionette shows for kids at its 19th-century Central Park Theater throughout the year.

## OTHER KID-FRIENDLY DIVERSIONS

In addition to the choices below, don't forget New York's fabulous theme restaurants, which are playgrounds unto themselves for visiting kids. New on the scene is the impressive new **ESPN Zone** and Mom's worst nightmare, **WWF New York.** See "Theme Restaurant Thrills!" in chapter 6.

**ZOOS & AQUARIUMS**    Bigger kids will love the legendary **Bronx Zoo** (p. 257), while the **Central Park Wildlife Center** with its Tisch Children's Zoo (p. 246) is particularly suitable to younger kids. At the **New York Aquarium** at Coney Island (p. 260), kids can touch starfish and sea urchins and watch bottlenose dolphins and California sea lions stunt-swim in the outdoor aquatheater. The **Prospect Park Wildlife Conservation Center** (p. 260) is a thoroughly modern children's zoo tucked away in Brooklyn's gem of an urban park.

**SKY-HIGH VIEWS**    Kids of all ages can't help but turn dizzy with delight at the incredible views from atop the **Empire State Building** (p. 232) and the **World Trade Center** (p. 210).

**ARCADES    Lazer Park,** in Times Square at 1560 Broadway, at 46th Street (☎ **212/398-3060;** www.lazerpark.com), has amusements ranging from good old-fashioned pinball to virtual-reality games and a full-on laser tag arena. There's also the brand-new, multi-level **Broadway City,** a Big Apple–themed "interactive amusement center" (read: video arcade), at 241 W. 42nd St., between Broadway and Eighth Avenue (☎ **212/997-9797;** www.broadwaycity.com).

# 11  Attractions in Upper Manhattan

## HARLEM

Over the past several years, the press has heralded Harlem's Second Renaissance, this one with more of an economic emphasis. With all kinds of development projects underway, Central Harlem—from about 110th Street to 155th Street, between St. Nicholas and Fifth avenues—is dispelling its reputation as a symbol of declining urban America. What's more, the revitalized area has become a kind of "sleeper" hit among outsiders—rediscovered first by visitors (especially Europeans and Japanese) and now by New Yorkers who head up on weekends to its music clubs (see chapter 9), something few would've even thought of just a few years ago. Still, because distances between Harlem's attractions are long and there are some unsafe areas between them, it can be a good idea to join a group tour, especially if it's your first time in New York. See "Organized Sightseeing Tours" earlier in this chapter for recommendations.

Harlem has always had more than its share of historic treasures. To find those that still grace Harlem, pay a call on the **Astor Row Houses,** 130th Street between Fifth and Lenox avenues, a fabulous series of 28 redbrick town houses built in the 1880s and graced with wooden porches, generous yards, and ornamental ironwork. Equally impressive is **Strivers' Row,** West 138th and 139th streets, between Adam Clayton Powell Jr. and Frederick Douglass boulevards, a group of 130 houses built in 1891 by developer David H. King, Jr., who'd already developed the base of the Statue of Liberty and the original Madison Square Garden. On the north side of 139th Street are neo-Italian Renaissance residences by McKim, Mead & White, and across the street are Georgian-inspired homes. Once the original white owners had moved out, these lovely houses attracted the cream of the Harlem population, the "strivers" (hence the name) like Eubie Blake and W. C. Handy.

Handsome brownstones, limestone town houses, and row houses are sprinkled atop **Sugar Hill,** 145th to 155th streets, between St. Nicholas and Edgecombe avenues, named for the "sweet life" enjoyed by its residents. In the early 20th century, such prominent African Americans as W.E.B. DuBois, Thurgood Marshall, and Roy Wilkins lived in the now-landmarked building at 409 Edgecombe Ave.

Besides its bounty of architectural wealth, Harlem has several important cultural institutions. The **Schomburg Center for Research in Black Culture,** 515 Malcolm X Blvd., between 135th and 136th streets (☎ 212/491-2200; www.nypl.org), a research branch of the New York Public Library, hosts changing exhibits related to black culture; see p. 230.

The **Studio Museum,** 144 W. 125th St. (☎ 212/864-4500; www.studiomuseum. org), is devoted to the historical and contemporary works of black artists; see p. 230.

The legendary **Apollo Theatre,** 253 W. 125th St. (☎ 212/749-5838), launched or abetted the careers of countless musical icons—including Bessie Smith, Billie Holiday, Dinah Washington, Duke Ellington, Ella Fitzgerald, Sarah Vaughan, Count Basie, and Aretha Franklin—and is in large part responsible for the development and worldwide popularization of African-American music. Since the 1980s, after years of deterioration, it has been revived, especially its famous Wednesday "Amateur Night at the Apollo" show. See "Major Concert Halls & Landmark Venues" in chapter 9.

In a mixed blessing for the congregations, **Sunday-morning gospel services** at Harlem's many churches have become so popular that bus tour groups sometimes outnumber parishioners. At **Abyssinian Baptist Church,** 132 W. 138th St., between Adam Clayton Powell Jr. and Malcolm X boulevards (☎ 212/862-7474), services are at 9 and 11am. Remember that these are religious services first, not gospel shows.

Another essential aspect of Harlem is its food, and it doesn't get any better than what drifts out of the soulful kitchens of **Sylvia's Restaurant** (see chapter 6). If the tourist crowds turn you off, head instead to the **Sugar Shack Cafe,** 2611 Frederick Douglass Blvd. (Eighth Ave.), at 139th Street (☎ 212/491-4422).

## IN WASHINGTON HEIGHTS & INWOOD

North of Harlem are these quiet multi-ethnic residential districts whose main attraction is the **Cloisters** (see "More Manhattan Museums" earlier in this chapter), the Metropolitan Museum of Art's uptown "castle," beautifully nestled in a bucolic setting with marvelous views and housing a magnificent medieval art collection.

Historic home–lovers might want to seek out the **Jumel Terrace Historic District,** west of St. Nicholas Avenue between 160th and 162nd streets, which is centered on the **Morris-Jumel Mansion,** and the Dutch Colonial **Dyckman Farmhouse Museum;** see the "In Search of Historic Homes" box earlier in this chapter.

## 12 Highlights of the Outer Boroughs

### IN THE BRONX

In addition to the choices below, literary buffs might also want to consider the **Edgar Allan Poe Cottage,** the final home for the brilliant but troubled author of *The Raven, The Tell-Tale Heart,* and other masterworks. See the box called "In Search of Historic Homes" earlier in this chapter.

○ **Bronx Zoo Wildlife Conservation Park.** Fordham Rd. and Bronx River Pkwy., the Bronx. ☎ 718/367-1010. www.wcs.org. Admission $7.75 adults, $4 seniors and children 2–12; discounted admission Nov–Mar; free Wed year-round. There may be nominal additional charges for some exhibits. Nov–Mar, daily 10am–4:30pm (extended hours for Holiday Lights late Nov–Jan 2); Apr–Oct, Mon–Fri 10am–5pm, Sat–Sun 10am–5:30pm. Subway: 2 to Pelham Pkwy.; then walk 2 blocks west.

Founded in 1899, the Bronx Zoo is the largest metropolitan animal park in the United States, with more than 4,000 animals living on 265 acres. Most of the old-fashioned cages have been replaced by more natural settings; this is quite a progressive zoo as zoos go.

One of the most impressive exhibits is the **Wild Asia Complex.** This zoo-within-a-zoo comprises the **Wild Asia Plaza** education center; **Jungle World,** an indoor re-creation of Asian forests with birds, lizards, gibbons, and leopards; and the **Bengali Express Monorail** (open May to October), which takes you on a narrated ride high above free-roaming Siberian tigers, Asian elephants, Indian rhinoceroses, and other non-native New Yorkers (keep your eyes peeled—the animals aren't as interested in seeing you). The **Himalayan Highlands** is home to some 17 extremely rare snow leopards, as well as red pandas and white-naped cranes. The new **Congo Gorilla Forest** is a 6¹/₂-acre exhibit that's home to Western lowland gorillas, okapi, red river hogs, and other African rainforest animals.

The **Children's Zoo** (open April to October) allows young humans to learn about their wildlife counterparts. Kids can compare their leaps to those of a bullfrog, slide into a turtle shell, climb into a heron's nest, see with the eyes of an owl, and hear with the acute ears of a fox. There's also a petting zoo.

If the natural settings and breeding programs aren't enough to keep zoo residents entertained, they can always choose to ogle the 2 million annual visitors. But there are ways to beat the crowds. Try to visit on a weekday or on a nice winter's day. In summer, come early in the day, before the heat of the day sends the animals back into their enclosures. You can schedule a free guide-led walking tour by calling ☎ 718/220-5141.

**New York Botanical Garden.** 200th St. and Southern Blvd., the Bronx. ☎ 718/817-8700. www.nybg.org. Admission $3 adults, $2 seniors and students, $1 children 2–12. Extra charges for Everett Children's Adventure Garden, Enid A. Haupt Conservatory, T. H. Everett Rock Garden, Native Plant Garden, and narrated tram tour; entire Garden Passport package is $9.50 adults, $7 seniors and students, $3.50 children 2–12. Apr–Oct, Tues–Sun and Mon holidays 10am–6pm; Nov–Mar, Tues–Sun and Mon holidays 10am–4pm. Subway: D, 4 to Bedford Park, then Bus Bx26 (use the MetroCard for a free transfer) or walk east 8 long blocks.

A National Historic Landmark, the 250-acre New York Botanical Garden was founded in 1891 and today is one of America's foremost public gardens. The setting is spectacular—a natural terrain of rock outcroppings, a river with cascading waterfall, hills, ponds, and wetlands.

Highlights of the Botanical Garden are the 27 **specialty gardens** (the Peggy Rockefeller formal rose garden, the Nancy Bryan Luce herb garden, and the restored rock garden are my favorites), an exceptional **orchid collection,** and 40 acres of **uncut forest** as close as New York gets to its virgin state before the arrival of Europeans. The **Enid A. Haupt Conservatory,** a stunning series of Victorian glass pavilions that recall London's former Crystal Palace, shelters a rich collection of tropical, subtropical, and desert plants as well as seasonal flower shows. There's also a **Children's Adventure Garden**. Natural exhibits are augmented by year-round educational programs, musical events, bird watching excursions, lectures, special family programs, and many more activities. Snuff Mill, once used to grind tobacco, has a charming cafe on the banks of the Bronx River.

There are so many ways to see the garden—tram, golf cart, walking tours—that it's best to call or check the Web site for more information.

## IN BROOKLYN

For details on walking the **Brooklyn Bridge,** see "Historic Lower Manhattan's Top Attractions" earlier in this chapter.

It's easy to link visits to the Brooklyn Botanic Garden, the Brooklyn Museum of Art, and Prospect Park, because they are all an easy walk from one another, just off **Grand Army Plaza.** Designed by Frederick Law Olmsted and Calvert Vaux as a suitably grand entrance to their Prospect Park, it boasts a grand Civil War memorial arch designed by John H. Duncan (1892–1901) and the main **Brooklyn Public Library,** an art-deco masterpiece completed in 1941 (the garden and museum are just on the other side of the library, down Eastern Parkway).

✪ **Brooklyn Botanic Garden.** 900 Washington Ave. (at Eastern Pkwy.), Brooklyn. ☎ **718/ 623-7200.** www.bbg.org. Admission $3 adults, $1.50 seniors and students, free for children under 16. Admission free to all Tues–Fri mid-Nov to mid-Mar and Sat 10am–noon year-round. Apr–Sept, Tues–Fri 8am–6pm, Sat–Sun 10am–6pm; Oct–Mar, Tues–Fri 8am–4:30pm, Sat–Sun 10am–4:30pm. Subway: 2, 3 to Eastern Pkwy./Brooklyn Museum; D, Q to Prospect Park.

Just down the street from the Brooklyn Museum of Art (below) is the most popular botanic garden in the city. This peaceful, 52-acre sanctuary is at its most spectacular in May, when thousands of deep-pink blossoms of cherry trees are abloom. Well worth seeing is the spectacular **Cranford Rose Garden,** one of the largest and finest in the country; the **Shakespeare Garden,** an English garden featuring plants mentioned in his writings; a **Children's Garden;** the **Osborne Garden,** a 3-acre formal garden; the **Fragrance Garden,** designed for the blind but appreciated by all noses; and the extraordinary **Japanese Hill-and-Pond Garden.** The renowned **C.V. Starr Bonsai Museum** is home to the world's oldest and largest collection of bonsai.

✪ **Brooklyn Museum of Art.** 200 Eastern Pkwy. (at Washington Ave.), Brooklyn. ☎ **718/ 638-5000.** www.brooklynart.org. Suggested admission $4 adults, $1.50 seniors, $2 students, children under 12 free; free to all first Sat of month 5–11pm. Wed–Fri 10am–5pm; first Sat of the month 11am–11pm, each Sat thereafter 11am–6pm; Sun 11am–6pm. Subway: 2, 3 to Eastern Pkwy./Brooklyn Museum.

One of the nation's premier art institutions, the Brooklyn Museum of Art rocketed back into the public consciousness in 1999 with the hugely controversial "Sensation: Young British Artists from the Saatchi Collection," which drew international media attention and record crowds who came to see just what an artist—and a few conservative politicians—could make out of a little elephant dung. Indeed, the museum is best known for its consistently remarkable temporary exhibitions, which have included "The Jewels of the Romanovs" and "Impressionists in Winter" as well as its excellent permanent collection. The museum's grand beaux-arts building, designed by McKim, Mead & White (1897), befits its outstanding holdings, most notably the Egyptian collection of sculpture, wall reliefs, and mummies. The distinguished decorative arts collection includes 28 American period rooms from 1675 to 1928. Other highlights are the African and Asian galleries, 58 works by Rodin, and a diverse collection of both American and European painting and sculpture that includes works by Homer, O'Keeffe, Monet, Cézanne, and Degas.

**First Saturday** is the museum's ambitious—and popular—program that takes place on the first Saturday of each month. It runs from 5 to 11pm and includes free admission and a slate of live music, docent talks, films, dancing, and other entertainment that can get pretty esoteric (think lesbian poetry, silent film, experimental jazz, Japanese taiko drumming, and disco). Weekly **Insider's Hour Gallery Tours** are offered at 1pm on weekends as well as on select Thursdays and Fridays.

**New York Aquarium.** 832 Surf Ave. (at W. 8th St.), Coney Island, Brooklyn. ☎ **718/265-3400.** www.nyaquarium.com. Admission $8.75 adults, $4.50 seniors and children 2–12. Daily 10am–5pm. Subway: D, F to W. 8th St., Brooklyn.

Because of the long subway ride (about an hour from midtown Manhattan) and its proximity to the Coney Island boardwalk, this one is really for summer. The aquarium is home to hundreds of sea creatures. Taking center stage are Atlantic bottle-nose dolphins and California sea lions that perform daily during summer at the **Aquatheater.** Also basking in the spotlight are seven beluga whales, gangly Pacific octopuses, and Bertha the sand tiger shark. Black-footed penguins, California sea otters, and a variety of seals live at the **Sea Cliffs exhibit,** a re-creation of a Pacific coastal habitat. Children love the hands-on exhibits at **Discovery Cove.** There's an indoor oceanview cafeteria and an outdoor snack bar, plus picnic tables.

If you've made the trip out, you simply must check out the human exhibits on nearby **Coney Island**'s 2.7-mile-long boardwalk. Not much is left from its heyday, and it can be a little eerie when the crowds aren't around. But you can still use the beach, drop some cash at the boardwalk arcade, and ride the famed wooden Cyclone roller coaster (still a terrifying ride, if only because it seems so . . . rickety). You can't leave without treating yourself to a Nathan's Famous hot dog, just off the boardwalk at Surf and Stillwell avenues. This is the original—where the term "hot dog" was coined back in 1906.

**Prospect Park.** At Grand Army Plaza, bounded by Prospect Park West, Parkside Ave., and Flatbush Ave., Brooklyn. ☎ **718/965-8951,** or 718/965-8999 for events information. www.prospectpark.org. Subway: 2, 3 to Grand Army Plaza (walk down Plaza Street West 3 blocks to Prospect Park West and the entrance) or Eastern Pkwy./Brooklyn Museum.

Designed by Frederick Law Olmsted and Calvert Vaux after their great success with Central Park, this 562 acres of woodland, meadows, bluffs, and ponds is considered by many to be their masterpiece and the pièce de résistance of Brooklyn.

The best approach is from Grand Army Plaza, presided over by the monumental **Soldiers' and Sailors' Memorial Arch** (1892) honoring Union veterans. For the best view of the lush landscape, follow the path to Meadowport Arch and proceed through to the Long Meadow, following the path that loops around it (it's about an hour's walk). Other park highlights include the 1857 Italianate mansion **Litchfield Villa** on Prospect Park West; the **Friends' Cemetery** Quaker burial ground (where Montgomery Clift is eternally prone—sorry, it's fenced off to browsers); the **carousel** with white wooden horses salvaged from a famous Coney Island merry-go-round; and **Lefferts Homestead** (☎ 718/965-6505), a 1783 Dutch farmhouse with a museum of period furniture and exhibits geared toward children. There's a map at the park entrance that you can use to get your bearings.

On the east side of the park is the **Prospect Park Wildlife Conservation Center** (☎ 718/399-7339). This is thoroughly modern children's zoo where kids can walk among wallabies, explore a prairie-dog town, and much more. Admission is $2.50 for adults, $1.25 for seniors, 50¢ for children 3 to 12. April through October, open Monday through Friday 10am to 5pm, to 5:30pm weekends and holidays; November through March, open daily from 10am to 4:30pm.

## IN QUEENS

For details on the **New York Hall of Science** and **Flushing Meadows–Corona Park** (also home to the Queens Museum of Art, below), see "Especially for Kids," earlier in this chapter.

**✪ American Museum of the Moving Image.** 35th Ave. at 36th St., Astoria, Queens. ☎ 718/784-0077 or 718/784-4777. www.ammi.org. Admission $8.50 adults, $5.50 seniors and college students, $4.50 children 5–18. Tues–Fri noon–5pm, Sat–Sun 11am–6pm. Subway: R to Steinway St.

If you truly love movies, this is the place to come. Unlike Manhattan's Museum of Television and Radio (see "More Manhattan Museums" earlier in this chapter), which is more of a library, this is a thought-provoking museum examining how moving images—film, video, and digital—are made, marketed, and shown; it encourages you to consider their impact on society as well. It's housed in part of the Kaufman Astoria Studios, which have hosted W. C. Fields, the Marx Brothers, Martin Scorsese (*The Age of Innocence*), Woody Allen (*Radio Days*), Bill Cosby (his *Cosby* TV series), and *Sesame Street*. (For details on getting tickets to a *Cosby* taping, see "Talk of the Town: TV Tapings" earlier in this chapter.)

The museum's core exhibit, **"Behind the Screen,"** is a thoroughly engaging two-floor installation that takes you step-by-step through the process of making, marketing, and exhibiting moving images. There are more than 1,000 artifacts on hand, from technological gadgetry to costumes, and interactive exhibits where you can try your own hand at sound-effects editing or create your own animated shorts, among other simulations. Special-effects benchmarks from the mechanical mouth of *Jaws* to the blending of past and present in *Forrest Gump* are explored and explained. And in a nod to Hollywood nostalgia, memorabilia that wasn't swept up by the Planet Hollywood chain is displayed, as are sets from *Seinfeld*.

The museum hosts free **film and video screenings,** often accompanied by artist appearances, lectures, panel discussions, or live music. The **Pinewood Dialogues** lecture series features renowned film and TV pros discussing their craft; past guests have included Spike Lee and Terry Gilliam, so it's definitely worth seeing if someone's on while you're in town.

**✪ Isamu Noguchi Garden Museum.** 32–37 Vernon Blvd. (at 33rd Rd.), Long Island City, Queens. ☎ 718/721-1932. www.noguchi.org. Suggested admission $4 adults, $2 seniors and students. Apr–Oct Wed–Fri 10am–5pm, Sat–Sun 11am–6pm. Subway: N to Broadway. Walk west on Broadway toward Manhattan until Broadway ends at Vernon Blvd.; turn left on Vernon and go 2 blocks; the museum is on the left. Shuttle: Sat–Sun, from outside the MoMA bookstore on W. 53rd St. (between Fifth and Sixth aves.) to museum hourly 11:30am–4:30pm (return trips noon–5pm); $5 round-trip.

No place in the city is more Zen than this marvelous indoor/outdoor museum showcasing the work of Japanese-American sculptor Isamu Noguchi (1094–88). The beautifully installed multi-gallery exhibit includes more than 250 works in stone, metal, wood, and clay; you'll even see Noguchi-designed theater sets, furniture, and models for public gardens and playgrounds.

A free guided tour is offered at 2pm, and short films about the artist and his work show continuously throughout the day in an intimate theater. A museum shop sells Noguchi's Akari lamps as well as books, cards, posters, and the like.

**P.S. 1 Contemporary Art Center.** 22–25 Jackson Ave. (at 46th Ave.), Long Island City, Queens. ☎ 718/784-2084. www.queensmuse.org. Suggested admission $4 adults, $2 seniors and students. Wed–Sun noon–6pm. (Hours vary in summer, so call ahead.) Subway: E, F to 23rd St./Ely Ave. (walk 2 blocks south); 7 to 45th Rd./Court House Sq. (walk 1 block south).

If you're interested in contemporary art that's too cutting edge for most museums, don't miss P.S. 1. Reinaugurated in 1997 after a 3-year, $8.5-million renovation of the

Renaissance Revival building that was originally a public school, this is the world's largest institution exhibiting contemporary art from America and abroad. You can expect to see a kaleidoscopic array of works from artists ranging from Jack Smith to Julian Schnabel; the museum is particularly well known for large-scale exhibitions by artists such as James Turrell.

**Queens Museum of Art.** Next to the Unisphere in Flushing Meadows–Corona Park, Queens. ☎ 718/592-9700. www.ps1.org. Suggested admission $4 adults, $2 seniors and children, free for children under 5. Wed–Fri 10am–5pm, Sat–Sun noon–5pm. Subway: 7 to Willets Point/Shea Stadium.

One way to see New York in the shortest time (albeit without the street life) is to visit the Panorama, an enormous building-for-building architectural model of New York City complete with an airplane that takes off from LaGuardia Airport. The 9,335-square-foot Gotham City is the largest model of its kind in the world, with 895,000 individual structures built on a scale of 1 inch = 100 feet. Also on permanent display is a collection of Tiffany glass manufactured in Queens between 1893 and 1938.

## 13 Spectator Sports

For details on the **New York City Marathon** and the **U.S. Open Tennis Championships,** see the "Calendar of Events," in chapter 2.

**BASEBALL**    With two baseball teams in town, you can catch a game almost any day from opening day in April to the beginning of playoffs in October. (Don't bother trying to get subway series tix, though; they're the hottest seats in town. Ditto for Opening Day or any playoff game.) Know that rooters for the **New York Mets** or the **New York Yankees** are fanatical and can't seem to understand why they don't win every year (perhaps a by-product of the Yankees' winning ways, which produced a 25th World Championship in 1999).

Star catcher Mike Piazza and the Amazin' Mets play at **Shea Stadium** in Queens (Subway: 7 to Willets Point/Shea Stadium). For tickets and information, call the **Mets Ticket Office** at ☎ 718/507-TIXX, or visit **www.mets.com**.

The Yankees play at the House That Ruth Built, otherwise known as Yankee Stadium (Subway: 4, C, D to 161st St./Yankee Stadium). For tickets, call **TicketMaster** (☎ 212/307-1212 or 212/307-7171; www.ticketmaster.com) or **Yankee Stadium** (☎ 718/293-6000; www.yankees.com). After the game, check into one of the rowdy sports bars across the street to down a brew and relive the action with fellow fans. Serious baseball fans might check the schedule and try to catch **Old Timers' Day,** usually held in July, when pinstriped stars of years past return to the stadium to take a bow. This is your chance to cheer for legends such as Whitey Ford and Reggie Jackson in person.

You can decide to catch a game a couple of hours before game time, hop on the subway, and buy your tickets at the stadium. At Yankee Stadium, upper tier box seats, especially those behind home plate, give you a great view of all the action. Upper tier reserve seats are directly behind the box seats and are significantly cheaper. Bleacher seats are even cheaper, and the rowdy commentary from that section's roughneck bleacher creatures is absolutely free. Most of the expensive seats (field boxes) are sold out in advance to season ticket holders. You can often purchase these very same seats from scalpers, but you'll pay a premium for them. Tickets can also be purchased at the teams' **clubhouse shops** in Manhattan; see p. 291 in chapter 8. If you're interested in taking a guided tour of the House that Ruth Built, call ☎ 718/579-4531 for details.

**BASKETBALL**    Two pro teams call **Madison Square Garden,** Seventh Avenue between 31st and 33rd streets (☎ 212/465-6741 or www.thegarden.com;

212/307-7171 or www.ticketmaster.com for tickets; Subway: 1, 2, 3, 9, A, C, E to 34th St.), home court: Patrick Ewing, Latrell Sprewell, Marcus Camby, and the rest of the **New York Knicks** (☎ **212/465-JUMP;** www.nyknicks.com); and the **New York Liberty** (☎ **212/564-WNBA;** www.wnba.com/liberty), who electrify fans with their tough-playing defense and star players such as Rebecca Lobo and Teresa Weatherspoon. Knicks tickets are hardest to come by, so plan ahead if you want a front-row seat near first fan Spike Lee.

**ICE HOCKEY**    The **New York Rangers** play at Madison Square Garden, Seventh Avenue between 31st and 33rd streets (☎ **212/465-6741** or 212/308-NYRS; www. newyorkrangers.com; Subway: 1, 2, 3, 9, A, C, E to 34th St.). The memories of the Mark Messier–led 1994 Stanley Cup team linger on, much to the chagrin of the present underachieving team, which suffered another serious blow when Wayne Gretzky retired in April 1999. Tickets are hard to get nevertheless, so plan well ahead. For tickets, call ☎ **212/307-7171,** or visit www.ticketmaster.com for online orders.

# 8

# Shopping for Big Apple Bargains

At first glance, the size and breadth of the city's shopping scene seems more overwhelming than anything else. The range of possibilities could test the limits of the most diehard shopaholic. Even as more and more big chains lay down roots in the city (what New Yorkers like to refer to as the "mallification" of Manhattan), the world's most unique crop of specialty shops continues to thrive right alongside them. And although you can easily go broke trying to keep up with what's new and haute, there's no need to. New York draws bargain-hunters from around the globe with its wealth of good values, wide range of merchandise, and unparalleled sales. As with anything, you just have to know where to look.

**OPEN HOURS** Keep in mind that open hours can vary significantly from store to store; even different branches of the Gap can keep different schedules depending on location and management. As a rule of thumb, stores open at 10 or 11am from Monday through Saturday, and 7pm is the most common closing hour (although sometimes it's 6pm). Both opening and closing hours tend to get later as you move downtown; stores in the East Village often don't open until 1 or 2pm, and stay open until 8pm or later.

All of the big department stores are open seven days a week. However, unlike department stores in suburban malls, most of these stores don't keep a regular 10am to 9pm schedule. The department stores, and shops along major strips like Fifth Avenue, usually stay open later one night a week (oftentimes Thursday), although not all shops comply. Sunday hours are usually noon to 5 or 6pm. Most shops are open seven days a week, but smaller boutiques might close one day a week, and some neighborhoods virtually shut down on a particular day—namely the Lower East Side on Saturday, the East Village on Monday, and most of the Financial District for the weekend. But during the holidays, anything goes: Macy's often stays open to midnight for the last couple of weeks before Christmas!

Your best bet is to **call ahead** if your heart's set on visiting a particular store.

**SALES TAX** City sales tax is 8.25%, but it was eliminated on clothing and footwear items under $110 as of March 1, 2000.

If you're visiting from out of state, consider having your purchases shipped directly home to avoid paying sales tax.

# 1 The Top Shopping Streets & Neighborhoods

Here's a rundown of New York's most interesting shopping areas, with some highlights of each to give you a feel for the neighborhood. **If addresses and phone numbers are *not* given here,** refer to the store's expanded listing by category under "Shopping A to Z" later in this chapter.

## DOWNTOWN

### LOWER MANHATTAN

The Financial District and environs are home to two kinds of shopping: discount shopping à la **Century 21** department store and **J&R** for electronics galore; and mall-style retail shopping.

National chains and standard mall stores are housed in **South Street Seaport** (☎ 212/732-7678; Subway: 2, 3, 4, 5 to Fulton St.) on Pier 17 and on Fulton Street, the Seaport's main cobbled drag, and on the ground level of the **World Trade Center** (☎ 212/435-2728; www.panynj.gov/wtc; Subway: 1, 9, N, R to Cortlandt St.; C, E to World Trade Center). The World Trade Center makes a good bet for standards like the **Gap,** the **Body Shop, Nine West,** the **Limited,** plus a terrific branch of **Borders Books & Music.**

### CHINATOWN

Don't expect to find the purchase of a lifetime on Chinatown's streets, but there's some fun browsing to be had. The fish markets along Canal, Mott, Mulberry, and Elizabeth streets are fun to browse for their bustle and exotica. Dispersed among them (especially along Canal), you'll find a mind-boggling collection of knock-offs: sunglasses, designer bags, and watches. **Mott Street,** between Pell Street and Chatham Square, boasts the most interesting of Chinatown's off-Canal shopping, with an antique shop or two dispersed among the tiny storefronts selling blue-and-white Chinese dinnerware. The definite highlight of Chinatown shopping is the three-story **Pearl River Mart** (see "The Department Stores," below).

### THE LOWER EAST SIDE

The bargains aren't quite what they used to be in the **Historic Orchard Street Shopping District**—which basically runs from Houston to Canal along Allen, Orchard, and Ludlow streets, spreading outward along both sides of Delancey Street—but prices on leather bags, shoes, luggage, fabrics on the bolt, and men's and women's clothes are still quite good. Be aware, though, that the hard sell on Orchard Street can be pretty hard to take. Still, the Orchard Street Bargain District is a nice place to discover a part of New York that's disappearing. Come during the week, because most stores are Jewish-owned and therefore close Friday afternoon and all day Saturday. Sundays tend to be a madhouse. Stop in first at the **Lower East Side Visitor Center,**

## Additional Sources for Serious Shoppers

If you're looking for a specific item or a special sale, your best bet is to peruse the online shopping listings; see the "**Planning Your Trip: An Online Directory**" (p. 46) for the best sites.

Hard information about current sales, new shops, and special art, craft, and antique shows is best found in the "Check Out" section of *Time Out New York* or the "Sales & Bargains," "Best Bets," and "Smart City" sections of *New York* magazine.

261 Broome St., between Orchard and Allen streets (☎ 212/226-9010) for a shopping guide.

The artists and other trendsetters who have been turning this neighborhood into a hopping club scene have also added a cutting edge to its shopping scene in recent years, too. You'll find a growing handful of alterna-shops in the area south of Houston between Allen and Clinton streets. In addition to **Foley & Corinna** (see "Clothing"), highlights include high-style **Cherry,** 185 Orchard St. (☎ 212/358-7131; www.erols.com/hotcherry), for modernist home accessories and retro-cool apparel; **TG-170,** 170 Ludlow St. (☎ 212/955-8660), for new designs in club-kid clothes; and **alife,** 178 Orchard St. (☎ 646/654-0628), for Gen-Y footwear and anime collectibles.

## SoHo

People love to complain about super-fashionable SoHo; it's become too trendy, too tony, too Mall of America. True, **J. Crew** is only one of many big names to have supplanted the galleries that used to inhabit the historic cast-iron buildings, but SoHo is still one of the best shopping neighborhoods in the city—and few are more fun to browse. You'll find few bargains here, as rents are too high for merchants to sell at anything but a premium. This is the epicenter of cutting-edge haute couture, with such designers as glammy Anna Sui, trend-busting British legend Vivienne Westwood, and golden boy Todd Oldham in residence. Most of these designer shops are likely to be *way* out of your price range (they're way outta mine, that's for sure), but the streets are chock-full of unique boutiques, some hawking more affordable wares, and the eye candy is tops. End-of-season sales, when racks are cleared for incoming merchandise, are the best bet if you actually want to buy.

SoHo's prime shopping grid is from Broadway east to Sullivan Street and from Houston down to Broome, although Grand Street, one block south of Broome, has been sprouting shops of late.

## NoLiTa

Less than a handful of years ago, Elizabeth Street was a nondescript adjunct to Little Italy and the no-man's land east of SoHo. Today it's the grooviest shopping strip in town, star of the neighborhood known as NoLiTa. Elizabeth and neighboring Mott and Mulberry streets are dotted with an increasing number of shops between Houston and Spring streets, with a few pushing one more block south to Kenmare. But don't expect cheap; NoLiTa is clearly the stepchild of SoHo. Its boutiques are largely the province of sophisticated shopkeepers specializing in high-quality, fashion-forward products and design. Still, this can be a good neighborhood to browse if you're looking for an exotic import or one-of-a-kind gift. It's an easy walk from the Broadway-Lafayette stop on the B, D, F, Q line to the neighborhood, because it starts just east of Lafayette Street.

Prince Street is probably the best stretch for affordable treasures. There's **Dö Kham** at no. 51 (☎ 212/966-2404), for Tibetan bags, rugs, hats, and other Himalayan imports; **Gates of Morocco,** at no. 8 (☎ 212/925-2650), for traditional Moroccan imports, and ✪ **kar'ikter,** at no. 19 (☎ 212/274-1966), which stocks New York's biggest collection of sleek and playful Alessi housewares from Italy as well as Tin-Tin animation cells and toys.

The boutique density is highest on Elizabeth. Some super-expensive vintage modern furniture dealers have taken roost here, but a few shops yield quirkier, more affordable gifts, particularly **Daily 235,** at no. 235 (☎ 212/334-9728), a quirky card and candy store for artsy grown-ups for creative under-$10 gifts.

# The Lowdown on Sidewalk Vendors

New York has a very active street culture. Along main thoroughfares throughout the city, you'll see street merchants selling everything from fresh fruit to knapsacks to art books to baseball cards. Many are legitimate, licensed vendors, but some aren't. Chances are, if there's a suitcase involved or a blanket that can be rolled up and carted away quickly, or the collection of stuff for sale is a little too eclectic (like it could be the contents of somebody's apartment or a traveler's bag, say), the vendor shouldn't be there.

The museum streets of **West 53rd and 54th** are peppered with vendors selling their own art. Book vendors line Broadway on the **Upper West Side,** especially on weekends. If you encounter a vendor selling just-published hardcover books on the street, chances are they've been stolen. And paperback books sold without covers are considered returned goods and aren't meant for resale. Hawkers with faux Chanel and Prada handbags and "designer" watches are most prolific in **Times Square** and in the **Flatiron District,** particularly along lower Fifth Avenue. The quality is questionable, so don't even think about shelling out more than $20 for a counterfeit watch. **SoHo** is popular with high-end street peddlers, mostly legitimate, hawking hand-crafted silver jewelry, coffee-table books, and their own art, mainly along Prince Street. **St. Marks Place** (8th Street) in the East Village is big on cheap sunglasses and goth jewelry.

At the city's immensely popular weekly **outdoor flea markets,** particularly those at 26th Street and Sixth Avenue, you'll find all kinds of stuff, from trashworthy junk to highly collectible antiques. (See the "Where the Fleas Are" box later in this chapter.) Most flea-market vendors are perfectly legitimate, but on occasion you'll run across one that's clearly hawking stolen goods.

When it comes to this type of alternative retail, the best rule of thumb is this: Use your best judgement, and let your conscience be your guide. But if you choose to buy what are clearly stolen goods, keep in mind that you're encouraging this kind of resale with your wallet—and the next set of stuff for sale on the street could be yours.

## THE EAST VILLAGE

The East Village remains the international standard of bohemian hip. It's one of the city's best neighborhoods for wallet-friendly shopping. The easiest subway access is the 6 train to Astor Place, which lets you out by **Kmart** and **Astor Wines & Spirits;** from here, it's just a couple blocks east to the prime hunting grounds.

✪ **East 9th Street** between Second Avenue and Avenue A has become one of my favorite shopping strips in the entire city. Lined with an increasingly smart collection of boutiques, it proves that the East Village isn't just for kids anymore. I'm happy to report that—so far, at least—prices have stayed within reach. Up-and-coming designers sell good-quality and affordably priced original fashions for women along here, including **Lisa Tsai,** 436 E. 9th St. (☎ 212/529-8231), a bright, cheery shop with wonderful retro-inspired designs and accessories; and **Mark Montano,** at no. 434 (☎ 212/505-0325), who harkens back to styles from Victoria to Jackie O. as inspiration for his line of wonderful wearables and handbags; plus the utterly fabulous **Jill Anderson** and a small branch of **Eileen Fisher** that's great for bargain hunters because it serves as the burgeoning chain's outlet store.

Vintage stays affordable on East 9th, too, and runs the gamut from pristine wearables at **Argosy** to kitschy collectibles at the charming **Cha Cha Tchatchka,** 437 E. 9th St. (☎ 212/674-9242) and **Atomic Passion,** at no. 430 (☎ 212/533-0718).

For stylish gifts and little luxuries, there's **Paper Rock Scissors,** 436 E. 9th St. (☎ 212/358-1555), for handmade treasures; **Ichak,** at no. 430 (☎ 212/673-0673), for funky, affordable handbags constructed from clear plastic, steel rivets, and images that range from Tide detergent labels to vintage pulp fiction covers; **Mascot Studio,** whose remarkable one-of-a-kind picture frames are sold at no. 328 (☎ 212/228-9090); and ✪ **H,** at no. 335 (☎ 212/477-2631), with wonderful Japanese-inspired and other collectibles, from slinky vases to rice-paper coasters.

If you're really enjoying this 'hood, check out the offerings on surrounding blocks, too, which aren't quite as mature yet, but it won't take long. Among the hidden treasures are **Kimono House,** 93 E. 7th St. (☎ 212/505-0232), for low prices on vintage kimono and yukata (cotton kimono, which make great bathrobes). The fabrics alone are worth the price.

If it's strange, illegal, or funky, it's probably available on **St. Marks Place,** which is 8th Street, running east from Third Avenue to Avenue A. This skanky strip is a permanent street market, with countless T-shirt and jewelry stands. The height of the action is between Second and Third avenues, which is prime hunting grounds for used-record collectors.

## LAFAYETTE STREET FROM SoHo TO NoHo

Lafayette Street has a retail character all its own, distinct from the rest of SoHo. It has grown into a full-fledged Antique Row, especially strong in mid-century modern furniture. The quality is high, but prices are even higher. Lafayette is great for browsing if you have a strong interest in design trends—the stretch to stroll is between Astor Place to the north and Spring Street to the south—but bargain hunters are better off elsewhere.

Dispersed among the furniture and design stores are a number of cutting-edge clothiers; this is where skateboard fashion moved from the street to the catwalks. Among the fashion outlets worth noting are **Bond 07,** just off Lafayette at 7 Bond St. (☎ 212/677-8487), and **Spooly D's,** 51 Bleecker St., at Lafayette (☎ 212/598-4415), both featuring artfully displayed collections of classic vintage fashions and accessories (Bond 07 often features homewares, too); and **Screaming Mimi's,** the city's most famous vintage clothing outlet. South of Houston is **X-Large,** 267 Lafayette St. (☎ 212/334-4480; www.xlarge.com), for upscale hip-hop wear (the Beasties' Mike D is a co-owner). And don't forget the wonderful **Pop Shop,** which sells cool casual wear emblazoned with Keith Haring's distinctive modern art (see "Logo Stores").

## GREENWICH VILLAGE

The West Village is great for browsing and gift shopping. Specialty book- and record stores, antiques and craft shops, and gourmet food markets dominate. The best **Tower Records** in the country is at West 4th Street and Broadway. Except for NYU territory— 8th Street between Broadway and Sixth Avenue for trendy footwear and affordable fashions and Broadway from 8th Street south to Houston, anchored by **Urban Outfitters** and dotted with skate and sneaker shops—the Village isn't much of a destination for fashion hunters.

The prime drag for strolling is bustling **Bleecker Street,** where you'll find lots of leather shops and record stores interspersed with a good number of interesting and artsy boutiques. Just a few of the highlights include **Barr-Magill,** at no. 333 (☎ 212/

741-0656), whose black-and-white photography—much of it featuring the city as subject—makes a great souvenir; **Condomania,** at no. 351 (☎ 212/691-9442), everybody's favorite creative condom store; and **Sleek on Bleecker,** at no. 361 (☎ 212/243-0284), featuring affordable fashions for working women with style.

Narrow Christopher Street is another fun street to browse, because it's loaded with genuine Village character. Those who really love to browse should also wander west of Seventh Avenue, where charming boutiques are tucked among the brownstones. Highlights include **House of Cards and Curiosities,** 23 Eighth Ave. (☎ 212/ 675-6178), the Village's own funky take on an old-fashioned nickel-and-dime, and any number of boutiques along Hudson Street.

## MIDTOWN
### THE FLATIRON DISTRICT & UNION SQUARE
The epitome of Uptown fashion more than a hundred years ago, the area has grown into the city's discount shopping center. Superstores and off-pricers now fill the renovated cast-iron buildings: **Filene's Basement, TJ Maxx,** and **Bed Bath & Beyond,** are all at 620 Sixth Ave., and witty **Old Navy** is next door; **Barnes & Noble** is just a couple of blocks away at Sixth Avenue near 22nd Street.

On Broadway just a few blocks north of Union Square is **ABC Carpet & Home,** a magnet for aspiring Martha Stewarts.

Upscale mall retailers such as **Victoria's Secret** have rediscovered the architectural majesty of **lower Fifth Avenue.** You won't find much that's new along here, but it's a pleasing stretch nonetheless.

### HERALD SQUARE & THE GARMENT DISTRICT
Herald Square—where 34th Street, Sixth Avenue, and Broadway converge—is dominated by **Macy's,** the self-proclaimed world's biggest department store, and other famous-name shopping, such as **Toys "R" Us** at 34th Street and Broadway. At Sixth Avenue and 33rd Street is the **Manhattan Mall** (☎ 212/465-0500), anchored by unremarkable Stern's department store and home to mall standards such as Foot Locker and Radio Shack.

A long block over on Seventh Avenue, not much goes on in the grimy Garment District. This is, however, where you'll find that quintessential New York experience, the sample sale; see "Scouring the Sample Sales," later in this chapter.

### TIMES SQUARE & THE THEATER DISTRICT
This neighborhood has become increasingly family-oriented: hence, **Warner Bros.** at the crossroads of Times Square; Richard Branson's rollicking **Virgin Megastore; The Gap** at 42nd and Broadway; and the mammoth new **E-Walk** retail and entertainment complex on 42nd Street between Seventh and Eighth avenues, which should be overflowing with mall-style retail shops by the time you read this.

West 47th Street between Fifth and Sixth avenues is the city's famous **Diamond District.** Apparently, more than 90% of the diamonds sold in the United States come through this neighborhood first, so there are some great deals to be had if you're in the market for a nice rock or another piece of fine jewelry. Be ready to wheel and deal with the largely Hasidic dealers, who offer quite a juxtaposition to the crowds that people the rest of the area. For an introduction to the district, including smart buying tips, go online to **www.47th-street.com.** For semiprecious stones, head to the **New York Jewelry Mart,** 26 W. 46th St. (☎ 212/575-9701). Virtually all of these dealers are open Monday through Friday only.

**Shopper's Alert:** You'll notice a wealth of electronics stores throughout the neighborhood, many suspiciously trumpeting GOING OUT OF BUSINESS sales. These guys have been going out of business since the Stone Age. That's the bait and switch; pretty soon you've spent too much money for not enough stereo. If you want to check out what they have to offer, go in knowing what going prices are on that PDA or digital camera you're interested in. You can make a good deal if you know exactly what the market is, but these guys will be happy to suck you dry given half a chance.

## FIFTH AVENUE & 57TH STREET

The heart of Manhattan retail is the corner of Fifth and 57th. Home to high-ticket names such as Gucci, Chanel, Cartier, and Van Cleef & Arpels, this tony shopping neighborhood has long been the province of the über-rich. In recent years, however, both Fifth Avenue and 57th Street have become more accessible as wallet-friendlier retailers such as the **Warner Bros. Studio Store, Niketown,** and the **NBA Store** have joined the fold. You'll also find kid wonderland **FAO Schwartz** as well as a number of national names such as **Banana Republic,** which have further democratized Fifth by setting up their flagships along the avenue.

Despite its more egalitarian profile, don't expect to find any bargains along these main drags. High traffic flow and real-estate costs keep prices up, and the flagships tend to send their sale merchandise to lower-profile shops around town. Still, the window shopping is classic. And if you, like Holly Golightly, always dreamed of shopping at **Tiffany & Co.,** 727 Fifth Ave., at 57th Street (☎ 212/755-8000; www.tiffany. com), the world's most famous jewelry store is well worth a stop. The multilevel showroom is so full of tourists at all times that it's easy to browse without having any intention of buying. If you do want to indulge, your best bet is to head upstairs to the gift level, where you'll find a number of gifts to suit a $50 or $75 budget.

## UPTOWN
### MADISON AVENUE

Welcome to Rich Man's Land. Madison Avenue from 57th to 79th streets has usurped Fifth Avenue as the toniest shopping stretch in the city. In fact, in 1998, it vaunted ahead of Hong Kong's Causeway Bay to become the most expensive retail real estate in the world. It's home to the world's most luxurious designer boutiques: Calvin, Prada, Versace, Valentino . . . the list goes on. Even the sales are ridiculous. ("This $1,200 sweater is on sale for just $575? I'll take it!" Yeah, right.)

For those of us with limited budgets, stores such as **Crate & Barrel,** at 59th Street (☎ 212/308-0011), and the fabulous **Ann Taylor** flagship, 645 Madison Ave., at 60th Street (☎ 212/832-2010), make untouchable Madison Avenue seem a little more approachable. Shoe freaks will want to check out wallet-friendly **Unisa,** 701 Madison Ave. (☎ 212/753-7474).

## THE UPPER WEST SIDE

The Upper West Side's best shopping street is **Columbus Avenue.** Small shops catering to the neighborhood's white-collar mix of young hipsters and families line both sides of the pleasant avenue from 66th Street (where you'll find an excellent branch of **Barnes & Noble**) to about 86th Street. For comfort over style (these city streets can be murder on the feet!), try **Aerosoles,** 310 Columbus Ave. (☎ 212/579-8659), or **Sacco** for women's shoes that offer a bit of both. Other highlights include **Elma Blint et al** at no. 453 (☎ 212/501-9577), for terrific contemporary jewelry designs that are worth browsing even if you can't buy; and **Maxilla & Mandible** for groovy natural science–based gifts (see "Museum Stores").

Boutiques also dot Amsterdam Avenue and Broadway, which is more notable for its terrific gourmet edibles at **Zabar's** and **Fairway** markets, both legends in their own right (see "Edibles").

## 2  The Department Stores

The stores I've outlined below are, to varying degrees, in keeping with the good-value mindset. There's also **Bergdorf Goodman,** 754 Fifth Ave., at 57th Street (☎ 212/753-7300), **Henri Bendel,** 712 Fifth Ave., at 56th Street (☎ 212/247-1100), and **Barney's New York,** 660 Madison Ave., at 61st Street (☎ 212/826-8900), all temples of haute couture—Bergdorf's largely in the classic style and both Barney's and Bendel's more on the cutting edge. Nothing comes cheap at these stores, and bargains are few and far between. Real fashion hounds might want to browse, but I feel like everything on the racks is just taunting me.

✪ **Bloomingdale's.** 1000 Third Ave. (Lexington Ave. at 59th St.). ☎ 212/705-2000. Subway: 4, 5, 6 to 59th St.

This is my favorite of the big department stores. It's more accessible than Barneys or Bergdorf's and more affordable than Saks but still has the New York pizzazz that Macy's and Lord & Taylor now largely lack. Taking up the space of a city block, Bloomie's has just about anything you could want, from clothing (both designer and everyday basics) and fragrances to a full range of housewares. Service is a step above lackluster Macy's. The frequent sales can yield unbeatable bargains; look for full-page advertisements in front section of the daily *New York Times.*

The main entrance is on Third Avenue, but pop up to street level from the 59th Street station and you'll be right at the Lexington Avenue entrance.

✪ **Century 21.** 22 Cortlandt St. (btw. Broadway and Church St.). ☎ 212/227-9092. Subway: 1, 9, N, R to Cortlandt St.; 4, 5 to Fulton St.; C, E to World Trade Center.

Just across from the World Trade Center, Century 21 long ago achieved legend status as *the* designer discount store. If you don't mind wrestling with the aggressive, ever-present throngs, this is where you'll find those $20 Todd Oldham pants or the $50 Bally loafers you've been dreaming of—not to mention underwear, hosiery, and ties so cheap that they're almost free. Don't see how $250 for an Armani blazer is a bargain? Look again at the tag; the retail on it is upwards of $800. The shoe department is an outlet-style madhouse, but the bargains can be incredible. The whole store's an utter hassle but always worth it. To avoid the bulk of the crowds, avoid lunch hour, after work, and weekends; weekday mornings are best.

**Kmart.** 770 Broadway (at Astor Place, btw. 8th and 9th sts.). ☎ 212/673-1540. Subway: 6 to Astor Place.

Kmart is so out of place in the East Village that it has turned the mundane into marvelous camp: Japanese kids stare at gargantuan boxes of laundry detergent as if they were Warhol designed, and multi-pierced and mohawked locals navigate the name-brand maze alongside stroller-pushing housewives. U2 even held a press conference/performance here to announce their consumption-minded *Popmart* tour back in 1998. Kitsch value aside, this multilevel megastore is a great bet for discount prices on practicals, from socks to shampoo. You'll also find a pharmacy, a sizable food department where you can stock up on Cocoa Puffs and other kitchenette supplies (sale prices on snack foods are rock-bottom), and even a photo studio.

There's a second Kmart in midtown at 1 Penn Plaza, on 34th Street between Seventh and Eighth avenues (☎ 212/760-1188).

**Lord & Taylor.** 424 Fifth Ave. (at 39th St.). ☎ **212/391-3344.** Subway: B, D, F, Q to 42nd St.

Okay, so maybe Lord & Taylor isn't the first place you'd go for a vinyl miniskirt. But I like its understated, elegant mien. Long known as an excellent source of women's dresses and coats, L&T stocks all the major labels for men and women, with a special emphasis on American designers. Their house-brand clothes (khakis, blazers, turtle-necks, and summer sportswear) are well made and a great bargain. Sales, especially around holidays, can be stellar. The store is big enough to have a good selection but doesn't overwhelm. I wish the lighting was better, but it's a minor complaint. The Christmas window displays are an annual delight.

**Macy's.** At Herald Square, W. 34th St. and Broadway. ☎ **212/695-4400.** Subway: 1, 2, 3, 9, B, D, F, Q, N, R to 34th St.

A four-story sign on the side of the building trumpets "MACY'S, THE WORLD'S LARGEST STORE"—a hard fact to dispute, because the 10-story behemoth covers an entire city block, even dwarfing Bloomie's on the other side of town. Macy's is a hard place to shop: The size is unmanageable, the service is dreadful, and the incessant din from the crowds on the ground floor alone will kick your migraine into action. But they do sell *everything*. Massive renovation over the past few years has redesigned many departments into more manageable "mini-stores"—there's a Metropolitan Museum Gift Shop, a Swatch boutique, and cafes and make-up counters on several floors—but the store's one-of-a-kind flair that I remember so well from my childhood is just a memory now. Still, sales run constantly, so bargains are guaranteed. And because so many feel adrift in this retail sea, the store provides personal guides/shoppers at absolutely no charge. My advice: Get the floor plan, and consult it often to avoid wandering off into the sportswear netherworld. At Christmastime, come as late as you can manage (the store is usually open until midnight in the final shopping days).

**Tips for Sale Seekers:** One-day sales usually occur on Wednesdays and sometimes on Saturdays. Extended hours are common on sale days. Call the store when you arrive to find out whether your visit overlaps with one. Or check the A (front) section of *The New York Times* any day of the week for full-page advertisements, which sometimes include clip-out coupons for additional 10% to 15% discounts.

✪ **Pearl River Mart.** 277 Canal St., at Broadway. ☎ **212/431-4770.** www. pearlriver.com. Subway: N, R to Canal St.

It doesn't look like much from the street, but this three-floor Chinatown emporium overflows with affordable Asian exotica. Cool goods run the gamut from colorful paper lanterns to Chinese snack foods to Mandarin-collared silk pajamas to mah jongg sets to Hong Kong action videos. This fascinating place can keep you occupied for hours, and it's a great source for cheap, creative souvenirs. The sibling **Pearl River Department Store,** 200 Grand St., between Mott and Mulberry streets (☎ **212/ 966-1010**), is equally enchanting.

**Saks Fifth Avenue.** 611 Fifth Ave. (btw. 49th and 50th sts.). ☎ **212/753-4000.** Subway: B, D, F, Q to 47–50th sts./Rockefeller Center; E, F to Fifth Ave.

There are branches of Saks all over the country now, but this is it: Saks *Fifth Avenue.* This legendary flagship is well worth an hour or two for real department-store afi-cionados, and the smaller-than-most size makes it manageable in that amount of time. Saks carries a wide range of clothing; departments err on the pricey designer side (stay out of the lingerie department if you're looking for fundamentals) but run the gamut to affordable house-brand basics. As department stores go, there's something for every-one, and every budget, here. The cosmetics and fragrance departments are justifiably noteworthy because they carry many hard-to-find and brand-new brands. And the store's location, right across from Rockefeller Center, makes it a convenient stop for those on the sightseeing circuit. Don't miss the holiday windows.

## 3  Shopping A to Z
### ANTIQUES & COLLECTIBLES

New York has a wealth of antiques shops, covering everything from ancient to Americana to art-deco to mid-century modern. The browsing almost qualifies as torture, however, because prices are astronomical across the board—much higher than virtually everywhere else in the country.

**Antique Addiction.** 436 W. Broadway (btw. Prince and Spring sts.). ☎ **212/925-6342.** Subway: N, R to Prince St.; C, E to Spring St.

This charming SoHo shop is chock-full of vintage genuine and costume jewelry (including a great selection of cufflinks), plus classic eyewear and lighters. Prices are decent, and collectors are bound to find something they like—or have lots of fun trying.

**Chelsea Antiques Building.** 110 W. 25th St. (btw. Sixth and Seventh aves.). ☎ **212/929-0909.** www.chelseaantiques.com. Subway: F to 23rd St.

Right around the corner from New York's best flea market, the Annex Antiques Fair and Flea Market (see box below), this 12-floor building filled with dealers is open not only during the weekend to coincide with the market but also during the week. Prices are so good that it's known as a dealer's source, and shoppers are the type who love to prowl, touch everything, and sniff out a bargain. Highlights include **Waves** (☎ 212/989-9284; www.wavesradio.com) for antique radios and phonographs, including a good selection of 78s and Edison cylinders; **Retro-Metro/The Missing Link** (☎ 212/645-6928) for cufflinks, handbags, and other vintage jewelry and accessories; and **Toys from the 50s** (☎ 212/352-9182; www.toys-50s.com), specializing in classic TV show toys and memorabilia.

**J. Fields Studio & Gallery.** 55 W. 17th St. (just east of Sixth Ave.), 6th Floor. ☎ **212/989-4520.** Subway: F to 14th St.

This terrific gallery is the place for vintage and contemporary film posters, both foreign and domestic. A limited supply of music posters is on hand, too (including a good selection of psychedelic "Bill Graham Presents" posters from the '60s). Prices are high, but with vintage lobby cards starting at $15, even those with small budgets can own a bit of movie history.

### BEAUTY

**Cosmetics Plus.** 1601 Broadway (at 48th St.). ☎ **212/757-3122.** www.cosmeticsplus.com. Subway: N, R to 49th St.

This chain sells a wide range of perfumes, health and beauty aids, cosmetics from Cover Girl to Lancôme and Borghese, and high-end hair-care products, all at discounted prices. Also at 1320 Sixth Ave., at 53rd Street (☎ 212/247-0444); 500 Lexington Ave., at 47th Street (☎ 212/832-5460); 79 Fifth Ave., at 16th Street (☎ 212/293-2482); and 170 Broadway, at Maiden Lane in the Financial District (☎ 212/843-6656). Check the Yellow Pages or visit the Web site to locate other branches throughout the city.

✪ **Kiehl's.** 109 Third Ave. (at 13th St.). ☎ **212/677-3171.** Subway: 4, 5, 6, N, R, L to 14th St.–Union Sq.

# Where the Fleas Are

For those in search of vintage treasures, the Big Apple is a flea-market bonanza. City fleas operate on weekends throughout the year, so even winter visitors can enjoy the prowl.

Usually called the 26th Street flea market, the famous **Annex Antiques Fair and Flea Market** (☎ 212/243-5343; www.annexantiques.citysearch.com) is an outdoor emporium of nostalgia, filling a few parking lots along Sixth Avenue between 24th and 27th streets on weekends year-round. The assemblage is hit or miss; some days you'll find treasures galore, and others it seems like there's nothing but junk. A few quality vendors are almost always on hand, though, and prices are usually negotiable. The truly dedicated arrive at 6:30am, but the browsing is still good as late as 4pm. Sunday is always best, because there's double the booty on hand. One lot charges $1 admission both days, but the rest are free. Diehards can continue the hunt at the **Garage,** an indoor two-story parking garage at 112 W. 25th St., between Sixth and Seventh avenues (☎ 212/647-0707), and then proceed to 26th Street and Seventh Avenue, where another lot fills up with dealers on Sunday.

Another popular weekend market is the **SoHo Antiques and Collectibles Market,** at Broadway and Grand Street (☎ 212/682-6200; www.sohoantiques.citysearch.com), Saturdays and Sundays starting at 9am. Knowledgeable fleabees don't consider this the prime hunting ground it once was, but prices are reasonable and real finds surface every so often. The collections tend toward mid-century kitsch, vintage clothes, old records, old-fashioned kitchen appliances, furniture odds and ends, and the like.

Uptown, the **Greenflea Market** (☎ 212/721-0900) operates at two different venues: on the east side on East 67th Street, between First and York avenues, on Saturday from 6am to 6pm; and on the west side on Columbus Avenue between 76th and 77th streets, Sundays from 10am to 6pm. Both markets operate as both green and flea markets (hence the name). I'm not a big fan, but some people just love the west side Sunday event, where goods run from used records to Turkish kilims to discount pet supplies. Costume jewelry hunters in particular should enjoy the east side Saturday event.

Kiehl's is more than a store: It's a virtual cult. This always-packed old-time apothecary is legendary for its simply packaged, wonderfully formulated products for women and men. Lip Balm no. 1 is the perfect antidote for the biting winds of city or slope. Now sold at Saks, too. But come to the original.

**Sephora.** 1500 Broadway (btw. 43rd and 44th sts.). ☎ **212/944-6789.** www.sephora.com. Subway: 1, 2, 3, 7, 9, N, R, S to Times Sq./42nd St.

This French beauty superstore took Manhattan by storm in 1999. You'll find everything you could want here, from scents to nail color to bath salts to makeup brushes to hair accessories . . . you get the picture. In addition to their own exclusive brand, they carry an extensive number of upscale lines, including Shu Uemura, Urban Decay, Bliss, and Elizabeth Arden. Testers galore. Also at Rockefeller Center, 636 Fifth Ave., at 51st St. (☎ 212/245-1633); in SoHo at 555 Broadway, between Prince and Spring (☎ 212/625-1309); and at the World Trade Center (☎ 212/432-1311).

# BOOKS

## THE BIG CHAINS

**Barnes & Noble Booksellers.** On Union Square, 33 E. 17th St. ☎ **212/253-0810.** www. bn.com. Subway: 4, 5, 6, N, R, L to 14th St./Union Sq.

With locations throughout the city, B&N is the undisputed king of city bookstores. This location is my favorite: The selection is huge and well organized, the store is comfortable and never feels too crowded, and you're welcome to browse—or nab a comfy chair and read—for as long as you like. There's a cafe, of course, and an extensive magazine stand.

There's another superstore at 1972 Broadway, at 66th Street (☎ **212/595-6859**), plus additional good-sized locations at 4 Astor Place, between Broadway and Lafayette Street (☎ **212/420-1322**); 675 Sixth Ave., near 22nd Street (☎ **212/727-1227**); 160 E. 54th St., at Third Avenue (☎ **212/750-8033**); 600 Fifth Ave., at 48th (☎ **212/765-0590**); 2289 Broadway, at 82nd (☎ **212/362-8835**); and 240 E. 86th St., at Second Avenue (☎ **212/794-1962**).

Call ☎ **212/727-4810** for the latest schedule of readings; the calendar is extensive, and recently featured luminaries have included Peter Jennings, David Byrne, and Elmore Leonard.

**Borders Books & Music.** 5 World Trade Center (at Church and Vesey sts.). ☎ **212/839-8049.** www.borders.com. Subway: 1, 9, N, R to Cortlandt St.; C, E to World Trade Center.

After several years with no decent bookstore representation anywhere in the neighborhood, Borders is a welcome addition to the Financial District. The selection is extensive, service is great, and the store hosts a wealth of in-store events, including appearances from best-selling authors to musicians such as Lou Reed. Also at 461 Park Ave., at 57th Street (☎ **212/980-6785**), and 550 Second Ave., at 32nd Street (☎ **212/685-3938**).

## SPECIALTY BOOKSTORES

New York has more terrific specialty bookstores than I can possibly recount here. These are just some of the best. Also consider **Tower Books,** a branch of the megamusic chain (see "Music," below).

**Academy Book Store.** 10 W. 18th St. (btw. Fifth and Sixth aves.). ☎ **212/242-4848.** Subway: 4, 5, 6, N, R, L to 14th St./Union Sq.

Academy is best known for its record store (see "Music"), but adjacent is this friendly neighborhood used bookstore. Their inventory is quite deep, focusing on literature, history, art, humanities, and philosophy. Prices are scrupulously fair.

**Archivia.** 944 Madison Ave. (btw. 74th and 75th sts.). ☎ **212/439-9194.** Subway: 6 to 77th St.

Here you'll find new, imported, and rare books on architecture, the decorative arts, gardening, and interior design. A book and design lover's dream.

**Argosy Books.** 116 E. 59th St. (btw. Park and Lexington aves.). ☎ **212/753-4455.** www.argosybooks.com. Subway: 4, 5, 6 to 59th St.

Antiquarian-book hounds should check out this stately 75-year-old store, with high ceilings, packed shelves, a quiet intellectual air, and an outstanding collection of rarities, including 18th- and 19th-century prints, maps, and autographs.

**Books of Wonder.** 16 W. 18th St. (btw. Fifth and Sixth aves.). ☎ **212/989-3270.** www.booksofwonder.com. Subway: 4, 5, 6, N, R, L to 14th St./Union Sq.

You don't have to be a kid to fall in love with this charming bookstore, which served as the model for Meg Ryan's shop in *You've Got Mail* (Meg even worked here a spell to train for the role). Kids will love BOW's story readings; call for a schedule.

**☻ Coliseum Books.** 1771 Broadway (at 57th St.). ☎ **212/757-8381.** www.coliseumbooks. com. Subway: 1, 9, A, B, C, D to 59th St./Columbus Circle.

This big, well-stocked independent is a must on any book lover's list—and it's well located for visitors, right on the edge of the Theater District and a stone's throw from Central Park. It may not be Barnes & Noble cozy, but you'll find an excellent selection of fiction and literature (both contemporary and the classics), along with great travel, art, and coffee-table books. Poised atop a raised platform in the middle of the store, the staff is on hand to answer questions or proffer a literary opinion.

**Complete Traveller.** 199 Madison Ave. (at 35th St.). ☎ **212/685-9007.** Subway: 6 to 33rd St.

Whether your destination is Texas or Tibet, you'll find what you need in this, possibly the world's best travel bookstore. There are maps and travel accessories as well, plus a rare collection of antiquarian travel books whose facts might be outdated but whose writers' perceptions continue to shine.

**A Different Light Bookstore.** 151 W. 19th St. (btw. Sixth and Seventh aves.). ☎ **212/989-4850.** www.adlbooks.com. Subway: 1, 9 to 18th St.

The city's largest gay and lesbian bookstore stocks just about every category—fiction, nonfiction, biography, travel, gay/lesbian studies, and more—plus cassettes, calendars, you name it. There's also a cafe. Check the Web site for a full calendar of readings and video nights.

**Forbidden Planet.** 840 Broadway (at 13th St.). ☎ **212/473-1576.** Subway: 4, 5, 6, N, R, L to 14th St./Union Sq.

Here's the city's largest collection of sci-fi, comics, and graphic-illustration books. The range of products can't be beat, and the proudly geeky staff really knows what's what. Great sci-fi-themed toys, too.

**☻ Gotham Book Mart.** 41 W. 47th St. (btw. Fifth and Sixth aves.). ☎ **212/719-4448.** Subway: B, D, F, Q to 47–50th sts./Rockefeller Center.

Paris may have had its Sylvia Beach, but New York was lucky enough to have Frances Steloff. She opened Gotham Book Mart in 1920 and quickly became a defender of the First Amendment rights of authors. She championed such once-banned works as Henry Miller's *Tropic of Cancer* and numbered among her admirers Ezra Pound, Saul Bellow, and Jackie Kennedy Onassis. Frances has since passed on, but her aura lives on. As always, the emphasis is on poetry, literature, and the arts. This is New York's undisputed literary landmark; look for the sign that says WISE MEN FISH HERE.

**Gryphon Bookshop.** 2246 Broadway (btw. 80th and 81st sts.). ☎ **212/362-0706.** Subway: 1, 9 to 79th St.

Here's the Upper West Side's best used bookstore. It's a browser's delight, stacked to the ceiling with used and rare fiction, non-fiction, and art books, plus the occasional new reviewer's copy at deeply discounted prices.

**Hagstrom Map & Travel Center.** 57 W. 43rd St. (btw. Fifth and Sixth aves.). ☎ **212/398-1222.** Subway: B, D, F, Q to 42nd St.

This bookstore sells travel guides and an incredible selection of cartography to meet just about any map need. Also in lower Manhattan at 125 Maiden Lane, between Pearl and Water streets (☎ **212/785-5343**).

❂ **Housing Works Used Books Cafe.** 126 Crosby St. (south of Houston St.). ☎ **212/334-3324.** Subway: B, D, F, Q to Broadway/Lafayette St.

Like the idea of your hard-earned dollars benefiting both you and others? Then buy your reading material at this spacious yet quietly cozy used bookshop. It's part of Housing Works, a not-for-profit organization that provides housing, services, and advocacy for homeless people living with HIV and AIDS. The sizable collection is terrific and well organized, with lots of well-priced paperbacks, hardbacks, advance copies, and coffee-table books. There's a comfortable cafe in back that serves up coffee and tea, sandwiches, sweets, and other light bites, plus beer and wine, and you're welcome to peruse the reading matter as you snack. The bookstore often hosts readings by well-known writers on Wednesday and Thursday evenings; look for an expanded calendar (not to mention almost twice as many books to buy) once a lower-level renovation is complete (it should be done by the time you arrive).

**Kitchen Arts & Letters.** 1435 Lexington Ave. (btw. 93rd and 94th sts.). ☎ **212/876-5550.** www.kitchenartsandletters.com. Subway: 6 to 96th St.

Foodies take note: Here's the ultimate cook's and food-lover's bookstore. You'll be wowed by the depth of the selection, which includes rare and out-of-print cookbooks. The staff will conduct free searches for hard-to-find titles. The shop is an overstuffed jumble, but if this is your bag, you'll be browsing for hours.

**Murder Ink.** 2486 Broadway (btw. 92nd and 93rd sts.). ☎ **212/362-8905** or 800/488-8123. www.murderink.com. Subway: 1, 9 to 96th St.

Murder, she wrote, he wrote, they wrote. This is the ultimate specialty bookstore—as much fun as a good mystery. They claim to sell every mystery in print and also carry a huge selection of out-of-print paperbacks, hard-to-find imported titles, and rare signed first editions.

**Mysterious Book Shop.** 129 W. 56th St. (btw. Sixth and Seventh aves). ☎ **212/765-0900.** www.mysteriousbookshop.com. Subway: B, D, E to Seventh Ave.

Mystery and true-crime fans will also enjoy this one, specializing in current and rare whodunits.

**Oscar Wilde Bookshop.** 15 Christopher St. (btw. Sixth and Seventh aves.) ☎ **212/255-8097.** www.OscarWildeBooks.com. Subway: 1, 9 to Christopher St.

The world's oldest gay and lesbian bookstore is still going strong. It's much smaller than A Different Light (above), but the nice staff makes this landmark a pleasure.

**Posman Books.** In Grand Central Terminal (at the base of the Vanderbilt Ramp), Vanderbilt Ave. and 42nd St. ☎ **212/983-1111.** www.posmanbooks.com. Subway: 4, 5, 6, 7, S to 42nd St./Grand Central.

This big, new store is a browser's delight, with smart and well-displayed fiction and non-fiction collections as well as a terrific art and cookbook inventory. Also at NYU, 1 University Place, across from Washington Square Park (☎ **212/533-2665**), where the emphasis is on literature and philosophy; and at the New School, 70 Fifth Ave., at 13th (☎ **212/633-2525**), specializing in art, architecture, fashion, and design.

**Rand McNally Travel Store.** 150 E. 52nd St. (btw. Lexington and Third aves.). ☎ **212/758-7488.** www.randmcnally.com. Subway: 6 to 51st St.; E, F to Lexington Ave.

Sheet maps, globe maps, city maps, international maps, laminated maps—so many maps, in fact, you might never get lost again. A wide range of travel guides, atlases, and travelers' aids such as voltage converters and inflatable pillows, too. Also at 555 Seventh Ave., between 39th and 40th (☎ **212/944-4477**).

**Rizzoli.** 31 W. 57th St. (btw. Fifth and Sixth aves.). ☎ **212/759-2424.** Subway: N, R to Fifth Ave.

This clubby Italian bookstore is the classiest—and most relaxing—spot in town to browse for visual art and design books, plus quality fiction, gourmet cookbooks, and other upscale reading. There's a decent selection of foreign-language, music, and dance titles as well. Also in SoHo at 454 W. Broadway, between Houston and Prince (☎ **212/674-1616**), and at 3 World Financial Center (☎ **212/385-1400**).

**Revolution Books.** 9 W. 19th St. (btw. Fifth and Sixth aves.). ☎ **212/691-3345.** Subway: 4, 5, 6, L, N, R to 14th St./Union Sq.

If you're looking for an alternative viewpoint, you'll find quite a few of them at Revolution. Books on Marxism, feminism, black nationalism, and just about any other "ism" make up the bulk of this earnest store. But it's not just political tracts; fiction, poetry, magazines, and newspapers are on hand as well. Stock is organized by such provocative categories as "U.S. Imperialism, Past & Present" and "Women's Oppression/Women's Liberation."

**Shakespeare & Co.** 716 Broadway (just north of 4th St.). ☎ **212/529-1330.** Subway: N, R to 8th St.

This boutique-like bookstore in the Village has a generally well-rounded inventory. The displays are quite enticing if you're looking for something new to read. Also at 939 Lexington Ave., between 68th and 69th streets (☎ **212/570-0201**).

✪ **St. Mark's Bookshop.** 31 Third Ave. (at 9th St.). ☎ **212/260-7853.** Subway: 6 to Astor Place.

Established in 1977, this left-of-center East Village bookshop is a great place to browse. You'll find lots of terrific alternative and small-press fiction and poetry, plus cultural criticism, Eastern philosophy, and mainstream literature with an edge. You'll also find art, photography, and design books as well as an alternative 'zine rack. Lots of spoken-word CDs and cassettes, too.

✪ **The Strand.** 828 Broadway (at 12th St.). ☎ **212/473-1452.** Subway: 4, 5, 6, N, R, L to 14th St./Union Sq.

Something of a New York legend, the Strand is worth a visit for its staggering "eight miles of books" as well as its extensive inventory of review copies and bargain titles at up to 85% off list price. It's unquestionably the city's best book deal—there's almost nothing marked at list—and the selection is phenomenal in all categories (there's even a rare book department on the third floor). Still, you'll work for it: The narrow aisles mean you're always getting bumped; the books are only roughly alphabetized; and there's no air-conditioning in summer. Nevertheless, it's a used-book lover's paradise. There's a smaller one downtown at 95 Fulton St., between William and Gold streets (☎ **212/732-6070**).

**Urban Center Books.** In the Villard Houses, 457 Madison Ave. (at 51st St.). ☎ **212/935-3592.** www.urbancenterbooks.com. Subway: 6 to 51st St.

The Municipal Art Society's bookstore boasts a terrific selection of books on architecture, design, and urban planning.

# CLOTHING
## RETAIL FASHIONS

Fashion hounds should check out "The Top Shopping Streets & Neighborhoods" earlier in this chapter for advice on prime hunting grounds for affordable original designs.

**FASHION FLAGSHIPS** Some New York flagship stores are an experience you won't catch in your nearest mall. These stores are display cases for the complete line of fashions, so you'll often find much more to choose from than in your at-home branch. These are meant to be the biggest and best: Check out the gorgeous **Ann Taylor,** at 645 Madison Ave., at 60th Street (☎ 212/832-2010); the brand-new **Banana Republic** flagship at Rockefeller Center, 626 Fifth Ave., at 52nd (☎ 212/644-6678; www.bananarepublic.com); **Eddie Bauer,** 1960 Broadway, at 68th (☎ 212/ 877-7629; www.eddiebauer.com), which also carries the AKA Eddie Bauer line and the sports and mountaineering line; **Liz Claiborne,** 650 Fifth Ave., at 52nd Street (☎ 212/956-6505; www.lizclaiborne.com), carrying all of Liz's lines; the **Original Levi's Store** at 3 E. 57th St., between Fifth and Madison (☎ 212/838-2125); and **Victoria's Secret,** 34 E. 57th St., between Madison and Park (☎ 212/758-5592; www.victoriassecret.com). **Old Navy** has a huge flagship featuring its affordable basics and signature sense of humor at 610 Sixth Ave., at 18th (☎ 212/645-0663; www. oldnavy.com). **J. Crew** has a big bi-level SoHo store at 100 Prince St., between Mercer and Greene (☎ 212/966-2739).

### For Men & Women

**Canal Jean Co.** 504 Broadway (btw. Spring and Broome sts.). ☎ **212/226-1130.** www.canaljean.com. Subway: N, R to Prince St.; 6 to Spring St.

This big, bright store almost single-handedly started the SoHo shopping revolution nearly two decades ago. You'll find scads of well-priced jeans (low-riders, bellbottoms, cropped, and just plain regular), midriff-baring T-shirts, and flannels, with the requisite vinyl purses/backpacks, and clunky costume jewelry thrown in. A new 15,000-square-foot juniors department adds even more of the same. Go downstairs for vintage wear, but know that the stuff they have is geared to the skateboard set and tends to be a tad shopworn.

**Patricia Field.** 10 E. 8th St. (btw. Fifth Ave. and University Place). ☎ **212/254-1699.** www.patriciafield.com. Subway: 6 to Astor Place.

Pat Field has been the doyenne of cutting-edge chic and downtown cool for more than two decades now, and she still is. Her shop sports the city's grooviest, most outrageous men's and women's clubwear. The store's wild makeup counter will appear tame once you see the outlandish 'dos in the wacky wig and hair salon. There is nothing understated about this place; it's a hoot to browse. The SoHo store, **Hotel Venus,** 382 W. Broadway, between Spring and Broome streets (☎ **212/966-4066**), is a bit more upscale, but no less funky.

**✪ Tristan & America.** 1230 Sixth Ave. (at 49th St.). ☎ **212/246-2354.** Subway: B, D, F, Q to 47–50th sts./Rockefeller Center.

This Canadian retailer sells affordable, nicely tailored clothing in muted palettes to men and women who love Banana Republic but need a break from the high prices there. Look for great men's sweaters, affordable women's suits, and nicely cut trousers and A-line skirts. Also in SoHo at 560 Broadway, between Prince and Spring (☎ **212/965-1810**).

**Urban Outfitters.** 628 Broadway (at Bleecker St.). ☎ **212/475-0009.** www.urbn.com. Subway: 6 to Bleecker St.

The store for basics is sort of a Gap for alternative guys and gals. Jeans, oversized and tiny T-shirts, and lots of bright velours and stretchy polyesters. There's a good selection of earrings and funky jewelry, as well as a wonderfully offbeat, affordable housewares section with batik bedspreads, candles, glassware, and mod bathroom accessories. You'll also find lots of silly gifts, from *Mad Libs* books to boxes of genuine *South Park* Cheesy Poofs. Also at 374 Sixth Ave., at Waverly Place (☎ 212/677-9350); 162 Second Ave., between 10th and 11th streets (☎ 212/375-1277); and 127 E. 59th St., between Park and Lexington avenues (☎ 212/688-1200).

## Just Women

**Anthropologie.** 375 W. Broadway (btw. Spring and Broome sts.). ☎ 212/343-7070. www.anthropologie.com. Subway: C, E to Spring St.

Funky-chic, exotic-tinged affordable wearables and accessories mix with fun gifts, furniture, and home decorating items—much like Urban Outfitters for grown-ups. Also at 85 Fifth Ave., at 15th Street (☎ 212/627-5885).

✪ **Eileen Fisher.** 314 E. 9th St. (btw. First and Second aves.). ☎ 212/529-5715. www.eileenfisher.com. Subway: C, E to Spring St.

Slowly making their way around the nation in her own shops and through outlets such as Saks and the Garnet Hill catalog, Eileen Fisher's separates are a dream come true for stylish women looking for easy-to-wear classic pieces that transcend the latest fads. She designs fluid clothes in a pleasing neutral palette with natural fibers that don't sacrifice comfort for chic. Prices are on the high side, but the superior quality, fabrics, and style make them worth every penny. The SoHo shop, at 395 W. Broadway, between Spring and Broome streets (☎ 212/431-4567), is Fisher's prime showcase, but bargain hunters should head straight for this closet-sized East 9th location, which basically functions as an outlet store, with lots of sale merchandise and seconds on hand.
     Also at 103 Fifth Ave., near 18th Street (☎ 212/924-4777); 521 Madison Ave., at 53rd (☎ 212/759-9888); 341 Columbus Ave., near 77th (☎ 212/362-3000); and 1039 Madison Ave., between 79th and 80th (☎ 212/879-7799).

**Foley & Corinna.** 108 Stanton St. (at Essex St.). ☎ 212/529-2338. Subway: F to Delancey St.

The Lower East Side's best boutique specializes in affordable original designs with a distinctly '70s flair that's beautifully retro, not kitschy. You'll find a few reconstructed vintage pieces mixed in (such as pristine vintage Ts with added lace for a sexier look), plus an excellent handbag collection.

✪ **Jill Anderson.** 331 E. 9th St. (btw. First and Second aves.). ☎ 212/253-1747. Subway: 6 to Astor Place.

Finally, a New York designer who designs affordable clothes for real women to wear for real life—not just for 22-year-old size-2s to match with a pair of Pradas and wear out clubhopping. This narrow, peaceful shop is lined on both sides with Jill's simple, clean-lined designs, which drape beautifully and accentuate a woman's form without clinging. They're wearable for all ages and many figure types (her small sizes are small enough to fit petites, and her larges generally fit a full-figured size 14). Her clothes are feminine without being frilly, retro-reminiscent but completely modern, understated but utterly stylish. If Jill's clothes sound appealing to you, don't miss her shop; you won't regret it.

**Liberty House.** 2878A Broadway (at 112th St.). ☎ 212/932-1950. Subway: 1, 9 to Cathedral Pkwy./110th St.

This Columbia University–area boutique is a real find. It specializes in comfy womenswear in easygoing styles that transcend age lines and figure types. Great casual sweaters, Ts, cotton pants and skirts, linen separates, and much more, all at affordable prices. You'll also find affordable ethnic gifts at the front of the store, neat jewelry and

# Scouring the Sample Sales

Welcome to the ultimate New York bargain: the sample sale, where top-notch fashion designers recoup some losses by selling off the sample outfits they make to show to store buyers. Often, they throw in canceled orders, overstock, and discontinued styles as well. Prices are rock-bottom, even better than what you'd pay at TJ Maxx. What's the drawback? Such sales aren't advertised because designers don't want to alienate the big retailers by stealing their customers.

So how do you get the inside scoop? The **weekly columns** "Sales & Bargains" in *New York* magazine and "Check Out" in *Time Out New York* list current and future sales. **CitySearch (www.newyork.citysearch.com)** lists new sample sales for the week on Monday; click on SHOPPING then EYES ON THE BUYS. **Style Shop (www.styleshop.com)** and **NYSale (www.nysale.com)** also post information about sample sales among their other sale news for New York. If you're in the Garment District (especially along Broadway and Seventh Avenue) in the morning or at lunchtime, you'll probably be handed several **flyers** advertising sales going on that day.

A few tips as you venture into bargain land:

• Don't go during the lunch hour; you'll be elbow-to-elbow with rushed office workers.

• Bring cash. Some designers do accept credit cards, but don't chance it.

• Few, if any, of these spaces have dressing rooms, so be prepared to try things on over your clothes (or cross your fingers and hope it fits). Furthermore, because these garments are samples, they don't always come in a wide array of sizes. A man who is a 40 regular, for instance, is in like Flynn. If you're a 46 extra long, you're going to have rougher going.

• All items are sold "as is," and every sale is final, so inspect merchandise carefully before you buy.

accessories under the glass-topped counter, and a great kids' shop in the back specializing in unique styles that don't cost a fortune.

**Nicolina.** 247 W. 46th St. (btw. Broadway and Eighth Ave.). ☎ **212/302-NICO.** Subway: 1, 2, 3, 9, N, R, S to 42nd St.–Times Square.

This charming and sophisticated shop is a Theater District anomaly. Come for fashionable basics in high-quality natural materials: wide-legged linen pants, flowing A-line and princess-cut dresses in silk and cotton, sweaters from labels such as Beyond Threads and Sarah Arizona in fine wools, cotton, and silk. Great accessories, too, plus a small selection of contemporary and vintage gifts. A joy to browse.

**Just Kids**

If you need the basics, you'll find branches of **Gap Kids** and **Baby Gap** all over town—it's harder to avoid one than find one—including 60 W. 34th St., at Broadway (☎ 212/643-8960). Call ☎ 800/GAP-STYLE to locate the branch nearest you. The department stores are also great sources, of course, and excel at mounting sales.

Also, don't forget **Liberty House,** which has a kids' boutique in back; see "Just Women," above. **Little O's** is the stop for vintage-minded kids; see "Vintage Clothing," below.

**OshKosh B'Gosh.** 586 Fifth Ave. (btw. 47th and 48th sts.). ☎ **212/827-0098.** www.oshkoshbgosh.com. Subway: E, F to Fifth Ave.

Wisconsin's most famous name in fashion has a store decked out with train compartments to display the clothes: infants in the rear, boys on the left, and girls on the right. Prices are affordable, especially for European shoppers who pay upward of $100 for overalls at home. The store gives away size-conversion charts at the center desk/cashier.

**Shoofly.** 465 Amsterdam Ave. (at 82nd St.). ☎ **212/580-4390.** www.shooflynyc.com. Subway: 1, 9 to 79th St.

This pleasing shop specializes in top-quality clothing, footwear, and accessories for kids from newborn through teen. You'll find lots of distinctive stuff here. The shoe selection, in particular, is terrific, and not too pricey. Also at 42 Hudson St., between Duane and Thomas streets, in TriBeCa (☎ **212/406-3270**).

## DISCOUNT FASHIONS

For discount mega-mart **Century 21,** see "The Department Stores" earlier in this chapter.

**Burlington Coat Factory.** 707 Sixth Ave. (btw. 22nd and 23rd sts.). ☎ **212/229-1300** or 212/229-2247. www.coat.com. Subway: F to 23rd St.

Burlington also has a stash of off-price and slightly irregular designer togs for men, women, and kids, but come for the coats. You'll find an exhaustive selection at excellent prices, as well as a fine selection of discounted leather bags and shoes. Also in lower Manhattan at 45 Park Place, between West Broadway and Church Street (☎ **212/571-2631**).

**Daffy's.** 111 Fifth Ave. (at 18th St.). ☎ **212/529-4477.** www.daffys.com. Subway: 4, 5, 6, L, N, R, to 14th St./Union Sq.

Long before any of these Johnny-come-lately discounters dropped anchor in Manhattan, Daffy's offered rock-bottom prices to the masses. They don't get the big-time brand names of Century 21, but you'll come across classic European sportswear (cashmere sweaters and the like) and reliable staples, especially for men. The kid's collection—much of it froufrou continental or trendy designer—is a well-kept secret among city moms. Also in SoHo at 462 Broadway, at Grand Street (☎ **212/557-4422**); at 335 Madison Ave., at 44th Street (☎ **212/557-4422**); across from Macy's at 1311 Broadway, at 34th (☎ **212/736-4477**); and 125 E. 57th St., between Park and Lexington avenues (☎ **212/376-4477**).

**Filene's Basement.** 620 Sixth Ave. (btw. 18th and 19th sts.). ☎ **212/620-3100.** www. filenes.com. Subway: F to 14th St.

This Boston-based bargain institution's Manhattan satellites pale when compared to the mother store. The stock can be hit-or-miss, but you will find discounts on men's and women's clothing, handbags, accessories, shoes, and a few brands of perfume. Every now and then a big-time European label pops up, but don't count on finding the current season's goods, especially in the downstairs men's store. Inventory turns over lightning-quick here, though, so you never know what a trip through can yield. Also at 2222 Broadway, at 79th Street (☎ **212/873-8000**).

✪ **H&M.** 640 Fifth Ave. (at 51st St.). ☎ **212/489-0390.** www.hm.com. Subway: E, F to Fifth Ave.

The Swedish super-discounter Hennes & Mauritz took New York by storm in early 2000 with its high-style fashions at budget-minded prices. The store is mammoth, the departments better organized than most full-retail department stores, the men's and women's wearables ultra-chic, and the prices low, low, low. Look for a second location at Broadway and 34th Street in late 2000.

✪ **Loehmann's.** 101 Seventh Ave. (btw. 16th and 17th sts.). ☎ **212/352-0856.** www. loehmanns.com. Subway: 1, 9 to 18th St.

This enormous outlet occupies a major chunk of the original Barneys, and it has really latched onto the stylish vibe. Unlike its progenitors, this Loehmann's is so fancy it even has its own personal shopper. Two chock-full floors of casual wear by makers such as Liz Claiborne and Laundry lead to one of the city's best discount finds: The top-level "Back Room," where styles by some of fashion's biggest names—think Versace, D&G, Donna Karan, Max Mara—are offered at a fraction of retail. There's also a whole floor of men's fashions, the best you'll find in the discount realm. Excellent shoes, too, with great prices on top-quality, high-fashion styles by the likes of Calvin Klein and Cole-Haan.

**Syms.** 42 Trinity Place (at Rector St.). ☎ **212/797-1199.** www.syms.com. Subway: 1, 9, N, R to Rector St.

Syms is the discount store for men and women who need career wear. Designer and brand-name clothes are slashed 40% to 60% off their original retail value. Fabulous deals on suits. Good buys on kids' clothes, too.

**TJ Maxx.** 620 Sixth Ave. (btw. 18th and 19th sts.). ☎ **212/229-0875.** www.tjmaxx.com. Subway: F to 14th St.

Located directly above Filene's Basement, TJ Maxx is yet another off-pricer of wearables for the entire family. If you're seriously into bargains, price check each store, as there's some crossover merchandise between Filene's Basement and TJ Maxx, and prices at TJ Maxx can be lower.

## VINTAGE & RESALE CLOTHING

✪ **Allan & Suzi.** 416 Amsterdam Ave. (at 80th St.). ☎ **212/724-7445.** Subway: 1, 9 to 79th St.

Make it past the freaky windows and inside you'll find one of the best consignment shops in the city. Allan and Suzi have specialized in gently worn 20th-century designer wear for well more than a decade now, and their selection is marvelous. Their extensive vintage and contemporary couture collection—which ranges from conservative Chanel to over-the-top Halston, Mackie, and Versace—is so well priced that it's well within reach of the average shopper looking for something extra-glamorous to wear. The wild one-of-a-kind pieces (for ogling only) are worth a look unto themselves.

**Argosy.** 428 E. 9th St. (btw. First Ave. and Ave. A). ☎ **212/982-7918.** Subway: 6 to Astor Place.

This narrow shop offers a small but utterly pristine collection of '60s and '70s fashions, including an excellent collection of stylish leather jackets. Prices are reasonable considering the quality.

**Encore.** 1132 Madison Ave. (at 84th St.), 2nd floor. ☎ **212/879-2850.** www.encoreresale. com. Subway: 6 to 86th St.

This is one of the city's best resale shops, with two floors of quality womenswear, plus a small men's department and some accessories, all sold at a fraction of the original cost. Periodic sales sweeten the deal even more: The Chanel suit I saw here for $650 was the buy of the century, but you don't have to bring that much cash to go home with a bargain.

✪ **Housing Works Thrift Shop.** 143 W. 17th St. (btw. Sixth and Seventh aves.). ☎ **212/ 366-0820.** Subway: 1, 9 to 18th St.

With consistently low prices (most pieces $25 or less), lots of designer names (Todd Oldham, Calvin Klein, Donna Karan, and friends), and clothes in excellent condition, why go anywhere else? Styles range from classic tweeds to funky pieces. There's also a good used-jeans area and a mini-boutique selling couture-ish items at slightly higher prices. There's furniture, too, but good pieces go very fast. A great place to shop—not only will you get a bargain, but sales benefit homeless people living with HIV and AIDS. Also on the Upper East Side at 202 E. 77th St., between Second and Third avenues (☎ **212/772-8461**), and across the park at 306 Columbus Ave., between 74th and 75th streets (☎ **212/579-7566**).

**Little O's.** 1 Bleecker St. (btw. Bowery and Elizabeth St.). ☎ **212/673-0858.** Subway: 6 to Bleecker St.

New York's first vintage clothing shop for kids is overflowing with little fashions of yesteryear, from hand-embroidered pre-war christening dresses to Speed Racer pjs. Everything is freshly cleaned and in good condition, so expect to pay more than you would at the Salvation Army.

**Love Saves the Day.** 119 Second Ave. (at 7th St.). ☎ **212/228-3802.** Subway: 6 to Astor Place.

This is the store made famous in Madonna's big film break, *Desperately Seeking Susan* (she bought those groovy boots here). LSD hasn't changed much since, except the prices keep going up. In addition to the big and entertaining collection of tacky vintage clothes, there's an impressive assortment of Donny and Marie memorabilia and other collectible kitsch.

**Metropolis.** 43 Third Ave. (btw. 9th and 10th sts.). ☎ **212/358-0795.** www. metropolisapparel.com. Subway: 6 to Astor Place.

It's rumored that some of the biggest names in the fashion world scout this clean, orderly vintage shop for street fashion ideas. With good reason, too: Some of the coolest old clothes in the world turn up here, from skater pants and micro-cords to gingham-checked Western shirts perfect for your very own hoe-down or hullabaloo.

**Michael's.** 1041 Madison Ave. (btw. 79th and 80th sts.), 2nd floor. ☎ **212/737-7273.** Subway: 6 to 86th St.

This boutique boasts top-drawer designer wear for women at a fraction of the original cost. The bridal consignment department is a real find for brides looking for a top-quality dress at an off-the-rack price.

✪ **Screaming Mimi's.** 382 Lafayette St. (btw. 4th and Great Jones sts.). ☎ **212/ 677-6464.** www.screamingmimisnyc.com. Subway: 6 to Astor Place.

Think you hate vintage shopping? Think again: Screaming Mimi's is as neat and well organized as any high-priced boutique. The clothes are a little pricier than in some competing shops, but it's worth paying for the well-chosen selection and top-notch display. The vintage housewares department offers a cornucopia of kitschy old stuff, and the selection of New York memorabilia is a real hoot. Good accessories, too.

# EDIBLES

New York boasts the finest gourmet markets in the world. Below are my favorites, but foodies will also have a ball at **Chelsea Market,** a big, dazzling food mall at 75 Ninth Ave., between 15th and 16th streets (☎ 212/243-5678). Grand Central now has its own gourmet foodhall, **Grand Central Market,** with such pleasing vendors as **Adriana's Caravan** (☎ 212/972-8804; www.adrianascaravan.com) for exotic spices and **Corrado Bread & Pastry** (☎ 212/599-4321), carrying loaves and pastries from Bouley Bakery. And don't forget about the **Union Square greenmarket;** see p. 248.

**☼ Balducci's.** 424 Sixth Ave. (at 9th St.). ☎ **212/673-2600.** www.balducci.com. Subway: A, B, C, D, E, F, Q to W. 4th St. (use 8th St. exit).

Although you'll need a yuppified income to afford anything here, this gourmet grocery is a foodie's dream come true. It's relatively small (the shopping carts are even scaled down) and always packed, but the store overflows with imported foodstuffs; the best and freshest meats, fish, and breads; picture-perfect fruits and veggies, including international exotica such as hard-to-find starfruit and enoki mushrooms; and deli, cheese, and dessert counters to die for. The knowledgeable staff manages to keep its collective cool even at the height of the bustle. You can put together a gourmet take-out meal at the prepared foods counter, but I suggest heading across the street to **Cafe Balducci,** where you can order from the extensive selection of sandwiches, salads, and other prepared foods and enjoy your meal at one of the pleasant cafe tables (see chapter 6). Balducci is scheduled to open a second market on the Upper West Side in the Phillips Club hotel, 155 W. 66th St., between Broadway and Amsterdam Avenue (☎ **212/835-8800**), in mid-2000.

**Dean & Deluca.** 560 Broadway (at Prince St.). ☎ **212/431-1691.** www.dean-deluca.com. Subway: N, R to Prince St.

This gourmet supermarket is a little too self-consciously hip, but it's hard to argue with quality. In addition to the excellent butcher, fish, cheese, and dessert counters (check out the stunning cakes and the great character cookies) and beautiful fruits and veggies, you'll find a dried fruit and nut bar, a huge coffee bean selection, a gorgeous cut-flower selection, lots of imported waters and beers in the refrigerator case, and a limited but quality selection of kitchenware in back. There's a small cafe up front, too.

Other **cafe-only** locations include a roomy branch at 9 Rockefeller Center, across from the *Today* show studio (☎ **212/664-1363**); in the Theater District at the Paramount hotel, 235 W. 46th St., between Broadway and Eighth Avenue (☎ **212/869-6890**); and in the Village at 11th Street and University Place (☎ **212/473-1908**).

**☼ Fairway Market.** 2127 Broadway (at 74th St.) ☎ **212/595-1888.** Subway: 1, 2, 3, 9 to 72nd St.

This completely unpretentious gourmet food mega-market is an excellent place to put together a sophisticated picnic for nearby Central Park or an eat-in meal. The fruits and vegetables are glorious, and prices are better than you'll find at similar quality markets. An excellent section of prepared and prepackaged foods, too—perfect for preparing in your in-room kitchenette.

**Gourmet Garage.** 453 Broome St. (at Mercer St.). ☎ **212/941-5850.** Subway: N, R to Prince St.

This SoHo store features a neighborhood-appropriate loft-like setting and some of the tastiest gourmet products in town. The Garage supplies many of the city's best restaurants, including Le Cirque 2000, and sells to the public at wholesale, about 40% off the retail of fancier stores. This location also boasts a surprisingly good selection of pre-made sandwiches and prepared foods. The Upper West Side store, at 2567 Broadway between 96th and 97th streets (☎ **212/663-0656**), features an extensive department of kosher foods.

✪ **Zabar's.** 2245 Broadway (at 80th St.). ☎ **212/787-2000.** Subway: 1, 9 to 79th St.

More than any other of New York's gourmet food stores, Zabar's is an institution. This giant deli sells prepared foods, packaged goods from around the world, coffee beans, excellent fresh breads, and much more (no fresh veggies, though). This is the place for lox, and the rice pudding is the best I've ever tasted. You'll also find an excellent selection of cooking and kitchen gadgets on the second floor and a never-ending flow of Woody Allen film stock characters that shop here daily. Prepare yourself for serious crowds.

## CHOCOLATES

**Black Hound.** 170 Second Ave. (btw. 10th and 11th sts.). ☎ **212/979-9505.** www. blackhound.com. Subway: 6 to Astor Place; L to Third Ave.

This charming shop specializes in beautifully made truffles, cookies, and cakes. This is a terrific choice for those who like their chocolates not too frilly or too sweet. Just about everything comes packaged in a blond-wood box tied with a velveteen ribbon, making them simple but elegant gifts for chocolate lovers.

**Li-Lac Chocolates.** 120 Christopher St. (btw. Bleecker and Hudson sts.). ☎ **212/ 242-7374** or 800/624-4784. www.lilacchocolates.com. Subway: 1, 9 to Christopher St.

Li-Lac is one of the few chocolatiers anywhere still making sweets by hand. In business in the same location since 1923, this supremely charming Village shop whips up its chocolate and maple-walnut fudge fresh every day. If fudge isn't your bag, they also make pralines, caramels, and other hand-dipped chocolates, including specialty sweets for the holidays (hollow bunnies and chocolate eggs for Easter, chocolate Santas for Christmas, and so on). Also at Grand Central Market in Grand Central Terminal (☎ **212/370-4866**).

**Teuscher Chocolates of Switzerland.** 620 Fifth Ave. (at the Channel Gardens in Rockefeller Center). www.teuscher.com. ☎ **212/246-4416** or 800/554-0924. Subway: B, D, F, Q to 47–50th sts./Rockefeller Center.

At $50 a pound, you'd think they were selling gold bouillon. Teuscher makes mints, pralines, and wondrous marzipan, but it's the truffles that folks write home about. Splurge on one or two justifiably famous champagne truffles, and you'll weep with joy. Also at 25 E. 61st St., just east of Madison Avenue (☎ **212/751-8482**).

## ELECTRONICS

**J&R Music World/Computer World.** Park Row (at Ann St., opposite City Hall Park). ☎ **800/221-8180** or 212/238-9100. www.jandr.com. Subway: 2, 3 to Park Place; 4, 5, 6 to Brooklyn Bridge/City Hall.

Midtown may be overrun with electronics dealers, but it's the Financial District's J&R that's the city's top discount computer, electronics, small appliance, and office equipment retailer. The sales staff is knowledgeable but can get pushy if you don't buy at once or know exactly what you want. Don't succumb; take your time and find exacly what you need. Or better yet, peruse the store's copious catalog or extensive Web site, both of which make advance research, mail order, and comparison shopping easy.

## GIFTS

If you're looking for a special gift for a creative spirit, be sure to check out the shops that line **East 9th Street** in the East Village; the side streets of **SoHo,** where a good number of unusual boutiques still survive; **NoLiTa;** and Greenwich Village, especially in the wonderful cadre of one-of-a-kind shops in the **West Village.** See "The Top Shopping Streets & Neighborhoods" earlier in this chapter.

**Alphabets.** 2284 Broadway (btw. 82nd and 83rd sts.). ☎ **212/579-5702.** Subway: 1, 9 to 86th St.

This playful, modern shop has two halves: one dedicated to wacky cards, toys, and Ts, the other to creative housewares, from colorful dishware to freeform vases. Everything's fun and affordable.

Also at 115 Ave. A., between 7th Street and St. Marks (☎ 212/475-7250), and in the West Village at 47 Greenwich Ave., between Perry and Charles streets (☎ 212/229-2966).

**Boucher.** 9 Ninth Ave. (near Little W. 12th St.). ☎ **212/206-3775.** www.badcow.com. Subway: A, C, E, L to 14th St.

This jewel box of a store sparkles on a gentrifying corner of the still-industrial Meatpacking District. Designer Laura Mady and her staff meticulously handcraft feminine, nature-inspired necklaces, earrings, and other jewelry using unusual gemstones in organic shapes and freshwater pearls in soft ice-cream hues. Very affordable, and ideal for dressing up or everyday wear.

**Card-O-Mat.** 2884 Broadway (at 112th St.). ☎ **212/663-2085.** Subway: 1, 9 to 110th St./Cathedral Pkwy.

This big, bright shop stocks the city's most diverse collection of creative cards, notepads, address and date books, photo albums, stationery, and other paper goodies. You'll find styles here you won't see anywhere else thanks to a wide range of European imports.

✪ **Extraordinary.** 251 E. 57th St. (just west of Second Ave.). ☎ **212/223-9151.** Subway: 4, 5, 6 to 59th St.

This warm, friendly gallery-cum–gift shop is well worth going out of your way to discover. Owner J.R. Sanders, an interior designer who has created lauded exhibits at many city museums, has directed his copious talents to assembling a gorgeous and beautifully displayed collection of gifts from around the world. Lacquered crackle–egg shell trays from Vietnam, carved mango bowls from the Philippines, clever rosewood serving utensils camouflaged as tree branches from Africa, charming cheese servers and wine goblets by American glassblowers—all eye candy for those who thrive on whimsy and good design. Best of all, prices are shockingly reasonable; you'd pay twice as much at any other gallery or boutique. Truly extraordinary! *Tip:* Pair your visit with a pint at the British Open pub (p. 330).

✪ **Felissimo.** 10 W. 56th St. (just west of Fifth Ave.). ☎ **800/565-6785** or 212/247-5656. www.felissimo.com. Subway: E, F to Fifth Ave.

This five-floor emporium is the spot for those who love beautiful things. Despite the Italian name, this is the only U.S. outpost of one of Japan's largest mail-order companies. The aesthetic is distinctively Asian, but far from exclusively so—rather, more in the simple, clean-lined, Zen-like display of the gorgeous housewares, accessories, and jewelry. Goods run the gamut from leather-bound picture frames to Moroccan slippers to the perfect pet accessories. Sure, lots of items are pricey, but on my last visit I walked out with a $14 barrette and a $30 set of sake cups, and I was in heaven. Simply fabulous and a must for shoppers looking for gifts of distinction. There's a Japanese tearoom on the fourth floor.

**Kate's Paperie.** 561 Broadway (btw. Prince and Spring sts.). ☎ **212/941-9816.** www.katespaperie.com. Subway: N, R to Prince St.

Three cheers to Kate's for keeping the art of letter writing alive in our computer age. I could browse for hours among this delightful shop's handmade stationery and wrap, innovative invitation and thank yous, imported notebooks, writing tools, and other creative paper products, including cool paper lampshades. Lovely art cards, too— perfect for writing the folks back home. A joy! The SoHo location is best, but also at 8 W. 13th St., between Fifth and Sixth avenues in the Village (☎ 212/633-0570), and 1282 Third Ave., between 73rd and 74th streets on the Upper East Side (☎ 212/ 396-3670).

**La Maison Moderne.** 144 W. 19th St. (btw. Sixth and Seventh aves.). ☎ **212/691-9603.** Subway: 1, 9 to 18th St.

This lovely little shop is filled with a beautiful, affordable mix of both vintage and contemporary gift items. Lots of care went into assembling this charming Parisian-inspired store, and it shows. My favorite part of the store is the basement, where you'll find one-of-a-kind homewares such as handcrafted velvet pillows and the cutest collection of teapots in town.

**Mxyplyzyk.** 125 Greenwich Ave. (at 13th St., near Eighth Ave.). ☎ **212/989-4300.** www.mxyplyzyk.com. Subway: 1, 2, 3, 9, A, C, E to 14th St.

Come to this unpronounceable Village shop for one of the city's hippest and most creative collections of one-of-a-kind housewares, officeware, and gifts.

**Old Japan.** 382 Bleecker St. (btw. Perry and Charles sts.). ☎ **212/633-0922.** Subway: 1, 9 to Christopher St.

Come to Old Japan for vintage silk kimonos and Japanese gifts, including scarves and handbags fashioned out of kimonos, as well as buckwheat pillows made of kimono cotton. Vintage kimonos can run from $300 to as high as $1,500, but there's always a year-round sale rack with prices under $100, and small antiques and collectibles are always affordable.

## HOME FASHIONS & HOUSEWARES

✪ **ABC Carpet & Home.** 888 Broadway (at 19th St.). ☎ **212/473-3000.** www.abccarpet. com. Subway: N, R, 4, 5, 6, L to 14th St./Union Sq.

This 10-floor emporium is the ultimate home fashions and furnishings department store, a dream come true for aspiring Martha Stewarts. Shopping ABC has often been compared to taking a fantasy tour of your ancestor's attic: The goods run the gamut from Moroccan mosaic-tile end tables to hand-painted Tuscan pottery to Tiffanyish lamps to distressed bed frames made up with Frette linens to·much, much more, all carefully chosen and exquisitely displayed. Prices aren't bad comparatively speaking, but these are high-end goods. Some of the smaller items are quite affordable, though, and their occasional sales yield substantial discounts. In back is the **ABC Parlour Cafe,** serving lunch fare, weekend brunch, tea, and elegant desserts. Across the street is the multi-floor carpet store, which boasts a remarkable collection of area rugs.

**Amalgamated Home.** 9–19 Christopher St. (btw. Sixth and Seventh aves.). ☎ **212/ 255-4160** (furniture and lighting), 212/989-6538 (hardware), or 212/691-8695 (household sundries). Subway: 1, 9 to Christopher St.

This trio of home shops stocks eye-catching household goods you won't see anywhere else. Looking for brushed metal switchplates for your groovy new stainless-steel kitchen? How about a purple velvet love seat straight out of a Looney Tunes cartoon? Or the hippest rice bowls in town? You'll find it all and more at Amalgamated, which has expanded its hardware and furniture lines in 2000. Don't miss the terrific matte-white dinnerware shaped like Chinese takeout containers from Swid Powell.

**Fishs Eddy.** 889 Broadway (at 19th St.). ☎ **212/420-9020.** www.fishseddy.com. Subway: N, R, 4, 5, 6, L to 14th St.–Union Square.

What a great idea—selling remainders of kitschy, custom-designed china leftover from yesteryear. Ever wanted a dish that *really* says "Blue Plate Special?" Or how about a coffee mug with the terse logo "Cup o' Joe To Go?" The store is Browse Heaven, and prices are low enough. Other items for sale include basic vintage and retro-inspired flatware, heavy crockery bowls, and classic restaurant-supply glassware that can be hard to find in regular stores, such as soda-fountain and pint glasses. Also at 2176 Broadway, at 77th Street (☎ **212/873-8819**).

✪ **Leader Restaurant Equipment & Supplies.** 191 Bowery (at Spring St.). ☎ **800/666-6888** or 212/677-1982. Subway: 6 to Spring St.

Bowery is the place to find restaurant-supply-quality kitchenware, and Leader is the best dealer on the block. This big, bustling, friendly shop is a particularly good source for Chinese and Japanese wares—chopsticks, rice and noodle bowls, sushi plates, sake cups, and the like. You'll see a lot of the same styles you'd find at the high-end home-stores in SoHo or the Village, but at a fraction of the prices (this is where they buy, too).

**Lighting by Gregory.** 158 Bowery (btw. Delancey and Broome sts.). ☎ **212/226-1276.** www.lightingbygregory.com. Subway: F to Delancey St.

The stretch of the Bowery (Third Avenue) from Houston to Canal streets is considered the "light-fixture district" for its huge selections and great bargains on light fixtures, lamps, and ceiling fans. This bustling store is, by far, the best of the bunch.

## LEATHER GOODS, HANDBAGS & LUGGAGE

Greenwich Village is the place to go for affordable leather looks, especially along Christopher and Bleecker streets in the West Village. Worth seeking out are **Bleecker House,** at 182 Bleecker St., between MacDougal and Sullivan (☎ 212/358-1440), for jackets, and the **Village Tannery,** a few doors down at no. 173 (☎ 212/673-5444), for bags, wallets, backpacks, and organizers.

**Jobson's.** 666 Lexington Ave. (btw. 55th and 56th sts.). ☎ **212/355-6846** or 800/221-5238. Subway: 6 to 51st St.

In business since 1949, Jobson's is a great discount source for name-brand luggage and small leather goods. Rather than simply offer a cut off the retail price, management marks most items at just 10% above cost, which usually amounts to a whopping 40% to 60% break for the buyer. The shop also does a huge airline and professional flyers business, and they'll be happy to tell you what the pros buy.

**Fine & Klein.** 119 Orchard St. (near Delancey St.). ☎ **212/674-6720.** Subway: F to Delancey St.

The Lower East Side's bargain district is a great source for discount handbags and luggage. The best of the bunch is this shop, offering good discounts (usually 20%) on name-brand handbags.

**Manhattan Portage Ltd. Store.** 333 E. 9th St. (btw. First and Second aves.). ☎ **212/995-1949.** www.manhattanportageltd.com. Subway: 6 to Astor Place.

Come here for the hippest nylon and canvas carry-alls in town. True to its name, Manhattan Portage manufactures all its bags right in the city, and they're made from hard-wearing materials that can stand up to an urban lifestyle. Popular styles include all-purpose messenger bags, DJ bags, and backpacks in a range of colors from irides-cent yellow to camouflage. Manhattan Portage bags are also sold through other out-lets, but you're unlikely to find such a complete selection elsewhere.

## LOGO STORES

In addition to the choices below, there's also the massive, new theme park–like **NBC Experience** store on Rockefeller Plaza right across from the *Today* show studio, at 49th Street (☎ **212/664-3700**).

**Coca-Cola Fifth Ave.** 711 Fifth Ave. (btw. 55th and 56th sts.). ☎ **212/418-9261**. Sub-way: E, F, N, R to Fifth Ave.

The one that began the Fifth Avenue theme-store invasion. T-shirts, jackets, baseball caps, keychains, glassware—if they can slap a Coke logo on it, it's probably for sale here. You'll also find vintage vending machines—and, of course, Coke.

**The Disney Store.** 711 Fifth Ave. (at 55th St.). ☎ **212/702-0702**. Subway: E, F to Fifth Ave.

Disney burst onto Manhattan's retail scene with this monster three-story emporium. You'll find another big branch on 34th Street between Fifth and Sixth (☎ **212/279-9890**). The Upper West Side store, at Columbus Avenue and 66th Street (☎ **212/362-2386**), is worth mentioning for its collection of ABC TV souvenirs (the studio is right next door), from *All My Children* Ts to goodies spouting those wry black-on-yellow "TV is Good" messages. Look for a new Times Square location in 2000.

**Mets Clubhouse Shop.** 143 E. 54th St. (btw. Lexington and Third aves.). ☎ **212/888-7508**. www.mets.com. Subway: E, F to Lexington Ave.

New York's other favorite baseball team has its very own logo store in Midtown. Stop in for goods galore—baseball caps, T-shirts, posters, Piazza jerseys, '69 Miracle Mets memorabilia, and much more. You can buy regular season game tix here, too.

**NBA Store.** 666 Fifth Ave. (at 52nd St.). ☎ **212/515-NBA1**. www.nbastore.com. Subway: B, D, F, Q to 47–50th sts./Rockefeller Center.

For all things NBA and WNBA, head to this three-level mega-store, a multimedia cel-ebration of pro basketball, complete with a bleacher-seated arena for player appear-ances and signings.

**Niketown.** 6 E. 57th St. (btw. Fifth and Madison aves.). ☎ **212/891-6453**. Subway: N, R to Fifth Ave.

More multimedia advertorial than sportswear store, Niketown is surprisingly low-key and attractive, with five floors of shoes and athletic wear displayed in stark, Lucite-and-polished-metal surroundings. "Museum" cases display Sneakers of the Rich and Famous, and everywhere you're assailed by images of celebrity pitchmen and women, with his Airness prevalent above all others, of course (retirement? what retirement?). No sales or bargains here—plan on paying top dollar for the high-style athletic wear. Somebody's gotta pay for this place!

✪ **The Pop Shop.** 292 Lafayette St. (btw. Houston and Prince sts.). ☎ **212/219-2784**. www.haring.com. Subway: B, D, F, Q to Broadway/Lafayette St.

For affordable and wearable art that makes super-cool souvenirs, come to the Pop Shop. This groovy store is chock-full of items based on designs by artist Keith Haring, who died in 1990. T-shirts, posters, calendars, stationery, toys, notebooks, neat trans-parent backpacks—all sport the vivid primary colors and loopy stick-figure drawings that Haring made famous. Best of all, the Pop Shop is a non-profit organization, offering continued support to the AIDS-related and children's charities that the young artist championed in life.

**Warner Bros. Studio Store.** 1 E. 57th St. (at Fifth Ave.). ☎ **212/754-0300.** Subway: N, R to Fifth Ave.

This mega-theme store sits right near both Van Cleef & Arpels and Tiffany; wouldn't Bugs have a field day in those joints! Another three-story shop with cartoon-character everything, including animation cels for sale. There's an equally monolithic branch at 1 Times Square, at 42nd Street and Broadway (☎ **212/840-4040**) as well as one in the World Trade Center (☎ **212/775-1442**).

**Yankees Clubhouse Shop.** 393 Fifth Ave. (btw. 36th and 37th sts.). ☎ **212/685-4693.** www.yankees.com. Subway: 6 to 33rd St.

For all your Bronx Bombers needs—hats, jerseys, jackets, and so on. Tickets for regular-season home games are also for sale, and there's a limited selection of other New York team jerseys. Also at 110 E. 59th St., between Park and Lexington avenues (☎ **212/758-7844**); and at 8 Fulton St. in the South Street Seaport (☎ **212/514-7182**).

## MUSEUM STORES

In addition to these standouts, other noteworthy museum shops worth seeking out include the **New York Public Library,** the **Museum for African Art,** the **Jewish Museum,** the **Museum of American Folk Art,** and the **Isamu Noguchi Museum;** see chapter 7.

**American Craft Museum.** 40 W. 53rd St. (btw. Fifth and Sixth Aves.). ☎ **212/956-3535.** Subway: E, F to Fifth Ave.

The nation's top showcase for contemporary crafts boasts an impressive collection of crafts in its museum store, too. Come for exquisite handblown glassware, one-of-a-kind jewelry, original pottery, and other artistic treasures, all beautifully displayed.

**Metropolitan Museum of Art Store.** Fifth Ave. at 82nd St. ☎ **212/570-3894.** www.metmuseum.org. Subway: 4, 5, 6 to 86th St.

Given the scope of the museum itself, it's no wonder that the gift shop is outstanding. Many treasures from the museum's collection have been reproduced as jewelry, china, and other objets d'art. The range of art books is dizzying, and upstairs is an equally comprehensive selection of posters and inventive children's toys. And you don't even have to go uptown to indulge: Other branches can be found on the plaza at Rockefeller Center, 15 W. 49th St. (☎ **212/332-1360**); in SoHo at 113 Prince St. (☎ **212/614-3000**), and on the mezzanine level at Macy's (☎ **212/268-7266**).

✪ **Maxilla & Mandible.** 451 Columbus Ave. (btw. 81st and 82nd sts.). ☎ **212/724-6173.** www.maxillaandmandible.com. Subway: B, C to 81st St.

This shop is not affiliated with the American Museum of Natural History, but a visit here makes a good adjunct to your trip to the museum (which is right around the corner). It might look like a freakshop at first glance, but it's really a fascinating natural history emporium. Inside you'll find unusual rocks and shells from around the world, luminescent butterflies in display boxes, even surprisingly affordable real fossils containing prehistoric fish and insects that come with details on their history and where they were excavated. There's also a good variety of natural history-themed toys for the kids.

✪ **MOMA Design Store.** 44 W. 53rd St. (btw. Fifth and Sixth aves.). ☎ **212/767-1050.** www.moma.org. Subway: E, F to Fifth Ave.; B, D, F, Q to 47–50th sts./Rockefeller Center.

Across the street from the Museum of Modern Art is this terrific shop, whose stock ranges from museum posters and clever toys for kids to *way* overpriced reproductions of many of the classics of modern design, including free-form Alvar Aalto vases and Eames recliners. Luckily, there are plenty of more affordable outré home accessories to choose from.

Across the street at the museum, the main gift shop has a stellar collection of gift books, posters, and the like, all with a modern twist.

## MUSIC & VIDEO

Music buffs will find a wealth of new-and-used shops in the West Village. Standouts include **Rebel Rebel,** 319 Bleecker St. (☎ 212/989-0770), for British and Japanese imports and New Wave and glam classics; and **Rockit Scientist,** just off Bleecker at 43 Carmine St. (☎ 212/242-0066), a tiny place with a huge folk and psych collection. **Vinyl Mania,** 60 Carmine St. (☎ 212/924-7223; www.vinylmania.com), and **Sonic Groove,** 41 Carmine St. (☎ 212/675-5172; www.sonicgroove.com), supply the sounds for many of the city's major raves. **Sam Goody,** 390 Sixth Ave. at 8th Street (☎ 212/674-7131), diverges from the mall-store norm with its cutting-edge in-house performance series. Unfortunately, **Bleecker Bob's Golden Oldies,** 118 W. 3rd St. (☎ 212/475-9677), has outlived its legend; it's now a dirty little hole-in-the-wall with lots of worn, badly organized vinyl and a rude staff.

Grungy **St. Marks Place** between Third and Second avenues in the East Village is another great bet. **Smash Records** (☎ 212/473-2200) is a standout, as are **Sounds** (☎ 212/677-3444), the dirt-cheap granddaddy of the St. Marks shops, and **Mondo Kim's** (☎ 212/598-9985; www.kimsvideo.com) for indie music, video, and 'zines.

In the Financial District, **J&R Music World** has a big selection of classical, jazz, and rock, and brand-new releases are almost always on sale; see "Electronics" above for details.

For musical instruments, see "Times Square & the Theater District" under "The Top Shopping Streets & Neighborhoods."

**Academy Records & CDs.** 12 W. 18th St. (btw. Fifth and Sixth aves.). ☎ **212/242-3000.** www.academy-records.com. Subway: 4, 5, 6, N, R, L to 14th St./Union Sq.

This Flatiron District shop has a cool intellectual air that's more reminiscent of a good used bookstore than your average used-record store. Academy is always filled with classical, opera, and jazz junkies perusing the extensive and well-priced collection of used CDs and vinyl. In addition to the extensive classical and jazz collection is a variety of other audiophile favorites, from rare '60s pop songsters to spoken word.

✪ **Bleecker St. Records.** 239 Bleecker St. (near Carmine St., just west of Sixth Ave.). ☎ **212/ 255-7899.** Subway: A, B, C, D, E, F, Q to W. 4th St.

This sizable, well-lit space is great for one-stop shopping. The clean, well-organized CD and LP collections run the gamut from rock, oldies, jazz, folk, and blues to Oi! punk. You'll find lots of imports, collectible, and out-of-print records (including singles), a terrific collection of used CDs, and a mix of casual listeners and serious collectors cruising the bins.

✪ **Colony Record & Tape Center.** 1619 Broadway (at 49th St.). ☎ **212/265-2050.** www.colonymusic.com. Subway: 1, 9 to 50th St.; N, R to 49th St.

This longlived Theater District shop is housed in the legendary Brill Building, basically the Tin Pan Alley of '50s and '60s pop, where legendary songwriters such as

Goffin and King and producers such as Don Kirschner and Phil Spector crafted the soundtrack for a generation. It's the perfect home for Colony, a nostalgia emporium filled with a pricey but excellent collection of vintage vinyl and new CDs. You'll find a great collection of Broadway scores and cast recordings, plus decades worth of recordings by pop song stylists both legendary and obscure. There's also one of the best collections of sheet music in the city (including some hard-to-find international stuff) and a great selection of original theater and movie posters. You can stock up your in-home karaoke machine here, too.

**Footlight.** 113 E. 12th St. (btw. Third and Fourth aves.). ☎ **212/533-1572.** www.footlight.com. Subway: 4, 5, 6, N, R, L, St to 14th St./Union Sq.

If you like Colony (above), also check out this dreamy collection of vintage vinyl, heavy on jazz and pop vocalists, soundtracks, and showtunes.

**✪ Generation Records.** 210 Thompson St. (btw. Bleecker and 3rd sts.). ☎ **212/254-1100.** Subway: A, B, C, D, E, F, Q to W. 4th St.

This tidy little store sells mostly CDs and is an excellent source for "import" live recordings. Originally specializing in hardcore, punk, and heavy metal, the new collection upstairs still has a heavy edge but has since diversified appreciably. Downstairs is a well-organized and well-priced used CD selection that's not as picked over as most and runs the genre gamut; there's also a good selection of used LPs. Despite the help's tough look, they're actually quite friendly and helpful.

**Jazz Record Center.** 236 W. 26th St. (btw. Seventh and Eighth aves.), 8th floor. ☎ **212/675-4480.** Subway: 1, 9 to 28th St.

Jazz Record Center is *the* place to find rare and out-of-print jazz records. In addition to the extensive selection of CDs and vinyl (including 78s), videos, books, posters, and other memorabilia are available. Prices can be high, as befits the rarity of the stock. Owner Frederick Cohen is extremely knowledgeable, so come here if you're trying to track down something obscure (Cohen does mail-order business as well).

**Kim's Video & Audio.** Kim's Underground at 144 Bleecker St. (at LaGuardia Place). ☎ **212/260-1010.** www.kimsvideo.com. Subway: A, B, C, D, E, F, Q to West 4th St. Kim's West at 350 Bleecker St. (at W. 10th St.). ☎ **212/675-8996.** Subway: 1, 9 to Christopher St. Mondo Kim's at 6 St. Marks Place (btw. Second and Third aves.). ☎ **212/598-9985.** Subway: 6 to Astor Place.

This funky mini-chain is New York's underground alternative to Blockbuster Video, but they also stock a decent selection of indie vinyl and CDs as well as books and 'zines. The staff at all three locations have a terrible reputation, but they've been friendlier than ever of late.

**✪ NYCD.** 426 Amsterdam Ave. (btw. 80th and 81st sts.). ☎ **212/724-4466.** www.nycd.com. Subway: 1, 9 to 79th St.

This neat, narrow little store is home to one of the city's best collections of used rock CDs, thanks to its off-the-beaten-track Upper West Side location. Downtown trollers simply don't make it this far uptown to prune the selection, so it's easy to find lots of top titles among the pickings.

**Other Music.** 15 E. 4th St. (btw. Broadway and Lafayette St.). ☎ **212/477-8150.** www.othermusic.com. Subway: 6 to Astor Place; B, D, F, Q to Broadway/Lafayette St.

Head to Other Music for the wildest sounds in town. You won't find a major label here (that's what Tower is for across the street). This shop focuses exclusively on small international labels, especially those on the cutting edge (you can find records on the Knitting Factory label here). The bizarro runs the gamut from underground Japanese spin doctors to obscure Irish folk; needless to say, the world music selection is terrific. Fascinating and bound to be filled with music you've never heard of. The sales staff really knows their stuff, so ask away.

**Throb.** 211 E. 14th (btw. Second and Third aves.). ☎ **212/533-2328.** www.throb.com. Subway: L to Third Ave.

Throb is home to CDs and 12" vinyls of not-even-close-to-mainstream genres: house, ambient, jungle, drum-and-bass, trance, and trip hop. Imports are also big business here. A popular stop for dance-club DJs: Test-drive the trippy sounds in a listening booth. You'll also find record bags and T-shirts.

**Tower Records.** 692 Broadway (at W. 4th St.). ☎ **212/505-1500.** www. towerrecords. com. Subway: N, R to 8th St.; 6 to Astor Place.

As mighty of a chain as it may be, it's hard to complain about Tower. Both the Village location and the Upper West Side branch (2107 Broadway, at 66th St.; ☎ 212/ 799-2500) are huge multimedia superstores brimming with an encyclopedic collection of music—classical, jazz, rock, world, you name it. The Village location also stocks a very good selection of indie and alternative labels. Just behind it at West 4th and Lafayette is **Tower Books** (☎ 212/228-5100), where you'll find videos, books, and magazines; and the **Tower Clearance Outlet** (☎ 212/228-7317), selling cut-out CDs for a song. Look for in-stores by big names in music, usually advertised in the *Time Out New York* and *Village Voice*.

**Virgin Megastore.** 1540 Broadway (at 45th St.). ☎ **212/921-1020.** www.virgin.com. Subway: 1, 2, 3, 7, 9, N, R to Times Square/42nd St.

Right in the heart of Times Square, this superstore bustles day and night. For the size of it, the selection isn't as wide as you'd think; still, you're likely to find what you're looking for among the two levels of domestic and imported CDs and cassettes. Other plusses are an extensive singles department, a phenomenal number of listening posts, plus a huge video department. There's also a bookstore, a cafe, and multiplex movie theater, and you can even arrange airfare on Virgin Atlantic with the on-site travel agent. The Union Square location, 52 E. 14th St., at Broadway (☎ 212/598-4666), is equally hopping. As at Tower, look for a busy schedule of in-stores at both locations.

## SHOES

Designer shoe shops are on **East 57th Street** and amble up **Madison Avenue,** becoming pricier as you move uptown. **SoHo** is an excellent place to search for the latest styles; the streets are overrun with terrific shoe stores. Cheaper copies of the trendiest styles are sold in the tiny shops along **8th Street** between Broadway and Sixth Avenue in the Village, which some people call Shoe Row. Most department stores have two sizable shoe departments—one for designer stuff and one for daily wearables. See "Discount Fashions," above; at both **Loehmann's** and **Century 21,** the women's shoe departments are well stocked and unbelievably priced. Also see "The Department Stores" earlier in this chapter. For **Niketown,** see "Logo Stores," above.

**Giraudon New York.** 152 Eighth Ave. (btw. 17th and 18th sts.). ☎ **212/633-0999.** www.giraudonnewyork.com. Subway: A, C, E, L to 14th St.

This French designer makes fashionable, well-made street shoes for hip men and women who want something clean-lined and stylish but not too chunky or trendy. Not cheap, but not overpriced, either—these shoes last forever. Prices run $115 to $200, and sales are excellent.

**John Fluevog Shoes.** 104 Prince St. (btw. Mercer and Greene sts.). ☎ **212/431-4484.** www.fluevog.com. Subway: N, R to Prince St.

John Fluevog's funky, chunky footwear has proven stylish enough to make the brand a mainstay among usually fickle young trendsetters. Some of the styles border on the ridiculous (check out the super-silly space-age Lift-Offs, with lucite heels) but others, such as the beautifully retro Buick loafers, are a dream. Offering a more stylized take on the Dr. Marten look, the longstanding Angels line is the ultimate in sturdy comfort for urban feet.

**Make 10.** 49 W. 8th St. (btw. Fifth and Sixth aves.) ☎ **212/254-1132.** Subway: A, B, C, D, E, F, Q to W. 4th St.

Make 10 sells good leather shoes (with some designer names) in trendy, up-to-the-minute styles. They're quite affordable for what you're getting; in fact, name brands are often a fraction of what you'd pay at a store like Barneys. Also at 1227 Third Ave., between 70th and 71st streets (☎ **212/472-2775**); and 1386 Sixth Ave., at 56th Street (☎ **212/956-4739**).

**Sacco.** 324 Columbus Ave. (btw. 75th and 76th sts.). ☎ **212/799-5229.** www.saccoshoes. com. Subway: B, C to 81st St.

This city chain specializes in mostly Italian-made women's shoes that cross style with supreme comfort. I especially love their fall and winter boots, comfortable enough to carry me around the city on even the most arduous of research days. Lots of terrific basic blacks and browns. Good prices and sales, too. Also at 111 Thompson St., at Prince, in SoHo (☎ **212/925-8010**); 94 Seventh Ave., at 16th, in Chelsea (☎ **212/675-5180**); and 2355 Broadway, at 86th (☎ **212/874-8362**).

**Stapleton Shoe Company.** 68 Trinity Place (at Rector St., 3 blocks south of the World Trade Center). ☎ **212/964-6329.** Subway: N, R to Rector St.

If Imelda Marcos had been a man, her first stop would have been this shoe store, right near the American Stock Exchange. Stapleton sells men's brands such as Bally, Timberland, and Johnston & Murphy, all at discounts so deep it'll feel like insider trading. The women's branch is **Anbar Shoes,** 93 Reade St., between Church Street and West Broadway (☎ **212/227-0253**).

## SPORTING GOODS

For Niketown, see "Logo Stores," above.

**Eastern Mountain Sports.** 611 Broadway (at Houston St.). ☎ **212/505-9860.** Subway: B, D, F, Q to Broadway/Lafayette St.

This one-stop sporting shop is famous for all-weather, high-tech camping, hiking, and climbing gear. This is an excellent, affordable source for Polartec pullovers, waterproof shells, and the like. You'll also find hardware such as compasses, cookwear, and Swiss Army knives. Also at 20 W. 61st St., between Broadway and Columbus on the Upper West Side (☎ **212/397-4860**).

**Paragon Sporting Goods.** 867 Broadway (at 18th St.). ☎ **212/255-8036.** www.paragonsports.com. Subway: 4, 5, 6, N, R, L to 14th St./Union Sq.

Paragon is an excellent all-purpose sporting goods store. The emphasis here is on equipment and athletic wear for virtually every sport, from tennis to biking to mountain climbing. End-of-the-season sales, especially on sneakers and outdoor clothing, bring serious discounts.

# TOYS

If your kids love to read, don't miss **Books of Wonder** under "Books" above. Vintage collectors should see the **Chelsea Antiques Building** under "Antiques & Collectibles."

**FAO Schwarz.** 767 Fifth Ave. (at 58th St.). ☎ **212/644-9400.** www.fao.com. Subway: N, R to Fifth Ave.

The best-loved toy store in America was designed with an eye for fun: The elevator is shaped like a huge toy soldier, and there are plenty of hands-on displays to keep the little ones occupied for hours. Entire areas are devoted to specific toy makers (Lego, Fisher Price, *Star Wars* action figures, Barbie). You and the kids will find plenty of affordable little gifts to take home as souvenirs (the front-left corner specializes in pre-wrapped gifts for Moms and Dads on business trips).

# WINE & SPIRITS

**Acker Merrall & Condit Co.** 160 W. 72nd St. (btw. Broadway and Columbus aves.). ☎ **212/787-1700.** Subway: 1, 2, 3, 9 to 72nd St.

This attractive little store is the Upper West Side's best wine source. There are no bad bottles here. The careful selection is well displayed, with opinionated cards attached to each bin to help you choose. A supremely knowledgeable staff is on hand for additional assistance.

**✪ Astor Wines & Spirits.** 12 Astor Place (at Lafayette St.). ☎ **212/674-7500.** www.astoruncorked.com. Subway: 6 to Astor Place.

This large store is the source for excellent values on liquor and wine; their stock is deep and ranges far and wide. The staff is always willing to recommend a vintage. Astor hosts an excellent slate of regular wine tastings Thursday and Friday from 5 to 8pm and Saturday from 3 to 6pm, often paired with edibles from local restaurants and gourmet shops.

**✪ Best Cellars.** 1291 Lexington Ave. (btw. 86th and 87th sts.). ☎ **212/426-4200.** www.best-cellars.com. Subway: 6 to 86th St.

Committed to stocking "Great Wines for Everyday," Best Cellars succeeds with èlan. I've never seen so many fine labels for $10 or less. Interestingly, the wines are stocked by taste (not by grape or region); look for fizzy, fresh, juicy, and other descriptors. It's hard to do better for the money—and the staff is terrific, too.

# New York City After Dark    9

New York's nightlife scene is an embarrassment of riches. There's so much to see and do in this city after the sun goes down that your biggest problem is likely going to be choosing among the many temptations.

There's no way that I can tell you in these pages what's going to be on the calendar while you're in town. So for the latest, most comprehensive nightlife listings, from classic and cutting-edge theater and performing arts to live rock, jazz, and dance club coverage, *Time Out New York* is my favorite weekly source; a new issue hits newsstands every Thursday. The free weekly *Village Voice,* the city's legendary alterna-paper, is available late Tuesday downtown and early Wednesday in the rest of the city. The arts and entertainment coverage couldn't be more extensive, and just about every live music venue advertises its shows here. Another great weekly is *New York* magazine; flip to the "Cue" section at the back for the latest happenings. *The New York Times* features terrific entertainment coverage, particularly in the two-part Friday "Weekend" section. The cabaret, classical music, and theater guides are particularly useful.

Some of your best, most comprehensive and up-to-date information sources for what's going on about town are in cyberspace, of course. For a complete rundown of Web sources, see pp. 46–58 in the "Planning Your Trip: An Online Directory."

## 1 The Theater Scene

Nobody does theater better than New York. No other city—not even London—has a theater scene with so much breadth and depth, with so many wide-open alternatives. Broadway, of course, gets the most ink and the most airplay and deservedly so: Broadway is where you'll find the big stage productions and the moneymakers, from crowd-pleasing warhorses such as *Phantom of the Opera* to phenomenal newer successes such as *Chicago* and *The Lion King.* But today's scene is thriving beyond the bounds of just Broadway; smaller, "alternative" theater has taken hold of the popular imagination, too. With bankable stars on stage, crowds lining up for hot tickets, and hits popular enough to generate major-label cast albums, off-Broadway isn't just for culture vultures anymore.

Despite this vitality, plays and musicals close all the time, often with little warning; witness the widespread shock (and the huge push to

---

## Worth Seeking Out

Legendary among off-Broadway theaters is **The Public Theater,** 425 Lafayette St. (☎ **212/260-2400,** or TeleCharge at 212/239-6200 for tickets; www.publictheater. org or www.telecharge.com), the legacy of visionary theater producer Joseph Papp. Now under the direction of George C. Wolfe, the Public draws top talent to the stage with its groundbreaking stagings of Shakespeare's plays—past schedules have featured F. Murray Abraham as Lear and Liev Schreiber as Hamlet—as well as new plays, classical dramas, and solo performances. The Public also produces Broadway shows on occasion, such as *Bring in 'Da Noise, Bring in 'Da Funk* and 2000's *The Wild Party*, and hosts New York's best annual free alfresco event, **Shakespeare in the Park** (see the "Park It!" box later in this chapter). The theater also offers **"Free at Three,"** a monthly series of free performances, readings, and symposia showcasing new and emerging talent. If that's not enough, it's also home to **Joe's Pub** (☎ 212/539-8777; www.joespub.com), a pricey but excellent showcase for traditional and alternative cabaret talent. Definitely worth seeking out!

---

grab up the remaining tickets) that accompanied the announcement of the closing of *Cats,* the longest-running musical on Broadway, in mid-2000. Even the most basic production is expensive to mount, and ticket sales must be robust to keep it in business. So I can't tell you precisely what will be on while you're in town. Your best bet is to check the **publications** listed at the start of this chapter—or the **Web sites** listed in the "Planning Your Trip: An Online Directory" at the back of this book—before you arrive, or even once you reach town, to get an idea of what you might like to see. A useful source is the **Broadway Line** (☎ **888/BROADWAY** or 212/302-4111; www.broadway.org), where you can obtain details and descriptions on current Broadway shows, hear about special offers and discounts, and choose to be transferred to TeleCharge or TicketMaster to buy tickets. There's also **NYC/Onstage** (☎ **212/ 768-1818;** www.tdf.org), providing the same kind of service for both Broadway and off-Broadway productions. (Don't buy tickets, though, until you read "Top Ticket-Buying Tips," below.)

Even though I can't guarantee what'll be on stage when you're visiting, the likelihood is good that you'll find lots of large-scale musicals and revivals on Broadway and more original drama and offbeat musicals on the off-Broadway stage. If you find new drama on Broadway, it's likely to be the transcontinental transfer of a London stage hit, similar to Yasmina Reza's for-thinking-theatergoers-only *Art* in 1998 and Michael Frayn's Bohr and Heisenberg atomic-science fantasy *Copenhagen* in 2000. If you're coming to see the big hits, chances are extremely good that you'll still find *Les Misérables* at the Imperial, *Miss Saigon* at the Broadway Theater (maybe), and *Phantom* at the Majestic. Kids will be enchanted by Disney's one-two punch of *Beauty and the Beast* and *The Lion King.* Off-Broadway is more volatile, but you're likely to still find the ridiculously fun *Blue Man Group: Tubes* at the Astor Place Theatre and the percussion sensation *Stomp!* at the Orpheum Theatre; both are performance art pieces that are more palatable than you'd expect and have been pleasing kids and grown-ups alike for years now. And I'd pretty much stake my life on the fact that the legendary show *The Fantasticks* will still be alive and kicking at the Sullivan Street Playhouse; it opened on May 3, 1960, and is now the longest-running musical in the world.

Keep in mind that although "Off-Broadway" might mean experimental and therefore might be riskier, it doesn't have to mean lower-quality in any way. These days, the best off-Broadway shows don't need to move to Broadway to be legitimized. In fact,

# The Theater District

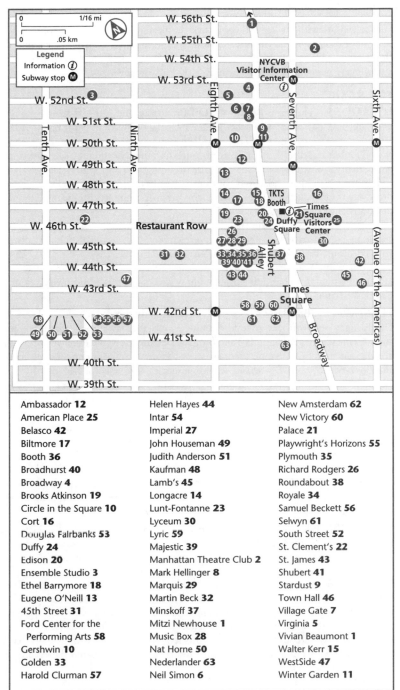

| | | |
|---|---|---|
| Ambassador **12** | Helen Hayes **44** | New Amsterdam **62** |
| American Place **25** | Intar **54** | New Victory **60** |
| Belasco **42** | Imperial **27** | Palace **21** |
| Biltmore **17** | John Houseman **49** | Playwright's Horizons **55** |
| Booth **36** | Judith Anderson **51** | Plymouth **35** |
| Broadhurst **40** | Kaufman **48** | Richard Rodgers **26** |
| Broadway **4** | Lamb's **45** | Roundabout **38** |
| Brooks Atkinson **19** | Longacre **14** | Royale **34** |
| Circle in the Square **10** | Lunt-Fontanne **23** | Samuel Beckett **56** |
| Cort **16** | Lyceum **30** | Selwyn **61** |
| Douglas Fairbanks **53** | Lyric **59** | South Street **52** |
| Duffy **24** | Majestic **39** | St. Clement's **22** |
| Edison **20** | Manhattan Theatre Club **2** | St. James **43** |
| Ensemble Studio **3** | Mark Hellinger **8** | Shubert **41** |
| Ethel Barrymore **18** | Marquis **29** | Stardust **9** |
| Eugene O'Neill **13** | Martin Beck **32** | Town Hall **46** |
| 45th Street **31** | Minskoff **37** | Village Gate **7** |
| Ford Center for the | Mitzi Newhouse **1** | Virginia **5** |
| Performing Arts **58** | Music Box **28** | Vivian Beaumont **1** |
| Gershwin **10** | Nat Horne **50** | Walter Kerr **15** |
| Golden **33** | Nederlander **63** | WestSide **47** |
| Harold Clurman **57** | Neil Simon **6** | Winter Garden **11** |

in many ways, especially with dramas, being away from Broadway can mean they're freer to be hits without being huge draws. Witness such recent powerhouse hits as Margaret Edson's *Wit* and the interactive performance-art hit *De La Guarda,* plus the aforementioned longrunners *Blue Man Group* and *Stomp!* And remember—*Rent* is just one of many phenomenons that made its debut off-Broadway.

## THE BASICS

**LOCATIONS**    The terms **Broadway, Off-Broadway,** and **Off-Off-Broadway** refer to theater size, pay scales, and other arcane details, not location. Most of the Broadway theaters are in Times Square, huddled around the thoroughfare the scene is named for but not directly on it: Instead, you'll find them dotting the side streets that intersect Broadway, mostly in the mid-40s between Sixth and Eighth avenues (44th and 45th streets in particular) but running north as far as 53rd Street. There's even a Broadway theater outside Times Square: the Vivian Beaumont in Lincoln Center, at Broadway and 65th Street.

Off-Broadway, on the other hand, is not that exacting an expression. With the increasing popularization of off-the-beaten-track productions, the distinction between off- and off-off-Broadway productions has become fuzzier. Off-off-Broadway shows tend to be more avant-garde, experimental, or nomadic. Off- and off-off-Broadway productions tend to be based downtown, but pockets show up in Midtown and on the Upper West Side.

**TIMETABLES**    Broadway shows tend to keep pretty regular schedules. There are usually eight performances a week: Evening shows Tuesday through Saturday, plus matinees on Wednesday, Saturday, and Sunday. Evening shows are usually at 8pm, and matinees are usually at 2pm on Wednesday and Saturday and 3pm on Sunday. Schedules do vary, however; *Les Misérables,* for instance, also stages a Monday show to accommodate the seemingly endless tourist demand. And times often vary depending on the show's length; the 1999 staging of *The Iceman Cometh* started nightly at 7pm to accommodate the marathon $4^1/_4$-hour running time. Shows usually start right on the dot or within a few minutes of starting time; if you arrive late, you might have to wait until after the first act to take your seat, which can really be a drag.

Off-Broadway shows tend to follow a similar daily schedule and time clock, but you'll find more variations. Off-Broadway theaters usually stage an additional Sunday evening show. Some also stage 11:30pm shows on Friday and Saturday to accommodate the downtown crowds who could care less about the late hour (this is the exception, not the rule).

**TICKET PRICES**    Ticket prices for Broadway shows vary dramatically. Expect to pay for good seats; the high end for any given show is likely to be between $60 and $100. The cheapest end of the price range can be as low as $20 or as high as $50, depending on the theater configuration. If you're buying tickets at the very low end of a wide price range, be aware that you might be buying obstructed-view seats. If all tickets are the same price or the range is small, you can pretty much count on all of the seats being pretty good. Otherwise, price is your barometer. Note that leg room can be tight in these old theaters, and you'll usually get more in the orchestra seats.

Off-Broadway and off-off-Broadway shows tend to be cheaper, with tickets often as low as $10 or $15. However, seats for the most established shows and those with star power can command prices as high as $50.

Don't let price be a deterrent to enjoying the theater. There are ways to pay less if you're willing to make the effort and be flexible, with a few choices at hand as to what you'd like to see. Read on.

## TOP TICKET-BUYING TIPS

**PURCHASING TICKETS BEFORE YOU LEAVE HOME**    If you want to guarantee yourself a seat at a particular show by buying them in advance, it's almost impossible to get around paying full price. (The only exception is to register for one or more of the online theater clubs, which offer advance-purchase discounts to members; see "Bargain Alert—How to Save on Theater Tickets," below.) Phone ahead or go online for tickets to the most successful or popular shows as far in advance as you can; with shows such as *The Lion King,* it's never too early.

Buying tickets can be simple, if the show you want to see isn't sold out. You need only call such general numbers as **TeleCharge** (☎ **212/239-6200;** www.telecharge. com), which handles most Broadway and off-Broadway shows and some concerts; or **TicketMaster** (☎ **212/307-4100;** www.ticketmaster.com), which also handles Broadway and off-Broadway shows and most concerts. If you're an American Express gold or platinum card holder, check to see whether tickets are being sold through **American Express Gold Card Events** (☎ **800/448-TIKS;** www.americanexpress. com/gce). You'll pay full price, but AmEx has access to blocks of preferred seating that are specifically set aside for gold-card holders, so you might be able to get tickets to a show that's otherwise sold out or better seats than you would be able to buy through other outlets.

Owned by Cameron Mackintosh (producer behind such megahits as *Cats, Phantom of the Opera, Les Misérables,* and *Miss Saigon*), **Theatre Direct International (TDI)** is a ticket broker that sells tickets to select Broadway and off-Broadway shows direct to individuals and travel agents. Check to see whether they have seats to the shows you're interested in by calling ☎ **800/334-8457** or pointing your Web browser to **www.theatredirect.com.** (Disregard the discounted prices, unless you're buying for a group of 20 or more; tickets are full price for smaller quantities.) With a service charge of $15 per ticket, you'll do a bit better by trying TicketMaster or TeleCharge first, but because they act as a consolidator, TDI may have tickets left for a specific show even if the major outlets don't.

Other reputable ticket brokers include **Keith Prowse & Co.** (☎ **800/669-8687** or 914/328-2357; www.keithprowse.com) and **Global Tickets Edwards & Edwards** (☎ **800/223-6108**). For a list of other licensed ticket brokers recommended by the New York City Visitor's Bureau, get a copy of the Official NYC Visitor Kit (see "Visitor Information" in chapter 2 for details). All kinds of brokers list ads in the Sunday *New York Times* and other publications, but don't take the risk. Stick with a licensed broker recommended by the NYCVB.

If you don't want to pay a service charge or if you want to secure tickets before you come to New York, try calling the **box office** directly. Broadway theaters don't sell tickets over the telephone, but a good number of off-Broadway theaters do.

**WHEN YOU ARRIVE**    Once you arrive in the city, getting your hands on tickets can take some street smarts—and failing those, good hard cash. Even if it seems unlikely that seats are available, always **call the box office** before attempting any other route. Single seats are often easiest to obtain, so people willing to sit apart might find themselves in luck.

You should also try the **Broadway Ticket Center,** run by the League of American Theaters and Producers (the same people behind the Broadway Line, above) at the Times Square Visitors Center, 1560 Broadway, between 46th and 47th streets (open daily 8am to 8pm). They often have tickets available for otherwise sold-out shows and only charge $4.50 extra per ticket.

# Bargain Alert—How to Save on Theater Tickets

If you employ a little patience, flexibility, and know-how, there are ways to pay less than full price for your theater tickets—sometimes a lot less.

Your best bet is to try before you go. You might be able to purchase **reduced-price theater tickets** in advance over the phone (or in person at the box office) by joining one or more of the online theater clubs. Membership is free and can garner you discounts of up to 50% on select Broadway and off-Broadway shows. I like the extensive list of offers that's always available from the **Playbill Club** (**www.playbillclub.com**) best, but great deals are also available to registered club-members at **TheaterMania** (**www.theatermania.com**); **Theatre.com's** Broadway Circle Club (**www.theatre.com**); and **Broadway.com** (**www.broadway.com**), a new site that should be up and running by the time you read this. And remember—there's no harm in joining more than one club. For further details, see p. 57 in "Planning Your Trip: An Online Directory."

The Theatre Development Fund runs two separate programs: a **Student Mailing List** that offers deep discounts—up to 75%—on individual theater tickets to college students, and a **Student Voucher Program,** in which students can pay $28 for four vouchers that they can use to attend any four participating performing arts events of their choosing—thus, it works out to just $7 per show. Visit the Web site (**www.tdf.org**) for details and to sign up.

Broadway shows—even blockbusters—sometimes have a limited number of cheaper tickets set aside for **students and seniors,** and they might even be available at the last minute; call the box office direct to inquire. *Rent* has offered all kinds of bargains to keep younger theatergoers coming.

The best deal in town on **same-day tickets** for both Broadway and off-Broadway shows is at the ✪ **Times Square Theatre Centre,** better known as the **TKTS booth,** run by the nonprofit Theatre Development Fund in the heart of the Theater District at Duffy Square, 47th Street and Broadway (open 3 to 8pm for evening performances, 10am to 2pm for Wednesday and Saturday matinees, from 11am on Sunday for all performances). Tickets for that day's performances are usually offered at half price, with a few reduced only 25%, plus a $2.50 per

---

If you want to deal with a licensed broker direct, **Global Tickets Edwards & Edwards** has a local office that accommodates drop-ins at 234 W. 44th St., between Seventh and Eighth avenues (☎ 212/398-1432; open Mon–Sat 9am–8pm).

If you buy from one of the **scalpers** selling tickets in front of the theater, you're taking a risk. They might be perfectly legitimate—a couple from the 'burbs whose companions couldn't make it for the evening, say—but they could be swindlers passing off fakes for big money. It's a risk that's not worth taking.

One preferred **insiders' trick** is to make the rounds of Broadway theaters at about 6pm, when unclaimed house seats are made available to the public. These tickets—reserved for VIPs, friends of the cast, the press, or other hangers-on—offer great locations and are sold at face value.

Also, note that **Mondays** are often good days to cop big-name show tickets. Although most theaters are dark on that day, some of the most sought-after choices aren't. Locals are at home on the first night of the work week, so all the odds are in your favor. Your chances will always be better on weeknights, or for Wednesday matinees, rather than weekends.

ticket service charge. Boards outside the ticket windows list available shows; you're unlikely to find certain perennial or outsize smashes, but most other shows turn up. Cash and traveler's checks only are accepted. There's often a huge line, so show up early for the best availability and be prepared to wait—but frankly, the crowd is all part of the fun. If you don't care much what you see and you'd just like to go to a show, you can walk right up to the window later in the day; something's always available.

Run by the same group and offering the same discounts is the **TKTS Lower Manhattan Theatre Centre,** on the mezzanine of 2 World Trade Center (open Monday to Friday 11am to 5pm, Saturday 11am to 3:30pm). All the same policies apply. The advantages to coming down here are that the lines are generally shorter; your wait is sheltered indoors; and matinee tickets are available the day before, so you can plan ahead.

Note that reconstruction is set to begin on the Times Square booth in mid-2000. Therefore, it's a good idea to call NYC/Onstage at ☎ **212/768-1818** and press "8" for the latest TKTS information, as there might be a temporary relocation or other news you should be aware of before you head to the booth.

Many shows, particularly long-running ones such as *Phantom of the Opera,* offer special **two-fers,** which allow you to purchase two tickets for the price of one for certain performances. You can find these coupons at many places in the city: hotel lobbies, in banks, even at restaurant cash registers. A guaranteed bet is the Times Square Visitors Center, 1560 Broadway, between 46th and 47th streets. They're also likely to be available at the new NYCVB Visitor Information Center at 810 Seventh Avenue, between 52nd and 53rd streets.

There are so many options for getting cut-rate tickets that virtually any visitor can fill up a week's vacation with shows seen on the cheap. But keep in mind that there is never any guarantee that last-minute tickets or discounts will be available to any given show, and they might not be. If your heart is set on seeing a specific show, save yourself the possible heartache and splurge on full-price advance-purchase tickets.

## 2 Opera, Classical Music & Dance

In addition to the listings below, check out what's happening at **Carnegie Hall** and the **Brooklyn Academy of Music,** two of the most respected—and enjoyable—multi-functional performing arts venues in the city. The marvelous **92nd Street Y** also regularly hosts events that are worth considering. I've listed the operatic and symphonic companies housed at **Lincoln Center** below; also check the center's full calendar for all offerings. See "Major Concert Halls & Landmark Venues" later in this chapter.

### OPERA

New York has grown into one of the world's major opera centers. The season generally runs from September to May, but there's usually something going on at any time of year.

In addition to the choices below, you might want to see what's on from the **New York Grand Opera** (☎ 212/245-8837; www.csis.pace.edu/newyorkgrandopera), which often puts on free Verdi productions at Central Park's SummerStage in July and August as well as workshop programs throughout the year at Carnegie Hall's Weill Recital Hall and the company's own hall.

Fans with an ear for experimentalism might want to consider **American Opera Projects** (☎ 212/431-8102), which develops new American operas and other innovative projects and showcases them at various venues around town. Tickets run $10 to $30, and discounts are usually available for students and seniors.

**Amato Opera Theatre.** 319 Bowery (at 2nd St.). ☎ **212/228-8200.** www.amato.org. Subway: 6 to Bleecker St.; F to Second Ave.

This cozy, off-the-beaten-track venue for mostly Italian opera, run by husband-and-wife team Anthony and Sally Amato, functions as a showcase for talented young American singers. The intimate 100-plus-seat house celebrated its 50th season last year amid a rising reputation and increasing ticket sales. The staple is full productions of Italian classics—Verdi's *La Traviata*, Puccini's *Madame Butterfly*, Bizet's *Carmen*, with an occasional Mozart tossed in—at great prices ($25). Performances, usually held on Saturday and Sunday, regularly sell out, so it's a good idea to reserve three weeks in advance. Once a month at the 11:30am show on Saturday, "Opera in Brief" offers fully costumed, kid-length versions of the classics interwoven with narration so Mom and Dad have a palatable forum in which to introduce the little ones to the music form. At $15 or so per ticket, these matinee performances are wallet-friendly, too.

✪ **Metropolitan Opera.** At the Metropolitan Opera House, Lincoln Center, Broadway and 64th St. ☎ **212/362-6000.** www.metopera.org. Subway: 1, 9 to 66th St.

Tickets can cost a small fortune (anywhere from $25 to $275), but for full productions of the classic repertory and a schedule packed with world-class grand sopranos and tenors, the Met Opera ranks first in the world. Millions are spent on fabulous stagings, and the venue itself is an acoustic wonder. To guarantee that its audience understands the words, the Met has outfitted the back of each row of seats with screens for subtitles—translation help for those who want it, minimum intrusion for those who don't. James Levine continues his role as the orchestra's brilliant and popular conductor.

The Met Opera has a number of programs that allow access to cut-rate tickets to operagoers; for details, see **"Last-Minute & Discount Ticket-Buying Tips"** on p. 306.

✪ **New York City Opera.** At the New York State Theater, Lincoln Center, Broadway and 64th St. ☎ **212/870-5570** (information or box office), or 212/307-4100 for TicketMaster. www.nycopera.com or www.ticketmaster.com. Subway: 1, 9 to 66th St.

This superb company has a delightful duality to its approach: It not only attempts to reach a wider audience than the Metropolitan with its more "human" scale and significantly lower prices ($20 to $95), but it's also committed to adventurous premieres, newly composed operas, the occasional avant-garde work, American musicals presented as operettas (Stephen Sondheim's *Sweeney Todd* is an example), and even obscure works by mainstream or lesser-known composers. Its mix stretches from the "easy" works of Puccini and Verdi and Gilbert & Sullivan to the more challenging oeuvres of Arnold Schönberg and Philip Glass.

**New York Gilbert and Sullivan Players.** At Symphony Space, Broadway and 95th St. ☎ **212/864-5400** or 212/769-1000. www.nygasp.org. Subway: 1, 2, 3, 9 to 96th St.

If you're in the mood for light-hearted operetta, try this lively company, which specializes in Gilbert and Sullivan's 19th-century English comic works. Tickets are relatively affordable, in the $25 to $50 range. The annual calendar generally runs from October through April and includes four shows a year.

## Bargain Alert—The Classical Learning Curve

The **Juilliard School,** 60 Lincoln Center Plaza (Broadway at 65th Street; ☎ 212/769-7406; www.juilliard.edu), the nation's premier music education institution, sponsors about 550 performances of the highest quality—at the lowest prices—throughout the school year. With most concerts free and $15 as a maximum ticket price, Juilliard is one of New York's greatest cultural bargains. In addition to classical concerts, Juilliard offers other music as well as drama, dance, opera, and interdisciplinary works. The best way to find out about the wide array of productions is to call, visit the school's Web site (click on CALENDAR OF EVENTS), or consult the bulletin board in the building's lobby. Watch for master classes and discussions open to the public featuring celebrity guest teachers.

The well-regarded **Manhattan School of Music,** at Broadway and 122nd Street (☎ 212/749-2802; www.msmnyc.edu) hosts regular student concerts as well as daily recitals during the academic year. Most performances are absolutely free, and the top ticket price is $20. In addition to orchestral and chamber music, the school is highly regarded for its contemporary music and jazz as well as musical theater programs, so performances run the gamut. Look for free master classes here, too. Call the box office weekdays between 9am and 5pm for the latest schedule.

## CLASSICAL MUSIC

**❁ Bargemusic.** At the Fulton Ferry Landing (just south of the Brooklyn Bridge), Brooklyn. ☎ **718/624-2083** or 718/624-4061. www.bargemusic.org. Subway: 2, 3 to Clark St.

Many thought Olga Bloom peculiar, if not deranged, when she transformed a 40-year-old barge into a chamber-music concert hall. More than 20 years later, Bargemusic is an internationally renowned recital room boasting more than 100 first-rate chamber music performances a year. Olga trawls from the pool of visiting musicians who love the chance to play in such an intimate setting, so the roster regularly includes highly respected international musicians as well as local stars such as violinist Cynthia Phelps. There are three shows per week, on Thursday and Friday evenings at 7:30pm and Sunday afternoons at 4pm. The musicians perform on a small stage in a cherry-paneled, fireplace-lit room accommodating 130. Bloom herself places name cards on the red-velvet cushions of the folding chairs, and there's bread and cheese, cakes and cookies, and wine and coffee. The barge might creak a bit and an occasional boat might speed by, but the music rivals what you'll find in almost any other New York concert hall—and the panoramic view through the glass wall behind the stage can't be beat. Neither can the price: Tickets are just $23 ($20 seniors, $15 students). Reserve well in advance.

**❁ New York Philharmonic.** At Avery Fisher Hall, Lincoln Center, Broadway at 65th St. ☎ **212/ 875-5030,** or Center Charge (212/721-6500) for tickets. www.newyorkphilharmonic.org. Subway: 1, 9 to 66th St.

Symphony-wise, you'd be hard-pressed to do better than the country's oldest orchestra, under the strict but ebullient guidance of music director Kurt Masur. Because he has announced that he'll retire in 2002, don't miss this final chance to see the maestro leading his orchestra. Highlights of the 2000–01 season include the Mendelssohn Festival in October; Bach's *Christmas* oratorio performed by the Choir of St. Thomas Church, the Leipzig choir Bach himself once directed; and Dame Felicity Lott singing an all-Strauss program conducted by Mazur to close the season in June.

## Last-Minute & Discount Ticket-Buying Tips

The majority of seats at **New York Philharmonic** performances are sold to sub-scribers, with just a few left for the rest of us. But there are still ways to get tickets. When subscribers can't attend, they can turn their tickets back to the theaters, which then resell them at the last moment. These can be in the most coveted rows of the orchestra. The hopeful form "cancellation lines" two hours or more before curtain time for a crack at returned tickets on a first-come, first-served basis. And periodi-cally, a number of **same-day orchestra tickets** are set aside at the philharmonic and sold first thing (10am weekdays, 1pm Saturdays, or noon if there's a matinee) for $25 a pop (maximum 2). **Senior/student/disabled rush tickets** might be available for $10 (maximum 2) on concert day, but never at Friday matinees or Saturday evening performances. To check availability for all performances, call **Audience Ser-vices** at ☎ **212/875-5656.**

Note that Lincoln Center's **Alice Tully Hall** (where the Chamber Music Society performs and other concerts are held), the **Metropolitan Opera,** the **New York City Opera,** and **Carnegie Hall** offer similar last-minute and discount programs (the **New York City Ballet** offers student rush tickets only). Call the box office first to check on same-day availability before heading to the theater—or, if you're willing to risk coming away empty-handed, be there at opening time for first crack.

If all else fails and your heart is set on seeing a sold-out performance, you can call or go to the box office to see if **standing room** is available (usually around $20). The best standing room is at the Met, where you get to lean against plush red bars. (Don't tell the ushers I told you, but if subscribers fail to show, I've seen standees with eagle eyes fill the empty seats at intermission.)

There's a summer season in July, when themed classics brighten the hall, as well as summer concerts in Central Park that are worth checking into.

Tickets range from $13 to $110; opt for a rush-hour concert or a matinee for the lowest across-the-board prices. The acoustics of the hall are such that, at the mid-range price points, I prefer the second tier (especially the boxes) over the more expensive rear orchestra seats. Go cheap if you have to; you're sure to enjoy the program from any vantage.

## DANCE

In general, dance seasons run September to February and then March to June, but there's almost always something happening. In addition to the major troupes below, some other names to keep in mind are the **Brooklyn Academy of Music,** the **92nd Street Y Tisch Center for the Arts, Radio City Music Hall,** and **Town Hall** (see "Major Concert Halls & Landmark Venues" below).

In addition to regular appearances at City Center (below), the **American Ballet Theatre** (www.abt.org), takes up residence at Lincoln Center's Metropolitan Opera House (☎ **212/362-6000**) for eight weeks each spring. The same venue also hosts such visiting companies as the Kirov, Royal, and Paris Opéra ballets.

For particularly innovative works, see what's on at the **Dance Theater Workshop,** in the Bessie Schönberg Theater, 219 W. 19th St. (☎ **212/691-8500** or 212/924-0077; www.dtw.org), a first-rate launching pad for nearly a quarter-century (tick-ets $15 to $20); and **Danspace Project,** at St. Mark's Church, 131 E. 10th St. (☎ **212/674-8194**), whose performances lean toward the seriously avant-garde, with ticket prices falling between free and $20, depending on the performance.

**City Center.** 131 W. 55th St. (btw. Sixth and Seventh aves.). ☎ **877/581-1212** or 212/581-1212. www.citycenter.org. Subway: N, R or B, Q to 57th St.; B, D, E to Seventh Ave.

Modern dance usually takes center stage in this Moorish dome-topped performing arts palace. The companies of Merce Cunningham, Martha Graham, Paul Taylor, Alvin Ailey, Twyla Tharp, and the American Ballet Theatre are often on the calendar. Don't expect cutting edge, but do expect excellence. Tickets generally run $25 to $65; sightlines are terrific from all corners, so you won't lose with cheaper tickets.

**Dance Theatre of Harlem.** Everett Center for Performing Arts, 466 W. 152nd St. (btw. Amsterdam and Convent aves.). ☎ **212/690-2800.** Subway: 1, 9, A, B, C, D to 145th St.

In addition to presenting a full slate of performances at City Center (above), the wonderful Arthur Mitchell–led Dance Theatre of Harlem hosts a open house the second Sunday of the month at 3pm. These creative and fun-filled afternoons are the bargain of the dance world at $8 ($4 for seniors) and often include both national and rising talents.

**۞ Joyce Theater.** 175 Eighth Ave. (at 19th St.). ☎ **212/242-0800.** www.joyce.org. Subway: C, E to 23rd St.; 1, 9 to 18th St.

Housed in an old art deco movie house, the Joyce has grown into one of the world's greatest modern dance institutions. You can see everything from Native American ceremonial dance to the innovative works of Pilobolus. In residence annually is Eliot Feld's ballet company, Ballet Tech, which WQXR radio's Francis Mason called "better than a whole month of namby-pamby classical ballets." The Joyce has a second space, **Joyce SoHo,** at 155 Mercer St., between Houston and Prince streets (☎ **212/ 431-9233**), where you can see rising young dancers and experimental works in the intimacy of a 70-seat performance space. Tickets are usually $32 to $35 at the main theater, $10 to $20 (often $15 or less) at the SoHo space.

**۞ New York City Ballet.** At the New York State Theater at Lincoln Center, Broadway and 64th St. ☎ **212/870-5570.** www.nycballet.com. Subway: 1, 9 to 66th St.

Highly regarded for its unsurpassed technique, the New York City Ballet is the world's best. The company renders with happy regularity the works of two of America's most important choreographers: George Balanchine, its founder, and Jerome Robbins. Under the direction of Ballet Master-in-Chief Peter Martins, the troupe continues to expand its repertoire and performs to a wide variety of classical and modern music. The cornerstone of the annual season is the Christmastime production of *The Nutcracker*, for which tickets usually become available in early October. Ticket prices for most events run $16 to $72.

# 3 Major Concert Halls & Landmark Venues

**Apollo Theatre.** 253 W. 125th St. (btw. Adam Clayton Powell and Frederick Douglass blvds.). ☎ **212/749-5838.** Subway: 1, 9 to 125th St.

Built in 1914, the Apollo had its heyday in the 1930s when Count Basie, Duke Ellington, Ella Fitzgerald, and Billie Holiday were on the bill. By the 1970s, it had fallen on hard times, but a 1986 restoration breathed new life into the historic Harlem landmark. Today the Apollo is again internationally renowned as a showcase for mainly African-American music, from hip-hop acts to Wynton Marsalis's "Jazz for Young People" events. Wednesday's "Amateur Night at the Apollo" are loud, fun-filled nights that draw in young talents from all over the country with high hopes of making it big (a very young Lauryn Hill started out here—and didn't win!). Tickets are $13 to $21, slightly higher for finalist shows.

# Park It! Shakespeare, Music & Other Free Fun

As the weather warms, New York culture comes outdoors to play.

**Shakespeare in the Park,** held at Central Park's Delacorte Theater, is by far the city's most famous alfresco arts event. Organized by Joseph Papp's Public Theater, the schedule consists of two summertime productions, usually one of the Bard's plays and a second revival (such as 1997's restaging of the 1944 musical *On the Town*). Productions usually feature big names and range from traditional interpretations (Andre Braugher as an armor-clad *Henry V*) to avant-garde presentations (Morgan Freeman, Tracey Ullman, and David Alan Grier in *Taming of the Shrew* as a wild-west showdown). Patrick Stewart's role as Prospero in *The Tempest* a few years back was so popular that the show was propelled onto Broadway for an award-winning run. The theater itself, next to Belvedere Castle near 79th Street and West Drive, is a dream; on a beautiful starry night, there's no better stage in town. Tickets are given out free on a first-come, first-served basis (two per person) at 1pm on the day of the performance at the theater. The Delacorte might have 1,881 seats, but each is a hot commodity, so people generally line up on the baseball field next to the theater about two to three hours in advance (even earlier if a big box-office name is involved). You can also pick up same-day tickets between 1 and 3pm at the Public Theater, at 425 Lafayette St., where the Shakespeare Festival continues throughout the year. For more information, call the Public Theater at ☎ 212/539-8500 or the Delacorte at ☎ 212/861-7277, or go online at **www.publictheater.org**.

Summer also brings the sound of music to Central Park, where the **New York Philharmonic** and the **Metropolitan Opera** regularly entertain beneath the stars; for the current schedule, call ☎ 212/360-3444, 212/875-5709, or 212/362-6000, or visit **www.lincolncenter.org**. But the most active music stage in the park is **SummerStage,** at Rumsey Playfield, midpark around 72nd Street, which has featured everyone from the Godfather of Soul, James Brown, to the angel poet of punk, Patti Smith. Recent offerings have included concerts by Hugh Masekela, the Sugarhill Gang, and the Jon Spencer Blues Explosion; and "Viva, Verdi!" festival performances by the New York Grand Opera; DJ sets;

---

✪ **Brooklyn Academy of Music.** 30 Lafayette Ave., Brooklyn. ☎ 718/636-4100. www.bam.org. Subway: 2, 3, 4, 5, D, Q to Atlantic Ave.; B, M, N, R to Pacific Ave.

BAM is the city's most renowned contemporary arts institution, presenting cutting-edge theater, opera, dance, and music. Offerings have included historically informed presentations of baroque opera by William Christie and Les Arts Florissants; Marianne Faithfull singing the music of Kurt Weill; dance by Mark Morris and Mikhail Baryshnikov; Philip Glass accompanying screenings of *Koyannisqatsi* and Lugosi's original *Dracula;* the Royal Dramatic Theater of Sweden directed by Ingmar Bergman; and many more experimental works by both renowned and lesser-known international artists as well as visiting companies. Tickets run anywhere from $5 to $95, depending on the performance.

Of particular note is the **Next Wave Festival,** from September through December, this country's foremost showcase for new experimental works (see the "Calendar of Events" in chapter 2). The **BAM Rose Cinemas** show first-run independent films, and cabaret nights; and more. The season usually lasts from mid-June to early August. Tickets aren't usually required (some big-name shows charge for admission, such as Lyle Lovett in the summer of '99); but donations are warmly accepted. Call the SummerStage hotline at ☎ **212/360-2777** or visit **www.summerstage.org**.

Central Park might be the most happening park in town, but the calendar of free events heats up throughout the city's parks in summertime. You can find out what's happening by calling ☎ **888/NY-PARKS** or 212/360-3456 or going online to **www.ci.nyc.ny.us/html/dpr**.

A full slate of free concerts, modern and classical dance, family events, and more are regularly offered year-round in Winter Garden and on the Plaza at the **World Financial Center** (☎ **212/945-0505;** www.worldfinancialcenter.com) in Battery Park City. Events are regularly held at the **South Street Seaport** (☎ **212/732-7678;** www.southstseaport.org) indoors at Pier 17 in winter, outdoors on Pier 16 in summer. You'll find free lunchtime and after-work alfresco performances on the plaza at the **World Trade Center** (☎ **212/435-4170**) from June through August.

Also in lower Manhattan, Trinity Church, on Broadway at Wall Street, hosts a chamber music and orchestral **Noonday Concert** series year-round each Thursday at 1pm and each Monday at noon at nearby St. Paul's Chapel, on Broadway at Fulton Street. This excellent program isn't quite free, but almost: A $2 contribution is requested. Call the concert hotline at ☎ **212/602-0747** or visit **www.trinitywallstreet.org**.

Additionally, most of the city's top museums offer free music and other programs after regular hours on select nights. The **Metropolitan Museum of Art** has an extensive slate of offerings each week, including live classical music and cocktails on Friday and Saturday evenings. There's lots of fun to be had at others as well, including the **Museum of Modern Art** and the **Brooklyn Museum of Art,** which hosts the remarkably eclectic **First Saturday** program monthly. For details, see the museum listings in chapter 7.

there's free live music every Thursday, Friday, and Saturday night at **BAMcafé,** which can range from atmospheric electronica from coronetist Graham Haynes to radical jazz from the Harold Rubin Trio to tango band Tanguardia! ($10 food minimum).

**Carnegie Hall.** 881 Seventh Ave. (at 57th St.). ☎ **212/247-7800.** www.carnegiehall.org. Subway: N, R or B, Q to 57th St.

Perhaps the world's most famous performance space, Carnegie Hall offers everything from grand classics to the music of Ravi Shankar. The 2,804-seat main hall welcomes visiting orchestras from across the country and the world. Many of the world's premier soloists and ensembles give recitals. The legendary hall is both visually and acoustically brilliant. There's also the intimate 284-seat **Weill Recital Hall,** usually used to showcase chamber music and vocal and instrumental recitals. Carnegie Hall has also reclaimed an ornate underground concert hall, occupied by a movie theater for 38 years, and is turning it into an intermediate-size third stage. For last-minute ticket-buying tips, see the feature on p. 306.

**✪ Lincoln Center for the Performing Arts.** 70 Lincoln Center Plaza (at Broadway and 64th St.). ☎ **212/546-2656.** www.lincolncenter.org. Subway: 1, 9 to 66th St.

New York is the world's premier performing arts city, and Lincoln Center is its premier institution. Whenever you're planning an evening's entertainment, check the offerings here—which can include opera, dance, symphonies, jazz, theater, film, and more, from the classics to the contemporary. Lincoln Center's many buildings serve as permanent homes to their own companies as well major stops for world-class performance troupes from around the globe.

Resident companies include the **Chamber Music Society of Lincoln Center** (☎ 212/875-5788; www.chamberlinc.org), which performs at Alice Tully Hall or the Daniel and Joanna S. Rose Rehearsal Studio, often in the company of such high-caliber guests as Anne Sofie Von Otter and Midori. The **Film Society of Lincoln Center** (☎ 212/875-5600; www.filmlinc.com) screens a daily schedule of movies at the Walter Reade Theater and hosts a number of important annual film and video festivals. **Jazz at Lincoln Center** (☎ 212/875-5299; www.jazzatlincolncenter.org) is led by the incomparable Wynton Marsalis, with the orchestra usually performing at Alice Tully Hall. The "Jazz at the Penthouse" program, where great jazz pianists such as Ellis Marsalis and Tommy Flanagan play in a spectacular candlelit setting overlooking the Hudson River, is the hottest jazz ticket in town. **Lincoln Center Theater** (☎ 212/362-7600; www.lct.org) consists of the Vivian Beaumont Theater, a modern and comfortable venue with great sightlines that has been home to much good Broadway drama, and the Mitzi E. Newhouse Theater, a well-respected off-Broadway house that has also boasted numerous theatrical triumphs. Past seasons have included excellent productions of Tom Stoppard's *Arcadia* and David Hare's one-man show, *Via Dolorosa.* For details on the **Metropolitan Opera,** the **New York City Opera,** the **New York City Ballet,** the **Juilliard School,** the phenomenal **New York Philharmonic,** and the **American Ballet Theatre,** which takes up residence here every spring, see "Opera, Classical Music & Dance" earlier in this chapter.

Most of the companies' **major seasons** run from about September or October to April, May, or June. **Special series** such as Great Performers and the new American Songbook, showcasing classic American show tunes, help round out the calendar. Indoor and outdoor events are held in warmer months: July sees **Midsummer Night's Swing** with partner dancing, lessons, and music on the plaza; **Mostly Mozart** attracts talents like Alicia de Larrocha and André Watts; the three-year-old **Lincoln Center Festival,** celebrating the best of the performing arts; **Lincoln Center Out-of-Doors,** a series of free alfresco music and dance performances; the **New York Film Festival,** and more. Check the "Calendar of Events" in chapter 2 or Lincoln Center's Web site to see what special events will be on while you're in town.

**Tickets** for all performances at Avery Fisher and Alice Tully halls can be purchased through **CenterCharge** (☎ 212/721-6500) or online at www.lincolncenter.org. Tickets for all Lincoln Center Theater performances can be purchased through **TeleCharge** (☎ 212/239-6200; www.telecharge.com). Tickets for New York State Theater productions (New York City Opera and Ballet companies) are available through **TicketMaster** (☎ 212/307-4100; www.ticketmaster.com), and tickets for films showing at the Walter Reade Theater can be bought via **Movie Phone** (☎ 212/777-FILM; www.777film.com; the theater code is 954).

For last-minute full-price and discount ticket-buying tips, see p. 306.

**Madison Square Garden.** On Seventh Ave. from 31st to 33rd sts. ☎ **212/465-MSG1.** www.thegarden.com. Subway: 1, 2, 3, 9, A, C,

Monsters of rock and pop ranging from KISS to the Backstreet Boys regularly fill this 20,000-seat arena, which is also home to the Knicks, the Rangers, and the WNBA's Liberty. A cavernous concrete hulk, it's better suited to sports than to concerts or in-the-round events such as the Ice Capades, Ringling Bros. Barnum & Bailey Circus, or the International Cat Show. End up in back, and you'd better bring binoculars.

You'll find far better sightlines at **The Theater at Madison Square Garden,** an amphitheater-style auditorium with 5,600 seats that has also played host to some major pop stars, from Barbra Streisand to Bob Dylan to Oasis. Watch for possibly annual stagings of *The Wizard of Oz* and *A Christmas Carol,* plus family shows such as *Sesame Street Live.*

The box office is located at Seventh Avenue and 32nd Street. Or you can purchase tickets through **TicketMaster** (☎ 212/307-7171; www.ticketmaster.com).

**❂ 92nd Street Y Tisch Center for the Arts.** 1395 Lexington Ave. (at 92nd St.). **☎ 212/996-1100.** www.92ndsty.org. Subway: 4, 5, 6 to 86th St.; 6 to 96th St.

This generously endowed community center offers a phenomenal slate of top-rated cultural happenings, from classical to folk to jazz to world music to cabaret to lyric theater and literary readings. Just because you see "Y," don't think this place is small potatoes: The greatest classical performers—Isaac Stern, Janos Starker, Nadja Salerno-Sonnenberg—give recitals here. In addition, the full concert calendar often includes luminaries such as Max Roach, John Williams, and Judy Collins; Jazz at the Y from Dick Hyman and guests; the long-standing Chamber Music at the Y series; the classical Music from the Jewish Spirit series; and regular cabaret programs. The lectures and literary readings calendar is unparalleled, with featured speakers ranging from Lorne Michaels to David Halberstam to Tim Koogle (CEO of Yahoo!) to Katie Couric to Susan Sontag to Charles Frazier to the Reverend Jesse Jackson to . . . the list goes on and on. The poetry center calendar has included V.S. Naipaul, E.L. Doctorow, and James Earl Jones reading from *American Slave Narratives.* There's a regular schedule of modern dance, too, through the Harkness Dance Project. Best of all, readings and lectures are usually priced between $12 and $20 for non-members (although select lectures can be priced as high as $30), dance is usually $15 to $20, and concert tickets generally go for $25 to $35—half or a third of what you'd pay at comparable venues.

**Radio City Music Hall.** 1260 Sixth Ave. (at 50th St.). **☎ 212/247-4777,** or 212/307-7171 for TicketMaster. www.radiocity.com or www.ticketmaster.com. Subway: B, D, F, Q to 49th–50th sts./Rockefeller Center.

This stunning 6,200-seat art deco theater, with interior design by Donald Deskey, opened in 1932. After an extensive renovation in 1999, legendary Radio City continues to be a choice venue, where the theater alone adds a dash of panache to any performance. Star of the Christmas season is the **Radio City Music Hall Christmas Spectacular,** starring the legendary Rockettes. Visiting pop chart-toppers, from Luis Miguel to Radiohead, also perform here. Thanks to perfect acoustics and uninterrupted sightlines, there's hardly a bad seat in the house. The theater also hosts dance performances, family entertainment, and a number of annual awards shows—such as the Essence Awards, the GQ Man of the Year Awards, and anything MTV is holding in town—so this is a good place to celeb-spot on show nights.

**Town Hall.** 123 W. 43rd St. (btw. Sixth and Seventh aves.). **☎ 212/840-2824,** or 212/307-4100 for TicketMaster. www.the-townhall-nyc.org or www.ticketmaster.com. Subway: 1, 2, 3, 7, 9, N, R, S to 42nd St./Times Sq.; B, D, F, Q to 42nd St.

This intimate landmark theater—a National Historic Site designed by McKim, Mead, & White—is blessed with outstanding acoustics, making it an ideal place to enjoy many kinds of performances. The calendar regularly includes such offerings as American tap and Brazilian tango exhibitions; Native American music and global rhythms; comedy from the Kids in the Hall Reunion Tour or Bill Maher; live tapings of "A Prairie Home Companion" with Garrison Keillor; lectures by luminaries such as Marianne Williamson and Frank Gehry; concerts by the likes of David Sandborn or the reunited Blondie; symphony, opera, and ballet companies from around the world; and much more. The grade is extremely steep, so unless Lurch sits in front of you, fellow audience members shouldn't block your view. Ticket prices vary depending on the show but are usually less than $35.

## 4  Live Rock, Jazz, Blues & More

For the latest goings-on at these top venues and others around town, check the publications discussed at the opening of this chapter as well as the online sources outlined in the "Planning Your Trip: An Online Directory."

For coverage of **Madison Square Garden,** the **Theater at MSG,** and **Town Hall,** see "Major Concert Halls & Landmark Venues," above. Another large venue that regularly hosts pop-music concerts is the 2,700-seat art-deco **Beacon Theatre,** 2124 Broadway, at 74th Street (☎ 212/496-7070; www.livetonight.com). General-admission halls that serve as popular stages for national rock, pop, and hip-hop acts are **Hammerstein Ballroom,** at the Manhattan Center, 311 W. 34th St., between Eighth and Ninth avenues (☎ 212/564-4882); and **Roseland,** 239 W. 52nd St., between Broadway and Eighth Avenue (☎ 212/777-6800 or 212/247-0200; www. roselandballroom.com).

### MIDSIZE & MULTIGENRE VENUES

Expect to pay a little more for shows at these venues than you would at smaller clubs—anywhere from $10 to $25, depending on the venue and the act.

**The Bottom Line.** 15 W. 4th St. (at Mercer St.). ☎ 212/228-7880 or 212/228-6300. www.bottomlinecabaret.com. Subway: N, R to Astor Place; A, B, C, D, E, F, Q to W. 4th St.

The Bottom Line built its reputation by serving as showcase for the likes of Bruce Springsteen and the Ramones, and it remains one of the city's most well-respected venues. With table seating, decent burgers and fries, and a no-smoking policy, it's one of the city's most comfortable, too. The Bottom Line is renowned for its excellent sound and bookings of the best rock and folk singer/songwriters in the business. Loudon Wainwright, Marshall Crenshaw, Robyn Hitchcock, Lucinda Williams, June Carter Cash, Jimmy Webb, and David Johansen (and alter-ego Buster Poindexter, natch) are among the many artists that make this their favored venue for area appearances. There are usually two shows nightly. Tickets run $15 to $25, with most $20 or less.

✪ **Bowery Ballroom.** 6 Delancey St. (at Bowery). ☎ 212/533-2111. www.boweryballroom. com. Subway: F, J, M, Z to Delancey St.

New in 1998, this marvelous space is run by the same people behind the pleasing Mercury Lounge (see below). The Bowery space is bigger, accommodating a crowd of 500 or so, and even better. The stage is big and raised to allow good sightlines from every corner. The sound couldn't be better, and art deco details give the place a sophistication that doesn't come easy to general-admission halls. My favorite spot is on the balcony, which has its own bar and seating alcoves. Quickly becoming a favorite with

## Ticket-Buying Tips

Tickets for events at all larger theaters as well as at Hammerstein Ballroom, Roseland, Irving Plaza, S.O.B.'s, and Tramps can be purchased through **TicketMaster** (☎ 212/307-7171; www.ticketmaster.com).

Advance tickets for an increasing number of shows at smaller venues—including CBGB's (and CB's 313 Gallery), Bowery Ballroom, Mercury Lounge, and the Knitting Factory—can be purchased through **Ticketweb** (☎ 212/269-4TIX; www.ticketweb.com). Do note, however, that Ticketweb sells out in advance of actual ticket availability. Just because Ticketweb doesn't have tickets left for an event doesn't mean it's completely sold out, so be sure and check with the venue directly.

Even if a show is sold out it doesn't mean you're out of luck. There's usually a number of people hanging around at showtime trying to get rid of extra tickets for friends who didn't show, and they're usually happy to pass them off for face value. You'll also see professional scalpers, who are best avoided; it doesn't take a rocket scientist to tell the difference. Be aware, of course, that all forms of resale are illegal.

---

alt-rockers such as Vic Chesnutt, Travis, Cracker, Shudder to Think, and the marvelous Toshi Reagon as well as more established acts (Warren Zevon, Neil Finn, Patti Smith) who thrive in an intimate setting. **Money-Saving Tip:** Save on the service charge by buying advance tickets at Mercury's box office.

**Irving Plaza.** 17 Irving Place (1 block west of Third Ave. at 15th St.). ☎ **212/777-1224** or 212/777-6800. www.irvingplaza.com. Subway: 4, 5, 6, L, N, R to 14th St./Union Sq.

This high-profile mid-sized music hall is the prime stop for national-name rock bands that aren't quite big enough yet (or anymore) to sell out Hammerstein, Roseland, or the Beacon. Think Lit, Ween, Elliott Smith, the Mickey Hart Band, Cowboy Junkies, and Cheap Trick. From time to time, top-shelf artists perform: Bob Dylan, Willie Nelson, Trent Reznor, Tom Petty, and A.J. McLean of the Backstreet Boys have all played sellout vanity shows here. All in all, a very nice place to see a show, with a well-elevated stage and lots of open space even on sold-out nights. There's an upstairs balcony that offers unparalleled views, but come early for a spot. You can also buy tickets to Roseland events at the box office here.

**The Knitting Factory.** 74 Leonard St. (btw. Broadway and Church St.). ☎ **212/ 219-3006.** www.knittingfactory.com. Subway: 1, 9 to Franklin St.

New York's premier avant-garde music venue has four separate spaces, each showcasing performances ranging from experimental jazz and acoustic folk to spoken-word and poetry readings to out-there multimedia works. Regulars who use the Knitting Factory as their lab of choice include former Lounge Lizard John Lurie; around-the-bend experimentalist John Zorn; guitar gods Vernon Reid, Eliot Sharp, and David Torn; innovative sideman (to Tom Waits and Elvis Costello, among others) Marc Ribot; and Television's Richard Lloyd. (If these names mean nothing to you, chances are good that the Knitting Factory is not for you.) The schedule is peppered with edgy star turns from the likes of Yoko Ono, Taj Mahal, Faith No More's Mike Patton, and Lou Reed. There are often two sets a night in the remarkably pleasing main performance space, so it's easy to work a show around other activities. The Tap Bar offers an extensive list of microbrews and free live music, often soundtracking obscure silent films.

# Free Music

**Arlene Grocery** and **Rodeo Bar** are the city's top no-cover clubs, but they're far from the only free shows in town.

Others worth checking out include the **Living Room,** 84 Stanton St., at Allen Street (☎ 212/533-7235), an unpretentious bar/restaurant that's particularly good for acoustic acts (the sound system isn't great for electric acts). The pass-the-bucket policy allows you to contribute as much or as little as you want to the performers' earnings for the evening; the only requirement is a one-drink minimum. Also on the Lower East Side is comfy **Luna Lounge,** 171 Ludlow St., between Houston and Stanton streets (☎ 212/260-2323; www.lunalounge.com), which usually hosts at least two bands per night (including the occasional act that has made an alt-blip on MTV, such as Nada Surf). Monday's comedy night has become so popular that there's $5 cover, but a free drink (at press time, at least) softens the blow.

East Village stalwart **Sidewalk Café,** 94 Ave. A, at 6th Street (☎ 212/473-7373), hosts live bands in the back room most nights. Pretty good cheap eats and a mere $3 drink minimum serve as additional attractions for the monetarily challenged. And—like sibling club **Manitoba's** (p. 316), where country-rockers Beat Rodeo hold free court on Monday night—**Lakeside Lounge,** 162 Ave. B, between 10th and 11th streets (☎ 212/529-8463), also regularly hosts free live music.

One of my favorite coffeehouses, **Eureka Joe,** 168 Fifth Ave., at 22nd Street (☎ 212/741-7500), stages a mix of eclectic acoustic acts and readings in its cozy, velvet-curtained environs. The cappuccino, sandwiches, and pastries are great, and there's also a beer and wine bar.

Jazz fans will want to try **Arthur's Tavern,** 57 Grove St., at Seventh Avenue South (☎ 212/675-6879), a comfortable club and piano bar attracting a mixed gay-and-straight crowd. Beware of the drinks, however, which can be pricey. Harlem's **Showman's Cafe** (p. 318) is another great bet for free jazz.

There's almost never a cover at **C-Note,** 157 Ave. C, at 10th Street (☎ 212/677-8142). This smart Alphabet City bar books mainly jazz performers in the contemporary vein but has been branching into rock, roots, Latin music, and other genres of late.

Blues fans should reserve Sunday night for **Tribeca Blues,** 16 Warren St., between Broadway and Church Street (☎ 212/766-1070), when there's no cover for the all-star jam.

World music fans should check out the spicy sounds at the **Blue Lounge** at **Gonzalez y Gonzales** 625 Broadway, just north of Houston Street (☎ 212/473-8787; www.gonzygonz.com), which regularly hosts hot Latin acts. The gringo-friendly Mexican food is mediocre at best, but the frosty piña coladas are terrific—and there's never a cover.

Also keep in mind that a number of clubs offer free music one or more nights a week, such as **Cafe Wha?,** the **Continental,** the **Cooler, Chicago B.L.U.E.S.,** the **Baggot Inn, Tonic, Tribeca Blues,** and the **Internet Café;** the **Knitting Factory** offers free music in its Tap Bar. The easiest way to check for free events while you're in town is to peruse the music calendar in the weekly *Time Out New York,* which announces no-cover shows with an easy-to-spot FREE! Sunday and Monday nights, in particular, are big nights for freebies.

Remember that schedules and no-cover policies can change at any time, so always confirm in advance.

## ROCK & MIXED-MUSIC CLUBS

In addition to the choices below, rock fans on the hunt for diamonds in the rough might also want to see what's on at folk rock's legendary **Bitter End,** 147 Bleecker St. in the Village (☎ 212/673-7030; www.bitterend.com), where the cover seldom tops $5 (only the occasional local name jacks it up to $10); **Brownie's,** in the East Village at 169 Ave. A, between 10th and 11th (☎ 212/420-8392; www.browniesnyc.com), which gets points for quantity with its nightly jam-packed lineup ($6 to $8); punk rock's proudly skanky **Continental,** 25 Third Ave., at St. Mark's Place (☎ 212/529-6924; www.nytrash.com/continental), where artists such as Joey Ramone and Spacehog occasionally surface among the unknowns (usually between free and $5).

**✪ Arlene Grocery.** 95 Stanton St. (btw. Ludlow and Orchard sts.). ☎ 212/358-1633. www.arlene-grocery.com. Subway: F to Second Ave.

Live music is always free at this Lower East Side club, which boasts a friendly bar and a good sound system. Arlene Grocery primarily serves as a showcase for hot bands looking for a deal or promoting their self-pressed record. On occasion, bigger names such as Mark Eitzel and Milla Jovovich take the stage to exercise their chops, but it's far more likely that the act on stage will be brand new to you. Still, there's little risk involved, thanks to the no-cover policy and bookers who know what they're doing. The crowd is an easygoing mix of club hoppers, rock fans looking for a new fix, and industry scouts looking for new blood.

**The Baggot Inn.** 82 W. 3rd St. (btw. Thompson and Sullivan sts.). ☎ 212/477-0622. www.thebaggotinn.com. Subway: A, B, C, D, E, F, Q to W. 4th St.

This nice, easygoing pub has become one of the best showcases in the city for unknown acts, especially if you like quality acoustic and folk-rock music. Blues, Irish music, poetry, and acoustic jams and open-mike nights also regularly pop up on the calendar. The cover is always bargain-priced—from free to $5—and Happy Hour and nightly drink specials round out the entertainment value.

**Cafe Wha?** 115 MacDougal St. (btw. Bleecker and 3rd sts.). ☎ 212/254-3706. Subway: A, B, C, D, E, F, Q to W. 4th St.

You'll find a carefree crowd dancing in the aisles of this casual basement club just about any night of the week. From Wednesday through Sunday, the stage features the house's own Wha Band, which does an excellent job cranking out crowd-pleasing covers of familiar rock-and-roll hits from the '70s, '80s, and '90s; comedians from sister club the Comedy Cellar warm the crowd on Friday and Saturday. Monday night is the hugely popular Brazilian Dance Party, and Tuesday night is Vintage Funk Night. Expect to be surrounded by lots of suburban kids and out-of-towners on the weekends, but so what? You'll be having as much fun as they are. Cover charges range from $5 to $10, and Wednesdays and Sundays are free. Reservations are accepted.

**CBGB.** 315 Bowery (at Bleecker St.). ☎ 212/982-4052, or 212/677-0455 for CB's 313 Gallery. www.cbgb.com. Subway: 6 to Bleecker St.; F to Second Ave.

Don basic black, not because you'll be doing the right thing fashionwise but because you'll leave without visible residue. The original downtown rock club has seen better days, but no other spot is so rich with rock-and-roll history. This was the launching pad for New York punk and New Wave: the Ramones, Blondie, the Talking Heads,

Television, the Cramps, Patti Smith, Stiv Bators and the Dead Boys—everybody got started here. These days, you've never heard of most acts who perform here. Never mind—CB's still rocks. Expect loud and cynical, and you're unlikely to come away disappointed. Come early if you have hopes of actually seeing the stage. Covers usually run $3 to $10.

More today than yesterday is **CB's 313 Gallery,** a welcome spin-off that showcases alternative art on the walls and mostly acoustic singer/songwriters on stage. Same goes for CB's new **downstairs lounge,** which has a more cerebral alt edge to its sounds. Within striking distance of the history, but much more pleasant all the way around.

**The Cooler.** 416 W. 14th St. (btw. Ninth Ave. and Washington St.). ☎ **212/229-0785.** www.thecooler.com. Subway: A, C, E to 14th St.; L to Eighth Ave.

A former meatlocker in the heart of the Meat-Packing District has been transformed into this marvelously moody alt music club with a discriminating taste for the experimental; anything goes, as long as it's good. Offerings run the gamut from reggae, roots, and punk rock to club parties, electronica, and video art; artists can range from Afrika Bambaataa to the acid-jazz Groove Collective to proto-hippies Royal Trux to any number of local boy Thurston Moore's numerous side projects (when he isn't busy with Sonic Youth, of course). DJ nights range from ambient to 100% hip-hop. There's no sign, so look for the metal doors and the staircase leading to the subterranean entrance. The cover can range from free to $10; advance tickets can be purchased at X-Large, 267 Lafayette St. (at Prince Street) in SoHo.

**Fez Under Time Cafe.** 380 Lafayette St. (at Great Jones St.). ☎ **212/533-2680.** www.feznyc.com. Subway: 6 to Bleecker St.

You have to reserve a seat a few days ahead for the wildly popular Thursday-night Mingus Big Band ($18), when the low-ceilinged basement performance space is filled with the cool sounds of jazz. The rest of the week brings an eclectic live music-and-performance art mix, which can range from Combustible Edison to esoteric local acts to fun lounge-lizardy tributes to acts such as Queen, ABBA, and the Monkees from Loser's Lounge. The stage is fronted by tightly packed picnic-style tables and a few coveted booths. Time Cafe's pleasing, well-priced menu is served (see chapter 6). I would love this space if it were just better ventilated; if you need to escape the rampant cigarette smoke, head upstairs to the relaxing lounge and bar. The cover ranges from $5 to $20, and a two-drink minimum might be required.

**Manitoba's.** 99 Ave. B. (btw. 6th and 7th sts.). ☎ **212/982-2511.** Subway: L to First Ave.

From former Dictators frontman Dick Manitoba comes this easygoing East Village hangout. The booker has been scoring top-flight entertainment of late; the occasional DJ party can run $5, but the bulk of it is free live music. Country-pop faves Beat Rodeo have a steady Monday-night gig that's well worth checking out.

✪ **Mercury Lounge.** 217 E. Houston St. (at Essex St./Ave. A). ☎ **212/260-4700.** www.mercuryloungenyc.com. Subway: F to Second Ave.

The Merc is everything a top-notch live music venue should be: unpretentious, extremely civilized, and outfitted with a killer sound system. The rooms themselves are nothing special: a front bar and an intimate back-room performance space with a low stage and a few tables along the wall. The calendar is filled with a mix of accomplished local rockers and up-and-coming national acts such as P.O.D. The crowd is grown-up and easygoing. The only downside is that it's consistently packed, thanks to the high quality of the entertainment and all-around pleasing nature of the experience. The cover can reach $15 but seldom does; it's more likely to be between $7 and $10.

○ **Rodeo Bar.** 375 Third Ave. (at 27th St.). ☎ **212/683-6500.** www.rodeobar.com. Subway: 6 to 28th St.

Here's New York's oldest—and finest—honky-tonk. Hike up your Wranglers and head those Fryes inside, where you'll find longhorns on the walls, peanut shells underfoot, and Tex-Mex on the menu. But this place is really about the music: urban-tinged country, foot-stompin' bluegrass, swinging rockabilly, Southern-flavored rock. Although bigger names such as Brian Setzer and up-and-comers on the tour circuit such as Hank Williams III occasionally grace the stage, regular acts such as Dixieland Swingers, the Flying Neutrinos, and the retro-rocking Camaros usually supply the free music, keeping the urban cowboys plenty happy. A ten-gallon hat full o' fun.

**Tonic.** 107 Norfolk St. (btw. Delancey and Rivington sts.). ☎ **212/358-7503.** www.tonicnyc.com. Subway: F to Delancey St.

This quirky Lower East Sider has become quite the avant-garde jazz/experimental rock spot in the Knitting Factory vein. Look for the "Klezmer Brunch" series on Sunday, plus Monday movie nights featuring cult classics. Tickets range from $4 to $15.

**Wetlands.** 161 Hudson St. (at Laight St.). ☎ **212/386-3600,** or 212/978-0838 for upcoming show info. www.wetlands-preserve.org. Subway: 1, 9, A, C, E to Canal St.

Now celebrating its 11th year, this environmentally conscious club isn't just for Deadheads anymore. Sure, Phish is worshipped by most of the crowd and you'll still find Haight-Ashbury scenesters such as Jorma Kaukonen on the schedule every once in awhile, but the club's musical focus has really broadened in recent years. Wetlands regularly offers hip-hop, soul, global funk, ska, and other groovy world music in addition to mind-bending jazz, indie, and roots rock. Covers range $5 to $15. A terrific venue.

## JAZZ, BLUES, LATIN & WORLD MUSIC

Be aware that a night at a top-flight jazz club can be expensive. For serious fans, it's worth splurging on a night at the **Blue Note, Birdland,** the **Village Vanguard, Iridium,** or **Sweet Basil,** all world-class showcases for top talents. However, cover charges can vary dramatically—from as little as $10 to as high as $65, depending on who's taking the stage—and there's likely to be an additional drink minimum (or a dinner requirement, if you choose an early show). Call ahead so you know what you're getting into; reservations are also an excellent idea at top spots.

For those of you who like your jazz with an edge, see what's on at the **Knitting Factory** (p. 313) and **Tonic** (p. 317). Trad fans should also consider the Thursday Mingus Big Band Workshop at **Fez Under Time Cafe** (p. 316). Those wearing their dancing shoes should check out the Brazilian Mondays and vintage funk Tuesdays at **Cafe Wha?** (p. 315) and the nightly parties at the **Greatest Bar on Earth,** where Monday is dedicated to funk, Thursday to Latin music, and Friday and Saturday nights to swing (p. 322). Look for groovy world music at **Wetlands** (p. 317). There's also worldbeat jazz every Friday and Saturday from 5 to 8pm in the rotunda at the **Guggenheim Museum;** see chapter 7. Also see **Arthur's Tavern, C-Note,** and the **Blue Lounge** in the "Free Music" box.

**Birdland.** 315 W. 44th St. (btw. Eighth and Ninth aves.). ☎ **212/581-3080.** www.birdlandjazz.com. Subway: A, C, E to 42nd St.

## Take the A Train

Harlem's jazz scene has taken on new energy in recent years, serving up top-notch music without the high cover charges and drink/food minimums that downtown clubs often require. These two first-rate clubs are Uptown's best bets for budget-minded jazz fans:

**Showman's Cafe,** 375 W. 125th St., between St. Nicholas and Morningside avenues (☎ 212/864-8941; Subway: A, B, C, D to 125th St.), hosts nightly music ranging from soulful jazz to funky bebop. No cover; two-drink minimum per person, per set.

**St. Nick's Pub,** 773 St. Nicholas Ave., at 149th Street (☎ 212/283-9728; Subway: A, B, C, D to 145th St.), is an older Sugar Hill closet has been rediscovered by a younger crowd, drawn in by its great jazz every night of the week except Tuesday. The Monday jazz jams with Patience Higgins and the Sugar Hill Quartet attract music lovers and players from all walks of life, and the service is just as friendly whether you come from the neighborhood, Downtown, or out of town. The cover charge is usually a wallet-friendly $5.

---

This legendary club abandoned its distant Uptown roost in 1996 for a more convenient Midtown nest, where it has established itself once again as one of the city's premier jazz spots. Although the legend of Parker, Monk, Gillespie, and other bebop pioneers still holds sway, this isn't a crowded, smoky joint of yesteryear. The big room is spacious, comfy, and classy, with an excellent sound system and a top-notch talent roster any night of the week. Expect lots of accomplished big bands and jazz trios, plus occasional appearances by stars such as Pat Metheny and Dave Brubeck. You can't go wrong with the regular Sunday-night show, starring Chico O'Farrell's smokin' Afro-Cuban Jazz Big Band. The Southern-style food is even pretty good. **Money-saving tip:** You might be able to save a few dollars on the cover and avoid a food minimum by posting yourself at the bar rather than taking a table.

**Blue Note.** 131 W. 3rd St. (at Sixth Ave.). ☎ **212/475-8592.** www.bluenote.net. Subway: A, B, C, D, E, F, Q to W. 4th St.

The Blue Note attracts the biggest names in jazz to its intimate setting, from Lionel Hampton to Manhattan Transfer to Oscar Peterson to B.B. King. The sound system is excellent, and every seat in the house has a sightline to the stage. A night here can get expensive, but how often do you get to enjoy jazz of this caliber? **Money-Saving Tip:** You'll likely save by attending a Sunday brunch or matinee show rather than a nighttime show. If you'd like to experience this legendary club but can't stomach the high charges that can accompany standard shows, consider the Friday- and Saturday-night **Late Night Jam Sessions,** which last until 4am ($5 cover, no minimum).

**Chicago B.L.U.E.S.** 73 Eighth Ave. (btw. 13th and 14th sts.). ☎ **212/924-9755.** www. chicagoblues.com. Subway: A, C, E, L to 14th St.

Here's the best blues joint in the city, with a genuine Windy City flair. The contrived decor makes the place feel more theme park than roadhouse, but the music is the real thing. The cover can go as high as $20 for acts such as Buddy Miles, Lonnie Brooks, and local powerhouse Popa Chubby (whose long sets are well worth the dough), but it's usually less than $10, and the Monday night blues jam is absolutely free.

**Iridium.** 44 W. 63rd St. (at Columbus Ave., below the Merlot Bar & Grill). ☎ **212/582-2121.** www.iridiumjazz.com. Subway: 1, 9 to 66th St.; 1, 9, A, B, C, D to Columbus Circle.

This well-respected and snazzily designed basement boîte features such top-flight acts as the Frank Foster Quintet and the excellent Jazz Messengers, plus the legendary Les Paul every Monday night. A $25 to $45 cover plus a $10 per-person food or drink minimum makes Iridium worth it only if you're a huge fan.

**55 Bar.** 55 Christopher St. (1 block south of Seventh Ave. and 10th St.). ☎ **212/929-9883.** Subway: 1, 9 to Christopher St.

This Village dive hosts high-quality jazz nightly, with guitarists a specialty. The house guitar trio is definitely worth a listen, and if saxist Ed Palermo is on the bill, go. The cover charge is a bargain-basement $3, with a two-drink minimum.

**Internet Cafe.** 82 E. 3rd St. (btw. First and Second aves.). ☎ **212/614-0747.** www. bigmagic.com. Subway: F to Second Ave.

Those looking for an affordable jazz fix should visit this casual online cafe, which features well-regarded jazz from up-and-coming acts nightly for a $5 cover (no minimum). Free film screenings Sundays at 8pm.

**The Jazz Standard.** 116 E. 27th St. (btw. Park Ave. South and Lexington Ave.). ☎ **212/576-2232.** www.jazzstandard.com. Subway: 6 to 28th St.

Boasting a sophisticated retro-speakeasy vibe, this basement lounge is one of the city's largest and most comfortable jazz clubs. The rule is straightforward, mainstream jazz by new and established musicians. Not cheap—a $15 to $25 cover, plus a $10 per-person minimum—but you really can't go wrong here. **Money-saving tip:** The cover charge is cheaper midweek and for the midnight sets on Friday and Saturday.

**✪ Small's.** 183 W. 10th St. (at Seventh Ave.). ☎ **212/929-7565.** www.smallsjazz.com. Subway: 1, 9 to Christopher St.

Here's a great destination for committed jazzophiles: This cozy basement hideaway stays open all night. Scheduled performers, which often include cutting-edge unsigned acts or overlooked talents, play from around 10pm to 2am, followed by a nightly jam session until 3:30 or 4am. No alcohol is served, but that doesn't keep the crowds away; they're happy to come just for the music. Drinks are free with the $10 cover, and all ages are welcome.

**✪ S.O.B.'s.** 204 Varick St. (at Houston St.). ☎ **212/243-4940.** www.sobs.com. Subway: 1, 9 to Houston St.

This is the city's top world-music venue, specializing in Brazilian, Caribbean, and Latin sounds. The packed house dances and sings along nightly to calypso, samba, mambo, African drums, reggae, or other global grooves, united in the high-energy, feel-good vibe. Bookings include top-flight performers from around the globe; luminaries from Astrud Gilberto to King Sunny Ade to Beausoleil have graced the stage. This place has real island-style pizzazz and is so popular that you might want to book in advance if you'd like table seating. At press time, free Latin dance lessons were offered before Monday's La Tropica party so you could be ready to strut your stuff once the band takes the stage. The cover ranges from free to $20 for dance parties, $10 to $25 if there's a performer in the house—and it's a worthy splurge for world-music lovers.

**Sweet Basil.** 88 Seventh Ave. South (btw. Grove and Bleecker sts.). ☎ **212/242-1785.** www.sweetbasil.com. Subway: 1, 9 to Christopher St.

The choice runs from fusion to traditional at this intimate but excellent jazz club, where you can count on finding top names playing top-notch music. Pricey—expect a $17.50 to $20 cover plus a $10 minimum—but you'll get your money's worth. The

Sunday brunch is so popular that they've added a Saturday version as well. Reservations are a must on weekends. **Money-saving tip:** You'll save $2 to $2.50 per person by attending a weeknight (Sunday through Thursday) set.

**The Village Vanguard.** 178 Seventh Ave. South (just below 11th St.). ☎ **212/255-4037.** www.villagevanguard.net. Subway: 1, 2, 3, 9 to 14th St.

What CBGB's is to rock, the Village Vanguard is to jazz. This legendary club is just as vital as ever. Expect a mix of established names and high-quality local talent, including the Vanguard's own jazz orchestra. The sound is great but sightlines are terrible, so come early for a front table. The crowd can seem either overly serious or overly touristy, but don't let that stop you; you'll always find great music. Covers range from $25 to $30 (drink minimums included). **Money-saving tip:** Sunday through Thursday, sets are $5 less per person.

## 5  Comedy & Cabaret

### STAND-UP & SKETCH COMEDY

Cover charges are generally in the $8 to $15 range, with all-star **Carolines on Broadway,** 1626 Broadway, between 49th and 50th streets (☎ 212/757-4100; www. carolines.com), running $18 to $26. Unless you're enamored with seeing a big name that's scheduled there, I suggest that those of you watching your wallets opt for a less-expensive club, where you're likely to enjoy just as many yuks. Keep in mind that most clubs have a two-drink minimum and might raise their covers if a famous name is in the house; be sure to ask about the night's cover and requirements when you reserve.

If it's Monday, also consider the weekly comedy night at **Luna Lounge,** 171 Ludlow St., between Houston and Stanton streets (☎ 212/260-2323), which is a bargain at $5.

**Boston Comedy Club.** 82 W. 3rd St. (btw. Thompson and Sullivan sts.). ☎ **212/ 477-1000.** www.thebostoncomedyclub.com. Subway: A, B, C, D, E, F, Q to W. 4th St. (use 3rd St. exit).

If you don't like the act here, wait a couple of minutes and it'll change. The M.O. here is to barrage the audience with a lineup of a dozen or so talents per set on the theory that someone will get a laugh. Jay Mohr is one of the Boston's breakthrough acts, and this is still his home club. The cover is $7 Sundays, $8 weekdays, $12 weekends, with a one- or two-drink minimum, depending on the night.

✪ **Comedy Cellar.** 117 MacDougal St. (btw. Bleecker and 3rd sts.). ☎ **212/254-3480.** www.comedycellar.com. Subway: A, B, C, D, E, F, Q to W. 4th St. (use 3rd St. exit).

This intimate subterranean spot is the club of choice for stand-up fans in the know, thanks to the best, most consistently impressive lineups in the business. I'll always love the Comedy Cellar for introducing me to an uproariously funny unknown comic named Ray Romano a few years back. $7 weekdays, $12 weekends (at press time, free admission with online reservations).

**Dangerfield's.** 1118 First Ave. (btw. 61st and 62nd sts.). ☎ **212/593-1650.** Subway: N, R to 60th St.; 4, 5, 6, to 59th St.

Dangerfield's is the nightclub version of the comedy club, with a mature crowd and a straight-outta-Vegas atmosphere. The comedians are all veterans of the comedy-club and late-night talk-show circuit. The cover is pricey—$15, $20 for Saturday's late show—but there's no food or drink minimum.

✪ **Gotham Comedy Club.** 34 W. 22nd St. (btw. Fifth and Sixth aves.). ☎ **212/367-9000.** www.gothamcomedy.com. Subway: N, R or F to 23rd St.

Here's the city's trendiest and most sophisticated comedy club. The young talent—Tom Rhodes, Jeff Ross, Lewis Schaeffer, Lynn Harris—is red-hot. Look for theme nights such as the lovelorn laugh riot "Breakup Girl Live!" and "A Very Jewish Thursday."

The cover is $10 weekdays, $15 weekends.

**New York Comedy Club.** 241 E. 24th St. (btw. Second and Third aves.). ☎ **212/696-5233.** www.newyorkcomedyclub.com. Subway: 6 to 23rd St.

With a $5 cover charge on weekdays ($10 Friday and Saturday), this small club offers the best laugh value for your money. Despite what the owners call their "Wal-Mart approach" to comedy, the club has presented Damon Wayans, Chris Rock, and Brett Butler, among others, in its two showrooms. Weekends set aside time for African-American and Hispanic comics. Come early for a good seat.

**Stand-Up New York.** 236 W. 78th St. (at Broadway). ☎ **212/595-0850.** www.standupny.com. Subway: 1, 9 to 79th St.

The Upper West Side's premier stand-up comedy club hosts some of the brightest young comics in the business, such as Joe DiResta and Paul Mercurio. Drop-in guests have included Dennis Leary, Joy Behar, and Robin Williams. $8 Sunday through Wednesday, $10 Thursday, $12 weekends.

✪ **Upright Citizens Brigade Theater.** 161 W. 22nd St. (btw. Sixth and Seventh aves.) ☎ **212/366-9176.** www.uprightcitizens.com. Subway: 1, 9 to 23rd St.

You've seen their twisted, highly original sketch comedy on Comedy Central; now you can see the Upright Citizen's Brigade, New York's premier sketch comedy troupe, live. The biggest success to come out of New York's late '90s alternative comedy explosion, the UCB now has its very own showcase. The best of the non-stop hilarity is *A.S.S.S.C.A.T.,* the troupe's extremely popular long-form improv show. You won't pay more than $5 for any show; phone reservations are a must.

## CABARETS

The city's top supper clubs and cabarets are not for the budget-minded. At **Cafe Carlyle,** in the Carlyle Hotel, 781 Madison Ave. (☎ **212/570-7189**), home to the legendary Bobby Short, and the Algonquin's **Oak Room,** 59 W. 44th St. (☎ **212/840-6800**), covers run $45 to $60, plus two-drink or dinner-check minimums and other qualifications. If you go, count on a $300 night on the town. Or try one of these more casual, less-expensive options.

**Danny's Skylight Room.** At the Grand Sea Palace, 346 W. 46th St. (btw. Eighth and Ninth aves.). ☎ **212/265-8133.** Subway: A, C, E to 42nd St.

You'll find this Theater District showroom tucked away in, of all places, the rear of a Thai restaurant. It regularly offers surprisingly strong lineups, as well as a cool piano bar up front. The cover ranges $12 to $20 (usually $15 or less), plus a $10 minimum; ask about money-saving dinner/show packages. There's no cover in the piano bar (they just ask that you drink).

**Don't Tell Mama.** 343 W. 46th St. (btw. Eighth and Ninth aves.). ☎ **212/757-0788.** Subway: A, C, E to 42nd St.

Singing waitresses go from tips to tunes when their turn in the spotlight comes. You'll find an evening of torch songs, comedy, and much more in a friendly, and affordable, atmosphere. Drinks only, no dinner. The piano bar is particularly lively. There's a $3 to $15 cover, depending on the show (two-drink minimum), but the piano bar is free.

**Duplex Cabaret.** 61 Christopher St. (at Seventh Ave.). ☎ **212/255-5438.** www. duplex.citysearch.com. Subway: 1, 9 to Christopher St.

Expect a high camp factor and lots of good-natured fun in this multilevel space. A mixed gay/straight crowd of locals and curious out-of-towners sit at outdoor tables for drinks, gather around the downstairs piano (sing-alongs from around 9pm), or head upstairs to the cabaret for shows that run from mini-musicals to drag revues to stand-up comedy. No cover in at the piano bar (two-drink minimum), $3 to $12 in the showroom.

## 6 Bars & Cocktail Lounges

### SOUTH STREET SEAPORT & THE FINANCIAL DISTRICT

Also consider the **North Star Pub,** at South Street Seaport, 93 South St., at Fulton Street (☎ **212/509-6757**), a genuine British pub boasting one of the finest single-malt scotch menus in the city in addition to hand-pulled British and Irish pints; see chapter 6.

**۞ The Greatest Bar on Earth.** 1 World Trade Center, 107th floor (on West St., btw. Liberty and Vesey sts.) ☎ **212/524-7000.** www.windowsontheworld.com. Subway: A, C, E to Chambers St.; N, R, 1, 9 to Cortlandt St.

High atop the World Trade Center sits the Greatest Bar on Earth, whose name is only a slight exaggeration. This is a magical spot for cocktails, decent gourmet munchies, and dancing. No matter how many times I come up here, I'm wowed by the incredible views, which are equal to those at the observation deck atop the other tower. The place is huge, but intimate nooks and a separate back room bring the scale down to comfortable proportions. The crowd is a lively mix of in-the-know locals and stylish out-of-towners. This is a great place to come with a group; the music is loud, and the joint really jumps as the night goes on. Quintessentially—and spectacularly—New York. GBOE is relatively affordable, too: Generous top-shelf martinis are just $8.50, but the same cocktail costs $10 to $12 at most trendy places about town. Look for swing on Friday and Saturdays, plus mambo, funk, and R&B other nights of the week. Wednesday is home to the hip Mondo 107 strato-lounge DJ party. **Money-saving tip:** Come Sunday through Wednesday to avoid a door charge ($15 on Thursday, $5 on Friday and Saturday).

**Wall St. Kitchen & Bar.** 70 Broad St. (btw. Beaver and S. William sts., about 1¹/2 blocks south of New York Stock Exchange). ☎ **212/797-7070.** www.wallstkitchen.citysearch.com. Subway: 4, 5 to Bowling Green; J, M, Z to Broad St.

Want to rub elbows with some genuine bulls and bears after a hard day of downtown sightseeing? Head to this surprisingly appealing and affordable bar, housed in a spectacular former bank. Wall St. Kitchen specializes in on-tap beers (around 50 are on offer at any given time) and "flight" menus of wines and microbrews for tasting. The familiar bar food is well prepared and affordable. Come on a weekday to enjoy the crowd.

## TRIBECA

**Grace.** 114 Franklin St. (btw. W. Broadway and Church St.). ☎ **212/343-4200.** Subway: 1, 9 to Franklin St.

This neighborhood newcomer has made itself right at home with a sophisticated yet down-to-earth vibe; a good selection of classic cocktails, single-malt scotches, and on-tap beers from the sweeping, welcoming bar; and an affordable menu of elegant yet unpretentious American regional dishes that make great late-night cocktail nibbles. There's a cozy dining room in back, too, if you'd like to reserve a nook for yourself.

**Riverrun.** 176 Franklin St. (btw. Greenwich and Hudson sts.). ☎ **212/966-3894.** Subway: 1, 9 to Franklin St.

Down-to-earth as ever, this neighborhood pioneer is now a refreshing find in an increasingly haute 'hood. Like a lot of vintage joints, the decor is more clutter than clean lines, but this friendly bar does a great job of keeping the easygoing crowd happy. There's a sensible wine list, a good selection of beers on tap, a respectable single-malt selection, and satisfying comfort food. The crowd morphs from traders to locals as the evening wears on.

**✪ The Sporting Club.** 99 Hudson St. (btw. Franklin and Leonard sts.). ☎ **212/ 219-0900.** www.thesportingclub.net. Subway: 1, 9 to Franklin St.

The city's best sports bar (rated no. 1 in the *Daily News*) is a guy's joint if there ever was one. The space is as big as a linebacker, with giant TV screens at every turn tuned to just about every game on the planet. (Wall Streeters bring their international cohorts here to catch everything from English football to Japanese sumo.) The menu is what you'd expect: wings, burgers, club sandwiches, and *lots* of beer. There's no better place for sports fans to get crazy at Super Bowl time and during March Madness. When the big games are over, this turns into a surprisingly popular singles place.

## CHINATOWN & LITTLE ITALY

**✪ Double Happiness.** 173 Mott St. (btw. Grand and Broome sts.). ☎ **212/941-1282.** Subway: 6 to Spring St.; B, D, Q to Grand St.

Thanks to its stylish speakeasy aura and low-key vibe, last year's new kid in town has outlived its initial buzz. The only indicator to the subterranean entrance is a vertical "watch your step" sign. Once through the door, you'll find a beautifully designed lounge with artistic nods to the neighborhood throughout. The space is large, but low ceilings and intimate nooks add a hint of romance (although the loud funkified music mix might deter true wooing). The green tea martini is an inspired house creation.

**Mare Chiaro.** 176$^{1}/_{2}$ Mulberry St. (at Broome St.). ☎ **212/226-9345.** Subway: 6 to Spring St.

This authentic corner of Little Italy now hosts a bizarro mix of slumming NoLiTa hipsters, uptown singles, and neighborhood holdovers from an age when this was just a drinkingman's bar. But Mare Chiaro still works its crusty magic, transporting you back to another era with its gentrification-resistant vibe. A great place for a cheap beer at a crossroads of city life.

## LOWER EAST SIDE

Also consider **Mercury Lounge,** 217 E. Houston St. (☎ **212/260-4700**), which has a casual, comfortable bar up front; see p. 316.

**Butcher Bar.** 93 Stanton St. (btw. Ludlow and Orchard sts.). ☎ **212/358-1633.** www.arlene-grocery.com. Subway: F to Second Ave.

With brick walls, a cozy open fireplace, and the same unpretentious atmosphere as its sister space, Arlene Grocery (see "(Mostly) Rock Clubs" above), this makes the ideal place to nurse a brew between bands. Sandwiches are served in daytime.

**Good World Bar & Grill.** 3 Orchard St. (btw. Division and Canal sts.). ☎ **212/925-9975.** Subway: F to East Broadway.

Don't worry about running into your fellow tourists here; this former Chinese bar-bershop is completely off the beaten track. Despite the location and utter lack of decor, it draws a young alterna-hip crowd with its refreshing lack of pretensions, low prices on good on-tap beers, and surprisingly good—and affordable—Scandinavian eats.

✪ **Idlewild.** 145 E. Houston St. (btw. First and Second aves., on the south side of Houston). ☎ **212/477-5005.** Subway: F to Second Ave.

It might look unapproachable from the street, with nothing but an unmarked stainless-steel facade, but inside, you'll find a fun, easygoing bar that's perfect for lovers of retro-kitsch. The interior is a larger-scale repro of a jet airplane, complete with reclining seats, tray tables, and too-small bathrooms that will transport you back to your favorite mid-air moments in no time. There are booths in back for larger crowds and an Austin Powers–style bar to gather around at center stage. The DJ spins a listener-friendly mix of light techno, groovy disco in the Funkadelic vein, and '80s tunes from the likes of the Smiths and the Cure.

**Lansky Lounge.** 138 Delancey St. (entrance on Norfolk St., between Rivington and Delancey sts.). ☎ **212/677-9489.** Subway: F to Delancey St.

A doorman stands on the sidewalk to point patrons down a flight of stairs, through an alley, and back up a staircase into this faux speakeasy. It's still one of the Lower East Side's coolest scenes, with a cool-as-a-cucumber zoot suit vibe that has outlived New York's flirtation with neo-swing. The special martinis and infused vodkas are terrific. Come on a weeknight, when the crowd is more local than bridge-and-tunnel. The food is kosher and comes from neighboring Ratner's. *Note:* The bar is closed on Friday night in observance of the Jewish Sabbath.

## SOHO

**Ear Inn.** 326 Spring St. (btw. Greenwich and Washington sts.). ☎ **212/226-9060.** Subway: C, E to Spring St.

This historic far-west SoHo pub has always been a local fave since before the Civil War, thanks to its casual ambiance, huge selection of beers, and old-style bartenders who aren't looking for their big break. This is the kind of place where tattooed bikers can pony up to the bar next to bankers, and everybody gets along. Live music and spoken-word events dot the not-too-ambitious calendar.

**Ice Bar.** 628 Canal St. (at Washington St., on the south side of the street). ☎ **212/226-2602.** Subway: 1, 9 to Houston St.

Here's a cutting-edge spot for those who don't mind going out of their way—really out of their way—for something completely different. Ice Bar is managing to draw a scene way out west (almost to the West Side Highway) by crossing an outrageously cool white-on-white retro-futuristic interior (blue-lit for ultimate effect) with an everybody's-welcome egalitarian attitude. Expect an electronica soundtrack (what else?).

✪ **Merc Bar.** 151 Mercer St. (btw. Prince and Houston sts.). ☎ **212/966-2727.** Subway: N, R to Prince St.; B, D, F, Q to Broadway/Lafayette St.

Notable for its long tenure in the fickle world of beautiful-people bars, upscale Merc Bar has mellowed nicely. You'll still find a good-looking crowd in this superbly appointed lounge, but now it's a confident rather than a trend-happy one. The decor

# The Final Word

**Nuyorican Poets Cafe,** 236 E. 3rd St., between avenues B and C (☎ 212/
505-8183; www.nuyorican.org), is a neat performance-art space with a persistent
boho spirit and a long history of showcasing fledgling creativity. The full calendar runs the gamut from experimental film to unstaged readings of original
screenplays to live Latin-infused jazz. The Wednesday and Friday poetry slams
can be a fun ride—a 1990s version of the *Gong Show,* where poets compete as
audience members score the performances. The cover runs $5 to $10, depending
on the evening.

On Sundays, two excellent East Village bars host highly acclaimed reading
series sans cover charge: **Temple Bar** (p. 327) hosts acclaimed writers such as
Colin Harrison (*Afterburn*) and Katherine Russell Rich (*The Red Devil: To Hell
with Cancer and Back*) in a loungey atmosphere at 7:30pm, and the 7pm series
at rough-and-ready **KGB Bar** (p. 326) has even spawned a collection of short stories, *The KGB Bar Reader.*

And don't forget **Barnes & Noble.** B&N might not be the first stop that
comes to mind when you're planning a tour of the Big Apple's nightlife circuit,
but the monthly events calendar is always chock full of compelling speakers, from
Rosemary Clooney to Michael Crichton to T-Boz from TLC, and all events are
absolutely free. Call ☎ 212/727-4810 or visit the store and events locator at
**www.bn.com** to see what's on while you're in town.

If film is more your thing, head to **Cinema Classics,** 332 E. 11th St., between
First and Second avenues (☎ 212/971-1015; www.cinemaclassics.com). Up
front is a casual coffee bar with cheap sandwiches and sweets, plus $2 Rolling
Rocks at happy hour (4:30 to 7:30pm). The back room serves as a screening
room for a cool calendar of oldies and alt classics from Howard Hawks's *The Big
Sleep* to Fritz Lang's *While the City Sleeps* to the Bowie concert film *Cracked Actor.*
Admission is a wallet-friendly $5.

bespeaks civilized rusticity with warm woods, a canoe over the bar, copper-top tables,
and butter-leather banquettes; think SoHo goes to Yosemite. A great place to nestle
into a comfortable couch with your honey and enjoy the scene. The European Martini
(Stoli raspberry and Chambord) is divine. Look carefully, because there's no sign.

**Soho Kitchen & Bar.** 103 Greene St. (btw. Spring and Prince sts.). ☎ **212/925-1866.**
www.sohokitchen.citysearch.com. Subway: N, R to Prince St.; C, E to Spring St.

This easygoing place is a nice antidote to the standard SoHo pretensions. The large,
lofty space attracts an animated after-work and late-night crowd to its central bar,
which dispenses 21 beers on tap, a whole slew of microbrews by the bottle, and more
than 100 wines by the glass or in "flights" for comparative tastings. The menu offers
predictable but affordable bar fare: buffalo wings, oversize salads, good burgers, and a
variety of sandwiches and thin-crust pizzas.

## THE EAST VILLAGE & NOHO

Also consider the magical **Fez,** 380 Lafayette St., at Great Jones St. (☎ 212/
533-2680), a dimly lit Moroccan-themed bar and lounge that I much prefer to the
downstairs performance space; see p. 316.

**Barmacy.** 538 E. 14th St. (btw. aves. A and B). ☎ **212/228-2240.** Subway: L to First Ave.

Barmacy is just what you'd guess—a bar housed in a vintage pharmacy, complete with shelves of classic toiletries and a drugstore counter that would make Lana Turner smile. On an otherwise desolate stretch of East 14th, it's really a fun place to spend an evening, complete with a youngish party-hearty crowd and DJs spinning tunes in the back room that range from earnest Britpop to modern funk to makeout music, depending on the evening.

**Burp Castle.** 41 E. 7th St. (btw. Second and Third aves.). ☎ **212/982-4576.** Subway: 6 to Astor Place.

This oddball theme bar is a must for serious beer lovers. It's styled as a "Temple of Beer Worship," complete with Medieval-inspired decor, choral music on the sound system, and soft-spoken waiters in monkish garb. Before you let the weirdness of it all sink in, you'll be distracted by the incomparable beer list. There are more than 500 bottled and on-tap beers to choose from—including a phenomenal collection of Trappist ales, of course. The staff is courteous but a bit too studiedly monkish; I couldn't wrest an actual recommendation out of them. Be prepared to choose, or head elsewhere if you think you'll just throw your hands in the air and order a Bud.

✪ **dba.** 41 First Ave. (btw. 2nd and 3rd sts.). ☎ **212/475-5097.** Subway: F to Second Ave.

Along with Temple Bar (below), this is my other favorite bar in the city. It has completely bucked the loungey trend that has taken over the city, instead remaining firmly and resolutely an unpretentious neighborhood bar. Most importantly, dba is a beer- and scotch-lover's paradise, with a massive drink menu on the giant chalkboards behind the bar. Owner Ray Deter specializes in British-style cask-conditioned ales (the kind that you pump by hand) and stocks a phenomenal collection of 90 single-malt scotches. The relaxed crowd is a pleasing mix of connoisseurs and casual drinkers who like the unlimited choices and egalitarian vibe. Excellent jukebox, too.

**Decibel.** 240 E. 9th St. (btw. Second and Third aves.). ☎ **212/979-2733.** www. sakebar.com. Subway: 6 to Astor Place.

This subterranean sake bar is a genuine Japanese refuge. The warren of little, dimly lit rooms draws a hip crowd with its long, excellent list of sakes (about 70 are on hand) and affordable Japanese nibbles. The menu explains everything you ever wanted to know about sake and then some; feel free to ask the bar's wise and tolerant staff for suggestions. Japanese beers and saketinis (martinis made with sake—an excellent invention) are also available.

**KGB Bar.** 85 E. 4th St. (btw. Second and Third Aves.) ☎ **212/505-3360.** Subway: 6 to Astor Place.

This former Ukranian social club still boasts its Soviet-themed decor, but it now draws creative intellectual types who like the low-key boho vibe. Sunday nights are the biggest draw, thanks to the success of KGB's excellent reading series, where an increasingly talented pack of up-and-coming and published writers read their prose to a receptive crowd starting at 7pm. Past readers have included Rick Moody (*The Ice Storm*), Catherine Texier (*Breakup*), and Kathryn Harrison (*The Kiss*). The Red Room also stages theatrical productions regularly.

**McSorley's Old Ale House.** 15 E. 7th St. (btw. Second and Third aves.). ☎ **212/ 473-9148.** Subway: 6 to Astor Place.

Shrine Time—and they want you to worship their way. In business for more than 140 years, McSorley's window proudly claims "WE WERE HERE BEFORE YOU WERE

BORN." Only McSorley's Ale is served, light or dark and two at a time. Come to bask in the old-time New York vibe, not to nurse a Diet Coke. This is an ale-sodden frat-boy madhouse most nights and an Irish Armageddon on St. Patrick's Day. Although it's also a McSorley's tradition to urinate on the wall outside, they prefer you honor that one in the breach, not in the commission.

✪ **Temple Bar.** 332 Lafayette St. (just north of Houston St., on the west side of the street). ☎ **212/925-4242.** Subway: B, D, F, Q to Broadway/Lafayette St.; 6 to Bleecker St.

Here's my favorite lounge in the city. Members of the It crowd will tell you it's passe, which only serves to increase its appeal as far as I'm concerned; it's easy to get in now and, on weeknights at least, you can even usually manage to find a comfy seat. This is a gorgeous art deco hangout, with a long L-shaped bar leading to a lovely seating area with velvet drapes, romantic backlighting, and Sinatra softly crooning in the background. Cocktails simply don't get any better than the classic martini (with just a kiss of vermouth, of course) or the smooth-as-penoir-silk Rob Roy (Johnnie Walker Black, sweet vermouth, bitters). Elegant finger foods provide a reason to never leave. Bring a date—and feel free to invite me along anytime. The entrance is a little inconspicuous, so look for the petroglyph-like lizards on the facade.

**Tom & Jerry's (288 Bar).** 288 Elizabeth St. ☎ **212/260-5045.** Subway: B, D, F, Q to Broadway/Lafayette St.; 6 to Bleecker St

Here's an extremely pleasing neighborhood bar minus the grunge factor that usually plagues such joints. The place has an authentic local vibe, and the youngish, arty crowd is unpretentious and chatty. The beer selection is very good, and the mixed drinks are better than average. Flea-market hounds will enjoy the vintage collection of "Tom & Jerry" punchbowl sets behind the bar, and creative types will enjoy the rotating collection of works from local artists. There's no sign, but you'll spy the action through the plate-glass window on the east side of Elizabeth Street just north of Houston.

## GREENWICH VILLAGE

Also consider the cheap-chic **Junno's,** 64 Downing St., between Bedford and Varick streets (☎ 212/627-7995), a sophisticated industrial-moderne restaurant that also hosts a red-hot bar scene until 4am on weekends; see chapter 6.

**artbar.** 52 Eighth Ave. (btw. Horatio and Jane sts.). ☎ **212/727-0244.** www.artbarnyc.com. Subway: A, C, E to 14th St.

This West Village hangout has a dual personality: It's a neighborhood bar up front, complete with after-work crowd and on-tap brews, and an artsy lounge in back, an ambiance enhanced by candlelight, Oriental rugs, and trendy cocktails. Come for the affordable drinks and the nice neighborhood vibe as well as the good collection of local art on the walls.

**Bar d'O.** 29 Bedford St. (at Downing St.). ☎ **212/627-1580.** Subway: A, B, C, D, E, F, Q to W. 4th St. (use 3rd St. exit).

This intimate space is home to the Village's best lounge scene—which unfortunately makes it crowded, but still cozy and appealing. A different DJ sets the scene for the mixed gay/straight crowd nightly in this low-slung, candlelit space; best is the exotic lounge music from In Hi-Fi on Thursdays. Drag diva Joey Arias wows the crowd twice weekly (Tuesdays, Saturdays, and Sundays at press time) with her spot-on Billie Holliday renditions.

**☺ Chumley's.** 86 Bedford St. (at Barrow St.). ☎ **212/675-4449.** Subway: 1, 9 to Christopher St.

A classic. Many bars in New York date their beginnings to Prohibition, but Chumley's still has the vibe. The circa college-age crowd doesn't date back nearly as far, however. Come to warm yourself by the fire and indulge in a once-forbidden pleasure: beer. The door is unmarked, with a metal grille on the small window; another entrance is at 58 Barrow St., which takes you in through a back courtyard.

**White Horse Tavern.** 567 Hudson St. (at 11th St.). ☎ **212/989-3956.** Subway: 1, 9 to Christopher St.

Poets and literary buffs pop into this 1880 pub to pay their respects to Dylan Thomas, who tipped his last jar here before shuffling off this mortal coil. Best enjoyed in the warm weather when there's outdoor drinking or at happy hour for the cheap drafts that draw in a big frat-boy and post-frat yuppie crowd.

## CHELSEA & THE MEAT-PACKING DISTRICT
**☻ Bongo.** 299 Tenth Ave. (btw. 27th and 28th sts.). ☎ **212/947-3654.** Subway: C, E to 23rd St.

This casual, comfortable mid-century–modern lounge is the place to come for cocktails that are well-made and a great value considering their x-large size ($7 to $10). Don't miss the French martini, made with Vox vodka and Lillet—yum! Even better: Bongo boasts a full raw-bar menu—a half-dozen varieties of oysters, cherrystones and littlenecks, even lobster and caviar—and an excellent lobster roll ($14.50, and worth every penny). The crowd is hip but, happily, not too trendy. Come early if you want to have space to sit and eat.

**Flight 151.** 151 Eighth Ave. (btw. 16th and 17th sts.). ☎ **212/229-1868.** Subway: A, C, E to 14th St.; L to Eighth Ave.

This friendly bar is full of great deals: Monday launches the week with dollar drafts and $2.50 margaritas. On Tuesday night, the bartender flips a coin to see whether you or the house is going to buy your next drink. Wednesday is "Let's Make a Deal" night: Pull a tab and pay what it says for your drink—full price, half price, or just 25¢. Thursday is trivia night: You be the first to call out the answer to a new trivia question every 15 minutes, and your drink is free. Even without the bargains, this popular aviation-themed hangout is affordable and very welcoming. There's now a second location, **Flight 1668,** on the Upper East Side at 1668 Third Ave., between 93rd and 94th streets (☎ 212/426-1416), offering the same bar specials.

**Gaslight.** 400 W. 14th St. (at Ninth Ave.). ☎ **212/807-8444.** Subway: A, C, E to 14th St.

The ideal cross between a cozy English pub and an elegant Victorian lounge. No taps, though—but a wonderful hangout nonetheless.

**☻ Serena.** In the basement level of the Hotel Chelsea, 222 W. 23rd St. (btw. Seventh and Eighth aves.). ☎ **212/255-4646.** Subway: 1, 9, C, E to 23rd St.

This plush new basement boîte is as hip as can be; I've even spotted mixmaster Moby here. It's relatively unpretentious considering its hotspot-of-the-moment status; still, dress the part if you want to make it past the doorman, especially on weekends. The crowd is young and pretty, and the music mix is a blast; think Fatboy Slim meets ABBA meets Foghat, and you'll get the picture.

## THE FLATIRON DISTRICT, UNION SQUARE & GRAMERCY PARK

Also consider the **Old Town Bar & Restaurant,** 45 E. 18th St., between Broadway and Park Avenue South (☎ 212/529-6732), a genuine tin-ceilinged, 19th-century bar that's a terrific place to soak up some old New York atmosphere; see chapter 6.

**Eureka Joe.** 168 Fifth Ave. (at 22nd St.) ☎ **212/741-7500.** Subway: N, R to 23rd St.

One of my favorite coffeehouses in the city also makes a great evening hang, too. It boasts comfy sofa nooks, a loungey stay-as-long-as you want vibe, and a good wine and beer bar in addition to the coffee counter. There's live entertainment most evenings.

**Dusk Lounge.** 147 W. 24th St. (btw. Sixth and Seventh aves.). ☎ **212/924-4490.** Subway: F to 23rd St.

This casual, arty lounge is a great choice for Anglophiles who relish the rise of Cool Britannia. There's a fab mirrored mosaic wall, comfortable banquettes opposite, a friendly bar serving up affordable drinks, a pool table, and British tunes—from drum-and-bass to Manic Street Preachers and Blur—on the sound system. Expect an easy-going, youngish crowd that stays relaxed and unpretentious into the evening.

**Heartland Brewery.** 35 Union Sq. W. (at 16th St.). ☎ **212/645-3400.** www. heartlandbrewery.com. Subway: 4, 5, 6, N, R, L to 14th St./Union Sq.

The food leaves a bit to be desired, but the house-brewed beers are first-rate. Great American Beer Festival three-time award-winner Farmer Jon's Oatmeal Stout is always on hand, as are three or four handcrafted ales and a lager or two. A good selection of single malts and tequilas, too. The wood-paneled, two-level bar is big and appealing, but expect a loud, boisterous after-work crowd, plus a good number of Germans and Brits (testament to the quality of the brew). Also in Midtown at 1285 Sixth Ave., across from Radio City (☎ 212/582-8244).

**Park Avenue Country Club.** 381 Park Ave. So. (at 27th St.). ☎ **212/685-3636.** Subway: 6 to 28th St.

More polished than your average beer-and-pretzels sports bar, this is a very comfortable place to hunker down over a club sandwich and a beer to watch the game. There are TVs at every turn, and a nice mahogany central bar serves up an extensive list of bottled and on-tap brews.

**Pete's Tavern.** 129 E. 18th St. (at Irving Place). ☎ **212/473-7676.** www.petestavern.com. Subway: 4, 5, 6, N, R, L to 14th St./Union Sq.

The oldest continually operating establishment in the city, Pete's opened in 1864—while Lincoln was still president! It reeks of genuine history—and, more importantly, Guinness on tap, a terrific happy hour, and a St. Patrick's Day party that makes the neighbors crazy. The crowd is a mix of locals from ritzy Gramercy Park and more down-to-earth types.

## TIMES SQUARE & MIDTOWN WEST

In addition to the choices below, also consider the genuinely terrific bar at the original theme restaurant, the **Hard Rock Cafe,** 221 W. 57th St., between Broadway and Seventh Avenue (☎ 212/459-9320), where you can groove to classic rock while you peruse a truly astounding collection of memorabilia. There's also **ESPN Zone,** the ultimate sports bar. See "Theme Restaurant Thrills!" in chapter 6. A second branch of **Heartland Brewery** (p. 329) is across from Radio City at 1285 Sixth Ave., at 51st Street (☎ 212/582-8244).

And don't forget terrific **Joe Allen,** the legendary Broadway pub on Restaurant Row, 326 W. 46th St., between Eighth and Ninth avenues (☎ **212/581-6464**), great for a after-theater cocktail even if you don't dine here; see chapter 6.

**⊙ The Algonquin.** 59 W. 44th St. (btw. Fifth and Sixth aves.), New York, NY 10036. ☎ **212/840-6800.** Subway: B, D, F, Q to 42nd St.

The past isn't just a memory anymore at this venerable literary landmark; a complete 1998 restoration returned it to its full Arts and Crafts splendor. The splendid oak-paneled lobby is the comfiest and most welcoming in the city, made to linger over pre- or post-theater cocktails. You'll feel the spirit of Dorothy Parker and the legendary Algonquin Round Table that pervades the room. Adjacent is the pubby, clubby **Blue Bar,** home to a rotating collection of Hirschfeld drawings that's well worth checking out.

**Mickey Mantle's.** 42 Central Park South (btw. Fifth and Sixth aves). ☎ **212/688-7777.** www.mickeymantles.com. Subway: B, Q to 57th St.

Of course, it's terribly sad that the Mick, who gave his life to the bottle, should have his name on a bar. But if you're a fan, it's definitely worth a visit to his classic mahogany-and-brass sports bar and restaurant, which chronicles his life and career in photos. The crowd is a laidback mix of white-collar after-workers and interested tourists. Classic moderately priced burger fare is available, plus the requisite souvenirs. A great place to watch the game.

**Tír Na Nóg.** 5 Penn Plaza (Eighth Ave. between 33rd and 34th sts.). ☎ **212/630-0249.** Subway: 1, 2, 3, 9 to 34th St./Penn Station.

Tír Na Nóg is a standout among the Irish pubs that line Eighth Avenue in the shadow of Penn Station. The handsome decor lends the place a genuine Celtic vibe, as does the Murphy's on tap and the lilt of the friendly bartender. The bar has quickly established itself among both locals and bridge-and-tunnel types for its unpretentious, lively air. There's good pub grub, a small dance floor, and live foot-stompin' Irish music Friday and Saturday nights.

**⊙ Russian Vodka Room.** 265 W. 52nd St. (btw. Broadway and Eighth Ave.). ☎ **212/307-5835.** Subway: C, E, 1, 9 to 50th St.

Here's a real Theater District find. It's not going to win any style awards—it's more hotel bar than chic boite—but this terrific old-school lounge is extremely comfortable and knows what's what when it comes to vodkas. There's more than 50 on hand, plus the RVR's own miraculous infusions; you can order an iced rack of six if you can't decide between such yummy flavors as cranberry, apple cinnamon, ginger, horseradish, and more (the raspberry makes a perfect Cosmo). The thirtysomething-and-up crowd is peopled with post-Soviet imports as well as New Yorkers in the know about this best-kept secret. The Russian nibbles are top flight, too. Come early if you want to snag a bar table.

**The View Lounge.** On the 48th floor of the New York Marriott Marquis, 1535 Broadway (btw. 45th and 46th sts.). ☎ **212/398-1900.** Subway: 1, 2, 3, 9, N, R to Times Square; N, R to 49th St.

If it's a clear night, head up to this aptly named three-story revolving rooftop bar and restaurant for great views and decent cocktails. Grab a window seat if you can; it takes about an hour to see the 360-degree view of Times Square go by.

# MIDTOWN EAST & MURRAY HILL

Also consider the **British Open,** 320 E. 59th St., between First and Second avenues (☎ 212/355-8467), a perfect pub for anybody who pines for a well-pulled pint and an easygoing vibe straight outta London; see chapter 6. There's also a comfy, and popular, bar underneath the sky ceiling at **Michael Jordan's–The Steak House,** on the mezzanine level at Grand Central Terminal (☎ 212/655-2300).

**Bull & Bear.** At the Waldorf-Astoria. 301 Park Ave. (btw. 49th and 50th sts.). ☎ 212/ 872-4900. Subway: 6 to 51st St.

The name speaks to its business-minded clientele; in fact, there's even an LED stock ticker in constant service for those three-martini lunches. The Bull & Bear is like a gentlemen's pub, with brass-studded red leather chairs, a waistcoated staff, and a grand troika-shaped mahogany bar polished to a high sheen at the center of the room. Still, it's plenty comfy for casual drinkers. Ask Oscar, who's been here for more than 30 years, or one of the other accomplished bartenders to blend you a classic cocktail. An ideal place to kick back after a hard day of sightseeing.

**Divine Bar.** 244 E. 51st St. (btw. Second and Third aves.). ☎ 212/319-9463. Subway: 6 to 51st St.; E, F to Lexington Ave.

This glowing hacienda-style wine bar is a big hit with a cute and sophisticated under-40 crowd (think up-and-coming media types and you'll get the picture), with a few older patrons in the mix who come for the excellent selection of wines and microbrews rather than the pick-up scene. I prefer the second, fireplace-lit level to the first floor. The DJ plays a familiar, radio-friendly mix, and there's live acoustic music on Sundays. Good tapas and an extensive humidor round out the appeal.

**The Ginger Man.** 11 E. 36th St. (btw. Fifth and Madison aves.). ☎ 212/532-3740. Subway: 6 to 33rd St.

The big bait at this appealing and cigar-friendly beer bar is the 66 gleaming tap handles lining the wood-and-brass bar, dispensing everything from Sierra Nevada and Hoegaarden to cask-conditioned ales. The cavernous space has a clubby feel, the limited menu is well prepared, and prices are better than you'd expect from an upmarket place like this.

## THE UPPER WEST SIDE

Amsterdam Avenue from 72nd to 86th streets has evolved into a major bar-hopping strip, dotted with yuppified bars and an ever-growing list of trendy lounges, plus long-standing neighborhood joints like the **Hi-Life Bar & Grill,** at 83rd Street (☎ 212/ 787-7199), which has a pleasant alfresco patio and makes a great (and affordable) martini. I suggest just strolling the avenue on a nice night and popping into the spots that suit your fancy.

Also consider **Fez** at **Time Cafe North,** 2330 Broadway, at 85th St. (☎ 212/ 579-5100), a second Moroccan-themed cafe from the people behind the ultra-groovy original Fez at Time Cafe in NoHo (p. 316). Closer to Columbia, there's also a terrific bar that rollicks well into the wee hours at **Nacho Mama's,** 2893 Broadway, between 112th and 113th streets (☎ 212/665-2800).

**All State Cafe.** 250 W. 72nd St. (btw. Broadway and West End Ave.). ☎ 212/874-1883. Subway: 1, 2, 3, 9 to 72nd St.

Despite its proximity to Broadway, this subterranean pub is one of Manhattan's undiscovered treasures. It's easy to miss from the street, and the regulars like it that way. The All State attracts a grown-up neighborhood crowd drawn in by the casual ambiance, the great burgers, and an outstanding jukebox. A fireplace makes it even more homey and inviting in cold weather.

## Additional Sources for Bar- & Club-Hoppers

If you want even more bars and clubs to choose from, pick up the pocket-sized *Shecky's Bar, Club & Lounge Guide; Zagat New York City Nightlife,* the first after-hours guide from the people who wrote the dining bible; or the annual ✪ *Time Out New York Eating & Drinking* guide, all available in most city bookstores. Hipster monthly *Paper* boasts opinionated coverage of the downtown bar scene online (**www.papermag.com**). You'll find additional online recommendations at **www.newyork.citysearch.com** and **www.digitalcity.com/newyork**.

**Evelyn Lounge.** 380 Columbus Ave. (at 78th St.). ☎ **212/724-2363.** Subway: B, C to 81st St./Museum of Natural History.

This basement bar is one of the more chic spots on the Upper West Side. Expect an attractive space outfitted with velveteen sofas and a stylishly dressed yuppie crowd on the make. There's the requisite cigar room, plus live music a few nights a week.

**The Heights.** 2867 Broadway (btw. 111th and 112th sts.), 2nd floor. ☎ **212/866-7035.** Subway: 110th St./Cathedral Pkwy.

This Columbia U. hangout is a great bet for bargain-hunters. It boasts an attractive, tree-lined view of Broadway (with open-air appeal in warm weather) and bargain drinks, from $7 10 oz. martinis to blended drinks in pint glasses ($6) to a wide world of beers. Ah, the joys of college life! The Heights doubles as a restaurant, so come late for the bar scene.

**Shark Bar.** 307 Amsterdam Ave. (btw. 74th and 75th sts.). ☎ **212/874-8500.** Subway: 1, 2, 3, 9 to 72nd St.

This perennially popular upscale spot is well known for its good soul food and even better singles' scene. It's also a favorite hangout for sports celebs, so don't be surprised if you spot a New York Knick or two.

## THE UPPER EAST SIDE

There's also **Flight 1668,** 1668 Third Ave., between 93rd and 94th streets (☎ **212/426-1416**), offering the same big-drinking bar specials as sibling hangout **Flight 151** (p. 328).

**Brandy's Piano Bar.** 235 E. 84th St. (btw. Second and Third aves.). ☎ **212/650-1944.** Subway: 4, 5, 6 to 86th St.

A mixed crowd—Upper East Side locals, waiters off work, gays, straights, all ages—comes to this intimate, old-school piano bar for the friendly atmosphere and nightly entertainment. The talented waitstaff does most of the singing while waiting for their big break, but enthusiastic patrons join in on occasion. An appealing and affordable night on the town.

**Subway Inn.** 143 E. 60th St. (just east of Lexington Ave.). ☎ **212/223-8929.** Subway: 4, 5, 6 to 59th St.

Now, here's a dive bar if there ever was one—and that's precisely the Subway Inn's charm. Every time I go to Bloomingdale's, I get a perverse joy at seeing this hole-in-the-wall surviving in the shadow of the great department store, as the high-rent neighborhood around it grows more and more upscale and out-of-reach to the average Joes inside. A great spot for hubbies to nurse a cheap beer while their wives exercise the plastic next door. Note to film buffs: This was Montgomery Clift's local bar; he lived just down the street for years.

# 7  Dance Clubs & Party Scenes

No slice of the New York nightlife pie is as mutable as the club scene. In this world, hotspots don't even get 15 minutes of fame; their time in the limelight is usually more like a commercial break.

First things first: Finding and going to the latest hotspot is not worth agonizing over. Clubbers spend their lives obsessing over the scene. My rule of thumb is that if I know about a place, it must not be hip anymore. Even if I could tell you where the hippest club kids hang out today, they'll have moved on by the time you arrive in town.

The tracking game is best left to the perennial party crowd who know the rest of the crowd as well as the guy at the door (who lets them in for free) and someone at the bar (who comps them drinks). You're just not likely to get that well-connected in your week of vacation. Just find someplace that amuses you, and enjoy the crowd that enjoys it with you.

In the listings below, I've concentrated on a wide variety of club scenes, from performance arty to perennially popular discos, most of which are generally easy to make your way into. You can find listings for the most current hotspots and moveable parties in the online sources listed in **"Planning Your Trip: An Online Directory"** and in the note called "Additional Sources for Bar- & Club-Hoppers" above. Another good bet is to cruise hip boutiques in SoHo, the East Village, and the Lower East Side, where party planners usually leave flyers advertising the latest goings-on.

In addition to the choices below, lovers of Brazilian, Afro-Caribbean, and other world music should seriously consider ✪ **S.O.B.'s** (p. 319), where top-notch live bands keep the dance party sizzling nightly; **Cafe Wha?** (p. 315) isn't quite so high quality, but it also steams up the dance floor. The **Greatest Bar on Earth** (p. 322) becomes a dance party extraordinaire for swingers; the Mondo-107 Strato-Lounge on Wednesdays is well worth catching. On the other side of the coin, certain bars, such as **Serena,** evolve into some of the hottest dance-free party scenes in town as the night wears on.

**MONEY MATTERS FOR NIGHTCLUBBERS**   New York nightlife starts late. With the exception of places that have scheduled live performances, it's almost useless to show up anywhere before 11pm. Don't depend on plastic; bring cash, and plan on dropping a wad at most places. Cover charges start out anywhere from $5 to $30 and often get more expensive as the night wears on. *Time Out New York* is a great source to check, as it lists cover charges for the week's big events and clearly indicates which are free.

**Always call ahead,** because schedules change constantly and can do so at the last minute. Even better: You might also be able to put your name on a guest list that will save you a few bucks at the door.

**Baktun.** 418 W. 14th St. (btw. Ninth Ave. and Washington St.). ☎ **212/206-1590.** www.baktun.com. Subway: A, C, E to 14th St.

This newish club, upstairs neighbor to the Cooler (p. xxx), has been hot, hot, hot since the word go. Sleek Baktun was conceived as a multimedia lounge and as such incorporates avant-garde video projections (shown on a clever double-sided video screen) into its raging dance parties as well as live cybercasts. The music tends toward electronica, natch. Best among the top-quality parties is N'Ice, a big, unpretentious, Friday-night house party. The cover runs $5 to $15.

## Getting Beyond the Velvet Rope

If your heart's set on getting into an exclusive club or lounge, here are a few pointers that might help to tip the scale in your favor:

- **Dress well and fashionably.** Like it or not, the doorman is sizing you up to decide whether you're hip enough to make the scene. If you want to get in, you have to play along.
- **Arrive early.** Frankly, the bouncers are just not as vigilant at 9pm, when the place is half empty, as they are at 11pm—and once you're inside, you're in for the night if you want. Weeknights are also a better bet. Clubbers might tell you that eager beavers are disdained for arriving too early, but I find earlier to almost always be more successful than later.
- **Be polite.** No matter how obnoxious the doorman might be, giving attitude back won't help. And who knows? You might just charm him with your winning personality.
- **Don't try to talk your way in.** Don't drop names or make up some story to get in the door. These guys have heard it all. If you're not wanted, why bother? Take your business to a friendlier establishment, where you'll be happier in the long run.

---

**Centro-Fly.** 45 W. 21st St. (btw. Fifth and Sixth aves.). ☎ **212/627-7770.** Subway: F to 23rd St.; N, R to 23rd St.

Anyone who remembers the old rock-and-roll joint Tramps won't believe the swank Op Art club that fills the space now. It's so fab, in fact, that Mary J. Blige used it as a video set. The sunken bar must be the coolest in town. Despite the fabulousness of the place, Centro-Fly is quite welcoming. Two mondo sound systems and a four-turntable booth are luring in top-notch DJ talent. Depending on the night, look for deep house, hip-hop, or another edgy music mix, and expect a $10 to $15 cover.

**Culture Club.** 179 Varick St. (btw. King and Charlton sts.) ☎ **212/243-1999.** Subway: 1, 9 Houston St.

Attention Karma Chameleons: This is where the Reagan 80s come to life in their full, big-haired glory. This silly dance club attracts a big bridge-and-tunnel and tourist crowd looking for some good, clean fun. Decidedly unhip, very accessible, and lots of retro enjoyment for those with a touch of nostalgia for Duran Duran, Pac Man, Boy Toy–era Madonna, Lita Ford, and *Miami Vice.* On occasion, the tides change and locals move in, as when DJ Grandmaster Flash himself takes to the turntables. The cover is $15 on Thursday, $20 on Friday and Saturday.

**Don Hill's.** 511 Greenwich St. (at Spring St.). ☎ **212/219-2850** or 212/334-1390. Subway: 1, 9 to Canal St.; C, E to Spring St.

This big and eclectic place draws a heavily integrated gay-lesbian/straight crowd that comes for top-notch local rock, glam, and punk talent some nights, campy party nights on others. The best of the party nights is Squeezebox on Friday nights, a rollicking gay/straight party with a drag edge. Ultimate groupie (and Liv Tyler's mom) Bebe Buell shows up on the bill occasionally. The cover is generally in the $5 to $10 range.

**Exit.** 610 W. 56th St. (btw. Eleventh and Twelfth aves.). ☎ **212/582-8282.** Subway: A, B, C, D, 1, 9 to 59th St./Columbus Circle.

If you want the biggest party in town, read no further. This brand-new, behemoth club is a doozy—and because it covers 45,000 square feet and is able to accommodate more than 5,000 partiers, any velvet rope scene is pure posturing. The main floor is a mammoth atrium with a DJ booth—usually housing the top talent of the moment spinning tunes—suspended above. The space was made for crazy carnival acts such as Antigravity, a bizarre clubland take on the Flying Wallendas. Upstairs is a warren of ultra-plush VIP rooms that have already drawn in celebs such as Sandra Bullock and Puffy. *Warning:* Most events are a pricey $25.

⊙ **Mother.** 432 W. 14th St. (at Washington St.). ☎ **212/366-5680.** www.mothernyc. com. Subway: A, C, E to 14th St.

A diverse crowd, both gay and straight, descends on this friendly, long-lived club for a variety of hugely popular events, thanks to the untiring talents of husband and wife Chi-Chi Valenti and Johnny Dynell (she's the hostess, he's the DJ). Saturday's Click + Drag, a futuristic techno-fetish party, is probably the most out-there of the regular events, but just about any night at Mother is a wild one. Friday's lesbian Clit Club is a club circuit institution. Performance art, poetry readings, and multimedia fun round out the goings-on. The cover runs $5 to $15.

⊙ **Nell's.** 246 W. 14th St. (btw. Seventh and Eighth aves.). ☎ **212/675-1567.** www. nells.com. Subway: A, C, E, 1, 2, 3, 9 to 14th St.

Nell's was the first to establish a loungelike atmosphere years ago. It has been endlessly copied by restaurateurs and nightclub owners, who have since realized that if people wanted to stay home, why not make "out" just as comfy as "in?" Nell's attracts everyone from homies to Wall Streeters, and it's as marvelous as ever. Most of the parties have a soulful edge. Look for the hugely popular laid-back Voices, sort of a sophisticated weekly *Star Search* that's a showcase for a surprising number of new talents as well as big names looking for an intimate moment. The cover runs $10 to $15 (free on Sundays). **Money-saving tip:** Check the Web site for reduced-admission passes.

**Roxy.** 515 W. 18th St. (at Tenth Ave.). ☎ **212/645-5156.** www.roxynyc.com. Subway: 1, 9 to 18th St.; A, C, E, L to 14th St.

This megaclub is still going strong, with inline roller disco on Wednesdays and an accessible dance mix on Fridays. But the reason to come is Saturday, when Roxy is home to the biggest gay dance party in the city, with legendary DJ Victor Calderone at the helm, spinning a terrific tribal house mix. **Money-saving tip:** The cover is generally $20, but you might be able to save by arriving before midnight; check the Web site for details.

**Shine.** 285 W. Broadway (at Canal St.). ☎ **212/941-0900.** Subway: A, C, E, 1, 9 to Canal St.

This new(ish) club draws a well-dressed crowd to TriBeCa with a loungey vibe and a few well-placed 21st-century twists—most notably, great cocktails and terrific DJ talent. The biggest club night is Thursday's Shag, when those Uptown yups loosen up and get down to a groovelicious mix; a committed hip-hop crowd takes over after hours. Don't overlook Giant Step Mondays, a weekly party that has seen such topflight international DJ talent as Ben Watt (Everything But the Girl). You'll also find cabaret and performance art that runs the gamut from classic to kooky. The cover varies but generally sticks close to $10 or so.

⊙ **13.** 35 E. 13th St. (btw. Broadway and University Place), 2nd floor. ☎ **212/979-6677.** Subway: 4, 5, 6, N, R, L to 14th St./Union Sq.

This little lounge is a great place to dance the night away. It's stylish but unpretentious, with a steady roster of fun weekly parties. I'm thrilled that Sunday night's no-cover Britpop fest Shout! lives on, as popular as ever. Thursday is '70s and '80s new wave and glam night, and DJ Cadet spins an appealing dance mix that ranges from 1970s disco to current hip-hop on Friday and Saturday. If there's a cover, it's usually just $5.

**2i's.** 248 W. 14th St. (btw. Seventh and Eighth aves.). ☎ **212/807-1775.** Subway: A, C, E, L, 1, 2, 3, 9 to 14th St.

This loungey club is finally getting the attention it deserves, thanks to its unique global spin on the party calendar. The place to come if you're looking for reggae, hip-hop, Latin, R&B, and other soulful sounds. The cover generally runs $7 to $15.

**Twilo.** 530 W. 27th St. (btw. Tenth and Eleventh aves.). ☎ **212/268-1600.** www.twilo. com. Subway: C, E to 23rd St.

Go west—way west—to this mega-size dance factory. Superstar DJ Junior Vasquez still spins pulsating dance music marathons, called Juniorverse, for an adoring, mostly gay crowd on Saturdays. Twilo Fridays draws an energized straight crowd with imported international DJs. The well-received new Wednesday party hosts live local and international talent for a dance crowd. The cover runs as high as $25.

**❍ Vinyl.** 6 Hubert St. (btw. Hudson and Greenwich sts.). ☎ **212/343-1379.** Subway: A, C, E to Canal St.; 1, 9 to Franklin St.

This commodious TriBeCa club welcomes a big, mixed black/white, gay/straight crowd to hip hop- and house-flavored party nights ruled by a first-rate crop of DJs. Best of all on an unimpeachable party calendar is the long-lived Body and Soul, a Sunday afternoon acid-garage-house party that's on its way to becoming a legend. Also try the weekly Dance Ritual, when DJ "Little Louie" Vega spins a house mix flavored with Latin, soul, and gospel for a committed crowd that comes to dance, not pose. The cover tops out at $15.

**Webster Hall.** 125 E. 11th St. (btw. Third and Fourth aves.). ☎ **212/353-1600.** www.webster-hall.com. Subway: 6 to Astor Place.

Five floors and a seemingly endless warren of rooms mean that there's something for everyone at this old warhorse of a club. Weekends are a great time to come if you're just looking for a straightforward crowd and music mix. Even though it's dominated by a bridge-and-tunnel crowd, Webster Hall is still a plenty interesting place to hang. Expect to wait in line to get in. **Money-saving tip:** The standard cover is $25, but add your name to the guest list via the Web, and you can enter for as little as $10. Ladies free on Thursdays.

## 8　The Lesbian & Gay Scene

For the latest on what's happening in gay and lesbian nightlife, pick up a free copy of *Homo Xtra (HX)* or *HX for Her,* by far the best guides to the gay scene. They're available for free in bars and clubs or at the Lesbian and Gay Community Center (see "Tips for Travelers with Special Needs" in chapter 2). *Time Out New York* also boasts a terrific gay section.

These days, many bars, clubs, cabarets, and cocktail lounges are neither gay nor straight but a bit of both, either catering to a mixed crowd or to varying orientations on different nights of the week. In addition to the choices below, most of the clubs listed under "Dance Clubs & Party Scenes," above, cater to a gay crowd, some predominately so. Be sure to see what's happening at **Mother, Twilo, Roxy, Exit, Don**

**Hill's,** and **Vinyl,** all of which regularly cater to gay and/or gay/straight mixed crowds. The **Duplex** (p. 322) is at the heart of the gay cabaret scene. Among the bars and cocktail lounges, consider **Bar d'O** (p. 327).

**◐ Barracuda.** 275 W. 22nd St. (btw. Seventh and Eighth aves.). ☎ **212/645-8613.** Subway: C, E, 1, 9 to 23rd St.

Chelsea is now central to gay life—and gay bars. This trendy, loungey place is a continuing favorite, voted "Best Bar" by *HX* and *New York Press* magazines, and *Paper* singles out the hunky bartenders. There's a sexy bar for cruising out front and a comfy lounge in back. Look for the regular drag shows.

**Big Cup.** 228 Eighth Ave. (btw. 21st and 22nd sts.). ☎ **212/206-0059.** Subway: C, E to 23rd St.

Big Cup isn't a bar, but a coffeehouse. Still, you'd be hard-pressed to find a cooler, comfier pickup joint or a more preening crowd. This is where all the Chelsea boys hang; just think of it as a living room-y lounge without the alcohol. By the way, it also happens to be a fab coffeehouse.

**Boiler Room.** 86 E. 4th St. (btw. First and Second aves.). ☎ **212/254-7536.** Subway: F to Second Ave.

This East Village bar is everybody's favorite gay dive. Despite the mixed guy-girl crowd, it's a serious cruising scene for well-sculpted beautiful boys who just love to pose and a perfectly fine hangout for those who'd rather play pool.

**The Cock.** 188 Ave. A (at 12th St.). ☎ **212/777-6254.** Subway: L to First Ave.

This gleefully seedy East Village joint is the most envelope-pushing gay club in town. A self-proclaimed "rock and sleaze fag bar," the Cock is dedicated to good, sleazy fun: Witness Foxy, a hugely popular regular game show-style party in which the participants compete for "Foxy dollars" from the crowd in increasingly creative ways; needless to say, there's a good deal of hardbodied nudity involved and a few ping-pong balls among the myriad accessories. Other outrageous antics spice the weekly brew. Head elsewhere if you're the retiring type.

**◐ Crazy Nanny's.** 21 Seventh Ave. South (at Leroy St.). ☎ **212/366-6312.** Subway: 1, 9 to Houston St.

This longstanding lesbian bar is capacious, friendly, hugely popular, and perpetually trendy. There's two floors, two bars, a groovy jukebox, dancing, video games, and a variety of theme nights, including Drag Kings and Queens on Thursday and no-cover Kasual Karaoke on Sunday and Wednesday (otherwise $7 to $8). Out-of-towners are welcome.

**g.** 223 W. 19th St. (btw. Seventh and Eighth aves.). ☎ **212/929-1085.** Subway: 1, 9 to 18th St.

Big crowds of muscular, designer-dressed men have made this lovely, relaxed lounge a popular style scene for meeting dream dates. There's a juice bar, too, and magazines that invite early-hours lounging.

**Hell.** 59 Gansevoort St. (btw. Washington and Greenwich sts.). ☎ **212/727-1666.** Subway: A, C, E to 14th St.

This glamorous lounge is a sexy haven for a predominately gay weekend crowd in the hipper-than-hell Meat-Packing District. The cocktails are well mixed, and plenty of comfy sofas are on hand for getting cozy. Ahead of its time in the 'hood, Hell is not quite as ultra-hot as it used to be, but that just means there's more room for you.

**Henrietta Hudson.** 438 Hudson St. (at Morton St.). ☎ **212/924-3347.** Subway: 1, 9 to Houston St.

This friendly and extremely popular women's bar is known for drawing in an attractive, upmarket lipstick lesbian crowd that comes for the great jukebox and videos as well as the pleasingly low-key atmosphere.

**Stonewall Bar.** 53 Christopher St. (at Seventh Ave. So.). ☎ **212/463-0950.** Subway: 1, 9 to Christopher St.

A new bar at the spot where the modern gay liberation movement got its start. A mixed gay and lesbian crowd—old and young, beautiful and great personalities— makes this an easy place to begin. At least pop in to relive a defining moment in queer history.

**Wonder Bar.** 505 E. 6th St. (btw. Avenues A and B). ☎ **212/777-9105.** Subway: 6 to Astor Place.

The "sofa look" has lent a loungier, more stylish tone to this packed-on-weekends East Village hangout. There's some male cruising, but fun, hip, and friendly Wonder Bar gets points for making straights feel welcome, too. DJs spin a listener-friendly mix in the back room nightly.

# Index

See also Accommodations and Restaurant indexes, below.